The
International
Economy

THE MACMILLAN COMPANY
NEW YORK • CHICAGO
DALLAS • ATLANTA • SAN FRANCISCO
LONDON • MANILA

IN CANADA
BRETT-MACMILLAN LTD.
GALT, ONTARIO

The
International
Economy, REVISED

P. T. Ellsworth

New York:

The Macmillan Company

PRINTED IN THE UNITED STATES OF AMERICA
SECOND PRINTING, 1959

LIBRARY OF CONGRESS CATALOG CARD NUMBER: 58-5211

PREFACE

I undertook a revision of *The International Economy* for two reasons. The first edition (1950) has been in print for some eight years. The passage of time and of the changes that come with it required that the chapters dealing with postwar events be brought up to date. More important than this matter of currency, however, was my own dissatisfaction with the 1950 volume. I became convinced that it could be greatly improved by condensing the historical sections and by making more coherent and systematic those concerned with theoretical analysis.

The revision undertaken for these reasons has been complete and thorough. Less than ten per cent of the earlier edition has been retained without substantial change.

Still adhering to my conviction that the incorporation of historical and institutional materials add to the usefulness of a text in this field, I have kept the original scheme of organisation. These materials have been greatly condensed, and increased emphasis has been given to the role of economic growth and change. Except in the initial presentation of the theory of international trade, factor proportions are not assumed to remain constant, but are shown to change, both as a result of the international movement of labor and capital, and as a result of internal growth. Greater stress is also laid on long-term shifts in the attitude of governments toward international trade, with a view to providing historical perspective for the evaluation of recent and current trade policies. I hope that the suppression of historical detail and the change in emphasis bring into sharper focus the more significant developments.

As for the theoretical portions of the text, I have tried to make these more systematic and rigorous, as well as clearer and more explicit. Here, too, the passage of time has suggested a change in emphasis. The factor-proportions theory of international trade is developed more fully, with more explicit attention to the problems raised by the existence of two or more alternative production functions. I have tried to bring out clearly the relation of a country's balance of payments to its national income, and to show the role this relationship plays in the adjustment mechanism. This treatment permits me to minimise the space devoted to consideration of the gold standard, whose virtual disappearance has greatly reduced the need for its detailed discussion. Devaluation and exchange control, as alternatives to balance of payments adjustment via income changes, are brought into juxtaposition with the latter. A concluding chapter to this section (Chapter 20) provides a comparative evaluation of all three methods of adjustment.

Since the preparation of students entering a course in international economics varies widely, I have reviewed the foundations upon which its subject matter rests. These reviews occur principally in Chapters 5 (price theory), 8 (competition, monopoly, inperfect competition), and 13 (national income accounting and the multiplier). Some may feel that these recapitulations of materials the students are supposed to have mastered are unnecessary. If so, they can omit them. Others—and I hope it will be the majority—may find them useful.

In addition to shortening a book that was over-long, and to improving the clarity of presentation, I have tried to stress the usefulness of economic theory and to show how it can be applied to the solution of practical problems. I hope the attempt has been successful.

In the preparation of the book, I have been greatly aided by my colleague, Professor Theodore Morgan, of the University of Wisconsin. He read the entire manuscript; his careful attention contributed immensely to improving both the material content and its form of presentation. Professor Bernard Goodman of Wayne State University also read the manuscript. Both he and I tried much of it, in mimeographed form, on our classes. Professor Goodman's comments and suggestions have also been very helpful. For the defects that remain, I can only blame my own shortcomings.

P. T. ELLSWORTH

Bangkok, Thailand
November 20, 1957

TABLE OF CONTENTS

1

WHAT INTERNATIONAL ECONOMICS IS ABOUT

Economics deals with man's daily activities in getting a living, in general with the problems of productivity, of depression and inflation, monopoly, and of inequality of incomes. The exact content of the subject, however, as with any broad field of knowledge, cannot be known until we have actually studied it. Economics is what economists do!

This is equally true of the branch of economics that we call international economics. Its name indicates that it concerns itself with the economic relations between nations. But what precisely do these relations include? Is a separate study of international economics necessary?

This first chapter gives a first-approximation answer to these questions— it surveys some of the principal problems we shall encounter, and shows how we will attack them. Here we will sketch the outlines only. You will get a fuller grasp of what it is all about as you become better acquainted with the critical problems and opportunities of our international economy.

WHY SHOULD WE TRADE?

The Role of Trade

Nations cannot live alone any more effectively than can individuals. A single family, living in isolation and providing for all its needs, can obtain only a meager and primitive living. So compelling is this fact that even among primitive peoples there is some rudimentary specialisation, together with an inevitable sharing or exchange of its fruits. With the progress of technology, from the discovery of fire and invention of the grinding stone and the wheel, down to the perfection of the latest electronic device, the scope of specialisation has increased—and with it the abundance of goods and services to satisfy our wants. The specialised producer uses only part— maybe none—of his own output. He exchanges his surplus for the things he wants of the specialised outputs of others. In other words, specialisation implies trade and cannot occur without it.

1

A large part of total trade, of course, is among the inhabitants of a single locality or region. In the Middle Ages, when perhaps nine-tenths of the world's population lived and worked on farms, when the techniques of production were relatively simple and incomes were correspondingly low, the volume of goods that travelled long distances—mainly luxuries of the rich—was only a minute part of total trade. Even today international trade, or trade that crosses national boundaries, represents only 5 to 6 per cent of the total exchange of goods. Yet that small percentage is crucial and amounts to many billions of dollars a year. Indeed, it is small percentage-wise only because of the immensity of the day-to-day transactions inside each country.

Trade or Perish

For many countries, as we shall see, international trade is a matter literally of life or death. Thus western Europe in the middle of the twentieth century consists of some 300 million people inhabiting a comparatively small land area with limited physical resources. This densely populated community cannot even feed itself. Most of its textile fibers—cotton, silk, jute, even wool—it must obtain from overseas. Without the rubber of Malaya and the petroleum of the Middle East and the Western Hemisphere, its cars and buses would be immobilised. Many of its luxuries, if they really can be called that—tea, coffee, cocoa, tobacco—would be unobtainable without far-reaching trade.

This point can be put in another way. Had Europe been unable to draw upon the resources of other continents for a constantly increasing flow of raw materials and foodstuffs, the industrial revolution—which transformed its industry and made western Europe by the end of the nineteenth century the workshop of the world—would either have been impossible or restricted within exceedingly narrow limits. Population might have increased some 50 per cent over the 100 million or so alive in 1800, instead of trebling. European people would be enjoying a standard of living half that available today, or less.

Trade or Be Poorer

At the other extreme from regions so dependent on international trade as Europe, are nations of huge area like the United States and the Soviet Union. Yet even to them, external trade is extremely important and in some respects essential. Were it not for foreign trade, the people of the United States, like Europeans, would have to do without many of their conventional comforts, such as coffee, tea, chocolate, bananas and other tropical fruits. Even sugar would be scarce and costly. Though formerly self-sufficient in iron ore, this country's deposits have been used up to such an extent that it is increasingly dependent on supplies from Canada, Venezuela, Brazil, and Chile. A Presidential Commission has estimated that by 1975, with consumption of iron ore up by more than 50 per cent, the United States will have to import nearly all its requirements of this most basic of industrial raw materials. We lack deposits of nickel and tin, and are entirely dependent on imports of these important materials. There are dozens of other materials for which we depend heavily upon foreign trade and will become increasingly dependent. But I have said enough for purposes of illustration.

Most of the commodities cited so far have been of a kind unobtainable in the importing countries, or obtainable in insufficient amounts. Such items, however, comprise only a part, though an important part, of world trade. Much the greater portion of its volume consists of articles which could be produced at home, but which instead are imported. They are imported because foreign producers can supply them more cheaply than home producers. As will be explained more fully later, foreign producers can quote low prices because the kind and quality of the resources available to them are more suited to the production of these exported goods than are the resources in the importing country. Not only does specialisation among individual producers within a country lead to more efficient and hence abundant output, but so also does geographical specialisation between countries.

The basic reasons for the importance of international trade should now be clear. Goods can be obtained from abroad that cannot be produced at home. Finally, also, goods that *could* be produced at home can be obtained at lower cost from other countries. In short, international trade permits more people to live, to gratify more varied tastes, and to enjoy a higher standard of living than would be possible in its absence.

THE INTERNATIONAL MOVEMENT OF RESOURCES AND TECHNIQUES

Trade between nations is important, but it does not exhaust even the purely economic ways in which their economies react upon one another. Not only goods, but also some of the resources that make them, move across national frontiers. So too does that vast accumulation of the product of man's intellect, knowledge of how to produce things. These movements bring about great changes in the world's economy. Thus during the middle half of the nineteenth century, the United States obtained large amounts of capital from Britain. These savings of the British people were transferred to us in the form of money, or unearmarked purchasing power. American borrowers chose to spend it in England on steel rails, railway rolling stock, and machinery for their growing factories. This foreign capital considerably hastened the transformation of our predominantly agrarian economy. Later the flow of British capital turned toward Canada, Latin America, and the colonies; the French invested heavily in Russia and the Germans in central and eastern Europe.

Along with the capital went engineers, construction workers, and some skilled labor. They built railways and factories, put new plants in operation, and trained local personnel to replace them. Besides these temporary migrants possessing technical qualifications, some proportion of the huge numbers of immigrants that left the relatively crowded nations of Europe carried with them skills that helped the expansion of mechanised industry in the newer countries.

Most of the labor that left Europe in search of better opportunities in the open areas of the world, however, was unskilled, or skilled mainly in agricultural practices. These workers brought with them little capital and not much technical knowledge. Their contribution to the equalisation of the productive power of nations, however, was immense. In the hundred years between 1830 and 1930, approximately 60 million people left Europe and Asia to take up residence abroad, mainly in North and South America and Australia. Lands that had been nearly empty became populated; their agricultural production expanded, providing ever more abundant supplies of wheat, corn, beef, and butter for the markets of Europe; cities and factories sprang up in hitherto deserted spots.

This was the era of the economic development of the "newer" regions of the world—the United States, Canada, Australia, New Zealand, Argentina, South Africa. Like the trade in goods that preceded and accompanied these movements of labor and capital, their flow benefited both the giver and the receiver. Emigration from Europe reduced somewhat the pressure of rising population on resources; as the emigrants arrived overseas, their additional labor permitted more effective use of the abundant resources awaiting them. European capital sent abroad earned a higher return for its lenders, and at the same time enhanced the productivity of the labor and land with which it was combined.

These great intercontinental movements of capital and labor, and of the technical knowledge that makes them productive, were a unique feature of the nineteenth century. Since the first World War, immigration has fallen to a mere trickle, and international investment has not yet recovered from the shock of the great depression of the 1930's. Yet some countries, notably Italy, have a surplus of population for which gainful employment cannot be found at home, while others, like Venezuela and Brazil, could benefit from additions to their labor force. More striking yet is the need for capital in the so-called "underdeveloped" areas—most of Asia, Africa, and Latin America—where a keen desire to share in the material progress of the more advanced nations has been awakened. Much effort and ingenuity are being devoted to discovering ways and means of enlarging and supplementing the sluggish flow of private capital, and of making available to the under-developed regions the technical knowledge of the West.

THE GROWTH OF RESTRICTIONS IN THE TWENTIETH CENTURY

During most of the nineteenth century, the world by and large gladly accepted the benefits of international trade and of the intercontinental flow of labor and capital and interposed few restrictions on this traffic. Subject only to relatively moderate and quite stable tariffs, buyers could seek out the cheapest and most suitable supplies of raw materials or manufactured goods, place an order, and expect to receive their purchase promptly and with a minimum of formalities. Travelers could obtain as large quantities of any currency as their means would allow and proceed to their destina-tion without passports, impertinent inquiries, or required declarations of political views. Immigrants were welcomed, while investors could invest their funds or remove them at will.

Since 1914, how times have changed! Tariffs are generally higher, and in many countries subject to sudden variation. Some nations prohibit altogether the import of particular commodities; many establish lists of goods for which import licenses are necessary and further buttress these restrictions by controls over spending abroad. Immigration is restrained by rigid national quotas and by various processes of screening the applicants. Even those countries most in need of capital often seem to do their best, by a variety of onerous restraints and limitations, to scare off foreign investors.

Passports and visas are the least of a traveler's worries. Most countries limit the amount of foreign currency he can acquire for his journey; upon entering others, he must declare how much of its money he has and account for it when he leaves. Suspicious customs officials paw through his luggage, and he may be subjected to close personal inquiries. Compare all this with the ease and freedom of trade and travel before 1914! It would appear that the world had deliberately turned its back on the gains to be obtained from international contacts—that is, that the world had lost its wits.

CHANGES IN THE STATUS OF NATIONS

British Dominance

During the nineteenth century, or more accurately, the hundred years (1814-1914) between the Napoleonic War and World War I, the role of outstanding leader among nations fell to Great Britain. After defeating Napoleon at Waterloo, Britain pursued the strategy of preserving a balance of power in Europe, shifting her weight from one side to another when it appeared that any single country might achieve a position of dominance. A century of uneasy peace resulted, broken—except for minor struggles— only by the Franco-Prussian War and the American Civil War.

If Britain was a movable counterweight in the politico-military sphere, in the economic sphere she could justly be called that century's stable but ever-expanding center. Her insular position, her role as the world's leading trader, her free institutions, and her rapidly growing population all combined to stimulate that revolution in the industrial arts which—at first slowly and imperceptibly, then with rapidly increasing tempo—made her by mid-century the outstanding industrial nation of the world.

Her economic predominance extended also to matters of trade and finance. British ships roamed everywhere, carrying British manufactures to the most distant markets and returning laden with wool, cotton, tobacco, sugar, and all the multitude of foods and materials required by a rapidly expanding industry and a multiplying population. London became a great central marketplace of the world, where anything known and desired could be bought or sold. Complementing this commercial preeminence was an equal financial preeminence, based on a currency fixed and stable in relation to gold and a financial market incomparable in its degree of specialisation and efficiency.

Until after 1914, Britain retained her outstanding position as trader and banker to the world, though her rank as industrial producer had been successfully challenged. First the United States, then Germany, surpassed Britain in manufacturing output. American industrial superiority, though it came as early as 1890, brought no threat to Britain's international position, for the United States, isolated by distance, was too busy with her own internal growth and expansion to have much concern for foreign markets. Germany, a keen rival, was thrust back temporarily by the war of 1914-1918.

American Leadership

It is in the four decades since that war that the United States has become —as a result of the growth of its own wealth and power and of the destruction in Europe of two major wars—the successor to Britain's role of leadership. We play this part, however, in circumstances far different and far more dangerous than those that confronted England. Though the nations of the nineteenth century were divided by conflicting rivalries, they operated within a framework of substantial agreement as to the desirable character of social organisation. Capitalism was dominant everywhere, and though challenged by socialist movements, it showed itself flexible and capable of accommodation to criticism.

Today there is no such agreement. Two rival philosophies divide the world. One acclaims the superior merits of the totalitarian state, where the state is everything, the individual nothing, and aspires to impose its views universally by force or by subversion. The other believes in the right of the individual to choose his government by a free vote, and in the economic field, in individual freedom tempered by controls and by varying degrees of democratically determined state action.

This cleavage would not be too disturbing were it not for the Communist aim of world domination. Given that aim, backed by the military and economic strength developed in the past thirty years by the Soviet Union, every decision on foreign affairs made by any government of the free world must inevitably be conditioned by its probable effect on the struggle against Communist expansion. This conclusion applies, of course, with particular force to the foreign policies of the United States.

The mid-twentieth century differs from the nineteenth not only in that ideological division has replaced agreement on the fundamentals of political and economic thought. There is also the economic fragmentation to which we have already alluded. A highly integrated world economy, based on relatively free trade focused upon the great center at London, has given way to restrictionism and separatism.

True, the situation has improved considerably from the chaos of the depressed 'thirties; the very pressure of adversity (and, perhaps of common sense) has compelled some degree of unification. Western Europe has taken a few tentative but important steps toward economic union. Allegiance to the pound sterling and the desire to retain the benefits of British commercial and banking connections link together the sterling area. Progress has been made toward lowering tariffs and removing trade restrictions.

Yet the international economy of today remains far less stable, less flexible, and less efficient compared to its possibilities than the pre-1914 international economy.

INTERNATIONAL ECONOMIC PROBLEMS OF THE MID-TWENTIETH CENTURY

In the preceding pages we have tried to show how nations depend on international trade, what they gain from it, and how, in spite of these gains, they have in the past half-century partially turned their backs on it. We have also examined briefly the effects of international movements of capital and labor, and the great change in the relative economic status of nations that these movements, together with the spread of modern industrial technology, have helped to bring about.

This review makes clear the divisions and instability that characterise the relations of nations today, and how this situation is the product of deep-seated changes during the past century and more. It also enables us to indicate the principal problems of today that arise out of the ways in which the economic activities and policies of different countries affect one another.

European Reconstruction

One of the most acute of recent international problems, and one that is still not completely settled, resulted from the destruction and disruption caused by World War II. Western Europe was hardest hit, and threatened to collapse in chaos if her abnormal postwar need for foreign supplies was not somehow met. American economic aid filled the gap and provided the essential margin to enable the western European nations to make a most remarkable recovery. There remains doubt, however, as to whether at least some of these nations can, without further adjustments, maintain their economic life. To pay for these supplies, an expansion of exports may be necessary, but for this to occur, their exports must be made more attractive as to price or quality. Can this goal be reached by increasing productivity, and if so, what internal social and economic changes will be required? Or must they lower prices by charging less for their services, which means accepting a decline in their standard of living?

European Union

Although great progress has been made toward the goal of economic unification of western Europe, many issues still remain in dispute, and the necessary institutional arrangements are far from complete. Concrete steps already taken include the economic union of Belgium, the Netherlands, and Luxembourg known as Benelux, and the formation of a single large market for coal and steel. Moreover, six western European nations—the three Benelux countries and France, Italy, and Western Germany—early in 1957 signed a treaty that when ratified will bind them to abolish duties on trade with members, to adopt a common external tariff, and to establish free movement of labor and capital inside the Common Market. Even this degree of union is to come only slowly, over a period of 12 to 14 years. And still to be decided is the question of whether a broader free trade area is to be created, including perhaps a dozen other European nations.

Removing Shackles of Trade
There is the still wider question of how the trade of the free world should be organised. Many countries place quantitative limits on their imports, and in doing so, discriminate against imports from the United States, while the only important currencies freely convertible into others are the dollar and the Swiss franc. Yet there is wide agreement, expressed explicitly in the Charters of the United Nations and of the International Monetary Fund, to work steadily toward the goal of the freest possible multilateral trade. But quantitative restrictions and inconvertible currencies are inconsistent with this goal. Must the latter be abandoned, or can quantitative restrictions be further reduced and additional steps taken toward making currencies convertible? Here is another set of problems likely to be with us for some time to come.

Economic Development
Another broad set of issues is presented by the desire and determination of the underdeveloped countries of the world to raise their national prestige and the welfare of their people by modernising and improving their stagnant economies. This concerns not only these countries themselves, but advanced countries of the West as well. The task confronting the under-developed regions is formidable. Should not the Western nations, and in particular the United States, share their burden even more fully than they have in the past, and thus help them achieve the desired advancement more rapidly? Perhaps that aid is the condition for any advance at all. What are the best ways of giving aid—by technical help, or by lending our capital, or by some combination of the two? And how will greater industrialisation in these countries affect the industrial nations of the West; what readjustments will they have to face?

These are some of the broader and more pressing economic problems of international scope. There are others of more limited concern to citizens of the United States. Among these is the ever-present question of the tariff.

Decade after decade the tariff question has stimulated more enthusiastic political battles than any other issue in American political history. And the issue is just as alive today as it ever was. Should tariffs be reduced, in our own long-range national interest, as a contribution to the increased viability of Europe and Japan? And if this were done, who would be injured, and how much? Another is the problem of reconciling our policy of maintaining an artificial level of agricultural prices, which requires restrictions on the entry of foreign farm products into our market, with our advocacy of a liberal international trade policy.

All of these problems would exist, and national decisions on relevant policies would be required, even if Communism had never been heard of. Yet the challenge Communism presents gives a special urgency to almost every international issue. Thus it may be that European Economic Union is not only desirable as a means to increased efficiency and prosperity, but in view of rising productivity in Russia, is perhaps even a necessity for western Europe's survival as part of the free world. Liberalisation of trade policies is also given added force as a possible contribution to the economic strength of the non-Communist nations. Finally, is not economic aid to underdeveloped countries, justifiable on independent grounds, made doubly necessary if they are not to succumb to the attraction of Communist planning and regimentation?

FIRST THINGS FIRST

The issues surveyed in the foregoing paragraphs are among the most vital of our age. It would be perfectly possible to attack them directly and immediately, and to make this book a survey of contemporary international economic problems. Many such books have been written, and good ones, too. Their purpose is to inform, and generally also to mold opinion in favor of a particular viewpoint or course of action. The best ones are written by experts, and the position they defend may well be the most sensible of the alternatives open. But because the problems in this field are complex and difficult, they have to take much for granted—in particular, the principles on which their specific analyses and conclusions are based.

Essential Tools Not Conclusions

Our purpose is to do something more than provide ready-made solutions to current international problems. It is to furnish you with the principles that underlie these vital issues, so that you can make up your own mind as to the relative merits of alternative ways of dealing with them. With proper study, you should acquire the tools essential to an informed judgment, rather than a ready-made conclusion, however well grounded. We will not avoid the problems; as the table of contents shows, we will get to them eventually. But the foundations come first.

Principles of Trade

Among these "first things" are a few, but only a few, basic theoretical principles. And the first of these shows the foundations on which the trade between nations rests. It explains what factors determine the commodities upon which a country can with greatest advantage specialise and thus export, and those which it should, in its own interest, import. An understanding of this theory is essential if we are properly to evaluate policies that alter the international flow of goods, such as protective tariffs or other import restrictions. It must also be given full consideration by a country engaged in economic development if that development is to lead to efficiency and not waste in the use of scanty resources.

This part of our theoretical study is mainly static in character; that is, it deals with what is true under given conditions. This is not to say that it cannot deal with changes; our reasoning will show how changes in costs and demands will lead to changes in a country's exports and imports.

Balance of Payments Analysis

Changes in the quantity of exports a country sells, or in the value of its imports, will clearly have an immediate effect on its international payments and receipts—its balance of payments. So too will a decline in its earnings from foreign investments, or in the volume of its borrowing or lending. But the effects do not stop here; they have substantial repercussions on the country's internal economy—on the level of employment and business activity, on prices, and hence on its ability to compete in international markets.

A second important area of theory deals with these phenomena. Since their impact differs a good deal when the currency of the country in question is fixed in value in terms of other currencies, as under the gold standard, and when it is free to fluctuate, we shall have to study balance of payments problems under both fixed and variable exchange rates. Such study should enable us to understand why the gold standard has been generally abandoned, why currency depreciation may sometimes be an effective remedy for a nation's international difficulties—and it should enable us to unravel the complex forces that underlay the much discussed "dollar shortage" which plagued the countries of western Europe after the last war and which some fear may reappear.

Knowledge of Institutions Also Needed

A firm grasp of international trade and balance of payments theory will go far toward providing you with the tools you need for attacking independently the major economic issues that transcend national boundaries. Most of this essential analytical equipment, however, is abstract in character. Yet it must always be applied to a concrete situation—a situation that has its roots in the past, and that can only be fully understood if one sees how it developed from its origins. Moreover, the general principles that emerge from theoretical analysis rest upon an unavoidable simplification of reality. When it comes time to apply them in the devising of a specific policy, allowance must be made for the differences between the simplified world of theory and the complex world of reality. Sometimes the differences will not be so great as to rule out a solution suggested by the most general principles. But sometimes the institutional environment will require substantial adjustments, and on other occasions it may render totally inapplicable a policy based on assumptions that do not fit the concrete case.

Let me illustrate. There are still some people, especially those concerned with the dangers of inflation, who would welcome the restoration of the gold standard. For this monetary system provides not only stable rates of exchange, but also (when allowed to work as it is supposed to do) automatic control over a country's money supply. It does this by establishing a fixed relationship between gold reserves and the total amount of money. An expansion of money and credit, especially if accompanied by inflationary symptoms, will lead to a loss of reserves and contraction of the money supply—that is, to automatic deflation. Though this system worked relatively well in the nineteenth century, its applicability to vastly different twentieth century conditions is at least dubious. To mention only one difference, many more people are affected today by any deflationary process, and for a number of reasons they have become far more sensitive to its impact. A type of policy that in an earlier day won public acceptance now encounters strenuous opposition. The reasoning underlying the gold standard (its theoretical foundation) is sound enough, but the environment it needs in order to work effectively no longer exists.

A second illustration shows how cultural and institutional differences affect a country's economic growth. In the early part of the nineteenth century, when most Latin American countries achieved their independence, their economic status was not radically different from that of the United States. Yet in the intervening century and a half, the United States has enjoyed a phenomenal increase in wealth and productivity, while until very recently the Latin American nations remained very much as they always had been—predominantly agrarian, static, and poor. This striking difference cannot be attributed mainly to a difference in resources, though that is certainly a factor. The explanation is to be found principally in the cultural characteristics of the two regions. The early settlers who came to North America were mainly from the lower middle classes—shopkeepers, artisans, small farmers. They brought with them a tradition of individual striving, a questioning of authority, and a desire for economic improvement. Except in the South, they established small farms suitable to operation with the labor of the family. The indigenous Indians, few and scattered, they exterminated or drove back into the interior.

The Spanish conquistadores, on the other hand, were either members of a feudal aristocracy or aspired to enter its ranks. This could be done by acquiring large estates, and these the crown granted liberally as a reward for the conquest of the New World. Along with the land went a labor force, supplied (in the principal areas of colonisation) by a settled and numerous Indian population. Here were the ingredients of the hacienda system, under which rich owners of huge estates monopolised the best land, dominated the political scene, and caused economic life to stagnate.

The significance of these striking differences is this: whereas in the United States a policy of laissez faire, of governmental inaction, produced rapid economic development, a similar policy could not, in the Latin American environment, be expected to have the same result. For there was no aspiring and energetic middle class to supply the business leadership that was such an important element in our economic growth. This agency of change either had to be created, or a substitute for it found. Its comparative absence today hampers the development of Latin America. Enough has been said to show why, if you are to be properly equipped to deal with the issues in question, a coupling of historical with theoretical analysis is essential.

Our study begins with a glimpse back in time, to the ideas of the Mercantilists of the sixteenth and seventeenth centuries. This starting point is chosen because their ideas, though often wrong, have led a hardy life—many are still with us today—and because an understanding of Mercantilist views serves to set in bold relief the accomplishments of the classical economists, who were the first to achieve a reasonably satisfactory understanding of international trade.

2

REGULATED TRADE: MERCANTILISM

Attitudes and policies of governments toward international trade have undergone sweeping changes within modern times. One of our major interests will be to understand present-day government trade policies and the arguments that support them. We should be able to throw light on this topic by contrasting what nations do today with what they have done in the past under circumstances in some respects similar, in some, different. Moreover, many views held in the past grew tenacious roots; they still live on and influence current decisions. It is important to show their origins and to see whether, if they suited conditions when they first arose, they still do so.

A Starting Point

We start with the era of Mercantilism. This period includes roughly the years 1500 to 1750, when western Europe emerged from the comparative stagnation of the Middle Ages, gradually discarded its feudal institutions, and acquired many of the characteristics of modern nationalism. We first review briefly the major characteristics of western European society at the beginning of the sixteenth century, together with the leading events that shaped its development during the next two and a half centuries.

SOCIAL AND ECONOMIC CHARACTERISTICS
OF THE MERCANTILIST PERIOD

In 1500: an Agrarian Society

In 1500, western Europe could probably count a population of between 55 and 60 million. Most of these people earned a meager living tilling the soil, either as serfs on the large estates of the nobility or as independent peasant farmers. Probably 80 to 90 per cent of them were so occupied. Of the remainder, most were employed as craftsmen, shopkeepers, or servants of the relatively small number of nobles, higher clergy, and well-to-do merchants who enjoyed ample incomes and who held the reins of political and economic power.

Household Manufacture

Society was thus preponderantly agrarian. Only a handful of cities had attained a population of close to or slightly above 200 thousand: London, Paris, Naples, Milan. A few more could count 100 thousand souls: Antwerp, Amsterdam, Lisbon, Seville, Rome, Palermo. There were a good many towns of a few thousand to 40 thousand or 50 thousand population, but even these were widely scattered. In these cities and towns, industry as we know it today did not exist. With few exceptions, manufacturing processes took place in the shop of the craftsman employing a few journeymen and apprentices, or in the home of the peasant. This was true of furniture, kitchen utensils, pottery, candles, hardware, and clothing. But in the manufacture of woolen textiles, which was the dominant industry of the thriving commercial cities of northern Italy and Flanders, and of England as well, the craft gild system had given way to the "domestic" or "putting-out" system. Here the trader or merchant-capitalist purchased raw wool; placed it in the homes of spinners and weavers to be worked up; collected the crude cloth and put it out with other workers for fulling, dyeing, and finishing; and marketed the completed product. In a few instances, an even more capitalistic method had been developed: the capitalist provided not only the raw materials but also the tools and a large building where he employed as many as several hundred workers on the various processes of textile manufacture. In some other industries, such as mining and the production of armor, the capitalist owner had achieved a position of dominance. Otherwise, the craft method of the Middle Ages continued relatively unchanged.

The Character of Trade

Because most people had an income sufficient only to provide the bare needs for food, clothing, and shelter, trade in the fifteenth century was confined mainly to the towns and their immediately surrounding countryside. Such trade as was carried on over greater distances could be divided into the movement of such staples as grains from the Baltic region and salt fish from the Baltic and North Seas to supplement the food requirements of city dwellers, and the flow of luxuries to supply the wants of the comparatively rich. The latter included the long established trade with the East in fine cotton and silk fabrics, spices, drugs, dyes, and perfumes, the movement northward of the wines and fruits of the Latin countries, and the exchange for these—and for other products such as armor, leather goods, Venetian glassware, and furs—of the famous woolens of northern Italy, Flanders, and England.

At about the turn of the fifteenth century, the earlier slow tempo of change became suddenly accelerated; in economic life, and especially in the scope and conduct of trade, it effected no less than a revolution. Though this relatively sudden speeding-up of man's way of life had many roots, three stand out as of primary importance. There was an intellectual awakening that advanced human understanding with a rapidity hitherto unknown; there occurred the great series of geographical discoveries that opened up an entire new world to exploitation and settlement; there was a sharp increase in population.

The Renaissance

The intellectual awakening that culminated in the sixteenth century represented a fundamental change in attitudes and ways of thinking. Starting in northern Italy in the fourteenth century, there occurred a rebirth of interest in the art, literature, and civilisation of Greece and Rome that differed radically from the medieval interest in Aristotelian logic and metaphysics. What now captured attention was the poetic and aesthetic aspects of Greek and Roman writings, the classical ideal of the full, well-rounded life. The literature that embodied these elements appealed to the wealthy burghers and princes who were the chief patrons of the arts. This was scarcely surprising, for although they were still loyal to the Church, their absorption in the affairs of business and the court bred a more secular view, while their greater wealth enabled them fully to enjoy pleasures not available to their medieval forebears. Concern with the after-life gave way to a concern with the here-and-now.

This secular influence was increasingly reflected not only in the literature of the times, but also in the work of scholars in many fields. Exhibiting a lively curiosity about the actual world, they began to examine the facts of nature instead of spinning out the logical implications of established doctrine. A number of important technical discoveries—the clock, the microscope, the telescope, the barometer—by making observation and experiment more accurate and even possible, immensely aided the increasingly popular study of the physical world. By the end of the sixteenth century, the foundations of modern science had been securely laid.

Effects of the Geographical Discoveries

Just when the leading intellects of the late fifteenth and early sixteenth centuries began to examine the world instead of what others had said about it, adventurous men commenced the series of geographical explorations that led to the discovery of the New World and of a new route to the East.

The discovery of the Americas was soon followed by the Spanish conquest of Mexico and Peru. From their art treasures and mines flowed a swelling stream of gold and silver that bulwarked Spain's power for over a century. Settlements, and with them the chance to sell European goods, grew first in the Spanish colonies. About a century later, emigrants from England, Holland, and France pitted themselves against the wilderness and the Indians to the north and gradually built up tobacco plantations, fisheries, lumbering, and the fur trade.

Vasco da Gama's voyage to India around the Cape of Good Hope (1498) brought Portugal to a position of affluence and power and established Lisbon rather than Venice as the central mart for trade with India and the Spice Islands. Together with the discovery and settlement of the Americas, da Gama's achievement meant that commerce was no longer confined to the Mediterranean galleys of Venice, to the camel caravans of the Near East, and to the pack trains winding their way northward over the Alps. Now commerce could take to the high seas in vessels of ever increasing size, ever diminishing cost of operation.

New opportunities for trade appeared over the widening horizon and under the very noses of the merchants. And this trade became increasingly profitable, for with the flow of the precious metals into Spain, whence they seeped out into the rest of western Europe, prices rose steadily if somewhat irregularly, while wages characteristically lagged behind. This is a situation made to order for business men. The mild but steady inflation continued until 1650 or later, reenforcing the tendency toward expansion caused by the opening up of new markets both at home and abroad. And with high profits, the accumulation of capital was greatly accelerated. Large individual fortunes became more common, their owners, increasingly powerful in political and economic affairs.

The Growth of Population

The third factor which operated to speed up the economic life of Europe, a rapid increase in population, paralleled the beginnings of science and the voyages of discovery. In 1300, the population of western Europe appears to have been about 53 million. It could scarcely have increased much in the next hundred and fifty years, for the Black Death and other plagues took a huge toll of lives, while the Hundred Years' War (1337-1453) kept France in a turmoil. Since the population of this area amounted to some 70 million in 1600, it follows that most of the increase of 17 million (nearly a third) took place after 1450.[1]

[1] Shepard B. Clough and Charles W. Cole, *Economic History of Europe*, pp. 98-9. Copyright 1941 by D. C. Heath & Co., Boston.

More people meant a more rapid migration from the country to the towns, thus furnishing more hands for the rising industries. It meant more men to man the ships, more recruits to fill the ranks of the armies, more colonists to settle overseas. It meant, in turn, a larger demand for fish, grain, and meat, for textiles, pottery, and muskets, for shoes, knives, and Bibles. It meant more profits for those who made and handled these goods, more capital from the profits that were saved, and an increased demand for the luxuries that the profits made possible.

Rise of the Commercial Class

One of the most significant developments of the period was the rise to positions of prominence and power of the new capitalist class. All the influences to which we have called attention worked in this direction: the new secular view, by creating a climate of opinion more favorable to commercial activity; the geographical discoveries and the growth of population, by providing expanding opportunities for men of enterprise; the fresh supplies of the precious metals by making profits more abundant and secure, and capital accumulation easy. The capitalist organiser expanded his activities in all directions. He increased his trade in such staples as grain, fish, and timber. The need for nails, chains, and miscellaneous hardware such as locks, keys, hinges, and lanterns stimulated the rise of many small industries making these articles in Birmingham as early as 1538. Sugar, which in the Middle Ages appeared only on the tables of the very rich, by the middle of the seventeenth century became a common article of diet for all but the poor. Sugar, molasses, and rum were mainstays of the trade with the West Indies at that time. The closely associated traffic in Negro slaves, which began in 1510, rose to a volume of 15 thousand a year in the seventeenth century and 30 thousand, in the eighteenth.

In his role as trader, the capitalist also introduced totally new commodities to Europe: tea, coffee, cocoa, and indigo from the East; tobacco, tomatoes, corn, and potatoes from the Americas. As organiser of industry, he invaded ever new fields. The putting-out system or the large but unmechanised "factory" became dominant, not only in woolen textiles, armor, and mining but also spread to firearms, cutlery, hardware, shipbuilding, and many other industries. The merchant-capitalist became an ever more important figure, both as investor and entrepreneur and as lender to and counselor of ruling kings and princes.

The Rise of National States

Quite as important as the economic expansion of the sixteenth century and the concomitant rise to a position of prominence and influence of the merchant-capitalist was the outstanding political fact of the period—the appearance in western Europe of powerful national states. Until after the middle of the fifteenth century, the terms "England," "France," "Spain," "Netherlands," had principally geographical and linguistic significance— they carried little political meaning. Although there had been kings of England and of France since at least the Norman Conquest, their power to command the loyalty of their subjects was constantly in dispute, ever challenged by the strong feudal nobility. Spain was divided into Castile, Aragon, and regions still dominated by the Moors, while the Low Countries were principalities of the dukes of Burgundy.

Yet during the late medieval period, even while authority remained dispersed among countless feudal nobles, the bases of their power were being gradually eroded. The slow but steady growth of trade brought with it and was supported by an increase in the supply of money. Towns grew and multiplied, expanding the numbers and influence of the wealthy burgher class. The use of money spread, invading even the institution of feudalism, where it led to the conversion of mutual rights and obligations between lord and vassal into contractual payments. With the spread of the money economy, royal monarchs no longer had to depend on feudal levies of armed knights for military support, but could hire mercenaries, using the proceeds of the taxes that replaced contributions in kind. And in the rising burgher class, they found men experienced in business and finance to administer their increasingly complex affairs and to provide, when needed, substantial loans. Finally, the introduction of gunpowder from China, together with the invention of muskets and cannon, destroyed the impregnability of the castle stronghold and relegated chain mail and plate armor to quiet corners of museums.

In spite of these developments favorable to centralised authority, it required the firm hand and strenuous efforts of Henry VII (1485-1509) to establish the royal power and to unify England. His work of national unification was strengthened and consolidated by his great successors, Henry VIII (1509-47) and Elizabeth (1558-1603). In France, it was not until the end of the Hundred Years' War in 1453, when the English claims to almost half of France were liquidated, that it became possible to weld the numerous duchies and counties into a national state subject to a single ruler. Then, building on the long struggle of his predecessors to subdue the feudal nobles, Louis XI (1461-83) used shrewdness and treachery to consolidate the kingdom. From his time on, the authority of the French king was never in serious doubt, and France became one of the major powers of Europe.

Spain's entry upon the international scene was sudden. Though the separate feudal kingdoms of Castile and Aragon spent several centuries in pushing back the Moors, national unity came all at once, with the marriage in 1469 of Ferdinand of Aragon and Isabella of Castile. In the same year that Columbus discovered America, his royal master's troops were engaged in the conquest of Granada, the last remaining stronghold of the Moors. Thereby all of the Iberian peninsula, with the exception of independent Portugal, came under the rule of a single Spanish king.

The Dutch Republic, the fourth of the great powers of Europe in the early modern period, did not emerge until more than a century later. By a succession of marriages, the Low Countries passed from the hands of the last of the dukes of Burgundy to those of Charles V, King of Spain. The intolerance and persecution that Charles's son Philip II visited upon the Dutch Protestants, culminating in the infamous cruelty and butcheries of his delegate, the Duke of Alva, provoked the Dutch into rebellion. For forty years, their bloody struggle against their Spanish oppressors continued, until in 1609 they won effective independence.

Less powerful and populous than the Big Four of the early modern period, yet important constituents of the emerging international community, were five other national states. Sweden achieved a position of power and influence in central Europe in the sixteenth and seventeenth centuries, while Norway and Denmark attained national unity by the beginning of the sixteenth century. The Swiss cantons shook off Hapsburg domination and became independent in 1499, though much time had to elapse before their confederation became strong and well organised. Portugal, as we have seen, had reached a vigorous nationhood by the time of the great geographical discoveries.

The rise of national states led not only to the subjugation of the feudal nobles and their transformation into courtiers of the king, but also to serious conflict with the Church. For the Church was a great landowner, and as such, it exerted temporal as well as spiritual authority, and was the recipient of large incomes. Moreover, as the sole unifying element in western Christendom, it had long exerted the strongest claim to men's loyalties. But the monarchs of the national states, faced with the need to raise large revenues and to enforce their authority over all their numerous subjects, asserted their right to tax the hitherto exempted clergy as well as Church lands. They insisted that temporal authority was theirs exclusively. The resulting struggle ended in victory for the crown. Together with the Reformation and the consequent transfer of religious affiliation in many of the northern countries to Protestantism, it brought an end to the universal authority of the Catholic Church.

THE BASES AND CHIEF ELEMENTS OF MERCANTILIST THOUGHT

We now have before us the chief elements that shaped the economic ideas of the sixteenth and seventeenth centuries. One of them was economic expansion, witnessed in ever-widening channels of trade bringing a growing volume of goods, both old and new, to the burgeoning ports of western Europe, in a flood of gold and silver from the New World boosting prices and profits and supporting rapid capital accumulation; and in a growing population supplying more customers to buy the goods, more workers to make them, more settlers to exploit the resources of the Americas. Another was the rise of the merchant-capitalist class, which furnished the organisers of commercial, shipping, and manufacturing enterprises, and financial advisers and financial sources to royal courts. A third was the new national states, each eager to augment its power, to expand its possessions, and to increase its trade.

Had these features sufficed to describe the main outlines of western Europe in their period, it might well have been an era of peaceful accumulation of wealth, peaceful settlement of the new lands to the west, and rising standards of living. For there was plenty of room for all, ample resources, and unbounded opportunity.

Accumulation and settlement there was, and improvement in living conditions. But there was no peace:

War was almost a normal relationship among national states. From 1494 to 1559 there was fighting nearly every year in some part of Europe; the seventeenth century enjoyed only seven calendar years of complete peace, and England was at war during eighty-four of the 165 years between 1650 and 1815.[2]

A Static View of the World

In part, no doubt, this prevalence of war can be attributed to the very human rivalry of ambitious monarchs, in part to religious zeal and intolerance. Yet in large measure, what was responsible was an essentially static view of the world and its resources. There was no conception, until relatively late, of the immense size of the American continents, of the room

[2] Herbert Heaton, *Economic History of Europe*, p. 228. Copyright 1936 by Harper & Bros., New York.

for expansion, of the increase in wealth that all could hope to share. Within each country, on the other hand, the desire for growth was strong. Merchants, manufacturers, and shippers all wanted to increase the scope of their activities. The kings and ministers of each of the new national states sought to build up its strength and to improve its position. But if the resources available for expansion were strictly limited, as they were thought to be, the desires of one nation were bound to collide with those of others. International conflict was inevitable.

One of the leading students of Mercantilism has described the situation this way:

Within the state, mercantilism consequently pursued thorough-going dynamic ends. But the important thing is that this was bound up with a static conception of the total economic resources in the world; for this it was that created that fundamental disharmony which sustained the endless commercial wars. Both elements together implied that the position of a particular country could change and was capable of progress, but that this could only happen through acquisitions from other countries. This was the tragedy of mercantilism. Both the Middle Ages with their universal static ideal and *laissez faire* with its universal dynamic ideal avoided this consequence. Without grasping this it is impossible to understand mercantilism either in theory or practice.[3]

The Doctrine of State Power

The common desire of the new states of western Europe to expand their wealth, their population, and their territory, combined with the conviction that the opportunity for such growth was severely circumscribed, set the overriding goal of national policy. To increase the power of the state by all possible means must be a nation's primary objective.

This goal, and the world view on which it rested, gave shape and content to Mercantilist ideas and practice. If national power was essential in a narrow and hostile world, how could it best be realised? Military strength is, of course, an important component of national power. Great stress therefore, was laid on the recruitment, training, and supplying of a sizeable army. A large navy was even more important, for the mines providing the vital flow of gold and silver lay overseas, and shipments of these precious metals had to be protected—as likewise the merchant vessels carrying the profitable cargoes of goods of all kinds. Colonies furnished an outlet for a growing population and could supply timber, ships' spars, and other naval stores, as well as an ever-widening variety of raw materials for processing by the skilled workers of the mother country. Colonies were

[3] August Heckscher, *Mercantilism*, Vol. II, pp. 25-6. Copyright 1936 by George Allen & Unwin Ltd., London.

therefore important in their own right, and they also required the protection of strong naval forces.

To feed and supply numerous and unproductive soldiers and sailors, one must be sure of a steady production of muskets, cannon, gunpowder, ships, clothing, and rations. A country therefore had to be economically strong. It must have available a wide range of manufactures and assured supplies of all the raw materials they need. National wealth, in other words, was seen to be the very foundation of national power.

The Necessity of Regulation

If all these things are necessary to ensure the strength of the nation, the question next arises: what is the best way of making certain you have them?

Of one thing Mercantilist statesmen were sure: their provision could not be left to chance, or to the unguided efforts of the individual. His activities must be regulated by the state—they must be subordinated and made to conform to the goal of national power. There was another reason for this preference for regulation of economic activity: no one had much experience with any other policy. Throughout the Middle Ages, the methods used by craftsmen and the quality of their product had been closely controlled by the craft gilds. Choice of an occupation by an individual was free for comparatively few; most people were compelled by tradition to follow in the footsteps of their fathers. Trade, too, had always been subject to jealous and detailed regulation. Thus, regulation of economic activity not only appeared to the statesman of Mercantilist times to be logically necessary; it also had the strong appeal of familiarity.

We can express the gist of the Mercantilist philosophy by describing it as *giving first rank to the goal of national power and adopting regulation of economic life as the preferred means of ensuring the desired increase of wealth.*

Expressions of this viewpoint are abundant in pamphlets and books that poured from the presses of Europe throughout the sixteenth and seventeenth centuries. Interest in economic affairs was keen, especially in matters of current government policy. Contributions to a lively discussion came from prominent merchants, lawyers, financial advisers to governments, and state officials. It is this miscellany of writers who later became known as Mercantilists. In spite of differences on details, they shared a substantial area of agreed opinion, which included the views we have just summarised as the core of Mercantilist doctrine. This concensus is not surprising, for their assumptions were based on the world situation they confronted and which, as members of the same social class, they tended to see in a common light.

The Balance of Trade Theory

In addition to their agreement on the goal of national power, on an abundance of riches as its essential support, and on regulation of economic activity as the best means of attaining national wealth, Mercantilists also shared—what is of particular interest to us—a common theory of international trade. This may be summarily stated as follows: *that a nation could only gain through foreign trade if it had a favorable balance, or an excess in the value of exports over imports.* Since this is the most typical and one of the most important of Mercantilist doctrines, let us examine it more closely.

Its origins are to be found in the peculiar concept of wealth that was all but universal among Mercantilist writers. To them, *wealth consisted above all else in gold and silver.* Only to a very few individuals could any other class of commodities compare in importance with these precious metals. As expressive as any of the nearly axiomatic character of this view is a statement by Antonio Serra:

> How important it is, both for peoples and for princes, that a kingdom should abound in gold and silver, and what great advantages this conveys, . . . I do not propose to discuss in this place; nor how great harm is caused by the lack thereof; for it is my opinion that this is understood by everyone, if not distinctly, at least vaguely.[4]

Other statements of this type abound. Two more will suffice. Thus, Clement Armstrong, an English Mercantilist of the early sixteenth century, asserted that it is "better to have plenty of gold and silver in the realm than plenty of merchants and merchandizes," and Monchrétien, a Frenchman writing a century later, said that: "We live not so much from trade in raw materials as from gold and silver."[5]

Why the Stress on the Precious Metals?

Today we think differently. We recognise that gold and silver are minor components of a nation's wealth, that what really counts is abundance of goods capable of satisfying human wants, and even more, of the productive resources that make a continued flow of such goods possible.

[4] Antonio Serra, *A Brief Treatise on the Causes Which Can Make Gold and Silver Plentiful in Kingdoms Where There Are No Mines,* reprinted in Arthur Eli Monroe, *Early Economic Thought,* p. 145. Copyright 1927 by Harvard University Press, Cambridge.

[5] Cited in Heckscher, *op. cit.,* ii, p. 187.

What led the Mercantilists to take their extreme and untenable position? Probably the most important reason was simply the use of imprecise terms, a practice that is almost unavoidable when a science is in its infancy, but which still plagues economics today. "Wealth" means many things, including the precious metals. But when the Mercantilists lived, money consisted almost exclusively of gold and silver; bank notes and bank credit were yet but little used. And since wealth is measured in money and is constantly being exchanged for it, their confusion is understandable, especially since many Mercantilists were themselves traders.

In addition to confusion as to the meaning of wealth, there were other reasons for according the precious metals a position of paramount importance. They are very durable, and thus serve well as a means of storing up or hoarding wealth. The Mercantilists highly approved saving as a means to the accumulation of wealth, but since their concept of saving was closely akin to hoarding, gold and silver naturally appeared in a preferred light. Again, business was observed to be good when money was abundant, slack when it was scarce.[6] Similarly, a low rate of interest stimulates trade and investment; since the Mercantilists believed there was a close connection between the supply of money and the rate of interest, this gave abundance of money an additional importance.[7] Most obviously of all, money could buy arms, supplies, and the services of troops; as a war chest it had a strong appeal to nations almost constantly engaged in or planning military campaigns.

Given the premise that gold and silver together comprise the most important form of wealth, the balance-of-trade doctrine follows logically and fits perfectly into the more general principles of Mercantilist thought. If the state must be powerful, if wealth is the necessary bulwark of such power, and if money is wealth *par excellence*, then ministers of state must bend every effort to ensure their country an abundant supply of the precious metals.

A nation without gold and silver mines can only obtain these metals from overseas by trade; it must export more than enough to pay for its ordinary imports. *An excess of exports, or a "favorable" balance of trade, is the essential means of acquiring the desired treasure.*

[6] Thus, Jacob Vanderlint, in his *Money Answers all Things* (1734): "Plenty of Money never fails to make Trade flourish; because, where Money is plentiful, the people in general are thereby enabled, and will not fail to be as much greater Consumers of every Thing, as such Plenty of Money can make them; Therefore Trade is always found to flourish as Money grows more plentiful amongst the People."

[7] For a suggestive discussion of this and related points, see J. M. Keynes, *The General Theory of Employment, Interest and Money,* Chapter 23.

An almost unlimited number of Mercantilist writers could be cited as having given expression to this doctrine. As typical as any is the following passage from Thomas Mun:

Although a Kingdom may be enriched by gifts received, or by purchase taken from some other Nations, yet these are things uncertain and of small consideration when they happen. The ordinary means therefore to increase our wealth and treasure is by Forraign Trade, wherein wee must ever observe this rule; to sell more to strangers yearly than wee consume of theirs in value. For suppose that when this kingdom is plentifully served with the Cloth, Lead, Tinn, Iron, Fish and other native commodities, we doe yearly export the over-plus to forraign Countries to the value of twenty two hundred thousand pounds; by which means we are enabled beyond the Seas to buy and bring in forraign wares for our use and Consumptions, to the value of twenty hundred thousand pounds; By this order duly kept in our trading, we may rest assured that the Kingdom shall be enriched yearly two hundred thousand pounds, which must be brought to us in so much Treasure; because that part of our stock which is not returned to us in wares must necessarily be brought home in treasure.[8]

Balance-of-Trade Corollaries

From this basic economic doctrine that the primary goal of economic policy should be the attainment of a favorable balance of trade there followed a number of corollaries. The value of exports should be made as great as possible; this meant that not only should the greatest possible amount of goods be exported, but also that exports of high value were to be preferred to those of low value. For this reason, exports of raw materials were decried; every effort was made to bring about their production at home, and to export the finished product. Imports, of course, must be kept to the minimum; raw materials were to be preferred to manufactures, as being of less value. Imports of the latter, especially of luxury manufactures, were to be severely restricted, if not completely prohibited.

Perhaps the clearest and most concise expression of these ideas is to be found in the work of an Austrian Mercantilist, Von Hornick (1638-1712):

. . . all commodities found in a country, which cannot be used in their natural state, should be worked up within the country; since the payment for manufacturing generally exceeds the value of the raw material by two, three, ten, twenty, and even a hundred fold . . .

The inhabitants of the country should make every effort to get along with their domestic products, to confine their luxury to these alone, and to do without foreign products as far as possible (except where great need leaves no alternative, or if

---

[8] Thomas Mun, *England's Treasure by Forraign Trade,* reprinted in Arthur Eli Monroe, *Early Economic Thought,* p. 171. Copyright 1927 by Harvard University Press, Cambridge.

not need, wide-spread, unavoidable abuse, of which Indian spices are an example). . . .
Such foreign commodities should in this case be imported in unfinished form, and worked up within the country, thus earning the wages of *manufacture* there. . . .

Opportunities should be sought night and day for selling the country's super-fluous goods to these foreigners in manufactured form, so far as this is necessary, and for gold and silver; and to this end, *consumption,* so to speak, must be sought in the farthest ends of the earth, and developed in every possible way. . . .

Except for important considerations, no importation should be allowed under any circumstances of commodities of which there is a sufficient supply of suitable quality at home; and in this matter neither sympathy nor compassion should be shown foreigners, by their friends, kinsfolk, *allies,* or enemies. For all friendship ceases, when it involves my own weakness and ruin. And this holds good, even if the domestic commodities are of poorer quality, or even higher priced. For it would be better to pay for an article two dollars which remain in the country than only one which goes out, however strange this may seem to the ill-informed.[9]

Get the foreigner to pay you as much as possible, pay him as little as you can—this rule extended not only to all goods traffic, but also to other kinds of international payments. The "invisible items," such as freight earnings, insurance payments, travelers' expenses, diplomatic and military expenditures abroad, and so on, were recognised early, and most of the leading Mercantilists urged the necessity of including these in the calculation of a country's favorable balance. The balance they had in mind was therefore a balance of international payments of all kinds, not just a balance of trade items. Thus Mun:

The value of our exportations likewise may be much advanced when we perform it ourselves in our own Ships, for then we get not only the price of our wares as they are worth here, but also the Merchants gains, the charges of ensurance, and fraight to carry them beyond the seas.[10]

MERCANTILISM IN ACTION: CONCRETE POLICIES

From the doctrine of state power and the derived theory of the balance of trade followed most of the concrete policies of Mercantilism.

Regulation of Trade

To anyone who regards trade principally as a means of obtaining a continuous inflow of the precious metals, it cannot be left to itself to develop naturally, but must be constantly watched and regulated. The

[9] Phillip W. Von Hornick, *Austria Over All If She Only Will,* reprinted in *ibid.,* pp. 223-5.
[10] *Ibid.,* p. 174.

Mercantilists developed a formidable apparatus of trade regulations; scarcely any measure that would promote exports or diminish imports, no matter how petty or annoying, was overlooked.

Bullionism. One of the earliest, and certainly the crudest, of Mercantilist restrictions consisted in the direct prohibition of exports of gold or silver bullion. The reasoning underlying bullionism, as it came to be called, was simple, obvious, and naive: if the precious metals do enter the country, keep them there.

Bullionist restrictions go back to the Middle Ages, but were common in the sixteenth and seventeenth centuries. Spain, the recipient of most of the gold and silver from the Americas, applied these restrictions over the longest period and with the greatest severity; it imposed the death penalty for the export of bullion or coin, established rewards for informers, and prohibited the purchase of bullion by foreigners. Yet so great was the appetite for goods in her growing colonies, and even among her own citizens, and so feeble the ability of her backward economy to produce them, that in the face of the flood of gold and silver, prices of commodities soared. Importing became so profitable, corruption of officials so common, that large amounts of specie moved surreptitiously into the hands of foreigners. Spain finally licensed limited exports of gold and silver. In England and Holland, bullionist restrictions virtually came to an end by about the middle of the sixteenth century.

The monopoly of trade. Prominent among Mercantilist measures were those designed to exclude all foreigners from certain areas of trade. Portugal made the monopoly of trade with the East the backbone of her policy throughout the sixteenth century, even going so far as to capture or destroy the ships of interlopers. The king, moreover, kept the trade in his own hands; private traders could carry on only petty dealings, being limited to what they could transport in their cabins on royal ships.

Spain, too, attempted to monopolise the trade with its colonies, though unlike Portugal, it did not try to keep all commerce in royal hands. Private traders bought goods in Spain, and shipped them to the colonies to an agent, who sold them and shipped back specie or colonial produce. All goods had to be carried, however, in royal ships, and traders' activities were subject to the closest inspection and regulation. To make this control more effective, colonial trade was confined to one port in Spain, Seville, and to a limited number of American ports. For protection against pirates, privateers, or organised attack by other nations, after 1560 all west-bound vessels sailed twice annually in great fleets accompanied by warships.

Arrived in the Indies, their shipments were sold at great fairs, the return cargo was loaded aboard, and the fleet sailed back to Spain.

This system worked quite well in the sixteenth century, in spite of considerable smuggling, but broke down in the seventeenth, owing to Spain's increasing economic weakness. Its land eroded by the over-grazing of sheep, its most industrious citizens and most skilled artisans—the Jews and Moors—expelled from the country, its economy ridden by inflation and by heavy taxation to support foreign wars, Spanish industry simply could not produce the goods demanded in its colonial markets. Dutch, English, and French traders, with the connivance of local governors, took over a large share of the trade with Spain's colonies by illegal methods.

Dutch Mercantilism revolved around the monopoly of the East India Company (founded in 1602). Its officials established trading posts in Java, Amboina, and other islands of the East Indies, drove out traders of other nationalities, and thereafter successfully bent every effort to keep them out. In addition to making the Indies its private preserve, the Company practiced every other device of monopoly. It limited the production of certain commodities, such as coffee, pepper, nutmeg, cloves, and indigo, to specific areas, destroying crops raised elsewhere; it used its strong bargaining power to hold to a minimum the prices it paid native growers. The artificially scarce but cheap goods were then sold at high prices in the European market. Small wonder that the Company established a dividend record unequalled in history.

Direct regulation of trade. Through their trading monopolies, the various nations sought to improve the balance of trade by obtaining needed supplies within an imperial area and by buying cheap—and selling dear—things needed by the rest of the world. This same objective was also pursued by the many detailed regulations applied to exports and imports. All the countries of western Europe, with the sole exception of Holland, used these measures extensively, but they were probably more widespread and more highly developed in England than elsewhere.

Thus British exports that could not meet foreign competition unaided were supported at the very least with refunds ("drawbacks") of taxes, internal or external, previously paid on raw materials. If more help was necessary, a subsidy was not hard to get. A more indirect stimulus to exports was sought in obstacles to the export of raw materials. It was thought that by keeping them at home, they would be made abundant and cheap, to the advantage of the exporter of finished products. Export duties were levied on a long list of raw materials and semi-fabricated articles, but total prohibition of such exports was common. The English woolen textile industry, accounting in 1700 for half the country's exports, was thus favored; we find sheep, wool, woolen yarn and worsted, as well as fuller's earth (used in cleaning wool) all on the list of prohibited exports. Enforcement of the law was Draconian in its severity; for the first offense the transgressor was to have his left hand cut off; the second offense carried the death penalty.

Measures aimed at imports paralleled those affecting exports. Instead of receiving a subsidy, practically every good imported into England paid a heavy duty, in a very large number of cases so high as to be prohibitive. As we might expect, direct prohibition of imports applied to England's most important manufactures, both woolen and silk textiles being so favored. Imports of raw materials, on the other hand, were permitted duty-free entry; some (principally naval stores and indigo from the American colonies) were even given bounties.

Each particular regulation, taken by itself, worked to the advantage of some specific industry. Special interests, therefore, worked unremittingly to maintain and extend the system that protected and favored them, yet in so doing they also worked to further the general interest, as it was understood in the Mercantilist economic philosophy.

Here, with a reverse twist, is that coincidence of selfish and public interests that Adam Smith later attributed to the working of laissez faire. He denied it to Mercantilism simply because he refused to accept either its principal goal, the increase of the power of the state, or its basic assumption, the supreme importance of the precious metals.

The Navigation System

If the complex system of trade regulation followed logically from the Mercantilist balance-of-trade doctrine, so likewise did the laws adopted by various countries to foster a native shipping industry. For as it was early recognised, ocean freights could substantially add to or subtract from a country's balance of international payments. Reenforcing this contribution of a merchant fleet to a nation's economic strength was its equally important contribution to its physical strength: merchant vessels—and the fisheries, too—reared up a force of seamen to man the navy, while the ships themselves could be converted into privateers or auxiliary men-of-war, or provide an assured means of bringing in needed foreign supplies. Laws affecting navigation, therefore, bulked large in Mercantilist economic policy. Nowhere did this aspect of national power receive closer attention or fuller expression than in England, whose insular position from early times aroused keen interest in matters relating to the sea.

Although England took her first steps in the regulation of maritime traffic as early as the late fourteenth century, and imposed increasingly exclusive controls as her colonial system developed, two and a half centuries passed before they were strengthened and consolidated in the famous Navigation Acts of 1651 and 1660. The motive leading to the adoption of these laws was the severe inroads on the British carrying trade made by the Dutch while England was preoccupied with the Civil War of 1642-46. Their purpose and effect was to reserve, with as few exceptions as possible, the carriage of freight to and from British and colonial ports to British (including colonial) vessels.

The Navigation Acts succeeded in excluding foreign ships from the British coastal trade, from trade between the colonies and Britain, and from carrying imports from Asia, Africa, or the Americas to Britain or her colonies. British ships, moreover, had to be British built and three-quarters British manned. It was felt unwise, however, to prevent foreigners from taking English exports to non-colonial destinations, for this could mean larger exports, a goal at least as important as a monopoly of the shipping trade. Yet if foreign ships were to be allowed to call at English ports, they must be allowed to bring goods in. Hence imports into the British Isles from the continent were permitted, though they had to pay double duties on arrival, and, to hold down the Dutch entrepot trade, they also had to come direct from the country of origin. Certain specific exceptions to the British monopoly of shipping also had to be granted for practical reasons. Thus, because they needed the spices produced in the Dutch East Indies, goods from the Spanish and Portuguese colonies, commodities coming to Holland overland from Italy, and naval stores, these could be brought to Britain from entrepot centers, even in the ships of their Dutch rivals.

Monopoly of the colonial trade was reenforced by the establishment of a list of "enumerated" commodities, comprising the most important colonial products, which the colonies could export only to other British possessions.[11] This regulation had particular relevance to the extremely profitable trade in sugar and molasses with the Spanish and French West Indies, which the sugar planters of the British West Indies wanted to reserve for themselves. These products went to the American colonies for conversion into rum, which in turn was shipped to Africa, there exchanged for slaves, who were transported to the West Indies. Since a single complete voyage yielded a

[11] At first including only sugar, tobacco, cotton, ginger, indigo, and dye-woods, this list was expanded by a score of commodities in the eighteenth century, and in 1766, all colonial exports to any port north of Cape Finisterre were forbidden.

profit as high as 1000 per cent, no wonder Yankee smuggling proved impossible to stop.

Although Spain and France also endeavored to enforce a monopoly of trade with their colonies, their policy was less rigorous than the British, and less successful.

The Dutch, on the other hand, showed a liberality unusual for this period. Except in the cherished East Indies trade, they relied not upon monopoly but upon competition. They developed the light, easily handled flyboat to replace the clumsy, armed tub in general use, standardised its design, bought construction materials in bulk, and built it by methods resembling the modern assembly line. Besides cheap construction, the need for a small crew and willingness to hire sailors of any nationality at the lowest possible wage—in contrast to the nationality requirements of their rivals—kept operating costs low and Dutch freight rates at levels half to two-thirds those of their competitors. No wonder that in the late seventeenth century perhaps half of Europe's shipping tonnage was Dutch, and that Holland was the shipbuilder to Europe.

The Old Colonial System

In the management of their colonies, the English felt that since they furnished the people and the capital needed for colonial development, they had a right to guide this development in such a way as to serve their major political objective, the increase of national power. According to Mercantilist doctrines, this meant using the colonies as a base of supplies needed by the mother country, as a source of raw materials that could be worked up into manufactures for export, and as a market for the products of English labor.

The means to this end of making colonies serve as the economic complement of the home country were numerous, and we have considered some of them already under other heads. Thus the navigation system, in addition to establishing a semi-monopoly of the carrying trade for British subjects, also formed an integral part of the colonial system. The principle of enumerated commodities, in particular, guaranteed that England would have her pick of these major products of the colonies and that her merchants would secure the profits to be gained from the reexport of any surplus.

In addition to the close regulation of colonial trade contained in the navigation acts, controls were established over the development of colonial industry. Positive encouragement of colonial production of articles wanted in England for consumption or reexport took the form of bounties or of preferential duties on their import into the British Isles. Negative measures of control aimed at the suppression of colonial manufactures in favor of producers in the mother country; these included the prohibition of colonial exports of woolen products and hats and of colonial processing of iron.

In spite of the burdens to which Britain's colonial subjects had to submit, we must remember that the special privileges possessed by English merchants and shippers were shared equally with colonials. The colonial system most injured the interests of consumers: English consumers, like colonial consumers, were sacrificed to the requirements of Mercantilism. Yet as the population and wealth of the colonies increased to the point where local manufacturing industries became significant, their suppression added one more element to the conflict of interests that led to the American Revolution.

The Internal Regulation of Industry

French Mercantilism stressed the guidance and control of domestic industry. Policy in this field followed two principal lines: the deliberate encouragement of manufactures, and the close regulation of almost every aspect of production.

In the seventeenth century, stimulation of manufactures first took the form of grants of tax exemptions, subsidies, and privileges and of the liberal investment of royal funds—as in the establishment of the raw silk and silk manufacturing industry and in many other luxury industries for which France is still famous.

Under Colbert, Louis XIV's great minister, the policy of fostering industrial development was intensified and expanded. Many businesses were made "royal manufactures" (the Gobelins' tapestry works is the best known), a title that carried with it the assurance of sales to the crown as well as the luster and prestige that went with royal patronage.

Colbert carried even further the second aspect of French industrial policy, the state regulation of industry. Building on existing gild controls, he drew up a comprehensive system of uniform regulations for each type of production, imposed them by decree, and tried—with indifferent success —to enforce them through local inspectors appointed from Paris.

England as well as France tried centralised regulation of industry. In the reign of Elizabeth, a major piece of legislation, the Statute of Artificers (1563), brought together and codified into a national system the workable parts of earlier national laws and local regulations. Its more important purposes were the provision of adequate training for industrial workers, who had suffered from the decay of the gilds and the spread of industry to villages and country districts; the ensurance of an ample supply of agricultural labor; and the establishment of greater security of employment. It met these goals by requiring, in every branch of industry, an apprenticeship of seven years; by prescribing in general terms a uniform training in each craft for all England; by making compulsory the employment in agriculture of all workers not engaged in some specific industry; and by setting up as the minimum hiring period the term of one year. In addition, it continued the regulation of wages, established in the mid-fourteenth century to cope with the great shortage of labor resulting from the Black Death.

Two other devices were also tried in England, though much less extensively than in France. Regulation of the quality of goods produced had been practiced in the woolen industry from its early days. To ensure the high quality of English exports, fabrics were subject to inspection by a royal official, the alnager; failure to meet standard specifications resulted in fines and confiscation of unsatisfactory goods. The first decades of the seventeenth century saw the extension of official supervision to the silk trade, to the smelting of iron, tin, and lead, and to the mining of coal.

Industrial policy was never as important in Holland or Spain as in either France or England. Holland, as we have seen, concentrated upon securing and maintaining a monopoly of the trade with the East Indies. At home, she followed a policy of relatively free trade and free conduct of industry. Spain likewise strove, though much less successfully, to rivet a monopoly control upon the trade of her American colonies; this implied the exclusion of foreign wares and merchants from Spanish markets. But Spanish industry simply could not deliver the goods, and her colonial markets were increasingly supplied by imports from other parts of Europe.

Labor Under Mercantilism

Trade, colonial, and navigation policies were, as we have stressed, shaped by the Mercantilist balance-of-trade theory. So too were the views and policies of Mercantilists toward labor, which in an age when capital equipment was limited mainly to comparatively simple tools, was clearly the chief factor of production, especially in manufacturing. Since exports of manufactures ranked high as a means of obtaining the precious metals, it is, therefore, only natural that Mercantilists stressed the need for a large and growing population to ensure an ample supply of labor, or that they advocated measures to stimulate its increase, such as rewards for marriage, bounties for children, and penalties on the unmarried. Indeed, they even

went so far as to concede labor "a position of strategic importance." [12]
Expressions such as the following were common:

The people are the riches and strength of the country. (Nicholas Barbon)

Is not that country richest which has the most labor? (Josiah Tucker)

That the strength and riches of a society consists in the numbers of the people
is an assertion which hath attained the force of a maxim in politics. (Henry
Fielding)

If the quantity of labor was important, its skill and industriousness were
equally so, for these qualities would enable it to produce more and better
exports. Almost without exception, economic writers of the Mercantilist
period emphasised the need for habits of industry and the acquisition of
manufacturing skills.

But what of wages? It would appear that those who hold that "the
people are the riches and strength of the country" should also want to
see them well paid, comfortable, and satisfied with their lot. Most Mercantilists, however, held quite the contrary view. In order to have a
favorable balance of trade, it was necessary to be able to undersell the
foreign rival. Labor, being the largest element in cost, therefore must be
cheap. Large numbers of workers were needed, not only to ensure a large
volume of manufactures for export, but also to guarantee low wages, low
cost, and strong competitive ability.

We know today that it does not necessarily follow that labor costs will
be low only if wages are low. High wages are consistent with low labor
costs if the productivity of labor is high. But among Mercantilists the
opinion was widespread that high wages induced, not greater industry,
but idleness and sloth. Thus, Arthur Young, a widely traveled and intelligent
observer of the middle of the eighteenth century, merely expressed the
common viewpoint of many other contemporary and earlier writers when
he said:

Every one but an idiot knows that the lower classes must be kept poor or they
will never be industrious; I do not mean, that the poor of England are to be kept
like the poor of *France*, but, the state of the country considered, they must (like
all mankind) be in poverty or they will not work.[13]

A low opinion of the motives that stimulated the workman to effort
thus combined with the balance-of-trade theory (and with the self-interest
of the employing classes) to establish the necessity of low wages as a firmly

[12] Edgar S. Furniss, *The Position of the Laborer in a System of Nationalism*, p. 31.
Copyright 1930 by Houghton, Mifflin Co., Boston. The quotations immediately following
are from p. 22n.

[13] Arthur Young, *Eastern Tour* (1771) iv, p. 361, cited in Furniss, *op cit.*, p. 118.

held doctrine. At the same time, it was believed with equal conviction that labor was of vital importance in the national economy. There is no inconsistency in the two ideas, however. An abundance of labor, as a source of exports and thus of treasure, was a necessary condition of national wealth and power. But this labor must be industrious and productive; if poverty is essential to make the laborer work, then low wages are just as much a necessary condition as an ample supply of labor.

Although it was easy for the Mercantilist to accord labor a position of great importance while at the same time denying it a reward much above mere subsistence, how could he possibly reconcile "the riches of the nation" with a people many of whom were in rags, and most of whom were poorly clad, badly housed, and ill fed? The reconciliation was simple. To the typical Mercantilist, the welfare of the common man had nothing to do with national wealth. That nation was rich which had, not a prosperous and well-fed population, but abundance of "treasure." To a person obsessed with the importance of gold and silver, convinced of the necessity of having a favorable balance of trade to obtain the precious metals, and sure that the only way to make people work hard was to keep them poor, the poverty of the common man was a national asset. A rich nation and a poor people were not incompatible, but actually complementary. To such paradoxical lengths were they led by a short-sighted view of the nature of wealth.

SELECTED REFERENCES

Clough, Shepard B., and Cole, Charles W., *Economic History of Europe* (D. C. Heath & Co., Boston, 1941).

Ferguson, W. K., *The Renaissance* (Henry Holt & Co., New York, 1940). An excellent brief statement of the major changes western society underwent in this exciting period.

Furniss, Edgar S., *The Position of the Laborer in a System of Nationalism* (Houghton, Mifflin Co., Boston, 1930). This book, especially Chapter II, contains a full and eminently readable account of the laborer in Mercantilist thought.

Heaton, Herbert, *Economic History of Europe* (Harper & Bros., New York, 1936). Both this and the text by Clough and Cole contain good chapters on the background of the Mercantilist period.

Heckscher, August, *Mercantilism*, 2 Vols. (Geo. Allen & Unwin, Ltd., London, 1936). This is the most comprehensive study of Mercantilism available, both with respect to theory and practice.

Lipson, E., *A Planned Economy or Free Enterprise*, 2nd edition. (Adam & Chas. Black, London, 1946). Chapter II is interesting for its argument that Mercantilism was a "planned economy."

Mosse, George L., *The Reformation* (Henry Holt & Co., New York, 1953). An excellent brief special study.

Viner, Jacob, *Studies in the Theory of International Trade* (Harper & Bros., New York, 1937). Chapters I and II provide the best discussion available of the Mercantilist theory of foreign trade as it was expressed in England.

3

THE TRANSITION TO ECONOMIC LIBERALISM

Any period of history is transitional, in the sense that it is not static, but is undergoing changes that foreshadow what is to come, while at the same time it clings to and only gradually sheds habits and institutions of an earlier age. Thus in the period from 1500 to 1750, Mercantilist views were dominant, but were themselves permeated and also in conflict with medieval doctrines and practices. Simultaneously, the theory and practice of Mercantilism underwent change, as the social class that spawned it, the merchant capitalists, became more numerous, more powerful, and more confident. The parallel institution of princely rule was also drastically modified, especially in England, as the national state to whose needs it ministered became more firmly established and secure in its power. And both economic ideas and the principles and practices of government reflected the influence of the spread of the scientific spirit and the changes it wrought in men's outlook on the world.

Continuity of History

In sum, the Middle Ages did not end in 1500, nor did the age of laissez faire begin with Adam Smith. The one extended its hold far into modern times, the other began as a seedling long before it came to flower. The historian G. M. Trevelyan clearly expresses this continuity of history in the following passage:

It is indeed useless to look for any date, or even for any period, when the Middle Ages "ended" in England. All that one can say is that, in the Thirteenth Century, English thought and society were mediaeval, and in the Nineteenth Century they were not. Yet even now we retain the mediaeval institutions of the Monarchy, the Peerage, the Commons in Parliament assembled, the English Common Law, the Courts of Justice interpreting the rule of law, the hierarchy of the established Church, the parish system, the Universities, the Public Schools and Grammar Schools. And unless we become a Totalitarian State and forget all our Englishry, there will always be something mediaeval in our ways of thinking, especially in our idea that people and corporations have rights and liberties which the State ought in some degree to respect, in spite of the legal omnicompetence of Parliament. Conservatism and Liberalism, in the broadest sense, are both mediaeval in origin, and so are trade unions. The men who established our civil liberties in the Seventeenth Century, appealed to mediaeval precedents against the "modernizing" monarchy of the Stuarts. The pattern of history is indeed a tangled web. No single diagram will explain its infinite complication.[1]

Just as no powerful social habits have suddenly lost their influence, so none has suddenly sprung into being. The individualistic age which was to follow Mercantilism was not the creation of the "classical" economists, but was germinating and slowly taking shape in an environment of state regulation and of restrictions aiming at the maximum favorable balance of trade.

The problem of this chapter is to trace the major strands out of which there grew a new philosophy of government and a new economic viewpoint that were to achieve dominance for a time, and then become modified, qualified, and eventually, perhaps, superseded by still other philosophies of government and economics more suited to the changed society they both shaped and mirrored.

THE INFLUENCE OF THE RISING CAPITALIST CLASS

The most important single contribution to the decline of the Mercantilist system of ideas and regulations and to the rise of economic individualism came from the growth in the numbers, wealth, and influence of the rising class of business men. Comparatively few and unimportant as a class in the late fifteenth century, by the eighteenth, they were numerous, rich, and powerful. They then dominated the affairs of cities and towns, were heavily represented in Parliament, and carried great weight in councils of state.

Challenge and Response

Their rise was made possible by the rapid expansion to whose increasing opportunities they responded vigorously and successfully. We have seen how the great geographical discoveries opened up a new world of trade, both in the Americas and in the East. To the stimulus of an expanding trading area was added the further stimulus of rising prices, supported by the seepage of the precious metals out of Spain and by occasional large leaks engineered by the daring piracy of men like Drake, Hawkins, and Frobisher. Trade offered rich rewards, capital accumulation proceeded in almost geometrical progression, and merchants, manufacturers, shippers, and bankers, English and Dutch above all, waxed prosperous and powerful.

[1] G. M. Trevelyan, *English Social History*, pp. 95-6. Copyright 1942 by Longmans, Green and Co., New York. Reprinted by permission of the publisher.

As the older industrial organisation of the craft gilds proved incapable of meeting the demands of an expanding economy, its place was taken, in industry after industry, by individual enterprise. The domestic system, with the merchant capitalist in the central guiding role, became common and eventually predominant, not only in the woolen trade, but also in ship-building, iron production and manufacture, mining, and in occupation after occupation, until by the eighteenth century, this system, supplemented and sometimes over-shadowed here and there by small factories, was typical, and gild organisation, an occasional survival of the past.

The substitution of the individual businessman for the corporate gild led to a radical change in the ideals by which men measured their accomplishments. The new aim of getting rich quick replaced the older ideal of a "suitable" income. The medieval notion of the regulation of economic activity according to moral principles gave way to the pursuit of wealth for its own sake.

At first this led, as we have seen, to the near-worship of the precious metals and to the regulation of trade so as to create a favorable balance of trade and an inflow of gold and silver.

Freedom Favors Expansion

Yet at the very time that these Mercantilist tendencies were strongest, individuals here and there perceived that their desire for gain would best be served by freedom. A free market, it became slowly but increasingly apparent, offered greater scope for individual initiative, and where individual initiative was least hampered, output could be most rapidly increased, costs could be lowered by using new methods and new sources of supply, and gain could be maximised. The desire of particular business men for freedom to expand their activities led to pronouncements and appeals in favor of the relaxation of Mercantilist restrictions.

This dislike of regulation appeared early. Thus, in 1550, a Sir John Masone, expressing himself with respect to a proclamation regulating the price of butter and cheese, said:

I have seen so many experiences of such ordinances; and ever the end is dearth, and lack of the thing that we seek to make *good cheap*. Nature will have her course, . . . and never shall you drive her to consent that a *penny*-worth of new shall be sold for a *farthing*. . . . For who will keep a cow that may not sell the milk for so much as the merchant and he can agree upon? [2]

[2] Cited in H. M. Robertson, *Aspects of the Rise of Economic Individualism*, p. 70. Copyright 1933 by Cambridge University Press.

Another illustration, a half century later in date, is furnished by the comment of Sir Walter Raleigh on a bill making compulsory the sowing of a certain proportion of hemp:

For my part, I do not like this constraining of men to use their grounds at our wills. Rather let every man use his ground to that which is most fit for, and therein use his own discretion.[3]

The slow accretion of such views as these went on steadily, building up, bit by bit, a widening sentiment in favor of freedom. At the same time, the belief that regulation and restriction of industry and of *internal* trade was necessary underwent gradual erosion.

Decline of State Control

The spreading dislike of regulation was strongly reenforced by experience, especially in England. For state control of industry, in particular the system of monopoly grants, had worked badly. Partly to domesticate industries that had grown up abroad or to develop new industries, partly to obtain revenue, the crown had adopted the system of granting monopolies to individuals or groups in return for a lump payment or a share of the profits. During the late sixteenth and early seventeenth centuries, such English industries as glass, salt, soap, alum mining, pin manufacturing, the production of wire, and the sale of coal came under this system. The result, quite generally, was high prices, poor quality, and inadequate supplies. "Nearly all the monopolists promised to supply a better quality more cheaply. In no single case was this promise fulfilled."[4] But not only were the monopolies grasping; they were also inefficient and corrupt, frequently being given, not to the most promising enterpriser, but to court favorites and their friends.

Public indignation mounted, became vocal, and expressed itself vigorously in meetings, pamphlets, and speeches in Parliament. Finally, with the establishment of that body's supremacy by the Revolution of 1688, the royal right of dispensation was abolished. Thereafter the individual was free to develop any industry to which he might be attracted.

But dislike of regulation did not stop at government-supported monopolies; it extended also to those survivals of the Middle Ages, wage and price regulations. The central agency that supervised and administered these ordinances was the Privy Council, a sort of super-cabinet. Their local enforcement was in the hands of the Justices of the Peace. With the abolition

---

[3] *Ibid.*
[4] Herman Levy, *Economic Liberalism*, p. 30. Copyright 1913 by The Macmillan Company, London.

of the Privy Council at the time of the Cromwellian Revolution (1642-46), the whole system of regulation lost its head; its hands and feet continued to function as before for a time, but showed increasing feebleness and lack of coordination. The Justices of the Peace were overburdened with a multitude of duties; where opposition to the wages and price legislation was strong, they tended to permit it to become a dead letter. Its enforcement became more and more sporadic. By the eighteenth century, the system of regulation was in an advanced stage of decay.

Other aspects of state control also declined or disappeared in the latter part of the seventeenth or in the eighteenth century. Thus the regulation of the quality of various kinds of goods, which had been enforced by agents of the crown, was abandoned when Parliament became the dominant institution of government. Even the Elizabethan Statute of Artificers, which regulated the conditions of apprenticeship, became more limited in its application, trade after trade being exempted by Parliament from its scope.

Thus, by the end of the seventeenth century there had been a strong growth of sentiment in favor of economic freedom and a great increase in the actual area of freedom. These tendencies were the result of the rise of an important capitalist trading and industrial class, itself the response of the individualist side of human nature to the expanding opportunities that appeared after the great geographical discoveries.

RELIGION

All during the Middle Ages, the influence of religion had been on the side of society against the individual. It had supported with its authority the medieval system of status, in which each person had his place, with established rights and established responsibilities, and it also contributed greatly to the framework of social organisation. The Church refused to countenance the taking of interest on loans, or usury, or the charging of more than the "just price." To do either was to be guilty of extortion and thus of the sin of avarice. Indeed, the Church and its ethical teachings permeated society and the daily lives of men.

As the opportunities for commercial activity increased and the commercial motive of gain became an ever more powerful force, the growing desire for individual freedom began to push against all obstacles that stood in its way. We have just seen how this force modified law and opinion in the sixteenth and seventeenth centuries. Religion was by no means excepted from its influence. Even in the Middle Ages, the doctrines of usury and of "just price" underwent a gradual softening which made them more agreeable to the investor and the trader. As the commercial and industrial classes became more numerous and more influential, their views, reflecting the changing facts of economic life, forced the Churches, both Catholic and Protestant, into a step-by-step retreat.

. . . The Churches, one and all, have had to accommodate themselves to an extraneous development of a busy commercial spirit, . . . capitalism has created, or found already existent, its own spirit, and set the Churches the task of assimilating it.[5]

Religion generally fought a losing battle with the individualism of the shop or the market place. In the case of the Protestant churches, individualism actually invaded the sacred precincts, turning them to its own purposes. Although, as Tawney shows, conservatism and communal discipline were strong in the early days of Protestantism, by the seventeenth century, they had succumbed to the demand for economic freedom.[6] The later Protestant church actively facilitated the spread of individualism. Thus the Puritan doctrine of work stressed the virtues of economic activity and regarded indolence as a sin. Puritanism ridiculed and abhorred sport, license, and loose living, and exhorted its members to frugality, close attention to business, and productive effort. Rather than being tolerated as necessary to life, business was exalted as a suitable calling for a Christian.

Protestantism strengthened the forces of individualism in another way. For an essential feature of Protestantism was its challenge to authority. By stressing individual freedom of conscience, it stimulated an individualist and anti-authoritarian attitude toward religion. It was no accident that the most numerous element in the prosperous English middle class was the Dissenters, nor that their opposition to the Church of England led them into opposition to its ally, the monarchy, and to the rebellion that ended in the supremacy of Parliament.

THE DECAY OF MERCANTILIST VIEWS

Our study of Mercantilism showed how a tendency to identify wealth with money led to undue stress on the importance of the precious metals, and how this fallacy, in turn, lay at the root of that unique Mercantilist doctrine, the need for a country without mines to have a favorable balance of trade.

With the passage of time, both these cornerstones of Mercantilist theory were subjected to criticism that eventually led to their overthrow. Thus,

[5] H. M. Robertson, *Aspects of the Rise of Economic Individualism,* p. 165. Copyright 1933 by Cambridge University Press.
[6] See Tawney, *op. cit.,* especially Ch. IV.

although the view that money was all-important continued to be expressed well into the eighteenth century, in the latter part of the seventeenth century, criticisms of this view became increasingly numerous and a broader understanding of the real nature of wealth, more general.[7]

Influence of Quantity Theory of Money

It was the development and acceptance of the quantity theory of money that finally provided the basis for the undermining of Mercantilism's most characteristic doctrine. This theory had been stated in simple form several times during the seventeenth century, but it had not been thoroughly incorporated into current thought, hence its inconsistency with the balance-of-trade doctrine was not perceived. Locke, writing in the 1690's, finally gave a clear and emphatic statement of the quantity theory,[8] but even he failed to see its relevance to the basic Mercantilist position. He went so far as to say that prices in different countries must be equal or close together, and that if they were not, a country with low prices would do a large volume of business, while industry would stagnate in a country with high prices, but there he stuck.

Dudley North, a critic of Mercantilism writing at the same time as Locke, stated that the supply of money adjusts itself automatically between nations according to the needs of trade.[9] But lacking a grasp of the quantity theory of money, he too failed to bring about the downfall of Mercantilism's main theoretical support.

The Price Specie-Flow Theory

This task fell to David Hume, who in a straightforward, effective passage brought the quantity theory of money and the balance-of-trade theory into direct juxtaposition, with a result that was logically fatal to the latter.

---

[7] Viner cites Mun (1621), Papillon (1677), Barbon (1696), Davenant (1698), and Jocelyn (1718) as critics of the more extreme Mercantilist position and as adherents of a more adequate view of wealth. (*Studies in the Theory of International Trade,* p. 20.) Also to be included are North (1691) and Clement (1695).

[8] "Money, whilst the same quantity of it is passing up and down the kingdom in trade, is really a standing measure of the falling and rising of other things, in reference to one another: and the alteration of price is truly in them only. But if you increase, or lessen, the quantity of money, current in traffic, in any place, then the alteration of value is in the money: and, if at the same time wheat keep its proportion of vent to quantity, money, to speak truly, alters its worth, and wheat does not, though it sell for a greater, or less price, than it did before. For money, being looked upon as the standing measure of other commodities, men consider and speak of it still, as if it were a standing measure, though when it has varied its quantity, it is plain it is not." (John Locke, *Some Considerations, etc., Works,* Vol. 5, p. 43.)

[9] See James W. Angell, *The Theory of International Prices,* pp. 16-18. Copyright 1926 Harvard University Press, Cambridge.

Suppose four fifths of all the money in Great Britain to be annihilated in one night . . . what would be the consequence? Must not the price of all labour and commodities sink in proportion . . . ? What nation could then dispute with us in any foreign market, or pretend to navigate or to sell manufactures at the same price, which to us would afford sufficient profit? In how little time, therefore, must this bring back the money which we had lost and raise us to the level of all the neighboring nations? Where, after we arrived, we immediately lose the advantage of the cheapness of labour and commodities; and the farther flowing in of money is stopped by our fullness and repletion.[10]

Here we have the essentials of what is known as the classical price specie-flow analysis. Prices in any one country are determined by the quantity of money; prices in different countries are interdependent—a low-price country can undersell a high-price country; such underselling will lead to a flow of specie to the low-price country, raising prices there and lowering them in the other country. Equilibrium is finally reached with some common relationship between national price levels.

After this, it remained for Adam Smith to add an explanation of the advantages of international trade, to dissect and expose the Mercantilist system in detail and with abundant ridicule, and to offer as a substitute for its restrictive philosophy the philosophy of individualism. This was in itself a great work, but the negative task of destroying the intellectual foundations of Mercantilism had already been accomplished by David Hume.

INDIVIDUALISM IN POLITICAL THOUGHT

Modern philosophy starts with Descartes, and with good reason. To him, writing at the time (the 1630's and '40's) when scientific inquiry was replacing reliance on authority as the source of knowledge, the universe appeared ruled by laws discoverable by human reason. Since the use of reason was an individual matter, the independence and importance of the individual as a discoverer and interpreter of the world about him were vastly stimulated.

Locke and Limits on Government
This modern view of the world was accepted by and applied to the problems of politics by John Locke. In the state of nature, governed by its own laws, he assumed all men were equal. Because of this equality, men were endowed with certain natural rights, which Locke identified—as a citizen of

---

[10] David Hume, *Essay of the Balance of Trade*, cited in Arthur Eli Monroe, *Early Economic Thought*, p. 325. Copyright 1927 by Harvard University Press, Cambridge.

seventeenth century England—with life, liberty, and the enjoyment of property. But since men, though equal in their rights, are unequal in intelligence, they will interpret natural law differently. The result is chaos and confusion. Government is necessary to ensure order and the peaceful pursuit by each man of his natural rights. Men instituted government by a social contract, endowing it with the power to make laws to secure life, liberty, and property, but no more. Government thus has a distinctly limited function—to permit individuals to live, not as they would in a state of nature, but according to the underlying laws of nature.

Revolution against a tyrannical government is implicit in such a concept, for a tyrannical government oversteps the limits of the social contract. But revolution, if necessary, should be the act of a majority. And to avoid tyranny, government should be democratic—it should reflect the will of the majority.

Thus Locke was the exponent of limited, democratic government, designed to serve the interest of individuals. His political liberalism, applied to the relations of Parliament and King in the English Revolution of 1688 and copied and elaborated by numerous followers, became the intellectual foundation of the British government, of the American Declaration of Independence, and as interpreted by Rousseau, of the French Revolution.

ADAM SMITH AND THE NEW ECONOMICS

Production for the Market

By the middle of the eighteenth century, the commercial and political revolutions of early modern times had completed their work. In England and Holland, and to a lesser extent in other countries, a simple agricultural society had been transformed into a complex economy with a thriving industry and commerce. Trade, no longer confined mainly to local markets, was conducted on a national and worldwide scale. Instead of wool and wheat, England now exported textiles, wares of iron and pewter, shoes, hats, leather goods, and coal. The domestic system of industry, supplemented here and there by small mills and factories, was now predominantly capitalistic. Labor received its raw materials, its orders, and often its tools from a capitalist employer; it received a money wage, fixed mainly by market forces, for its skill and effort. A developed system of banking, involving the widespread use of bills of exchange and the issue of bank notes, and headed by the Bank of England (established 1694) had come into being to serve the needs of industry and trade.

Above all, the guidance of economic activity was no longer subject to the control of gild, town authority, or church, or king. The questions of what to produce, by what methods, and at what price were now decided by the individual enterpriser serving an impersonal and ever-growing market.

Even in agriculture, production for the market had replaced the old communal system of the manor. Transfer of property had become increasingly free, and many small holdings had been bought up and consolidated by the more enterprising peasants. Serfdom had ceased with the reign of Elizabeth, and farming was now carried on by small freeholders and by tenants working the large- and medium-sized farms of the gentry. The numbers of the latter were steadily augmented by the purchase of farms by well-to-do businessmen desirous of acquiring the status of landowners. The enclosure movement, involving the union into a few large properties of the scattered small holdings of the manorial open-field system, had begun with the scarcity of labor after the Black Death (1348-49). As the English woolen industry became more important, the demand for its raw materials became steadily greater, sheep-raising became more profitable than arable farming, and enclosures increased rapidly under the Tudors. Yet the amount of land enclosed by the end of the seventeenth century was probably only a small proportion of the total.[11] The disappearance of the old open-field system awaited the tremendous burst of enclosures in the latter half of the eighteenth century.

The modern state, no longer new and untried, but secure and well established, had less need to shape every policy with an eye to the increase of its power. It could tolerate greater freedom of the individual to pursue his own interests. Moreover, in Holland, the machinery of government had been taken over by the commercial classes, while in England they shared its control with landed proprietors. Mercantilist restrictions on internal trade and industry, together with those medieval survivals that Mercantilism supported, disappeared with the declining interest of government in their retention and the rising interest of traders and manufacturers in their abolition. With the progress of economic inquiry, even that pillar of the Mercantilist ideology, the favorable balance of foreign trade—a concept not unwelcome to the exporting classes—was rudely shaken.

Adam Smith and "the Invisible Hand"

Though the spirit of individualism was already dominant in the mid-eighteenth century and had received its political expression in the writings of Locke, it still awaited formulation as a rounded economic philosophy. This

---

[11] On the enclosure movement, see W. H. R. Curtler, *A Short History of English Agriculture*, especially Ch. VII, IX, and XI. Clarendon Press, Oxford, 1909.

it was the great task of Adam Smith to perform. What Locke had done for government, he did for economics. Taking the prevalent view of the universe as ruled by natural law, and of individual enterprise as the most efficient means of getting goods produced, he constructed a thorough-going, individualist economic system. The central core of his ideas may be summarised in the following propositions:

Each man is best fitted to be the judge of his own actions.

Individual interests are not in conflict, but are subject to a natural harmony.

Therefore, the selfish actions of individuals lead to the welfare of all, and the continuous regulation of government is unnecessary. The best results can be obtained if the state follows a policy of let-alone, of laissez faire.

But let Adam Smith speak for himself:

As every individual endeavors as much as he can both to employ his capital in the support of domestic industry, and so to direct that industry that its produce may be of the greatest value; every individual necessarily labours to render the annual revenue of the society as great as he can. He generally, indeed, neither intends to promote the public interest, nor knows how much he is promoting it. By preferring the support of domestic to that of foreign industry, he intends only his own gain, and he is in this, as in many other cases, led by an invisible hand to promote an end which was no part of his intention. Nor is it always the worse for the society that it was no part of it. By pursuing his own interest he frequently promotes that of the society more effectually than when he really intends to promote it.[12]

From this reasoning comes a major conclusion. The "Wealth of Nations" is best served, not by minute regulation—of which there were many survivals, especially in the field of foreign trade—but by the greatest possible freedom of enterprise. The business man's yearning for economic freedom is now entirely justified. Full release of his energies is the right prescription for a prosperous society.

No wonder that Adam Smith's philosophy of laissez faire received wide acceptance, becoming the ruling economic doctrine of the nineteenth century. For it told the rising commercial and industrial classes, who were soon to achieve political dominance, to do what they wanted to do.

Protection Survives

Adam Smith did not confine his recommendation of freedom to internal economic affairs—he also vigorously advocated a policy of free trade.[13] But

---

[12] Adam Smith, *The Wealth of Nations*, p. 400, Modern Library Edition.
[13] For a brief discussion of his theory of international trade, see below, Chapter 5.

his prescription had little in the way of immediate, practical results. Beneficiaries of protection were loath to give it up, even though they did not need it, and even though they agreed with his basic philosophy. Moreover, the most significant restrictions on foreign trade, the very core and center of English protectionism, were the duties on grain, or, as they were generally known, the Corn Laws. The landowning classes, whose interests these served, were still the numerically dominant group in Parliament.

Not until the Reform Act of 1832, which gave wider representation to the urban middle class, was a frontal assault on the Corn Laws politically possible. And not until the interests of merchants and manufacturers in free trade were more clearly apparent than in 1776, when Adam Smith wrote, could a powerful body of opinion be marshaled behind a free-trade movement. The growth of this opinion had to await the impact of the Industrial Revolution.

THE INDUSTRIAL REVOLUTION: TECHNICAL ASPECTS

Although individualism was the dominating philosophy in politics, economics, and religion by the time Adam Smith wrote *The Wealth of Nations*, the full consequences of the unleashing of the individual's energies were not brought out until the Industrial Revolution had transformed England from an economy of household industry, based on skilled labor adept in the use of tools, to an economy of factories and mills, based on machines and steam power.

Inventions: A Chain Effect

On the technical side, the Industrial Revolution was a series of interrelated inventions, each meeting some immediate and pressing industrial need, but upsetting the balance of industry so that additional inventions became an urgent necessity. Consider, for example, the sequence of development in the cotton textile industry. The production of cotton fabrics (actually fustians, a cloth half linen and half cotton) had first been established in England about 1600, on the same household basis as its older rival, the woolen industry. For a century, its growth was very gradual until, in the opening years of the eighteenth century, the importation of cotton prints, and even their wear, was prohibited. These colorful prints, a product of Indian hand looms, had become so popular that they aroused the strenuous opposition of the woolen and silk industries. English-made fustians, however, met no such obstacles; with the elimination of the competition of pure cotton fabrics, for which they were a fairly satisfactory substitute, their production expanded swiftly.

The first of the textile inventions was a simple improvement in the old loom designed to remedy a defect that hampered the expansion of production. Hitherto, the width of the fabric that could be made by a single workman had been limited by the length of his arms, for he had to throw the shuttle containing the cross thread, or woof, from one hand to the other. For wider fabrics, two or more men had to be employed. In 1733, John Kay, a weaver with mechanical talent, developed the flying shuttle, fitted with wheels and propelled mechanically with sufficient force so that a much wider stretch of warp threads could be traversed.

Because the flying shuttle permitted a considerable expansion in the output of the weaving branch of the textile industry, it upset its balance. The spinning process had always required five or six men to supply one weaver with thread. Now the spinners found it impossible to keep up with the demand. The need for improvement in this stage of the industry became acute. The Society for the Encouragement of Arts and Manufactures offered a prize for a suitable invention,[14] and many men worked intensely on the problem.

Finally, between 1769 and 1779, three inventions revolutionised spinning —Hargreaves' spinning jenny, Arkwright's water frame, and Crompton's mule. The jenny made possible the spinning by one operator of several threads, of fine quality, but too weak to replace linen in the warp. Arkwright's water frame furnished a coarser but stronger thread which could be spun by power-driven machinery and which permitted for the first time the manufacture in England of pure cotton goods.[15] The mule combined the principles of the jenny and the water frame and made a thread that was both fine and strong. It soon came to be fitted with three to four hundred spindles, so that a single machine did the work of that many individual spinners, each working with a single spinning wheel. Fortunately, at about the time that these advances in spinning made it possible to work up much larger quantities of the raw material, an American, Eli Whitney, developed his cotton gin (1793). By permitting the easy extraction of the rough seeds from the boll, his invention enabled the processing of enough cotton to keep up with rapidly expanding demand.

[14] Paul Mantoux, *The Industrial Revolution in the Eighteenth Century*, p. 220. Copyright 1927. Harcourt, Brace & Co., New York. This book contains one of the best accounts available of the role played by inventions in the Industrial Revolution. I am much indebted to it.

[15] It was Arkwright's defense of his industry before Parliament that resulted in freeing it from the prohibition against cotton manufactures.

The new spinning machines gave a great impetus to factory production, since they could be operated most economically by water (later steam) power, and thus had to be brought together in large numbers where the power was available. Arkwright, whose claims as an inventor are at least dubious, was above all else a man of great business ability. He succeeded in raising capital, training workmen, and building and setting into operation a large number of factories, employing from 150 to 600 hands. His fame thus has a legitimate basis mainly in the fact that he was the first of the new class of industrial capitalists who, seizing upon the inventions of others, were to transform Britain's cottage industry in the next hundred years. Even in the cotton textile industry, his example was soon followed by many others, while similar men-of-business made over the iron and steel trades.

By 1790, when the inventions in spinning were widely used, the different parts of the textile industry were again badly out of balance. Whereas thirty years earlier, thread had been scarce, now there were not enough weavers to work up all the thread streaming out of the spinning mills. A chance discussion set a country parson named Cartwright to proving that a power loom was not, as the company present had alleged, an impossibility. After several years of effort, he proved his point in 1785. But it took years more for his invention to make its way in industry, owing mainly to the violent opposition it met from handloom weavers. Not until about 1810 was the power loom widely used, but within a few years more, it was universal in the cotton industry.

In the manufacture of wool, the spinning inventions took hold rapidly, especially in Yorkshire, where wages rose from the competition of the neighboring Lancashire cotton districts and where abundant water power was to be found. The power loom, partly because of strenuous opposition to its introduction, partly because it was less adapted to weaving woolen fabrics, made much slower progress. In 1803, according to Mantoux, only one-sixteenth of the cloth production of the main Yorkshire woolen district was factory-made. Large numbers of handlooms continued to be operated until late in the nineteenth century.

As in the textile industries, a succession of inventions upset the balance of the iron industry, each leading to further development. Thus the opening years of the eighteenth century found the English iron industry quite incapable of meeting the demands of the Midland iron workers for pig iron; it was even on the point of disappearing. Ever since prehistoric man discovered how to extract the metal from its ore, its manufacture had been dependent on charcoal for smelting. By 1720, almost all wooded areas near enough to iron mines to permit economic production had been destroyed. In that year, but sixty blast furnaces, producing only some 17 thousand tons of pig iron annually, were in operation in England.[16] The country was becoming increasingly dependent on imports of pig iron from Sweden, Germany, Spain, and the American colonies. Coal was abundant and was widely used as a fuel in many countries, but it could not be combined with iron ore to smelt pig iron because its sulphur content made the product too brittle for use. A method of making coal into a serviceable smelting agent had to be devised and was actively sought throughout the seventeenth century. Finally, about 1709, an English iron-master named Abraham Darby succeeded in making a coke that could be used in the smelting process.

Apparently, in spite of its great utility, the manufacture of pig iron with coke did not become common until some seventy years had passed. By that time, the supply of pig iron outstripped the ability of refiners to make it into malleable iron, the type necessary in the many uses requiring a low carbon content. Research became actively stimulated, and in 1784, the process of "puddling," or heating and stirring molten pig iron mixed with iron oxide to burn out the carbon left by the coke, was invented by a contractor named Cort, together with a rolling mill that eliminated the tedious labor of hammering the refined metal.

Along with these basic discoveries, there were many auxiliary ones, such as the development of air pumps to deliver an adequate blast in the blast furnace, the invention of the steam hammer, and of metal-turning lathes. They made possible a rapid expansion in the output of iron and a lowering of its cost, as well as greater precision in machine manufacture. The use of machines made of iron grew rapidly; the iron industry itself furnished an increasing number of applications of the new technique, while the superior strength, accuracy, and durability of machinery made of this material led, after a beginning was made in 1785, to the rapid replacement of the early wooden spinning mules and water frames.

Advent of the Steam Engine

But the invention which removed all limitations to the spread of machinery, and which, combined with the chemical discoveries of coking and puddling, laid the foundations of England's industrial greatness, was the steam engine. At about the beginning of the eighteenth century, two primitive steam engines had been developed in England, and these became quite widely used. Owing to mechanical defects, however, and to the lack of any means of transmitting power from the engine to a driving wheel, their use was limited mainly to pumping water.

[16] Mantoux, *op. cit.*, p. 278.

The problems of designing an engine of sufficient power and accuracy and of translating the straight thrust of a piston into rotary motion were solved by James Watt. His person united scientific training, intelligence, and a rare intellectual curiosity. A maker of scientific instruments at the University of Glasgow, a student, and the friend of distinguished scientists, he devoted years of study and patient research to making the inefficient Newcomen engine an effective source of motive power. Success came in 1769 when he registered his first patent. A great gap, however, separates an invention from its effective application to industry. In Watt's case this gap was overcome by a fortunate partnership with Boulton, a Birmingham manufacturer of small metal wares. His financial aid brought the new engine past the test stage, his business connections established its first market, and his exceptionally well-equipped and well-managed shops furnished the accuracy of construction required for a satisfactory engine. After initial difficulties, the partnership throve, and the firm of Boulton and Watt became the producer of steam engines for all of Britain. By 1800, when their patents expired, steam power was really beginning to displace water power.

With this new great event, the invention of the steam engine, the final and most decisive stage of the industrial revolution opened. By liberating it from its last shackles, steam enabled the immense and rapid development of large-scale industry to take place. For the use of steam was not, like that of water, dependent on geographical position and local resources. Wherever coal could be bought at a reasonable price a steam engine could be erected. England had plenty of coal, and by the end of the eighteenth century it was already applied to many different uses, while a network of waterways, made on purpose, enabled it to be carried everywhere very cheaply: the whole country became a privileged land, suitable above all others for the growth of industry. Factories were now no longer bound to the valleys, where they had grown up in solitude by the side of rapid-flowing streams. It became possible to bring them nearer the markets where their raw materials were bought and their finished products sold, and nearer the centres of population where their labour was recruited. They sprang up near one another, and thus, huddled together, gave rise to those huge black industrial cities which the steam engine surrounded with a perpetual cloud of smoke.[17]

THE INDUSTRIAL REVOLUTION: SOCIAL AND ECONOMIC ASPECTS

The mechanical inventions in the textile and iron industries, the chemical discoveries in the use of coal and the manufacture of iron, set in motion a

[17] Mantoux, *The Industrial Revolution in the Eighteenth Century*, pp. 344-5. Copyright 1927 by Harcourt, Brace & Co., New York.

technological revolution, a revolution that was to alter completely the physical bases of industry. From its dependence for thousands of years upon wood as a material and as a fuel, upon water, animals and men for power, upon human dexterity and skill for the scope of its processes, it now became liberated. Coal, iron, and machinery replaced these less reliable, less accurate resources and opened up a century of industrial growth and progress that made earlier periods of expansion look stagnant.

The Factory System

If the Industrial Revolution had had no other effects than these, it would have earned its title. But it was at least as revolutionary in the social and economic sphere as in the purely technical. The new industrial machinery and methods could be used effectively only in establishments where large numbers of machines could be assembled, both because of the close relationship of the various processes of manufacture and because of the large volume of power made available by a single steam engine. This meant, of course, the grouping together under a single roof of hundreds of workmen and the development of a system of factory discipline that tolerated little deviation from a standard norm, whether in the matter of hours, of shop practice, or of quality of performance. Paradoxically, the industrial changes that gave the freest rein to the individual, provided he belonged to the managing and directing class, imposed an iron conformity of behavior on the great mass of the workers.

The new working environment came gradually, since the factory system supplanted the old cottage industry only in the course of decades. But by 1830, the cotton textile industry had become thoroughly mechanised, the production of iron was a relatively large-scale operation, and even in iron manufacturing, the small shop of the skilled craftsman was fast disappearing. Not until after the middle of the century, as we have noted, were the hand-loom weavers of woolen fabrics finally vanquished.

What is important is not the time required for the spread of the factory system, but its inevitability. With minor exceptions, the progress of the steam engine, the machine, and the new factory discipline was remorseless. Within the span of a century, most men who earned their living by making things ceased to work in their own homes, at hours they themselves set, and often with their own tools, and instead, entered the factory gates at a set hour, took their places before expensive machines in which they had no share of the ownership, and worked for a period, in a manner, and at a speed determined by the iron constitution of an inhuman engine. Machines and steam power spawned a new class, the industrial proletariat, with a new way of life, and in so doing gave a tremendous impetus to the growth of cities.[18]

Industrial Leadership

Urbanisation and the growth of an urban industrial proletariat were two of the social consequences of the Industrial Revolution. Still another was a tremendous increase in the importance of capital and the capitalist. We have seen that even the earlier cottage or domestic system of industry was dominated by the capitalist, who organised and directed the various processes of manufacture. He was, however, essentially still a merchant, and was generally so called, even though he might direct extensive manufacturing operations. With the replacement of tools by machines, and of hand or water power by the steam engine, thousands of pounds or dollars had to be invested in plant and equipment where hundreds or tens had formerly sufficed. The men who raised these vaster sums and who directed their use were a very different type from the earlier merchants.[19] Besides a knowledge of markets, they had to know a good deal about the technology of industry, they had to possess organising ability, and, if they were to succeed, they had to have, or to understand how to raise, large amounts of capital. Men like Arkwright, the cotton manufacturer, and like the ironmasters Boulton and Wilkinson, were typical of the new "captains of industry" who became the innovators, the entrepreneurs of the new age of iron and coal.

What made the innovating activity of this class of industrial capitalists possible was an inheritance of the previous century—the "liberal" view of society that had arisen out of the constant pressure of business interests seeking to take advantage of expanding opportunities, and out of the

[18] If we put the figure for the population of a town at 2,000, in 1801 there were in England and Wales 283 towns containing approximately 31 per cent of the total population. By 1841 these towns contained 46 per cent of the people. This later figure may exaggerate the situation somewhat, but it is probably not excessive. [G. P. Jones and A. G. Pool, *A Hundred Years of Economic Development in Great Britain*, p. 19, Gerald Duckworth and Co. Ltd., London.]

For the United States, comparable figures are available for the period 1820-1940. In 1820, 82 per cent of the country's labor force was engaged in agriculture, only 18 per cent in non-agricultural pursuits. In 1940, the figures were exactly reversed—18 per cent of the labor force was employed in agriculture, 82 per cent in non-agricultural pursuits. (These latter include, besides industry, also transportation, trade, government, the professions, etc., all of which have expanded with the expansion of industry.)

[19] At first, the capital came from accumulations already made in trade or industry, frequently pooled in partnerships containing from two to several partners. As the profits of the new enterprises mounted, large sums were ploughed back into the expansion of old, or the erection of new plants. It was not until after the middle of the nineteenth century that the corporate form of organisation, with its limited liability and its power of attracting many small streams of savings, became at all common in England.

stimulus to individual freedom of thought and action furnished by the rise of scientific thought and the parallel decline in the hold of religion and authority. Without the favorable climate of opinion known today as political and economic liberalism (formulated in the writings of Locke, Hume, Adam Smith, and Jeremy Bentham), the freedom necessary for introducing the radical changes in industry required by the mechanical inventions would have been lacking. Bound by old rules of handicraft manufacture, industry would have continued along lines laid down in the Middle Ages. Evasion of these rules had made possible the rise of the domestic system; their continued evasion, and the repeal of the restrictions introduced during the Mercantilist period, was essential to the rise of the new industry.

The Combination Act

So far had the philosophy of individualism gone by the end of the eighteenth century that intervention by the state was largely discredited, and laissez faire widely accepted as the foundation of economic relations. In the Combination Act of 1799, all combinations of workmen to improve their conditions of labor were outlawed. Henceforth, it was assumed, individual pursuit of individual interest would ensure economic justice to all. Forbidden to unite their strength to offset the greater bargaining power of the employer, workers tried to obtain remedy for low wages, long hours, and wretched working conditions by appealing for enforcement of such old laws as the Elizabethan Statute of Artificers. But though many such laws remained on the books of Parliament or were technically in force in various towns and trades, the spirit that had created them was dead. Besides, fixed numbers of apprentices and regulation of methods of production were inconsistent with the needs of a rapidly changing industry and with the interests of its owners and directors. The old laws were suspended, then repealed.[20] The "simple system of natural liberty" had prevailed. The character of industry and the status of labor were to be determined in a free market by free competition. Government was to combat ignorance by providing instruction, to stimulate progress by encouraging science and invention, and to protect the unsuspecting against fraud. With government thus limited, all restraints on the spread of the factory system vanished.

[20] The Statute of Artificers was repealed in 1809, thus finally doing away with national regulation of apprenticeships and of wages.

SELECTED REFERENCES

Halévy, Elie, *The Growth of Philosophic Radicalism*. (Faber & Gwyer, Ltd., London, 1928). Chapter III, Section I, has a good discussion of the views of Adam Smith, especially his principle of the natural identity of interests.

Mantoux, Paul, *The Industrial Revolution in the Eighteenth Century*. (Harcourt, Brace & Co., New York, 1927.) One of the outstanding studies of the Industrial Revolution.

Polanyi, Karl, *The Great Transformation* (Farrar & Rhinehart, New York, 1944). A provocative study of the development of the market economy in the eighteenth and nineteenth centuries, and of its subsequent decline.

Robertson, H. M., *Aspects of the Rise of Economic Individualism*. (Cambridge University Press, 1933.) This book contains a full account, with many illustrations, of how individualism displaced the philosophy of state regulation.

Smith, Adam, *The Wealth of Nations*, Chapters I-III, on the division of labor, and its relation to the extent of the market, are well worth reading.

Tawney, R. H., *Religion and the Rise of Capitalism*. (Harcourt, Brace & Co., New York, 1926) See especially Chapter IV, Sections II & III, for a discussion of religion, trade, and the economic virtues.

Trevelyan, G. W. *English Social History*. (Longmans, Green & Co., New York, 1942.) Chapters VI to XIII provide a vivid picture of the social background of this period.

4

THE DEVELOPMENT OF
INTERNATIONAL TRADE THEORY

State regulation of internal industry and trade within England had, as we have seen, a limited scope and a relatively short life. After the Cromwellian Revolution it expired. By the end of the eighteenth century, business men possessed almost unlimited freedom in the choice of their field of activity and the manner in which they carried it out; the philosophy of individualism permeated the intellectual classes and was beginning to influence both statesmen and leaders of industry.

From this time on, the controls of Mercantilism affected chiefly the country's external trade by means of tariffs, bounties, prohibitions, and the Colonial and Navigation systems. Although a beginning had been made, in the Eden Treaty of 1786 with France, toward the relaxation of restrictions on foreign trade, commercial and industrial opinion was divided on this topic; during the long interval, from 1793 to 1815, of the wars with France, further progress in this direction was impossible.

Yet during these war years expansion and mechanisation of England's newer industries, cotton, iron and steel, coal, and engineering, continued rapidly, and the new machine processes began to take hold in the old woolen textile industry. On the continent of Europe, the war retarded development in these lines. With the end of the military conflict, therefore, Britain's leading industries held an unchallengeable position. No one anywhere was in a position to offer them effective competition. On the other hand, the termination of the war brought with it a collapse of markets. Steel was no longer needed for muskets and cannon, the demand for soldiers' uniforms and blankets vanished, and prostrate Europe was in no position to buy large quantities of English goods. Concern for markets, therefore, caused a strengthening of sentiment in favor of freer trade among merchants and manufacturers, a change in opinion which was to have important consequences, as we shall see.

ADAM SMITH

At the same time that economic developments were preparing the ground for an attack on Mercantilist foreign trade policies, the intellectual weapons necessary for this attack were being sharpened and improved. Adam Smith stressed the absurdities of Mercantilist restrictions and had laid the groundwork for the free trade argument when he showed that trade between nations enables each to increase its wealth—in the sense of real income— by taking advantage of the principle upon which all increase of wealth rests, the division of labor.

It is the maxim of every prudent master of a family, never to attempt to make at home what it will cost him more to make than to buy. The taylor does not attempt to make his own shoes, but buys them of the shoemaker. The shoemaker does not attempt to make his own clothes, but employs a taylor. The farmer attempts to make neither the one nor the other, but employs those different artificers. All of them find it for their interest to employ their whole industry in a way in which they have some advantage over their neighbours, and to purchase with a part of its produce, or what is the same thing, with the price of a part of it, whatever else they have occasion for.

What is prudence in the conduct of every private family, can scarce be folly in that of a great kingdom. If a foreign country can supply us with a commodity cheaper than we ourselves can make it, better buy it of them with some part of the produce of our own industry, employed in a way in which we have some advantage. . . .

The natural advantages which one country has over another in producing particular commodities are sometimes so great, that it is acknowledged by all the world to be in vain to struggle with them. By means of glasses, hotbeds, and hotwalls, very good grapes can be raised in Scotland, and very good wine too can be made of them at about thirty times the expense for which at least equally good can be bought from foreign countries. Would it be a reasonable law to prohibit the importation of all foreign wines, merely to encourage the making of claret and burgundy in Scotland? But if there would be a manifest absurdity in turning towards any employment, thirty times more of the capital and industry of the country, than would be necessary to purchase from foreign countries an equal quantity of the commodities wanted, there must be an absurdity, though not altogether so glaring, yet exactly of the same kind, in turning towards any such employment a thirtieth, or even a three hundredth part more of either. Whether the advantages which one country has over another, be natural or acquired, is in this respect of no consequence. As long as the one country has those advantages, and the other wants them, it will always be more advantageous for the latter, rather to buy of the former than to make. It is an acquired advantage only, which one artificer has over his neighbour, who exercises another trade; and yet they both find it more advantageous to buy of one another, than to make what does not belong to their particular trades.[1]

Absolute Advantage Assumed

This statement, vigorous and clear though it was, lacked something in

[1] Adam Smith, *Wealth of Nations*, Modern Library Edition, pp. 424-6.

sharpness. Excellent as far as it went, it did not go far enough. For it assumed without argument that international trade required a producer of exports to have an *absolute* advantage, that is, an exporting industry must be able to produce, with a given amount of capital and labor, a larger output than any rival.

But what if a country had *no* line of production in which it were clearly superior? Suppose a relatively backward country whose "capital and industry" in the broadest sense (compared with its more advanced neighbors) were inefficient, capable of producing less in all lines of activity—a not too hypothetical case. Would it be forced to insulate itself against more efficient outside competition or see all its industry and agriculture subjected to ruinous competition? Adam Smith's analysis was incapable of dealing with this kind of situation, and it was not until David Ricardo undertook a more precise formulation of the theory of international trade (*Principles of Political Economy*, 1817) that a *general* theory of the subject became available.

DAVID RICARDO

Labor Cost Determines Domestic Value

The logical point of departure for considering Ricardo's explanation of international trade is his theory of value. According to this, the value of any commodity depended upon its labor costs: "it is the comparative quantity of commodities which labour will produce that determines their present or past relative value." [2] In the domestic trade of a country, this rule held good. Thus suppose that in Yorkshire, a certain quantity of cloth (*x* yds.) could be produced at a cost of 60 days' labor, in London at a cost of 100 days, while in Yorkshire the labor cost of cheese (*y* lb.) was 30 days, in London 90 days. Both commodities would be produced in Yorkshire, since the costs there are lowest, and they would exchange in the proportions of 1 unit of cloth for 2 units of cheese.

If these were the only commodities that could conceivably be produced in either region (or if the costs of producing all other commodities were lower in Yorkshire,) labor and capital would desert London for the more productive Yorkshire area. In reality, however, other possibilities would doubtless exist in London for a more effective application of labor and capital than in Yorkshire. Suppose one of these to be the manufacture of hardware, at a cost of 20 days' labor as compared with 60 in Yorkshire. A table of costs would look like this:

[2] David Ricardo, *Principles of Political Economy*, Everyman's Edition, p. 9.

| | Labor Costs of Producing | | |
	Cloth (x yd.)	Cheese (y lb.)	Hardware (z units)
Yorkshire	60	30	60
London	100	90	20

The hardware industry would then locate in London, the cloth and cheese industries in Yorkshire, and their products would exchange for one another in the proportions of 1 cloth for 2 cheese for 3 hardware.

In international trade, however, the labor-cost principle does not govern value in exchange, according to Ricardo.

The same rule which regulates the relative value of commodities in one country does not regulate the relative value of the commodities exchanged between two or more countries. . . . The quantity of wine which (Portugal) shall give in exchange for the cloth of England is not determined by the respective quantities of labour devoted to the production of each, as it would be if both commodities were manufactured in England, or both in Portugal.[3]

What, then, does determine values in international exchange? Ricardo assumes the following figures for labor costs of producing wine and cloth in Portugal and England:

| | Labor Costs of Producing | |
	Wine (x bbl.)	Cloth (y yd.)
Portugal	80	90
England	120	100

Costs of producing both commodities are lower in Portugal. In spite of this, it will pay Portugal to specialise in the production of wine and to exchange it for cloth made in England. For by so doing, Portugal would procure for an outlay of 80 days of labor (in Ricardo it is man-years) what would cost her 90 days to produce at home. England would also gain from the exchange. For by concentrating on the production of cloth and exchanging it for wine, she could get for a cost of 100 days labor what would, in the absence of trade, cost her 120 days.

International Immobility of the Factors

Why should there be such a remarkable difference in the principles regulating exchange within and between countries? The explanation is simple.

The difference in this respect, between a single country and many, is easily accounted for, by considering the difficulty with which capital moves from one coun-

---

[3] *Ibid.*, pp. 81-2.

try to another, to seek a more profitable employment, and the activity with which it invariably passes from one province to another in the same country.

It would undoubtedly be advantageous to the capitalists of England, and to the consumers in both countries, that under such circumstances the wine and the cloth should both be made in Portugal, and therefore that the capital and labour of England employed in making cloth should be removed to Portugal for that purpose. . . .

Experience, however, shows that the fancied or real insecurity of capital, when not under the immediate control of its owner, together with the natural disinclination which every man has to quit the country of his birth and connections, and intrust himself, with all his habits fixed, to a strange government and new laws, check the emigration of capital. These feelings, which I should be sorry to see weakened, induce most men of property to be satisfied with a low rate of profits in their own country, rather than seek a more advantageous employment for their wealth in foreign nations.[4]

In more modern terms, it is the immobility of labor, capital, and enterprise which tends to keep them at home, and thus to prevent production from taking place where labor costs are absolutely lowest. The localisation of production as between different countries follows the principle of *comparative cost:* each country will tend to specialise in the production of those commodities for which its (labor) costs are comparatively lowest.

At bottom this is simply an extension of the principle of the division of labor. In general terms, applicable to both nations and individuals, competence should specialise where competence counts most, and incompetence where incompetence counts least. As Ricardo expressed the matter in an illustration:

Two men can both make shoes and hats, and one is superior to the other in both employments, but in making hats he can only exceed his competitor by one-fifth or 20 per cent., and in making shoes he can excel him by one-third or 33 per cent.;—will it not be for the interest of both that the superior man should employ himself exclusively in making shoes, and the inferior man in making hats? [5]

It is clear that the doctrine of comparative cost marks a real advance over Adam Smith's statement of the basis of international trade. For it is more general; it explains situations not covered by Smith's formulation and includes the latter as a special case, one where a country's *comparative* cost advantage is also an absolute advantage.

Yet as it left the hands of Ricardo, though the principle gave a more convincing and adequate proof of the benefits of trade, it left the actual ratios of international exchange, or international prices, undetermined. For

[4] *Ibid.*, p. 83.
[5] *Ibid.*, footnote, p. 83.

Ricardo simply assumed that Portugal would exchange wine costing 80 units of labor (*x* bbl.) for English cloth costing 100 labor units (*y* yd.) Perhaps he failed to go further and establish the precise terms of profitable exchange because he was mainly interested in showing that only a comparative and not an absolute difference in labor costs is necessary for gainful international trade. Or it may have been because the way in which he set up his illustration tended to obscure the problem of the terms of trade. Whatever the reason, this further step awaited the attention of Ricardo's illustrious successor, John Stuart Mill.

JOHN STUART MILL

When, after restating Ricardo's doctrine of comparative cost in a clearer fashion, Mill proceeded to examine the question of international values, he used an illustration whose very form focused attention upon this problem. Instead of taking as *given* the output of each commodity in two countries, with the labor costs different, he assumed a given amount of labor in each country, but differing outputs. Thus his formulation ran in terms of comparative advantage, or comparative effectiveness of labor, as contrasted with Ricardo's comparative labor cost.

Mill's contribution can be illustrated as follows:

Input of Labor (days)	Country	Output of:	
		Tin cans (gross)	Cotton cloth (yards)
10	U.S.	50	15
10	G.B.	10	10

For the same input of labor, the United States and Great Britain produce widely differing outputs of tin cans and cotton cloth. The United States has an absolute advantage in the production of both commodities (50 tin cans against 10, and 15 cotton cloth against 10), but a clear comparative advantage in tin cans (5 to 1, as compared to 1½ to 1). Great Britain's least comparative disadvantage is in cotton cloth. It is *comparative advantage* that indicates the lines of profitable specialisation if trade is permitted to develop.

Possible Terms of Trade

In the absence of trade, 10 units of tin cans will exchange in Britain for 10 units of cloth, since these quantities represent an equal labor cost. In the U.S., 10 cans will command only 3 units of cloth, each of these quantities being the product of 2 days of labor. Clearly, however, trade will benefit the U.S. if for 10 units of tin cans anything more than 3 units of cloth can be obtained, while Great Britain will gain if it can get 10 of tin cans by exporting any less than 10 cloth. That is, *the limits to the possible barter terms of trade* (the international exchange ratio) *are set by the domestic exchange ratios established by the relative efficiency of labor in each country.*

The range of possible barter terms can be shown as:

Tin cans   Cloth

10   3+   10—

Within this range, any single ratio may rule. The question Mill sought to answer was: What factors determine *the actual terms* on which the commodities will trade?

Reciprocal Demand

Stated briefly, Mill's answer was: The actual ratio at which goods are traded will depend upon the strength and elasticity of each country's demand for the other country's product, or upon reciprocal demand. This ratio will be stable when the value of each country's exports just suffices to pay for its imports.

The operation of Mill's principle of reciprocal demand can be shown most clearly if we introduce money wages into our illustration.[6] Let us assume that wages in the United States are $10 a day, and in Great Britain $5. (It will do no violence to our analysis and will keep the exposition simple if we consider both countries to be using gold currency and if we express prices in a common unit, the dollar.) We now obtain determinate money costs from which the barter terms can easily be computed.

Input of Labor	Daily Wages	Total Cost	Country	Tin Cans Output	Tin Cans Unit Cost	Cotton Cloth Output	Cotton Cloth Unit Cost
10	$10	$100	United States	50	$2.00	15	$6.67
10	$ 5	$ 50	Great Britain	10	$5.00	10	$5.00

[6] Mill's answer took a somewhat different form from the presentation given here, which is chosen for the purposes of clarity. He did not introduce money wages, but reasoned in terms of barter trade. Thus he would say that the ratio of 10 tin cans for 4 cloth would be stable provided each country's requirements are a common multiple of the terms of trade, say when the U.S. wants 1,000,000 x 4 units of cloth or 4,000,000 cloth and when Great Britain at the same time wants 1,000,000 x 10 tin cans or 10,000,000 tin cans.

At these costs, 10 units of tin cans will come to $20. For this sum, 4 units of cotton cloth can be obtained in Great Britain (at $5 a unit). If, at these barter terms of 10 tin cans for 4 cloth, total American demand for cloth is, say, 4 million units or $20 million worth, and British demand for tin cans is 10 million units, also $20 million worth, the value of each country's exports is just equal to the value of its imports, its trading account is in balance, and the barter terms of trade will be stable.[7]

Suppose, however, that at these prices and barter terms, Great Britain's demand amounted to 12 million units of tin cans, with a total value of $24 million. Great Britain would have to send the United States a net sum of $4 million in gold. This would cause wages and prices to rise in the United States and to fall in Great Britain. Suppose American wages were to go up to $12, British wages to fall to $4. Our illustration changes as follows:

Input of Labor	Daily Wages	Total Cost	Country	Tin Cans Output	Tin Cans Unit Cost	Cotton Cloth Output	Cotton Cloth Unit Cost
10	$12	$120	United States	50	$2.40	15	$8.00
10	$ 4	$ 40	Great Britain	10	$4.00	10	$4.00

At the now higher price of $2.40 for tin cans, British buyers will reduce their purchases somewhat, while American purchases of cotton cloth will expand at the lower price of $4. If British demand now amounts to 9 million units of tin cans, the total value of their imports will be $21.6 million. Should American demand for cloth at a price of $4 a unit chance to be 5.4 million units, the value of American imports would also be just $21.6 million. Trade would be in balance, and so would the barter terms, which now stand at 10 tin cans = 6 cotton cloth. If, however, American demand at this new price were smaller or larger, the adjustment of wages and prices to international demands would have to continue until a stable position was reached.

In summary, (1) the possible range of barter terms is given by the respective domestic terms of trade as set by the comparative efficiency in each country; (2) within this range, the actual terms depend on each country's demand for the other country's product; (3) finally, only those barter terms will be stable at which the goods demanded by one country are equal in value to the goods demanded by the other.

Limits to Wage Differences

It is convenient to go one step further. At the same time that the com-

[7] In this simplified illustration, trade is, of course, assumed to be confined to these two countries and these two commodities. We are also abstracting from transport costs.

parative efficiency of labor in each country establishes the limits to the barter terms of trade, it also sets bounds on relative wages. Consider the illustration we have been using. The ratio of labor efficiency in producing tin cans is 5 to 1, in producing cotton cloth only 1.5 to 1. Wages in the U.S. could never be 5 times as high as in Great Britain, for this would fully counteract the U.S. comparative advantage in tin cans and make their export impossible. Britain would make her own tin cans, at the same cost as in the U.S., and would export cotton cloth, for which the U.S. would pay with gold. Nor could the ratio of American to British wages ever fall as low as 1.5 to 1, for at that ratio U.S. money costs for cotton cloth would be equal to costs in Great Britain. The U.S. would produce both cloth and tin cans, and export the latter, receiving gold in payment.

In both instances, balanced trade is impossible. The price specie-flow mechanism would operate to reduce wages and prices where they were high, raise them when they were low, until prices were such that reciprocal demands just balanced.

ELABORATION AND REFINEMENT OF THE CLASSICAL DOCTRINE

From the time of Ricardo and Mill down to the present, the essentials of their theory of international trade have remained relatively intact. The theory has, however, been elaborated and refined in a number of ways. Of most importance have been the refinements introduced by Taussig to deal with the problems raised by non-competing groups of labor and by the existence of capital charges.

Non-competing Groups

In the basic theory, labor in each country is assumed to be homogeneous, and to differ between countries only in productivity. Yet it has long been recognised that any country's labor force consists of many different groups of labor (technical, skilled, semi-skilled, and unskilled, to mention one common classification) among which mobility is far from perfect. These distinct categories of labor, with rather well-marked and enduring differences in wages, became known as "non-competing" groups.

Now the mere existence of such groups would nowise affect the theory of international trade provided that in each country the relative scale of wages were the same. But if, for example, wages of unskilled labor were especially low in one country, because this kind of labor was unusually abundant, that country could produce some commodity or commodities at a lower money cost than its competitors, even though it had no comparative advantage. The same would be true were skilled labor, or any other of the non-competing groups, the one with abnormally low wages, or if wages of *all* groups were especially depressed in some particular industry. Abnormally low wages for a particular kind of labor, in other words, act as a substitute for *real* comparative advantage.

Taussig developed this point at some length. Yet he thought non-competing groups served to explain only special situations, such as existed in the German chemical industry and in the U.S. iron and steel industry before 1914. In the former, employers could obtain highly-skilled chemical workers at abnormally low rates of pay, while in the latter, an unusually large supply of unskilled immigrant labor reduced its wage level to an extraordinary degree. To a considerable extent, Taussig felt, the ability of both industries to export rested upon these facts. Barring a few such exceptional cases, however, the basic doctrine of comparative advantage required no modification. This was because—at least in the Western nations—the hierarchy of non-competing groups and the relative differences in their wages were about the same.[8]

Capital Charges

Taussig treated capital charges in a similar manner. While admitting interest on capital as an element in money costs, he held that it would have no effect on the relative prices of commodities unless it bore with *unequal weight on different goods.*

For this to be true, (1) interest rates have to differ among countries, and (2) the relative use made of capital as compared with labor would have to vary from one industry to another. Thus a country enjoying low interest rates would have a price advantage equivalent to one caused by the basic principle of comparative costs only in industries in which capital was used in relatively large quantities. Since national differences in interest rates were judged to be "not considerable," and since Taussig implied that the relative use of capital did not vary greatly between industries, the range of influence of interest rates "is restricted to a special set of circumstances." As with non-competing groups, its introduction "does not lead to a radical modification of our first conclusions."[9]

By permitting diversity of wages between different groups of labor and

[8] See F. W. Taussig, *International Trade*, Ch. 6. The trade between Western nations Taussig regarded as determined by the principle of comparative costs, whereas in the trade with the tropics and other overseas areas, differences in costs or advantage were absolute rather than comparative only.

[9] *Ibid.*, pp. 67-8.

differences in interest rates to play a role only in exceptional circumstances, Taussig was able to retain the doctrine of comparative labor costs as the dominant principle explaining international price differences and thus the direction of specialisation and trade.

Defects of Classical Theory

While one cannot deny that this principle has served well as a tool of analysis for more than a century, and that with the necessary qualifications it can be applied to a wide range of problems, it remains true that it suffers from serious defects.

First, the theory rests on weak foundations. Its starting point—the explanation of commodity prices (or the exchange ratio between goods) within a country—is the discredited labor theory of value. The values of commodities in one country are presumed to be proportional to absolute labor costs. But in international trade, their proportionality no longer holds. There is a different theory of value. *Comparative* labor costs set the limits within which the exchange ratio must lie, but its precise position is determined by reciprocal demand.

Second, the stress laid on a single factor, labor, flies in the face of well-known facts, that there are many factors of production, and that even labor is not a single, homogeneous factor. To take these facts into account by treating them as exceptional fails to do them justice; moreover, this method has the defect of being roundabout and cumbersome.[10]

One further point with respect to the shortcomings of the principle of comparative cost: unless one is to leave this principle hanging in the air, it is essential to give some explanation of *why* the labor of one country is more efficient than that of another in various lines of production. When this is attempted, one is inevitably driven to appeal to such factors as superior natural resources, the use of elaborate machinery, or the presence

---

[10] Another approach attempts to meet the problem posed by the existence of numerous factors by resort to the concept of "real costs." These are the subjective costs attached to different kinds of inputs of human origin—the effort or disutility of various kinds of labor and the abstinence involved in saving. Since these costs are incommensurable (the disutility of labor and the disutility of saving are different in kind and therefore cannot sensibly be added), either one must assume that the proportions in which capital and different kinds of labor are combined are the same in all industries, or that the valuations given them by the market (wages, interest) are proportional to the disutilities involved (so that the sum of their prices accurately reflects the sum of real costs). Since it is impossible to admit the realism of either of these alternatives, the real costs approach cannot be justified. Furthermore, it cannot take into account costs which are "real" but involve no disutility, such as the necessity of using land to produce tobacco instead of cotton.

of more abundant and better managerial talents.[11] But this is to introduce the abundance of *other* factors of production to explain the greater productivity of *one* of them—labor.

Would it not be more fitting and overcome, at the same time, the objection to the stress on a single factor involved in the comparative cost theory, if we founded our explanation of international trade on the striking differences with which different nations are endowed with *all* the productive agents? The next chapter begins an analysis based precisely on this fact.

SELECTED REFERENCES

Ellsworth, P. T., *International Economics* (Macmillan, New York, 1938). Chapter II reviews the contributions of the classical economists to the development of international trade theory. Chapter III is a synopsis of the modern classical position, with all its qualifications.

Haberler, G., *The Theory of International Trade* (Wm. Hodge & Co., Ltd., London, 1936). Chapters IX-XI contain an excellent elaboration of the classical theory. A much briefer statement is to be found in the same author's *A Survey of International Trade Theory, Special Papers in International Economics*, No. 1, Sept. 1955 (International Finance Section, Princeton University).

Marsh, Donald B., *World Trade and Investment* (Harcourt, Brace & Co., New York, 1951). Chapters 19 and 20 give a a rigorous statement of the theory of international trade in terms of real cost. Difficult, but rewarding.

Mill, John Stuart, *The Principles of Political Economy*. Book III, Ch. XVIII contains Mill's theory of reciprocal demand.

Ohlin, Bertil, *Interregional and International Trade* (Harvard University Press, Cambridge, 1933). Appendix III is a vigorous criticism of the classical theory.

Ricardo, David, *The Principles of Political Economy and Taxation*. Chapter VII contains the famous statement of the doctrine of comparative cost.

Viner, Jacob, *Studies in the Theory of International Trade* (Harper & Bros., New York, 1937). See Chapter VIII, Sections I, VII, VIII, X, XI, and XII for a defense of the real-cost approach to international trade.

[11] See, for example, the numerous illustrations of this sort given by Taussig in his *International Trade*, Chs. 15 and 16.

5

THE MODERN THEORY OF
INTERNATIONAL TRADE

THE SIMPLE MODEL

Explaining International Prices

The immediate reason for international trade and specialisation is that some countries can produce certain goods at prices so much lower than other countries that even after costs of transporting them are added, they can deliver them in foreign markets at a lower price than can local producers. A satisfactory theory of international trade must explain *why* such price differences exist.

The theory of comparative cost is one attempt to provide such an explanation. We have rejected it because it is expressed in terms of a single factor of production, labor, whereas it is clear that there are many factors to be reckoned with. Varying combinations of labor and capital, and of different types of labor—when the classical theory recognises their existence—are treated as exceptional. It is a matter of everyday observation, however, that the proportions in which the various productive factors are combined differ greatly from industry to industry. A more modern theory, which we shall use as our guide, begins by recognising these facts: (1) that there are several factors of production, and (2) that they can be combined in varied proportions. As a start, we shall assume three factors—land, labor, and capital. This will serve very well for dealing with the broader aspects of international specialisation. When it becomes necessary to consider more complex and detailed problems, we can readily modify our simple model by adopting a more refined and adequate factor base.

This approach not only has the advantage of starting with recognised facts. It also provides a common explanation for both national and international prices. The comparative cost doctrine, on the other hand, distinguished sharply between domestic and international values or prices. Within a single country, the value of commodities depended upon their *absolute* labor cost. But in international trade, there was a different rule. *Comparative* labor costs set the limits to exchange ratios, while the actual terms of exchange, or relative value, depended upon reciprocal demand.

The modern theory of international trade starts where conventional price theory leaves off—with the analysis of prices in a single market. It simply broadens this theory to include many markets.

Now in explaining any class of phenomena, it is always desirable to minimise the number of explanatory principles. The resulting model will be simpler and more understandable, and thus easier to use. We shall adhere throughout to modern price theory, which analyzes price determination in terms of the forces underlying the demand and the supply sides of the market. Starting with this theory as the accepted explanation of pricing in a single market, we simply extend its application to interconnecting markets.

SINGLE VERSUS MULTIPLE MARKETS

In discussing price theory, the usual elementary text starts by discussing a single market, within which raw materials, finished products, and the factors of production are assumed to move with perfect freedom and without cost. Such a market must be assumed if the usual conclusions— a uniform price for each product, equal returns to each factor in all uses— are to be justified. And even when geographical distances between different parts of a nation-wide market are taken into account, they are generally given insufficient emphasis. Not until one reaches the chapters on international trade is geographical specialization stressed.

Yet a moment's reflection will show that specialisation and trade between different regions of a single country, especially if it is a large one, are just as much facts as specialisation and trade between nations. The Detroit area in the United States specialises in the production of automobiles and accessories, shipping them to all parts of the country, while the New York garment industry fills shops from Maine to California with women's dresses, blouses, suits, and skirts; the employees of both these localised industries obtain their breakfast grapefruit from Florida and Texas, the flour for their bread from western mills and wheat fields, the lumber to build their homes from the pine woods of the South or the fir and spruce forests of the Pacific Northwest.

What this all adds up to is that an entire nation is not a single, homogeneous market, within which all commodities are produced and exchanged and within which each commodity and each factor has a uniform price, but a series of connecting markets. The concept of a single market must be limited to an area or region within which the mobility of goods and factors, if not so perfect as to yield absolute uniformity of commodity and factor prices, is at least so great as to reduce any such price differences to relative insignificance. Regional specialisation and trade, in other words, is just as much a fact to be explained as its international counterpart. Moreover, the latter is only a special case of the former, to be explained by the same set of basic principles. There are differences, to be sure, that make international specialisation and trade more complex, and these differences have attracted special attention to its problems. But in fundamentals, interregional and international trade are indentical.

The discussion of the foundations of interregional and international trade will be greatly simplified if we first review the basic principles of pricing in a single market.

REVIEW OF THE PRICING PROCESS IN A SINGLE MARKET

Use of Factors in Production

Within any market area, a wide variety of goods and services is continually being produced. Such production requires the use of scarce factors— labor, capital in the form of tools, machines, buildings and stocks of goods, and natural resources. Thus to produce a simple commodity like cotton, the farmer must apply his own labor, employ field hands, and obtain the services of tractors, plows, cultivators, and possibly mechanical pickers, as well as of the land on which the cotton grows. All these productive agents or factors are combined in appropriate proportions according to an established method and are transformed, after ginning, into cotton fibre. Of course the farmer must also buy other commodities that are used up in the production of cotton, such as gasoline, fertilizers, and insecticides. But each of these commodities, like cotton, has gone through a productive process that required the use of land, labor, and capital. All production, accordingly, can be expressed as a process of transforming the services of resources into finished commodities. The latter may be regarded as a sort of reincarnation of the services rendered by the productive agents. From the reverse point of view, one may say that each finished commodity can be broken down or decomposed into its elemental parts, and that these parts are the services contributed by the factors of production.

Factor Prices are Costs

Parallel with the physical processes of production, there occurs a process of pricing. All the scarce resources required in production can command a price for their services. Labor obtains wages, capital a return called interest, and land, rent. To our cotton farmer, these payments to the various factors are costs, which he must recoup from his sales proceeds if he is to stay in business. Therefore he charges a price for his cotton. If the price he gets per bale is just sufficient to pay for the services contributed to its production by each of the factors used, including wages for his own labor and interest on capital and rent of the land he owns, he will have no incentive either to increase or decrease output. His economic situation is one of stability, or equilibrium.[1] If all producers of raw cotton were in similar circumstances, we would say that the entire industry was in equilibrium. And if in all industries each producer were receiving from his sales proceeds just enough to cover costs as defined, the entire economy would be in equilibrium.

Competitive Conditions

This statement assumes a competitive economy, in which the number of producers and consumers is so great that no single one can by his action affect price. Each producer or consumer takes price as a given fact, determined by the actions of numerous other producers and consumers whom he cannot control. He adjusts as best he can to it. Only in such a competitive economy do total receipts just cover total costs, including, for the producer himself, only wages for his labor and the usual return for the services of any non-human factors he may contribute. Later, in Chapter 8, we shall take into account the fact that competition may be imperfect. This may be because there are only a few producers in an industry, each of whom can influence price—and thus profits—by his action. Or it may be because producers, even though numerous, split the market into segments by advertising and selling devices that differentiate their products.

Payments to Factors are Income

From the point of view of the factors of production, the payments they receive for their services are income. The appended table shows, for the United States, how the total national income for 1956 was divided. Far the greatest share went to labor, a share that includes the specific item

**NATIONAL INCOME IN THE UNITED STATES AND ITS
MAJOR COMPONENTS, 1956**

(in billions of dollars)

Wages and Salaries	239.1
Proprietorships	40.8
Interest and Rent	21.6
Corporate Profits	40.9
Total	342.4

Source: Federal Reserve Bulletin, February 1957.

[1] At the next stage of production, the processing of the raw cotton into textiles, a similar analysis would hold. To the textile industry, of course, raw cotton is a cost, but as we see here, its cost may be broken down into payments for the services of productive factors. Similarly with the gasoline and fertilizers used by the farmer.

"Wages and Salaries," and an estimated two-thirds of the return labelled "Proprietorships." This sector comprises the earnings of independent professional workers like doctors, lawyers, and accountants, together with the earnings of farmers and small businessmen. Most of their incomes reflect the contribution of their own labor, the remainder a return on capital or land they have put into their business. If we add to the $239.1 billion earned by hired employees two-thirds of the $40.8 billion income of the self-employed, or $27.2 billion, we obtain a total of $266.3 billion or 78 per cent of all income. The remaining 22 per cent consists mainly of interest and rent—the $21.6 so stated, together with that (larger) part of corporate profits which consists of the going rate of return (interest) on capital and on land (rent) owned by corporations. Only a relatively small portion of corporate profits could be regarded as true profits, or a return in excess of competitive earnings.

Incomes are the Source of Demand

The income received by the productive factors, or more accurately, by their owners, since the earnings of capital and land are received by those who own them, are in turn the source of demand for the commodities and services the factors cooperate to produce. Factor incomes are passed on, through retail shops, landlords, the box offices of theaters, cinemas and racetracks, to the producers of commodities and services, in whose hands these funds are again used to employ the productive factors. The flow of income is circular and continuous, ever repeating itself.

Demands Induce Production

Returning now to the problem of the pricing of goods and services and of the productive factors, it should be apparent that, like the flow of income, it is a circular phenomenon. Assume a given total of income is being currently earned in a particular market area from determinate payments to the factors, and focus your attention for the moment upon the markets for goods and services. Here are funneled the demands of individuals and organised groups with money in their pockets or their bank accounts. Their wants, backed by purchasing power, comprise the demand for each of a whole host of things—shoes and clothing, foods of many kinds, automobiles, houses, recreation. The demand for each commodity or service provides an opportunity for some producer or entrepreneur to earn an income, perhaps only enough to cover his wages and the going return on non-human factors, but possibly (he hopes) something more—profits. Each commodity or service on which buyers are willing to spend money attracts a number of entrepreneurs who employ labor, borrow capital and invest it in productive equipment, and rent land [2]—a large amount of land in relation to capital and labor if they engage in farming, a relatively unimportant amount if their line is manufacturing or trade.

Price Equals Cost

The strength of demand for a particular commodity—the prices buyers are willing to pay for it—justifies the allocation of a larger or smaller total volume of productive resources to its production. A widely consumed article like wheat would call for the use of large amounts of the different factors, a rarity like *paté de fois gras* very little. Each line of production attracts entrepreneurs, who offer employment to the factors, combining them in each industry in proportions determined by existing technology. Payments to the factors at the going rates, together with the output obtained in each "plant," determine unit costs. Under competitive conditions, these will be the same for all producers.[3] Total output of each industry tends toward that level at which the price buyers are willing to pay is just equal to average unit cost. Commodities that require a relatively small input of scarce factors per unit (like cotton, corn, or wheat in a land-rich country) will sell for a few cents or dollars per unit, whereas those calling for a large input of the factors per unit, or requiring the use of particularly scarce and costly factors, (like diamonds, uranium, or vicuna cloth) will command a very high price.

Real Costs vs. Money Costs

A distinction needs to be made here between money costs and real costs. The money costs of a unit of a given commodity, as we have just indicated, are the money payments that have to be made to the factors required to produce a unit of that commodity. These are the costs that interest the producer, who must make sure, if he is to stay in business, that his money costs are at least as low as those of his competitors. It is money costs, as we shall see, that determine where geographical specialisation will take place, for in international markets the country with the lowest costs will get the business.

Often, however, it is important to consider, not the money cost of pro-

---

[2] Or purchase it, in which case their accounts must include a charge for rent equal to what the land would earn were it hired out to someone else.

[3] If some entrepreneurs are abler and more efficient than others, they will earn a higher return (wages of management), equal to what they could earn if they hired out their services. This counts as a cost, and serves to equalise the costs of the more and the less efficient producing units.

ducing an article, but the real cost to society of obtaining it. This is the alternative product foregone by society when that article, rather than something else, is produced. *Real* cost is *opportunity* cost. Thus the real cost of the radar network, the planes, and other components of the American defense effort is the schools, roads, houses, and industrial plant that could have been produced with the resources actually devoted to defense.

If we bear in mind that scarce resources (factors of production) can be used to produce a variety of alternative products, we can express the same idea briefly by saying that the real cost of producing anything is the resources used up.

Economy in the use of resources implies a reduction in real cost because the sacrifice of alternative production, or opportunity cost, is diminished. The resources released can be devoted to the satisfaction of other wants.

This review of real cost has nothing in common with the classical notion of real cost. To the classical and neo-classical economists, real cost was and is the effort or sacrifice of the labor required to produce a commodity, and the sacrifice involved in providing the necessary capital. Aside from the fact that the two kinds of sacrifice are of different kinds, hence incommensurable, and thus incapable of being added, the classical concept of real cost cannot encompass the cost of using land, since no human sacrifice is involved in its use.[4]

Factor Prices

We began our inquiry into the pricing process by assuming the income of the community as given. Since this income is simply the sum total of the payments to the factors, this involves assuming their rates of pay, or factor prices, as known. But factor prices, like the prices of the commodities they jointly produce, are subject to determination by the forces of demand and supply. The demand for their services is derived from the demand for commodities and is transmitted through the entrepreneurs who organise and carry on the processes of production. Fundamentally, what each entrepreneur is able and willing to pay for the services of a given factor depends on what that factor contributes to the value of his output. As any good elementary text shows, it will tend to equal the value of its marginal product, or the amount of output contributed by the last unit of the factor employed (marginal physical product) multiplied by the unit value of the product.

Whether the marginal value product, or marginal productivity for short,

---

[4] There is, however, a real cost to society of using land: the output foregone when it is applied to one purpose rather than to another.

of any single factor is high or low will depend on the supply of that factor. If a given factor, say labor, is scarce relative to the other factors, the last or marginal worker will make a substantial contribution to output. Entrepreneurs, each eager to obtain an adequate working force, will compete for labor's services and wages will be high. If the labor force increases, through immigration or a high natural rate of population growth, while capital and land remain constant in amount, the employment of the additional workers will encounter diminishing returns; the marginal productivity of the augmented labor supply will decline and with it labor's rate of pay.

It is differences in the relative supply of labor, with corresponding differences in its marginal productivity, that mainly account for the great differences in wages in various parts of the world. Thus in India and Egypt, where labor is exceptionally abundant in relation to capital and land, wages are extremely low, the returns to the scarcer factors, land and capital, comparatively high. Wages in the United States and Canada, where relatively little labor is combined with much capital and land, are many times higher.[5]

In accord with our definition of a region as a geographical area within which factor mobility, if not perfect, is nonetheless very great, it is easy to see that the return to any factor is going to be the same, or nearly the same, in all uses to which it is put. Mobility makes competition throughout the region possible, and competition will ensure equality of returns to all units of a factor.

Summary

We have now closed the circle of the pricing process, and it is possible to see it as a system in which all the elements are mutually and simultaneously determined. From the incomes received by the owners of factors are derived the demands for goods and services; these demands authorise, in effect, the payment of a scale of prices for the goods and services that satisfy them. The precise point reached on each demand scale depends

[5] Marginal productivity is not, of course, the only force affecting the return to a factor. A strong union, by restricting the number of workers available for a given employment, can force the payment of a wage above the competitive level. It is still equal to the value of the marginal worker's product, but since fewer workers are employed than would be under fully competitive conditions, that value is greater. Employers, on the other hand, may take advantage of the weakness and ignorance of unorganised labor, and hold wages below the value of labor's marginal product.

Changes in consumer demand, by increasing or decreasing the value of particular goods, can—at least for a time—raise or lower the value productivity of the labor employed in their production. Changes in technology may increase the need and thus the demand for a specific factor, thus raising its marginal productivity. Or such changes may (as with labor-saving or capital-saving inventions) reduce the need for a factor, release it for other employment, and thus tend to depress its marginal product in all uses.

on the terms on which the commodity is supplied, and this in turn is determined jointly by the production function or required factor combination together with the prices of the factors. Factor prices result from the interaction of the demands for factor services (derived from the demand for commodities) with the supply of the various productive agents. Each factor obtains a return equal to its marginal contribution to the value of output in each line of production. Thus we are back at the starting point, the incomes of the owners of productive resources. The pricing process, seen as a whole, is a system of mutually determined general equilibrium such as is encountered in many other fields of human inquiry—in the solar system, in the structure of the atom, and in the political realm when stability results from the successful reconciliation of the interests of conflicting political groups.

FACTOR PRICES AND INTERNATIONAL SPECIALISATION

With this review of the pricing process in a single region as a point of departure, the fundamental basis for interregional and international differences in commodity prices becomes readily apparent. Since prices, under competitive conditions, are equal to costs of production, and costs can be reduced to payments to the factors of production, any cause that leads to the emergence of varying rates of factor pay, or to factor price differences between regions or countries, will result in differing scales of commodity prices.

Factor Price Differences and Factor Endowments

Ample reason for the existence of international factor price differences is to be found in the marked differences in the way in which nations are endowed with the productive agents.[6] We have already noted how the relatively low wages in India and Egypt, the relatively high wages in the United States and Canada, are explainable mainly in terms of the relative abundance of labor in the first pair of countries, its relative scarcity in the second. Similar differences characterise the geographical distribution of all the factors. Some countries, like Australia, possess ample land; the United

---

[6] We shall concentrate upon international differences from now on, since our major concern is with international trade, and for the sake of brevity drop the term "interregional" from the discussion. The argument in the text applies, however, to regions as well as nations. Interregional differences in factor prices are likely, though, to be less marked and less enduring than similar international differences, simply because the mobility of factors is greater between regions than between countries.

States is well endowed with both capital and land, Great Britain, with capital and skilled labor.

Demand for the services of the factors, as well as their supplies, is of course also relevant. We can say with some assurance, however, that barring exceptional circumstances, the supply of the factors dominates in the determination of relative factor prices. Although it is conceivable, for example, that the inhabitants of a nation richly endowed with land might have such a strong preference for food and other agricultural products as to make rents as high, in comparison with wages and the return on capital, as they were in a densely populated country with relatively little land, such an outcome is most improbable. Human demands for the services of the various factors differ, in general, far less than the supplies of those services.

It is important to note that it is *relative* differences in factor supplies that are significant. Thus India, with an area of approximately a million and a quarter square miles, has *absolutely* more land than Argentina, with its 1,079,000 square miles. But India's population is 346 million, that of Argentina only 20 million; relative to its immense population, land in India is scarce, labor abundant, while the reverse is true of Argentina. Expressed in per capita figures, available land in India amounts to 2.3 acres per capita, in Argentina to 34.5. No reliable estimate of capital supply in either country exists, but probably their relative supplies of capital are much closer together.

Even with differences in factor supplies less striking than these, measurable and even significant international factor price differences are bound to emerge. In general, we can say with confidence, that if in two countries or regions, the relative supplies of land, labor, and capital are different, their prices will also be different. If much land is available relative to labor and capital, land rents will be low, whereas with much labor but little land or capital, labor will be cheap; if capital is the relatively abundant factor, interest rates will be low.

Differing Production Functions

In international factor price differences, we now have one of two important bases for the emergence of international differences in commodity prices. The other, and one which is a common fact of observation, is that the way in which the factors are combined in production shall vary from commodity to commodity. *Methods of production,* or in more technical language, the production functions, *must not be identical for all goods, but must differ from one commodity to another.* This condition will be met if some goods require relatively large amounts of labor, others relatively large quantities of land, and still others relatively much capital.[7]

Automobiles, for example, are produced with immense quantities of capital, substantial amounts of labor, and very little land. They are a capital-intensive product. So are steel, machine tools, synthetic fibers, and refined petroleum products. Compared with these, fine watches, photographic and scientific equipment, and high-grade cutlery require the use of relatively large amounts of labor, especially of skilled labor. Even more conspicuously labor-intensive are hand-blown glass, lace, the finest types of rugs, and mink coats. Most agricultural products are, of course, land intensive, though the relative use of land varies widely from one crop to another. The livestock industry, with its need for extensive grazing areas, very little labor or machinery, provides the most extreme example. Wheat cultivation is not too far behind in its relative use of land. At the other end of the scale is the cultivation of rice in the Orient, typified by the intensive application of labor to small areas of land, and with capital limited to simple implements and a team of bullocks or water buffalo.

International Commodity Price Differences

We can now show very simply how, given (1) a variety of production methods or techniques, and (2) international differences in the prices of the productive factors, international commodity price differences are bound to emerge. We shall confine our attention to essentials by assuming that exchange rates between currencies are known and fixed, so that we can express prices in units of a single currency, say dollars.

To illustrate, let us assume two countries, with A, like Argentina, possessed of abundant land, labor in moderate supply, and capital scarce, while B, similar to Burma, is endowed with a relatively large labor supply, but has comparatively little land and very little capital. Factor prices such as those registered in the following table would not be too unrealistic.

Factor Prices

	in A	in B	
Land	$ 1	$ 20	(unit: 1 acre-year)
Labor	600	100	(unit: 1 man-year)
Capital	80	150	(unit: use of $1,000 for a year)

[7] This reasoning transforms Taussig's exceptional case into the general rule. For in his treatment of capital charges, Taussig held that international differences in interest rates have no effect on international trade and specialisation unless the relative use made of capital varies from industry to industry. He regarded such varying use of capital as exceptional. But the theory we are presenting considers it (and the relative use of land and labor as well) to be quite normal. See the illustrations which follow in the text.

Land, being abundant in A, is cheap, but expensive in B, where it is scarce. Labor, B's abundant factor, is cheap there, but six times as costly in A, where it is comparatively much scarcer. And capital, being less plentiful in B, is almost twice as dear there.

Our next step is to introduce production functions. Let us take, for illustrative purposes, beef and rice. The former calls for the use of an extensive land area, while rice is produced by a method in which land is economised, labor applied in relatively large amounts. Suppose production requirements are as follows:

QUANTITY OF FACTORS REQUIRED TO PRODUCE:

	BEEF (1 million lbs.)	RICE (10,000 lbs.)
Land	100,000 units	10 units
Labor	20 units	5 units
Capital	70 units	1 unit

(Note: the factor units are the same as those in the table of factor prices.)

By combining these two tables, we can see what it would cost to produce beef and rice in each of our two countries.

	FACTOR PRICES IN A	IN B	FACTOR REQUIRE-MENTS	Beef COSTS IN A	IN B	Rice FACTOR REQUIRE-MENTS	Costs IN A	IN B
Land	$ 1	$ 20	100,000	$100,000	$2,000,000	10	$ 10	$200
Labor	600	100	20	12,000	2,000	5	3,000	500
Capital	80	150	70	5,600	10,500	1	80	150
Cost of 1,000,000 lbs.				$117,600	$2,012,500	Cost of 10,000 lbs.	$3,090	$850
Cost per lb.				$0.118	$2.01	Cost per lb.	$0.309	$0.085

Beef, the land-intensive product, costs only about 12¢ a pound to produce in A, where land, the factor weighing most heavily in costs, is abundant and cheap. In B, because land is scarce and expensive, its cost is prohibitively high. Clearly, as between these two countries, A would specialise in the production of beef. In rice, on the other hand, B achieves a low cost of 8½¢ a pound because labor, the factor contributing most heavily to costs, is cheap there. A's costs, at approximately 31¢ are nearly four times as high, because even though land is cheaper, labor, the factor used most intensively, commands far higher wages. B would specialise in rice production, even exporting it to A unless transportation charges and other costs of transfer exceeded some 22¢ a pound.

MORE THAN ONE PRODUCTION FUNCTION

Up to this point, our argument has been based on the tacit assumption that for each commodity, only one method of combining the factors, or production function, is available. This is enough, if the prices of the factors differ from country to country, to ensure international specialisation and trade. For the costs and prices of labor-intensive commodities will be relatively low in countries where labor is abundant and wages are low, and similarly with capital-intensive and land-intensive products.

In fact, however, most commodities can be produced by two or perhaps even several methods. Rice, for example, has in recent years become an important crop in the United States, owing to the development of machinery that can be combined with relatively small quantities of labor to cultivate and harvest large areas. This method economises in the use of labor, the expensive factor in this country, but uses the relatively cheap capital and land liberally. As a result, rice can now be produced in the United States at a cost comparable to that achieved by the labor-intensive type of cultivation typical in Japan, Burma, and Thailand. The following hypothetical exmple shows how the two techniques compare.

COST OF PRODUCING RICE BY ALTERNATIVE METHODS

	Labor-intensive			Capital-land-intensive		
FACTORS	FACTOR PRICES (BURMA)	FACTOR REQUIREMENTS	COST	FACTOR PRICES (U.S.)	FACTOR REQUIREMENTS	COST
Land	$ 20	10	$200	$ 10	1,000	$10,000
Labor	100	5	500	2,000	10	20,000
Capital	150	1	150	50	400	20,000
	* Cost of 10,000 lbs.:		$850		* Cost of 600,000 lbs.:	$50,000
		Cost per lb.:	$0.085		Cost per lb.:	$0.0833

* As with the previous illustration, the yield per acre has been assumed to be 1,000 lbs., or 10,000 lbs. for 10 acres, using the labor-intensive method. With the capital-land-intensive method, yield is assumed to be 600 lbs. per acre, or 600,000 lbs. for a land input of 1,000 acres. This is in accord with the general principle that the yield per acre will be less, the lower the proportion of the other factors (labor and capital) is to land.

Costs per pound by the capital-land-intensive method are approximately the same as by the labor-intensive method. Although, with wages twenty times as high in the United States as in Burma, the wage bill still comprises a large share of total costs (40 per cent as compared with nearly 60 per cent in Burma), by combining with a *relatively* small quantity of labor very large amounts of capital and land, output is so increased as to bring unit cost down to the Burmese level.

This point can be clarified, and the role of factor proportions made more apparent, if we reduce the capital-land-intensive method to the same scale as the labor-using method. Total output on the large (1,000 acre), mechanically cultivated farm is 600,000 lbs.; on the small (10 acre), intensively cultivated farm it is 10,000 lbs. If we divide the factor requirements of the extensive farming method by 60, they become—for 10,000 lbs. of output—16⅔ acres of land, 0.167 units of labor, and 6⅔ units of capital. The capital-and-land-using method requires two-thirds more land and 6⅔ times as much capital as the labor-using method, but the latter requires 30 times as much labor.

Prediction

The existence of alternative methods of producing a single commodity has interesting implications for international trade theory. Production of a good, instead of being concentrated solely in those countries possessing a factor endowment suited to a single method, will spread to others whose quite different factor supplies and prices make economical other, competing methods of producing this good.

From this it follows that the predictive value of our reasoning is reduced, since the number of variables that have to be taken into account has now been increased from one to two. If a commodity can only be produced by a labor-intensive method, we can predict with relative ease where its production will be economical: we need only look for regions or countries where labor is relatively abundant and cheap. But if a capital-intensive method can be used to produce the same good at a comparable cost, a wider range of possible production sites is opened up. We must now also look for countries where capital is the cheap factor. Although the location of production is just as fully determined as before, in the sense that the site of an industry is fixed by objective, measurable forces, with alternative production methods these determining forces become more complex and their outcome less easy to predict in advance.

Our difficulties are compounded if, instead of two alternative methods of production, we have to admit of a multiplicity, say three or four. The extreme would be represented by a single continuous production function subject to an unlimited and smooth variation in the proportions in which the factors could be combined.[8] Yet even with this situation, although

---

[8] The diagrammatic discussion in the Appendix is helpful here. Instead of yielding separate rays representing distinct production methods with rigidly fixed proportions and rectangular isoquants, the continuous production function would give a single, smooth, curved isoquant (or equal output curve), starting high up and close to the capital axis and moving downward and to the right until it approached the labor axis. It is to be interpreted as meaning that a given output could be obtained by means of an unlimited and very gradually changing series of combinations of capital and labor.

the *physical* combinations of the factors potentially capable of yielding a given output would be without limit, the number that would actually need to be considered would be finite. It might even be limited to a single specific method (i.e., combination of the factors), with only minor variations in the use of the factors practically realisable. For what is significant from the point of view of geographical specialisation is not that a variety of production methods may be *technically possible,* but that only a very limited number of them are likely to be *economical.*

For example, petroleum refining is carried out everywhere in the world according to methods that are almost identical, involving the use of huge amounts of capital invested in cracking plants, distillation units, great storage tanks, miles of pipes, thousands of valves, and hundreds of gauges. It is also possible to produce petroleum products by techniques using relatively large amounts of labor and very little capital, and such methods were used prior to the development of the modern technique. But they are now obsolete and unused because they are uneconomical: they would require so much labor to attain an output comparable to that of even a small modern plant that wages would have to be a fraction only of what they are in the poorest and most densely populated parts of the world.[9]

Fortunately for the practical usefulness of our theory, the range of alternative factor combinations that are economically feasible appears, in most industries, to be rather limited. Especially in those of relatively recent origin, such as petroleum refining, rayon and other synthetic fibers, automobiles, antibiotics, heavy industrial chemicals, and many others, capital-using techniques are highly productive—to achieve a given output by labor-intensive methods would require such a great increase in the input of labor to offset the decreased use of capital as to render them extremely costly unless wages were unimaginably low. Alternative methods are simply not worth considering. Even the old established cotton textile industry appears now to be approaching this pattern, else why would Japanese manufacturers, with abundant labor available at very low wages, have built plants whose machinery is practically 100 per cent automatic?

In many other industries, and agriculture and mining as well, the range of practicable alternatives is certainly not unlimited, and in most cases would appear to be confined to two or three. We have already mentioned

[9] In technical terms, which you can only understand after reading the Appendix, the outlay curve that is the tangent to the production isoquant in its labor-intensive sector is of a higher order than the one that is tangent to the isoquant in its capital-intensive sector.

rice production. Cotton is similar: its production in Egypt and India is labor-intensive; in the United States, most is produced at least with the aid of tractors, expensive plows and other cultivating equipment, with relative economy in the use of labor, while a large proportion is harvested with the mechanical cotton picker. Machinery, tools, optical goods, and many other products permit the adoption—depending on factor prices—of either a capital-intensive or a comparatively labor-intensive technique. In the United States, Germany, and other western countries, the production of such goods takes place in large, highly mechanised plants, in which the relative use of the factors is closely similar. In Japan and some other low-wage countries, skilled labor working in small, poorly equipped shops turns out comparable products at competitive prices. Yet the range of alternatives that must be considered is not unlimited. In most cases two or three fairly sharply demarcated choices appear to be all that are indicated.

Simplicity Versus the Facts

Even this wide a range, it must be admitted, destroys the neatness and clarity of our simple, single-production-function model. It makes prediction more hazardous and difficult. But if more facts must be taken into account, the model must be modified to deal with them. If this modification can be made successfully, the explanatory value of the theory is retained. We shall find that even further qualifications have to be introduced, all of which complicate our theory. But the facts of life are complex. It would be most convenient and gratifying if we could explain them by reference to a single touchstone of limpid clarity and unequalled simplicity. If this is impossible, if simple explanations are misleading, we must reconcile ourselves to using an elaborate kit of tools to deal with complex problems.

APPENDIX

Some students find graphic methods helpful. For those of you of whom this is true, the issues raised by the existence of two or more production functions for a single commodity can be clarified by the following presentation.

On the accompanying diagram, units of capital are measured along the vertical axis, units of labor along the horizontal axis. Different production functions or processes may be represented by rays, such as those marked I and II, radiating outward from the origin at zero. I represents a capital-intensive process, involving the use of 3 units of capital with 1 unit of labor, while II, requiring 4 labor for each unit of capital, is labor-intensive.[10]

Output can be measured by distances from the origin along each of the rays. The point *a*, for example, might represent 10 units of output, obtainable by method I by using 3 units of capital and 1 of labor, while point *b* reflects the same output obtainable via method II when 1 unit of capital is combined with 4 units of labor.

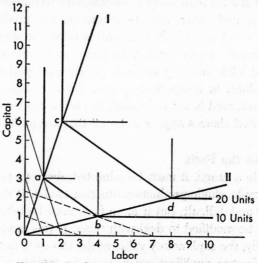

Fig. 5.1: Production Functions and Relative
Prices of Factors.

If we connect *a* and *b* and extend this connecting line horizontally from *b* and vertically from *a*, we obtain an "equal product" line, or isoquant. Any point on this isoquant represents the same output, 10 units, obtainable by combining the factors in the proportions corresponding to the point in question. Points of the vertical portion of the isoquant above *a* stand for an output of 10, the same as at *a* itself, and reflect the fact that the production function is assumed to be fixed. That is, it is assumed that the addition of more capital to that already in use at point *a* will not increase output. Similarly with the horizontal portion of the isoquant beyond *b*—the addition of more and more labor will leave output unchanged. Points between *a* and *b*, on the other hand, indicate that an output of 10 can be obtained by a combination of the two methods. At the mid-point between *a* and *b*, for example, 10 units of output could be obtained by using half the available resources according to method I, the other half according to method II.

[10] Only two factors can be considered at a time, since we have only two axes available.

Additional isoquants, representing still larger outputs, can be drawn farther out along the production rays. Thus the isoquant *cd*, twice as far from the origin as *ab*, stands for an output of 20 units.[11]

Now introduce factor prices into the picture. Suppose that in country A, capital is plentiful and cheap, labor, scarce and dear. Then a given sum spent on each of these factors in turn will command a relatively large amount of capital, a relatively small amount of labor. Let us assume that for $10, we can buy 1 unit of labor or 3 units of capital. A diagonal line drawn between the 3 unit point on the capital axis and the 1 unit point on the labor axis will then reflect the fact that $10 will buy either 3 capital or 1 labor, or a combination of the two determined by the slope of the line. A higher line, indicating, say, an expenditure of $20 or $30, will show that these sums will buy 6 units of capital and 2 of labor or 9 of capital and 3 of labor. At the same time, the slope of these lines, or of any parallel line representing a greater expenditure, tells us that 3 units of capital will exchange for 1 labor, at a price of $3.33⅓ per unit of capital and $10 per unit of labor. Such lines are therefore called "exchange" or "price" lines as well as "total expenditure" lines.

Given this ratio of exchange between labor and capital (the relative prices of these factors), which production function will be most economical for A? To discover this, we need merely find the total expenditure or price line that just touches (is "tangent" to) a point representing a determinate amount of production according to one of the two production functions, say at *a* or *b*. The $20 line is just "tangent" to *a*. Since this outlay will give an output of 10 units, cost per unit is $2. (Factor costs for this output will be $10 for 3 units of capital and $10 for 1 unit of labor, as required by the production function at this point.) Were A to try to use production method II, it would have to employ 4 units of labor, costing $40, and 1 unit of capital, costing $3.33⅓, for a total cost of $43.33⅓, or $4.33⅓ a unit. Clearly, for A, the most economical method is the capital-intensive method, which is what one would expect since in A capital is the abundant and cheap factor. Our diagram tells us not only this, but also precisely what unit costs will be by each method.

Turn now to country B, where we may assume labor to be the abundant and capital the scarce factor. Suppose that an outlay of $10 will command either 1 unit of capital or 3 units of labor, thus giving prices for capital

---

[11] This assumes constant returns to scale, i.e., that doubling all inputs results in a doubling of output. Were diminishing returns to scale assumed, *cd* would have to be drawn proportionately farther from the origin than is *ab*.

and labor, respectively, of \$10 and \$3.33$\frac{1}{3}$ per unit. This outlay and exchange ratio are shown by the dashed line connecting the appropriate points on the two axes. The lowest such total expenditure line (parallel, of course, to the one just mentioned) that is "tangent" to *a* or *b* is the one connecting 7 units of labor and 2$\frac{1}{3}$ units of capital. It represents an outlay of \$23.33$\frac{1}{3}$ and therefore a unit cost of \$2.33$\frac{1}{3}$. (The factors will be combined, in line with the production function, in the proportions of 1 capital and 4 labor, which at \$10 and \$3.33$\frac{1}{3}$ a unit each come to \$23.33$\frac{1}{3}$.)

Should country B try to use production method I (at *a*), the total cost, for 3 capital and 1 labor, would be \$43.33$\frac{1}{3}$, or \$4.33$\frac{1}{3}$ a unit. Clearly, if B is to produce the commodity in question at all, it will have to use method II. But if trade is unrestricted and if we neglect transportation costs, A will be able to undersell B, with a minimum production cost of \$2.00 a unit. This is because, given these two production functions, the price of labor is not low enough in B to offset the relatively great use of labor required by method II.

If now the price of labor relative to capital in A falls, owing say to an increase in the population, this could be represented by rotating A's price or expenditure lines in a counterclockwise direction, reflecting an exchange ratio of a smaller number of units of capital for a larger number of units of labor. When would it pay A to begin using production method II? As soon as one of the entire family of expenditure or price lines coincided with the line *ab*. If we extend this line to the axes, it appears that a line of this slope would represent an exchange of 3$\frac{2}{3}$ capital for 5$\frac{1}{2}$ labor. If we assume that the price of capital remains at \$3.33$\frac{1}{3}$ a unit, and that only wages have fallen, then the line coinciding with *ab* would represent a total expenditure of \$12.22$\frac{2}{9}$ (3$\frac{2}{3}$ $\times$ \$3.33$\frac{1}{3}$). Used to buy 5$\frac{1}{2}$ units of labor, we find wages would be \$2.22$\frac{2}{9}$ a unit.

Now it would be a matter of indifference whether method I or II were used, or some combination of the two. A similar outcome would be reached in country B if wages were to rise relative to the cost of capital until one of its price lines coincided with *ab*, also giving a ratio of exchange of 3$\frac{2}{3}$ capital for 5$\frac{1}{2}$ labor.

SELECTED REFERENCES

Haberler, G., *The Theory of International Trade* (Wm. Hodge & Co., Ltd., London, 1936). Chapter XII is noteworthy in showing how, when the single (labor) factor model of the classical economists becomes transformed into a multi-factor model, costs must be measured in terms of opportunities foregone.

Haberler, G., *A Survey of International Trade Theory,* Special Papers in International Economics, No. 1, Sept. 1955. (International Finance Section, Princeton University). Chapter III reviews and evaluates Ohlin's and more recent contributions to the theory of international trade.

Kindleberger, Charles P., *International Economics* (Richard D. Irwin, Inc., Homewood, Ill., 1953). Chapters 5 and 6 use a diagrammatic analysis to present the classical and the factor-proportions versions of international trade theory.

Leontief, W. W., "Domestic Production and Foreign Trade; the American Position Re-Examined," *Proceedings of the American Philosophic Society,* April 24, 1953 (Philadelphia); also in *Economia Internazionale, VII* (1954). Leontief challenges the usual assumption that capital is the abundant and labor the scarce factor in the United States.

Ohlin, Bertil, *Interregional and International Trade* (Harvard University Press, Cambridge, 1933). Part I contains the gist of the author's formulation of the general equilibrium theory of international trade. Appendix I presents a statement in mathematical form.

Robinson, Romney, "Factor Proportions and Comparative Advantage," *Quarterly Journal of Economics, LXX* (May, August, 1956). A trenchant criticism of the factor-proportions analysis.

Snider, Delbert A., *Introduction to International Economics* (Richard D. Irwin, Inc., Homewood, Ill., 1954). Chapters 2 and 3 are an excellent brief statement of the modern theory of international trade. The appendix to Chapter 3 provides a brief introduction to the indifference curve analysis.

6

INTERNATIONAL TRADE THEORY: MODIFICATIONS OF THE SIMPLE MODEL

The model of international trade whose construction we have just completed is a very simple one. It rests explicitly upon the assumption that there are only three factors and that all industries are perfectly competitive. It assumed constant unit costs for any volume of output. Moreover, it neglected the role of costs of transporting goods between markets and it postponed consideration of the function of exchange rates.

Although this simple model is useful as a first approximation, to make it more realistic and hence more applicable to actual conditions, we must relax the restrictive assumptions upon which it rests. We shall deal first with the three-factor assumption.

MANY FACTORS OF PRODUCTION

The need for introducing a more elaborate classification of the factors of production may be made clear by an illustration. Switzerland is relatively well supplied with skilled labor; its wages are therefore comparatively low. This accounts, in considerable part, for Switzerland's specialisation in high-grade watches, whose production requires the use of relatively large amounts of this factor. Unskilled labor, on the other hand, is not particularly abundant in that country; hence it is not noted for the production of commodities that use it in large quantities. In India, however, unskilled labor is plentiful and cheap, and one of that country's specialties is the (unskilled) labor-intensive product, jute. Labor, in other words, is an abundant factor in both Switzerland and India, but it is not the same kind of labor.

Perhaps even more obviously, land is not a single, homogeneous factor; there are many kinds of land, each capable of producing different types of product. Relatively infertile, semi-arid land is well suited to stock-raising and poor for growing crops, whereas fertile areas in the tropics may give good yields of sugar, pineapples, or coconuts, but be relatively unproductive in growing potatoes or wheat.

Clearly, in making international comparisons, we need a more detailed classification of factors than the traditional land, labor, and capital. But how many factors, or better, sub-factors? What criteria shall we use in differentiating one from another?

Two criteria are relevant. One is that to characterise a particular collection of productive agents as a sub-factor, it must be suited to the performance of a specialised function. Thus for a given area of land to be so classified, it should be especially suited to the production of a particular kind of output, say grains or citrus fruit. Secondly, all units of any such sub-factor must be of the same quality, which means that their inherent productive efficiency in their special function must be at least approximately the same. It would not do, for example, to compare good grazing land in one country with poor grazing land in another; even though the latter were considerably cheaper, its lower quality might more than offset the lower price.

We are now ready to show how these criteria can be applied to the three major factors of production. Let us begin with land.

Land

When we speak of the factor "land," what we have in mind is the contribution to production made by natural resources of any kind. Their varieties are obviously numerous. Most specialised of all are mineral deposits, and for the production of any mineral, availability of the relevant natural resource factor—deposits of the mineral in question—is uniquely necessary. The cooperation of labor and capital is also required, but a country without deposits of iron ore, nickel, or copper simply cannot produce these minerals, although many other production alternatives, depending upon less specialised natural resources, may be open to it.

Of all natural resources, minerals are the most unevenly distributed. Most of the world's nickel comes from Ontario, smaller amounts from New Caledonia and northern Finland. Copper is derived principally from Ontario, Chile, the Belgian Congo, and the United States. Iron ore is more widely distributed. Outstanding in this respect are the Soviet Union and the United States, though our best iron reserves are approaching exhaustion and we are having to rely increasingly upon imports from South America and Canada.

Forest resources, another highly specialised category, are also very unevenly distributed. Softwoods, such as the fir and spruce so important for building purposes, today come principally from British Columbia and the north-western United States, though vast, untapped stands exist in southern

Alaska and Siberia. Most of the pulpwood to meet the ever-growing demand for paper is produced in Canada, the northern Scandinavian countries, and our southern states. Hardwoods, as yet of minor industrial importance, are available in vast quantities in Central America, the Amazon Valley, central Africa, and Malaya.

Fisheries are another widely dispersed natural resource, of which the most famous are the Dogger Bank of the North Sea, the Newfoundland Banks, and the salmon fisheries of the northwest Pacific region. The seas around Japan have for centuries contributed an important share of its people's diet and in more recent years of its exports.

Another specialised natural resource not to be overlooked is water power. Potentially best endowed in this regard are the U.S.S.R., India and Pakistan, the United States, western Europe, Canada, and China, in that order. Potential is one thing, however, accessibility another. Many of the finest power sites are so remote from markets as to render them unusable. This is particularly true of South America.

Agricultural land is the most abundant and ubiquitous of all resources, yet its amount in relation to the world's total land area is surprisingly small. Out of 52 million square miles in all, only 3.7 million, or about 7 per cent, are now cultivated. A somewhat larger area, 4.2 million square miles, now too dry or too swampy to be used, could be rendered arable by heavy expenditures on irrigation or drainage, while another 2.1 million square miles of pasture land could be cultivated. In all, not more than 20 per cent of the earth's land surface could be brought under crops; the rest is mountain, desert, hopelessly swampy, frigid, or suited only for grazing or forestry.

Enough has already been said to indicate that from the point of view of accounting for international specialisation, "agricultural land" is too broad a category to be very serviceable. Land areas differ tremendously with respect to fertility, character of terrain, and the three components of climate: insolation (exposure to the sun), humidity, and rainfall. Various combinations of these elements are suited to different kinds of crops. Depending upon the degree of refinement desired, a number of sub-factors could be distinguished. A simple classification would certainly list the following:

(1) the temperate, well-watered, and comparatively fertile areas that are the world's great grain-producing regions;

(2) "Mediterranean" type lands—fertile, warm, but with relatively little rain and much sun (accounting for olives, citrus fruits, grapes, avocados);

(3) the tropical lowlands (sugar, bananas, pineapple, cacao, coconuts);
(4) the medium-altitude lands of the tropics, whose equable, warm climate especially suits them for growing tea and coffee.

These four categories of arable land, together with pasture (dairying) and grazing land (stock-raising), should provide sufficient detail for most purposes. In comparing costs of producing a given crop in different countries, allowance for qualitative differences will of course have to be made. We reserve treatment of this problem for the next section (pp. 98-9).

Labor

We can distinguish at least four labor sub-factors.

(1) Technical and managerial labor requires, in general, the highest degree of intelligence and the most prolonged training or experience. In this class are technicians of all kinds: engineers, architects, scientists, agronomists, plant superintendents and business managers, accountants, and professional people generally.
(2) Skilled labor demands, in varying combinations, intelligence, manual dexterity, artistic talent, and other special qualities, usually together with an apprenticeship of considerable duration. In this group are printers, plumbers, electricians, machinists, loom-fixers, draftsmen, commercial artists, and the like.
(3) Semi-skilled labor, though not divided from skilled labor by a sharp line, comprises those occupations in which skills and the human qualities that support them are less important. In this category fall such occupations as bus and truck drivers, tractor operators, loom operators, lumber workers, and most types of machine operatives.
(4) Unskilled labor includes all those whose work requires little or no specialised skill. Here we find delivery men, janitors, sweepers, hand truckers, assembly line workers, and common labor generally.

Because the human attributes needed to perform the more exacting tasks are possessed by relatively few, and because lengthy training requires a financial outlay that relatively few can afford, we find the lower ranks of these non-competing groups relatively crowded. Hence there is generally a fairly close correlation between the degree of skill and training and the level of pay, though exceptions are not hard to find. (Teachers, especially in the United States, though in terms of qualifications they fall in the technical group, have for many years earned a smaller average income than many in the skilled labor category. The growing shortage of teachers may in time correct this anomaly.) These groups are found in practically all countries; they are called non-competing because although there is some movement from one group to another, it is slow and gradual and is mainly restricted to adjacent groups.

Capital

When labor and natural resources are combined with capital in a productive enterprise such as a factory, as many as four different kinds of labor may be required in proportions that vary with the kind of article being produced. The capital with which the labor works is likely to be equally or even more diverse. It includes buildings, machines, tools, and probably trucks, as well as typewriters and other types of office equipment. The capital, in other words, is in the form of extremely varied, concrete producers' goods. Each particular capital good—even the factory building—is suited to the performance of a specialised productive task; indeed, there is a good chance that some of the equipment was specially designed for this particular factory's operations. In line with our second criterion of a productive factor, all units of a given type of capital good (except those specially designed), whether used in this or any other factory in the industry, are likely to be identical or at least closely similar.

Now if capital goods were "on all fours" with labor and natural resources, the tremendous specialisation that characterises these aids to production would require us to admit of a bewildering variety of capital sub-factors. This would be true even if we were able to lump together all equipment performing a single type of operation, such as the dozens of kinds of lathes. As with labor, we would have non-competing groups of capital goods, though instead of four, the number of such groups would be many times greater. Each of these types of capital goods would command a price for its services determined by its marginal productivity, as fixed by a supply which could be increased only slightly via competition from other analogous though distinct groups.

Capital goods differ from labor (and natural resources), however, in one crucial respect: they are not an original productive agent given by nature (though considerably modified by training and experience), but are a produced means of production. Unlike labor or natural resources, capital goods must be created by the cooperation of labor, natural resources, and previously existing capital goods.[1] Now this creation of capital goods can take place quite rapidly—even a large office building or a petroleum refinery

---

[1] It is true that the skills of labor are also in part created by training and experience; their acquisition, however, is restricted by limitations of inherent ability and by the barriers, financial and other, to obtaining the required training.

can be constructed in a matter of two or three years at most. Hence the prices of the services of different types of capital are on a different footing from those of non-competing groups of labor; in a competitive economy, they cannot for long differ, since a high return to a particular type of capital good will be driven down by the production of an increased supply.[2] There is a strong operative tendency toward equality of return to all units of capital, or toward a uniform supply price for capital.

The answer to the question, "Into how many sub-factors are we to classify capital?" is perhaps best reached by raising first the further question, "What is the supply price of capital a payment for?"

With a natural resource, its supply price (rent) is the payment necessary to command its services—its contribution to production. In the case of labor, we have seen that its supply price, the wage earned by one of the non-competing groups, is a payment for the services of this particular kind of labor, the point at which the margin falls being determined by the proportion of the total labor force possessing the requisite abilities and training. In a competitive economy, profits need not concern us, for they are short lived. They constantly tend to disappear, leaving the producer no return over cost, which includes normal wages of management.

As for capital, a payment—in this instance of interest—is necessary in the long run, not to command the services of capital goods, but to get them produced. Interest must be paid, in other words, to cause people to perform the function necessary to bring capital goods into existence. This function is the postponement of consumption, or saving.

Initially, savings are provided in the form of freely investible funds, or money capital, which later becomes embodied (through the employment of existing resources) in various kinds of concrete capital goods. Those who perform this function of supplying investible funds are unwilling to do so "for free," but exact a premium; when this premium is expressed as a percentage of the funds advanced, it becomes the familiar rate of interest. Payment of this premium is *possible* because indirect or roundabout methods of production, involving the use of capital goods to aid labor, are more productive than direct, non-capital-using methods.

---

[2] For the time it takes to increase the supply of a particular capital good, its return may exceed the normal, being, like the rent of land, determined by demand over against a (relatively) fixed supply. On the other hand, when the demand for an existing type of capital good contracts (as for office space or homes in a decaying section of a city), its return may fall below the normal for a relatively long period—as long as the life of this particular property. For these reasons, the short-period income from fixed capital assets is often characterised as a quasi-rent.

It is *necessary* to overcome the unwillingness of savers to divert resources from consumption to the production of capital goods.[3]

The rate of interest—the payment necessary to permit the use of roundabout methods—is determined in the market for capital funds. These funds are in the first instance, as equivalent units of purchasing power, all alike. In the absence of complicating factors, they would receive a uniform return. But loans to different borrowers present different degrees of risk, depending on the creditworthiness of the borrower and whether the funds are invested in a safe or speculative venture. We must therefore distinguish between the pure rate of interest on riskless loans (i.e., to governments and perhaps large corporations with a top credit rating), and rates of interest that include varying premiums for risk. It is the former that we shall have in mind when we make international comparisons.

Since the supply of long-term capital is not completely homogeneous, but is differentiated according to the amount of risk attaching to different kinds of loans, logically, we should classify capital into as many sub-factors as there are degrees of risk. These are very numerous, however, ranging in an ascending scale from investments in the bonds of a financially sound government to outright speculations. We shall not be doing too great violence to the facts if we assume that, in the absence of contrary evidence, the relative supply of funds for investments of varying risks is the same in different countries. We can then treat capital *as if* it were homogeneous, and take the "pure" rate of interest in different countries as our measure of the relative abundance of capital. If, in any given country, there are no riskless investments, then it will be necessary to compare the return on investments with a similar degree of risk.

Where there is objective evidence indicating exceptional abundance or scarcity of funds for risky investments, this fact will have to be taken into account separately. Treatment of this problem requires careful judgment, however, for a tendency to shy away from risky investments in favor of the

---

[3] There would probably be *some* savings even at a zero rate of interest. The point is that these would be insufficient to satisfy the demand for capital (at a zero rate of interest) to be embodied in productive capital goods. *Additional* savings must be coaxed forth by offering a positive return.

Over short periods, the interest rate is not closely related to thrift, but is determined by the supply of liquid capital available. And the supply made available for active use, and the price or interest rate it can command, depends upon the attitude ("liquidity preference") of holders of idle balances. This attitude, however, is strongly influenced by what is felt to be a "normal" level of the interest rate. And this "normal" level is subject to determination by the long-run forces of productivity on the one hand, and the resistances to savings on the other.

safer kinds (which appears to exist in some underdeveloped countries) may merely reflect an extremely high degree of risk. Although lenders might be willing to advance funds for projects comparable in riskiness to ventures in other countries, unstable political conditions or the absence of basic investment in community facilities such as transport and power may make investment in manufacturing, for example, particularly hazardous.

Over the long run, the rate of interest as such, discounting risk, depends principally on the level of income, which is the source of savings, and on the savings habits of the public, together with the demand for investible funds as determined by the productivity of the roundabout method.[4] Since savings are made in the form of money, the supply of money capital can be augmented by the expansion of credit, i.e., by banking policy. This, however, is essentially a short-run factor—in the long run, productivity and thrift assert themselves.

If we can treat capital as homogeneous, we need not concern ourselves about classifying it into sub-factors. Unlike labor or natural resources, it can be regarded as a single, undifferentiated factor. Like these other factors, its relative supply or abundance in different countries varies. It is plentiful and cheap in countries with a large per capita income and a relatively high propensity to save, scarce and dear where incomes are low and/or the propensity to save is low.

It might be urged that we should regard short-term capital as a factor distinct from long-term capital. It does, indeed, generally receive a substantially lower return. Yet because the markets for short-term and long-term capital are interconnected, with a constant flow of funds between the two, the differential in returns tends to be fairly stable. This means that in countries where one kind is abundant, the other is almost certain to be, too. Thus for international comparisons, the distinction between short- and long-term capital is unimportant.

One further point: the immense variety of concrete capital goods is a technological fact. And since technology changes rather rapidly, so does the composition of the stock of capital goods, which are producible in relatively short order. The diversity of character of concrete capital goods is unrelated to the problem of the supply of capital, or what it is that requires

---

[4] There is an element of circularity here, since the level of current income is in part what it is because of the existing stock of capital goods, which are the result of past saving. The productivity of additional capital also depends on the size and existing stock of capital. At any point in time, however, this stock is a given datum.

a payment for its use. This diversity is a matter to be considered in connection with technology.

QUALITATIVE DIFFERENCES IN THE FACTORS

You will recall that the classical theory of international trade formulated its explanation in terms of the comparative effectiveness or efficiency of a single factor, labor. One of our objections to this theory was that the superior efficiency of labor in one country as compared to another might be largely due to the fact that it was combined with superior resources, greater amounts of capital, or better management. By taking these productive agents into account only indirectly—giving them, so to speak, only an off-stage part—the theory gave to a single factor an importance it does not possess in reality. It is, I believe, a strong point of the relative factor-supply approach that it avoids this fault by according each of the cooperating factors general equality of status. Then, by recognising explicitly that factor combinations vary widely for different commodities, and that different countries are very variously endowed with the different factors of production, it points the correct conclusion: that in some circumstances one factor, in others another, will be of preponderant importance in providing a cost advantage for a particular commodity in a particular country.

The shift in emphasis is from the *quality* of a single factor, labor, to the *quantity* of all the factors. Although this is a step in the right direction, since it expresses correctly, in terms of quantities of the cooperating factors, what were earlier taken to be qualitative attributes of labor, it would be a mistake to rule out qualitative considerations altogether. For these, too, can be important, even though their role is more restricted than it was formerly thought to be.

What we are now concerned with is international differences in the efficiency or productivity of a given factor, combined with similar (theoretically, identical) amounts of the cooperating factors. If, under such circumstances, the given factor is of poorer quality in one country than another, this fact will offset partially, or wholly if the qualitative differences are great enough, a cost advantage provided by relative abundance and cheapness of the factor in question. Thus in our earlier beef-rice illustration (p. 81), country B was able to produce rice by a labor-intensive method at a cost of 8½¢ a pound, while the cost to A was 31¢. B's cost advantage rested on the availability of abundant and cheap labor—wages in B were one-sixth those in A. But suppose B's labor is much less efficient than A's, say only one-sixth as efficient. Then to accomplish the same amount of work, six times as many laborers would have to be used.[5] The labor cost in the two countries would then be equal, and since land and capital costs in B are higher than in A, so would the cost of producing rice be higher— 33¢ in B as against 31¢ in A. B's advantage of cheap labor would be wiped out by its relative inefficiency.

Qualitative Differences in Labor

Evidence as to qualitative differences in labor is contradictory. Some appears to indicate approximately equal productivity, under similar conditions of production, of labor in different countries.[6] Many other comparisons, however, point to substantial disparities.[7] Moreover, the differences in productivity appear to be greatest (with some exceptions) between countries that differ most markedly as to culture and social institutions. The difference between Canadian and American labor is slight, relatively small between British, German, Swedish, and American labor, and in general very great as between the latter groups and labor in India, Egypt, Indonesia, and Brazil. Qualitative differences in labor are important, whatever their cause.

Qualities of Land

The case of land is even more conspicuous. Rich Kansas wheat land is far superior to the infertile and arid land of Montana or northern Alberta or Saskatchewan. And Chile's rich central valley produces far more, acre for acre, than the poor and stony soil of Greece, although the climate and crops are very similar.

---

[5] This involves relaxing the assumption that the combination of the factors is rigidly fixed. This appears reasonable, since with any given method of production, there is usually some possibility of varying the proportions of the factors. Such variation would appear to be greater for labor-intensive methods than for highly capital-intensive, such as quasi-automatic types of manufacture, where the labor (and land) requirements are confined within narrow limits.

An alternative to relaxing the fixed-factor-combination assumption would be to count each A laborer as the equivalent of six B laborers, and then to reckon the labor requirements of the combination in terms of "efficiency units."

[6] Thus, Chinese workers in an American electric bulb factory in Shanghai before World War II are asserted to have been as efficient as American workers in the U.S. (D.K. Lieu, *China's Economic Reconstruction and Stabilisation*, p. 53, Rutgers University Press, 1948.) Filipino men and women operated American shoe machinery in Manila with efficiency equal to that in the U.S. (Daniel H. Buchanan, *The Development of Capitalist Enterprise in India*, p. 361, Macmillan, 1934.)

[7] Thus Buchanan found that operation of an electric crane in India required three workers as against one in the U.S., while the output of coke per man ("working with new and wholly up-to-date American equipment") was less than one-sixth and that of pig-iron about one-fifth that of the American worker. (*Ibid.*, pp. 364-5.)

Capital vs. Management

Capital presents a different face. If a given method of production (say capital-intensive, which may involve output on a relatively small or a very large scale) is suited to a country's factor endowment and market area, there is nothing to prevent management from obtaining the most up-to-date machinery, tools, power plant, and other equipment. Producers of these artifacts are eager to sell their wares, not only to domestic buyers, but to consumers in all parts of the world. Failure to install modern equipment could be due only to one of two things. Management may be stubbornly conservative, refusing to keep abreast of the times, and adhering to outdated equipment and antiquated methods. But this is tantamount to saying that management has failed to adopt the factor combination best suited to the country's factor endowment, choosing (irrationally) instead to use one that is more labor-intensive and hence less efficient.[8] It is the quality of management (a labor sub-factor) that is at fault, not the quality of capital.

Alternatively, management may deliberately choose to install a poor grade of equipment (for instance, second-hand machinery) because it is cheaper. In other words, management rationally chooses a less capital-intensive method as being better adapted to its country's factor supply and price situation. Our initial assumption, that a production method of given capital-intensity is suited to the country's factor endowment, does not apply. Management is correct in its decision, and efficient, and the low physical productivity of the used equipment is offset by its lower cost.

Whether management is efficient and rational, or stubbornly conservative and irrational, we need make no allowance for international differences in the quality of capital. Fundamentally, this is because in its original state, capital consists of uninvested funds, which are alike everywhere. The quantitative element—the relative supply of capital in different countries—is the only one we need consider.

With land and labor, however, allowance must be made for qualitative differences. How can we best do this? The simplest way would seem to be to say that, where the cheapness of a factor is due, not just to its greater abundance, but to its inferior quality (as indicated by yield per acre or output per man hour under comparable conditions), a larger number of units of this factor will be required. Thus if in the production of pig iron by modern techniques, the wages of an Indian worker are one-twentieth of the

---

[8] In this situation, the proportion of labor to capital would be *greater* than were modern equipment used, since the *value* of the antiquated equipment would be less; therefore the total investment for a given labor force would be smaller.

American worker's but his efficiency is only one-fifth as great, then labor costs in India are one-fourth those in the U.S. (This advantage might or might not be offset by the availability of cheaper capital in the U.S. This would depend upon the relative importance of capital in the production function.)

SOCIAL CONDITIONS OF PRODUCTION

One of the striking differences between nations, and one that is generally far less marked between different regions of the same country, lies in the realm of social habits, attitudes, and institutions. These features, which the anthropologist summarises under the heading of culture, cover an immense range. They would include caste distinctions, racial or class prejudice, attitudes toward work in general and toward specific occupations in particular, religious convictions, arrangements with respect to land-holding, and the character of family relationships. An attempt to explore this subject in any detail would take us far afield. Yet it is essential that we acquaint ourselves with some of the more important ways in which a nation's culture can influence its people's economic activities and thereby its position in the international economy.

Speaking generally, a country's social environment affects its productive system chiefly by distorting the relative supply of its factors or by influencing their efficiency. A few illustrations should make these relations clear.

Class Distinctions

Thus India's caste system divides the Hindu population into over a thousand occupational groups whose techniques are prescribed by tradition.[9] Mobility between groups is therefore negligible; the relative supply of any particular class of worker changes only very slowly. The traditional disdain among upper class Brahmans for material production or pursuit of gain has handicapped and continues to handicap the development of industrial leaders and of the technical and managerial staff so essential to industrial expansion. Similarly, where racial projudice is strong, members of certain races may be denied access to preferred occupations. Thus in South Africa, skilled labor, of which there is a shortage, is the preserve of the white race; employment of Negroes is limited mainly to unskilled jobs in industry, to household service, and to agriculture. Though the lines are much less

[9] The caste system in India is undergoing rapid change, partly from deliberate pressure by the Government, partly from the needs of modern industry. Yet it is still strong enough to exert great influence upon industrial and agricultural organisation and practices.

sharply drawn in the United States, racial discrimination is sufficient to push a disproportionate number of Negroes into semi-skilled and unskilled occupations. Wages of groups thus swollen are depressed, while those of the higher categories are raised above the level that would be attained with fuller mobility.

Land Tenure Systems

Land tenure systems, or the laws and customs affecting land-holding, can strongly influence the character of a nation's agriculture. Where by primogeniture (sole inheritance by the eldest son) or other means, the accumulation and maintenance of huge estates is encouraged, as in many countries of the Near East and Latin America, production of crops suited to large-scale agriculture with an established market is encouraged. The latifundia of Chile run to cattle and wheat, of Brazil, to coffee and cotton, of Iran, to sheep and wheat. Were the landholdings smaller, many different crops would doubtless be grown, especially fruits and vegetables for domestic consumption. Efficiency as well as the type of crops grown is also involved: large landholdings provide the owner a satisfactory income even when inefficiently cultivated; the land tends to be wastefully used, and there is little incentive to introduce improved methods or more plentiful crops. At the opposite end of the scale, extreme fragmentation of holdings, as in parts of India, Ceylon, and under the land distribution program of Mexico, can result in uneconomically small farms, dedicated to the inefficient production of subsistence crops.

Political Features

Unstable and corrupt governments, especially if their instability is accompanied by public disorder and if government policies are changeable and unpredictable, can exert a powerful influence on the direction and character of investment. Investments promising a quick return will be preferred to those requiring many years to yield their benefits, small-scale operations will be preferred to large, and capital will avoid normally risky investments like the plague. The results of these political considerations may be seen in the enduring preference among the peoples of the East for the embodiment of their savings in precious metals and jewels, and in the tendency in Latin American countries for a large proportion of investment to go into real estate and inventories of goods, or to move abroad into the securities of more stable countries. Such practices starve industry and other productive activities of the capital needed for their expansion and create an artificial scarcity of investible funds.

Among special laws that discriminate against particular kinds of business, especially against foreign enterprise, we should mention tax laws and those that require majority stock control by citizens of the country in which the business is located, or that prescribe the employment of a high proportion of its citizens.

"Climate of Productivity"

Similar in its all-pervasive character to a country's political structure is what has been called "the climate of productivity." This phrase sums up the attitudes of a people toward production—attitudes that are the result of the interaction of a wide range of complex and subtle forces. This "climate" appears to be most favorable in northern and western Europe, the United States, and the British Dominions settled and developed by British immigrants. These were the areas most deeply affected by the Renaissance and the Reformation, which led to the release of the spirit of inquiry, stress on individual freedom and the dignity of the individual, and emphasis on the virtues of thrift and work. It would appear that these and related social values have been preserved most intact in the Scandinavian countries and the United States, which may account in considerable part for the relative strength in these lands of competition as an economic force, of the willingness to innovate, and of the social esteem accorded to economic success.[10] Though Britain shares the values of freedom and individualism, she also inherited an aristocratic social structure that stressed the values of social position, pleasant living, and cultural attainment. The resulting blend softened the force of competition and the urge to get ahead, to the detriment of Britain's industrial leadership. In France, dominance of the small, family-centered firm has tended to place security ahead of profits as a business motive, with the result that preservation of the status quo has become more important than the exercise of initiative and enterprise.

Poverty

Widespread poverty, though not an aspect of a nation's culture, but rather a result of that culture as it affects the utilisation of resources, has a clear and obvious connection both with the supply of factors and with their efficiency. Capital originates in the savings of a community; if incomes are generally low, there is little surplus over living requirements; savings will be small and capital scarce and dear. Moreover, since entry into the

[10] For an interesting discussion of the "climate of productivity," with special reference to the United States, see the chapter with this title in Graham Hutton, *We Too Can Prosper*, George Allen & Unwin, Ltd., London, 1953.

ranks of technical and managerial labor generally necessitates a long period of training and education which few in a poor community can afford, such labor is also likely to be scarce and to command relatively high wages. Owing to the pressure to put children to work at the earliest opportunity, even the acquisition of skills may be beyond the reach of most. Unskilled occupations tend to be overcrowded and wages there especially low.

But this is not all. Poverty means crowded and unsanitary living conditions and an inadequate diet. From these follow undernourishment and a high incidence of contagious disease. Much time is lost from work, the worker lacks energy, and his productivity is low. Ignorance and illiteracy also usually accompany poverty; they too reduce the efficiency of labor.

If poverty places obstacles in the way of individual advancement, widespread educational opportunities help to overcome them. Countries that place a high value on education—which means those that stress the dignity and worth of the individual—can, by making cheap and easy the acquisition of knowledge, both general and technical, minimise the barriers to advancement.[11] The ready availability of educational opportunities in the United States certainly goes far toward explaining the relatively large numbers of skilled workers, managerial staff, and technicians in this country. The same is true of Germany.

SUMMARY

Our simple three-factor model of international trade has now been made considerably more sophisticated. Without altering it in any essential way, we have allowed for the fact that labor and land do not consist of identical homogeneous units, but of a number of sub-groups distinguished from one another by the productive purposes they serve. The precise number to be considered will vary with the problem at hand. If we wish to make a very detailed analysis, we shall need a highly specific classification. But for most purposes, only a rather small number of sub-factors need be distinguished.[12]

[11] Communist doctrine depreciates the individual, accords primary importance to the state. Yet the U.S.S.R. has greatly expanded its educational facilities, and now provides education free up to the limits of an individual's capacities. It is doubtful that this represents a change in communist ideology. Rather it reflects a realisation of the importance to the state of a body of well-trained citizens, especially of those with technical training, which Russia's educational program has been emphasizing heavily.

[12] The advantage of a theory is that it permits us to generalise—to comprehend a large number of individual instances by means of a single general principle. The more we have to qualify and particularise a theory, the less becomes its explanatory value. As Samuelson has said, "But if one is forced ultimately to work with dozens of grades of labor, hundreds of grades of land, and innumerable grades of capital equipment, the explanations become rather *ad hoc* and not very helpful." P. A. Samuelson, "International Trade and the Equalisation of Factor Prices," *Economic Journal*, LVIII (1948), p. 181 n.

And for dealing with broad categories of commodities, the simple three-factor model is adequate.

Qualitative differences in the productive factors also had to be taken into account. Making allowance for these differences is not difficult—it merely requires increasing the input of an inefficient factor sufficiently to compensate its low productivity—but it blurs the sharp outlines of our basic theory, which originally ran solely in terms of relative quantities (and hence prices) of the productive factors.

Introducing social conditions of production into the picture implies no further qualifications. Rather it broadens the scope and realism of our discussion by exposing some of the forces determining the supplies of the factors and their efficiency. Factor supplies are not given once for all. They may increase or decrease, and the character of a country's culture can strongly influence the direction and degree of change. And by providing an environment favorable or adverse to a factor's operation, it can augment or diminish its efficiency.

SELECTED REFERENCES

Buchanan, Daniel H., *The Development of Capitalist Enterprise in India* (Macmillan, New York, 1934). This book is still worth reading for its account of India's development while still a colony. It has many comparative illustrations, though admittedly these are now out of date.

Ohlin, Bertil, *Interregional and International Trade* (Harvard University Press, Cambridge, 1933). Chapters V and VI discuss in some detail the problems of factor classifications and of qualitative differences in the factors.

Woytinsky, W. S., & Woytinsky, E. S., *World Population and Production* (Twentieth Century Fund, New York, 1953). A rich source for information on world resources, physical and human, and their relation to human needs.

Zinkin, Maurice, *Economic Development for Free Asia* (Blackwell, Oxford, 1956). The first few chapters contain many illustrations of the social conditions of production typical of the countries of Southeast Asia.

Zimmerman, Erich W., *World Resources and Industries,* Revised edition (Harper & Bros., New York, 1951). A good source for information on the distribution of the world's resources.

7

INTERNATIONAL TRADE THEORY:
FURTHER MODIFICATIONS

A country will produce and export a commodity if its costs are lower than those of its competitors. In our search for an explanation of *why* costs for some things are lower in one country, for others in another, we now know that a cost comparison must be computed in more complex terms than those of our illustrations in Chapter 5. Instead of just three factors, we must distinguish and make separate entries for several different grades of labor and several different kinds of natural resources. Allowance must also be made for differences in the efficiency of any single factor. Enough more of an inefficient factor may compensate for its lower productivity.

A table of costs for the production of pig iron in two countries might look like this:

FACTOR PRICES:	FACTOR PRICES In A	In B	FACTOR REQUIREMENTS	COSTS In A	FACTOR REQUIREMENTS ADJUSTED FOR INEFFICIENCY	COSTS In B
Site land	$ 400	$ 200	10	$ 4,000	–	$ 2,000
Managerial labor	10,000	5,000	3	30,000	6	30,000
Skilled labor	5,000	300	10	50,000	50	15,000
Semi-skilled labor	3,000	200	5	15,000	25	5,000
Unskilled labor	2,500	150	20	50,000	100	15,000
Capital	50	100	2,000	100,000	0	200,000
Cost of 10,000 tons:				$249,000		$267,000
Cost per ton:				$24.90		$26.70

Note: Factor units assumed are: Site land, 1 acre-year; all types of labor, 1 man-year for each; capital, use of $1,000 for a year. Management in A is assumed to be twice as efficient as in B, labor of all grades, five times as productive.

These, we may assume, would be the costs of typical plants operating at normal capacity. In the short run, if they (and the entire industry as well) faced conditions of slack demand, sufficient to justify only less than optimum output, unit costs would be higher, since part of the labor cost alone could be reduced—charges for capital, land, and management would continue unabated. If demand were very strong, enough to justify the temporary employment of additional labor, including perhaps some overtime, unit costs would also be likely to rise, owing to operation of the plant beyond its rated capacity.

But the adaptation of a country to its factor endowment, or to changes therein—the problem that concerns us—does not take place immediately, or even quickly. It requires years. Therefore our interest is in the long run. The question is: after allowing time for an industry to adjust to a stable level of demand, will its unit costs be the same whether it operates at a high or a low level of total output? In particular, starting from a stable level of output, will unit costs rise, fall, or remain constant as output increases? We shall see that the answer depends on the conditions under which production takes place.

VARIABLE AVERAGE COSTS

The problem we are here confronting has to do with the response of a *single* industry to an increase in demand for its product. To deal with it properly, we must assume that total expenditure in the economy remains constant, so that as demand for a given industry's output rises, the demand for other things is reduced by an equal amount. In other words, we are *not* concerned with the expansion of the economy as a whole.

Constant Costs

If under these conditions we have constant returns to scale, whereby increased input of all the factors results in a proportional increase in output (e.g., doubling the use of *all* the factors leads to a doubled output), and if the additional factors needed are drawn from the declining industries with no increase in their prices, unit costs will remain constant.

These results would be most likely to follow if the industry in question were small in relation to the entire economy, and if efficient plants were typically small in size. For then its demand for highly specialised factors would put no great pressure on their supply,[1] while economies of scale (see below) would be unlikely to play a significant role.

Many small industries appear to meet these conditions: ladies' garment making, custom-tailoring, dry-cleaning, fine watch-making, and handicraft-type industries generally.

Increasing Costs

Unit costs of production will rise with increasing output if one or more

---

[1] And if the "run" were long enough, needed special skills, for example, could be imparted to the labor released from other industries.

of the factors required in the expanding industry is limited in supply, or if additional supplies of a factor (though obtainable at a constant price) are of inferior quality. Since almost any kind of labor can be trained, given sufficient time, and any type of capital good can be produced, whereas the best agricultural land and mineral resources are limited in amount by nature, this means that increasing costs are most typical in agriculture and mining. Most other industries probably operate under conditions of constant costs over a wide range of output—though, especially if the industry is large, eventually an increase in its output is likely to encounter limited or inferior supplies of one or more factors important to its operation.

Thus an increased demand for lead, for example, would require more miners, more machinery and equipment, more intensive working of existing deposits, and the opening up of additional deposits of lead. The factor most severely limiting long-run expansion of output is clearly the deposits of the mineral. More intensive mining of existing deposits would require an input of capital and labor relatively greater than in the past for a given increase in output, since deeper shafts would have to be sunk. The royalties payable to the owners of the mining property would also rise, unless previously fixed in long-term contracts. And the opening of new deposits would entail recourse to less accessible or poorer veins of ore, which would also mean greater inputs of capital and labor for a given output, and hence increased unit costs.[2]

Decreasing Costs

Decreasing costs of production will arise if, when we increase the input of all the resources in an industry, output increases by a greater proportion. In other words, economies of scale, or increasing returns to scale, are present. (There is another cause of decreasing costs—external economies—to be explained shortly.)

During its early stage of development, while its market is small, almost any industry is likely to consist of a number of small-scale producers. If the market expands sufficiently (owing, say, to increased popularity of its product, or to the opening up of foreign markets) to justify the installation of large, complex, and expensive machinery in place of simpler tools and machines, unit costs of production may fall, even though the input of all factors has increased by the same proportion. Advantage can be taken of

[2] Since all factors cannot be increased equally, the factor proportions have to be altered. The result is not diminishing returns to scale, but diminishing returns in the use of a scarce factor. Diminishing returns to scale would arise only if, as the input of *all* factors was doubled, for example, output increased less than 100 per cent.

the superior efficiency of indivisible units of capital goods, whose use would have been uneconomical at lower volumes of output. Thus holes can be punched in sheet steel far more rapidly by using a big, expensive punch press than by the same capital outlay on smaller-scale equipment, such as drills. The punch press is "indivisible" in that it comes only in a large size; small presses cannot exert the necessary pressure. It is economical to use, however, only when output is large, so that its cost can be spread over many units.

It is almost certain that economies of scale are obtainable only over a limited range of output of an industry. Costs will cease to decline and become stable when increasing the scale of operations yields no further economies. An indefinite continuance of economies of scale would mean that the industry, as its output grew, would consist of a constantly smaller and smaller number of larger and larger plants, until one giant plant emerged, with a monopoly of production.

Another source of decreasing costs may, and often does, appear as an industry grows. This source is found in the phenomenon known as *external economies,* so-called because they are external to the individual plant, whereas economies of scale occur *within* the plant, or internally. External economies are principally the consequence of increased specialisation within an industry. Thus, with annual sales of, say, $1 million, each firm in the industry might have to perform all productive operations itself. With sales of $10 million, special parts producers might set up shop, and by introducing specialised machinery and more highly trained workers, produce the part in question at lower cost. With output at the $100 million mark, it might pay someone to establish a research organisation to provide a service hitherto not performed at all by the firms in the industry, or performed only intermittently or inefficiently. Or a trade journal might be established, furnishing the producer with information on the availability of managerial staff or of skilled labor, on market conditions, and on technological developments.

VARIABLE COSTS IN RELATION TO INTERNATIONAL TRADE

The outstanding effect of international trade is to bring about specialisation among nations. If trade were free from all restraints, and if, further, there were no costs of transport, each country would concentrate upon the production of those commodities for which its relative costs were lowest. Resources would clearly be allocated very differently than if each country were isolated, trying to supply all its requirements from domestic production.

Constant Costs: Complete Specialisation

How far would specialisation and the consequent reallocation of resources go? Would it be complete, meaning that any single country would devote itself to producing only those goods in which it had a comparative advantage in cost, while importing everything else from other specialised producers? Clearly costs of transport play a major role here; we shall consider them in some detail in the next section. But independently of this factor, even were international trade quite costless, the degree of specialisation and the corresponding allocation of resources would be strongly affected by the kind of cost conditions encountered in different industries.

With constant costs, complete specialisation would be the rule. Figure 7.1 represents two countries, A and B, both producing a commodity (watches) at constant costs. The vertical (price) axis is common to both countries; on the horizontal (quantity) axis, quantities are read from O to the right for country B, from O to the left for A. In isolation, A would produce OD for domestic buyers at a price of $50. In B, where costs are assumed to be higher, a domestic demand for the amount OH would be satisfied at a price of $75. If trade is opened up between the two, A could undersell B's producers and would capture the entire market. The resources

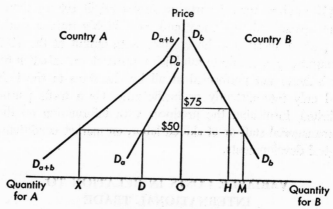

Fig. 7.1: International Trade: Different Levels of Constant Cost in Two Countries.

thus freed from the production of watches in B would move into some other line of production in which B had a cost and price advantage. In A, resources similarly released in some other industry by the new international competition would be drawn into the production of watches. Assuming the new market in B represents A's entire foreign market, output in A would expand to OX, or by the amount DX. Of A's total production, DX would be exported; these exports would of course equal OM, the amount imported by B at a price of $50.

Increasing Costs: Partial Specialisation

The situation is very different with a commodity, such as wheat, produced under conditions of increasing cost. In Figure 7.2, the (increasing) cost of producing wheat is shown for A in its supply curve, C_a, and in B, which is A's potential foreign market, by C_b. A is assumed to be the more efficient wheat producer, so its supply curve starts at a point below B's and is lower for every volume of output. The demand in each country is shown by the respective demand curves, D_aD_a and D_bD_b.

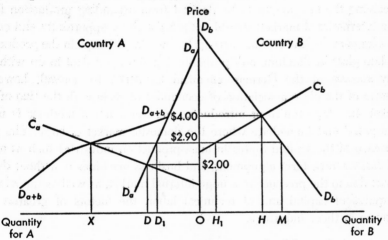

Fig. 7.2: International Trade: Different Levels of Increasing Cost in Two Countries.

In isolation, each country would produce for domestic sale that amount at which price and unit cost were equal. This would be OD at a price of $2.00 in A, OH at a price of $4.00 in B. With free trade, buyers in B, finding the price of wheat lower in A, would begin to import. Owing, however, to the necessity in A of resorting to poorer land or of intensifying the cultivation of land already in use, costs would rise as output increased, while with the decline in output and reduced pressure on scarce resources in B, costs would decline. Equilibrium would be reached at a price of $2.90, common to both countries. At this price, production in B would continue in the amount OH_1, with this supplemented by imports of H_1M. Country A would produce a total of OX, of which OD_1 is sold to home consumers, while D_1X ($= H_1M$) would be exported.

Specialisation is not complete, but only partial, under conditions of increasing cost. B continues to produce that part of her total consumption which can meet foreign competition (OH_1).

Decreasing Costs: Complete Specialisation

With decreasing costs (whether due to economies of large scale or to external economies), complete specialisation again would tend to be the rule. If there were several countries, each with similar but unrealised possibilities of producing a larger output at lower costs, where specialisation would occur would depend upon where entrepreneurs first saw these possibilities and acted upon them, by introducing larger-scale operations. A headstart gives a great advantage, which it would be difficult for others to overcome. There is no reason why foresighted producers in a small country, perceiving the advantages to be derived from expanding production for a wide international market, should not seize such an opportunity and establish a large-scale, low-cost industry. (This may in part explain the production of plate glass in Belgium, and probably it had a good deal to do with the early success of the German chemical industry.) In general, however, because of the close association of economies of scale with the size of the market, the opportunity of introducing mass-production methods is more widespread and immediate where the domestic market is large. The preeminence of the United States in mass-production industries such as automobiles, tractors, farm equipment, and business machines is without doubt in part due to the presence of a huge internal market, as well as the relative cheapness of capital and of technical labor, the factors of greatest importance in these industries.

International Demands

Until this chapter, our analysis of international prices was based on the assumption of constant costs. This permitted us to ignore demand, and to explain international price-cost differences in terms of supply conditions alone—in terms, that is, of prices of the factors and alternative ways of combining them. For if unit costs do not vary with output, demand determines *how much* of any commodity will be produced, but not *where* it will be produced. Production will take place wherever costs are lowest. Nor does demand have any influence on price, which remains constant regardless of output.

All this is changed if costs are variable. Suppose a larger output costs more per unit than a smaller. Then the price and cost of a commodity will depend upon demand as well as upon supply conditions. This is also true if unit costs decrease as output expands. Moreover, with increasing costs, whether and how much of a good competing with imports will be produced domestically will depend upon the relative size of domestic and foreign demand as well as upon the position and shape of home and foreign cost curves.

The important point is that demand comes back into the picture again as one of the determinants of the level of international prices. Thus in a world of multilateral trade the prices of exports produced at increasing costs will be higher, of those produced at decreasing costs lower, than in a world of isolated national units. With multilateral trade, the average level of a single country's export prices, given the cost conditions in its export industries, will depend upon the size of its own and the world's demand for these products. The same is true of every other country. Therefore the average of our country's import prices will also depend in part upon its own and upon other countries' demands for these goods.

Now the demand of one country for the products of other countries, and of those countries for the products of the first country, is simply our old friend, reciprocal demand. It is set, however, in a broader framework than when Mill stated it, for he applied it only to the simple case of two countries and two commodities. And like Mill, we can say that reciprocal demand determines the terms of a country's trade, meaning by this the relative height of its export prices as compared with its import prices. If, as with Mill, we assume that the transactions between one country and the rest of the world are confined to commodity trade, then we can go on to say that the prices of this country's exports and imports will be in a stable or equilibrium relationship with one another when the total value of its exports and of its imports are equal.

TRANSPORT COSTS

Up to now we have deliberately pushed aside consideration of transportation costs, so that we could focus attention upon the basic role played by factor prices in determining costs of production and thus where different commodities would be produced and which commodities would be traded between nations. We have also considered the ways in which the basic factor price explanation of international trade has to be modified because of the varying response of production costs to increasing output. We can now take account explicitly of the fact that the movement of goods involves costs, often heavy, that exert a strong influence upon the course of trade and upon the location of industry.

General Effects

The mere existence of transport costs affects trade in two general ways: (1) the prices of imported commodities will be raised; (2) because import prices are higher, the volume of international trade will be reduced. When transport costs exceed the difference in production costs in the (potential) exporting and importing centers, no trade will take place.

The effect of transport costs upon the prices of internationally traded goods can be stated very simply: the price in the importing center will differ from the price in the exporting center by the amount of the charges for freight, insurance, loading and unloading, etc., that comprise the costs in question. Whether this difference is great or small will depend upon the level of these transport costs, and these costs in turn will vary with the difficulties to be overcome in transporting goods and therefore the resources required to surmount them. It costs more to carry freight by rail across high mountain ranges than across level plains, more to carry it by land than by sea. In each case the reason is that more resources must be employed in the task of transportation. During the past two centuries, great advances in methods of transportation have tremendously lowered transport costs. It is only necessary to mention the transition from pack-horse to horse-drawn wagon and coach and then to steam- and diesel-powered train, from sailing vessel to screw-propelled steamship.[3] Distance itself is an impediment to trade, since other factors being equal, the greater the distance the goods must be carried, the higher the total of freight charges.

Anything that increases the level of freight charges—be it the need to cross difficult terrain, to use inefficient methods of transport (a camel caravan), or to go a long distance—increases the *economic distance* between two points, and therewith increases the price differentials and reduces the volume of goods traded. Accordingly, both the range of goods traded and the volume of trade in goods that move tend to be least between countries separated by great distances or connected by costly means of transport.

In our earlier, simpler model of international trade, when we concerned ourselves solely with production costs proper, it is clear that *all* goods would be either exported or imported. Any country that could produce

---

[3] "In the 1790's, freight in wagons over the bad roads from Philadelphia to Pittsburgh cost from $5 to $10 a hundred pounds (30 to 60 cents per ton-mile), with the result that salt sold at $5 a bushel in Pittsburgh and iron and steel from 15 to 20 cents a pound. Around 1800-25 long land movements of bulky freight in the United States were said to cost, on the average, about 33½ cents per ton-mile, but were rarely attempted." Eugene Staley, *World Economy in Transition*, p 17. Copyright 1939 by Council on Foreign Relations, New York. By 1910, the average freight rate per ton-mile on the principal American railways had been reduced to less than 1 cent.

a commodity at a cost lower than others would export it, and in turn would import all commodities for which costs were lower elsewhere. The only justification for domestic production of an article not exported would exist in increasing-cost industries, where at some point the rising costs of the principal supplier (exporter) would permit limited production in the importing country.

The introduction of transport costs changes this model materially. Even when production occurs under conditions of constant or decreasing costs, if the transport cost per unit of a commodity exceeds the difference between the home cost and the cost in the exporting center, the entire supply of this article will be produced domestically. Transport costs furnish "natural protection" that justifies the establishment of certain industries.[4]

Differential Effects

We must now take into account the fact that transport costs are not the same for equal weights of different goods, nor always proportional to the distance a given commodity is carried.

Differential rates for the same weight of different commodities are partly the result of the fact that costs of carriage themselves differ. Thus the additional investment in refrigeration equipment raises the cost of transporting perishables, while fragile freight requires careful and hence costly handling. Much more important, however, is the additional fact that a very large proportion of the costs of carrying various kinds of freight cannot be specifically allocated to any particular shipment, but are joint costs of all goods shipped. This is obvious so far as concerns overhead costs—those costs that continue regardless of the volume of traffic, such as the capital charges on the investment in railway rolling stock, terminal, and roadbed, or the salaries of management or wages of maintenance employees. But a considerable part of operating costs is also jointly shared by all types of traffic, as for example, the wages of switchmen and repairmen.

Since, by their very nature, joint costs cannot be traced back to specific shipments, their allocation leaves great room for discretion. This inevitably means discrimination, which can be completely arbitrary. As a general rule, shippers or regulatory agencies follow the principle of charging "what the traffic will bear." This results in the setting of relatively low rates per ton-mile on bulky or heavy items with a low value per unit of weight, such as coal, lumber, iron ore, grains, and crude oil, and relatively high rates on

---

[4] This is not true, of course, of such artificial costs of transfer as man-imposed tariffs. These may make possible but do not justify—in the sense of affording an alternative to be preferred on economic grounds—the establishment of an industry.

compact, highly fabricated, and valuable articles such as typewriters, cameras, watches, and jewelry. Rough equity is thereby achieved and the volume of paying traffic increased.

Joint costs are also responsible for the phenomenon of low "back haul" rates. From every major shipping center, there radiates outward a network of rail, ship, plane, and truck lines. Each type of conveyance must make an outward and a return voyage. If the volume of traffic carried in each direction were normally about the same, freight rates on the outward and the inward journey would be approximately equal. But often over any given route, more tonnage is carried in one direction than the other. Without some specific inducement, such as especially low rates, trains or ships will have to make one voyage empty, or partially so. Their loads may be increased if transport charges are lowered. Hence the low rates on coal shipped from Cleveland or Erie to Duluth, as against the much higher rate on iron ore moving in the opposite direction.

A particularly interesting illustration is provided by the overseas shipments of dry cargo from London. Before 1930, the weight of outward freight, of which some four-fifths was coal, considerably exceeded the weight of inward freight and bore the major part of the joint costs of both voyages. The cumulative effects of a structural change in British trade made themselves felt at just this time. Because of growing depletion of the coal mines and the rising costs associated therewith, the British industry found itself unable to compete with other fuels in extra-European markets. In addition, the use of coal as a source of power had been declining since at least 1913. Between 1929 and 1931, while the weight of dry-cargo imports fell only 8 per cent, that of exports (predominantly coal) dropped 31 per cent. The major burden of costs shifted to the inward voyage; outward rates dropped sharply, while inward rates rose.[5]

Many other aspects of differential freight rates are of importance; we shall mention only one or two. There is of course the practice of quoting lower rates for the long haul than the short haul, which may result from the desire to stimulate increased traffic to outlying points, from the need to meet competition (as between rail and ship between Atlantic and Pacific coast ports of the United States), or simply because the long haul spreads some overhead costs thinner. And there is the advantage afforded by canal and river barges of exceptionally low rates on long-distance traffic as

[5] Freight rates in May, 1931, to South America were 38 per cent lower than a year earlier, to India 20 per cent, while inward rates from these regions rose by 75 per cent and 34 per cent, respectively. All data for this illustration are taken from the interesting article by Carl Major Wright, "Convertibility and Triangular Trade as Safeguards Against Economic Depression," *Economic Journal*, LXV (September 1955).

compared with rail or truck transport. Operating as compared with overhead costs are unusually low for barges; once goods are loaded, the cost of transporting them by barge is relatively little greater for a long than for a short journey. The opposite is true of trucks, while railways are in an intermediate position.

Transport Costs and Localisation

Before attempting to assess the role of transport costs in determining the location of industry (broadly conceived to include all types of production) and thus the course of trade, let us recapitulate briefly.

We saw that in the absence of transport costs, the production of a commodity is determined principally by the relative supply of the factors of production taken together with the factor requirements established by various methods of production. If only one method is available for a given commodity, it will be produced in and exported from the country or countries where the supply of the factor most important to its production is relatively most abundant and hence cheapest. With two or more productive techniques available, say one labor-intensive and one capital-intensive, factor supplies and prices still determine the locus of production, but in a more complex way: the commodity is produced both where labor is abundant and cheap and where the same is true of capital. Supplementing these basic considerations, we saw that where economies of scale are important, a country may specialise in some line of production provided its businessmen appreciate these opportunities and establish a mass-production industry before this is done elsewhere.

The existence of transport costs as such, bearing uniformly on all goods, raises delivered prices and reduces the volume of trade, but affects the location of industry only insofar as such costs exceed international differences in production costs. As we have seen, however, transport charges vary widely from commodity to commodity and are not always proportionate to distance. Of particular importance is the fact that all commodities require raw materials for their production, and that freight rates are generally lower on raw materials than on finished articles. Moreover, the manufacturing processes may by their very character eliminate much of the weight of the materials used or, on the other hand, they may add to the weight or bulk of the finished goods at a rather late stage of processing.

These complexities increase the difficulty of determining the most economical point at which to locate production, and they lend themselves poorly to generalisation. Nonetheless, even though one can derive no broad, simple rule, yet one can arrange commodities into three groups in terms of where their processing will tend to take place. Commodities may be materials oriented, market oriented, or neutral in their orientation.[6]

Materials-oriented commodities. When the cost of transporting the raw material (or fuel) to the market exceeds the cost of transporting the finished good, the processing or finishing industry will tend to locate near the site of raw materials production. This will generally be the case if the raw material loses much weight in processing, for there is no sense in shipping waste matter to the point of manufacture. Thus lumber manufacture usually takes place near the timber stands—the bark, sawdust, and other waste are left behind, and only the finished lumber is shipped to the market. Vancouver, B. C., is an important lumber-milling center. Spruce trees are felled in the woods some hundreds of miles to the north, formed into huge rafts at tidewater, and towed (cheaply) to Vancouver. There an adequate supply of labor and external economies available in an industrial city provide excellent conditions for milling. The finished lumber is then loaded on ships and carried to markets all over the world.

Cotton ginning and baling (but not spinning and weaving), the extraction of cane and beet sugar and turpentine and rosin, vegetable canning, and pottery manufacture are further illustrations of materials-oriented processes. Aluminum refining requires immense quantities of electric power (the fuel factor). Hence the processing occurs not at the source of the raw material (bauxite) in Jamaica and British Guiana, but near the Grand Coulee Dam in the state of Washington, and in British Columbia.

Coal has immense drawing power, especially for the iron and steel and engineering industries, which are heavy users of this important fuel.[7] The greatest industrial area in western Europe arose in the coal deposits of the Ruhr—first iron and steel manufacture, drawing its ore from Lorraine and then northern Sweden, then industries fabricating heavy iron and steel products and needing coal for fuel as well as heavy steel sheets, rods, and bars as raw materials.

[6] By "materials" are meant the principal raw materials to be processed or the fuel required for processing operations. The production of raw materials (primary production) must, of course, occur where the essential natural resources are located.

[7] Coal rather than iron ore exerts a more compelling attractive power on the smelting process (manufacture of pig iron in blast furnaces), since the weight of coal used exceeds that of the iron ore, and the coal loses all its weight during the operations. (Formerly, many tons of coal were required for each ton of iron ore. As a result of many improvements, the ratio of coal to iron ore has been reduced to about 2:1 in the most modern blast furnaces.) Although other fuels are available, such as oil or electric or atomic power, they are unlikely to displace coal (in the form of coke) in the blasting process. The coke is more than a fuel: it is a deoxidizing agent as well. Its carbon unites with the oxygen in the iron ores to form carbon monoxide and carbon dioxide, gases that are carried away, leaving molten iron in the furnace

The steel industry of the Pittsburgh area got its start with the discovery of iron ore in the region about 1790. These deposits were near exhaustion by 1860, when the rich Superior ores of upper Michigan, later of Minnesota, were opened up. Because of the weight-losing feature of coal, the steel industry remained in the coal-producing Pittsburgh district, the ore being brought by boat from Duluth and Superior to lake ports such as Cleveland and Erie, and thence by rail. Rather than send the ore cars back empty, the rail companies offered low rates on return shipments of coal, so coal and iron ore began to meet at the lake shore, and steel mills were established in Gary, Cleveland, Erie, Toledo, Detroit, and other intermediate points. A similar combination of forces led to the establishment of the Bethlehem Steel Corporation's plant at Sparrow's Point, Maryland, and the new U.S. Steel plant near Philadelphia: the nearness of Norfolk coke, low ocean freight rates on iron ore shipments (coming from Chile and Venezuela), and the proximity of the great eastern markets.

Market-oriented commodities. Just as weight-losing commodities tend to be attracted to the supply of raw materials or fuel, so commodities that gain weight or bulk in processing are attracted to the market.[8] Automobile assembly is of this character. Parts are made principally in Detroit or Flint, attracted originally by the availability of capital and enterprise and held there by ready accessibility of raw materials and fuel; but assembly in this area is only for nearby markets. To serve more distant markets (both domestic and foreign), unassembled parts, concentrated in small space, are shipped to widely scattered plants. Coca-cola extract is made in Atlanta; this is carried all over the world to local bottling companies, where carbonated water is added and the product bottled. Beer and ink, like soft drinks, are weight-adding products; they, too, tend to be produced near their market areas.

Also market-oriented are perishable commodities, such as bread and baked goods, flowers, ice, and fresh milk. Fresh vegetables in season are in this category, though competition from frozen foods shipped large distances is increasing.

Services, which must be rendered directly to the customer, must of course be produced in the market area. Among these are laundries, dry-cleaning establishments, theaters, and gasoline filling stations.

---

[8] If the processing adds bulk rather than weight, this amounts to the same thing as adding weight, for the greater bulk displaces shipping space and will involve a higher freight charge than a smaller, more compact shipment. The same is true if the article in question breaks easily in shipment, since a given delivered amount will require more cargo space than a sturdier object.

Neutral commodities. Some commodities, or more accurately, processes, are neutral or indifferent to the pull of supply or of the market, and hence may locate at either point (or occasionally at intermediate points). This will be true where transport costs are unimportant in relation to processing costs, or where there is little gain or loss in weight or bulk during processing. In the former category are matches, plastic novelties, photographic equipment, cigarette lighters, and other small metal objects; in the latter, cotton and woolen textiles, cement, boots and shoes, and furniture.

Where transport costs exert little influence, either because they are unimportant or because they exert a roughly equal pull toward materials and market, other elements will be decisive in determining industrial location. The relative supply and prices of factors tend to become dominant, just as they are in determining the location of crop production, lumbering, fisheries, and mining.

One cannot, however, rule out sheer accident as unimportant. A number of industries in which the availability of special types of skilled labor is vital can attribute their period of growth and expansion to the drawing power of a supply of specialised labor. But how did this particular kind of labor happen to be there in the first place? Where did the first skilled workers come from? They may have appeared simply as the result of gradual specialisation in a center of large population, thus providing a specific illustration of the attraction of a large labor supply. Yet they may have migrated from some other center, settling where they did for capricious or at least non-economic reasons.

Thus a small number of lens grinders from Germany migrated to Rochester, New York, in the first half of the nineteenth century, choosing this place to settle quite accidentally. With the outbreak of the Civil War, orders for telescope and binocular lenses poured in, requiring the training of additional workers and bringing prosperity and renown to Rochester. After the war, it was only natural that the photographic industry should locate in this city.

Or it may be that the man or men who conceive the idea of starting an industry happen to live in a particular place. Their natural attachment to their home town tends to keep them there, as well as the industry they establish. This attraction may be reenforced if the capital they need can only be obtained locally. The American automobile industry appears to have been initiated in Detroit for such personal reasons, for when it began, many other cities had equal advantages in most other respects.

SELECTED REFERENCES

Hoover, Edgar M., *The Location of Economic Activity* (McGraw-Hill Book Co., New York, 1948). A comprehensive discussion of transfer costs and other factors affecting the location of industry.

Kindleberger, Charles P., *International Economics* (Richard D. Irwin, Inc., Homewood, Ill., 1953). Chapter 7 has a somewhat more extended treatment of transport costs and their relation to industrial location than that given here.

Ohlin, Bertil, *Interregional and International Trade* (Harvard University Press, Cambridge, 1933). Chapter X. A more extended discussion of transport costs and problems of localisation, with illustrations.

8

COMPETITION AND MONOPOLY

Perfect competition was a useful assumption to make in constructing a theoretical model to serve as a first approximation, for it enabled us to treat all producers as equals and thus to focus upon the features common to all. But having relaxed our other assumptions—only three factors with no qualitative differences among them, constant costs, and trade without costs of transport—we must now eliminate this remaining major unrealistic aspect of our model. We should then be able to approach the problems of international trading with a set of concepts sufficiently flexible and realistic to permit accurate detailed analysis.

Competition

It is well to begin a discussion of the role of competition and monopoly by reviewing some of the fundamentals of price theory. First, let us make explicit what perfect competition means. For an industry to be thoroughly competitive, it must meet two conditions. First, the number of producers must be so large that no single one can, by increasing or decreasing his output, exert any influence on price. Each firm is but a single unit, in a market made up of innumerable such units on the supply side.[1] The second condition is that the product of the industry should be homogeneous. If all units are alike, then no buyer will have any reason for preferring the product of one producer over that of another, and there will be no basis for price differences. A single price will rule throughout the industry's market. With both these conditions—atomistic competition and a uniform price—the result is that each seller confronts a demand curve *for his own output* which is infinitely elastic—a horizontal straight line.

Under these conditions, the position of any firm could be represented by Figure 8.1. Here we have the typical average and marginal cost curves of an individual producer, with the marginal curve cutting the average curve at its minimum point. The demand for this producer's output is represented by the horizontal line **ar**, so labelled because it measures

---

[1] The number of buyers is also assumed to be similarly large. Our main concern here, however, is with the supply side. Perfect knowledge of market conditions is, of course, postulated of both buyers and sellers.

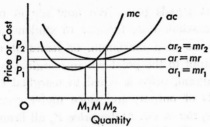

Fig. 8.1: The Individual Firm Under
Perfect Competition.

average revenue.[2] It is horizontal because under the conditions assumed
—atomistic competition and a uniform price for a homogeneous product—
if this producer raised his price by the slightest amount, demand for his
product would fall to zero, all sales being transferred to his competitors.
Likewise, were he to reduce price infinitesimally, he could expand his
sales to the limit of his productive capacity. It is also true (as indicated
in the diagram) that average revenue is equal to marginal revenue, or the
revenue from each additional unit sold. For since this firm cannot in any
way influence the price, it can obtain the same revenue from each additional unit sold (starting, say, at output OM) as it obtained from all
previous units.

Long-run equilibrium would be reached when the total number of firms
in the industry was just sufficient to establish the price at P. For then,
price (or average revenue) for each firm would be exactly equal to average
cost, and total revenue ($OP \times OM$) would just equal total costs, including
normal competitive returns to capital invested and to management.

In the short run, price could be below or above the equilibrium level,
as at P_1 or P_2. At P_1 output would be reduced to OM_1, where marginal
costs were equal to price, since any units beyond this amount would cost
more to produce than the price yielded by their sale. (Output would not
be reduced below OM_1, since for smaller outputs price would exceed
marginal cost and total revenue could be increased by expanding output
to OM_1. Though the firm is losing money at a price of P_1, its losses are
minimised at this output.) With the passage of time, some firms would
be eliminated from the industry, and the price would gradually rise to the
equilibrium position at P.

The price could also, in the short run, rise above the normal or equilibrium level, say to P_2. The individual firm would increase output to OM_2,

[2] A demand curve, whether for an individual firm or an entire industry, *always*
measures average revenue, since each point on it—the price at which a specific amount
could be sold—indicates the return to the producer or producers for each unit of output
sold. Demand curves are therefore sometimes referred to as average revenue curves.

where marginal cost equals price. We now see in operation the basic principle of profit maximisation, familiar to students of elementary economics: profits will be at a maximum, or losses at a minimum, if the producer adjusts output to the point where marginal cost equals marginal revenue. In our diagram, price is equal to marginal cost at each of the three possible levels of output; and since under competitive conditions **ar** (or price) = **mr, mc** = **mr.** At the price P_2 all firms would be making abnormal profits; this would attract new firms into the business and encourage existing firms to expand, thus bringing price down to P, where profits were normal once again.

Monopoly

At the other extreme from perfect competition is perfect monopoly. Here there is a single producer responsible for the entire output of a homogeneous product: the monopolist *is* the industry. Therefore the demand curve for the firm and the industry are one and the same. Although the product of the monopolist may confront competition from substitutes (as steel must compete in industrial uses with aluminum and other light metals, plastics, lumber and fibreboard), there are no *close* substitutes. A typical monopoly situation is illustrated by Figure 8.2. The marginal and average cost curves are similar to those for a competitive firm, reflecting average costs that diminish until the point of optimum plant utilisation is reached, with marginal costs crossing average costs at this minimum point.

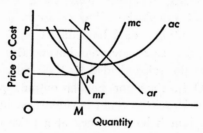

Fig. 8.2: Monopoly Price.

The differences from the competitive firm's position show up in the average and marginal revenue curves. The demand, or average revenue, for the output of the firm is no longer horizontal: it has a negative slope, with an elasticity determined by the tastes of the buyers of the product. Being the sole producer, variations in the monopolist's output will affect price, or average revenue. Under atomistic competition, as we have seen, the small individual firm can vary its output over the widest possible range without altering price in the slightest. This means that marginal revenue, or the addition to revenue derived from the sale of an additional unit of output, is always identical with average revenue.

Not so with monopoly: when the price is lowered by selling additional output, not only is the average return on each unit sold reduced, but the revenue yielded by the additional unit or units sold falls even more. Thus if at a price of $100, 10 units can be sold, total receipts will be $1,000. If at a price (average revenue) of $99, buyers will take one more unit, or a total of 11, total receipts will be $1089. The amount added to receipts from the sale of the additional unit, or marginal revenue, is $89. It is less than the average revenue of $99 obtained for each of the 11 units because, although the 11th unit brings $99, the 10 units previously sold for a total of $1,000 now yield only $990. Because of this depressing effect of additional sales upon the yield from goods previously sold, marginal revenue will always be less than average revenue. Thus the marginal revenue curve in the diagram lies at all points below the average revenue curve.

If the monopolist follows the principle of maximising profits, he will determine his most profitable output in the same manner as the individual firm in a competitive industry. He produces that output at which marginal cost equals marginal revenue. This is the output *OM*, at which marginal cost and marginal revenue are both equal to *MN*. The price at which this output can be sold is *OP* (= *MR*), and monopoly profits are equal to *PRNC*. At any smaller output, marginal cost would be less than marginal revenue; by increasing output, the monopolist would add less to costs than he added to revenue. If he increased output beyond *OM*, he would add more to costs than he added to revenue.

In real life, instances of complete monopoly are rare, and even these are subject to the competition of fairly close substitutes. On the national level, one thinks of aluminum metal before World War II in the United States, when the Aluminum Company of America was the sole producer, and du Pont's monopoly of cellophane. In the international field, the outstanding illustration is the de Beers' diamond syndicate.

Perfect competition is also exceptional. Most illustrations that come to mind are in agriculture. Wheat, corn, wool, cotton, and many other crops meet the requirements quite well when the government does not intervene; producers are very numerous, and the product (or at least any given grade) is homogeneous. But in most lines of industry, firms operate under conditions somewhere between perfect monopoly and perfect competition. These are generally described by the term "imperfect competition," indicating a situation that is partly competitive, partly monopolistic.

Imperfect Competition

The degree to which, in actual practice, elements of competition and monopoly are intermingled varies widely. Some industries include a very large number of firms, each with very little power to affect price, while others consist of only a handful of sellers, each capable of exerting a great influence on price.[3] In between lies a host of intermediate cases.

Thus, in the United States and in other countries with a sizeable market, producers of textiles, women's dresses, and plastic manufactures, and the printing and the fruit and vegetable canning industries, should be placed at the competitive end of the scale, where the number of firms is quite large and competition is keen. Somewhat removed from this end of the scale would come producers of men's suits and coats, shoes, cement, paper, and machine tools. "Competition among the few" would characterise aluminum, steel, automobiles, industrial chemicals, ethical drugs, petroleum refining, heavy electrical equipment, and banana imports. With the declining relative number of producers that is the basis of this rough classification, there corresponds a rising volume of investment in plant and equipment, a feature that increases the difficulty new firms have in entering the ranks of the "monopolistic competitors."

If the products of individual firms in one of these imperfectly competitive industries were completely undifferentiated, it would be very difficult to maintain a price above the competitive level and to earn monopoly profits. This would be especially true if the number of firms were large, or even sizeable. For with a homogeneous product, customers would have no reason to show preference to one firm over another. Price would be the only consideration, and all firms would have to adopt the same price tag.[4] Even with oligopoly (a very small number of competitors), unless there is collusion in the form of an agreement, either tacit or explicit, maintenance of a price close to the monopoly level is very difficult—the threat of a price war is always present. "Competition among the few," when the product of the industry is homogeneous, tends to be unstable, periods of high prices alternating with periods of cut-throat competition.

[3] It should be noted that a very strict definition of an industry would include only a group of firms selling in a single market area, within which, if competition were perfect, a single uniform price would rule. This would confine an "industry" to a single geographical region, and exclude those firms separated from this market by distance and the necessity of incurring transport costs. This is rather unrealistic, since all firms must incur transport costs, even for goods sold in the city where they are produced. We shall consider an industry to include all sellers of a given product who do in fact compete effectively for sales in a given area, which of course will vary in size from industry to industry.

[4] If entry into the industry were difficult, the price might remain above the competitive level for some time. All firms, however, would receive the same price.

It is for reasons such as these that we find firms in practically every industry making strenuous efforts to differentiate their product. For each and every producer wants to ensure for himself a good level of profit, and there are only two ways in which he can do so, short of collusion. First, he can approach the problem from the supply side and attempt to reduce his costs below those of his competitors. If the industry is already reasonably efficient, this is difficult; in any event, others can and will imitate him. Eventually, the general level of costs of the entire industry will be lower and will be reflected in a lower price, with profits no greater than the competitive norm.

Second, the individual firm can try to differentiate its product favorably in the minds of the consumers. To the degree to which it is successful, competing products become imperfect substitutes for that of the differentiating firm. In other words, it insulates its market from competition to some extent, and the demand curve for its produce ceases to be horizontal and acquires some downward slope. (In non-technical terms, this means that this firm can charge a higher price without losing all its sales.)

To differentiate its product, our firm can adopt one or both of two strategies. (1) It can improve the quality of its product. Attempts to do this are going on all the time. Witness the introduction in the automobile industry in recent years of such "improvements" as automatic transmissions, power brakes and steering, streamlining, larger bodies, or merely more and more chromium. Similar in character is attractive or convenient packaging.

But any differential advantage established by this means is also subject to erosion by imitation. Hence (2) it is common to resort to sales strategy. A firm employs salesmen and buys advertising space to impress upon the minds of its customers the real or trumped-up advantages of its product. Sales efforts are expensive, and will of course raise the firm's cost curve. But they may pay off, by raising the demand curve more than the cost curve.

Again, success breeds imitation. If one firm by these devices manages to expand its sales at the expense of its competitors, they are almost certain to follow suit. But if all the members of an industry engage in competitive selling and advertising, each will partly offset the efforts of the others. Individual demand curves move downward. Where ease of entry is great, the end result is not very different from that of perfect competition. Quality and sales competition will push individual demand curves downward and to the left until each is tangent or almost tangent to the average cost curve of the individual producer. Price will be equal to or only slightly above average cost, though (because the average revenue curve is downward sloping) a bit above the minimum point, with profits little if any greater than competitive returns. (See Figure 8.3.)

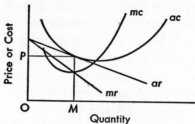

Fig. 8.3: Monopolistic Competition
with Intensive Quality and
Sales Competition.

Where the number of competitors is small, owing to economies of scale, and especially where the realisation of such economies requires heavy investment and thus keeps numbers small, successful product differentiation may make it possible for firms to charge prices well above the competitive level. If each firm pursued only the short-run goal of profit maximisation, high prices would be the outcome.

Longer-run considerations, however, may and often do lead producers in such an industry to adopt a policy of moderation, charging a price not much higher than would exist under competition. Profits are then positive, but not huge. Each producer might be concerned lest high prices and high profits attract new competitors into his field, or elicit the unwanted attentions of government attorneys. Rapid technological progress in the economy as a whole, ensuring the frequent appearance of fairly close substitute goods, helps to reenforce this tendency toward moderation.

There is another aspect of technological progress that should be allowed for. A partially insulated market and the higher profits that go with it may establish the sort of financially secure base needed if the firm is to engage in active research, improve its product, and lower its costs. Paradoxically, an element of monopoly can be the prerequisite of more effective competition in the longer run. If this is true, then although at any moment in time successful product differentiation, achieved by not too strenuous sales competition, results in a price that is substantially higher than the competitive level, in the long run, the price can be brought even lower than had the industry been marked by intense competition.

The Temptation of Collusion

Although there are many reasons for doubting that, even under conditions of imperfect competition, price or profits will differ much from those established under pure competition, there is no guarantee of such a happy outcome. A small number of competitors selling highly differentiated products may not be deterred from exerting their monopoly power—their government, like many in Europe, may not be hostile to monopoly, or perhaps the high initial investment necessary to establish a new business may effectively limit new entrants. Their fear of stirring up competition from existing firms may be eliminated by an agreement to hold competition within defined bounds.

The temptation to reach such an agreement is especially great in an industry producing a standardised product with few natural differentiating characteristics, such as sheet metal, industrial chemicals, or raw materials. For then the regulation of competition may be the only practicable means of avoiding recurring and destructive price wars.

Effective collusion (agreement to avoid competition) is the surest means to the universal goal of high profits. Understandably, therefore, it is widely practised, both on the national and the international level. We shall therefore conclude our discussion of imperfect competition by considering briefly some of the typical ways in which it is deliberately organised.

CARTELS

Agreements to restrict competition, whether formal or informal, explicit or merely tacit understandings, may be classed together under the general term, "cartels." Since explicit agreements are both more definite and more capable of enforcement than looser arrangements, cartel members commonly are linked in some form of organised association.

The purpose of cartels is to ensure members higher profits than would be possible without agreement;[5] their means, one device or another to limit competition.

Scope of Cartels

According to each of several estimates of the international importance of cartels, something between a third and a half of world trade was subject to some degree of cartel control during the inter-war period.[6] A very large

[5] In self defense, members of cartels sometimes plead that their objective is merely "stable profits." It is safe to say, however, that these stable profits are invariably higher than they would be even under stable but truly competitive conditions.

[6] Machlup estimated the figure to be "at least 32 per cent." Mason gives 42 per cent as a "minimum estimate" for the share of world trade "cartelized or influenced by loosely knit associations or conferences." Fritz Machlup, "The Nature of the International Cartel Problem," in Corwin D. Edwards and others, *A Cartel Policy for the United Nations* (Columbia University Press, New York, 1945), p. 11; Edward S. Mason, *Controlling World Trade* (McGraw-Hill Book Co., New York, 1946), p. 26n. Postwar estimates are not to my knowledge available.

number of commodities falls within this range, including both important raw materials such as the principal metals and minerals, and a long list of manufactured goods, of which the more important have been chemicals and dyestuffs, pharmaceutical products, and electrical equipment.

Owing to the decartelisation policy put into effect in Germany during the period of occupation and to the emergence in Britain of a policy less friendly to monopoly, the area of cartelisation probably has diminished somewhat since the war. Of particular importance has been the substitution of public for private control over the production and sale of European coal and steel, with the establishment in 1950 of the European Coal and Steel Community. (See Chapter 27.) The mere fact that the war itself forced the dissolution of many agreements has—at least temporarily—also reduced their importance.

Means of Control

Cartel devices used to restrict competition can be classified in three groups: (1) direct control over the prices charged by members; (2) restriction of output; (3) allocation of markets.

Although in some instances, prices to be charged by members have been fixed by a cartel, real power to control prices rests upon limitations of output. Price policy therefore has more often been applied to effect discrimination in different markets (see below) or among different classes of buyers, or to eliminate competition through an actual or threatened price war. To restrict output, thus indirectly but effectively raising price, cartels have commonly imposed quotas on members, enforcing their observation by a system of penalties and bounties for over- or under-production. Since patents give the exclusive right to manufacture the patented object, agreements limiting the amount to be produced by licensees are another widespread cartel practice. Allocation of markets has been a favorite cartel device. Each member of an international cartel (often itself a national cartel) agrees to keep out of markets cherished by another member in exchange for a similar agreement on the part of other members.

A few illustrations:[7]

Price policy. In 1927-28, tungsten carbide, an important hard-metal composition used for cutting and wear-resistant surfaces, sold in the United States for $50

[7] Except where noted, these illustrations are taken from Corwin D. Edwards, *Economic and Political Aspects of International Cartels.* (Senate Committee Print, Monograph No. 1, 78th Congress, 2nd Session. Government Printing Office, Washington, D. C., 1944.)

a pound. General Electric and the Krupp organisation then pooled their patents, with G. E. given the right to establish the price in the U. S. and on imports into Germany. The U. S. price then rose to $453 a pound; it remained above $200 throughout the thirties. After an anti-trust indictment in 1942, the price ranged between $27 and $45 a pound.

In 1936, Bunge & Born, an Argentine company, began the production of sulphuric acid. An Argentine subsidiary of du Pont and Imperial Chemical Industries announced that it intended to keep its existing share of the market "irrespective of the level to which prices might decline during the ensuing period of competition."

It gave this information in order that Bunge & Born "might visualise the effect on their own prospective returns from sulphuric acid manufacture."

Restriction of output. A government sponsored International Tin Committee in 1931, covering 95 per cent of world output, made production of tin in excess of prescribed quotas a criminal offense. With demand and prices declining, it set an initial quota of 78 per cent of 1929 production. This proved ineffective; in 1933 the quota was cut to ⅓ of capacity. The price of tin promptly jumped from 27 to 46¢ a pound. By juggling the quota to conform to changes in demand, the price was raised still further, and kept fairly stable around 60¢ until 1937.[8]

Imperial Chemical Industries and du Pont established jointly owned subsidiaries in Argentina and Brazil under the name Duperial, which it was agreed would be the exclusive sales agents for the products of both firms in these countries. Each Duperial company was instructed to divide its purchases equally between the parent companies unless one charged a higher price than the other.

In 1929, I. G. Farben and Standard Oil of New Jersey agreed that I. G. Farben would stay out of the oil business, while Standard Oil would refrain from selling chemicals that had no bearing on the oil business.

Price Discrimination

When a firm has a monopoly of its product in its own domestic market, it is in a position to charge one price in that market, a different one in one or more foreign markets. This is due to the fact that these markets are separated from one another by transportation costs, and possibly also by tariffs or differences in tastes, customs and business practices. If the commodity in question is sold at a lower price in a foreign market, it cannot —within the limits set by the costs of reentering the high-priced domestic market—be reexported at a profit. On the other hand, if the price is lower in the domestic market, the monopolist's control of production there gives him control also of exports to the foreign market.

Price discrimination will be profitable provided the elasticity of demand

[8] George W. Stocking and Myron W. Watkins, *Cartels or Competition?*, pp. 164-5. Twentieth Century Fund, New York, 1948.

in the two markets is different. For if the monopolist sells at the same price (f.o.b. plant) in the two markets, the marginal revenue in the market with an inelastic demand will be less than the marginal revenue in the market with an elastic demand. Total revenue will be increased if he shifts some sales from the market in which marginal revenue is low into the market in which it is high. It will pay to continue thus shifting sales until marginal revenue in both markets is equal; at this point of maximum profits, marginal revenue will be equal to marginal cost for the entire output.

The argument can be visualised in a diagram (Figure 8.4). A and B represent two separate markets with the vertical axis (average and marginal revenue) in common, but with distinct horizontal (quantity) axes, amounts of the commodity being read from 0 to the right for B, to the left for A.

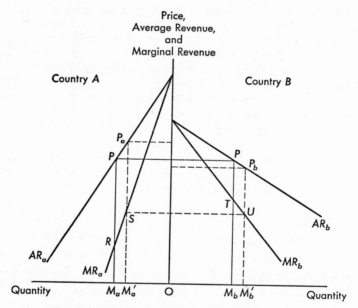

Fig. 8.4: Discriminatory Pricing in Two Markets.

If the same price, P, is charged in both markets, marginal revenue will be lower in A, where the demand is relatively inelastic, than in B, where it is comparatively elastic. By shifting a part of the output sold in A ($M_a M_a'$, equal to $M_b M_b'$) to B's market, marginal revenue in A is raised from R to S, while the price is increased from P to P_a. In B marginal revenue is lowered from T to U, price from P to P_b.

Either A or B could be the home market, with the other the foreign market. If A is the home market, where the seller has his original monopoly, demand may be more elastic abroad (as in B of the diagram) because of the presence of some competition, though of differentiated products, or because of the character of buyer's tastes. (In the extreme case of perfect competition abroad, our seller would sell at the competitive price there and charge a monopoly price at home.) On the other hand, if B is the home (monopoly) market, a more inelastic demand in the foreign market (A) would have to be accounted for in terms of differences in tastes or of the availability of fewer indirectly competitive substitutes.

EFFECTS OF MONOPOLISTIC PRACTICES

Whenever producers can wield effective monopoly power, whether as a result of collusion or merely because competitors are few and entry is difficult, price is generally higher and output smaller than it would be under competition. The allocation of resources is therefore different from, and socially less desirable than it would be in, a competitive system.

We have seen that in a freely competitive market, price and cost are equal for each commodity, with price equal to both marginal and minimum average cost. Costs just cover the prices paid for the services of the various factors needed to produce a unit of each commodity, while the factors receive an equal return in all uses.

Allocation of Resources

Resources are therefore allocated in the most efficient possible manner.[9] If more resources were devoted to any use, costs would rise while the price fell, and consumers would be paying for the commodity less than the services of the factors were worth in other uses. Allocation of fewer resources to any use would lower marginal cost and raise price; consumers would be paying a premium over the value of factor services.

Optimum results are ensured by the existence of perfectly competitive conditions, when price, and average revenue and marginal revenue of the individual producer, are all equal. (See Figure 16.1.) He maximises his returns by producing an output at which marginal cost is equal to marginal revenue and thus to price. With perfect mobility of the factors, the price of each will be the same in all uses, and equal to the value of its marginal product.

When some degree of monopoly is present, whether because producers are few in numbers, because they collaborate, or because they differentiate

---

[9] There is the possible exception of the monopoly or oligopoly that is "well-behaved" in the long run, and that uses its financially secure position to engage in research, improve its product, and reduce its costs.

their product, price tends to exceed marginal cost. This will be so if producers exercise their monopoly power by limiting output to the amount that equates marginal cost and marginal revenue. For under monopoly conditions, the individual firm's demand or average revenue curve is no longer infinitely elastic, but is negatively inclined, and average revenue exceeds marginal revenue.

But if price exceeds marginal cost, it follows that resources are allocated uneconomically. For if marginal cost is equal to the value of the services of the factors, then the consumer is paying the monopolist more than the value of the resources used in production. If additional resources were devoted to producing the monopoly product, the satisfaction of consumers —which is the goal of production—could be increased. Moreover, with the restricted output produced by the monopoly, average costs are above their minimum level, indicating that resources are being used inefficiently. With increased output, not only would consumer satisfaction be increased, but, with average unit costs lowered, resources would be used more efficiently.

Where monopoly is deliberately enforced by collusion among producers, the inefficient use of resources is likely to be magnified. This is so because to make a collusive agreement effective, it is usually necessary to include a number of high-cost, inefficient producers. Their output is not needed; if production were concentrated in the most efficient plants, their resources could be transferred to other, more productive uses. But to obtain their consent to the agreement, it is essential to allot them some part of the output.

Income Effects

Monopoly, especially if it is widespread, can also adversely affect the incomes of the factors. For by restricting their employment in the monopolised industries, it forces them to seek employment in the remaining competitive sectors, where both their marginal product and its value will be reduced.

When a monopoly is confined to a single country, with no exports of its product, nothing need be added to the above. The universal objection to monopoly holds: resources are allocated uneconomically, too few being used to produce the monopolised product, and as a consequence, domestic consumers derive less satisfaction than they should.

Price Discrimination

When a monopolist exports part of his output, he may practice price discrimination between his home and his foreign market. The price will be lower in the foreign market if its demand is more elastic than demand in the home market, either because of differences in tastes or because the monopolist has to meet competition abroad. Price will be lower at home if home demand is more elastic. *Total* resources used will be the same whether uniform or different prices are charged; on this score, there is no advantage or disadvantage in price discrimination. The parties discriminated against will naturally resent the discrimination. If we regard home and foreign buyers as equally important, however, there is no reason to prefer flat pricing to discrimination.

Effects on Trade

Even when confined to a single country, a monopoly tends to diminish the volume of international trade. This follows from the fact that monopoly depresses the earnings of the factors by restricting job opportunities in the monopoly area, thus causing overcrowding elsewhere. With reduced incomes, they have less to spend on everything, including imports.

When a monopolist in one country sells abroad at a higher price, the volume of trade is still further reduced. On the other hand, if he discriminates against the home buyer, *his* exports may be larger than they would be under pure competition.

The reduction of international trade is clearest when several markets are controlled by an international cartel, and these markets are allocated among the members. Potential international trade is then simply stopped at its source.

Adaptation to Change

Also to be noted is the tendency of monopoly to increase the rigidity of prices and to decrease the mobility of resources as compared with competition. At least in the short run, there is less flexibility of costs in the face of changing conditions, and unless a monopolist (or a group operating as a monopoly) is alert to his long-run interest in improving processes and lowering costs, costs may be rigid in the long run too. This consequence can be important when changed international conditions require an expansion of exports and an increase in productive efficiency.

PUBLIC POLICY TOWARD MONOPOLY

There are three ways in which governments can respond to monopoly, whether it extends across international boundaries or is confined to a government's own territory. They can leave it alone, they can attempt to destroy it, or they can regulate it.

Something can be said in favor of each policy. Spokesmen for international cartels contend that they stabilise prices, prevent destructive, cut-throat competition, and stimulate technical improvement through the exchange of information and patents. If this and nothing else were true, laissez faire would be the correct policy.

Such a view of cartels is highly idealised, and is unsupported by the facts. Prices are certainly raised by cartels, usually to a level sufficient to permit operation of the least efficient plants. Since this stimulates the competition of outsiders, as well as increased production by the more efficient cartel members, the history of many cartels has been a period of high prices followed by a collapse to a low level. Rather than preventing cut-throat competition, restrictive agreements have encouraged its use, or the threat of its use, to eliminate potential competition. Cartels are designed, moreover, not to avoid cut-throat competition, but to eliminate *all* competition. As for technical advance, exchange of patents has more often than not been accompanied by restrictions on their use. And with some justice, cartels have been accused of suppressing new inventions rather than encouraging their adoption.

Prohibition of monopoly, though it has more to recommend it as an abstract proposition, is too undiscriminating. It fails to distinguish between monopoly, or more accurately, oligopoly, that rests on economies of scale and that which depends on collusion. If all oligopoly positions were destroyed, say by limiting any single firm to a small percentage of its industry's output, important economies of scale might be lost. So far as this is true, a policy of prohibition would be self-defeating, for it would bring about a more uneconomic allocation of resources, the very feature of monopoly to which objection can legitimately be made.

As we saw earlier, collusion is the surest means to output below and price above the competitive level. This suggests regulation or prohibition of collusive practices, rather than prohibition of monopoly or oligopoly, as a preferable policy. Practices to be banned would include the establishment of production or sales quotas, price fixing, allocation of markets, or restrictive patent agreements. The problem, however, is to achieve international agreement on such a program. The attitude of different governments toward monopolistic practices differs widely; attempts to reach agreement in the past have brought these differences sharply to the fore. Although agreement to prohibit such practices as those mentioned above was reached in the proposal to establish an International Trade Organisation (see Chapter 24), enforcement was to have been left to each country. At this level, the basic difference in attitudes would probably have re-asserted itself.

SELECTED REFERENCES

Boulding, Kenneth, *Economic Analysis*, 2nd edition (Harper & Bros., New York, 1955). Stonier, Alfred W., and Hague, Douglas C., *A Textbook of Economic Theory*, 2nd edition (Longmans, Green & Co., London, 1955). These are two of the many good texts in intermediate economic theory that provide a statement of the theory of imperfect competition and monopoly.

Edwards, Corwin D., *Economic and Political Aspects of International Cartels*, Committee Print No. 1, Senate Subcommittee on War Mobilisation of the Committee on Military Affairs, 78th Congress, 2nd Session (Washington, D. C., 1944). This study contains an unusually large number of illustrations of cartel practices.

Hexner, Ervin, *International Cartels* (University of North Carolina Press, Chapel Hill, 1945). An excellent, full-scale discussion of the cartel problem.

Machlup, Fritz, *The Political Economy of Monopoly* (The Johns Hopkins Press, Baltimore, 1952). Chapters 4 and 5 provide an especially detailed, descriptive discussion of the types of business practices used to enforce monopoly.

Marsh, Donald B., *World Trade* and *Investment* (Harcourt, Brace & Co., New York, 1951). Chapter 21, in which monopoly and imperfect competition are treated with special reference to their impact on international trade, is excellent.

Mason, Edward S., *Controlling World Trade* (McGraw-Hill Book Co., New York, 1946). Chapter I provides an excellent brief statement of the issues raised by cartels. Part II is devoted to a discussion of the attempt to regulate trade by intergovernmental commodity agreements.

Morgan, Theodore, *Introduction to Economics*, 2nd edition (Prentice-Hall, Inc., New York, 1956). Chapters 15 and 16 cover monopoly and competition rather thoroughly for an elementary text.

Samuelson, Paul A., *Economics*, 3rd edition (McGraw-Hill Book Co., New York, 1955). Chapter XXV gives a good brief review of imperfect competition.

Schumpeter, Joseph A., *Capitalism, Socialism,* and *Democracy*, 3rd edition (Harper & Bros., New York, 1950). Chapters VII and VIII have an especially interesting discussion of monopolistic practices as a protection against the blasts of competition and as giving rise to a "process of creative destruction" that constantly revolutionises the economic structure.

Stocking, George W., and Watkins, Myron W., *Cartels or Competition?* (Twentieth Century Fund, New York, 1948). This is another full-scale discussion of the cartel problem.

9

SOME EFFECTS OF TRADE

RECAPITULATION

Our effort to expose to view the foundations upon which international trade and specialisation rest is now complete. We have seen that the most basic of these is the relative endowment of the different countries with the productive factors, taken together with the alternative methods of combining these factors that are at any time available. Considering these elements alone, each country would specialise upon those products best suited to its factor endowment, which means those using little of its scarce factors and drawing heavily upon the cheap and abundant ones. In determining which commodities each country can produce most economically, allowance must be made for any qualitative differences in its factors. Cheapness or dearness might be offset by qualitative inferiority or superiority, which we saw could be explained principally in terms of the social conditions under which production takes place.

For most of its exports, there would be competitors—either from countries with comparable factor endowments or from countries with endowments suited to a different production function. All goods and services adapted to a country's factor supply and price situation and therefore producible at relatively low cost would be exported. The only exceptions would be those tied to the local market by such considerations as perishability, the need for personal service, and the like. All other commodities would be imported, although part of home consumption might be met from local production, if a commodity were subject to conditions of increasing cost.

Transport costs alter this picture in important respects. By raising the delivered price of a country's exports, they reduce the volume sold, and if they exceed the difference in production costs between the home country and a potential market, they rule out trade altogether. Beyond this, they may determine (with respect to industries that process raw materials or foodstuffs) whether that industry locates at the source of supply or near the market. It will tend to be materials-oriented if the cost of transporting the raw material to the market exceeds that of transporting the finished product, market-oriented if the opposite is true.

Where there is some degree of effective monopoly, prices will be raised above the competitive level. This tends, as with any cause that raises price (like transport costs), to diminish the volume of trade. The income effects of monopoly, which will only be serious if it is extensive, work in the same direction. Trade may also be reduced directly, as when an international cartel allocates markets among its members. It is doubtful, however, if imperfect competition, whose most restrictive form is the collusive agreement, must be regarded as a major obstacle to international trade.[1]

This group of principles should enable us to explain the composition of a country's exports, to account for the pattern of world trade, and even to determine why a particular industry is located as it is or whether a particular industry is likely to be an economical proposition for a given country. A working model based on these principles makes no allowance for interference with its operation, in the form of government subsidies, tariffs, special tax favors, and the like. In any detailed analysis such distorting factors would, of course, have to be taken fully into account.

Our concern up to this point has been with the forces underlying international trade and with the nature of trade, which we have seen to be essentially the exchange of the products of specialised resources. It is time now to consider how trade affects the people who engage in it—how and why they benefit from it, how the incomes of different groups are influenced, and what kind of relationships are established between nations that trade with one another. We shall begin with the gains from trade.

THE GAINS FROM TRADE

Specialisation Means a Larger Income

Trade in its essentials is a very simple thing: it is merely an exchange of one kind of goods for another. Yet it is one of the most important of man's social inventions, for it freed the isolated individual from the need to produce all his own requirements. Instead of being a "jack-of-all-trades and master of none," as the old saying goes, he could become a specialist. Specialisation enables those with particular aptitudes to make full use of them; it permits everyone to perfect his skill by constant practice in a

---

[1] Thus Mason advances as his opinion that "the injury inflicted by tariffs on domestic competition and American foreign trade has been several times greater than the effect of cartels." Edward S. Mason, *Controlling World Trade*, McGraw-Hill Book Co., New York, 1946, p. 28.

single occupation. The waste of time involved in changing from one job to another can be eliminated, while the constant repetition of a single task often suggests ways of simplifying it or stimulates the invention of tools to make it easier or of machines to take it over.

Because of these advantages, a community whose members specialise will have a far larger total income than one where each person (or family) produces everything. But since a specialised worker produces far more of his particular product than he can use and nothing at all of all the other things he needs, it must be possible for each to exchange his surplus production for some of the surplus of others. Trade is an essential condition for specialisation, and the gain from trade is the increased income it makes possible.

Specialisation can occur under various conditions. It may be regulated by tradition, as during the Middle Ages; it may be controlled by the state, as during the Mercantilist period; or it may develop spontaneously in accordance with the choice of individuals. It can be shown that it yields the best economic results under a free price system; that is, a system where the mobility of both labor and capital is unfettered and where producers are effectively competitive.[2] For such a system results in a single uniform price for each commodity that is the minimum the competing producers can charge and stay in business. Faced with a list of minimum prices, consumers can allocate their expenditures until each dollar spent yields the same satisfaction; since nothing further can be gained by shifting expenditure from one use to another, consumers' satisfaction is maximised. The price of each factor will also be uniform in all its various uses; this makes the return to each factor a maximum. If labor, for example, could earn more in some occupations than others, its movements from the poorly paid to the better paid jobs would lower wages in the latter and raise them

[2] The assumptions of perfect competition and mobility imply full knowledge of alternatives by buyers and sellers of commodities and of the factors, the absence of important costs of moving from one occupation to another, and prompt but not excessive response to price changes. These are strong assumptions, and the conclusions of this brief summary would have to be considerably qualified in practice, since it is clear that these assumptions are by no means fully realised. Yet it seems worth while to set up this strong case as the ideal which a reasonably efficient price system will approximate.

The above is not meant to imply that socialism need be inefficient. But if it is to be efficient, its managers must act like perfect competitors—they must follow the rule of equalising the value of each factor's marginal product and its price. This is essential to maximise output and minimise cost. On this point see Oskar Lange & Fred M. Taylor, *On the Economic Theory of Socialism* (edited by Benjamin E Lippincott), University of Minnesota Press, 1938; and Abba P. Lerner, *The Economics of Control*, Macmillan, New York, 1944.

in the former, thus improving the earnings of labor as a whole. Moreover, equalisation of each factor's returns would mean that it was being put to the most important uses, as measured by the free choice of consumers. In summary, we can say that a free price system leads to the most efficient use of a community's resources; that is, to the highest possible income.

International Trade Extends Specialisation

International trade is simply the extension of trade beyond the boundaries of a nation. It therefore extends the range of specialisation and the gains derivable therefrom. Just as local trade enables advantage to be taken of the special aptitudes of individuals, so international trade makes it possible for each country to draw upon the special aptitudes of other countries and to utilise its own resources more efficiently. A region poor in land, where land-using products are consequently scarce and costly, though unable to import land to aid its labor, can import the products of land-rich areas, while the latter, with relatively little labor or capital, can obtain by exchange products requiring large amounts of these factors. Each region benefits in so far as trade enables it to obtain at low cost commodities that it could produce only at higher cost.

From the viewpoint of the people of the world as a whole and of any single country in it, both as consumers and as the owners of factors of production, international trade thus permits a better allocation of resources. Some countries have the right factor combination for the low-cost production of tropical agricultural products, others can produce grains and meats cheaply, and still others special types of manufactured goods. With international trade and specialisation, a wide range of commodities can therefore be made available at lower prices to everyone. Consumers' money incomes will stretch farther, and satisfaction can be increased.

Instead of being used unproductively in home production for home use, the factors can be transferred to more efficient uses where their marginal return is higher. Instead of using its relatively abundant labor to raise high-cost wheat on scarce land, Britain combines it to better effect with capital in the production of manufactures. Rather than lying idle, the prairies of Canada and Australia are put to work growing the wheat Britain needs.

Note that this means that Britain indirectly uses the abundant land of Canada and Australia, while they are enabled to use the relatively abundant labor and capital of Great Britain. Similarly, India and other countries that lack capital in effect obtain the use of the abundant capital of the United

States by importing capital-intensive products, while the United States supplements its short labor supply by obtaining labor-intensive goods from India.

Measuring Gain

The concrete gain of any country from international trade may now be expressed as follows: imports, which if produced at home would require an uneconomical and costly use of resources, can be obtained more cheaply abroad. A given quantity of import goods can therefore be acquired for a smaller outlay of resources if those resources are used to produce exports and these are exchanged for the imports. Or, a given expenditure of resources will yield more import goods if devoted to export production than if used to produce the import goods directly.

To compute the gain from trade for any country would involve immense labor, even if it were possible to estimate with any accuracy what its imports would have cost had the country produced them itself instead of buying them from a cheaper foreign source.

Terms of Trade

A method widely used to estimate, not the total gain from trade at any moment, but the trend of the gains from trade, does so by measuring changes in the terms of trade. The terms of trade, as we noted in Chapter 7, measure the *relation* between the prices a country gets for its exports and the prices it pays for its imports. If, as compared with this relation in a given or base year, its export prices rise or its import prices fall, its terms of trade are said to have improved. If, on the other hand, the prices of its exports decline or the prices of its imports rise, its terms of trade are said to have worsened.

To make such comparisons, index numbers are used. For the base year, an average of a country's export prices is computed, with each commodity in the average weighted according to its importance in total trade. For a later year, a similar average is computed; it will reflect the average change in export prices. The same procedure is followed for imports. The change in the country's terms of trade can then be measured by obtaining a ratio of the change in export prices to the change in import prices.

$$T_c = \frac{P_{x_1}}{P_{x_0}} \bigg/ \frac{P_{m_1}}{P_{m_0}}$$

In this expression T_c stands for the commodity terms of trade, the subscripts x and m for exports and imports respectively, and the subscripts 1 and o for the given year and the base year.

Thus, taking 1937 as the base year and expressing both British export and import prices for that year as 100, we find that in 1956 the index of export prices had risen to 339, that for import prices to 385. The terms of trade, consequently, had changed as follows:

$$T_c = \frac{339}{100} \Big/ \frac{385}{100} = 88$$

Since Britain's import prices had risen more than its export prices, the terms of trade had deteriorated, by 12 per cent as compared with 1937. This can be interpreted as meaning either that for a given amount of exports, Britain could obtain 12 per cent less imports, or that to purchase a given amount of imports, Britain had to give up 13.6 per cent more exports.

Changes in the commodity terms of trade, as we said, are taken to indicate the direction of the gains from trade. This interpretation, however, is only acceptable provided there are no offsetting considerations. In fact, we must note at least two important reservations.

(1) If changes in export prices are the result of changes in productivity, we must adjust our interpretation of a movement of the terms of trade. Thus suppose that, while a country's import prices, on the average, remain constant, the costs and prices of its exports fall 10 per cent because of an increase in productivity. An index of the commodity terms of trade would then indicate that these had worsened by the percentage decline in costs. There would be no real worsening of the country's position, however, for although a given value of exports can now command 10 per cent less imports, the exports required to obtain the imports can be produced for a correspondingly reduced expenditure of resources. The real cost of imports, in terms of resources used, is unchanged.

(2) The usual interpretation placed on changing commodity terms of trade must also be qualified if there have been changes in the quality of imports or exports. This point is particularly important in connection with recent discussions of the terms of trade of primary producing countries. Thus a United Nations' publication shows that according to the price indices used, the terms of trade between primary products and finished industrial goods deteriorated substantially (from 100 to 64) between 1876-80 and 1936-38. This proves, it is claimed, that only 64 per cent as large a

value of manufactured goods could be purchased with a given amount of primary products at the end of this period as at the beginning.[3]

Besides other defects, this interpretation of the statistical results completely ignores the fact that while the primary exports of 1938 were substantially the same as primary exports in 1875, manufactured imports had improved tremendously in quality.[4] Consider the nylon stockings of today as contrasted with the cotton stockings in 1875, or the mercury vapor lamp as compared with the kerosene lamp. Moreover, many commodities, such as the automobile, the television set, and the radio, were unknown in 1875 and hence cannot be given any weight in index numbers covering such a long span of years.

Because changes in the quality of goods are constantly taking place, and because changes in productivity must be reckoned with, the conventional conclusion drawn from variations in an index of the commodity terms of trade must be limited to short periods. Even then, the evidence must be treated with care. As for long periods—say more than ten years—any statement about changing terms of trade will in all likelihood have to be highly qualified.

Different Cost Conditions

We know that commodities may be supplied under conditions of increasing, decreasing, or constant cost. Does the gain from trade in any way depend upon which of these conditions holds good? We have seen that if the imports are produced at constant or decreasing cost, production in the importing country will cease. But if conditions of increasing cost hold, some home production may continue. Imports will be limited to that volume for which marginal cost is equal to the marginal cost of domestic supplies of the good. The intra-marginal gain is still there.

Holland, for example, imports some of its grain, though it raises some itself. Were that country unable to procure wheat, rye, and other grains from abroad, the resources now used to produce the exports exchanged for grain would have to be shifted onto its scanty agricultural land, marginal costs would rise sharply, and the additional grain obtained would be far less than current imports. (Reference to Figure 3 may be helpful here.)

But what if a country's exports are also produced at increasing cost?

[3] United Nations, Economic Commission for Latin America, *The Economic Development of Latin America and Its Principal Problems.* (E/CN.12/89/Rev. 1. 1950.) Table I.

[4] For a discussion of the issues at stake, see J. Viner, *International Trade and Economic Development* (The Free Press, Glencoe, Ill., 1952), pp. 143-4; also P. T. Ellsworth, "The Terms of Trade Between Primary Producing and Industrial Countries," *Inter-American Economic Affairs,* X (Summer, 1956).

Then if it withdraws from international trade, it can reduce production of these commodities to the smaller amount required for home consumption, and their marginal cost will be substantially lower. Is it not possible that the loss from higher-priced export goods, some of which are consumed at home, will offset the gain from lower-priced imports?

The answer is "no." For remember that exports embody large amounts of a country's abundant factors, while its imports contain large quantities of factors that are scarce at home. To produce domestic substitutes for imports would increase the demand for scarce factors and drive up costs sharply. Producing export-type goods with which to buy imports would increase demand primarily for factors that are abundant, and costs would rise more moderately. Resources can be more efficiently used to produce exports than to produce substitutes for imports.

EFFECTS OF TRADE ON FACTOR PRICES

Seeking profitable employment of their energies and their capital, individual businessmen, firms, and farmers undertake, in each country, the production of a wide variety of goods and services. If they exercise good judgment, they take into account as best they can the competitive situation they are likely to face, the cost of materials, the availability and wages of the kinds of labor they will need, and the availability and cost of capital and suitable land. These bases of each decision to produce or not to produce are determined, in an economy linked to others by the ties of trade, by such forces as the strength of demands in the various economies, relative factor supplies, alternative production methods, economies of scale, and transport costs. Under the guidance of these forces, an immense number of individual decisions to invest capital and employ labor results in the emergence, in each country, of many different industries, some producing for a sheltered home market, others sending their goods to the far corners of the world.

Prices of Traded Goods

Concerning goods that cross national borders, these sell everywhere at the same price, after allowing for costs of transport and other obstacles to trade. (The existence of monopoly, of course, may lead to price discrimination in different markets.) The effect of international trade, in other words, is to equalise prices which, in the absence of such trade, would differ very substantially.

Factor Price Equalisation

But international trade does more than equalise the prices of traded goods. It also exerts a strong influence toward equalising the prices of the factors that make these goods. For the corollary of one country's specialisation on its cheap-factor products is the concentration of world demand for that factor's services on the abundant supply available in that country and in others similarly situated. Similarly, the demand of this country for its scarce and expensive factors is shifted to other countries, where they are abundant and cheap. As a consequence of this reshuffling of demands, the price of each country's abundant factors tends to rise, of its scarce factors, to fall. Factor prices throughout the world therefore tend to become more uniform and equal.

To illustrate: Canada possesses abundant and relatively cheap land suited to producing wheat. Its production costs are low and it exports large quantities. The demand in more populous nations for this land-intensive product and therefore for the services of land is focussed upon Canada (and also upon Australia, Argentina, and the prairie states of the United States). Land rents in Canada are, in consequence, higher than they would be had Britain and other western European countries been forced to depend for their wheat supplies upon their own scanty agricultural land; rents are correspondingly lower in the latter.

Need for Factor Mobility

Complete factor price equalisation throughout the world, and, therewith, the most efficient use of its factors, could be attained only if the factors were fully mobile. Although natural resources cannot move to achieve this result, it would be closely approximated if capital and labor could be freely redistributed. Then, infertile regions of the earth would be deserted, and food production would be concentrated in the most fertile regions, together with most of the population and most of the industry. Each of these settled areas would be comparatively self-sufficient, requiring imports only of such special products as minerals, lumber, and fish, coming from those scattered small centers of economic activity where the relevant natural resources were located. Wages would be the same for comparable skills in China, India, the United States, and Europe, and the entire world would share a common rate of interest.

Obstacles to Factor Price Equalisation

Although international trade works in the same direction as international mobility of the factors—toward equalising factor returns everywhere—for a number of reasons it cannot achieve the complete equalisation that mobility would bring. For one thing, transport and other costs of trading prevent the equalisation of commodity prices that would be necessary were factor returns also to be equalised.

In addition, where there is great inequality of factor endowments, the concentration of the world's demand for specific factors upon those regions where they are most abundant is not sufficiently powerful to offset the initial great disparity in supply. To illustrate, it is inconceivable that even if the rest of the world bought all its labor-intensive goods from such areas as China and India, this would suffice to raise wages in the latter and lower them in the former until they were equal. Countries in which labor is the scarce factor can shift only *part* of their demand for labor onto countries in which labor is abundant, since the demand for the factors is a joint demand. *Some* labor must always be combined with capital and natural resources.

Thirdly, the equalising effect of the channeling of world demands toward abundant factor supplies is reduced when alternative methods of production can be used. When a capital-intensive process was developed for producing rice, for example, part of the demand hitherto directed especially toward the labor of Burma and Thailand was shifted toward U.S. capital.[5]

Injury to a Scarce Factor

In spite of these obstacles to complete equalisation of factor prices, international trade unquestionably works in this direction. Any country's abundant factor receives a higher, its scarce factor, a lower return, than it would in the absence of such trade. From the point of view of the entire world supply of the factors, the average reward of each is raised. Yet from the national point of view, a country's scarce factor is injured.

In a country where labor is the scarce factor, this effect of international trade might be socially important, and justify, in terms of a desirable distribution of income, the protection of labor-intensive industries. Its

[5] Theoretically, if any country specialised *completely* on a certain product, this alone would be sufficient to prevent factor price equalisation, since it would eliminate contact between the ratio of commodity exchange and the ratios of factor reward. Practically, this case is unimportant, since the argument rests on the assumption of two countries and two commodities, with one or both countries devoting all its resources to specialised production. With the numerous lines of production actually open to any country, complete specialisation on one or even a few becomes almost inconceivable.

practical significance, however, is doubtful. The entire argument is based upon the static assumption that the supply of each factor is fixed and unchanging. In the real world, this is not true; factor supplies can and do change. If capital is the abundant factor, the growth of trade will cause its return to rise. Moreover, as we have already shown in the last section, even though the real income of one factor may decline, that of the entire community will be raised by international trade. With a larger total income, and with capital receiving an increased reward, it is probable that savings will increase. Over a period of years, labor would then stand to gain by having a larger total complement of capital to assist it in production. Nor should we overlook the possibility that an expanding supply of capital, by holding down the interest rate, will encourage the growth of capital-intensive industries, a development that is likely to stimulate technological advance, to the benefit of all elements in the community, including labor.

Even if none of these things happens, the disadvantage to which scarce labor is subjected may be counteracted by a deliberate act of government policy. Taxes may be levied on those who gain because of trade, and the proceeds distributed to labor, either directly or as a supplement to wages, or by the socially more acceptable method of financing social security, recreation facilities, or simply a larger share of ordinary government operations.

FACTOR ENDOWMENTS AND THE PATTERN OF TRADE

If the model of international trade we summarised at the beginning of this chapter really works, we should be able to show that trade actually does proceed in accordance with its principles. There should be some sort of system in the trading relations of the world, with the flow of goods dominated by international disparity in endowments with the major categories of factors—land, labor, and capital. We should expect to see a large volume of exports of agricultural products moving from land-rich countries in exchange for the manufactures, handicrafts, and other goods produced in countries where capital or labor is abundant. Within this broad schema, of course, there would be many cross currents. For as we know, the division of the productive factors into three main categories is only valid as a first approximation—in a more detailed account we have to consider at least three or four different kinds of labor and several kinds of agricultural land, in addition to specific types of natural resources such as mineral deposits.

Factor Endowment and Specialisation: 1870-1890

To obtain the broad view here in question, let us look first at the much simpler world of the 1870's and 1880's, just after the expansion of railways had opened up the major grain-producing or Great Plains regions (Argentina, Australia, Canada, Russia, and the United States). At that time the more important trading nations of the world could have been grouped into four main regions in accordance with the test of relative factor supply. In the tropics, particularly in the parts for which trade was of considerable importance (India, Ceylon, and the Dutch East Indies), population was relatively dense, capital very scarce, and land, as compared with the other regions, in moderate supply. In the United Kingdom, transformed by the Industrial Revolution into the world's premier manufacturing nation, capital was far more abundant than elsewhere, land scarce, and labor in an intermediate position. Continental Europe, with a dense population, was behind the United Kingdom in the accumulation of capital and in industrial development, but like it in the possession of a relatively small area of usable land. In the Great Plains area, of course, land was far and away the most abundant factor, capital in short supply, and labor only moderately abundant. Thus the relative factor supply structure in these major trading regions looked approximately like this:

RELATIVE FACTOR SUPPLY	TROPICS	GREAT PLAINS REGIONS	CONTINENTAL EUROPE	UNITED KINGDOM
Ample	Labor	Land	Labor	Capital
Moderate	Land	Labor	Capital	Labor
Scarce	Capital	Capital	Land	Land

Now consider the main features of trade in this period. The records are inadequate to permit us to state with any precision the direction or size of net export or import balances, but they are perfectly clear as to the character of the goods exchanged between the various regions. The United Kingdom was the great exporter of manufactures to the rest of the world. These ranged from light consumer goods such as cotton and wool textiles, pottery, notions, and hardware to heavy capital goods like railway rails and rolling stock, stationary engines, pumps, and mining equipment.

The Great Plains regions, of course, supplied the United Kingdom and Continental Europe principally with meats, wheat, wool, and (from the United States alone) cotton. Except in the United States, even the production of manufactures for local use was in its infancy, and although the

United States exported some specialised manufactured goods, they totalled only a little more than one-tenth of all its exports.

The Tropics, with labor as the abundant factor, exported such labor-intensive agricultural products as rice, raw silk, tea, cocoa, coffee, and spices and fine handicrafts such as lacquer ware, silk fabrics, and fine cotton goods.

Continental Europe stood in a position intermediate between industrial Britain and the predominantly agricultural areas. Production of wheat, in the face of competition from the prairies overseas, declined (except in Russia), and farmers increasingly turned to more labor-intensive commodities, in particular, butter and cheese, eggs, ham and bacon, perfumes, and temperate and subtropical varieties of fruits. Lumber exports also grew in importance, and manufactures, especially those demanding close attention by skilled labor (watches, jewelry, fine leather goods, lace), expanded steadily.

These results may be portrayed in tabular form:

TYPE OF PRODUCT	TROPICS	GREAT PLAINS REGIONS	CONTINENTAL EUROPE	UNITED KINGDOM
Labor-intensive	Tropical agricultural products; handicrafts		Dairy products; skilled labor manufactures	
Land-intensive		Grains, meats wool, cotton		
Capital-intensive				Light and heavy manufactures

Changes in Relative Factor Endowment

During the generation between 1890 and the 1920's the relatively simple factor-supply structure of the 1870's and 1880's changed appreciably. There were large international movements of labor and capital, and internal growth through capital accumulation and the increase of population was substantial.

The most striking case is that of the United States. Between 1880 and 1914, the international movement of population totalled approximately 40 million, of whom most came from Europe. Over half proceeded to the United States, meeting the demand for labor for its expanding factories and farms without, however, changing the status of labor as the relatively scarce factor. Since productivity continued to be high and rising as North America's natural resources were exploited, and entrepreneurs reaped large gains therefrom without hindrance from progressive income taxes, capital accumulation was rapid. By the 1920's, it would appear to have become relatively more abundant even than the land factor.

The Great Plains regions shared in the growth of population from European immigration, and benefited also from large capital movements, principally from the United Kingdom, as well as from rapid domestic accumulation. Land remained the abundant factor, but a more rapid rise in the supply of capital than of population enabled it to displace labor as the factor in moderate supply.

In the Tropics, the benefits of trade were largely taken out in the form of population increases, while in spite of sizeable investment of European funds, the general poverty kept the supply of capital relatively scanty.

In Europe, large-scale emigration held down the growth of population, while at the same time its increasing industrialisation and urbanisation slowed down the birth rate in the more advanced countries. Population continued to increase, though less rapidly than formerly. Meanwhile, the profits from its expanding industry, especially prominent in Germany, Belgium, France, Switzerland, and Sweden, were invested in this very expansion. As capital accumulated, it ceased to be the scarce factor and became at least moderately abundant.

By the 1920's the relative position of the major trading regions of the world with respect to factor supplies appears to have assumed the following pattern:

RELATIVE FACTOR SUPPLY	TROPICS	UNITED STATES	GREAT PLAINS	CONTINENTAL EUROPE	UNITED KINGDOM
Ample	Labor	Capital	Land	Labor	Capital
Moderate	Land	Land	Capital	Capital	Labor
Scarce	Capital	Labor	Labor	Land	Land

Factor Endowments, Pre-World War II

This conclusion is supported by such data as are available. These include fairly reliable estimates of agricultural land and of the working population and very rough estimates of the value of capital stock in five major regions of the world. The land and capital figures for each region were divided by those for the working population, thus converting them into the amount of land and capital per worker. These data are shown in columns (1) and (3) of Table 9.1. The working population is given a value of 1 in each region (column 2), since the figure for land and capital is relative to each region's working population.

Table 9.1

RELATIVE SUPPLIES OF CAPITAL, LABOR, AND LAND
IN MAJOR REGIONS, 1935-38

REGION	(1) CAPITAL PER WORKER	(2) WORKING POPULATION	(3) LAND PER WORKER
United Kingdom	5,024	1	0.94
Western Europe	2,500	1	1.08
United States	4,365	1	9.0
Great Plains	4,290	1	43.9
Tropics	510	1	4.57

Note: The data on capital were derived from Colin Clark, *The Economics of 1960* (London: Macmillan, 1942), p. 80, and are expressed in "international units," defined as the amount of goods and services that could be purchased for $1.00 in the United States over the average of the decade 1925-34. Figures for working populations used in the computations are from the same source. The data on agricultural land are based on materials in Food and Agriculture Organisation of the United Nations, *Yearbook of Food and Agricultural Statistics*, 1952, Vol. VI, Part I (Rome, Italy), pp. 3-7. Both arable and pasture land are included; they are expressed in hectares.

The capital data relate to the years 1935-38; those for the working population are for the same period. The figures for land are for the year 1951. Since land areas changed inappreciably between 1937 and 1951, the various data may be regarded as closely comparable. The same countries are included in each region for all three factors compared. They are: Western Europe — Germany-Austria, France, Belgium-Luxembourg, Italy, Switzerland, the Netherlands, Sweden, Norway, Denmark, and Czechoslovakia; Great Plains—Argentina, Uruguay, Australia, Canada, New Zealand; Tropics—India, Pakistan, South Asia, Africa, and Oceania other than Australia and New Zealand.

To determine which factor is relatively the most abundant and which the scarcest in each region, we must look at the figures for the three factors in each region in relation to their values in all the other regions. Doing this, we see that in the United Kingdom, capital has the highest value for any region, land the lowest, clearly indicating that these are the abundant and the scarce factors in the U.K., with labor in the intermediate position. The data for the Great Plains stand out equally sharply; its figure for land is the highest of all, that for capital is relatively large. Land is abundant, capital in relatively moderate supply, labor is relatively the least abundant.

In the United States, capital and land are both abundant relatively to the other regions. But the capital figure is higher than the average of 3,336 for all regions, while the land figure is below the overall average (11.9), though exceeded only by that for the Great Plains. The abundant factor is capital, labor the scarce one, with land in between.

As for Western Europe, both capital and land show values that are below the average. That for land, however, is relatively much lower. Land is the scarce factor, capital is in moderate supply, and labor (with a value that *relative* to the others is highest) is the abundant factor. Similar reasoning shows that in the Tropics, labor is relatively abundant, capital scarce, while land falls in between.

World Trade in the Inter-War Period

Consider now the trade between these areas. Empirical studies have shown that, as of 1928, it fell into a well-defined multilateral pattern, illustrated by the following diagram.[6] The arrows point in the direction of net

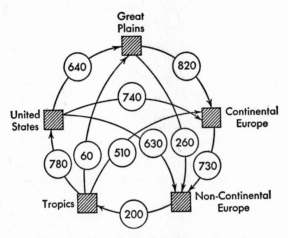

Fig. 9.1: The System of Multilateral Trade.

export balances of merchandise trade, whose values in millions of dollars are inscribed in the circles. The countries represented in the diagram in 1928 accounted for nine-tenths of total world trade.[7]

The Tropics had a large export balance with the United States, reflecting heavy U.S. purchases of tropical produce (coffee, tea, rubber, fruits, vegetable oils) and minerals (petroleum, copper, manganese). Based on relative abundance of labor and of tropical land (as well as specific mineral deposits), these exports provided a large proportion of the raw materials

[6] The original study is *The Network of World Trade* (League of Nations, 1942). The detailed data of this study are summarised and discussed in Folke Hilgerdt, "The Case for Multilateral Trade," *American Economic Review*, XXXIII, No. 1, Pt. 2 Supplement (Mar. 1943). The diagram used here is the modified one in the article by Karl-Erik Hansson, "A General Theory of the System of Multilateral Trade," *American Economic Review*, XLII, No. 1 (March 1952). I have also used Hansson's simplified method of stating relative factor-supply structures.

[7] The Great Plains include, besides the four countries in Table 9.1, Paraguay and South Africa. Continental Europe comprises all continental European countries except the U.S.S.R., and is thus more inclusive than the region, "Western Europe," used in that table. Non-Continental Europe is the United Kingdom plus Ireland and Iceland and a few small islands. The Tropics is much more representative than the table, since it is limited to truly tropical countries, whereas in Table 9.1 many countries are included that are not in the tropics.

needed by American industry and of highly specific consumption requirements.

Next, the capital-rich United States economy complemented the land-rich economies of the Great Plains by shipping large quantities of tractors and other agricultural machinery, automobiles, and industrial goods generally—some $640 million worth more than its imports of wool, leather, meat, and minerals.

The Great Plains region, in turn, exported a large net balance of its land-intensive products—principally wool, grains, and meat—to Continental Europe. This region, though its factor structure resembles that of non-Continental Europe (substantially the U.K.), nonetheless exported to the latter, on balance, more specialised manufactures than it received, as well as large amounts of such relatively labor-intensive commodities as dairy products, bacon, eggs, and wines, together with lumber and wood-pulp from the northern European forests.

Finally, non-Continental Europe, like the United States, drew upon the land and labor of the Tropics for many raw materials and consumption items, but unlike the United States, exported a still larger value of manufactured goods.

In addition to the direct movement of trade balances around the circle, which if equal in amount would permit each region to cancel its import balance to the preceding member by its export balance to the next, large net balances ran from the United States direct to both European regions, and from the Tropics to Continental Europe. Settlement of these balances, and of the gap in the circular flow caused by the relatively small export balance from non-Continental Europe to the Tropics was made possible by an opposite movement of service items, such as freight charges, insurance, and interest and dividends for which the United States and the Tropics were indebted to Europe. (U.S. loans, especially to Germany, were also important at this time).

Taking the pattern of trade shown by the diagram together with the factor-supply structure indicated by the table, we see that theoretical expectations based on the latter are by and large borne out by the actual movement of trade. The major trading regions of the world complemented one another in terms of factor supplies, and their trade corresponded fairly well to factor endowments in broad terms of the three main categories. A more detailed account, of course, would have to use a narrower classification, and consider as well other relevant determinants of trade such as transport costs, economies of scale, monopolistic restrictions, and government policies as embodied in tariffs, subsidies, and the like.

SELECTED REFERENCES

Hansson, Karl-Erik, "A General Theory of the System of Multilateral Trade," *American Economic Review*, **XLII** (1952). Well worth consulting for a more elaborate statement of the application of the theory of international trade to the system of world trade.

Hilgerdt, Folke, "The Case for Multilateral Trade," *American Economic Review*, **XXXIII**, Supplement (1943). A pragmatic and well-documented formulation.

Kindleberger, Charles P., *International Economics* (Richard D. Irwin, Inc., Homewood, Ill., 1953). Chapter 14, "The Case for Free Multilateral Trade," has an excellent though brief discussion of the price system in relation both to efficiency and to general welfare considerations.

Leontief, W. W., "The Use of Indifference Curves in the Analysis of Foreign Trade," American Economic Association, *Readings in the Theory of International Trade* (The Blakiston Co., Philadelphia, 1949), chapter 10. Shows how indifference curves may be applied to international trade, and in particular, how the gain from trade may be demonstrated by this method.

Meade, James E., *Problems of Economic Union* (Geo. Allen & Unwin, Ltd., London, 1953). Pp. 56-72 contain a brief statement of the factor-price equalisation argument, and of the principal obstacles to its operation. A less difficult version than Samuelson's.

Samuelson, Paul A., "The Gains from International Trade," American Economic Association, *Readings in the Theory of International Trade* (The Blakiston Co., Philadelphia, 1949), chapter 11. This is the definitive proof of the gain from trade, expressed in mathematical language and in terms of the general equilibrium theory.

Samuelson, Paul A., "International Trade and the Equalisation of Factor Prices," *Economic Journal*, **LVIII** (1948); **LIX** 1949). These two articles provide the fullest discussion of the tendency toward factor-price equalisation.

Scitofsky, Tibor, "A Reconsideration of the Theory of Tariffs," *Readings in the Theory of International Trade*, chapter 16. Provides an advanced though non-mathematical discussion of the gains from trade and of the possible use of tariffs by a single country to maximise its advantage.

Viner, Jacob, *Studies in the Theory of International Trade* (Harper & Bros., New York, 1937). Chapters VIII and IX contain an exhaustive discussion of the issues and the literature of the gains from trade, in the setting of a real costs approach to international trade theory.

10

THE GROWTH OF AN
INTERNATIONAL ECONOMY

The body of theory whose study we have just completed explains the bases on which international trade rests and indicates in what ways nations can benefit from the specialisation trade makes possible. In pointing to these gains, the theory serves as a policy prescription that has found wide though not universal acceptance. As a model that describes reality, however, it can be valid only if a number of critical assumptions are at least approximated in practice.

The more important of these are that capital and labor shall be highly mobile within a single country, substantially less so between countries; and that production and merchandising shall be effectively competitive. But for competition to be effective, buyers and sellers must be able to communicate readily with one another. This implies that trade shall be free, especially of direct quantitative restrictions, and that currencies shall be at least partially convertible into one another, for without convertibility contact between national markets is lost.

Europe in 1815

Conditions in the real world of the early nineteenth century were far different from those postulated in the theoretical model. Only in Great Britain and Holland was it comparatively easy for capital and labor to seek out those industries or occupations in which returns were highest, owing to the fact that in these countries alone had thoroughgoing national unification been achieved. Internal barriers to trade were nonexistent, the feudal order was a thing of the past, and in Holland a good canal system, in England canals, coastal shipping, and recently improved roads quickened the movements of goods and people. Men of commerce had long dominated the political and economic affairs of the Netherlands. In Great Britain, energetic and enterprising businessmen had already revolutionised the production of iron and cotton textiles and were spreading the new techniques over an ever-widening range of industry. Although the landed aristocracy still dominated Parliament, the political influence of the business class was steadily increasing. British agriculture, too, had but recently undergone a revolutionary change in technology and provided a prosperous and efficient model for others to copy.

On the Continent, on the other hand, local tariffs, dues, and tolls impeded commerce, even in countries as united as France. Germany and Italy were still divided into petty kingdoms and principalities. ("Germany" consisted of some 300 independent territories, each with its own customs and currency system, and using a bewildering variety of weights and measures.) The feudal system, binding the peasant to the land and concentrating its ownership in the hands of a favored few, had only recently been demolished in France; over most of the rest of Europe, it retained a shaky dominance. Capital was scarce and the enterprise to use it even scarcer.

As for international trade, the complex Mercantilist structure of tariffs, prohibitions, bounties, and shipping regulations continued unimpaired. Even in Britain, the Navigation Acts were still in force, and what Adam Smith said in 1776 could have been repeated in 1815 with little change.

During the nineteenth century all this changed. Northwestern Europe became industrialised, its agriculture was improved, people and investment funds flowed from Britain, France, and Germany to the Americas and other regions new and old, and the Mercantilist structure was thoroughly dismantled. From about 1860 until the outbreak of the first World War, one could say that the world of fact reasonably approximated the world of our theoretical model. It will be the task of this chapter to trace the main changes that occurred and to sketch the principal features of the international economy they brought into being.

Three aspects of change in the nineteenth century will be stressed. First, there is the rise of Great Britain to a position of economic and political pre-eminence, and the accompanying emergence of London as the world's economic nerve center. Second is the rapid economic growth of western Europe and then of the overseas regions settled by Europeans. And finally, there is the demolition of the surviving remnants of Mercantilism, the restrictions on foreign trade. These strands of history were, of course, closely interwoven; it is possible to distinguish them only for purposes of analysis. Together they produced the institutions and the forces that constituted a truly international economy.

THE RISE OF BRITAIN

Industry

During the sixty years between 1815 and 1875, the Industrial Revolution continued its work of transforming the predominantly agrarian economy of Britain into the workshop of the world. The weaving of cotton textiles, still a hand-loom operation at the turn of the century, gradually gave way to machinery. By 1875 the hand-loom was extinct. A few years later the woolen industry, too, succumbed to mechanisation. With this technical progress, costs fell, and British textiles, even with expanding output in Europe and the United States, dominated markets from Shanghai to Buenos Aires. Iron had become liberated from its dependence on charcoal and was now processed with coke from the rich British coalfields; it found ever expanding uses as new machines were perfected and took over more and more operations. From less than a quarter of a million tons in 1800, pig-iron production expanded fifty times in the next seventy-five years. By 1875, Great Britain accounted for more than all the rest of the world put together. The factory system, with its clanking machines, its soot and smoke, its sprawling slums, but also with its ever cheaper and more abundant stream of cottons, woolens, glass, pottery, leather goods, and the tools and machines to make them, attracted more and more workers from farms and fields. City dwellers, from a mere 31 per cent in 1801, came by 1871 to comprise 61 per cent of the population. Though rivals were emerging, they presented as yet no serious challenge. Britain stood out alone as the world's sole industrial nation.

It was the displacement of manual by mechanical operations in industry after industry that mainly accounted for the phenomenal growth in the output of coal and iron, the dominant materials of the age. No other product of the nineteenth century even began to compare with machines as a consumer of iron and steel. And the greatest pressure on these resources came when the steam engine acquired mobility by land and sea with the appearance of the locomotive and the steamship. These early nineteenth century inventions [1] not only required iron and steel to build them and coal to drive them; far larger quantities of iron and steel were needed for rails, wheels, carriages, and miscellaneous gear, and later (especially after 1850) in the construction of ships.

Transportation

Although the railway and the steamship gave a tremendous impetus to the growth of the iron and steel industry, their real importance lay in their true function—that of providing rapid, reliable, and cheap transport

---

[1] Although preceded by earlier experimental models, the first successful steamboat was Robert Fulton's *Clermont* (1807), and the first successful locomotive, George Stephenson's *Rocket* (1825).

of goods and people. Within a quarter century after the first short line opened in 1825, Great Britain had acquired its main trunk lines. The dray, the carriage, and the canal boat became, instead of the sole means of transport, supplements to the railroad—supplements of ever declining importance. By 1880, some 18 thousand miles of lines crisscrossed the country with a dense network.

Though the steamship antedated the railway as a new form of transport by some twenty years, technical problems delayed its extended use by several decades. Not until 1865 did steamships become quantitatively important; they then comprised some 15 per cent of total British shipping tonnage. In the meantime, greatly increased numbers of sailing vessels served the needs of expanding world trade. British ships and sailors maintained and extended their earlier lead; by 1850, about 60 per cent of world shipping tonnage was of British registry. Toward the end of the century, when steamer tonnage far exceeded that of sailing vessels, Britain's share of the world's merchant fleet reached a peak of 73 per cent.

Trade

As her railways ensured speedy and cheap delivery of raw materials to processors and of finished goods to shipping ports, as her expanding fleet furnished ready means of carrying her industrial products to overseas markets and of bringing back raw materials and foodstuffs of every kind, Britain's trade mounted ever higher. Exports tripled in the first half of the nineteenth century, and almost tripled again in the second half. Imports grew even more rapidly, reflecting the country's increased dependence on foreign raw materials and foods; they expanded nearly fivefold by 1850, and trebled again by 1900. Textiles and textile products continually exceeded all other exports; in the early 1880's they accounted for just over half the value of total exports. Taken together, coal, and iron and steel and their products comprised another quarter. The remaining exports were scattered among a wide variety of industries.

As Britain's population moved into the cities and as the nation specialised increasingly in the production of manufactures, her dependence on foreign farms, plantations, and mines grew constantly. At the end of the Napoleonic Wars, the country was still largely self-sufficient as to foods; as for raw materials, it needed no foreign wool nor iron ore, but had to import all its cotton and most of its timber. With the needs of her growing population (15 million in 1800, 44 million in 1900) constantly rising, and with her expanding exports, Britain rapidly lost most of her relative independence. By the close of the century, close to 60 per cent of the wheat and flour consumed in the country came from overseas. Imports of meat began in the seventies; with the introduction of refrigeration after 1876, cheap Argentine beef and Australian mutton steadily displaced the products of local slaughterhouses. To ever-growing imports of cotton and timber were added wool from Australia, which with later supplies from Uruguay and South Africa eventually furnished practically all of this fiber. After 1860, imports of rich Spanish iron ores began to supplement those of native origin; by 1885 imports amounted to almost a quarter of domestic ore production. In addition to these most basic imports, purchases of innumerable other products—hemp, jute, and flax; tin, copper, lead, and nickel; tea, coffee, and cocoa—also reflected the growing specialisation of Britain and of her suppliers.

Specialised Market Facilities

An interesting and important result of expanding imports of highly specialised products was the emergence one after another of specialised marketing facilities. Some of these were of long standing, such as the markets for spices and sugar, in which specialised dealers and brokers had carried on an active import and reexport business since at least Elizabethan times. After 1846, with the steady increase in wheat imports that followed the repeal of the Corn Laws, specialised trading in this and other grains coming from Russia centered in the Baltic Coffee House in London, long a rendezvous for general traders. Simultaneously, Liverpool began to develop specialised facilities for dealings in imports from America. With the flood of cheap American wheat after 1870, when railways opened up the western States, Liverpool came to outrank London as a market. Liverpool, as the port nearest the cotton manufacturing towns, also became the outstanding cotton market, with organised exchanges dealing in both "spot" and "futures" transactions in standardised grades. London had long been the country's chief market for transactions in wool; as imports outdistanced domestic production in importance, it became the great distributing center for the world.

The London Money Market

Of all the specialised markets that developed in Great Britain as that nation rose to a position of commercial and industrial pre-eminence, none was as important in its contribution to the country's leadership as the London money market. For it was the gradual perfection of London's banking and financial facilities that made the pound sterling a true world currency, and the entire world a sterling area.

London had for centuries been the commercial and financial metropolis of the kingdom. By the end of the Napoleonic Wars, its banking business was conducted by over 800 private, unincorporated banks, the sixty strongest being located in London, the rest scattered throughout the country. To finance the stream of commodities moving to London for local use, for redistribution to other parts of the nation, or for export, provincial traders and manufacturers drew bills of exchange on their London customers, ordering them to pay the sum due to some city bank. These bills they discounted with a local country bank, from which they received the amount owed less a discount. The country bank then forwarded these bills of exchange to the London bank of its choice, which either held the bill for collection, say thirty or sixty days later, or rediscounted it immediately for cash itself or with some other bank with funds to invest. Immediately or later, the country bank acquired deposits in London to compensate it for its payments to local clients.

Simultaneously, goods moved from London to the provinces. For these, provincial buyers had to make payment in London. They did so by purchasing bills of exchange drawn on its London correspondent by a local bank. These ordered the former to pay the sum specified to the London merchant. In this way the deposits built up in London by country banks were constantly being depleted. Buyers and sellers in the provinces paid their bills to and received payment from local banks; their opposites in London received or paid London funds. Little gold or currency had to move in either direction, the great bulk of transactions being cleared against one another.

Bill brokers and dealers. If this mechanism was to work efficiently, someone had to stand ready to discount the large numbers of country bills of exchange constantly being drawn, ordinarily not for immediate but only for a later payment. As the volume of this business increased, specialised agencies arose to put up the money, or find someone who would. The first to appear, just as the struggle with Napoleon ended, was the bill broker. For some time, he was just what his name implies—a financial go-between, seeking out the bills of country merchants and bankers, locating banks with surplus funds, and persuading the latter to invest in the bills in his care. For his trouble and his knowledge, he exacted a small commission.

About 50 years later, the bill broker began to give way to the dealer. The bill dealer was himself a principal, not just an agent. Using sizeable funds of his own or borrowing for short periods at the big London banks, he took up bills on his own account. Still later came the so-called discount house, which was simply the dealer writ large; it had more capital of its own, it took deposits from the public and paid interest on them, and it did a greater volume of business.

Acceptance houses.   The acceptance function, the second task to be taken over by a highly specialised group, was from the latter part of the eighteenth or the early part of the nineteenth century performed by various leading London mercantile firms. Because of the great knowledge they acquired as to the credit-worthiness of an immense number of merchants and manufacturers with whom they did business, they could afford to underwrite, as it were, the bills of exchange of reliable individuals and firms whose names were less well known than theirs. This they did by simply writing "accepted," together with their signature, across the face of a bill. For this act, which amounted to guaranteeing the bill, they received a small commission. The effect was that:

In plain English the man with second-class credit paid a commission to the possessor of first-class credit and thereby secured an improvement in the discount terms which was equal to an amount far in excess of the small commission paid for the accommodation.[2]

As the volume of their business increased, and as England waxed wealthier and began to invest in the securities of foreign governments and railways, some of the more prominent of these trading firms dropped their mercantile transactions and specialised in the business of acceptance and of security issues. Because of their foreign connections and because of the phenomenal growth of British foreign trade, the bulk of their acceptance business had to do with international transactions. Down to about 1850, these great acceptance and issue houses also had a near monopoly of the foreign exchange business, i.e., the purchase and sale of bills and drafts running in terms of foreign currencies. Later, they began to leave this part of their operations to be carried out by a new class of financial institutions, the branches of foreign banks that appeared in London after the Franco-Prussian War.

At the same time that some of these more important houses were turning their attention increasingly to the issue of securities, others, together with newcomers, specialised entirely in the acceptance business. By the end of the nineteenth century, the function of accepting, as well as that of discounting, was very largely in the hands of highly specialised firms and

[2] Ellis T. Powell, *The Evolution of the Money Market,* p. 374. Copyright 1915 by the Financial News, London.

companies. Some part of each type of business, however, was undertaken by the commercial banks, particularly by the branches of foreign and colonial banks that came to London after 1870.

The Bank of England. Occupying a central position in this banking system was the Bank of England. Privately owned, its directors insisted on regarding it as in no essential different from any other private bank. Nonetheless, it had even by the end of the eighteenth century come to perform certain of the functions typical of a central bank: (1) it carried on all of the banking business of the government, and during the Napoleonic Wars had been its financial right hand; (2) it maintained the only gold reserve of importance in the kingdom; and (3) it kept in the form of deposits a large part of the reserves of all other London banks.

Nowadays it is a commonly accepted duty of a central bank to provide commercial banks with additional reserves in time of need by rediscounting certain types of commercial paper. This duty the Bank of England came to accept only grudgingly and reluctantly. In a whole series of early crises, when extraordinary demands for currency or gold caused a drain on the reserves of the commercial banks, refusal of the Bank to play the role of "lender of last resort" forced the government to take the initiative. It did so either (as in 1793 and 1811) by advancing Exchequer bills to merchants against the security of goods, or (as in 1847 and 1857) by promising the Bank legislation indemnifying it for issuing its notes liberally, in excess of the legal limit.

Finally, in 1866 the Bank on its own initiative lent freely to meet the demands upon it, and in a letter to the Chancellor of the Exchequer, laid the facts before him. His reply authorised free lending to stem the crisis. Following this action, there was considerable dispute as to the wisdom of the Bank's accepting the duty of acting as "lender of last resort." The issue was finally settled by the publication of Bagehot's *Lombard Street,* whose

lucid common sense . . . was itself decisive. Since then the responsibilities of the Banking Department as the lender of last resort have been unequivocally recognised.[3]

Summary. We are now in a position to see the London money market as a whole and to examine its operation. The London banks, including the branches of foreign and colonial banks, furnished the principal source of funds for financing the short-term requirements of industry and commerce. This was supplemented to some extent by the capital of bill dealers and

[3] R. G. Hawtrey, *The Art of Central Banking,* p. 126. Copyright 1932 by Longmans, Green & Co., London.

discount houses and by money deposited by the public with the latter. The ultimate borrowers of these funds were traders and manufacturers in London, in various parts of the United Kingdom, and—increasingly as the nineteenth century wore on—exporters and importers all over the globe. British borrowers obtained part of their short-term working capital by direct loans fom one or more of the London or country banks; the rest they raised by offering their bills of exchange on the discount market, which furnished practically all the funds supplied to foreigners. Bills coming on the discount market, if from a well-known and established firm, whether domestic or foreign, would either be discounted directly by a bill dealer or a discount house, or parceled out among the banks by the bill brokers. If the borrowing firm was not outstanding, it had its credit validated by one of the specialised acceptance houses before placing it on the discount market.

In normal times the supply of funds lent at short-term by the banks to their clients, together with those available in the discount market, was adequate to finance smoothly the conduct of Britain's domestic and foreign trade, as well as a large part of the foreign trade of the rest of the world. All the loans and bills discounted ran for short periods of time, usually from sixty to ninety days, and since some were coming due every day, there was a steady stream of repayments and issuance of new credits. The entire resources of the London money market were therefore a gigantic revolving fund, constantly being depleted and as constantly, replenished.

Of course the demands varied from time to time in relation to the supply of funds available; these changes were reflected in movements of the discount rate. When the demands became exceptionally large, or when the capacity of the London banks to make advances was strained by having to draw upon their reserves to ship gold abroad or to meet unusually heavy internal needs for currency, it became necessary for the market to have recourse to the Bank of England. Then the discount houses, rather than the banks, obtained the additional reserves necessary to avoid a disastrous contraction of credit.

We have already referred to the fact that dealings in foreign exchange proper, that is, the purchase and sale of bills of exchange drawn in foreign currencies, came to be concentrated in the hands of foreign banks. The volume of this business was never large in London before World War I. British exports were in demand everywhere, the pound sterling was as good as gold and more convenient, and British exporters and importers preferred to draw and to be drawn upon in pounds sterling. Hence sterling bills of exchange were used to finance the exports and imports of the United Kingdom, and those of a large part of the rest of the world as well.

The volume of sterling bills constantly coming into the London money market was immense. They arose, as we have seen, out of the financial requirements both of purely domestic economic activities and of foreign trade, including in the latter remittances for shipments which never saw English shores. The reasons for this worldwide preference for the pound sterling as a medium of international payments were numerous. In part it was Great Britain's paramount position as exporter of manufactured goods and importer of raw materials and foodstuffs and her equally great pre-eminence as international investor. In part, also, it was the stable value of the pound sterling in terms of gold, resulting from the rigorous adherence to the gold standard from 1821 until 1914. But certainly of great importance was the high standing of the British acceptance houses and the assurance that any bill receiving their endorsement could be readily discounted, at the world's most favorable rates, on the London discount market. As Powell expressed the matter:

The effect of this system, from the point of view of our national economy, is that we are able to take toll of a vast aggregate of foreign trade in which we have no direct concern whatever, by lending our acceptances to finance it. A draft on New York or Berlin may be imagined as negotiable in Canton against shipments of silk to New York itself; but if the silk exporter is to get the best rate for his drafts, he will see that they are drawn on London.[4]

From the operation of these compelling forces, London became the world's great financial center, furnishing short-term credits to foreign as well as to British importers, to overseas borrowers needing funds to meet a temporary excess of foreign claims over foreign credits, and providing, through the capital-raising activity of the security-issuing houses, sterling loans for foreign long-term capital requirements.

WESTERN EUROPE CATCHES UP

With a lag of several decades, western Europe went through a phase of development similar to Britain's, though with certain important differences.

Agriculture

Before appreciable progress could be made, the feudal landholding system had to be abandoned. The Revolution had freed the peasant in France. His inbred conservatism remained, however, and it required both

[4] *Op. cit.*, p. 375.

official prodding and the competition brought by the railway to persuade him to adopt new crops and new methods. In Prussia, the defeat at Jena in 1806 forced the large landholders to recognise the need for reform. Emancipation edicts followed, which, by freeing the serfs and permitting land transfers and choice of occupations, created the mobility essential for progress. Similar reforms spread to other parts of western Europe.

Improvements in agriculture now became possible. Leadership in some countries, notably Prussia, came from the more progressive landowners, who saw in the modernised large-scale commercial farms of England a model to emulate. With population increasing and the towns and cities growing, markets were good, and new crops—especially potatoes, sugar beets, and linseed—afforded good returns and required a break with old methods. Government sponsorship of change helped, both in France and Germany; agricultural societies were formed, new techniques and new machinery demonstrated, and competitive exhibits organised. After 1840, the expansion of the railway network added the stimulus of intensified competition to force the abandonment of antiquated methods and the less profitable crops.

Industry

European industry in 1815 remained almost completely in the handicraft stage. Its progress thereafter varied widely. Change was negligible in Italy and Spain until late in the century. In France, for a variety of reasons, it lagged badly until about 1860, when railway mileage was substantial. Advance came sooner and was most rapid in Germany and Belgium.

German industrialisation exhibited a sharp contrast with that of Britain. There was no revolution in thought or attitudes such as occurred in England between the fifteenth and nineteenth centuries. Prussia, the dominant state, carried down into modern times a spirit of medieval submission to authority and of looking to the state for leadership. From the very first, the state took an active part in fostering the growth of industry, both from choice and from necessity.

In 1816, a staff member of the Prussian Department of Commerce, Industry, and Public Works established the Industrial Institute (*Gewerbeinstitut*), which began training engineers and machine builders in 1821. Both Prussia and other German States sent industrial spies to England, where they used various stratagems to evade the numerous British laws (repealed in 1842) restricting the export of machines, models, and blueprints. Prussia also displayed a keen interest in and careful attention to education, with special solicitude for the teaching of science.

Lack of a numerous class of enterprising business men concerned with manufacture, as well as a shortage of capital, also handicapped industrial development on the Continent. As additional remedies for these deficiencies, Prussia granted a number of subsidies to industry, admitted imports of machinery duty free, and encouraged the migration of skilled British workers and engineers. After the formation in 1834 of the German Customs Union *(Zollverein)*, which brought the German states behind a single tariff, new industries were sheltered by protective duties. The Prussian State took an active part in the planning and construction of railways. Their stimulating effect became especially important after 1860, when Germany possessed nearly seven thousand miles of track.

Any account of the early stages of industrialisation on the Continent would have to give an important place to the aid provided by British capital, labor, and enterprise. It was less in Germany than elsewhere, but even here British workers and engineers installed machinery and demonstrated its operation in the cotton, woolen and jute industries, in machine manufacture, gas works, mines, and railways. In France and Belgium, most of the early railways were built by British engineers and navvies, manned by British engine drivers, and financed in part by British capital. Many industrial plants, too, owed their origin or their modernisation to British skills and capital.

By 1870, the leading nations of western Europe had gone through the first stages of the Industrial Revolution. They had a well-developed railway system, factory methods of production were well entrenched in the textile industries, and modern engineering establishments were producing most of their own requirements of machinery. They still lagged far behind Great Britain, however. Measured by the output of pig-iron, the most important industrial raw material, Britain was far out in front, with over 6 million tons. Germany produced a little less than a quarter of this amount (1.4 million tons), with France somewhat behind with 1.2 million tons. Britain also stood far ahead in manufactures, with almost a third of world production. The United States was coming to the fore, accounting for about a fifth, Germany was responsible for some 13 per cent and France, for about 10 per cent.

ECONOMIC DEVELOPMENT OVERSEAS

Many volumes have been written about the economic development of the United States, Canada, Australia, Argentina—the "regions of recent settlement" outside Europe. It would be impossible to deal in brief scope with this phenomenon—to trace the effect of differing government policies, the relative importance of specific natural resources, and the exertions by which the citizens of these areas peopled the empty spaces, built cities, and founded and developed important industries. We shall, therefore, limit ourselves to an account of the international contributions to overseas growth—the tremendous migration of labor and capital of the nineteenth century—and to some of the more important social conditions surrounding that growth.

Overseas Investment

British capital not only helped to get the Industrial Revolution under way in Europe; it also aided greatly in inaugurating the process of economic development overseas. Here its main contribution was to provide what has come to be called *social overhead capital*—the facilities without which specific industries and even agriculture cannot function efficiently, but which they are incapable of furnishing themselves; railways, roads, harbor works, power plants, telephone and telegraph systems. Of total British foreign investment of some $18,500 million outstanding in 1913, 40 per cent was in railways, 5 per cent in other utilities, and 30 per cent in loans to governments, most of which probably went into one form or another of social overhead capital. This is three-fourths of the total. The rest was scattered in mining, finance, manufacturing, and plantations. Moreover, about two-thirds of all British overseas investment went to the newly settled lands; only a quarter was directed to the tropical or semi-tropical economies with large populations and widely differing cultures. Europe obtained the rest, mainly before 1870.

British capital began to move abroad in sizeable amounts soon after the Napoleonic Wars. By 1850, it amounted to £200 million, most in western Europe and the United States, and the larger part in railways. During the next twenty-five years the destination of Britain's surplus funds remained the same; the rate of flow increased. Between 1875 and 1913, Canada and the Empire came to the fore, though the United States and Latin America also received substantial amounts. At the end of this period, nearly $9,000 million was invested in the Empire (principally in the great Dominions), while the United States and Latin America shared some $7,500 million almost equally.

Beginning with the second half of the nineteenth century, France and Germany also became foreign lenders. Both countries at first invested mainly in Europe; political considerations strongly influenced the direction of their loans. Thus France, with strong diplomatic ties with Russia, lent heavily to the Russian government. Germany, to counter Russian expansion, concentrated on southeastern Europe. Later investments of both countries helped finance overseas development. France directed large sums to Latin America and the French Empire, Germany to Latin America and the United States. By 1914, French investments abroad totalled approximately $9,000 million, of which about 60 per cent was in Europe. Germany had lent some $6,000 million, half of it to European borrowers, and a sixth each to the United States and Latin America.[5]

Results of Investments

Although some of the funds invested came from governments, the great bulk derived from private savings. The decisions that directed them to their destinations were made by individuals, banks, and business firms. Frequently these decisions were strongly influenced by fanciful misrepresentation by the banks that distributed the securities. With few exceptions, however, their motivation was gain. Investors expected a higher return than they could get at home. By and large, in spite of numerous defaults, they do not appear to have been disappointed. On comparable home and foreign investments (government bonds, or railway securities, for example), British investors did rather better on their foreign ventures.[6] Frenchmen came off worse; any advantage on the side of foreign investments was very small, for French banks gave bad advice, and the native caution of the French investor was outweighed by his credulity.

The most important gains from the international investment were not those received by the investors themselves, but those accruing to the entire community, both at home and abroad. In the lending countries, export industries enjoyed larger markets and bigger orders; their expansion permitted them to achieve economies of scale. Investments in foreign mines, plantations, and means of transport assured the industrial countries of needed supplies of raw materials and foodstuffs; they also, especially those in railways and shipping, made them cheaper. In the borrowing countries, foreign investment provided the social overhead capital so necessary for economic growth. It opened up new regions, thus making possible the combination in more effective proportions of labor and hitherto unexploited

---

[5] Figures from William Ashworth, *A Short History of the International Economy 1850-1950*, p. 173. Copyright 1952 by Longmans, Green & Co., London.

[6] Excluding about one-tenth of total British investments between 1870-1880 in government bonds on which losses from defaults outweighed gains from interest payments, returns from foreign government bonds exceeded those on British consols by amounts ranging from 0.7 per cent to 10.7 per cent. The differentials on railways stocks and bonds were comparable. Figures are from A. K. Cairncross, *Home and Foreign Investment, 1870-1913*, (Cambridge University Press, 1953), pp. 229-30.

resources, while freeing domestic capital to provide such direct aids to labor as farm implements and machinery, factory equipment, and all the array of producers' goods so badly needed in a growing economy.

People on the Move

One of the outstanding features of nineteenth century investment was that it was accompanied by, even correlated with, a large migration of labor. Between 1820 and 1930, gross migration amounted to 62 million people, some three-fourths of it occurring in the half century before World War I. Europe contributed much the greater part of these immigrants. Until 1890, most of them came from Ireland, Germany, and the Scandinavian countries; thereafter southeastern Europe, especially Italy, supplied the majority. The United States exerted the greatest drawing power; it attracted over three-fifths. Another fifth went in about equal proportions to Canada and to Australia, New Zealand, and South Africa, while Argentina and Brazil between them claimed most of the remainder.

In the earlier stages, the immigrants moved from relatively unproductive farms in the old countries to more productive agricultural employment in the newer countries, or they provided the labor to open mines and build railways. Later, an increasing proportion went into industry; in the United States, the steel industry, the women's dress industry, and the building industry took large numbers.

With a few exceptions, factors—both labor and capital—moved from areas where they were abundant and cheap to regions where they were scarce and dear. (It will be recalled that the movement of goods, which may be regarded as a substitute for factor movements, is similar in character.) In the nineteenth century, too, the migration of labor and capital was complementary; both entered the new countries together, to be combined with the relatively rich, virgin resources of the new lands in proportions that were more productive than those formerly attainable either there or in the old countries. Economic growth resulted—the appearance of new industries, better communications, the settlement of empty plains, the emergence of new towns, and all with rising per capita incomes— probably at a faster rate than ever before witnessed.

Conditions Favorable to Development

One aspect of the economic development of western Europe and of the regions of recent settlement overseas merits special attention. This is the *social environment* in which that development took place. Feudalism had been destroyed early, either before or on the threshold of the great economic changes of the nineteenth century. With the elimination of the relatively rigid social relations of feudalism, the class structure became fluid, ensuring the social mobility and the freedom to exploit resources so essential to the new industrial society. (The contrast is sharp between the rate of economic development in Latin America, where a feudal land tenure system and social structure were imported by the Spanish and Portuguese, and in the United States, Canada, and Australasia.)

More positively, western Europe and the regions settled mainly in the nineteenth century by its emigrants possessed a set of institutions uniquely favorable to rapid economic growth. High on the list is a tradition of orderly government and all that implies; the supremacy of the law and a corresponding willingness to abide by the decisions of courts, respect for prescribed methods of transferring political power between contending parties, and a reasonably efficient and honest bureaucracy. Given this tradition, changes in government could be peaceful, continuity and stability were assured, and transactions involving the government could be guided by reason and common sense.

Western Europe also acquired, as a result of the stimulus to secular and scientific interests given by the Renaissance, of the emphasis on individual efforts generated during the Reformation, and of the vigorous political, economic, and philosophical disputes of the eighteenth century Age of Enlightenment, a high respect for the role of the individual, for the experimental approach, and for the material rewards of effort. The importance of these considerations for the successful operation of a private enterprise system are clear.

Finally, the prior accumulation of capital in England, the creation in London of an international capital-market open to European borrowers, and its later widening to include western Europe itself, provided financial resources vital to rapid overseas development. The tradition of order and stability carried overseas by the settlers in turn guaranteed their access to these sources of capital.

TRADE IS MADE FREE

An efficiently functioning international economy would have been impossible without the third of the great changes of the nineteenth century—the release of trade from its burden of Mercantilist restrictions. Here, as in the growth of industry and the creation of an international market for goods and capital, Britain led the way. We have repeatedly called attention to the increasing numbers and wealth of the English manufacturing and mercantile class, whose desire for economic freedom resulted in the gradual repeal or nullification of various domestic regulations of Mercantilism. After the Napoleonic Wars they were ready for an attack on its still intact foreign ramparts. Both their interests in and their ideas on foreign trade had been altered by recent or current developments.

The Need for Wider Markets

Although the long years of war with France had intensified rather than relaxed the regulation of trade, they had also speeded the growth of Britain's newer industries—cotton, iron and steel and coal, and engineering. After Waterloo, though their position was unchallenged abroad, their markets were in a state of collapse. The government stopped buying fire-arms, cannon, and naval vessels. Supplies of uniforms, blankets, and tents were no longer needed. Nor was Continental Europe, for years overrun by marauding armies, likely for some time to be a heavy buyer of British goods. Concern for markets, therefore, led merchants and manufacturers to look more favorably on measures to increase the freedom of trade.

Changing Ideas

At the same time that sagging sales aroused an interest in broader markets, ideological weapons useful in the coming fight against trade barriers were being sharpened. Adam Smith had made a good beginning, with his exposure of the absurdities of Mercantilism and his limited demonstration of the gains from trade. Now Ricardo, himself a business man and a recognised spokesman for business groups, strengthened the argument for the liberalisation of trade with his famous doctrine of comparative costs. Followers in England and France, and popularisers too, soon took it up, clarified it, and developed a well-reasoned case for free trade. This became part of the standard intellectual equipment of liberal statesmen and crusading reformers. One of the former, Huskisson, brought some order into the chaotic jumble of Britain's Mercantilist and wartime duties, paring down the most exorbitant, substituting moderate tariffs for import prohibitions, and abolishing bounties. The Corn Laws, the core of British protectionism, remained sacred so long as an archaic distribution of Parliamentary seats gave unqualified political control to the landed gentry.

The Reform Bill of 1832 abolished at a stroke the numerous rotten or pocket boroughs that permitted many great landowners to appoint members of Parliament, and at the same time enfranchised half the middle class. Though still far from representative, Parliament reflected more accurately the views of the governed. Its reform furnished an essential ingredient for repeal of the Corn Laws.

Repeal of the Corn Laws

Sir Robert Peel (Prime Minister, 1841-46), who became the great parliamentary leader of the free trade movement, began the dismantling of protection by obtaining adoption of the income tax. This provided assured revenues hitherto derived from a mass of duties on exports of manufactures and imports of raw materials, which with the support of the manufacturing class were now dropped or greatly reduced. On the issue of agricultural protection, however, he at first sided with his party. But a rising tide of opposition to the Corn Laws outside Parliament, together with eloquent representation of the free trade interest within, finally caused him to desert it.

The opposition was the work of the Anti-Corn Law League, an organisation of manufacturers founded in 1839 to promote repeal. The prospect of cheaper bread had a strong appeal to the laborer, whether on the farm or in the factory, while the manufacturer saw in cheaper food, according to the Ricardian theory of the day, the possibility of lower money wages and higher profits. Backed with plenty of money, organised with extraordinary efficiency, and supported with the eloquence of Richard Cobden and John Bright, the League

accomplished the miracle of uniting capital and labour. It combined argument and emotion, bringing both to perfection in meetings that began with Cobden and ended with Bright. It appealed equally to self-interest and to humanity. In an age when political literature was limited in quantity and inferior in quality, the League, in 1843 alone, distributed nine million carefully argued tracts by means of a staff of eight hundred persons. In an age when public meetings were rare, when finance and government were regarded as mysteries appertaining to the political families and to well-born civil servants, the League lecturers taught political economy, and criticised the year's budget, to vast audiences of merchants and clerks, artisans and navvies, farmers and agricultural labourers.[7]

Within Parliament, Cobden's lucid economic arguments, combined with Peel's own study of the facts, finally converted the Prime Minister to free trade. In 1845 he seized the opportunity afforded by the Irish potato blight to suspend the Corn Laws. Popular opposition to their restoration was so strong that in 1846 repeal was inevitable.

[7] G. M. Trevelyan, *British History in the Nineteenth Century*, p. 270. Copyright 1922 by Longmans, Green & Co., London.

The Spread of Freer Trade

In ensuing years, Great Britain completed her movement toward free trade and other countries followed her lead. In 1860, Parliament removed all but 60 of 400 articles from the dutiable list; gradually even these fell by the wayside and the British market became and remained open to imports without restriction until 1914. France, under the leadership of the liberal emperor Napoleon III, replaced her highly protective tariff with a very moderate one in a series of international negotiations beginning with the Cobden-Chevalier Treaty of 1860. After 1850, Holland and Belgium adopted distinctly liberal tariffs. Even the United States, which had pursued a protective policy since 1816, substantially moderated its duties in the tariff of 1857. And during the 1860's the German *Zollverein*, whose original mild tariff of 1834 had been raised thereafter, succumbed to free trade pressures and lowered its duties from protective to purely revenue levels.

In addition to their liberality, two features of these mid-nineteenth century tariffs that were to endure until after 1914 are well worth noting. These were their stability and their generality. Even though rates of duty tended to move upward again after 1870, tariffs changed very gradually, usually being left in force for a decade or more. By reducing the risks and increasing the calculability of trade, this feature facilitated its steady expansion. And by the insertion into commercial treaties of the now famous "most-favored-nation" clause, which extended to all treaty partners concessions granted in each treaty, the benefits of tariff reductions were generalised throughout the world.

Stimulated by its release from restrictions, international trade grew apace. Rough estimates, which are all that are available, suggest that its value doubled between 1830 and 1850. In the next thirty years world trade at least trebled and may have nearly quadrupled. From being a relatively unimportant adjunct of domestic activity, foreign trade loomed increasingly large where it did not dominate economic life altogether. Australia, New Zealand, Argentina, and Uruguay became specialists in the production of wheat, wool, and meat. Britain, their principal market, permitted its agriculture to go through a sharp phase of contraction while the nation concentrated its energies on specialised manufactures. In the face of cheap supplies of western wheat, Denmark transformed its economy from a grain growing and exporting basis to one that imported grain and exported bacon, ham, eggs, and dairy products. All over the globe, specialisation matched the growth of trade.

AN INTERNATIONAL ECONOMY

With the adoption of the gold standard in the early 1870's by all the important countries of Europe and by several Latin American nations, currencies became firmly linked at stable exchange rates and were made fully convertible.[8] The expanding needs of the rising industrial countries for imported raw materials and foodstuffs and for markets for their manufactures could be met by purchases from one group, sales to another, the balances being cleared through a complex multilateral network centering in London. There the highly developed and efficient money market attracted funds from all over the world and made them available to finance the major part of world trade and an important share of the capital requirements of growing national economies.

Disturbances and consequent adjustments were inevitable. Yet because it was an era of rapid growth, the disturbances could be assimilated without too great dislocation. For such as remained, the gold standard provided an effective mechanism of adjustment which, though it tended toward deflation, was politically acceptable and therefore allowed to work.

Although socialist doctrines— both "utopian" and Marxist—had their adherents, neither they nor any other rival seriously challenged the combination of industrial capitalism and political democracy that spread throughout the western nations. Reliance could be and was placed upon market forces to regulate production, the flow of raw materials and finished goods, the movement of capital and even in large part of labor. By the late nineteenth century, an international economy not too unlike the theoretical model actually existed.

(For references, see end of Chapter 11.)

[8] The United States had legally established the gold standard in 1873, after being on a paper currency basis since 1861. Specie payments, however, were not resumed until 1879.

11

THE REVIVAL OF NATIONALISM

From the vantage point of the mid-twentieth century, there can be no doubt that the nineteenth, or more accurately the hundred years between the Napoleonic Wars and World War I (1814-1914), constituted a unique period in many respects. From our own focus of interest, it stands out as the century during which deliberate governmental regulation of trade gave way to regulation by market forces. Nations became free to specialise in production according to the dictates of relative costs, and did so. A large and constantly growing volume of international trade linked the various regions of the world into a smoothly functioning, integrated economy of global scope. The developments that brought this about began soon after 1815 and reached a crescendo in the fifties and sixties in the free trade movement.

By the early 1870's, the liberalising forces reached their peak of accomplishment. From then on, though far from spent, they had to fight a rear-guard action against a rising tide of nationalism. Though most of the gains remained intact, events of the late nineteenth and early twentieth century established a trend which foreshadowed the future. These include a revival of nationalism with its anti-cosmopolitan policies, and a great shift in the balance of economic power. This chapter will examine these developments.

THE CHALLENGE TO BRITAIN'S LEADERSHIP

The Rise of Germany

At the time Germany achieved political union in the Empire (1871), she was no better than a poor third in economic weight, whether this be measured in manufacturing production, the output of iron and steel, or the volume of trade. But within forty years, she outdistanced the United Kingdom, became the strongest European power, and made a bid for world domination!

Germany's rapid economic growth began immediately after the Franco-Prussian War and the attainment of political unity. With a strong central government replacing the numerous small and ineffectual principalities, a coordination of hitherto independent and sometimes conflicting policies became possible. The billion dollar indemnity from France enabled Germany to adopt the gold standard; the acquisition of Alsace-Lorraine, with its textile mills and iron ore deposits, provided additional resources for expansion. Coal and iron production, which had increased slowly until now, rose sharply. Between 1870 and 1900, the output of both minerals grew fivefold. Still behind at the turn of the century, in the next decade Germany rushed forward, surpassing Britain in the production of pig-iron and coal and outranking her in her share of world manufacturing output.

Nor was Germany's growth exclusively internal. Her exports grew steadily, but more slowly than industrial production up to 1900, then increased sharply. In 1872 they totalled $500 million; in 1900, $1,132 million, and in 1913, $2,494 million. The principal export items were manufactures—hardware, chemicals, cotton textiles, beet sugar, and one major mineral, coal—while the leading imports were raw materials and foods—grain, wool, cotton, and timber.

Because of the similarity of Germany's exports to those of Britain, their expansion depended partly upon the ability of German producers to undersell the British. Germany's advance unquestionably introduced a strong element of direct competition. But these exports were by no means wholly competitive. There was considerable specialisation within products; Germany concentrated on the coarser textiles, Great Britain on the finer grades; German producers made principally cheap watches and clocks, the British (and later the Swiss) the more expensive types. Some German goods, too, were relatively non-competitive, even being exported to England; among these were chemicals and electrical equipment. Moreover, in eastern Europe, Germany found a market to which British exporters had paid little attention and in which she had the advantage of location. The increase of her exports in this area, especially, represented a net increase in world trade rather than a loss to Britain.

Lulled into complacency by their long enjoyment of an unchallenged position, the commercial interests of Britain were stunned when confronted, in the eighties and nineties, by German and to a lesser degree by French, Belgian, Swiss, and Austrian rivalry. British goods had always been superior. They had required little pushing. If they were not precisely suited to the foreigner's needs, then the foreigner had had to adapt himself to what was available!

To get a foothold in foreign markets in the face of British dominance, the German trader exploited his rival's every weakness. He adapted products to his customers' wishes; he packaged his wares attractively; he took pains with even the smallest orders, hoping that larger ones might follow. His representatives abroad became more numerous than the British, and unlike the latter, learned the local language and often married local girls and took root in the community. Cash on demand, or at the most, sixty to ninety days' credit, was sound British practice. But the upstart Germans did not hesitate to give six to nine months or even longer.

These new, unpleasant facts aroused acute alarm, notably in the mid-eighties and -nineties, years of severe depression. But as world trade recovered, it became apparent that although British manufactures had lost ground in some markets, especially on the Continent, the development of new, together with the growth of old, provided more than an offset. Expansion overseas required steadily increasing imports, while exploitation of the mass market for cheap textiles in Asia furnished a new outlet. The net result of the new competition was not, as some had feared, England's collapse as an industrial power. British traders had to work harder and producers had to relinquish some lines of production to new, low-cost rivals, and to specialise where their resources and skills counted most.[1] Channels of trade altered, some diminishing, some swelling. And with the emergence of Germany and other western European nations as important producers of manufactures, an increasing proportion of trade took the form of an exchange of manufactured specialties—German electrical and mining machinery for English agricultural and textile machines, coarse grades of textiles for finer, dyestuffs for heavy industrial chemicals.

The United States

The economic progress of Germany was far exceeded by that of the United States. The contrast was but natural, considering the fact that the transition from a predominantly agrarian to a modern industrial nation took place in a country of continental size, possessing immense resources of land, minerals, power, and timber. Rapid development of these resources was assured by their very richness, which gave the profit-seeking business man the prospect of high returns; by the prevalance, as in England, of an individualist philosophy; by the rapid growth of population; and by the relatively high level of incomes attributable to a favorable ratio of population to resources.

The high proportion of resources to population, or the relative scarcity of labor, together with the rapid growth of population, played a most

---

[1] Some branches of British industry met sharp German competition in the home market, notably sugar refining, chemicals, iron and steel, and cotton and woolen textiles. Exports of woolen fabrics declined absolutely, from 324 million yards per annum in 1870 to 174 million in 1909-13.

important role in the speedy development of American industry. With abundant fertile land available almost for the asking down to the end of the nineteenth century, farming offered rich rewards for the enterprising and provided a growing market for products of industry. Continued expansion of this market was assured by the phenomenal growth of population, which nearly doubled between 1870 and 1900.

Not only did the high productivity of American agriculture furnish a large and growing market for industry among the farming population, but also by offering an attractive alternative to work in mine or mill it forced the payment of high wages in industry. And because of the basically democratic character of the American people, they were ready to spend their high per capita earnings on mass-produced goods. Thus the tendency toward the production of standardised commodities with a broad, mass market received a strong impetus from the nature of the buying public.[2]

The economies attainable when industry can concentrate upon the production of large quantities of identical goods were partly responsible for the rapidly increasing efficiency of American industry. Probably of equal importance was the high level of wages caused by the scarcity of labor. This forced manufacturers to adopt labor-saving devices, the invention of which has been a unique feature of "Yankee ingenuity."[3] Thus necessity compelled the use and stimulated the development of the most advanced technology of any of the industrial nations.

The presence of mass markets and the need for labor-saving machinery

[2] This explanation of the prominence of mass-production industries in the United States is advanced by Erwin Rothbarth in a brilliant and suggestive article, "Causes of the Superior Efficiency of U.S.A. Industry as Compared with British Industry," *Economic Journal,* LVI (1946), p. 383. By way of contrast with the United States he cites the United Kingdom, where "there remains an aristocracy and a middle class impregnated with aristocratic ideas, who reject mass-produced articles and insist on articles with individual character." (P. 386.)

We may add to what Rothbarth says, that in addition to the relative abundance of land, our comparatively enlightened land policy (as embodied in the Homestead Act of 1862), by making land accessible to would-be-buyers, "put purchasing power in the hands of those . . . ready to buy large quantities of standardised goods." Had the concentration of land-holdings been permitted on a wide scale, as in many Latin American countries, great extremes of income distribution such as characterise those nations might have resulted here as well.

[3] "The American display of machinery at the Vienna International Exhibition of 1873 was, according to the contemporary reporter, 'the richest in new forms of apparatus, and contained by far the most striking examples of the special adaptation of machines to peculiar varieties of work, and of what is commonly described as "labor-saving machinery."' . . . As an English observer noted in 1885: 'The tools and processes which we are inclined to consider unusual are the commonplaces of American shops, and the determination to do nothing by hand which can be done by machinery is the chief characteristic.' " Samuel Rezneck, "Mass Production Since the War Between the States," in *The Growth of the American Economy,* (Harold Williamson, ed.), p. 502. Copyright 1944 by Prentice-Hall, Inc., New York.

made their effects evident early. Before 1850, guns and pistols were manufactured from interchangeable parts. After the Civil War, this system was applied to sewing machines and to clocks and watches, agricultural machinery, the typewriter, and the bicycle. The machine tool industry, located first in the eastern States, later spreading to Ohio, furnished the technical basis for the precision manufacture of interchangeable parts.

In spite of the early introduction of mass-production methods, American industry remained until the very end of the nineteenth century well behind British, though advancing rapidly. The figures for both pig-iron production and for share of manufacturing production reflect this fact. (See Tables 11.1 and 11.2.) In 1870, U.S. output of iron was just over a quarter of British. It is doubtful if manufactures at this date amounted to more than half the production of the U.K.[4] By 1900, the United States ranked first as a producer of pig-iron and of coal. It also apparently was the premier manufacturing nation. By 1913, there was no question as to relative position. U.S. output of pig-iron was as large as that of the United Kingdom, Germany, and France together, while its share of world manufactures (35.8 per cent) was only slightly less than that of these three industrial nations (36.1 per cent). In other words, just before the outbreak of World War I, the United States had replaced Britain as the world's principal industrial power.

Table 11.1

PIG-IRON PRODUCTION IN LEADING COUNTRIES

(in millions of metric tons)

	GREAT BRITAIN	UNITED STATES	GERMANY	FRANCE	RUSSIA
1870	6.1	1.7	1.4	1.2	0.4
1900	9.1	14.0	7.6	2.7	2.9
1910	10.2	27.7	13.1	4.0	3.0
1920	8.2	37.5	6.4	3.3	0.1
1930	6.3	32.3	9.7	10.0	5.0
1940	8.4	43.0	21.0	4.6	15.5

Source: W. Nelson Peach and Walter Krause, *Basic Data of the American Economy*, p. 59. Copyright 1948 by Richard D. Irwin, Inc., Chicago. Reproduced from *The Metal Industry During 1941*, edited by G. A. Roush (McGraw-Hill Book Co., New York).

[4] While Table 11.2 shows the U.S. in 1870 as accounting for 23.3 per cent of world manufacturing production, as against the U.K.'s 31.8 per cent, the figure for the U.S. is almost certainly too high. It includes a large proportion of articles produced by handicraft and neighborhood "industries." In addition, prices were very low in 1870, and there is no indication that this factor is taken into account. Even the 1900 figure for the U.S. is probably too high, owing to the fact that almost a fourth of total manufactures were of the handicraft variety.

Table 11.2

PERCENTAGE DISTRIBUTION OF THE WORLD'S MANUFACTURING PRODUCTION

	U.S.	GER-MANY	U.K.	FRANCE	RUSSIA	ITALY	BEL-GIUM	SWEDEN	JAPAN
1870	23.3	13.2	31.8	10.3	3.7	2.4	2.9	0.4	—
1896/1900	30.1	16.6	19.5	7.1	5.0	2.7	2.2	1.1	0.6
1913	35.8	15.7	14.0	6.4	5.0	3.1	2.1	1.0	1.2
1926/29	42.2	11.6	9.4	6.6	4.3	3.3	1.9	1.0	2.5
1936/38	32.2	10.7	9.2	4.5	18.5	2.7	1.3	1.3	3.5

Source: League of Nations, *Industrialization and Foreign Trade*, p. 13.

A large growth in our foreign trade accompanied our phenomenal expansion. Just after the Civil War, United States exports barely exceeded $300 million (1866-70 average). A few years before the outbreak of World War I, they were nearly six times as large, or $1,750 million (1906-10 average). Despite their growth, however, our exports were much more complementary to than competitive with British production. As late as 1910, nearly three-fourths consisted of crude materials and foods, manufactured foods (of which flour is by far the most important), and semi-manufactures, and only about a quarter (26.7 per cent) of finished manufactures. Moreover, although our exports exhibited rapid growth, they remained a relatively small proportion of our total production. In 1870, exports were 7 per cent of gross national product; in 1913, 8 per cent.

We were so busy developing a continent and satisfying the needs of our immense free-trade area that the development of export markets, except as an outlet for the abounding production of our farms, forests, and mines, was comparatively unimportant. As our production of manufactures grew, we became, it is true, more capable of taking care of our requirements of finished goods. This is reflected in the decline in imports of finished manufactures from over 40 per cent in 1866-70 to just under 25 per cent in 1906-10. In spite of this trend toward industrial self-sufficiency, reenforced by rising tariff rates, our total imports increased so rapidly—from $408 million to $1,345 million—that imports of finished manufactures doubled in the period under review. Europe, moreover, remained by far our greatest market and our principal source of imports. In 1870, that continent (including the United Kingdom as a major customer) took 80 per cent of our exports; in 1910 the figure was still 65 per cent. As for imports, we obtained 55 per cent of these from Europe in 1870; by 1910, its share had dropped only to 52 per cent.

Britain's Position in 1913

Although the economic growth of Germany and the United States had vital implications for power politics, as the events of 1914-18 were to show, it made little difference to the average citizen of the British Isles. Real wages increased steadily throughout the last half of the nineteenth century, owing to the fact that money wages either rose more rapidly than prices, or fell less rapidly. From 1901 to 1914, the rise of real wages was reversed; they fell an average of 0.7 per cent per annum during this period. Prices were now rising rather rapidly, and especially the prices of raw materials and foods. Yet even then, hours of labor continued to be shortened, and the extension of social services worked to labor's advantage. According to another estimate, which covers not only labor but all gainfully employed, real income continued to rise right up to 1913, though less rapidly than during the last half of the nineteenth century.[5]

The British balance of payments had been under no strain from 1870 onward. Not only was a large and somewhat irregularly growing excess of imports over exports paid for out of the earnings of British foreign investments, the merchant marine, and insurance and banking establishments, but there was also a substantial surplus available each year for additional investment overseas. For the period 1873-96, it is true, investment turned more toward internal improvements, and the rate of foreign lending declined. It increased again, however, after 1900, and by 1913, British total foreign investment stood close to £4,000 million, yielding an annual income of £210 million. At the close of our period, the balance of payments surplus was larger than ever before, and still growing.

There was, in short, nothing unsound about Britain's position on the eve of World War I. Though forced, by the fact of world economic expansion, to share markets with relative newcomers, she herself benefited from this expansion. Some adjustments to competition had been necessary, but the industries that had been the backbone of her own development were still growing and were still the world's largest exporters. Real income per head of the population had been rising for two generations and was exceeded only moderately by that of the United States and Canada. A huge stake in foreign investment yielded a substantial annual revenue. Together with

---

[5] From 1850 to 1873, when prices and wages were both rising, the annual increase in real wages, after allowing for unemployment, was 1.3 per cent. From 1873 to 1900, the annual increase averaged 1.85 per cent. (W. W. Rostow, *British Economy of the Nineteenth Century,* Chapter IV.) The data for the period after 1900 show that income per head of the occupied population, in constant prices, stood at £175.8 in 1894-1903; by 1913 it was £195.4, or 11 per cent higher. (Colin Clark, *The Conditions of Economic Progress,* 1940 edition, p. 83.)

large earnings from services, this enabled the country to import each year far more than it exported, and in addition to export a large sum of capital.

NATIONALISM AND PROTECTIONISM

The rivalry for markets that arose in the eighties and nineties reflected the attainment of maturity by continental industry and its consequent release from British tutelage. Since this successful industrial development had been achieved during an era of relatively low tariffs, one might have expected the liberal attitude toward trade to persist. Indeed, in view of the challenge to Britain's exports and the invasion even of her domestic market, a revival of protectionist sentiment in the United Kingdom would have been understandable. And though there was such a revival, it never acquired sufficient strength to alter Britain's commitment to free trade. On the contrary, it was on the Continent that a rising spirit of nationalism took root, one of whose fruits was a renewed campaign for protection which reversed the earlier downward trend of tariffs.

The resurgence of nationalism appears to have been partly the perverse outcome of liberal doctrine and partly the aftermath of wars. Liberalism, the dominant political philosophy of the nineteenth century, stressed the supremacy of the individual and the natural harmony of individual and social interests under a regime of free competition. It took the existence of national states for granted—they were the necessary agency for eliminating obstructions to economic and political freedom and for establishing the minimum rules of a free society. But if the individual was to be free, he must not only be free from excessive government intervention. His freedom implied also freedom from foreign oppression. National self-determination was an essential ingredient in the liberal system of thought.

Enforcement of the doctrine of self-determination by local leaders resulted in the formation, by peoples who were by and large homogeneous as to language and culture, of several new nations. Greece, with British aid, threw off Turkish rule in 1829. Belgium became an independent nation in 1830. In the 1850's, Garibaldi led the Italian people against their Austrian oppressors, and with the help of French troops and British diplomacy, Italy achieved national unity in 1860. Self-determination had little to do with the creation of the German Empire, which was more the result of the assertion of Prussian military hegemony, yet the Empire did bring together peoples who were linguistically and culturally similar.

When a new nation is born, it tends to assert its new-found nationality.

This is especially true when it is large and powerful and when its birth is attended by military struggle. Germany and Italy provide good examples. And one of the characteristic forms of nationalist self-assertion is the imposition of protective duties on imports. In the revival of nationalism in the mid-nineteenth century we have a force providing at least a predisposition toward protection.

History also records that protection is a legacy of war and a common expression of national rivalry. We have already noted the growing rivalry of the eighties and nineties; as for war, there was the Crimean War, the bitter struggle between the Northern and Southern States of the American Union, and conflict between France and Prussia. All these influences together were surely enough to generate a reaction against the earlier, liberal trade policies.

What actually set the protectionist movement under way was, however, none of these broad political factors, but two specific economic developments of the 1870's. One was the invasion of the Continent by cheap American and Russian grain, made accessible by the activities of railway builders. The other was the depression of 1873-79, the longest and deepest period of stagnant trade the world had yet experienced. Peasants and manufacturers alike were full of lamentations; their clamor for relief gave the initial stimulus to protection.

Another influence was at work over the whole latter half of the nineteenth century. To meet rising expenditures on armaments, education, public health, and social insurance, greater revenues became necessary. And since customs duties provided, during the nineteenth century, the larger part of the revenue of many nations, it was natural to turn the screw a bit tighter.

Once the swing to protection started, the deeper force of nationalism supported and maintained it. There is also a tendency for a rise in duties to continue, as vested interests grow and gather political strength. They also tend to spread over an ever wider range of commodities, since it is difficult to deny to others what has already been granted to some. The operation of these forces is illustrated in the history of tariff policy from 1870 to 1913.

Tariff Policy to 1913

Even in the face of serious depression, German tariffs continued to fall in the 1870's. Duties on grain had been abolished in 1865, those on iron and on shipbuilding materials followed in 1873, and the tariff on iron manufactures was to go in 1877. Despite the pressure of distressed farmers and worried industrialists, Bismarck resisted; the iron duties were dropped according to schedule. His need for funds, however, helped win him over. In the tariff of 1880, moderate duties were imposed on various iron products, while grains and a number of other items received considerably more protection. Further upward revision of the iron and food duties occurred in 1902, when rising tariffs elsewhere and the lapse of various treaties which had frozen German duties furnished the motive and the opportunity. Even then, though the tariff on grains was highly protective, that on manufactures averaged only a rather modest 25 per cent.

In France, inability of agricultural and industrial groups interested in protection to unite promptly postponed for two decades any action to reverse the low duty treaties of the 1860's. Not until 1892, when these groups controlled Parliament, was tariff revision undertaken, but when it came it was thorough. Duties on agricultural products were set at new high levels, and those on manufactures were raised to an average of about 34 per cent. Another increase came in 1910, when protection was also extended to many newly developed products, among them chemicals and electrical and rubber goods.

For the beginning of that policy of protection always associated with the Republican party in the United States, we have to go back to the eve of the Civil War. Victory in the elections of 1859 brought them to power on a platform calling for the encouragement of industrial development by tariff protection. The tariff of 1861 embodied this principle; it repealed the low duties of 1857 (24 per cent on most imports, with maximum rates of 30 per cent) and restored these current in 1846, when most dutiable articles paid 30 per cent, a few 40 per cent, and brandy and spirits, alone, a maximum of 100 per cent. Rising financial requirements of the Union government led to further increases and extensions until 1864, when rates averaged 47 per cent, a record level. After a brief lowering of duties by a flat 5 per cent in the 1880's, owing to a constant surplus in government revenues, the tariff was hiked twice in rapid succession, in 1890 (average rate of duties, 50 per cent) and in 1897 (average rate of 57 per cent).[6]

Some idea of the intellectual level of tariff discussion of these times may be gained from the following excerpt from the Republican platform of 1896, which wrapped the tariff in the American flag and propounded most of the conventional arguments in its support:

We renew and emphasize our allegiance to the policy of protection as the bul-

[6] These percentages are very approximate, owing to the difficulty of estimating the ratio of duties to dutiable imports when some rates effectively prohibit imports. Nonetheless, they probably give a fairly accurate impression of the upward trend.

wark of American industrial independence and the foundation of American development and prosperity. This true American policy taxes foreign products and encourages home industry; it puts the burden of revenue on foreign goods; it secures the American market for the American producer; it upholds the Amercan standard of wages for the American workingman; it puts the factory by the side of the farm, and makes the American farmer less dependent on foreign demand and price; it diffuses general thrift, and founds the strength of all on the strength of each.[7]

No further change of general importance in the U.S. tariff occurred until 1913, when the new Democratic administration, the first since 1892-96, undertook in the Underwood Tariff a thoroughgoing revision. Over 100 items, including sugar and wool, were added to the free list, rates on nearly 1,000 classifications were reduced and relatively few raised; the ratio of duties to dutiable imports fell to the extremely low average of 16 per cent. Unfortunately, this new tariff had little opportunity to be tested; within a year, war broke out in Europe.

With the sole exception of Great Britain and the Netherlands, European countries generally followed the lead of Germany and France by adopting protective tariffs. Russia even preceded them. Before 1868, the Russian tariff had been comparatively moderate, aiming chiefly at revenue. That year, however, marked the introduction of a deliberate policy of protection. Recurrent and substantial increases in the duties from then until 1914 gave her one of the highest, if not the highest, tariffs in the world.

Upon the unification of Italy in 1860, the moderate tariff of Sardinia became the law of the new kingdom. Parliament adopted a policy of industrial protection in 1878, extending the program to agriculture in the following year. In 1887, rates were raised to a high level and remained in effect until after the war. Switzerland first embarked upon a policy of mild protection in 1891, then stepped the rates up sharply fifteen years later.

Though increasing foreign competition stimulated the rise of strong internal opposition to Britain's liberal trade policy, its practical effect was to divide the Conservative party and to unite the free trade forces. In the election of 1906 the Liberals enjoyed an overwhelming victory, and little more was heard of protection as a general alternative to free trade until the economic collapse of the 1930's.

IMPERIALIST EXPANSION, 1880-1913

Just as during the liberal era governments showed an antipathy toward protection, so too they exhibited at least a passive attitude toward colonies.

[7] Cited in Asher Isaacs, *International Trade: Tariff and Commercial Policies*, pp. 207-8. See below, Ch. 12, for a discussion of these arguments.

There was little interest in subjugating native peoples and thus extending the dominion of the metropolitan countries. If the practice of governments thus coincided with the liberal doctrine of self-determination, it is doubtful if this resulted from deliberate intent. More likely, it was the consequence of preoccupation with internal problems of growth and development, as well as recent experience with colonies. Thus in Britain, the value of colonies was seriously questioned, partly as a reaction perhaps to the rebellion of her American possessions, partly because larger and more accessible markets for her rising production were available in Europe and abroad. To England's experience of 1776, buttressed by claims for and achievement of self-government by Canada and Australasia, was added that of Spain and Portugal, which between 1810 and 1825 witnessed the loss of all but shreds of their former empires. Even Bismarck as late as 1868 regarded the advantages of colonies as illusory. Small wonder then that "colonies were looked upon as an antiquated encumbrance from the past." [8] France alone sought overseas possessions, acquiring Algiers in 1830 and parts of Indo-China and Somaliland in 1862.

All this changed suddenly. Beginning in the 1880's a wave of colony grabbing began that continued right down to the outbreak of war in 1914. Its principal results were the division of Africa among the European powers, the spread of Britain's dominion over Burma and Malaya, the extension of France's Indo-Chinese empire over an area half again as large as the mother country, and the economic if not the political partition of China. The Americas were exempt from this land-grabbing fever—apart from the earlier, ill-fated attempt of Louis Napoleon to conquer Mexico—because of the Monroe Doctrine, the presence of the British fleet, and the growing strength of the United States.

How shall we explain this burst of imperialist expansion? Although it was a manifestation of the intensified national rivalry of the late nineteenth century, it can no more be explained by nationalism than can protection. Nationalism is a pervading sentiment that is conducive to certain types of action, but it contains no mechanism capable of generating change. It may provide the intellectual climate needed for change, but it is not itself a moving force.

It would appear that the planting of national flags in alien territory was closely related to the industrial growth of the metropolitan countries. This growth created a voracious appetite for raw materials—for copper, tin, manganese; for sisal, hemp, and jute; for ivory, teak and mahogany; for

---

[8] L. C. A. Knowles, *The Industrial and Commercial Revolutions in Great Britain During the Nineteenth Century* (Routledge, London, 1922), p. 321.

palm oil, copra, and rubber. Demand for these and other raw materials was high and rising; traditional sources of supply were inadequate, and new ones needed to be opened up.[9] Traders on the spot at the source of raw materials could make handsome profits—profits that were enhanced by the superior knowledge and sophistication enjoyed by the trader in his dealings with primitive people.

But to obtain the raw materials on which his profits depended, together with sales to the native population of cotton cloth, liquor, beads, and trinkets, the trader required trading ports with an assured food supply, protection for his own and his employees' lives, and safe conduct for his goods to and from the interior. And when, as with rubber, cacao, tea, and palm oil, careful cultivation of crops in large plantations became necessary, substantial funds had to be invested.

All this implied a reasonably stable and effective government, capable of keeping the peace, of disciplining outlaw and criminal elements, and of providing assurances against the destruction or expropriation of property. Since backward and warring tribes could provide none of this, the trader had to do it himself. Very often the first political penetration of an area came about in this way, as an additional function of private enterprise in primitive surroundings. Later, as traders of rival nationalities threatened to invade his preserves, he appealed to his government. Supported by the industrial interests to which he ministered, and reenforced by the pervading sense of national rivalry, his appeals seldom fell on deaf ears. The "white man's burden" was accepted. And like protection, once started, land-grabbing tended to continue of its own weight, since unappropriated territory probably contained resources of value that someone else might get first.

This sequence of events could be observed in many parts of the world, but nowhere more clearly or consistently than in Africa.

The Partition of Africa

Africa stood alone as a comparatively empty, vast, and defenseless area, and it was in Africa that the new imperialism found its main outlet. Before 1875, nearly nine-tenths of this continent was a primitive wilderness. The Ottoman Empire controlled, after a fashion, a fringe along the Mediterrean

[9] Although the London prices, both of finished manufactures and of raw materials and foodstuffs, followed a downward trend from 1875 to about 1900, there is considerable evidence to show that at the source, primary products prices remained constant or even rose. They fell in London owing principally to the large reduction in transportation costs brought about by the extension of railways, the substitution of steam for sailing vessels, and improvements in warehousing and handling facilities. See P. T. Ellsworth, "The Terms of Trade Between Primary Producing and Industrial Countries," *Inter-American Economic Affairs*, Vol. 10, No. 1. (Summer 1956).

coast including Egypt, with the French-conquered territory of Algeria to the west. At the extreme southern tip, Great Britain had acquired the Cape Colony (1806) and Natal (1843). Apart from these substantial European and Turkish possessions, there was no trace of foreign domination except for scattered and largely forgotten trading posts established long before by the Spanish, Portuguese, French and British along the west coast and by the Portuguese and French on the east.

The new imperialism began, strangely, as an international venture. After Stanley's exploration of central Africa brought news of its wealth in 1878, Leopold II of Belgium formed an international company that sent Stanley back into the Congo basin to stake out claims and establish trading posts. In 1885, the company transformed itself into the Congo Free State, with Leopold as its private sovereign and business manager. Later, in 1908, after mounting indignation over the brutal methods of exploitation used in the ivory, rubber, and slave trades, it was taken over by Belgium.

Simultaneously with Stanley's activities, the French got busy. De Brazza pushed inland from the French coastal settlement at Gabun, preceded Stanley's arrival at a point which later became Brazzaville, and established claims that were rapidly enlarged into French Equatorial Africa.

On the heels of de Brazza's and Stanley's exploits, rivalry between French, English, and German trading companies began in and around the basin of the Niger, which lies at the base of the west African bulge. The Germans also, with the support of Bismarck, now converted to imperialism, made a start in carving out German Southwest Africa, far down the coast next to Cape Colony. Typical methods were to buy small tracts or to make treaties (containing unintelligible text but accompanied by appropriate gifts) with native chiefs, and then to set up trading and missionary posts. Later the areas were extended by a wider network of "treaties" or by outright conquest, railways were built, and direct rule over large territories became a reality.

The partition of east Africa occurred simultaneously with that of the west, and by identical methods. Cecil Rhodes built an empire in Rhodesia and Bechuanaland, while other Englishmen were busy acquiring British East Africa and British Somaliland. Germany absorbed Tanganyika, France picked a quarrel with the native queen of Madagascar and added this huge island to her domain. Even the Italians entered the race, to gain their slice of Somaliland, together with Eritrea.

Meanwhile Britain, after a period of joint supervision of Egypt's finances with France, had taken control of the country in the process of putting down a nationalistic revolt (1882). Using dubious Egyptian claims to the

Sudan as a legal basis, Lord Kitchener pushed up the valley of the Nile, conquering the native dervishes as he went, until he reached Fashoda in 1898. There he met a Captain Marchand, who, after a two-year trek across the jungle from the French Congo, had hoisted the French flag. A diplomatic wrangle in London and Paris settled the question of sovereignty in favor of the British; the Sudan became nominally an Anglo-Egyptian condominium, and the British were well on their way to establishing their rule over a solid belt of territory from Cape to Cairo. Thus after two decades of exploring, land purchase or conquest, and economic assimilation, all Africa except Abyssinia and the Negro Republic of Liberia had fallen under foreign rule.

Imperialism in the Far East

French imperialism, checked at Fashoda, found more scope in the Orient. The acquisition in 1862 of Cochin-China, at the tip of the Indo-Chinese peninsula, had only whetted France's appetite. By intervention to avenge the murder of (non-French) Christians, by conquest, by war with China, the French during the decade of surging imperialism extended their rule over all of what came to comprise Indo-China. After an ultimatum to the King of Burma (demanding revocation of trading rights granted the French), followed by invasion, British India annexed Burma in its entirety (1886).

At the end of the 1880's the era of imperialistic land grabbing was almost at a close. There was little unpopulated or weakly held territory not already under the dominion of one or another of the major powers, except in China. And it was to China that the scene of imperialistic rivalry shifted in the nineties.

Both China and Japan had been forcibly opened to commerce between 1840 and 1880. And even though Britain, as a result of the Opium War (1839-42), had obtained Hong Kong, as well as five "treaty ports" where traders were to be free to reside and do business under their own laws, the rights so acquired were not to be exclusively British, but were to be enjoyed equally by other nations. The liberal principles of trade, not imperialistic exclusiveness, became the rule.

It was Japan, rapidly modernising on western lines, which in 1894 began the race for foreign domination of the mainland. Rivalry in Korea between Japanese and Chinese factions unleashed the Sino-Japanese War, which resulted in Korean "independence" under Japanese tutelage, and the cession to Japan of Formosa and various smaller islands. Fearing Japan's expansion, Russia, joined by France and Germany, intervened to prevent her taking south Manchuria. For their "friendship," and at their urging, China granted important concessions. The battle for concessions was on, and with the concessions came economic penetration and trade dominance as the preludes to possible territorial partition.

Thus matters stood when in 1904 Japan challenged the presence of Russian troops in Manchuria. The success of the well-trained Japanese troops in the war which followed gave Japan bases in Port Arthur and Dairen, together with important railway and mining rights hitherto held by Russia.

After the Russo-Japanese war, the parceling out of the earth had about come to an end. Only a few changes occurred before the frictions bred of imperialism broke out in World War I.

Dollar Diplomacy

Somewhat belatedly, the United States also became caught up in the wave of nationalist expansion. During our war with Spain, military strategy had dictated the seizure of the Philippine Islands. Since there was danger that they might fall into Germany's hands, since they had great economic and strategic value, and since there was also the "white man's burden" to consider, it was decided to keep them. In the same year, 1898, sugar interests in the Hawaiian Islands fomented a rebellion, established a Hawaiian Republic, and succeeded in getting it adopted by the United States as a territory. Hawaiian sugar thereby became a domestic American product, with duty-free entry to the mainland.

Barring these two episodes, our imperialist phase involved no acquisition of foreign real estate, but what came to be called "dollar diplomacy"—intervention in the affairs of our near neighbors in support of previous commercial or financial penetration. Thus in Mexico a struggle between British and American oil interests for control of the Mexican oil fields brought their governments to their support, with each backing a rival Mexican political group. The outcome was not too happy for either of the big powers, however, since the Mexican constitution of 1917 vested all subsoil rights in the Mexican people, and furnished the legal basis for Mexico's expropriation, in 1938, of all foreign oil holdings. A similar conflict between British and American oil interests in Costa Rica led to United States support of a rebellion which established in power a regime that recognised American and cancelled British oil concessions.

Threatened losses to American bondholders led to direct armed intervention in the Caribbean republics. In 1905, our government insisted that the Dominican Republic appoint an American receiver-general to collect customs and to allocate to American and foreign bondholders the amounts necessary for interest payments. Political interference followed a few years later and culminated in 1916 in armed intervention and the establishment of an American military dictatorship, which lasted until 1924. In Haiti, other means of imposing an unwelcome treaty having been unsuccessful, American armed forces in 1915 took over administration of the country.

Strategic rather than commercial or financial interests lay behind our armed support of the Panamanian "revolution" of 1903, which pried Panama loose from Colombia and gave us a perpetual lease of the Canal Zone. In Nicaragua, strategic and financial interests merged in American support, by loans and by armed intervention, of a rebellion (1909) friendly to our purposes. In the end, a treaty gave to our government the right to build a canal and a naval base and to American bankers, control over Nicaragua's finances, banking and railways.

SELECTED REFERENCES

Ashworth, William, *A Short History of the International Economy* (Longmans Green & Co., London, 1952). An excellent brief study of the spread of the Industrial Revolution during the past century, of the emergence of an international economy, and of the course of international economic relations since 1914.

Bagehot, Walter, *Lombard Street* 14th edition (Murray, London, 1915). A nineteenth century work which had great influence on the formation of central banking policy.

Buchanan, Norman S., and Ellis, Howard S., *Approaches to Economic Development* (Twentieth Century Fund, New York, 1955). Chapters 7 and 8 contain a good, brief account of the expansion of the western economy.

Clapham, J. H., *An Economic History of Modern Britain*, Vol. II. (Macmillan, New York, 1932). A standard work on the subject.

Feis, Herbert, *Europe the World's Banker 1870-1914* (Yale University Press, New Haven, 1930). The best single source for data on international investment in this period.

Henderson, W. O., *Britain and Industrial Europe, 1750-1870* (Liverpool University Press, 1954). Contains much illustrative material on Britain's role in the industrial expansion of Europe.

Jones, G. P., and Pool, A. G., *A Hundred Years of Economic Development in Great Britain* (Gerald Duckworth & Co., London, 1940). An interesting and readable account of Britain's economic growth in the nineteenth century.

Knowles, L. C. A., *The Industrial and Commercial Revolutions in Great Britain in the 19th Century* (Routledge & Kegan Paul, London, 1922), Noteworthy for its emphasis on the role played by transportation in Britain's development.

12

THE TARIFF ISSUE

We have now analysed the forces that determine international specialisation and trade, and have traced the emergence of a highly integrated international economy which gave wide scope to those forces. Our next major task will be to consider the various ways in which the operation of the international economy may be disturbed and the manner in which such a disturbance is assimilated or adjusted.

But before we commence this study, let us consider the grounds on which free international trade is opposed. For we have noted that the era of thoroughgoing liberal trade was brief, being succeeded by a gradual swing toward protective tariffs between 1870 and 1914. The initiation of this change can be accounted for by the sharp increase in European grain imports during the lean years of the eighties and nineties, reinforced by the rising spirit of nationalism. But the spread of protection required action by national legislatures. To obtain the necessary changes in laws, protagonists of protection had to prepare and argue their case.

First we must distinguish between tariffs for revenue and for protective purposes and indicate the more important effects resulting from the imposition of a tariff.

EFFECTS OF A TARIFF

Protection or Revenue?

Duties on imports may be imposed with a view to raising revenue, or to give protection to producers of the commodity taxed.[1] But unless a protective duty is so high as to exclude all imports, it is bound to have some revenue effect.

Is there such a thing as a tariff providing revenue, but no protection? The best candidate is a tariff on imports of a commodity not produced in the

---

[1] In this chapter our sole concern will be with import duties. Other kinds of duties are also levied: transit duties and export duties. Transit duties are imposed on goods traversing a country en route from the country of origin to the country of consignment. They were of considerable moment before the early part of the nineteenth century, but are no longer important. Export duties are of greater significance, and are used principally by primary producing countries either to raise revenue or to stimulate domestic processing of the primary products (i.e., as a protective measure). To conserve space, we shall omit any further discussion of these duties.

country at all. But even such a tariff does give some protection by diverting demand to other products. It appears that the intent of legislators provides no clear criterion for distinguishing between duties for revenue and duties for protection.

It is best to leave the matter as follows: A duty is purely protective only if it is so high as to prohibit all imports of the taxed commodity. And a duty can be made to have no net protective effects if domestic production of the commodity subject to duty also has imposed on it a domestic excise tax equal to the import duty. All duties lower than prohibitive and unaccompanied by equivalent excise duties have both revenue and protective effects.

Let us examine the impact of a customs duty and see how its influence is spread.[2] In Figure 12.1, SS is the supply curve of domestic producers of a commodity (their long-run average cost curve), DD the domestic demand curve. In the absence of a tariff, foreign competition sets the price at P_1. (Factor prices in some other country or countries are assumed to be more suited to the optimum production function for this commodity, since imports are available at a lower cost than can be attained except on a relatively small amount of domestic production.) Domestic production is OM_1, while imports amount to M_1M_4.

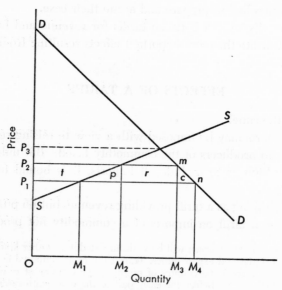

Fig. 12.1: Effects of a Tariff.

[2] The analysis which follows is similar to, though it differs in some respects from, that used by Kindleberger in his *International Economics*, pp. 182-3.

A duty equal to P_1P_2 is now levied on imports of this commodity. To simplify the argument, let us assume that the foreign price of this article remains unchanged. The price in the domestic market now rises to P_2. At this price, domestic output expands from M_1 to M_2, while consumption shrinks from M_4 to M_3. Imports decline from a total of M_1M_4 to the smaller amount M_2M_3.

Revenue Effect

Since not all imports are excluded (to be prohibitive, the duty would have to be equal to P_1P_3), there is a revenue effect; the government collects customs revenue equal to the duty times the volume of imports. This is reflected in the rectangular area **r**.

Protective Effect

In terms of domestic production alone, the protective effect may be seen in the expansion of output from M_1 to M_2. This is made possible by the fact that the higher price, P_2, enables producers to cover their rising marginal costs on the larger output. The wherewithal to do this comes from that part of producers' increased receipts represented by the triangular area **p**, which measures the purely protective effect of the duty. It is that part of increased receipts necessary to pay for the increasingly inefficient use of factors to obtain the additional output M_1M_2.

Transfer Effect

The remaining portion of the larger producers' receipts, measured by the area **t**, is a surplus over costs on all but the last unit of output produced. It is an economic rent extracted by producers from consumers of the commodity, and represents a mere transfer of income. This can be called the transfer effect of the duty. (Kindleberger calls it the redistribution effect.)

If we assume that resources were fully employed before the imposition of the duty, the protective effect measures the loss to the country from the uneconomic reallocation of its productive resources. Before the duty was introduced, these were employed in other lines of production, where they earned the going rates of return. They earn no more in their new, protected employment, so they gain nothing, whereas the country loses from their more costly, less efficient use.[3]

---

[3] To attract resources (e.g., labor) from their old employment into the protected industry, however, they may have to be offered higher pay. If so, then since their remuneration is a cost to producers, its increase will be reflected in a more steeply rising cost curve. Their increased earnings are a partial offset to the loss to the community due to rising costs,

Consumption Effect

Let us look at matters from the viewpoint of consumers of the protected commodity. Before the imposition of the duty, their total satisfaction from consumption is measured by the area under the demand curve to the left of the vertical line M_4n. The cost of obtaining this satisfaction, on the other hand, is measured by the price paid times the amount consumed, or by the rectangular area OP_1nM_4. On all units consumed other than the marginal one (at n), they obtained a consumers' surplus measured by the triangular area between P_1n and the demand curve.

After the duty is imposed, total consumers' satisfaction is measured by the area under the demand curve to the left of the vertical line M_3m. The cost of obtaining it is consumers' outlay, or the area OP_2mM_3. Consumers' surplus is now the area between P_2m and the demand curve. Since this is smaller than the previous consumers' surplus (by the area P_1P_2mn), consumers have suffered a net loss in satisfaction as the result of protection.

Partially offsetting the loss to consumers is the revenue received by the government (r) and the surplus transferred to producers (t). The net loss to the community as a whole is measured by the two triangular areas, p (less efficient use of resources) and c (loss to consumers not offset or otherwise accounted for).

The loss of consumers' satisfaction is not imaginary, but very real, though it may not be consciously realised by consumers who are not aware of the existence of particular customs duties. It is the difference between the enjoyment consumers would get from having the use of a larger quantity of Swiss watches, for example, at a lower price, and the enjoyment they actually get from a smaller quantity bought at a higher price.

Tariffs and Prices

In all the foregoing discussion, we adhered to the assumption that the introduction of an import duty would have no effect on the foreign price of the import, and that hence the price in the protected market would rise by the full amount of the duty. This may occur, or price may not rise at all, or it may rise by less than the amount of the duty.

The price in the protected market will rise by the full amount of the duty only if the commodity is produced abroad at constant cost. Then imports come in at an unchanged price at the customs house; to this the duty must be added to get the domestic price.

No change in price will occur if the commodity taxed is exported from the country imposing the duty. The price at home will then be (barring discriminating monopoly) the world price less cost of transport. If, after protection, the home price should rise, domestic sales would be increased at the expense of exports until the home and foreign prices were brought into line again.

Whenever foreign production of the taxed import takes place under conditions of increasing cost—and in the long run, this is probably the typical case—the reduction in sales of foreign producers will force a contraction of production, and with it a decline of cost to a lower level. To a new, lower, landed price of imports the duty is added. The price in the protected market is higher than the foreign price by the amount of the duty, but not higher than the *old* pre-tariff price by this amount, owing to the decline in foreign costs.

FREE TRADE VERSUS PROTECTION

The case for free trade is very simple. It consists in the fact that, if trade is free, goods and services can be obtained at lower cost abroad than if domestic substitutes are produced in their stead. By producing exports and exchanging these for imports, fewer resources are required than if the imported goods were produced at home. If this were not true, the goods would not be imported, but would be obtained from home producers, as are those commodities that *are* produced more economically at home.

In other words, free trade permits full advantage to be taken of the possibilities of geographical specialisation. Some countries have endowments of the factors that enable them to achieve economical production of one group of commodities, others are suitably endowed for the production of another group. Left alone, each country will specialise in producing those goods for which its factor endowment best suits it, and will exchange these specialties for those of other countries, to the mutual benefit of all.

The gain to any country from free trade can be expressed in terms of increased real income. By using a given amount of resources to produce imports, or import substitutes, a certain quantity of these goods can be obtained. But this quantity will be larger, and national income correspondingly greater, if the same resources are first used to produce exports, which are then exchanged for the cheaper foreign imports.

Protection wipes out, or at least reduces, the gains from trade. As our analysis has shown, its net effects are two in number: (1) It causes resources to be shifted from a more efficient to a less efficient use; (2) By raising the price of goods and services, it restricts the consumer's freedom of choice, arbitrarily forcing him to reduce his consumption of things of which, with uninhibited choice, he would prefer to buy more.

The case for free trade has never been successfully refuted, nor even has an intellectually acceptable argument for long-run, enduring protection, based on economic considerations, ever been devised, though much ingenuity has gone into the attempt. The arguments for protection that do have validity are either short-run or non-economic in character, or require the realisation of very special conditions. Yet most of the arguments advanced by protectionists are unqualified, asserted with great conviction, and what is more important, are widely believed.

Professor Viner concludes:

The contrast is striking between the almost undisputed sway which the protectionist doctrine has over the minds of statesmen and its almost complete failure to receive credentials of intellectual respectability from the economists. The routine arguments of the protectionist politician differ somewhat in quality from country to country. In my own country they are often magnificent achievements of sustained and impressive oratory, capturing their audiences in spite of—or perhaps because of—the absence of any visible means of intellectual support. . . . They are fairly adequately disposed of in any one of a large number of elementary textbooks, and what importance they have is due mainly to the fact that the general public does not read economic textbooks.[4]

SERIOUS ARGUMENTS FOR PROTECTION

Infant Industry

Protection can be an effective means of stimulating the development of an industry that is well suited to a country but which finds it impossible to get started unless it is sheltered for a time from the blast of competition from established foreign producers. The only advantage possessed by the foreign industry is that of an early start; in all other respects—especially suitability of factor prices to the combinations required, availability of raw materials, and nearness to market—the two are on a par. This means that established producers, because of their early beginning, have been able to acquire internal and external economies not available to the potential producer in another country. These economies would develop gradually if he were given the temporary shelter of a tariff, and the newcomer would become equally or more efficient than his older competitors, since he suffers from no other disadvantage.

[4] Jacob Viner, *International Economics,* Ch. 6, "The Tariff Question and the Economist," p. 109. The Free Press, Glencoe, Ill., 1951.

Suppose, for example, a new producer finds his domestic market pre-empted by existing foreign firms. He would have to start on a small and uneconomic scale, and could not possibly meet the low costs of his competitors. But with the shelter furnished by protection, he could expand gradually until, having attained optimum size, he could confront them on an even footing. In more technical terms, growth, as the years go by, permits the new producer to acquire internal economies of scale which are unattainable in the infant stage of development.

External economies, or those economies that accompany the growth not of a single plant but of an entire industry, are also at stake. As more domestic firms enter the field, the labor force grows and becomes able to supply specialised workers to fill vacancies on short notice; service and repair establishments arise to provide their specific contributions; research may be taken over by a special agency, and so on. All these developments help to bring costs down and to hasten the day when the infant industry becomes mature and capable of standing on its own feet.

A moment's reflection will show that this argument in no way conflicts with the goal of the free trader: maximum international specialisation on the basis of relative national advantage. Its proponents correctly believe that this result may not always be achieved without intervention. At bottom, intervention is justified because one of the assumptions on which the free trade case rests—perfect competition—is not realised in practice. Imperfections in competition, in the form of unequal access to internal and external economies, make temporary protection necessary to equalise competitive conditions.

But notice that the infant industry case is definitely circumscribed. Protection is only warranted if the industry in question is clearly suited to the country's factor endowment, market prospects, and facilities for obtaining raw materials, so that it can reasonably be expected one day to stand on its own feet. Moreover, the grant of protection should be for a limited period only; the day of the industry's maturity should be foreseeable in the reasonably near future.

In the practical application of infant-industry protection, these limitations are seldom observed. Infants are selected for nurture without the careful exercise of parental judgment necessary to determine their chances of survival. "Infant industry" becomes a slogan to justify promiscuous protection without regard to merit. And when the indiscriminately chosen infants fail to become vigorous adults, the protection that keeps them unhealthily alive is rarely removed. Their anemia may even be treated to fresh doses of protection.

Before leaving this topic, notice that when infant industry protection is applied to several industries at once, the argument acquires added force —always assuming that due care was used in choosing the recipients of aid. For to the external economies that arise with the growth of a *single* industry are added others of a broader character, such as accompany a country's total industrial expansion. Roads are improved, railways constructed, power plants erected, and technical and engineering training provided—facilities which are needed by all industries, but many of which cannot be economically justified until a certain stage of development is attained or within sight. These are what Friedrich List, a German economist of the early nineteenth century, had in mind when he wrote:

Manufactories and manufactures are the mothers and children of municipal liberty, of intelligence, of the arts and sciences, of internal and external commerce, of navigation and improvements in transport, of civilisation and political power. They are the chief means of liberating agriculture from its chains, and of elevating it to a commercial character. . . . If restrictions on the importation of raw products hinder . . . the utilisation of the natural resources and powers of a State, restrictions on the importation of manufactured goods, on the contrary, call into life and activity (in the case of a populous country already far advanced in agriculture and civilisation) a mass of natural powers; indeed, without doubt, the greater half of all natural powers, which in the merely agricultural State lie idle and dead for ever.[5]

Diversification of Industry

Among the battery of protectionist arguments, one that has frequently been prominent urges the diversification of industry as a goal. A highly interdependent international economic system, made up of individual nations specialising upon a rather narrow range of exports and depending upon others for a much wider range of imports, is very unstable. Its members are subject to the recurrent shock of worldwide depression and to serious economic disruption in the event of war or of major industrial change. These disturbances could be avoided or minimised, it is held, if the nation deliberately set out, through protection, to create a more balanced and self-sufficient economy. Insulated from these outside disturbances, the country would gain more in the long run from greater stability than it would lose from the higher cost of its protected production.

The argument has a strong popular appeal—everyone prefers a "balanced" to an "unbalanced" economy, safety to danger, and national pride is stirred by the thought of being economically independent. Moreover, there is no

[5] Friedrich List, *The National System of Political Economy*, pp. 115, 175. Copyright 1922 by Longmans, Green & Co., London.

denying the fact that between World War I and World War II the international economy was very unstable, and that these wars, by cutting off markets and sources of supply for many years, seriously disrupted the economies of many countries. These effects fell with particular harshness upon the more specialised producers of foodstuffs and raw materials, such as Australia, Argentina, Mexico, and Chile, where they strengthened the case for diversification of industry.

But let us be clear about the nature of this argument. It applies only to highly specialised economies, in practice especially those which export a narrow range of primary products and which depend upon imports for most of their supplies of manufactured goods. And if diversification in these conditions is to be warranted, it should provide, without excessive cost, substantial insulation against depression and wars.

Thus qualified, the argument has little to recommend it. Highly specialised economies export from a fourth to a third or more of their national incomes. Their dependence on imports is equally great. Sufficient independence to give effective insulation against international shock would probably require that these proportions be brought down to around 5 per cent, close to the figure for the United States. To do so would mean such a huge reallocation of resources and such a wholesale denial of the benefits of international trade as to make the goal prohibitively costly. It would be much more sensible to rely on infant industry protection, legitimately applied, to achieve—together with conscious efforts at economic development—a greater degree of industrialisation, and to meet the problems of war and depression in other ways. (As a matter of fact, the war years, though they brought serious disturbance to primary producing countries, also brought great prosperity and rapid economic advance.)

Maintenance of Employment

During periods of severe unemployment, as in the 1930's, much use has been made of the argument that protection can furnish an effective remedy. By reducing imports, a tariff stimulates employment directly in the import-competing industries; from this focus, the employment-creating effect spreads to other industries in ever-widening though diminishing waves. Investment in facilities for producing substitutes for imports may also result, setting in motion a second force to increase employment.

Taken by itself, the argument is valid. Whether it is the best means of dealing with the problem, however, is questionable. First, it may not be very effective. If one country reduces its imports by a newly imposed tariff, the exports of its trading partners are thereby reduced in like amount. A decline in employment is set in motion abroad; as employment and incomes fall there, less is spent on imports, which are our country's exports. Even though this foreign repercussion is likely to be of smaller magnitude than our country's initial reduction of its imports, it may well constitute a substantial offset. Second, our country's exports are almost certain to be reduced, directly and drastically, by retaliation on the part of other countries. A country attempting to increase employment at home by means of a tariff is in effect exporting its unemployment. This sort of beggar-my-neighbor policy is sure to arouse resentment and prompt counter measures abroad. Finally, the stimulation of employment by a tariff involves a permanent reallocation of resources for what may be at best a temporary gain. The remedy is a costly one.

An alternative is to use monetary and fiscal policy to relieve unemployment. If successful, the accompanying rise in income will bring with it an increase in imports, which may lead to a deficit in the balance of payments and a loss of international reserves. A good deal depends upon whether the unemployment is purely local or is part of a worldwide phenomenon. If the former, and income and employment are merely restored to a pre-existing level, there need be no ensuing balance of payments difficulties. If the latter, and other countries also adopt expansionary monetary and fiscal policies, incomes and imports of the several countries will rise together and no country need lose reserves. Even if our country has to go it alone, it would be preferable to combine an internal policy of expansion with direct quantitative restrictions on imports. For then imports may remain constant, any tendency to increase with rising incomes being held in check by quotas, whereas a tariff alone depresses imports and makes economic conditions worse abroad. Moreover, there is a better chance that direct restrictions can later be removed, especially if they are adopted for the specific purpose of safeguarding the balance of payments. Tariffs, once imposed, are very difficult to dislodge.

Improving the Terms of Trade

Some economists have urged the use of tariffs to take advantage of their tendency to force down prices in the exporting country. If this occurs, the tariff-raising country gains from obtaining its imports on better terms: a given amount of exports will exchange for a larger amount of imports than formerly.

As we have seen, the degree to which the landed price of imports will fall depends upon the conditions under which they are supplied. If their supply in the country of origin is highly elastic (approaching infinity, or

constant cost), a tariff on imports will cause their prices to decline little
or not at all. Only if their supply is inelastic (steeply rising costs) will a
reduction in imports push their costs down appreciably.[6]

There is, moreover, no assurance that there is any net gain at all. We
must remember the two certain adverse effects of a tariff: its diversion of
resources to a more uneconomic use, and the loss in satisfaction it imposes
on consumers. These offsets to any gain from lower-priced imports must
be taken into account. When they are, if there is any benefit to the country
as a whole, it is likely to be very small.

Nations being sensitive to the action of others in tariff matters, we must
reckon with the possibility of retaliation. If other nations retaliate, and the
prices of our country's exports fall, its terms of trade (the ratio of its export
prices to its import prices) revert to or approximate their previous position.
Even the fancied gain—which ignores the offsets to which we have called
attention—is lost. Nothing remains but the reduction in consumers' satisfaction and the worsened allocation of resources.

Tariffs for Bargaining

A country which already has a tariff can, and frequently does, use it as
a means of bargaining to obtain from other countries lower duties on its
exports. The trade agreements program of the United States amounted in
effect to using our tariff as just such an instrument of bargaining; it consisted essentially in a swapping of duty reductions.

Such a course is not open to a free-trade country or one with only a
revenue tariff. It is therefore sometimes argued that adoption of protective
duties would benefit the country by giving it a lever with which to pry open
foreign markets for its goods. There is some merit in this argument, but
only for a free-trade or very low-tariff country. And there is the off-setting
disadvantage that duties introduced for bargaining purposes cannot fail
to create vested interests which will oppose the use of the tariff for the
purpose originally intended. Indeed, the bargaining lever, instead of
being used to gain tariff concessions from foreign powers, may be employed
by others to extract additional protection from the home government.

Anti-dumping

The tariffs of many nations contain special provisions against "dumping,"
a practice which arouses the indignation, real or feigned, of producers in
the market where dumping occurs.

---

[6] Moreover, if *foreign* demand for these goods is elastic, any decline in their price will
be checked by expanding purchases abroad.

What is "dumping"? Contrary to a widespread impression, dumping is not selling abroad below costs of production. It means instead *sales in a foreign market at a price below that received in the home market,* after allowing for transportation charges, duties, and all other costs of transfer. Discrimination between the home and foreign price is the essential mark of dumping. Thus, sales abroad below cost of production would not constitute dumping *unless* the foreign were lower than the domestic price.

The problem is complicated by the existence of different kinds of dumping. It may be *persistent,* continuing indefinitely because the exporter is in a position to practice discriminating monopoly. (See Chapter 8.) Selling in two separate markets, if the elasticity of demand is greater in the foreign than in the (monopolised) home market, he will gain by selling at a lower price abroad. Such dumping may continue indefinitely. On the other hand, dumping may be *intermittent* rather than continuous, with price-cutting undertaken for the purpose of destroying foreign competition.

From the point of view of the country in which the dumping occurs, it is clear that intermittent dumping can be most disturbing, even ruinous, to local firms. The gains of consumers are at best purely transitory, while the effects on business can be lasting. If care is taken to define dumping precisely, and not simply as selling below costs, anti-dumping duties can be justified. Such duties appear to have worked reasonably well in the United States and Canada.

Persistent dumping, on the other hand, is no different in its effects from sales by a low-cost foreign producer. Year in and year out, buyers get their supplies at low cost; competing producers, if there are any, can adjust to a stable situation. There is no special case for protection because of dumping; if a case can be established, it must rest on other grounds.

National Defense

Protection of certain industries is often supported by appeal to the needs of national defense. If the products of a particular industry are essential to military strength, it is argued, then, if that industry cannot survive without protection it should by all means be maintained by protective duties. The desirability or necessity of providing for the national defense involves ends, such as security, power, or even the survival of the nation, that lie outside the scope of economics.

Notice, however, that nowadays, when war is total, practically any industry necessary for the operation of an economy is essential to the national defense. Hence the argument implies that military security can be guaranteed only by establishing nearly complete self-sufficiency. *Complete* self-sufficiency is a goal impossible to any nation. It can be substantially realised only by the United States and the Soviet Union.

Even near self-sufficiency, moreover, would for most nations require massive protection. But protection means inefficiency, and inefficiency is certainly no aid to defense!

If "essential industries" are defined very narrowly, to include only those engaged in producing technical military goods, such as optical instruments, radar equipment, explosives, and airplanes, then we should remember that there are less expensive ways than protection to ensure their survival. The industries in question may be carried on by the government as part of a national defense program, or they may be supported by bounties from the public treasury. The former alternative means that they would be included with other ordnance works, supplying the needs of the government. The requirements of the public for optical instruments, etc., would continue to be met by imports or by such domestic private enterprise as might exist without protection. Alternately, bounties might be held down to a level only just adequate to provide for military needs, or expanded to support industries supplying the entire population.

Either of these alternatives would be superior to protection on grounds of justice (and possibly of cost as well), since the benefit of possessing an industry essential to the national defense accrues to the entire population, and it should therefore be paid for out of general taxation rather than supported by the consumers, as it would be under a protective policy.

NONSENSE ARGUMENTS FOR PROTECTION

All the protectionist arguments so far considered are relatively sophisticated. So far as any is valid, it is so only under narrowly circumscribed conditions. And to deal with the situations toward which some of them are directed, clearly superior alternatives are at hand. Being sophisticated, none of these arguments is popular (barring perhaps that for national defense) except the infant industry argument, whose very popularisation has brought its corruption. It is a striking fact that the arguments for protection that carry the greatest political weight contain the least economic sense. Maybe because economics is a difficult subject that few understand?

The case for protection one commonly encounters is loaded, not with rational argument, but with appeals to prejudice and to vested interests. This is especially true where the retention or increase of existing protection is at stake, rather than the introduction of new duties. For when an inefficient industry is threatened with more intense foreign competition, either from the removal of duties or the worsening of its competitive position, a good many people are likely to be at least temporarily hurt. Their probable injury is exaggerated, the sympathies of their fellow citizens are invoked, and consideration of the national as opposed to special interest is ignored. Bear these things in mind as you examine the arguments that follow.

The Pauper Labor Argument

Everyone knows that wages in different countries vary tremendously. The average level in the United States, for example, is 2½ times as high as in Great Britain, approximately 6 or 7 times that of Italy, and perhaps 15 or 20 times the average Japanese wage. With only these facts to go on, it is natural to conclude that the products of "pauper labor" can undersell those of high-wage labor. The tariff is extolled as "protecting the American standard of living" or "sheltering the American worker from the competition of pauper labor."

As a generalisation applying to *all* the labor of a country, this view is patent nonsense. It is possible to advance it seriously only if one is completely ignorant of both the principles and the facts of international trade. As for the facts, every day, year in and year out, the products of high-wage American labor are sold abroad in competition with goods made by low-paid workers. High wages are clearly no bar to low-cost production, at least in many important lines.

These facts, and the fallacy in the pauper labor argument, can only be explained by an appeal to the principles underlying international trade. There are two reasons why high-wage labor can without difficulty compete with low-wage labor. One is that labor is not the only factor of production. It is always combined with capital and natural resources. But the proportions in which the different factors are combined varies enormously from one product to another. And we know that the prices of the factors differ greatly between countries. Hence commodities embodying much capital can be produced at low cost in countries where capital is cheap, land-intensive products will be cheap in countries abundantly endowed with land, whereas labor-intensive commodities will be cheap where wages are low.

Low-wage countries, in other words, have an advantage over high-wage countries *only* with respect to commodities whose production requires the combination of much labor with relatively little capital or land—that is, where the wage bill is the preponderant element in costs. It is senseless for a high-wage country to try to compete in the production of such commodities. But is equally senseless to contend, as the pauper labor argument does, that a high-wage country is at a disadvantage in *all* lines of production.

But there is an additional element of fallacy to deal with. Even if labor *were* the only factor, a high-wage country could still meet the competition of a low-wage country wherever its relative productivity were higher than its relative wages. To take a simple case, suppose wages in A are 3 times as high as in B, but that in the manufacture of shoes its labor is 3 times as efficient as B's. It could then produce shoes at the same cost. If its ratio of efficiency were higher than its ratio of wages, say 4 or 5 to 1, its costs would be lower than B's.

The causes of such superior efficiency could be better management, better fed or better educated labor, access to a more advanced technology, or any of the social conditions of production which give rise to qualitative differences in the labor of different countries. These causes of efficiency would explain labor's higher average wages in A. Wherever they operated with particular force, A's labor efficiency would be relatively high, its costs relatively low. In industries in which A was less than three times as efficient as B, the latter country would have a cost advantage.

Taken together, differing factor combinations and conditions affecting labor efficiency go far toward explaining the ability of a high-wage country such as the United States to meet the competition of low-wage countries. It cannot compete, of course, where labor dominates the factor combination unless its labor is disproportionately productive. But the pauper labor argument makes no such qualifications. It is a sweeping generalisation, and as such, wrong.

Protection of the Home Market

An argument sometimes encountered claims that if a country's manufactures are protected, this will expand the market for agricultural products by increasing the purchasing power of industrial workers.

> Agriculture derives large benefits not only directly from the protective duties levied on competitive farm products of foreign origin but also, indirectly, from the increase in the purchasing power of the American workmen employed in industries similarly protected.[7]

The implication, of course, is that there will be a net expansion of the market for agricultural products. But if the purchasing power of industrial workers is increased because more are employed, the purchasing power of foreign customers will be reduced, since domestic manufactures replace

---

[7] Cited in Asher Isaacs, *International Trade: Tariff and Commercial Policies*, p. 229. Copyright 1948 by Richard D. Irwin, Inc., Chicago.

imports. A domestic market is substituted for a foreign market. This is no gain to the farmer, and he suffers a certain loss in the higher prices he will have to pay for protected manufactures.

Keeping Money at Home

One of the crudest protectionist fallacies is well expressed in the form of a remark falsely attributed to Abraham Lincoln: "I do not know much about the tariff, but I know this much, when we buy manufactured goods abroad we get the goods and the foreigner gets the money. When we buy the manufactured goods at home we get both the goods and the money."

Except for its occasional currency, this argument scarcely deserves consideration. The classically appropriate comment has been made by Beveridge: "It has no merits; the only sensible words in it are the first eight words." [8] The view represents, of course, the crassest form of mercantilism, with its emphasis upon money as a form of wealth. It is only necessary to point out that in international trade goods pay for goods, and that international money (gold) moves only to perform the function of adjusting disturbances to trade. Our money—that is, the money of our country—will not be useful to the foreigner unless he spends it in our country!

Equalising Costs of Production

Proponents of protection often contend that a truly "scientific" tariff is one which equalises costs of production at home and abroad. This principle of cost equalisation is not, properly speaking, an argument for protection; it is rather a way of dressing up the case to make it more palatable.

The doctrine has an engaging appearance of fairness. It seems to say, no favors, no undue rates. Offset the higher expenses of the American producer, put him in a position to meet the foreign competitor without being under a disadvantage, and then let the best man win. Conditions being thus equalised, the competition will become a fair one. Protected producers will get only the profit to which they are reasonably entitled and the domestic consumers are secured against prices which are unreasonable.[9]

The doctrine's apparent fairness is only skin deep. To appreciate this, one needs only to realise that a tariff is essentially discriminatory. It picks out for special advantage at the cost of the public precisely the least efficient of a country's industries. By keeping out imports, this protection

[8] Sir William Beveridge, *Tariffs: The Case Examined*, p. 27. Copyright 1931 by Longmans, Green & Co., London, where the quotation above is also cited.

[9] In the course of criticising the argument, F. W. Taussig, *Free Trade, The Tariff, and Reciprocity*, p. 134 (Copyright 1920 by the Macmillan Company, New York).

reduces foreign markets for the country's most efficient (export) industries, and so injures them. Legislation that discriminates in favor of inefficient producers, against efficient ones, and against the general body of consumers, can hardly be given high marks for common sense, let alone for fairness.

If there were such a thing as a "scientific" tariff, it should provide an unambiguous set of criteria for determining what commodities to protect and how far protection should be extended in each case. Apply this test to the principle of equalising costs of production. Should any producers who want to establish an uneconomic industry, or who have already established such an industry, be granted sufficient protection to meet foreign competition, even if this requires a duty of 100 per cent—or 1,000 per cent? If not, where shall the line be drawn? Shall cost equalisation apply only to the most efficient 10 per cent of firms in the industry, to 90 per cent, or to all, including the least efficient? Where shall we draw the line? Where *can* the line be drawn except between those who have the political power to exact discriminatory treatment and those who do not?

Upon closer inspection, therefore, this "scientific" principle of tariff-making turns out to be a completely unscientific and irrational appeal to national prejudice against the foreigner. Its disarming character, and its lack of any criteria for limiting protection, are its most dangerous features.

SELECTED REFERENCES

Beveridge, Sir William, *Tariffs: The Case Examined,* 2nd edition (Longmans, Green & Co., 1932). Still one of the best general discussions of the tariff in all its aspects.

Isaacs, Asher, *International Trade: Tariffs and Commercial Policies* (Richard D. Irwin, Inc., Homewood, Ill., 1948). A detailed study of tariffs, with much useful illustrative material.

Kindleberger, Charles P., *International Economics* (Richard D. Irwin, Inc., Homewood, Ill., 1953). Chapter 10 has a somewhat fuller discussion of tariffs to improve the terms of trade, to increase employment, and to redistribute income in favor of the scarce factor than is given here.

Lloyd, Lewis E., *The Case for Protection* (Devin-Adair Co., New York, 1955). A frankly partisan book, which tries to make protection seem in the national interest.

Scitovsky, Tibor, "A Reconsideration of the Theory of Tariffs," *Readings in the Theory of International Trade.* Chapter 16. Besides its discussion of the gains from trade (above, Ch. 9), this article contains an exhaustive analysis of the terms-of-trade argument and of retaliation, with some interesting closing comments on infant industry protection.

Stolper, Wolfgang F., and Samuelson, Paul A., "Protection and Real Wages," American Economic Association, *Readings in the Theory of International Trade* (The Blakiston Co., Philadelphia, 1949). Chapter 15. Shows that a country's scarce factor's return is raised, both relatively and absolutely, by protection.

Taussig, Frank W., *Some Aspects of the Tariff Question*, 3rd edition (Harvard University Press, Cambridge, 1931). Examines the growth of the protected sugar, steel, and textile industries in the United States to determine the role played by the tariff in their development.

Towle, Lawrence W., *International Trade and Commercial Policy*, 2nd edition (Harper & Bros., New York, 1956). Chapters 17 and 18 contain a discussion of transit and export duties, as well as the different kinds of tariff systems. Chapter 21 describes the various forms of indirect protection.

13

NATIONAL INCOME AND
FOREIGN TRADE

Our study so far has shown the forces determining international specialisation and trade, and we have traced the main lines of historical development during the nineteenth century. We have seen that international trade,
by extending the range of specialisation, makes it possible for a country
to enjoy a larger total income of goods and services, and that this larger
income also involves a wider range of commodities and services to choose
from. In other words, both the level of income and its composition are
affected by trade.

Little has been said, however, about how *changes* in the amount of a
country's trade, or in other transactions in which nations engage, such as
lending and borrowing, react upon its economy. When a nation's exports
expand, owing to an increase in demand abroad, will its imports also rise
by an equal amount, as Hume appears to have thought, thus preserving
balance in its external trade? Or will the increase in imports be smaller,
thus leaving it with an export surplus to be settled in some other way?
And what of the internal effects of such a rise in exports? Are they significant, or can we afford to neglect them? Similar questions arise in connection with variations in imports resulting from a change in home demand.

This chapter will consider how changes in the level of a country's
exports or imports affect the level of employment and output within the
country, and how variations in the latter react upon exports and imports.
In succeeding chapters, we shall concentrate upon a country's external
relations, bringing together into a balance of payments all of its international transactions, examining the problems of how they are disturbed and
how such disturbances may be adjusted. Since our immediate concern will
be the relation between a country's income and output and its foreign trade,
we must first attend to the forces which govern the level of national income.

THE TOTAL VALUE PRODUCED BY A FIRM

A nation's economy is made up of a multitude of producing units—firms
engaged in manufacturing, trade, and transportation; government agencies

like the post office department or the department of defense; farms of many kinds; and individuals rendering services, such as doctors, lawyers, dentists, and the like. These units, of which we shall take the firm as typical, employ the factors of production in varying combinations to create goods or services which are sold on the market. The income generated by this productive activity may be looked at from the point of view of its source—the proceeds of a firm's sales to its customers—or from the viewpoint of its allocation to costs and profits. These two points of view may also be expressed as the value of the firm's production, on the one hand, and the money income generated by that production, on the other.

In a private enterprise economy, the volume of a firm's output and thus, the income it generates, is closely geared to sales. Yet it is not exclusively tied to sales; the production of any period may exceed sales by the amount added to inventory or fall short thereof by the stock drawn out of inventory.[1] The value of the production undertaken in response to market demand and adjusted for inventory changes, and therefore the money income generated, will be equal to the proceeds of sales at market prices plus or minus inventory changes at the same valuation.

Now consider the value of a firm's total production, not from the viewpoint of its source, but in terms of how it is allocated among the factors responsible for its creation, or in terms of the money income generated by the firm's productive activity. The following statement shows the value of the production of a typical firm, the United States Manufacturing Corporation, in both its aspects. (In the light of the foregoing discussion, the "sources" side should be self-explanatory). The first and largest item, "wages and salaries," is simply that part of the cost of producing output worth $1,616,000 chargeable to labor of all kinds employed in its production. "Interest" represents the payment for the use of capital lent to the corporation by banks or other outsiders. "Materials and services purchased from other firms" comprises raw materials, fuel, power, insurance, etc. All these goods and services were necessary to get the final product of the corporation; payments for them are legitimate and typical elements of cost. "De-

[1] There is no uniform relation between sales and inventory changes for the economy as a whole. Although it is generally true that when sales rise, producers will also try to increase inventories, and when sales are falling, to reduce them, they may for a time be frustrated. For the increase in output necessary to expand inventories raises employment and income, and therewith stimulates increased sales, which keeps inventories low. The same forces operate in reverse when producers generally try to lower inventories in the face of declining sales. As the rate of expansion or contraction of sales slows down, however, inventory accumulation or reduction can begin. Hence at times, sales and inventories may move together, at others—especially at the beginning of a rise or fall in sales—in opposite directions.

PRODUCTION STATEMENT OF THE
UNITED STATES MANUFACTURING CORPORATION
FOR 19—.

(in 000's)

ALLOCATIONS		SOURCES	
Wages and salaries	$ 700	Sales to Company A	$ 500
Interest	20	Sales to Company B	380
Materials & services purchased		Sales to Company C	320
from other firms	620	Sales to Company D	120
Depreciation	80	Sales to Company E	110
Taxes other than corporate		Other sales	80
profits taxes	45	Inventory increase	106
Social insurance contributions	30		
Provision for corp. profits tax	41		
Dividends paid	50		
Undistributed profits	30		
Total allocations of value			
of production	$1,616	Total value of production	$1,616

preciation" shows how much the value of plant and equipment declined during the year in question; it reflects the amount contributed to the value of output by the physical transformation of capital goods into finished manufactured products. Depreciation must be charged against gross income as a cost if the firm is to be able to replace its physical capital when it is worn out, and thus stay in business. "Taxes other than corporate profits taxes" is the cost incurred by payment of property taxes, excise or sales taxes, and fees and licenses to governmental units. The corporate profits tax is recorded separately, since it is not a cost of production, but is levied on the profits of the business; in effect, it represents a sharing of the corporation's profits with the government. Another tax shown separately is "social insurance contributions," which include both the employer's and the workers' contributions, the latter being paid by the employer and deducted from the worker's pay. "Dividends paid" and "undivided profits," together with the amount set aside to provide for the corporate profits tax, comprise the total profit of the firm, which is the difference between the total value of current production and the costs incurred in producing it.

Such a production statement as this thus shows how the value of a firm's total production originated—from sales to various buyers and from additions to inventories[2]—and how this value was allocated to costs and profits. Costs and profits comprise the incomes earned by the factors, together with that

[2] Had sales been made out of inventories, with a resultant decline in the latter, there would have been a minus sign in front of this entry. If correctly computed, total costs would be less than total sales by the amount of inventory reduction; the cost of goods sold out of inventory would have been incurred in an earlier period.

part of the value of output which must be set aside to replace plant and equipment and to pay taxes.

If we were to add together all such production statements for all producing units in the economy, the resulting aggregate statement would show the value of total national output and its allocation, or gross national income and product. An important but simple correction of the individual production statements would, however, first be necessary. From each such statement we would have to subtract (on both sides) the entry for "materials and services purchased from other firms".[3] The corrected statements would then show the value contributed to total output by the productive efforts of each firm, thus avoiding double counting, since the value of the output of the firms supplying these materials and services would be recorded in their own production statements.

GROSS NATIONAL INCOME AND PRODUCT

Just as with the production statement of a firm, an aggregate statement for the whole economy would have two sides, one showing the value of gross national product from the viewpoint of its source in sales and changes in inventories, the other its allocation to costs and profits. Now the sales, for firms and individuals in the aggregate, may be conveniently classified according to the type of purchaser to whom the sales are made. A significant classification of this sort lists sales to final consumers, to business firms, to government, and to foreigners.[4] These are shown in the accompanying skeleton statement of GNP, on the side of sources, together with changes in inventories and the deduction essential to avoid double counting, "goods purchased for use in current production."

GROSS NATIONAL PRODUCT ACCOUNT

ALLOCATIONS	SOURCES
	Sales to consumers
	Sales to business firms
	Sales to government
	Sales to foreigners
	Net change in inventories
	Minus: Goods & services purchased for use in current production

[3] This item would then disappear from the allocations side and reappear, with a minus sign, on the sources side.

[4] More appropriately, to *residents* of other countries, whether they are of foreign nationality or not.

Certain simplifications can now be introduced which both make the GNP account easier to read and cause it to correspond with the form in which that account (for the United States) is actually published. First, we split the entry for "sales to business firms" in two, to reflect the fact that firms buy, not only goods and services for current production, but also plant, machinery, and equipment which are not for current use but represent investment in capital goods. Second, we can also divide the adjustment item, "goods and services purchased for use in current production," into two parts, reflecting the fact that some are bought from domestic firms, while some are purchased abroad. These change the gross national product account into the following form:

GROSS NATIONAL PRODUCT ACCOUNT

ALLOCATIONS   SOURCES

Sales to consumers
Sales to business firms on current account
Sales to business firms on capital account
(Investment)
Sales to government
Sales to foreigners

Net change in inventories

Minus: Goods & services purchased from firms on current account
Goods & services purchased from abroad on current account

It is now possible to eliminate two entries altogether. "Sales to business firms on current account" are obviously identical with "goods and services purchased from firms on current account," so that instead of showing the latter as a subtraction, we simply allow it to cancel out the corresponding positive item. We can also subtract "goods and services purchased from abroad on current account" (imports) from "sales to foreigners" (exports of goods and services), leaving "net foreign sales." The sources side of the gross national product account now takes the following simplified form:

GROSS NATIONAL PRODUCT ACCOUNT

ALLOCATIONS   SOURCES

Sales to consumers
Investment
Sales to government
Net foreign sales

Net change in inventories

These items are also shown in the accompanying complete statement of the gross national income and product for the United States in 1955. Except for minor differences in terminology, the entries on the sources or product side correspond to those we have already encountered. The most striking such difference is the use of the term "net foreign investment" (in this case negative, since in 1955 imports exceeded exports) instead of "net foreign sales." The reason for this change in terminology need not concern us here; it will be explained in the next chapter.

Gross national product in this year amounted to almost $391 billion. This was also the gross income of the nation, shown on the left side of the account as "charges against gross national product." Net income, or actual money payments to the factors for their contribution to production, amounted to $324 billion; its components are shown above the parenthetical entry for "net income." These consist of wages and salaries, together with supplements such as bonuses; rent ("rental income of persons"), corporate profits, and interest. Corporate profits are shown as they were distributed— the share going to the government, that paid out to stockholders in dividends, and that withheld by corporations. ("Inventory valuation adjustment" is an adjustment made necessary by price changes). "Income of unincorporated enterprises" is a mixture of wages, rent, interest, and profits which cannot be divided into these shares because the accounting procedures of these enterprises do not permit it.

The difference between gross income and net income appears in the deductions at the bottom of the table. Gross income, or gross national product, is the value at market prices of total national output. These deducted items appeared in the market value of the nation's output, but did not result in the payment of income. We are already familiar with "capital consumption allowances," which includes provision for depreciation and other forms of capital consumption and represents capital used up in the creation of the gross national product. Indirect taxes and business transfer payments are other elements included in the price paid for current output by consumers and other buyers. Business transfer payments consist of gifts to non-profit institutions, cash prizes, etc., which are not income resulting from productive activity, but mere transfers of purchasing power derived from sales proceeds. Indirect taxes (sales, excise, and property taxes) are similar transfers to the government. If the government used these tax proceeds to hire employees, this would be reflected in "government purchases of goods and services" on the product side, and also in "wages and salaries" on the income side.

Table 13.1

NATIONAL INCOME AND PRODUCT ACCOUNT, 1955

(in millions of dollars)

Compensation of employees:		Personal consumption expenditure	253,971
Wages and salaries	210,354	Gross private domestic investment	60,557
Supplements	12,838	Net foreign investment	470
Income of unincorporated enterprises and inventory valuation adjustment	39,019	Government purchases of goods and services	76,802
Rental income of persons	10,076		
Corporate profits and inventory valuation adjustment:			
Corporate profits tax liability	21,533		
Dividends	11,218		
Undistributed profits	9,915		
Inventory valuation adjustment	− 1,738		
Net interest	10,833		
(National income	324,048)		
Indirect business tax and non-tax liability	32,521		
Business transfer payments	1,430		
Statistical discrepancy	1,820		
Less: Subsidies minus current surplus of government enterprises	297		
Capital consumption allowances	31,338		
Charges against gross national product	390,860	Gross national product	390,860

Source: Survey of Current Business, July 1956.

THE EQUATIONS FOR GROSS NATIONAL PRODUCT

Our discussion of changes in the national income and product, upon which we are about to embark, can be considerably simplified and abbreviated if we formulate what we now know about gross national product and its components in terms of symbols. Take first GNP in terms of its sources, or how it is generated. "Sales to consumers" we shall represent by C (consumer expenditure), sales to government, by G. Since any addition to (or subtraction from) inventories is a form of investment (or disinvestment), we can lump this item together with the ordinary investment item (sales to business firms on capital account) under the symbol I, for total investment. And since net sales to foreigners consist of exports minus imports, we can express this entry as $X - M$. We can now equate GNP to its sources as follows:

$$GNP = C + I + G + X - M$$

Let us consider this equation. If imports were not subtracted, so that the equation read: $GNP = C + I + G + X$, it would be false. For sales to consumers (C) include some goods purchased from foreign firms, either as raw materials or as finished goods (as in the case of articles imported by department stores). Similarly, many of the investment goods produced and sold, many of a country's exports, and even the items purchased by government, contain imported goods and services as components—they have an "import content." Hence failure to subtract imports would overstate the value of national production.

Allocation of GNP

Turn now to the gross national product looked at in terms of its allocation. Far the larger part of GNP is allocated as income to the owners of the factors of production. This is only natural, since the goods and services produced and sold result mainly from the contribution to production of factor services. Personal incomes of factor owners would include wages and salaries, income of unincorporated enterprises, net interest, and dividends. The other elements of GNP according to allocation can be classified under two heads: savings and taxes. Savings would include capital consumption allowances and undistributed profits (profits not distributed to stockholders and hence saved). Under taxes would fall indirect taxes, social insurance contributions, and corporate profits taxes.

Let us push the principle of allocation of GNP one step further, and consider what happens to personal incomes. These are allocated by their recipients to one of three purposes: the major part is spent on consumer goods, some is saved, and some goes to pay income taxes. The allocation of GNP can now be expressed in terms of three symbols. Total savings (S) would include savings out of personal income plus the items specified above. Under taxes (T), we have those already listed plus personal income taxes. Finally, there is consumption expenditure (C), which is equal to the value of sales to consumers on the sources side. Another equation is available:

$$GNP = C + S + T$$

But since it is also true that $GNP = C + I + G + X - M$, we can write:

$$C + S + T = GNP = C + I + G + X - M$$

For the analysis which follows, it is convenient to have imports on the allocations side. It is also realistic, since part of any country's income is allocated to the purchase of imports. Your high school algebra taught you that the same thing may be added to both sides of an equation without altering its equivalence. By adding M to each part of the last equation, we get:

$$C + S + T + M = \text{GNP} + M = C + I + G + X$$

This expresses the fact that the total value of a country's production, before allowing for its import content, is allocated to consumption expenditure, savings, taxes, and imports.

The reason why it is convenient to eliminate imports as a subtraction from the sources of GNP and to include it as an addition to the allocation or disposal of GNP is that thereby we segregate, on the sources side, all the positive, income-generating forces, while on the disposal side we segregate all the income-retarding forces or leakages out of income (S, T, and M). The importance of this arrangement will soon be made clear.

CHANGES IN GROSS NATIONAL PRODUCT

We are now ready to consider the effect of a change in any sector of GNP upon its total. Any change in any income-generating sector (C, I, G, or X) will affect *GNP* unless it is offset by an equal and opposite change in another sector. Thus if investment increases by \$10 billion, GNP—which includes investment—will rise by that amount unless at the same time either C, G, or X decrease.

The "Multiplier" Effect

Now it is most unlikely that a change in one sector will be offset by an opposite change elsewhere; as a general rule, a change in one sector will be reinforced by a similar movement in another part of the economy.[5] The reason for this is to be found in the repercussions of the initial change. If there is some slack in an economy in the form of unemployment, a \$10 billion increase in investment outlays will put some people back to work—construction workers, employees in machine tool plants, and others normally engaged in the production of capital goods. They will spend some part of their new incomes, and this expenditure will put still more people back to work supplying their wants. The additional incomes of these latter workers

---

[5] One exception should be noted that at times may be important. If business men are frightened by government spending, then an increase in government outlays may, through its effects on business confidence, induce an offsetting (partial or complete) decline in private investment.

will have the same effect, and employment and income will go on increasing in ever-diminishing amounts, very much like the series of wavelets set off by throwing a stone into a still pool.

An opposite sequence of repercussions would follow from an initial decline in investment: reduced employment and income in the capital goods industries, reduced expenditure by those now unemployed, an induced fall in employment and income in the trades supplying their wants, and so on.

The total effect on national income and GNP of such a change (positive or negative) in investment depends on what proportion of the initial increase in incomes is passed on by its recipients in the form of consumption expenditure, what part leaks away into savings, tax payments, and imports. The relations between investment, consumption, and income will follow the pattern described unless, as they change, variations are induced in the other components of income—government outlay and exports. It seems reasonable to regard these components as substantially independent. Government decisions as to expenditure are made by a different group of men acting independently of the business men who decide to increase investment or the production of consumption goods. As to exports, changes in these result from decisions made by foreign business men, consumers, and governments, which are external or exogenous to the economy in question.[6]

It will simplify our discussion if we state it not in terms of GNP, but of national income, for which we shall use the symbol Y. This has the advantage of brevity; also, the behavior of consumption is more closely related to national income than to gross national product, which includes depreciation, tranfer payments, and indirect taxes.

Derivation of the Multiplier

Whether national income rises by twice the initial increase (ΔI), or by more or less, depends, as we have said, on the *proportion* of the rise in income that is allocated to domestic expenditure on consumer goods. Economists have adopted a technical term for this: they call it the *marginal propensity to consume,* that is, the proportion of any increase in income that is spent on consumer goods, or $\Delta C/\Delta Y$. Since this concept refers to expenditure on consumer goods in general, whether foreign or domestic in origin—and thus includes expenditure on imports—let us first give it a workout in a simple model of a closed economy (one without foreign

[6] Later we shall see that the increase in imports resulting from the increase in incomes in our economy stimulates a rise in employment and income abroad. Since some part of this larger foreign income will be spent on imports, which are our economy's exports, there will be a minor secondary repercussion on its income. But this is a refinement we can postpone for the moment.

trade). This enables us to avoid the complication raised by imports, which can easily be introduced later.

We shall assume the marginal propensity to consume is ½, meaning that one-half of any increase in income is allocated to the purchase of consumer goods, and the other half to savings and taxes. If investment increases by 10, the total effect on income and national product can be shown by the following table, in which each column represents one of the successive stages or waves of diminishing increments of income, each row an income payment period. (The latter may be defined as the average time required for a dollar of income to flow from the hands of one recipient into the hands of the next. A number of estimates place this period for the United States at about three months.)[7]

Table 13.2

THE PROPAGATION OF INCOME:
A SINGLE INJECTION OF INVESTMENT

INCOME PAYMENT PERIOD	I	C_1	C_2	C_3	C_4
1	10				
2		5			
3			2.5		
4				1.25	
5					0.625

During the interval of, say, fifteen months for which this table gives definite figures, the total increase in income is equal to the sum of all the increments shown:

$$10 + 5 + 2.5 + 1.25 + 0.625 = 19.375$$

This can also be expressed in the form:

$$10 \ (1 + 1/2 + 1/2^2 + 1/2^3 + 1/2^4) = 19.375$$

[7] For his own and several other estimates, see Fritz Machlup, "Period Analysis and Multiplier Theory," *Quarterly Journal of Economics,* LIV (1939); reprinted in American Economic Association, *Readings in Business Cycle Theory,* The Blakiston Co., Philadelphia, 1944, pp. 213-5.

At each stage after the first, you will note that the original increment in investment, ΔI, is multiplied by an increasing power of the marginal propensity to consume ($\Delta C/\Delta Y$, or for brevity, c), which we have assumed to be $\frac{1}{2}$, but which could conceivably have any value between 0 and 1. Formulated in general terms, the total effect on income of an intial increase in investment, over an indefinite number (n) of income payment periods, can be expressed in the following equation:

$$\Delta Y = \Delta I \left(1 + c + c^2 + c^3 + c^4 \ldots + c^n\right)$$

The expression in parentheses may be reduced by mathematical manipulation to the following much simpler form: [8] $\dfrac{1}{1 - c}$

This is known as the "multiplier" (k) for a closed economy. From it we can tell immediately by how much income will be increased as a result of an initial change in any one of its components, such as I. For the current example, it is:

$$\Delta Y = \Delta I . \frac{1}{1 - c} = 10 . \frac{1}{1 - \frac{1}{2}} = 10 . 2 = 20$$

This means that with $c = \frac{1}{2}$, over an indefinite (infinite) period of time, any increase in I will cause Y to increase by twice that amount. Far the greater part of this effect will be felt, however, within a fairly short time. In our table, which covers only some 15 months, 19.375 out of a total increase of 20 will have been experienced; this is 96.875 per cent. If we lengthened our table to two years, the total effect would be 19.921875, which is 99.61 per cent of the ultimate total of 20. For practical purposes, therefore, we can ignore the very small changes that occur after eight or ten income periods.

Any Multiplicand Will Do

An expansion of income need not start with an increase in investment. It could equally well be initiated by a change in any other sector of income

---

[8] The derivation of the multiplier, k, or $\dfrac{1}{1-c}$, is as follows:

$k = 1 + c + c^2 + \ldots\ldots c^n$
$kc = c + c^2 + c^3 + \ldots c^n + 1$
$k - kc = 1 - c^n + 1$
$k(1 - c) = 1 - c^n + 1$
$k = \dfrac{1 - c^n + 1}{1 - c}$
When n is infinite,
$k = \dfrac{1}{1 - c}$

—in C, G, or X. A spontaneous increase is most likely to occur either in investment, because of a change in business men's estimates of the future; in government outlays, as when it is decided to expand public works to combat a depression; or in exports, following a reduction in foreign tariffs, or increased expenditure abroad out of rising incomes. These components of national income are more subject to independent change than is consumption, which is dependent upon or a function of income rather than independently determined.

Changes in the volatile components of national income may be down as well as up. Thus a decline of exports can inaugurate a multiplied contraction of income. The mechanism is the same as for expansion, but in reverse.

A Continuing Multiplicand

In our illustration, we have introduced only a single, once-for-all injection of increased investment, occurring in the first of our three-month income periods. We have seen that (with $c = \frac{1}{2}$) the total increase in income is twice the initial increment of investment, but that this effect is distributed over time, and that it gradually wears off and disappears. Suppose, however—and this is more realistic—that whatever change in the investment climate caused business men to expand their investment outlays leads them to maintain this increased investment. Our table would then look like this:

Table 13.3

**THE PROPAGATION OF INCOME:
A CONTINUING INJECTION OF INVESTMENT**

INCOME PAYMENT PERIOD	I	C_1	C_2	C_3	C_4	C_5	C_6	C_n
1	10							
2	10	5						
3	10	5	2.5					
4	10	5	2.5	1.25				
5	10	5	2.5	1.25	0.625			
•								
•								
n	10	5	2.5	1.25	0.625	0.3125	0.15625	 0

National income rises steadily in each period. By the fifth (after 15 months) it is higher than its starting level by 19.375; eventually its rise will reach the limit of 20 and remain there as long as investment stays at its new higher level.

The Import Leakage

We are now ready to take into account the leakage into imports and apply our analysis to an open economy. The required alteration is very simple. If the marginal propensity to consume includes, as it is usually taken to do, expenditure on imported goods as well as on domestic goods, in arriving at a value for the multiplier we must correct it for the expenditure that spills over into imports. We do this by introducing a further concept, the *marginal propensity to import,* that is, the proportion of any increase in income spent on imports.

Thus suppose that, continuing our illustration with a marginal propensity to consume of ½, the marginal propensity to import (m) is ¼. Then out of every $10 of additional income, $5 will leak off into savings and taxes, $5 will be spent on consumer goods. But if the marginal propensity to import is ¼, $2.50 out of the $10, or half the sum spent on consumer goods, will be directed toward the purchase of imports. The series of increments of income will be, not $10 + 5 + 2.5 + 1.25 + 0.625$ etc., as in Table 12.1, but $10 + 2.5 + 0.625 + 0.15625$ etc.

The total increase in income will be substantially less than when there was no leakage into imports. How much less? This depends upon the multiplier. For the closed economy, it was $\dfrac{1}{1 - c}$, which with $c = \frac{1}{2}$ gave a value of 2. But we must now diminish c by the value of m, the proportion of increased income directed toward imports, so our multiplier becomes: $\dfrac{1}{1 - (c - m)}$. Removing the parentheses, this is $\dfrac{1}{1 - c + m}$.

With $c = \frac{1}{2}$ and $m = \frac{1}{4}$, the multiplier takes the value of

$$\frac{1}{1 - \frac{1}{2} + \frac{1}{4}} = \frac{1}{\frac{3}{4}} = \frac{4}{3} = 1.33.$$

For each dollar of investment injected into the economy, national income will increase by a total of $1.33. Or take the values, $c = \frac{2}{3}$, $m = \frac{1}{3}$. Then the multiplier is

$$\frac{1}{1 - \frac{2}{3} + \frac{1}{3}} = \frac{1}{\frac{2}{3}} = \frac{3}{2} = 1.5.$$

With $c = \frac{3}{4}$, $m = \frac{1}{8}$, we get:

$$\frac{1}{1 - \frac{6}{8} + \frac{1}{8}} = \frac{1}{\frac{3}{8}} = \frac{8}{3} = 2.67.$$

A large value of the marginal propensity to consume will increase the multiplier, a large value of the marginal propensity to import will diminish it. For that part of increased income which is spent on domestic goods goes on generating a further rise in income, while that part which leaks abroad has no such (direct) effect.

Simplification of the Multiplier

The formula for the multiplier can be still further simplified. We do this by substituting for $1 - c$, the symbol "s." Since $1 - c$ represents the difference between a dollar of income and what is spent on consumption, or that part of a dollar of income that is diverted into domestic leakages (savings and taxes), we can say that s stands for these domestic leakages. The multiplier now becomes: $\frac{1}{s + m}$, of which the denominator may be said to stand for the sum of the leakages.

THE SIGNIFICANCE OF THE MULTIPLIER

Let us get away from the mechanical details of the multiplier for a moment, and see what its economic significance is. We start with a more favorable investment outlook, which stimulates business men to increase their outlay on capital goods. There occurs a direct increase in income and product, equal to the expenditure on investment. But the rise in income does not stop here; it goes on increasing, to an extent determined by the value of the marginal propensity to consume and the marginal propensity to import. Put in the alternative form of leakages, the total multiplying effect, or the value of the multiplier, depends on the proportion of increased income that is drained off into domestic and foreign leakages. The smaller are these leakages, the larger is the value of the multiplier.

Balance of Payments Effects

Another consequence of an increase in investment—or for that matter, in government expenditures, or exports—is also important. As national income increases, some part of the increase will be spent on imports. This is only to be expected, since with rising production, more foreign raw materials will be required, while out of the additional incomes, some part will be allocated to imports of bananas, coffee, and other items that are attractive to consumers. But this alters the country's balance of trade and services; with larger imports, its obligation to make international payments increases. Thus, suppose investment rises by 10. If the marginal propensity to consume is $\frac{3}{4}$ and the marginal propensity to import is $\frac{1}{4}$, the value of the multiplier is 2. National income will increase by 20. With a marginal propensity to import of $\frac{1}{4}$, the rise in imports will be 5. Thus an induced increase in income and production also causes an increase in a country's international payments.

A Word of Caution

Now for a word of caution. We must beware of using the marginal propensities to consume and to import too mechanically, and in particular of assuming that their values remain constant regardless of circumstances. Statistical data for the United States covering the period from the early 1920's to World War II, for example, give a marginal propensity to consume of approximately 0.8. This value, however, is an average for some twenty years. *Within* this period, the marginal propensity to consume fluctuated widely—it was much lower in the early years of the great depression of the thirties, when fear of unemployment afflicted those who were still employed, and higher in the late twenties, when business was buoyant and optimism ruled unchecked. The propensity to import, too, varies with circumstances. It will be high as an economy approaches full employment, when the possible increase in domestic output is small and any sizeable additional purchases must be made abroad. It will also tend to be high if the investment which stimulates a rise in income is predominantly in inventories, in which imported raw materials bulk relatively large, as contrasted with investment in building, which uses mainly domestic materials. The multiplier, the marginal propensity to consume, and the marginal propensity to import are all useful analytical tools, but unlike the tools of a craftsman, their size can change without our being aware of it. Practitioners making use of them in a concrete situation must recognise this possibility and always take it into account.

Finally, although the multiplier analysis can always be applied to a contraction of income, it is only valid for an expansion if there is room to expand. That is, if there is to occur a rise in real incomes as contrasted with money income and prices, there must be a reasonable amount of slack in the economy, in the form of unemployed resources. If there is not, then any force, such as increased exports or a rise in investment, which tends to raise income and employment, will merely cause an inflationary rise in prices. For then, total expenditure will exceed the value at current prices of the productive resources available, which is how we define an inflationary situation.

USES OF THE MULTIPLIER

Subject to the foregoing reservations, the multiplier, together with such related concepts as the marginal propensities to save and to import, can be a useful tool. In the first place, we can clarify the relation between a country's income and its imports and exports. If an increase in investment or in government expenditure stimulates a rise in income, we know that this expansion will continue until a limit, given by the value of the marginal propensity to consume and of the marginal propensity to import, is reached. And this increase in income in turn will affect the country's balance of payments. Imports will increase by the product of the marginal propensity to import and the increase in income.

Exports Generate Imports

Or suppose the rise in income originates with an expansion of exports. Income will rise by more than just the additional income payments in the export sector. $\Delta Y = k \Delta X$. Moreover, accompanying the rise in exports will be an indirect increase in imports. $\Delta M = m \Delta Y$. Except under very special conditions, the induced imports will be less than the rise in exports that set the whole process in operation. We can specify these special conditions precisely: imports will increase in an amount equal to the additional exports only if there are no domestic leakages; that is, only if none of the increased income is diverted into savings or taxes. Then our multiplier will have the value of $\dfrac{1}{m}$ instead of $\dfrac{1}{s + m}$. And imports will be the same proportion of the increase in income as are exports. Algebraically:

$$\Delta Y = k \Delta Y = \frac{1}{m} \Delta X$$
$$\Delta X = m \Delta Y$$
$$\Delta M = m \Delta Y$$

Use in Prediction

A second use of these concepts is practical rather than analytical. If after careful investigation we obtain values for c and m that we have good reason to believe reliable, we can use them for prediction. Since, as we have noted, these variables are likely to be unstable in the short run, we must use them with great caution. It is safer to apply them to long-run problems, as for example predicting the effect upon a country's balance of payments over a five- to ten-year period of a planned development program.

Propagation of the Business Cycle

Finally, the multiplier mechanism provides a basis for explaining the international transmission of business fluctuations. Suppose a depression occurs in an important country, owing perhaps to a collapse of domestic investment. Income declines sharply, and with it the country's imports. Since its imports are the exports of other countries, a decline of income is inaugurated abroad, its extent depending in each case upon the value of the multiplier (together, of course, with the amount of the shrinkage in exports). This induced decline of income in many countries means a decline in their imports, so the forces of contraction spread ever more widely, though with diminishing effect, since the induced decline in imports is in each instance smaller than the initial decline of exports.

A similar analysis can be used to show how a boom, starting in one country, is communicated to the rest of the world.

THE MULTIPLIER ALLOWING FOR FOREIGN REPERCUSSIONS

Our formal presentation of the multiplier has reckoned only with the changes in expenditure occurring within the borders of a single country. But we have just noted that a change in the income of one country is transmitted abroad through the induced change in its imports. If income in the United States rises, its imports will also rise, and stimulate an increase in income in the rest of the world. But if incomes abroad increase, imports there will rise, too, and some of these imports will come from the U.S., further reenforcing the rise in its income. We must take this foreign repercussion, or "play-back" effect, into account. To do so, we need merely expand our formula for the multiplier.

Since its derivation is rather complex, I shall give only the end result here.[9] The full multiplier, expressed in terms of leakages both at home and abroad is:

$$\frac{1}{s_a + m_a + m_b \cdot \dfrac{s_{a \cdot}}{s_b}}$$

[9] The derivation of the full multiplier is given in Machlup, *International Trade and the National Income Multiplier,* pp. 76-9, and in Kindleberger, *International Economics,* pp. 178-90.

The subscript "*a*" refers to the country in question, "*b*" to the rest of the world, while "*s*" and "*m*" have the now familiar meaning of domestic and foreign leakages.

SELECTED REFERENCES

Gordon, R. A., *Business Fluctuations* (Harper & Bros., New York, 1952). Chapters 2–4 provide an excellent statement of the relations between national income and its components, and a more detailed discussion of the multiplier than is given here.

Kindleberger, Charles P., *International Economics* (Richard D. Irwin, Inc., Homewood, Ill. 1953). Ch. 9 has a somewhat more elaborate presentation of the multiplier in relation to international trade than is given here, with numerous diagrammatic illustrations and a derivation of the foreign repercussion formula.

Machlup, Fritz, *International Trade and the National Income Multiplier* (The Blakiston Co., Philadelphia, Pa., 1943). This is still the most thorough and detailed discussion of the multiplier and its relation to foreign trade that is available. It takes into account many points omitted in this chapter for the sake of brevity.

Meade, James E., *The Balance of Payments* (Oxford University Press, 1951). Part II describes in detail the income and price effects of changes in domestic expenditures.

Nurkse, Ragnar, "Domestic and International Equilibrium," Ch. XXI of *The New Economics*, edited by Seymour E. Harris (Alfred A. Knopf, New York, 1947). A lucid account of the two-way relationship between national income and foreign trade, followed by a discussion of the issues that arise from the pursuit of full employment in a world of international trade.

Polak, J. J., "The Foreign Trade Multiplier"; Haberler, G., "Comment"; Polak and Haberler, "A Restatement," *American Economic Review*, **XXXVII** (1947). This discussion is chiefly concerned with the question of the suitable multiplicand to use when a change in exports causes national income to change.

Ruggles, Richard, *An Introduction to National Income and Income Analysis* (McGraw-Hill, New York, 1949). This is one of the clearest treatments of the topic that I know. I have followed its presentation in the early pages of this chapter.

14

THE BALANCE OF INTERNATIONAL PAYMENTS

One of the most important sources of information about a country's international economic position is its balance of international payments. This is a *summary statement of all the transactions between the residents of one country and the rest of the world.* It covers a given period of time, usually a year.

From the balance of payments, we can tell whether a country is having difficulty in meeting its international obligations and is being forced to draw on its reserves or to borrow, or whether its position is one of comparative ease. A good deal, too, can be learned about the character of a nation's economy from its balance of payments. In this chapter, we shall become acquainted with this important accounting statement and acquire some practice in using it.

THE BALANCE OF PAYMENTS ON CURRENT ACCOUNT

A country's balance of payments is intimately related to its gross national income and product. As we have seen, the latter includes, on the product side, only current production of goods and services, and on the money income side, the allocation of the income resulting from the production of these goods and services. Among the components of GNP is net foreign sales $(X - M)$, which reflects that part of total national product destined for foreign shores (exports) less the contribution to overall output that resulted from the productive efforts of foreigners (imports).

Taken by itself, this item $(X - M)$, of GNP is part of a country's total foreign transactions—that part derived from current production. This portion of the balance of payments is appropriately called the balance of payments on income or current account. As the name implies, it is set up in the form of a bookkeeping account. The various export items, which entitle the country to receive payments from others are on the "credit" side, and the import items, which oblige it to make payments to other countries, are on the "debit" side.

To acquaint you with how these items are classified and with the terms applied to them, the following schedule will be helpful. It lists under the headings of "debits" and "credits" the various goods and service items distinguished in the current account of the balances of payments published by the International Monetary Fund.

Components of Balance of Payments
on Current Account of Country A

DEBITS (PAYMENTS)

Merchandise imports (all goods imported from foreign sources).

Foreign travel (goods sold and services rendered to normal residents of A who are temporarily residing or traveling abroad).

Transportation (passenger or freight services rendered to residents of A by international carriers).

Insurance (premiums on insurance policies issued to residents of A by companies domiciled abroad, and indemnities on insurance policies issued to foreigners by companies domiciled in A).

Investment income (interest and dividends on securities of or property in A owned by residents of other countries).

Government (purchases of goods or services from foreigners by A's diplomatic or military establishments abroad, and any other government outlays abroad).

Miscellaneous (payments of account of motion picture royalties, telephone and telegraph service, management, engineers' and contractors' fees, etc.).

CREDITS (RECEIPTS)

Merchandise exports (all goods shipped to foreign destinations).

Foreign travel (goods sold and services rendered to foreigners travelling in or temporarily residing in A).

Transportation (passenger or freight services rendered to foreigners by firms in A engaged in the international carrying trade).

Investment income (interest and dividends on foreign securities or property owned by residents of A).

Insurance (premiums on insurance policies issued to foreigners by companies domiciled in A, and indemnities on insurance policies issued to residents of A by companies domiciled abroad).

Government (sales of goods or services to foreign diplomatic or military establishments in A, and other sales of goods or services to foreign governments).

Miscellaneous (earnings abroad on account of motion picture royalties, telephone, telegraph service, management, engineers' and contractors' fees, etc.).

A balance of payments tells us what international transactions a nation's residents carried out during a given period. It does not give this information in all the detail that characterised the original transactions, for to do so would require a statement of bewildering detail and complexity. A summary statement, which condenses a large number of individual transactions into categories such as those listed above, is much more comprehensible and therefore useful.

Balance of Payments Accounting

In constructing a balance of payments, the principles of double-entry bookkeeping are followed. The fundamental rule of bookkeeping is that every business transaction has two sides, both of which must be recorded. This simply reflects the economic principle underlying all business dealings: you pay for what you get, or, one never gets something for nothing. (Gifts present a special problem, to be considered shortly.) The balance of payments, which is simply the sum or aggregate of all of a nation's international transactions, therefore reflects this rule.

It is a convention of bookkeeping to charge, or debit, the owner of an account for everything he gets, and to credit him for everything he gives up. Thus if a merchant sells goods worth $100 and is paid in cash, his account would look like this:

Dr.	Merchant's Account		Cr.
Cash	$100	Merchandise	$100

He is credited for the merchandise with which he has parted, and debited for the cash he got in exchange.

Let us apply these rules to the balance of payments on current account of a country, with all the various service items listed above condensed, for the sake of simplicity, into a single entry. We shall assume that the country is one, like Venezuela, whose residents transact their foreign business mainly through New York banks, and that they pay for what they buy and are paid for what they sell with bank deposits in that city. Assume that the country (more accurately, its residents) imports goods to the value of $1,800 million, exports goods worth $2,300 million, that it renders services (shipping, foreign travel, etc.) amounting to $200 million and receives services from others totalling $300 million. The country's balance of payments on current account would then appear as follows:

Table 14.1

Dr.	Balance of Payments on Current Account of Country A, 1958		Cr.
	(million)		(million)
Increase in New York balances	$2,300	Merchandise exports	$2,300
Merchandise imports	1,800	Decrease in New York balances	1,800
Increase in New York balances	200	Services	200
Services	300	Decrease in New York balances	300
	$4,600		$4,600

The account balances, since each item is entered on both the debit and the credit side. The entries are few, since each condenses into an aggregate numerous individual transactions. (In practice, the "service" entries should be shown in at least the detail we used in our classification.) But we can usefully carry condensation one step further. To a large extent, the payments into and out of New York banks offset one another. In-payments total $2,500 million, out-payments $2,100 million. Since both kinds of payments refer to the same thing, deposits in New York banks, it will suffice if we subtract the smaller item from both sides and show only the net change.

A's international account would then take the following form:

Table 14.2

Dr.   Balance of Payments on Current Account of Country A, 1958   Cr.

	(million)		(million)
Merchandise imports	$1,800	Merchandise exports	$2,300
Services	300	Services	200
Net increase in New York balances:	400		
	$2,500		$2,500

Balance, Surplus, Deficit

The balance of payments still balances, as it must, since each side is the sum of equal opposing entries from which the same amount has been subtracted. But since total money payments received (in the form of New York deposits) as a result of the country's exports and services rendered to others exceed payments made on account of imports and services from the residents of other countries, A has something left over—a surplus. When, as in this instance, a country earns more from its exports and services than it spends for imports and similar services, it is common to speak of it as having a surplus on current account. When the imports or expenditures side exceeds the exports or earnings side, so that financial payments are larger than financial receipts, it is said to have a deficit on current account.

Foreign Balances in General

Had country A conducted part of its international business through London, or other financial centers, some of its in-payments for export items and of its out-payments for import items might have been made in pounds sterling or other currencies. Bank deposits in London, owned by banks in A, would then have been increased or diminished. Unless for some special reason it was desired to distinguish these from New York deposits, the balancing financial entry, or surplus in the current account would then be called by a more general name, such as "Net increase in foreign balances." (This, and all the items in the balance of payments, can be expressed in terms of dollars or of the country's own currency. For our purposes, it is immaterial.)

Foreign-Owned Domestic Balances

One more detail. Suppose A itself, like France or Switzerland, possessed an international financial center of some importance. Then it is likely that part of its transactions would have been settled in its own currency. This creates a difference, about which it is well to be clear. Imports of goods and services for which payment was made in A's currency would require importers in A to add to deposits held in A's banks by foreign banks. Exports similarly handled would require a transfer from those deposits to A's exporters, and thus a reduction of foreign-owned deposits. Whereas with transactions carried out through foreign financial centers, exports would increase A's foreign assets (bank deposits held abroad) and imports would *diminish* them, with transactions carried out in A's currency— through banks in its financial center—exports would *diminish* A's foreign *liabilities* (foreign-owned deposits in A's banks) and imports would increase them.

Transactions carried out in foreign currencies and in a country's own currency are usually distinguished in the balance of payments. Thus suppose that of A's exports of goods and services, $200 million had been paid for in its own currency, and of its imports, $100 million. This would have left a net reduction in the liability of A's banks to foreigners to be recorded. The increase in A's foreign balances would have been that much smaller, and its current account would take this form:

Table 14.3

Dr.   Balance of Payments on Current Account of Country A, 1958   Cr.

	(million)		(million)
Merchandise imports	$1,800	Merchandise exports	$2,300
Services	300	Services	200
Net increase in foreign balances	300		
Net decrease in balances due abroad	100		
	$2,500		$2,500

Change in Capital Position

Because payments received by country A for its export items exceed payments made to foreigners for import items, its foreign assets (bank balances abroad) have increased, its liabilities to foreigners (foreign-owned domestic balances) have decreased. When a change occurs in the net assets or liabilities of an accounting entity (a person, a corporation, or a nation), its capital position has altered.

This change can be expressed in a manner that throws additional light upon the country's international financial position. In the illustration before us, it is A's short-term capital position that has changed. It has extended $300 million in short-term loans to foreigners, since the increase in A's bank balances abroad are promises of foreign banks to pay money on demand. (Bank deposits are not money, but substitutes for money.) At the same time, A's banks have repaid $100 million of foreign short-term loans, since their promises to pay foreigners money on demand have been reduced by this amount. We can therefore say, as is often done, that A's short-term capital position had improved by $400 million, consisting of $300 million increase in short-term loans to foreigners and $100 million repayment of short-term debt to foreigners.

What if A's exports of goods and services, instead of exceeding similar imports by $400 million, had been smaller than the import items by $400 million? Instead of having something left over to improve its short-term capital position, A would have been short of meeting its required payments out of the receipts to which it was entitled. It would have a deficit on current account. This could be met by its banks drawing down their foreign balances (say by $300 million) and by their increasing domestic deposits held by foreigners. In place of the balancing debit entries shown above, there would be two balancing credit entries:

	Cr. (million)
Net decrease in foreign balances	$300
Net increase in balances due abroad	$100

A's short-term capital position would be worsened by $400 million through the repayment by foreign banks of $300 million of short-term debt to A's banks and the increase in the debt of A's banks to foreigners of $100 million.

DONATIONS OR GIFTS

We began this chapter by defining a balance of payments as a summary statement of all the transactions between the residents of one country and the rest of the world. We have surveyed those transactions that are directly related to the national income and product accounts. But nations (that is, their residents) also engage in lending and borrowing, and in the last twenty years especially, many transactions, both private and public, have been of the nature of gifts, or donations.

Accounting for Donations

Donations differ from ordinary business transactions such as are included in the current account in that they do not reflect an exchange of goods or services for money (or perhaps for goods, as in barter transactions, or for evidences of debt, as when exports are financed by long-term credits). Donations involve no *quid pro quo*. A person or a government transfers commodities or services or money to some other person or government, but receives nothing in exchange. Yet since in any system of accounts, all transactions must be accounted for, if any items have been given away, it is necessary that that fact be recorded. The method of doing so is to make an entry indicating the character of the gift on the side of the account opposite to the entry for the thing given or received. This not only "accounts" for the gift, but preserves balance in the accounts.

Thus suppose that a wealthy individual gives his daughter, on her marriage, a house and lot. This would be shown in his personal account as follows:

Dr.	Account of Mr. Wellfixed	Cr.
Gift to daughter $35,000		Real estate $35,000

This records the fact that (1) Mr. Wellfixed has parted with real estate valued at $35,000, and that (2) he has received no cash or other *quid pro quo*, but instead has made a gift of this property.

Donations in the Balance of Payments

The category of donations in a nation's balance of payments includes a wide variety of transactions: military aid, economic aid, technical assistance, immigrants' remittances, charitable contributions of churches or organisations such as CARE, and also such compulsory donations as reparations and indemnities. Frequently the term "unilateral transfers" is applied to these transactions to indicate their one-sided character.

Such transfers are recorded in a country's balance of payments in the manner already indicated. If the country has furnished military or capital equipment to another nation on an aid basis, those goods will be entered among its exports on the credit side, and an offsetting entry will be made on the debit side, to indicate that no payment was received for them, but that they were gifts. Thus suppose that of country A's exports of $2,300 million, $100 million were machinery and equipment donated as economic aid to underdeveloped countries. This would reduce by a like amount the net receipts from exports and would require a debit entry to record the fact that a donation had been made. A's balance of payments would be altered to look like this:

Table 14.4

Dr.   Balance of Payments on Current Account of Country A, 1958   Cr.

	(million)		(million)
Merchandise imports	$1,800	Merchandise exports	$2,300
Services	300	Services	200
Net increase in foreign balances	200		
Net decrease in balances due abroad	100		
Donations:			
Official	100		
	$2,500		$2,500

Where the donation consists, not of goods or services, as in the preceding illustration, but of money, as is the case with immigrants' remittances and some government transfers, the transaction is treated in the same way. Thus, if A's donations had all been made by private individuals or organisations, the only change in the balance of payments would be that the donations would be entitled "Private" instead of "Official." If all of these gifts consisted of remittances of foreign deposits to relatives or charitable organisations abroad, the entry would record the fact that $100 million of the $400 million surplus in the current account, which otherwise would improve A's short-term capital position by this amount, had been purchased by residents of A for transfer to foreigners.

THE CAPITAL ACCOUNT

Whereas the current account records all transactions relating to a country's current international income and current expenditures (including donations), the capital account records transactions that affect its international debtor-creditor position.

Current Account Balance Goes to the Capital Account

A few pages earlier we noted that when the payments received for goods and services exported exceeded the payments made for goods and services imported, A's current account had a surplus. This took the form of an increase in foreign balances owned by A's banks, together with a decrease in the indebtedness of A's banks to foreigners. We also called attention to the fact that this meant that A's position as an international debtor or creditor had altered; its international capital position (short-term) had changed.

If we are logical with respect to the classification of the various items in A's balance of payments, the net change in its capital position should be recorded in the capital account. Since this is the practice generally followed, we shall bring the net change in A's short-term capital position (net increase in foreign balances, $200 million, plus net decrease in balances due abroad, $100 million) down into the capital account. A's balance of payments now takes on the following appearance:

Table 14.5

Dr.	Balance of Payments of A, 1958		Cr.
CURRENT ACCOUNT			
	(million)		(million)
Merchandise imports	$1,800	Merchandise exports	$2,300
Services	300	Services	200
Donations:			
Official	100		
	2,200		2,500
CAPITAL ACCOUNT			
Short-term Capital			
(net change)	300		
	$2,500		$2,500

Normal Capital Movements

In addition to such capital transactions as this (which we may note in passing is the *result* of all the other transactions), individuals, corporations, and governments frequently engage deliberately in international borrowing, lending, and investing. Normally these transactions result from ordinary calculations of gain or loss; therefore the movement of funds tends to be from countries where the return on capital (after allowing for the element of risk) is low, toward countries where the return is higher. Owing, however, to the fact that different individuals may evaluate returns or the risks to be taken differently, and also to the fact that some may prefer security to a high return, capital is usually observed moving into and out of a country simultaneously. The net movement, however, is generally from nations relatively well-supplied with capital, where the return on investments is comparatively low, and toward countries where capital is scarce and the yield high.

Long-Term Loans or Investments

When the residents of a nation lend or invest abroad at long-term, they exchange their liquid money capital for foreign bonds, stocks, or physical assets (plant and equipment) with a maturity or term until repayment that is either indefinite or longer than a year. When, on the other hand, they borrow abroad or attract foreign investment, they acquire liquid money capital in exchange for their own bonds, stocks, or physical capital of long-term or indefinite maturity.

Foreign investment by the residents of a given nation, say A, thus results in their importing securities, for which—at the time they are acquired—they have to pay. A perfectly appropriate entry in the balance of payments would be a debit in the capital account to "security imports," which has the advantage of referring specifically to what is being imported and thus has to be paid for. The corresponding credit is to foreign balances (decreased) or to foreign-owned domestic balances (increased). Since we have already characterised these balances as short-term capital, what occurs in this kind of a transaction is that long-term assets of the investors are increased, their short-term assets decreased (or short-term liabilities increased).

Although debiting "security imports" would be an appropriate way of entering a long-term loan or investment, it is not the usual one. Many writers prefer to use the term "long-term capital export." This has the advantage of calling attention to the direction of the capital flow, but it tends to be confusing, since exports of commodities entitle the exporter to receive a payment, whereas exports of capital require the exporter to make a payment. The International Monetary Fund uses the neutral term "long-term capital" as a general heading, then lists under this the different kinds of capital transactions (see below). If the country in question is lending or investing abroad—exporting capital—the entries appear on the debit side of its balance of payments. If the transactions involve borrowing, or importing capital in any manner, they of course appear as a credit.

Types of Long-Term Investment

There are three main types of long-term investment: direct investment, portfolio investment, and amortisation. Direct investment includes the acquisition of stocks or bonds of firms abroad in which the investors own a controlling interest, as well as real estate or physical assets which become the property of such firms. Portfolio investment covers all other stocks and bonds, such as the obligations of governments or the securities of firms in which the investor does not have a controlling interest. Amortisation refers to the repurchase or retirement of securities previously sold to foreigners. As with direct or portfolio investment, there is an import of securities and an export of capital by the investors; the securities imported, however, are not foreign issues, but domestic issues previously sold abroad and now being retired.

One special type of direct investment deserves attention. Suppose a firm in the United States exports equipment for installation in a branch plant abroad. These goods will be recorded in the U.S. balance of payments among exports; this implies that the exporting firm is entitled to receive a payment. It receives no such payment, however. Instead, it increases the value of its assets abroad. This should be shown as a debit entry under direct investment.

Short-Term Capital Movements

We have already encountered short-term capital movements in the net increase or decrease in a country's short-term capital position resulting from a surplus or deficit in the current account.[1] But short-term capital movements are also undertaken for their own sake, just as are long-term capital movements.

Three types of short-term capital transactions may be distinguished in terms of the motives that cause them: (1) An individual may be stimulated to purchase foreign short-term securities (treasury bills, commercial bills, bankers' acceptances) because he can earn a higher return on them than he can on similar short-term investments at home. Such capital transactions may be said to be income-motivated; (2) Anticipated changes in the international value of a particular country's currency (i.e., changes in the exchange rates on this currency) may lead some people to seek gain from buying it when they think it is cheap, or selling it when they believe it to be dear. Such transactions are speculative in nature; (3) Fear of war, of political instability, or of inflation may lead the residents of a country, or foreigners holding assets in that country, to seek to liquidate fixed assets

---

[1] Actually, every transaction in the current account, or for that matter, any transaction, involves a short-term capital movement if it is currently settled, or paid for. This is because the means by which transactions are settled is bank deposits, either foreign or domestic, and bank deposits are a liability of the bank in which they are held, an asset to the person who holds them. Since the greater part of payments and receipts resulting from current account transactions offset one another, our attention was focussed upon the net receipts or net payments, which reflect the net change in the country's short-term capital position.

and to transfer these and other liquid assets abroad. Such transactions are fear-motivated.

Short-Term Capital Movements and the Balance of Payments

Whatever the motive underlying a short-term capital movement, the effect on a country's balance of payments is the same. If residents of France, for example, acquire short-term assets in the United States (Treasury bills, or perhaps just dollar deposits), the purchase of these assets will be entered in France's balance of payments as a debit to short-term capital, to indicate what has been acquired. (This is the Fund's practice; some would call the debit entry "short-term capital export.") The corresponding payment made will be a credit in the balance of payments; it will consist of a reduction in French-owned deposits in New York or an increase in foreign-owned deposits in Paris. Thus, the end result of a short-term capital movement would appear to be a mere swapping of one kind of short-term foreign asset for another, or possibly of a foreign asset for a domestic liability to foreigners.

There is more to it than this, however. Who owns the foreign assets can be important, and short-term capital movements may cause changes in the ownership of those assets that will be to a country's disadvantage. To clarify this point, let us again introduce A's balance of payments into the discussion.

As we last left it, the only item in the capital account was a debit of $300 million, representing a net improvement in A's short-term capital position ($200 million increase in foreign balances, $100 million decrease in foreign-owned domestic balances). Before proceeding with short-term capital transactions, let us assume that investors in A have made long-term loans or investments abroad to the amount of $300 million, and that foreigners have invested in $50 million of long-term assets in A. The purchase by A's residents of foreign securities is a debit to long-term capital (private); the payment for these may be presumed to have been made by exhausting A's $200 million of foreign balances and by adding $100 million to foreign holdings of domestic deposits. This import of securities (or export of capital) would wipe out the net change in short-term capital, replacing that entry in the balance of payments. If the foreigners who are investing $50 million in A pay for the exported securities by turning over foreign balances to A's banks or by drawing down their holdings of A balances, a short-term capital debit of $50 million will reappear, along with a $50 million credit to long-term capital (export of securities, or import of capital). A's revised balance of payments will now appear as follows:

Table 14.6

| Dr. | | Balance of Payments of A, 1958 | | Cr. |

CURRENT ACCOUNT

	(million)		(million)
Merchandise imports	$1,800	Merchandise exports	$2,300
Services	300	Services	200
Donations:			
Official	100		
	2,200		2,500

CAPITAL ACCOUNT

Short-term capital			
(official)	50		
Long-term capital	300	Long-term capital	50
	$2,550		$2,550

The net change in short-term capital for the year 1958, as a result of the additional long-term capital transactions, is now only $50 million. If in the form of foreign balances, these are presumably held by A's central bank. Although originally acquired by commercial banks in A from exporters of goods and securities, who in turn will have been paid by these banks in domestic currency or deposits, it is the practice for commercial banks doing a foreign business to maintain minimum working balances abroad. When these balances rise, owing to an excess of exports over imports or to the sale abroad of domestic securities, the commercial banks will generally turn them over to the central bank, receiving for them the equivalent in central bank deposits. The central bank of a country is much more likely to allow its holding of foreign balances to vary widely.

Movements of Short-Term Capital

Suppose now that, owing to a rise in short-term interest rates in some foreign financial center (say B) above the level current in A, A's commercial banks decide to lend $50 million in that money market. They will purchase foreign balances from the central bank with a check drawn against their reserve deposit, then invest the B funds so acquired in treasury bills or other suitable short-term assets.

The effect on A's balance of payments is nil; there has been a transfer of ownership of foreign short-term assets from the central bank to commercial banks, that is all. Since in most countries today the commercial banks engaging in foreign transactions are subject to the control of the monetary authorities, this change in ownership is seldom important. That the foreign assets are now in the form of B's treasury bills instead of bank deposits is of little moment, for such bills are almost as liquid as deposits.

It is different if the export of capital is undertaken, not by banks, but by private persons. For then, foreign balances hitherto under the control of the monetary authorities pass into the hands of individuals over whom they have no control. Those balances cease to be part of the country's international reserves (see below) and thus available to the authorities in case of need.

Commercial banks are by all odds the most important exporters and importers of short-term capital to take advantage of interest-rate differentials. Short-term capital movements by private individuals are far more likely to be speculative or fear-motivated. If they are so small that they do not seriously deplete the central bank's holdings of foreign balances, they can be ignored. If large, they may raise serious problems.

Assume, for example, that serious inflation got under way in A during 1958, the year to which our balance of payments refers, and that as a consequence a flight of capital develops. Individuals and firms in A want to transfer $500 million of domestic funds into balances in foreign centers that are free of inflation. To do so, they surrender domestic currency and deposits to their commercial banks, which—if they adhere to the practice of maintaining only working balances abroad—will have to obtain the desired foreign balances from the central bank. If A's international transactions are free of controls, that institution will provide the desired balances to the extent of its ability. But suppose that, in addition to the $50 million of such balances previously acquired during 1958, it has only $250 million in foreign deposits available. It surrenders these, and to supply the remaining $200 million, must withdraw gold from its reserves and ship it abroad, where it is deposited. These deposits, too, are turned over to the persons who are exporting capital. A's balance of payments is changed as follows:

Table 14.7

Dr.	Balance of Payments of A, 1958		Cr.
	CURRENT ACCOUNT		
	(million)		(million)
Merchandise imports	$1,800	Merchandise exports	$2,300
Services	300	Services	200
Donations:			
Official	100		
	2,200		2,500
	CAPITAL ACCOUNT		
Short-term capital		Short-term capital	
(private)	500	(official)	250
Long-term capital	300	Long-term capital	50
		Gold exports	200
	$3,000		$3,000

Private individuals have transmitted capital of $500 million, as is shown by the debit entry of this amount. It represents the foreign balances acquired by these individuals. The former entry, "Short-term capital (official), $50 million," on the debit side, has disappeared. This addition to the central bank's foreign holdings, acquired earlier in 1958, has been turned over to the private exporters of capital. The credit entry of $250 million under "Short-term capital (official)" reflects the reduction in the central bank's previously held foreign assets, now transferred to private individuals in A. Gold exports of $200 million are a credit, since they require a payment of this amount to residents of A. The payment is $200 million more of foreign balances; it appears as part of the $500 million of the debit to private short-term capital.

This large fear-motivated movement of capital has two important consequences: it seriously reduces the country's international reserves, and it changes a balance of payments with a modest surplus to one with a substantial deficit. Both these topics require further examination. Let us begin by explaining more fully the meaning of a deficit and a surplus in a country's balance of payments.

DEFICIT, SURPLUS, AND RESERVES

Meaning of Deficit and Surplus

We first encountered these terms when discussing the current account of the balance of payments. A surplus in the current account was said to arise when receipts from exports of goods and services exceeded payments for similar items. Similarly, a deficit was taken to mean an excess of such payments over corresponding receipts.

To make these concepts unambiguous when applied to the balance of payments as a whole, *it is well to distinguish between transactions that are undertaken for their own sake,* for the profit they entail or the satisfaction they give (autonomous transactions) *and those that result from these* (induced transactions). Thus, referring again to the current account, exports and imports of goods and services are undertaken for the sake of the profit to be made—they are autonomous transactions. When they differ, there is an induced increase or decrease in foreign balances—a short-term capital movement—that is *not* undertaken for its own sake, but which results from the relative size of exports or imports. Depending upon which set of autonomous transactions is larger, the induced capital movement is a surplus or a deficit.

Of the other balance of payments transactions considered, donations are voluntary and deliberate in character. So too are long-term capital movements, whether exports or imports. Short-term capital movements motivated by the desire to earn a higher return, to make a speculative gain, or to get one's capital into a safer place must also be classed as autonomous or made for their own sake.

This leaves, in the illustration before us, only gold movements and official short-term capital movements. These clearly are the result of the other transactions. A's central bank reduced its foreign balances, not from any decision of its own, but because of the pressure on the balance of payments. It exported gold, too, in response to the balance of payments situation.

We conclude that *a deficit appears in a balance of payments when autonomous transactions requiring payments exceed autonomous transactions involving receipts.* By the same token, a surplus exists when autonomous transactions giving rise to receipts exceed autonomous transactions requiring payments.

International Reserves

The *induced* transactions, in our illustration, were movements of reserves. This is always the case. International reserves serve the purpose of filling in a gap in a balance of payments. And we can measure the size of a surplus or a deficit by the volume of reserve movements. This makes it necessary to be clear as to what constitutes such a movement. The following descriptive list uses the concept of reserve movements developed by the International Monetary Fund.[2]

Components of International Reserve Movements

Monetary gold. Only movements of gold into or out of the holdings of the monetary authorities (treasury, central bank, or exchange stabilisation fund) are counted. Shipments of gold by producers (e.g., South African mines) or to manufacturers, or movements into or out of private hoards, are classed as ordinary commodity exports and imports.

Foreign currency or bank deposits held by the monetary authorities, or by commercial banks subject to their control (official holdings).

[2] Since we are concerned here with international reserves as they are used to finance a deficit or a surplus in a country's balance of payments, it is appropriate to limit ourselves to defining reserve movements rather than the total of international reserves in a country's possession at any time. This approach also avoids the need for an elaboration of such distinctions as that between a country's total gold holdings and the portion required by law to be held as a currency reserve, and that between total short-term liabilities to foreigners and the actual or probable use of them in financing balance of payments deficits or surpluses. For a discussion of these problems, see International Monetary Fund, *Balance of Payments Yearbook 1938-1946-1947* (Washington, D. C., 1949), pp. 4-23.

Short-term foreign claims, officially held, which can be readily liquidated at a stable price (such as treasury bills and bank acceptances). Both this item and foreign bank deposits are reserves in the fullest sense if they are in convertible currencies. When they are in currencies subject to limited transferability their reserve quality is of course impaired.

Domestic bank deposits held by foreign monetary authorities and banks.

Domestic short-term claims, similarly held. These two items are the counterpart of foreign reserves; changes in them serve to finance a deficit or surplus.

Sale of long-term securities officially held (including any requisitioned from private owners by the Government). Purchases would not appear here, since purchases of long-term securities would merely represent a shift of foreign assets of low yield into a higher yielding form.

Use of International Monetary Fund resources.

The Financing of Deficits and Surpluses

The method by which a deficit or surplus in the balance of payments is financed varies with the kind of currency and exchange system in force.

Under the international gold standard of pre-1914 days, deficits or surpluses and the means of financing them appeared simultaneously. The financing was automatic, and took the form, almost exclusively, of gold movements. Commercial banks maintained convenient working balances of foreign deposits, which they allowed to vary very little. When the United States, for example, had a surplus in its international account, and the United Kingdom a deficit, bank balances accumulated in London to the credit of New York banks. Ordinarily the latter would convert these into gold for import into the United States.[3] This gold movement financed the U.S. surplus, and at least part of the U.K. deficit.

On such occasions, the Bank of England frequently took action to check the outflow of gold by raising its discount rate, thus forcing up market rates. At the higher level of interest rates in London, New York banks found it profitable to leave their accumulating balances there, and lend them in the market. An American export of short-term capital (import of British short-term obligations) replaced the gold flow. From the viewpoint of the United States, this capital movement was undertaken for its own sake, to earn a higher return. As an additional autonomous item in the U.S. balance of payments, it reduced or perhaps eliminated the surplus needing to be financed. From the viewpoint of the United Kingdom, however, there can be no doubt that the import of capital was deliberately engineered as a preferred alternative to gold exports as a means of financing the

---

[3] The actual procedure was more indirect than this, but came to the same thing. It is explained in Chapter 17.

deficit. Britain's short-term borrowing was undertaken not for its own sake, but because the deficit had to be financed.

A second and very different situation with regard to unbalanced international payments arises when exchange rates are free to fluctuate, instead of being held steady through the linkage of currencies to gold. For then, any tendency toward an excess of autonomous receipts over payments, with a consequent accumulation of foreign balances, would be counteracted by a fall in the value of foreign currencies. Imports are cheapened, exports become more expensive to foreign buyers, and the surplus simply disappears. No compensatory financing is needed.

Another kind of situation arises when, as in most of the world today, governments exercise effective controls over international payments. They do so through quantitative restrictions on imports, together with controls over the uses to which foreign receipts may be put. Nations equipped with such regulatory apparatus can, within broad limits, have a deficit as small as their control authorities wish to make it. Whatever deficit arises is then deliberately planned; it is the task of the monetary authorities to determine how it is to be financed. Their action, which is called "compensatory official financing," involves choosing between the different kinds of reserve movements to be permitted—for example, drawing upon foreign balances, liquidating officially held foreign assets, exporting gold, or acquiring a drawing right from the International Monetary Fund. Compensatory official financing may also include, in addition to use of various components of international reserves, loans specifically arranged for the purpose of meeting a deficit in a country's balance of payments. The Anglo-American loan of 1946 was of this character; so were most of the loans of the Export-Import Bank and of the International Bank to European governments after the last war, as well as a large proportion of American aid to Europe.

WHAT A BALANCE OF PAYMENTS SHOWS

As we noted at the beginning of this chapter, a balance of payments is an extremely useful aid to economic analysis, for by examining it, we can learn much about the strength or weakness of a country's international position. Particularly revealing is a series of balances of payments for successive years, or a pair of statements at the beginning and end of an interval of time during which important changes have occurred; by comparing these statements we can perceive in some detail both the character and the magnitude of the change. Even though the balance of payments itself may not tell us *why* the change took place, examination of its components may suggest where we can obtain further information as to the causes.

Table 14.8

BALANCE OF INTERNATIONAL PAYMENTS OF THE
UNITED STATES, 1955

DEBIT		CURRENT TRANSACTIONS	CREDIT
Merchandise imports	$11,516	Merchandise exports	$14,264
Foreign travel	1,155	Foreign travel	645
Transportation	1,202	Transportation	1,336
Investment income	512	Investment income	2,512
Government	3,190	Government	333
Insurance & miscellaneous	489	Insurance & miscellaneous	825
Sub-total	18,064	Sub-total	19,915
(Net credit balance on current transactions	1,851)		
Donations:			
Private	456		
Official	1,865		
		(Net debit balance before capital transactions	470)
	CAPITAL AND MONETARY GOLD		
Short-term capital	537	Short-term capital	560
Long-term capital	918	Long-term capital	873
		Monetary gold	41
		Errors and omissions	451
Total	$21,840	Total	$21,840

Source: International Monetary Fund Balance of Payments Yearbook, February 1957. In addition to the above, goods and services totalling $2,134 million were transferred under military aid programs.

Looking at the United States balance of payments for 1955, we see that exports of goods and services substantially exceeded similar imports, providing an apparent surplus on current transactions of $1,851 million. This surplus was fictitious, however, since not only were exports and services of this amount provided to foreigners without payment (principally as military aid), but an additional net sum of $470 million was turned over as a donation.

This amount, plus an autonomous debit of $45 million for net long-term capital movements (U.S. investment abroad, $918 million, less sales of U.S. government bonds and other securities to foreigners, $873 million), or $515 million in all, had somehow to be covered by compensatory financing. Relatively little of this financing is actually accounted for: $23 million from net short-term capital movement,[4] and $41 million from gold exports. All the rest—$451 million—is unexplained; it shows up in "errors and omissions." This is in all likelihood to be traced mainly to unreported changes in short-term capital items, since these are the most subject to error, although a considerable part of the error may be scattered among the other elements of the balance of payments.

In spite of the current account and over-all deficit in the U.S. balance of payments for 1955, that nation's position was, to say the least, comfortable. It was able to donate the entire surplus from current transactions and to finance an additional half billion dollars in gifts mainly, it would seem, by changes in bank balances at home and abroad.

Contrast with the comfortable U.S. balance of payments that of France in 1947. At that time France desperately needed imports of many kinds

Table 14.9

BALANCE OF PAYMENTS OF FRANCE (FRANC AREA), 1947

DEBIT	CURRENT TRANSACTIONS		CREDIT
Merchandise imports	$2,497	Merchandise exports	$1,093
Foreign travel	51	Foreign travel	57
Transportation	427	Transportation	104
Investment income	68	Investment income	148
Government	48	Government	2
Insurance & miscellaneous	159	Insurance & miscellaneous	158
Sub-total	3,249	Sub-total	1,562
		(Net debit balance, goods and services	1,687)
	MOVEMENT OF CAPITAL AND MONETARY GOLD		
Private		Private	
		Short-term capital	81
Long-term capital	15	Long-term capital	5
Government and banking institutions:		Government & banking institutions:	
		Short-term capital	744
Long-term capital	361	Long-term capital	794
		Monetary gold	438
		Errors and omissions	1
Total	$3,625	Total	$3,625

Source: International Monetary Fund, *Balance of Payments Yearbook, 1938-1946-1947.* As presented here, the data have been rearranged and consolidated to a minor extent.

---

[4] Short-term capital credits or imports of $560 million were principally in the form of an increase in the liabilities of U.S. banks to foreigners, while short-term capital debits or exports of $537 million represented mainly increases in U.S. balances in foreign banks.

to keep her economy going. On the other hand, her ability to produce exports was at low ebb, owing to the destruction and disorganisation caused by World War II. These facts are reflected in a total for imports almost two-and-a-half times as great as the value of exports, which in large part accounts for the deficit in current transactions of $1,687 million.

To obtain France's total deficit, we add to this the private and public long-term capital exports of $376 million, and subtract the $86 million of private capital imports, for a net addition of $290 million. Together with the deficit on current account, this makes the over-all deficit $1,977 million. To meet this deficit, France was forced to borrow heavily and to export gold. The large ($794 million) debt item under long-term capital reflects, in the main, loans to France by the Export-Import Bank of the United States and by the International Bank for Reconstruction and Development, made for the purpose of financing France's deficit. Official short-term borrowing (net) of $744 million is accounted for principally by French borrowing from the International Monetary Fund and by a reduction of foreign balances.

Contrast France's international position in 1954 with this unfavorable state of affairs. Imports have increased only moderately over 1947, while

Table 14.10
BALANCE OF PAYMENTS OF FRANCE (FRANC AREA), 1954

DEBIT		CURRENT TRANSACTIONS	CREDIT
Merchandise imports	$2,724	Merchandise exports	$2,545
Foreign travel	121	Foreign travel	182
Transportation	211	Transportation	137
Investment income	146	Investment income	121
Government	65	Government	582
Insurance & miscellaneous	310	Insurance & miscellaneous	261
Sub-total	3,577	Sub-total	3,828
(Net credit balance, goods and services	251)		
Donations	10	Donations	509
(Net balance, current transactions	750)		
		CAPITAL AND MONETARY GOLD	
Private, short-term capital	121	Private, long-term capital	55
Official & banking institutions:			
Short-term capital	581		
Long-term capital	136		
Monetary gold	6	Errors and omissions	39
Total	$4,431	Total	$4,431

Source: International Monetary Fund, *Balance of Payments Yearbook*, Vol. 6, 1953-54.

exports have expanded almost two-and-a-half times. Foreign travel in France has recovered, providing net earnings of $61 million, transportation charges have been cut in half, and income from this source has risen slightly. Only "insurance and miscellaneous" and payments on investment income have moved unfavorably. Moreover, France is earning $582 million from foreign government expenditures in the country, chiefly U.S. outlays on military projects and military equipment.

As a result of these favorable changes, in 1954, France's goods and services account shows a surplus of $251 million instead of a deficit of $1,687 million. When to this is added $509 million of donations (chiefly U.S. economic aid, but also including a special grant of $89 million from the European Payments Union), there is a surplus of credit on current transactions of $750 million.

France used this credit balance for investment abroad; this took the form of repayment of long-term loans to the United States, the United Kingdom and Canada, repayment of a large short-term debt to the European Payments Union, and the acquisition of foreign balances and the reduction of franc balances in the hands of foreigners. Everything considered, France's balance of payments in 1954 was in good shape, even though most of the loan repayments undertaken depended in large part on donations of a half-billion dollars.

WHAT A BALANCE OF PAYMENTS DOES NOT SHOW

Effects of Controls

As the preceding illustrations demonstrate, a country's balance of payments can be highly informative. It shows clearly whether it is paying its way internationally on its current transactions, so to speak, or whether to balance its imports of goods and services it is being forced to borrow abroad heavily or to export large amounts of gold. But it may not always reveal whether a country is having difficulty in balancing its imports and exports. For example, imports may be subject to artificial controls. Then a country's balance of payments might show current transactions in substantial balance, with no increase in its international indebtedness. Yet it might be maintaining an apparently satisfactory position only by the imposition of rigorous restrictions on its imports. To analyse and understand a situation such as this, it is necessary to go behind the balance of payments and acquire information as to its trade policy and how it affects its international payments.

Lack of Detail

For many analytical purposes, balances of payments, as published, provide insufficient detail. Thus merchandise trade, both exports and imports, is shown in aggregate form; there is no breakdown as to types of commodities or as to origin or destination of the goods-movements. Yet often such information can be revealing. Changes in the composition of a country's exports may stem from a deep-seated change in its economic structure, or they may simply reflect a shift in commercial policy. It is important to trace such changes, and to know what lies behind them. To obtain a commodity classification of a country's trade, one has to go to the detailed trade figures published by many nations. These must also be consulted if one needs to know a good deal about origins and destinations of trade, although the IMF *Balance of Payments Yearbook* publishes supplementary balances of payments giving a breakdown of all transactions by major areas. When currencies are inconvertible, as most of them have been since about 1931, whether a country sells to the United States or to Argentina or Egypt may be just as important as whether it has a credit or a debit balance on current account.

The Balance of International Indebtedness

One thing a balance of payments does not show, and that it may be important to know, is a country's over-all balance of indebtedness. This is the total of its investments in securities and property in other countries, less the total of such investments by foreigners in the country in question. Such information can be useful for estimating a country's net earnings from overseas investment income or for calculating what liquid funds it could raise in a crisis, as on the outbreak of war. Together with known investment income, it provides a check on the average yield on the country's foreign investments. Such information has to be obtained through a separate inquiry or inventory of foreign long-term assets and liabilities. We cannot expect to get it from the balance of payments, since that includes, on the one hand, that part of the gross national product derived from net sales abroad, and on the other hand, *changes* in the country's foreign assets and liabilities, both short- and long-term.

SELECTED REFERENCES

Badger, Donald G., "The Balance of Payments: A Tool of Analysis," *IMF Staff Papers*, Vol. II, No. 1 (Sept. 1951). A detailed discussion of the International Monetary Fund's method of presenting balances of payments, together with a reply to Machlup's criticism (see below) of the concept of compensatory official financing.

"The Adequacy of Monetary Reserves," *IMF Staff Papers*, Vol. III, No. 2 (Oct. 1953). A discussion of the meaning of international reserves and the concept of adequacy.

International Monetary Fund, *Balance of Payments Manual* (Washington, D. C., 1950). Detailed instructions for preparing balance of payments statements.

International Monetary Fund, *Balance of Payments Yearbook 1938-1946-1947* (Washington, D. C., 1949). In addition to the balances of payments of member countries, this number of the yearbook contains an extended discussion of the concepts underlying the Fund's presentation of balance of payments data.

Machlup, Fritz, "Three Concepts of the Balance of Payments and the So-Called Dollar Shortage," *Economic Journal*, **LX** (Mar. 1950). Draws a careful distinction between a market balance, a program balance, and an accounting balance of payments, on the basis of which the concept of compensatory official financing is criticised.

"Oskaloosa vs. the U. S.," *Fortune*, April 1938. An interesting application of the concept of a balance of payments to the trade and financial relations of this Iowa town.

U. S. Department of Commerce, *Balance of Payments of the United States, 1949-1951*. Contains a detailed discussion of the methods used in balance of payments accounting, how the data are collected, the sources of data, and how data are arranged in the Department's presentation.

15

FOREIGN EXCHANGE

One of the features that distinguishes international trade from trade within a country is that each nation has its own currency and its own banking system. Prices in each country are reckoned in the country's own currency units—in dollars, pounds, francs, marks, lire, pesos, rupees, and so on. To the inhabitants of one country, the currencies of others are usually almost as unfamiliar as their languages.

Within a single country, its currency moves freely. Purchasing power can be transferred over considerable distances through the use of checks on a local bank, and the great bulk of these payments are cleared against one another, assisted either by relationships established between banks in different parts of the country or by the central bank acting as a clearing agency.

It is the necessity of making payments at a distance *and* in different currencies that raises the problem of foreign exchange. Exporters, as they sell their goods abroad, acquire claims in an alien currency. But since they must pay wages and other costs in their own national money, they need a means of exchanging the foreign money for their own. Importers confront the same problem—they must pay for goods from foreign lands, but they have only local currency to do it with.

THE FOREIGN EXCHANGE MARKET

It is the foreign exchange market that in any country provides the needed facilities. This is not a place, like a produce market, where buyers and sellers confront one another face to face. The people who participate in it have highly specialised jobs in the foreign departments of banks, or in the offices of brokers or dealers, and they are in constant touch with one another by telephone. Because communication is so easy, all dealers quote the same price for each currency, which is the test of a unified market.

Dealings, of course, are in foreign currencies. Into the foreign exchange market comes a supply of all the currencies on which a country has claims —from exporters, borrowers who are selling domestic securities abroad, sellers of services, and at times, speculators. The demand comes from those having to make foreign payments—importers, buyers of services or foreign securities, and perhaps speculators as well. Either in the market of the particular country or in some related foreign exchange market abroad, depending upon the specific method used to finance an international trans· action, both sides of the country's balance of payments meet in day-to-day purchases and sales of foreign exchange.

Different Exchange Rate Quotations

As the accompanying table (taken from *The New York Times*) shows, a number of different rates are quoted on a single currency in the same market on the same day. This scarcely corresponds to our concept of a

Sterling Exchange Rates
(Wednesday, November 21, 1956)

Cables 2.78¼
30 days' .... 2.77¹⁄₁₆
60 days' 2.77
90 days' .... 2.76¹³⁄₃₂
Transferable 2.7435

market as giving rise to a single price for a given item, or of an exchange rate as the price of a specific currency.

There is no inconsistency, however, for the various exchange rates, though all are dollar prices of sterling, are for different kinds of sterling. The cable rate is for sterling to be made available immediately in London, and is the highest in price. The 30-, 60-, and 90-day rates are for sterling to be delivered at later dates. Each is slightly below the next highest rate, reflecting mainly the discount rate in London. Whoever buys sterling to be made available in London, for example, only after 30 days, cannot expect to get his funds there immediately unless someone makes an advance, for which he will charge the going rate of discount. The buyer of sterling therefore pays a lower rate the more distant the date of delivery.

Transferable sterling, the cheapest of all, is quite a different kind, one which is subject to certain controls, in contrast to "free" sterling, to which the other rates apply.

THE MECHANISM OF FOREIGN PAYMENTS

Two components are required to transfer purchasing power across national boundaries and from one currency to another. One is an instrument, the bill of exchange (or its more speedy counterpart, the telegraphic transfer); the other is an institution, the bank, of which one is needed in both the paying and the receiving country. The way in which these two operate to effect international monetary transfers can be most clearly presented by an illustration.

Financing Exports

Sight bills. Suppose a Brazilian coffee exporter has entered into a contract with a New York importer to deliver a shipment of coffee worth, at the price agreed upon, $100 thousand, payment to be made upon arrival of the shipment in New York. The coffee is put aboard ship, and the exporter receives from the shipping company a bill of lading, which carries title to the shipment, as well as documents certifying its insurance and clearance through customs. If the exporter can afford to wait the two weeks or so it takes the coffee to reach New York, he will delay until just before it is to arrive, and then—in accord with arrangements made when the deal was settled—draw a bill of exchange on the New York importer. This is an order by the "drawer" (the exporter) on the "drawee" (the importer) to pay a "payee" (a New York bank) $100 thousand at sight —that is, on presentation of the bill. Since the exporter has no use for dollars, but wants cruzeiros with which to buy coffee from growers and to pay his other expenses, he takes this bill of exchange to a local bank with a foreign department and obtains immediate payment.[1] He receives the value of the bill in cruzeiros at the current rate of exchange for dollar-sight-bills. This will be the same as, or very close to, the rate for cable transfers, since in these days of fast airmail service, the bank purchasing a sight bill will have the use of its money in the foreign financial center within a very short time. Assuming the sight rate of exchange is 37 cruzeiros per dollar, the exporter's receipts will be 3,700,000 cruzeiros.

The Brazilian bank mails the bill of exchange, together with the bill of lading and other documents relevant to the shipment, to a bank in New York with which it has "correspondent" relations. Presumably this is one of the large banks with a foreign department, say the Guaranty Trust Company. It will present the bill of exchange to the importer, who pays its face value with a check on his own bank and receives the bill of lading, with which he can obtain the coffee at dockside.

Observe now the results of this financial transaction. The exporter has

[1] The bank is protected in such a purchase by the fact that, so long as the importer has not guaranteed payment of the bill by accepting it, the drawer remains primarily liable. Sometimes an advance guarantee is provided by the importer's bank, in the form of an "authority to purchase" issued to the exporter's bank.

obtained payment in cruzeiros. The Brazilian bank has paid out 3,700,000 cruzeiros, either in currency or in the form of a checking deposit in the exporter's name. In either case, the supply of money in Brazil is increased by this amount, just as it would be had the bank made a new loan. To compensate this reduction in its assets or increase in its liabilities, the bank now has a deposit of equivalent value in New York.

Time bills. Had the exporter wanted his payment as soon as the coffee was put aboard ship in Santos, or had the New York importer needed time to dispose of the coffee before making payment, an extension of credit for a more or less extended period would have been involved. Assuming that the bill of exchange is drawn as of the date of shipment and is not to be collected for sixty days, it would be a "time" bill instead of a "sight" bill. The exporter would sell it, as before, to his bank, but at the lower rate for 60-day bills, say 36.8 cruzeiros per dollar, which would yield the exporter a total of 3,680,000 cruzeiros.

The Brazilian bank would now forward the bill to its New York correspondent bank, which would present it to the importer for "acceptance." The bill now becomes a *commercial acceptance;* depending upon instructions from the Brazilian bank, the New York bank will either discount it in the money market or hold it until maturity. If the former, the Brazilian bank would obtain the discounted value of the bill, which it had paid the exporter. The credit to carry the transaction is then provided by the money market. Had it ordered the bill held, the Brazilian bank would provide the credit and earn the discount, since it advanced only the discounted value of the bill and would obtain its face value upon payment. At the end of sixty days, of course, the bill would be presented to the importer for payment.

But, in all probability, since there is no ready market for commercial acceptances in New York, a *bankers' acceptance* would have been used instead. In this instance, the American coffee importer would have arranged for his bank to issue a letter of credit. This instrument authorises the Brazilian exporter to draw a bill on this bank—say the Chase Manhattan Bank—for the sum specified. Upon receipt of this letter of credit, he would draw such a bill and cash it in the usual fashion. His bank would mail it to its correspondent, the Guaranty Trust Company, which would present it to the Chase Manhattan Bank for acceptance and then either hold it until maturity, if the Brazilian bank elected to earn the interest, or discount it in the New York money market. At the end of sixty days, it would be presented by its holder for payment, the funds necessary for this purpose having been turned over to the Chase Manhattan Bank by the importer.

Financing Imports

To pay for an import into Brazil, the importer would initiate action, just as the Brazilian exporter did in the preceding transaction, for the good reason that New York is a great international financial center with whose banks those of many other countries maintain correspondent relations and in which they keep substantial dollar balances.

Sight drafts. Consider a Brazilian importing firm which has bought a $100,000 shipment of machine tools from an American manufacturer. The shipment has arrived and the arrangement is that he is to pay on delivery. He goes to his bank (let us suppose it is the same one used by the coffee exporter) and purchases a sight bill of exchange (a sight draft) on the drawee (Guaranty Trust Company) to pay the payee (the American exporter of machine tools) the sum specified. The importer pays for the draft with cash or a check in cruzeiros, mails it to the exporter in the United States, who presents it to the Guaranty Trust Company for payment.

The results of this transaction are plain to see. The importer has received the goods and paid for them in the money of his country, while the exporter has received payment in dollars. The Brazilian bank's assets in New York have diminished, its cash holdings have increased or its demand deposits have diminished. A contraction of the supply of money in Brazil has therefore occurred, since either currency has been retired from circulation or checking deposits have been extinguished. Finally, purchasing power has been transferred over a great distance and from one currency to another. This is made possible by the practice of Brazilian banks of keeping deposits in New York, which are augmented by Brazilian exports and diminished by Brazilian imports.

Time payments. Our import illustration, involving a cash payment on delivery of the goods, is the simplest type of transaction. But suppose the importer had wanted sixty days in which to dispose of the machine tools before settling his bill. The necessary extension of credit could have been arranged in any one of a number of ways. One of the simplest would be for the American exporter to sell the shipment on *"open book account"*—thereby undertaking to wait perhaps sixty days or more before expecting the importer to purchase and remit a draft. This method would only be used, however, if the seller was well acquainted with the buyer and if the latter had a first-class credit rating.

A more common procedure would involve the use of a *dollar export bill*. Here the importer would arrange through his bank to have its New York correspondent, the Guaranty Trust Company, issue a letter of credit to the American exporter, authorising him to draw a *dollar* bill of exchange upon it for the $100,000. This would order the Guaranty Trust Company to pay this sum at the end of sixty days to the bearer, i.e., whoever held it at that time. The machine tool exporter, located let us say in Cleveland, would discount it at his local bank and obtain immediate payment, while the Cleveland bank would send it to its correspondent in New York and have it accepted by the Guaranty Trust Company. The bill has now become a bankers' acceptance, and would probably be rediscounted in the money market, the proceeds being deposited to the credit of the Cleveland bank with its New York correspondent. Just before the sixty days expired, the Brazilian importer, according to terms prescribed when the letter of credit was arranged, would purchase a dollar sight draft in favor of the Guaranty Trust Company for $100 thousand. This would be mailed to New York and would transfer to the Guaranty Trust Company this amount of the Brazilian bank's deposit with it. Even more simply, the funds could be transferred by telegraph.

The economic results of this more complicated transaction would be precisely the same as those of our first and simpler one, which involved the purchase by the Brazilian importer of a sight draft on New York. Only the details differ.

THE ROLE OF INTERNATIONAL FINANCIAL CENTERS

Practically every country in the world has economic transactions of one kind or another with many other countries. If each country's banks maintained correspondent relations with banks in each and every country with which its residents did business, the number of such correspondents and hence the number of separate foreign balances to be kept would be unconscionably large. Such complexity is made unnecessary by the concentration of international payments in a small number of financial centers.

Two such—London and New York—are of outstanding importance. British Commonwealth countries, and a number of others comprising the sterling area or more or less closely linked with it, use London as their principal

financial and clearing center. Their banks maintain balances there and
finance most of their transactions with the rest of the world through bills
of exchange drawn in favor of or against these balances, in a manner identical or similar to those of our Brazil-U.S. illustrations. New York, on the
other hand, is the established clearing center for the countries of the
so-called dollar bloc—those bordering on the Caribbean, Canada, the Philippine Republic, and Japan.

These two currency areas are by no means sealed off from one another;
the banks of most countries maintain balances in both New York and
London, using the one center or the other as the occasion demands. In
addition, a number of other cities—Paris, Berne, Rome, Cologne, Amsterdam, and Tokyo, to mention the more important ones—also perform similar
clearing and financing functions, though on a smaller scale.

For any group of nations whose banks have balances in a center like
New York, it is a simple matter to carry out their transactions, not only
with the United States, but also with one another, in dollars. Thus Brazil
can export to Greece and receive payment in dollars, while paying for its
imports from that country in the same currency. Both Brazilian and Greek
exporters, under letters of credit issued by correspondents of their banks
in New York, draw bankers' acceptances on these New York banks, discount them at their local banks, which then have them rediscounted when
they reach New York. When the time comes for the respective importers
in each country to pay, each buys a sight draft or a cable transfer from
his local bank, and therewith transfers Brazilian- or Greek-owned dollars
in New York to the banks in that city which have to meet the acceptances
as they come due. The Brazilian and Greek exporters receive payment in
cruzeiros and drachmas respectively, the importers pay in these currencies, and so far as the exports of the two countries offset one another, they
are cleared in dollars in New York. So far as Brazilian-Greek trade is concerned, that country whose exports are larger will wind up at the end
of a given period with an increased dollar balance, the other with a
diminished one.

Why London and New York?

The reason why London and New York are such important centers,
financing and clearing a large proportion of the trade of many countries,
is that they provide abundant and expert banking facilities, together with
ample funds from their respective money markets for the discounting of
bills of exchange at low rates of interest. We saw in Chapter 10 that during
the nineteenth century, a variety of specialised brokers, dealers, and bank-

ers arose in London who were ready to provide or to find the funds for discounting an ever-increasing volume of commercial or bankers' acceptances. Funds in this money market were so plentiful that discount rates ruled generally lower than anywhere else in the world. No wonder that importers, who have to pay the cost of carrying their transactions, preferred to have bills drawn on London, where the cost of the needed credit was low.

Not until after the establishment of the Federal Reserve System in 1915 and the growth of a market for bankers' acceptances that its existence aided, did New York become an important international financial center. With the growth in importance of U.S. trade and of the United States as a source of investment funds and a safe haven for capital seeking security, it has since come to rival London.

Even though the great bulk of dealings involving New York or London is carried out in dollars or pounds sterling, this does not mean that, even in these centers, other currencies are never used. A part of the trade with such countries as France and Italy, for example, is transacted in francs and lire, and there is always a demand for the currencies of a large number of countries for the remittance of dividends and charitable contributions. A demand for dollars arises in these countries from similar needs. Hence, New York and London banks maintain balances in a large number of countries, often in branches of the great metropolitan banks, and stand ready to discount or sell bills of exchange, buy or sell telegraphic transfers, on these balances.

FOREIGN EXCHANGE RATES

In our discussion of the foreign exchange market and its operation, we have taken the rate of exchange between two currencies as given, since the method of its determination, or even fluctuations in that rate, did not immediately concern us. It is now time to consider these matters.

Importance of Exchange Rates

The rate at which a country's currency exchanges for those of other countries measures its external value. It provides a direct link between the domestic prices of commodities and productive factors and their prices in the rest of the world. With prices at home and abroad at a given level, a low set of rates of exchange (low prices, in home currency, of foreign currencies) will hamper exports and stimulate imports, and thereby tend to bring about a deficit in the balance of payments. On the other hand, high exchange rates will stimulate exports and restrict imports, thus tending to bring about a balance of payments surplus.

This central role of exchange rates in determining a country's ability to export can be illustrated as follows: We choose a list of commodities produced both in the United States and in the United Kingdom; we arbitrarily take as the *unit* of each of these commodities the *amount that costs $1 to produce in the United States.* This cost of a given amount of each commodity in the U.S. appears as column one in the following table. Column two shows the (assumed) cost of producing the same amounts of each of these products in the United Kingdom in shillings and pence. Whereas the price of each commodity is the same ($1) in the U.S., because we chose an amount that cost $1 to produce, the prices vary widely in the United Kingdom, ranging from a minimum of 4 shillings for margarine to a maximum of 10 shillings for tin cans.

These relative price differences reflect, of course, differences in factor prices and in the proportions in which the factors are combined, as well as differing economies of scale. Since wages in the United States average approximately 2½ times as high as in the United Kingdom, while costs of using capital are possibly slightly lower in the United States, commodities at the top of the list—relatively cheap in the U.K.—comprise relatively labor-intensive products, those at the bottom of the list—relatively cheap in the U.S.—are capital-intensive, as well as prone to economies of scale.

PRICES AND EXCHANGE RATES

COMMODITY	(1) COST IN U.S. IN $	(2) IN SHILLINGS AND PENCE	(3) @£1=$5	(4) IN DOLLARS @£1=$4	(5) @£1=$2.80
			Cost in the United Kingdom		
Margarine	$1	4/—	$1.00	$0.80	$0.56
Wool cloth	1	4/3	1.06	0.85	0.60
Cotton cloth	1	4/8	1.16	0.93	0.65
Cigarettes	1	5/—	1.25	1.00	0.70
Linoleum	1	5/6	1.38	1.10	0.77
Paper	1	6/—	1.50	1.20	0.84
Glass bottles	1	7/—	1.75	1.40	0.98
Radio tubes	1	8/—	2.00	1.60	1.12
Pig iron	1	9/—	2.25	1.80	1.26
Tin cans	1	10/—	2.50	2.00	1.40

The various British prices are then converted into dollars and cents at three different rates of exchange. Column three shows the prices British producers would have to charge American and other foreign buyers at a rate of exchange of £1 = $5. Columns four and five show the very different prices corresponding to rates of exchange of £1 = $4 and £1 = $2.80.[2]

If the pound had a value or rate of exchange as high as $5, the United Kingdom could sell in competition with the United States, ignoring transport costs, only the first commodity in the list, margarine.[3] In all the others, the United States would be able to undersell British products. The volume and value of British exports would be very small, while without serious restrictions on imports, their value would far exceed that of exports. The United Kingdom would confront a serious imbalance in its international payments.

At a rate of exchange of £1 = $2.80, on the other hand, the U.K. could undersell the U.S. in all but the last three commodities. This would ensure large exports, while imports would be much reduced. Instead of a deficit in its balance of payments, the U.K. might well enjoy a large surplus. With an intermediate exchange rate of $4 to the pound, the United Kingdom could undersell the United States in the first three products and compete on an even basis with respect to the fourth, while the U.S. could underbid British producers on the other six commodities.

From this illustration, it is easy to see that the rate at which a country's currency is quoted on foreign exchange markets is a matter of crucial importance. Since it is by means of the exchange rate that home prices are translated into foreign prices, and vice versa, the exchange rate occupies a key position with respect to a country's international transactions. Close atttention to how exchange rates are determined and what causes them to vary is therefore warranted. The next chapter is devoted to a discussion of these problems.

Some Technicalities

An exchange rate is frequently defined as the price, in domestic currency, of a unit of foreign currency. It might equally well be defined as the price, in a foreign currency, of a unit of domestic currency. For an exchange rate is simply the value or price of one currency in terms of another, and it makes no difference in which currency the price ratio is

---

[2] For those not familiar with British monetary units, there are 20 shillings to the pound, 12 pence to each shilling. Thus at an exchange rate of £1 = $5, a shilling would be worth 1/20 of $5, or 25¢, and a penny 1/12 of 25¢ or approximately 2¢. At £1 = $4, 1 shilling = 20¢, 1 d. (pence) = 1.67¢; at £1 = $2.80, 1 shilling = 14¢, 1 d. = 1.167¢.

[3] If the value of the pound in dollars was high, its value in other currencies of given dollar values would also be high. Therefore we can ignore price comparisons with other countries, which would be similar in nature, though the list of commodities compared would presumably be different.

expressed. In practice, exchange rates are sometimes quoted in one manner, sometimes in the other. The British are in this respect consistent: exchange rates on all currencies are quoted as the price of the pound in terms of foreign currency units. In New York, the opposite practice is commonly followed; foreign currencies are expressed in terms of dollars and cents per unit. The rate on the pound, since its devaluation in 1949, has been slightly above or below $2.80. The official dollar/franc rate (for the French franc) is $0.02857. Because small fractional numbers are inconvenient, however, the rate on the French franc and other currencies is sometimes quoted as the foreign price of dollars. For the franc, this is 350 francs per dollar.

Which practice is followed is unimportant. What *is* important is that you be conscious, in any particular instance, of just which way this relationship is expressed. This is of particular significance when changes in a rate of exchange are involved. Thus, if the dollar/sterling rate should rise from $2.80 to $2.90, this would represent a higher price of the pound in dollars, and thus a rise in the value of the pound, but a fall in the value of the dollar. On the other hand, should the franc/dollar rate go up from 350 to 360 francs, this would mean that the dollar was dearer and hence more valuable in terms of francs. The higher rate, however, would represent a lower value of the franc.

It is this two-sided relationship between currencies that is the source of much confusion with respect to foreign exchange problems. To minimise difficulties, always make sure you know (1) in which currency, domestic or foreign, an exchange rate is expressed, and (2) from which country's point of view the rate or a change in it, is being considered.

Arbitrage

When foreign exchange markets are free from or subject to only very limited controls,[4] the rate of exchange between two currencies in one of the markets must be the same in the other market. Thus if the pound is quoted at $2.80 in New York, it must also stand at $2.80 in London. For if dealers were free to buy or sell dollars and pounds without limit, then if the rate were $2.80 in New York and $2.85 in London, they would acquire pounds with dollars in New York at the lower rate, sell these pounds for dollars in London at the higher rate, and make 5¢ profit on each pound bought and sold. The increased demand for pounds in New York would raise the rate there, while the additional supply of pounds sold against dollars in London would lower it, and the two rates would converge. They

---

[4] As they were before World War I, in the later 1920's and it is hoped will be again.

could differ only by the very small cost (which is low per pound because transactions would be in large sums) of carrying out these operations, which are known as "arbitrage."

But arbitrage is not limited to operations in two currencies, or to two-point arbitrage. Three-point (and even wider) arbitrage is also common when currencies are free. Thus suppose the dollar/sterling rate is $2.80, the franc/dollar rate is 350 francs per dollar, and the cross rate between the pound and the franc is 1020 francs per pound. Arbitragers will buy pounds with dollars, convert each pound into 1020 francs in London, and then sell the francs thus obtained for dollars in New York. For an investment of $2.80 they will obtain slightly more than $2.91 (1020/350 = 2.9143). Assume, to simplify the arithmetic, that the dollar/sterling and the franc/dollar rates remain unchanged. Then arbitraging will continue until the value of the franc in pounds is consistent with its value in dollars. This will be when the pound/franc rate is 980 francs per pound. Continuing purchases of francs in London would drive up the value of the franc, which means lowering the number of francs obtainable for a pound. The result of arbitraging is to link the three exchange markets virtually into one, and to bring into being consistent cross rates. To the extent to which foreign exchange markets are free, arbitraging of this kind unifies all the markets of the world.

When the purchase and sale of foreign exchange are subject to effective and tight control, arbitrage becomes impossible. Exchange controls usually require the surrender to the authorities of all foreign currencies acquired by residents, and limit purchases thereof to specific approved purposes. If, in our illustration, France had such controls, arbitragers would be unable to buy francs with pounds at the cheap franc/sterling rate. This would effectively block the operation of selling francs at the relatively higher franc/dollar rate. The rate between the franc and the pound could then be inconsistent with the dollar/sterling and the dollar/franc rates. Such "disorderly" cross rates are a common accompaniment of exchange controls.

APPENDIX

FORWARD FOREIGN EXCHANGE

The Risk of Exchange Rate Fluctuations

Individuals or firms engaged in the export business make their profit from the spread between their buying price and their selling price, like any other trader. If they are manufacturers, the necessary profit comes out of the markup over costs. But if the exporter carries on his business in terms of a foreign currency, that is, if he normally finances a shipment by drawing an export bill in a foreign currency, a fall in its value occurring between the time he contracts the shipment and undertakes to obtain payment could wipe out or seriously reduce his profits as a trader. Risks arising from exchange rate fluctuations are at a minimum under gold standard conditions, but they can be very serious in the case of fluctuating exchange rates. These risks can be avoided by the trader, and he can concentrate on his normal functions and the risks attendant thereto, if there exists a market for forward foreign exchange, where the exporter can obtain an advance assurance of a guaranteed price for the foreign exchange he will have at his disposal at a later date.

To illustrate, suppose that a French exporter of wine to the United States knows in the late spring that he will be shipping wine to buyers in this country in the autumn, and about how much. If he can obtain a contract from his bank to accept, say ninety days later, a stipulated amount of dollars, at an exchange rate specified in advance, he will thereby avoid all risk of fluctuations in the franc/dollar rate of exchange. The existence of a forward exchange market enables him to "hedge" against the risk that the sum of dollars for which he has contracted to deliver the wine will yield him a reduced sum in francs, owing to a fall in the franc/dollar rate of exchange. The bank, of course, will take over the risk, but as we shall see, it has at its disposal means of offsetting this risk or of passing it along to someone else.

Similarly with the importer: After placing his orders with foreign exporters, he knows he is going to have to buy foreign exchange in the near future, say in sixty or ninety days. He too can avoid a possible increased cost of imports resulting from a rise in the exchange rate if he can hedge by obtaining a contract from his bank to deliver foreign exchange when he needs it, at a rate specified in advance.

Thus suppose a French importer of tobacco places an order for a shipment of $10 thousand with an American exporter, shipment to be made in ninety days, payment to be by sight draft upon arrival. If the importer thinks it possible that dollars may cost him more in francs at that time than when he places the order, he will welcome the opportunity to buy $10 thousand forward from his bank.

Of course both exporter and importer might gain rather than lose if the exchange rate moved favorably. In the case of the exporter, a rise in the franc/dollar rate would net him more francs and a profit larger than his normal trading profit. With the importer, a fall in the franc/dollar rate would put him ahead. But the point to be stressed is that if there is uncertainty as to the probable movement of the exchange rate, there is a risk of loss over and above the normal trading risks. So far as a foreign trader concentrates upon his purely trading activities, he will shift this risk to someone else. Only if he wishes to speculate on the future of the exchange rate will he fail so to shift this risk.

The Role of Banks in the Forward Exchange Market

The bank that undertakes to provide forward exchange to importers will at the same time be contracting to purchase forward exchange from exporters. So far as any bank succeeds in matching forward purchases and sales, it avoids "taking a position" and assumes no risk. For both its buying and selling rates are known to it in advance, and they will differ only by an amount sufficient to assure the bank of a commission on its dealings. Whether they are above or below the spot rate at the time the forward contracts mature is immaterial, since the purchases of exchange provide the means for deliveries on sales.

There is, however, no particular reason to expect that the needs of exporters and importers for forward exchange will exactly coincide at any one point in time. If a bank undertook to deliver forward exchange in amounts greater than its purchases, this would result in its taking an uncovered position. But this would mean that the bank was speculating on the course of the foreign exchanges, and normally banks do not engage in speculation, but confine themselves, so far as they are foreign exchange dealers, to the normal activities of dealers, making their profit (like exporters and importers) on the spread between the buying and selling prices of the commodity in which they trade. A bank can, however, avoid taking an uncovered forward position by adjusting its spot position with the future in mind.

Thus suppose that a French bank has contracted to sell 90-day forward exchange to importers in excess of its purchases from exporters. At the end of this period, it will have to make available more foreign exchange, say dollars, than is coming to it from the execution of exporters' forward contracts. Foreseeing this situation, it can, at the time of making the forward contracts, supplement its dollar resources by buying 90-day bills currently coming on the market. When these mature in New York, they will provide the dollars needed to meet the excess forward sales. Alternatively, the bank can buy spot dollar exchange (currently available sight drafts) from exporters, or it may be able to purchase additional dollar balances from banks which have surplus dollar resources. Adoption of these latter alternatives will mean holding dollars in New York for ninety days. If the supply of 90-day bills, sight drafts, and exchange available from other banks is inadequate, the bank may simply refuse to make additional forward commitments. There remains only one alternative—the purchase by the bank of additional forward exchange from speculators, who, since they are speculators, are willing to take an open position. This alternative, however, is present only with respect to a limited number of currencies—those in which the volume of trading is sufficient to create a market of proportions such as to attract the activity of speculative dealers.

The Forward Market and International Capital Movements

When banks buy spot exchange and hold it until needed to meet forward commitments, they pay out domestic currency. On such investments of their funds, they lose interest which they might earn by making loans. But the foreign currency acquired can be lent out in the foreign money market. Thus the French banks we have used in our illustrations will forgo interest on the francs they pay out for spot dollars, but these dollars can be lent in New York. The difference in interest rates in the two money markets will be an important element in determining whether the forward rate is at a premium or a discount relative to the spot rate.

Let us suppose that the short-term rate of interest in Paris is 1 per cent, in New York 2 per cent. If at the time of entering into forward contracts, the spot and forward exchange rates are the same (say 350 francs per dollar), then the covering of any excess forward commitments to French importers by spot purchases of dollars will yield 1 per cent per annum extra income for ninety days. Banks will then compete in selling dollars forward, and in buying spot dollars too. Competition in the sale of forward dollars will drive down the forward rate, while the spot rate will be forced up. A discount on forward relative to spot exchange will tend to arise. These opposite price movements, resulting in an increased cost of dollars to transfer to New York and a decreased yield from their sale when they are brought back to France, will tend to eliminate the gain from lending in New York, leaving only a commission available to the banks.

Purchases of spot exchange of this kind, which result in the transfer of funds from one market to another, are undertaken not only to provide cover for (or a hedge against) excess sales of forward exchange, but also on their own account. When interest rates abroad are higher than at home, banks will want to lend overseas. A forward exchange market provides the mechanism by which they can do it without risk.

From the point of view of the French lender, a spot purchase of dollars must be covered by a simultaneous sale of dollars forward.[5] Otherwise the return of dollars to France at a later date—implicit in the fact that these are *short-term* loans—will involve an exchange loss if francs appreciate, that is, if a given dollar loan yields at maturity less francs than it cost. The possibility of appreciation will always exist under inconvertible paper currency conditions, and it will be present under the gold standard if at the time the foreign loan is made the spot rate is above the gold import point. In the absence of a forward market, short-term foreign lending will be hazardous except when, under gold standard conditions, the spot rate stands at or very close to the gold import point for the lending country.

How small a fluctuation in the exchange rate may convert a gain in interest into a loss is shown by the following example. It is assumed that the short-term rate of interest in New York exceeds that in Paris by 1 per cent, that a 90-day loan of $100 thousand is made by a French bank when the spot rate is 350 francs per dollar, and that when the loan expires the spot rate has fallen to 349 francs per dollar. Instead

Purchase of spot dollars @ 350 frs./$:	$100,000	= 35,000,000 frs.
Excess interest @ 1% for 90 days:	250	
Sale of dollars at end of 90 days @ 349 frs./$:	$100,250	= 34,987,250 frs.
Loss		12,750 frs.

of earning $250, the French bank suffers a small loss of 12,750 francs. In the assumed circumstances, lending by Paris in New York would be unprofitable in the absence of a forward market unless there were no possibility of a fall in the franc/dollar rate of exchange of something less than 1 in 350. Even with a forward market, if the interest differential were only 1 per cent, the discount on the forward rate would have to be sufficiently less than $\frac{1}{4}$ per cent (= 1 per cent for ninety days) to provide a commission adequate to compensate the bank for its trouble.

When lending operations were profitable in Paris, they would be duplicated by simultaneous borrowing operations in New York. New

---

[5] This type of operation is called "interest arbitrage," since arbitrage, or simultaneous purchases and sales in each of two markets, is being carried out to take advantage of an interest differential.

York banks would sell spot francs for dollars, and lend these out in New York. Spot francs would be available either from (1) existing balances of New York banks in Paris or (2) balances in Paris established by drawing 90-day drafts on Paris banks. Repayment of borrowed balances (and probably restoration of depleted balances) would be necessary at the end of ninety days. To avoid exchange loss on this operation, New York banks would have to purchase forward francs simultaneously with the sale of the borrowed balances. Therefore in New York the forward rate on francs would rise, the spot rate would fall, and forward *francs* would go to a premium.

If, on the other hand, the interest rate were higher in Paris than in New York, then dollars would be converted into francs, to be lent in the Paris money market. French banks would sell spot dollar bills (and cables) against their New York balances, and would borrow dollars. To borrow, they would draw long dollar drafts, which would be accepted by New York banks, and discounted in the New York money market. Against the dollar balances so established in favor of French banks, the latter would then sell spot dollar exchange, lending the franc proceeds in Paris. To avoid exchange loss when these loans matured, they would have to buy forward dollars simultaneously.

Competition to sell spot dollars would depress the spot rate, while the increased demand for forward dollars would put the forward rate at a premium. Competition to buy forward dollars would stop when, after allowing for a commission on spot sales of exchange by the banks, the premium on forward dollars was equal to the excess earnings in Paris.

With respect to the relationship between forward and spot rates, we can say that, in the absence of speculation, the forward rate will tend to be at a discount from the spot rate on a given country if interest rates there are higher, and at a premium if interest rates in that country are lower. Thus in our first illustration, with interest rates higher in New York than in Paris, forward dollars were at a discount. In the second illustration, with interest rates higher in Paris, forward dollars were at a premium.

Speculation

In addition to exporters wanting to hedge against exchange loss by selling forward exchange and importers wanting to buy forward exchange for similar purposes, together with banks desiring to earn commissions or to take advantage of interest rate differentials, there may be other important buyers and sellers of forward exchange: the speculators. As we have already seen, these individuals deliberately take an open position. Because they anticipate a fall or a rise in the (spot) exchange rate for a specific currency, they will enter into contracts to sell or buy forward exchange at rates slightly higher or lower than their estimate of the future spot rate. They hope to gain from gambling on the future level of the spot rate.

Thus a French speculator who anticipates that the franc will appreciate, or that the franc price of dollars will fall, will sell forward dollars. When, say ninety days later, he has to deliver, he will make a speculative profit if he can buy spot dollars with which to fulfill his forward contract at a rate below that specified in this contract.

Suppose, for example, that speculators at a given date are optimistic or "bullish" with respect to the franc, "bearish" with respect to the dollar. Assume the spot rate at that date is 350 francs/dollar, and that competition to sell forward dollars has driven the forward rate to 348 francs/dollar. An individual speculator sells $100 thousand forward, that is, he undertakes to deliver this sum in dollars, ninety days later, for a total sum in his own currency of 34,800,000 francs. If the spot rate at that time is 347 francs/dollar, he will purchase the dollars to meet his forward contract for a total outlay of 34,700,000 francs, clearing 100 thousand francs profit on the deal. If the spot rate were then above 348 francs/dollar, he would of course lose on his speculation.

So far as the forward rate of exchange is determined by the activities of speculators, the fact that the dollar stands at a discount in Paris does not mean that no speculators will be willing to buy, rather than sell, forward dollars at this rate. One of the characteristics of a speculative market is that there is usually a division of opinion among speculators. In the illustration we have just given, those who were "bullish" with respect to the dollar would be buyers rather than sellers of that currency. And they would gain if, when their forward contracts came due, the spot rate stood above 348 francs/dollar. The fact that, on the initial date, dollars were at a discount reflects a preponderance of "bearish" opinion relative to the dollar, not unanimity.

Had speculators been preponderantly "bullish" instead of "bearish" relative to the dollar, total forward purchases would exceed forward sales, and competition to buy dollars forward would drive the rate to a premium, say to 352 francs/dollar. If, at the delivery date, speculators could buy spot dollars for 351, the "bulls" would make a profit, the minority of "bears" would lose.

Influence of Speculation on the Spot Rate

When the opinion of speculators with respect to the future value of foreign currencies is strongly "bearish" (or "bullish" with respect to their own), they will on balance *sell* forward exchange, thus depressing the forward rate. Those who buy from them, principally banks and foreign exchange dealers, *not* being speculators, will have to cover their purchases by spot sales. The increased volume of spot offerings will push down the spot rate, thus reflecting *in the present* the opinion of speculators as to the *future* course of exchange rates. (The forward rate will, however, remain at a discount, owing to the continued pressure of speculation.)

On the other hand, if speculators are preponderantly "bullish" with respect to foreign currencies ("bearish" with respect to their own), they will on balance *buy* forward exchange, thus driving the rate up. Those who sell to them, to cover their position, will have to buy spot exchange. This forces up the spot rate, again reflecting *in the present* fears or hopes about the *future*.

If "bull" speculators have difficulty in buying forward exchange, the premium over spot rates will tend to be substantial. As the premium rises, however, it becomes more attractive for banks to buy spot exchange, transfer their funds abroad, and by simultaneously selling this exchange forward, to ensure the return of their funds at a profit.

To illustrate, suppose the spot rate in Paris is 350 francs/dollar, the forward rate 355, and to eliminate capital movements induced by interest rate differentials, let us assume interest rates in New York and Paris are identical. A Paris bank can then transfer $100 thousand to New York by purchasing spot exchange at a cost of 35 million francs, lend the proceeds out there, and by simultaneously selling these dollars forward to a speculator, be sure of obtaining from its loan a total sum of 35,500,000 francs. By undertaking such an exchange arbitrage,[6] the bank gains 500 thousand francs.

A large premium on forward dollars would indicate lack of confidence in the future of the franc. This would be the first manifestation of such pessimism, stemming from the competition of speculators to buy forward dollars. By making capital movements profitable, however, it would induce (1) additional supplies of forward dollars to match the speculators' desire to buy and (2) additional purchases of spot exchange to

[6] That is, the simultaneous purchase and sale of dollars in different markets, to take advantage of exchange rate rather than interest rate differentials.

transfer funds abroad. The additional supplies of forward exchange would tend to moderate the rise in the forward rate, while the additional demand for spot exchange would tend to force the spot rate up, thus reflecting in the present the lack of confidence in the future of the country's currency.

It is clear that when forward dollars are at a sufficient premium in Paris to induce exchange arbitrage, or capital movements of this type, banks will gain regardless of whether, when their loans mature, the spot rate is above or below the rate specified in their forward contracts. For they buy dollars at a specific (spot) rate, and sell them at a higher (forward) rate. Speculators, in such a situation, will gain only if, when they acquire dollars from their prior forward contracts, the spot rate is *above* the rate specified in these contracts. Then they will gain by selling dollars acquired at, say, 355 francs/dollar for a price of 356 or 357 francs.

Moreover, it should also be noted that a speculative capital movement may be profitable even though interest rates are *higher* in the lending than in the borrowing market. This will be true provided the gain from buying spot exchange at one rate and selling the proceeds forward at a higher rate (exchange arbitrage) exceeds the loss from transferring funds from a market where the interest rate is high to one where it is low.[7]

SELECTED REFERENCES

Crump, Norman, *The ABC of the Foreign Exchanges* (Macmillan & Co., Ltd., London, 1951). An excellent, simple discussion of the mechanism of international payments.

Holgate, H. C. F., *Foreign Exchange, an Introductory Outline* (Pitman, London, 1936). Has a vivid account of the London foreign exchange market, as well as a readable discussion of the foreign exchange mechanism.

Rosenthal, Morris S., *Techniques of International Trade* (McGraw-Hill Book Co., Inc., New York, 1950). Covers this topic thoroughly from the business point of view.

Southard, Frank A., Jr., *Foreign Exchange Practice and Policy* (McGraw-Hill Book Co., Inc., New York, 1940). A good account of the mechanism of foreign payments. Chapter IV has an illuminating discussion of various types of credit management.

von Klemperer, Alfred H., "Present Foreign Payments Practices in the United States," *IMF Staff Papers*, Vol. II, No. 2 (April 1952). A brief treatment of methods of payment now in use, including non-traditional practices.

[7] On this point, see Frank A. Southard, Jr., *Foreign Exchange Practice and Policy*, p. 101 (McGraw-Hill Book Co., Inc., New York, 1940). For a fuller discussion of the forward exchanges, as well as other aspects of foreign exchange problems, this book is an excellent source, to which the presentation in this Appendix owes much.

16

FOREIGN EXCHANGE RATES
IN FREE MARKETS

From our numerous references to the demand and supply of foreign exchange, the foreign exchange market, and the exchange rate as the price of one currency in terms of another, it should be apparent that the determination of an exchange rate is a pricing problem, to which the usual demand and supply analysis presumably applies.

Many Rates of Exchange

That analysis applies, however, with some differences. One is that whereas in a commodity market there is a single price for a given grade of a commodity, in the foreign exchange market there is no one price for foreign exchange of a certain kind (e.g., spot or cable transfers). Instead, there are as many prices as there are currencies traded. Yet just as a country's balance of payments includes all its transactions with the rest of the world, so its foreign exchange market brings together all its demands for foreign currencies and all its supplies of those currencies. These are merged in a common market.

Which of the numerous rates of exchange are we to take as reflecting the interaction of the forces of demand and supply? Actually, if a free market exists, the problem is not serious. We can take the rate on any currency as representative of all the rest. For arbitrage operations keep the rates on different currencies in line. If the price of one rises or falls, the prices of all the others must move in the same direction and in the same proportion.

Balance of Payments and the Foreign Exchange Market

The parallelism between a country's balance of payments and its foreign exchange market extends beyond the fact that each encompasses a total of that country's relations with the rest of the world. This total to which each concept refers is the same—it is all of a nation's economic transactions with all other nations. Yet there is a difference. A balance of payments refers to all such transactions as *actually occurred* during a given period, at whatever exchange rate or rates ruled during that interval. It is a record of accomplished fact.

The demand and supply that meet in the foreign exchange market, on the other hand, tell us what a country's autonomous payments and receipts *would be* at each of a whole series of exchange rates. Demand and supply of foreign exchange are schedules that interact to determine the exchange rate, and therewith the transactions actually undertaken. If these market forces can be taken to have remained comparatively constant over a given balance of payments period, say a year, then we can say with reasonable accuracy that the actual payments and receipts recorded reflect the size of market demand and market supply at the ruling exchange rate.

Another distinction, too, must be noted. A balance of payments is complete; it shows, not only the autonomous payments and receipts, but also the amount and sources of compensatory financing. The demand and supply of foreign exchange, however, include only the autonomous transactions —the imports of goods, services, and securities that would be undertaken and the exports of similar items that would be forthcoming at each of a series of exchange rates. Under stable conditions, therefore, a deficit or surplus in the balance of payments indicates the amount by which the demand for exchange exceeds the supply of exchange, or vice versa, at the ruling rate.

Composite Demand and Supply

A second difference between commodity markets and foreign exchange markets results from the fact that the demand and supply of a commodity are homogeneous, whereas the corresponding foreign exchange schedules are composite. The demand, say, for cotton reflects the wants of buyers for a single commodity with distinctive characteristics. The demand for foreign exchange, it has just been suggested, is a mixture of many different demands—for many types of commodities, for a great variety of services, for a wide range of securities. The supply of foreign exchange is similarly composite.

If the components of demand and supply in the foreign exchange market differ so radically from those that operate in commodity markets, how can we be sure they will not produce different results? Is there not a danger that foreign exchange rates are inherently unstable—in the sense that a rise or fall, once started, will go unchecked? Commodity prices tend to vary widely only when demand and supply conditions themselves change substantially. Even then, the resultant price changes are generally self-limiting. A rise in price calls forth additional supplies, which bring the rise to a halt; a price decline stimulates additional purchases, which check any further fall.

Stable and Unstable Markets

A market is said to be stable when at any price above the one at which demand and supply are equal and the market is cleared, supply exceeds demand, and when at any lower price demand exceeds supply. These conditions are generally met in commodity markets. But if, at prices above the one that clears the market, demand is greater than supply, any rise in price above the "equilibrium" level will continue without limit, since demand exceeds supply by ever-increasing amounts. Similarly, if below this "equilibrium" price supply is greater than demand, a drop in price will go on unchecked because of the depressing effect of an increasing excess of supply.

It is possible that foreign exchange markets tend to behave in this unstable fashion. Certainly there have been periods of wild fluctuations in exchange rates, notably just after the first World War, when the German mark, the Austrian crown, and the Russian rouble, after violent gyrations, ended by losing virtually all their value. One of our tasks will be to determine whether the peculiar composition of the demand and supply of foreign exchange predisposes exchange rates toward excessive fluctuations, or whether this is true only under exceptional circumstances.

Crucial Role of Exchange Rates

We observed in the last chapter that because changes in exchange rates alter the scale of relative prices between countries, exchange rates play a role of crucial importance in international trade. Because a rise in the price of foreign currencies raises the prices of a nation's imports and permits it to lower the foreign prices of its exports, thus retarding the former and stimulating the latter, variations in a nation's exchange rates afford a potential means of eliminating a deficit in its balance of payments without recourse to costly compensatory financing. This is a further reason for discovering how exchange rates are determined.

In this chapter we shall explore this topic. In doing so, we shall consider only the case of a country confronting a balance of payments deficit, for only such a country has a real problem. A country enjoying a surplus accumulates foreign balances and gold; it is under no strain to find such means of compensatory financing. Hence our analysis will be confined, with only incidental exceptions, to the effects of exchange depreciation. To determine the impact of appreciation, or a decline in exchange rates, you need only reverse both the analysis and the conclusions. The following chapter will apply our findings to the solution of balance of payments problems, and contrast the very different solution provided under the gold standard with the use for this purpose of exchange rate variations. Finally, we shall consider a third alternative: combating a balance of payments disequilibrium with direct controls.

If exchange rates are to be effective in altering international price relationships, they must be free to move. This obviously implies the absence of controls over the purchase and sale of foreign exchange. But exchange rates cannot move freely if currencies are anchored to a common standard, such as gold. We shall therefore assume not only uncontrolled exchange markets, but also independent currencies. That is, each country's monetary authority determines the supply of its currency and thus the level of internal prices in accordance with a policy independently arrived at.

A Deficit Reflects the Foreign Exchange Situation

A few pages ago, we noted that the demand and supply of foreign exchange include only the autonomous transactions in a nation's balance of payments. If this is true, then over a period during which demand and supply conditions remain stable, a deficit in the balance of payments indicates the amount by which the demand for foreign exchange exceeds the supply at the ruling rate of exchange. For a deficit *is* the difference between autonomous receipts and autonomous payments, and the supply of exchange actually delivered during the period in question corresponds to these receipts, the demand for exchange to these payments.

Thus when a country has a balance of payments deficit, this gives the location of one point on both the foreign exchange demand and supply curves, namely, the demand for and supply of exchange at the ruling rate. Of what the demand and supply would be at higher or lower rates, the country's monetary authorities have no indication. This depends upon the relative steepness of these curves, or their elasticity.

Relevance of Foreign Exchange Elasticities

But if these authorities are contemplating exchange depreciation, or a rise in exchange rates, as a means of eliminating the deficit, the elasticities of demand and supply of foreign exchange are of vital importance. An illustration will clarify this point.

Figure 16.1 portrays an imagined situation in France's foreign exchange market. The franc/dollar rate is taken as representative of all exchange rates, and the total amount of foreign exchange demanded and supplied is expressed in dollars. We assume that the demand and supply of foreign exchange have been reasonably stable over the past six months. During this period, autonomous balance of payments receipts from exports of goods, services, and long-term securities amounted to $400 million. Corresponding payments were $700 million. The resulting deficit we may assume was financed by exports of gold, reduction of official foreign balances, and short-term official borrowing abroad. By such means alone, in the absence of controls, would it be possible to maintain the exchange rate stable at 350 francs/dollar.

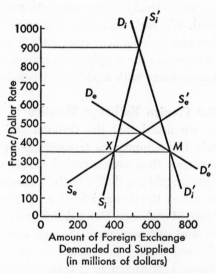

Fig. 16.1: Adjustment via
Free Exchange Rates.

From our knowledge of the value of autonomous exports and imports and of the ruling exchange rate, we obtain one point on the foreign exchange demand curve, at *M*, and one on the supply curve, at *X*. What the position of these curves is at other rates of exchange, we have no idea, since transactions have been effected only at the ruling rate of 350 francs/dollar.

If the monetary authorities have good reason to believe that for the foreseeable future, underlying conditions will continue about the same, they can expect the current deficit to be repeated. To avoid the need for further compensatory financing, they are considering whether it may not be advisable to let the exchange rate rise. But by how much is it likely to go up? A moderate rise, say of 20 or even 30 per cent, might not create serious problems, whereas depreciation of 50 or 100 per cent might be unsupportable.[1]

Two possibilities are illustrated in the diagram, where we have drawn two sets of demand and supply curves, one (D_eD_e' and S_eS_e') relatively elastic, the other (D_iD_i' and S_iS_i') relatively inelastic. If demand and supply were as elastic, or as responsive to an increase in the exchange rate, as the first pair, the supply of exchange would expand and the demand contract quite rapidly, clearing the market at a rate of exchange of 450 francs/dollar—representing an appreciation of the dollar in terms of francs of approximately 28 per cent, a depreciation of the franc of slightly over 23 per cent.

If, however, demand and supply were as inelastic as the second set of curves (D_iD_i' and S_iS_i'), the exchange rate would have to rise to 900 francs/dollar before an equilibrium position was reached. This involves a 157 per cent appreciation of the dollar in francs, or a 61 per cent depreciation of the franc.

Clearly, it is important for the monetary authorities of a country for which depreciation is being contemplated to have some idea, even if only approximate, of how far depreciation is likely to have to go before the deficit is eliminated. The purpose of what follows is to explore this problem.

THE DEMAND FOR FOREIGN EXCHANGE
FOR GOODS AND SERVICES

Since the demand and supply of foreign exchange are made up of quite different components that react differently, as we shall see, to changes in the exchange rate, it is necessary to consider these components separately. We shall begin with goods and services, leaving capital movements for later consideration. Moreover, we shall also take the point of view of the short-run, meaning by this a period long enough for producers to adjust output to changed demands, but not so long as to permit any change in productive capacity.

Elasticity of Demand for Imports

Let us continue our illustration, and suppose the French franc is allowed

---

[1] We shall postpone consideration of the problems raised by exchange depreciation until the following chapter, concentrating in this upon what factors determine how severe it is likely to be.

to depreciate. The franc price of dollars rises, and if we may assume for the time being that the dollar price of France's imports remains constant, their price in francs will increase in direct proportion to the rise in the exchange rate. What will determine whether the demand for foreign exchange is elastic or inelastic, and thus whether this side of the market contributes much or little toward eliminating the deficit? Clearly, this elasticity will directly reflect the elasticity of demand for imports, since we are considering the demand for foreign exchange (i.e., dollars) with which to acquire these goods and services.

So far as concerns imports none of which is produced in France, the demand for goods in general of the kind imported and the demand for imports proper will be identical; their elasticities are therefore also the same. The demand for foreign exchange will mirror the demand for imports. The only difference is that the demand for foreign exchange is expressed in rates of exchange and amounts of foreign exchange, whereas the demand for imports is stated in terms of import prices and quantities of the goods (or services) demanded.

Supply of Import-Competing Goods

If, however, goods that compete with imports are produced in France, a distinction must be drawn between the demand for goods such as are imported, or import-type goods for short, and the demand for imports. The former demand is directed toward and can be satisfied by supplies from French or from foreign producers; the latter is directed toward imports alone.

The demand for import-type goods, being the general demand for a particular good, say shoes, has an elasticity, or responsiveness of sales to price, determined by the tastes of consumers, just as with any other commodity. The *demand for imports* of shoes, on the other hand, will be *more elastic* than the demand for shoes in general, since as the price of imported shoes is reduced (increased), competing domestic producers will contract (expand) their output in the face of the intensified (reduced) competition. Sales of imported shoes increase as their price is reduced, not only because of the normal inclination of buyers to purchase more at lower prices, but also because the higher cost portion of competing domestic production is eliminated, leaving a larger share of the market to be taken over by imports.

These reactions are shown in Figure 16.2. DD' is the demand (say in France) for some commodity such as shoes. C_hC_h' is the short-run supply curve of domestic producers. If for the sake of simplifying our argument we leave aside costs of transport, then at a price of P_n or above, home producers can supply the entire market. If imports can be landed only at

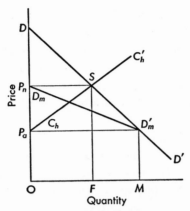

Fig. 16.2: Elasticity of Demand
for Import-type Goods
and for Imports

a higher price, they cannot compete. If, owing to a reduction in foreign costs or to appreciation of the franc (a lower franc price for the dollar), the import price is lowered, imports will begin to enter the country. The highest cost portion of French production will be discontinued. Successive reductions of the import price will cause more and more competing French supplies to be displaced, until at a price of P_a, they disappear completely. The demand for imports, as distinct from the demand for the goods imported (DD') is represented, within the price range of P_nP_a, by the curve D_mD_m'. Below P_a, imports supply the entire market; the demand for imports becomes the same as the demand for the commodity in question.

Elasticity of Demand for Foreign Exchange

Having established this peculiarity of a country's demand for imports when import-competing goods are available, we can continue our discussion of the demand for foreign exchange. This will be a carbon copy, as it were, of the demand for imports, with only the difference that rates of exchange are substituted for prices and amounts of foreign exchange for quantities of imports.

How elastic a given country's demand for imports (and thus for foreign exchange) is, depends (1) on the elasticity of demand for import-type goods, (2) on the proportion of imports that encounter local competition, and (3) on the rapidity with which such local competition withdraws (expands) when confronted with declining (rising) import prices (the elasticity of supply of import-competing goods).

The elasticity of demand for imports, and thus of the demand for foreign exchange, will naturally be high in a country whose imports are principally luxuries, for whose imports there are many domestic substitutes, and whose import-competing production expands and contracts rapidly in response to price changes. Contrariwise, this elasticity will be low where imports are mainly necessities, where few domestic substitutes are produced, and where these substitutes are relatively fixed in supply.

Elasticity of Supply of Imports

Somewhat less important, though certainly to be included in a complete account, are conditions in the country where the imports are produced. To enable us to concentrate on what happens in the importing country when its currency depreciates, we have assumed up to now that the price of imports remains constant in their country of origin. We have assumed constant costs, or infinite elasticity of supply. This condition is likely to be approximated in the short run in periods of depression, when many resources lie idle. And then it is likely to apply most fully to goods whose production is continuous, like manufactures.[2] In these circumstances, what we have said about the elasticity of demand for foreign exchange requires little modification.

Even under conditions of full or near-full employment, prices of manufactured goods in the exporting center are likely to change little or not at all, if, because of depreciation, foreign demand is reduced. This curious result is due to the fact that most manufactures are produced under conditions of highly imperfect competition. When plants are working at capacity, producers seldom raise their prices to the full extent justified by the high level of demand. Unless wages and other costs are rising, they accumulate backlogs of orders, while keeping their prices relatively constant, thus rationing their customers via a waiting list rather than by the competitive device of a higher price. And if foreign demand falls off owing to depreciation, these producers need not lower their price—they merely see their backlog of orders dwindle somewhat. With respect to a country's manufactured imports, one is not wide of the mark if he assumes that with either severe depression or full employment in their country of origin, prices there will remain comparatively stable. Depreciation of the import-

---

[2] A wide range of behavior in different industries is possible. Hence generalisation is dangerous. But resistance to price cuts is likely to be especially great when production has fallen to a low level.

ing country's currency then will be reflected in a parallel rise in the prices of manufactured imports.

Agricultural products, which become available only intermittently, at the end of the growing season, tend to react differently to depreciation of an importer's currency. Between one season and the next, the supply is fixed. If sales in the import market decline as a result of depreciation there, unsold stocks will accumulate. To maintain sales and dispose of the supply, the price in the producing country must be lowered sufficiently to keep the price in the depreciating country constant.[3]

Thus if the franc depreciates, the price of imported tobacco will rise, French imports will decline, and stocks in the supplying country (say the United States) will accumulate. To prevent this, growers in the United States will have to reduce the dollar price enough to offset the rise in the franc/dollar exchange rate. This will leave the price of tobacco in France unchanged, and French buyers will maintain their purchases.

But if Frenchmen buy the same amount of this import at the same price, their outlay in dollar exchange will remain constant. What does this mean? When total outlay on a commodity is constant at all prices, we say the elasticity of demand is unity. Here, with the rate of exchange rising, outlay on foreign exchange stays the same. The elasticity of demand for foreign exchange, in these circumstances, has a value of 1. The elasticity of demand for imports, whether high or low, has no opportunity to make itself felt, since with the price of imports constant, it is simply not brought into play.

Thus, so far as concerns the conditions under which a country's imports are supplied, we have two extremes: (1) when the exporter's price remains constant and the price in the importing country's currency rises with the exchange rate and (2) the opposite, when the price in the importing country's currency remains constant, while the exporter reduces the price in his currency. When the first condition holds good, the demand for foreign exchange has an elasticity identical with that of the demand for imports. Under the second condition, the elasticity of demand for foreign exchange is unity, regardless of what the elasticity of import demand may be.

Intermediate cases, where import prices rise, though not in proportion to the exchange rate, are not hard to imagine. They will occur when the elasticity of supply of imports is neither zero nor infinite. This will be true when, for example, as producers of French imports respond to reduced sales in France by contracting output, they encounter decreasing unit

---

[3] This conclusion is valid only if there are free markets for farm products. When, as in many countries today, price support schemes are in force, the outcome is more like that suggested in the preceding paragraphs.

costs. With manufactures, this will be most likely when capacity is neither stretched to its limit, with orders backed up, nor seriously under-utilised. With agricultural products, it will be over periods longer than a single growing season.

Foreign Demand for a Country's Imports

Until now, we have ignored the fact that the imports of a given country, such as France, are sold in other parts of the world, too. If the prices of French imports remain constant abroad, this foreign demand will not be called into play and can be ignored. But if those prices are depressed as a result of France's declining purchases, foreign buyers will increase their purchases. This will support foreign prices. The price-maintaining effect of foreign demand will of course be greater the more elastic is this foreign demand.

SUPPLY OF FOREIGN EXCHANGE FROM GOODS
AND SERVICES

We now turn to the supply side of the foreign exchange market, and consider the supply of foreign exchange derived from the export of goods and services. Our task is made easier now that we have covered the demand side, for most of what we shall have to say about the supply side is analogous in character.

Foreign Exchange Supply, and Demand for Exports

The supply of foreign exchange, or the amount of foreign exchange that will be forthcoming at different rates of exchange, is simply the foreign demand for a country's exports seen in reverse. A rise in the franc/dollar exchange rate, if the franc price of a given export remains constant, will permit a lowering of its foreign price and thus stimulate increased sales abroad.

Consider a French export costing 350 francs to produce, say an inexpensive pair of gloves. At an exchange rate of 350 frs./$, these would sell for $1 in the American market (and at equivalent prices in other currency markets). At 400 frs./$, to realise his 350 francs, the exporter would need to charge the American buyer only $0.875. At a rate of 450 frs./$, the price abroad could be further reduced to $0.778, at 500 frs./$, to $0.70, and so on.

Other things equal, the volume of exports and therewith the supply of foreign exchange will expand more rapidly the more elastic is foreign demand. To obtain a benchmark to which we can refer, let us first assume an elasticity of demand for exports of 1. In the following table, which assumes an export whose home price remains constant at 350 francs, franc/dollar rates are shown for 50 franc intervals, and in column three, the price which would have to be charged in the American market, at each exchange rate, to yield 350 francs.

Table 16.1

DEMAND FOR EXPORTS AND SUPPLY OF FOREIGN EXCHANGE

(1) PRICE OF EXPORT IN FRANCS	(2) FRANC-DOLLAR EXCHANGE RATE	(3) PRICE OF EXPORT IN $ $(1 \div 2)$	(4) QUANTITY OF EXPORT DEMANDED (ELAS. $= 1$)	(5) AMOUNT OF FOREIGN EXCHANGE SUPPLIED (3×4)	(6) QUANTITY OF EXPORT DEMANDED (ELAS. $= 2$)	(7) AMOUNT OF FOREIGN EXCHANGE SUPPLIED (3×6)
350	700	$0.50	2,000	$1,000	4,000	$2,000
350	650	0.538	1,859	1,000	3,455	1,859
350	600	0.583	1,715	1,000	2,942	1,715
350	550	0.636	1,572	1,000	2,472	1,572
350	500	0.70	1,429	1,000	2,041	1,429
350	450	0.778	1,285	1,000	1,652	1,285
350	400	0.875	1,143	1,000	1,306	1,143
350	350	1.00	1,000	1,000	1,000	1,000
350	300	1.167	857	1,000	734	857
350	250	1.40	714	1,000	510	714

Column four gives the quantity of exports that will be demanded if, over the range of American prices listed, the elasticity of demand is 1. This requires that price times quantity, or total outlay, shall be constant.[4] But note what this means from the point of view of the supply of foreign exchange: If total outlay in the United States on our export remains constant, the supply of foreign exchange will also be a constant. When such a supply is represented graphically, it takes the form, as in Figure 16.3, of a vertical straight line $(S_1S'_1)$. Such a curve is said to have an elasticity of zero. Thus when the foreign elasticity of demand for our exports is unity, the elasticity of supply of foreign exchange is zero.

An elasticity of demand greater than unity exists when the quantity demanded increases more than in proportion to the decrease of price. Column six introduces figures appropriate to such an elasticity of demand for exports. But this means that as price falls, total outlay will increase. Column seven shows the total expenditure in the United States on the export in question corresponding to the prices of column three and the

[4] The quantities demanded are inaccurate to the extent that the introduction of decimals was avoided. Therefore price times quantity does not quite meet the test of constancy.

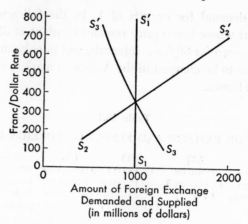

Fig. 16.3: Supply of Foreign Exchange Under
Different Conditions of Elasticity.

quantities of column six; this is the same thing as the supply of foreign
exchange derived from this export. Portrayed graphically (curve S_2S_2'
of Figure 16.3), this gives a supply curve of positive inclination. To an
elasticity of demand for exports greater than unity, there corresponds
a positively inclined supply curve of foreign exchange. A similar process
of reasoning could easily show that when the foreign elasticity of demand
for exports is less than unity, the corresponding supply curve of foreign
exchange will be negatively inclined (S_3S_3' of Figure 16.3).[5]

Supply of Export-Competing Goods

Just as in the case of demand for foreign exchange we had to take
account, along with the elasticity of demand for imports, of the elasticity
of supply of import-competing goods, so in dealing with the supply of
foreign exchange we must allow for the competition exporters are almost
sure to meet abroad. That is, we must reckon with the elasticity of supply
of export-competing goods.

[5] There is a limit, however, to the negative inclination of such a curve. It cannot rise
(from right to left), as the exchange rate rises, so slowly as to reflect a declining yield
in francs (rate of exchange times supply forthcoming at each rate). For this would
imply, as the quantity of exports increased, that they were being sold at a constantly
diminishing price in francs. But this cannot be. For the pressure to expand output as
exports increase will put pressure on productive resources. In the short run, this is
almost certain to result in rising costs and prices.

If a supply of foreign exchange reflecting a declining franc-yield is an impossibility,
this means that the limit to the negative inclination of the foreign exchange supply curve
is that which represents a constant franc-yield. But this corresponds to an elasticity
of — 1. Therefore this is the most adverse supply of foreign exchange conceivable—from
the point of view of the exporting country, and so far as this supply is derived from
exports of goods and services.

Since a rising franc/dollar exchange rate induces a decline in the dollar price of French exports, sales abroad will expand more rapidly just to the extent to which French price competition causes foreign competitors to contract output and to retire from the field. And the rapidity with which their output contracts is simply the elasticity of supply of these export-competing products.

The outcome may be stated in terms of the effect on the elasticity of demand for the exporting country's, say France's, exports. This demand is distinct from the more general demand for goods such as are being exported. Its elasticity depends upon the commodity elasticity of demand for such goods, as modified by the elasticity of supply of export-competing goods. Since a single nation (particularly if it is a small one) is almost certain to meet extensive competition for its exports, this modification is likely to be substantial. Even though the underlying elasticity of demand for export-type goods may be less than unity, the displacement of foreign production from export markets may well be great enough to transform a negatively inclined supply curve of foreign exchange into a positively inclined one.[6]

A Range of Export Goods

This conclusion is reenforced when we consider, not merely the goods that were already on an export basis at a given rate of exchange, but also those additional commodities that become exportable as a currency depreciates. The range of such commodities may be very sizeable; it is particularly likely to be so for a large and diversified economy. Therefore even though the elasticity of demand for a country's existing exports might be only moderate, perhaps no more than unity, when this factor is taken into account, there is a strong presumption that it will be greater than unity, and that as a consequence the aggregate supply curve of foreign exchange will be positively inclined.

Elasticity of Supply of Exports

So much for the forces operating abroad to determine exports. But we must also reckon with domestic factors—the ease or difficulty with which the output of exports can be expanded, and the extent to which domestic customers reduce their purchases and release goods for export as their

[6] With only minor changes, Figure 16.2 could be transformed to portray the demand for exports. DD' would represent the demand for goods such as are exported (export-type goods), $C_hC'_h$ (perhaps relabeled $C_fC'_f$) foreign production of export competing goods, and $D_mD'_m$ (relabeled $D_xD'_x$) the demand for French exports within the price range P_aP_h.

prices rise. These forces determine whether the home prices of exports remain constant, as we have assumed up to this point, or whether, and to what degree, they will be raised.

Distinguishing, as before, between manufactured and agricultural products, it would seem that, as to the former, much will depend upon the state of employment and the effectiveness of competition in the exporting country. With many resources idle, output can be increased with little if any increase in cost and price. With full employment, if producers sacrifice short-run gain to longer-run considerations, they may hold prices constant and allow unfilled orders to accumulate. Under either of these circumstances, with prices unchanged in the exporting country, no qualification of our conclusions is necessary. The supply of foreign exchange will reflect the foreign elasticity of demand for the country's exports.

If, at full employment, manufacturers of exports react competitively, they will raise their prices, since production facilities are being stretched to the limit, approximately in proportion to the exchange rate. Prices abroad will then remain unchanged, sales will not vary, and total foreign outlay on the depreciating country's exports will be constant. This gives an unvarying supply of foreign exchange, with elasticity of zero.

Over a period of no more than a year, the same conclusion would apply to agricultural products, unless there were large accumulated stocks whose release would moderate the price increase. Over a period of more than a year, increased supplies of agricultural commodities could presumably be made available, though probably only at some increase in cost. This would also tend to be true of manufactures when some, but not excessive, idle resources were present. Such intermediate conditions would, of course, give intermediate results. With some increase in export prices, but less than in proportion to the rise in the exchange rate, prices paid by foreign buyers would decline somewhat. The elasticity of demand would not be called fully into play, and the supply of foreign exchange would have an elasticity between zero (with a constant foreign price) and that reflecting the elasticity of demand for exports (with a constant home price).

With pressure from increasing foreign sales tending to raise prices, domestic demand for exports would act as a safety valve, releasing goods for export as prices rose and thus moderating this rise. This moderating influence would be more powerful, the more elastic were these domestic demands.

Summary

We have now come to the end of a long and difficult road. It may be helpful, in view of its tortuous course, if we recall the principal landmarks we have encountered.

There is a symmetry in the forces determining the demand and supply of foreign exchange. This symmetry helps one remember them. Four elasticities are involved on each side of the market, and of these, two are domestic in origin, two foreign.

The demand for foreign exchange. The domestic determinants of the demand for foreign exchange are the demand for import-type goods and the supply of import-competing goods. Their interaction determines the demand for imports, whose elasticity will vary *directly* with the elasticity of each of these determinants.

The two foreign elasticities involved are the elasticity of supply of imports and the elasticity of home demand for these goods. Together they determine whether the foreign price of imports will remain constant in the face of declining imports in the depreciating country, or whether that price will fall, and how much. If the foreign price of imports stays the same, price in the importing country will follow the rate of exchange and the elasticity of import demand will determine the demand for foreign exchange. If the foreign price of imports falls sufficiently (in proportion to the exchange rate), price in the import market will remain unchanged, total outlay on imports will be constant, and the elasticity of demand for foreign exchange will be unity. Intermediate price changes abroad will produce intermediate results.

The supply of foreign exchange. The supply of foreign exchange derives from the demand for the depreciating country's exports. Underlying this demand are the demand for export-type goods (goods such as our country exports) and the supply of export-competing goods. Their interaction determines the demand for exports, whose elasticity will vary directly with the elasticity of each of these determinants.

The two domestic elasticities are the elasticity of supply of exports and the elasticity of home demand for these goods. Together they determine whether the home price of exports remains constant as the exchange rate rises, or whether the home price goes up, and how much. If this price stays unchanged, the foreign price of exports will vary with the exchange rate, and the elasticity of demand for our country's exports will be fully reflected in the supply of exchange. If the home price of exports rises in proportion to the exchange rate, the foreign price will remain constant, foreign outlay on our country's exports will not change, and the elasticity of supply of foreign exchange will be zero. Intermediate price changes will produce intermediate results.

INTERACTION OF THE DEMAND FOR AND SUPPLY OF FOREIGN EXCHANGE

Having terminated our examination of the forces determining the elasticity of demand for and supply of exchange, so far at least as these are dependent on imports and exports of goods and services, we are now in a position to give an answer to two questions raised early in this chapter: (1) Are elasticities in the foreign exchange market likely to be sufficiently large so that a deficit in a country's balance of payments can be eliminated by a moderate depreciation, or will it have to be excessive? [7] (2) Is the foreign exchange market, so far as it depends on exports and imports, likely to be stable?

With respect to the first question, our analysis entitles us to be fairly optimistic, with the reservation that some countries may be subject to an especially adverse combination of circumstances. In general, however, the foreign exchange elasticities should be sufficiently great to make it possible to eliminate a "reasonable" deficit by a depreciation that is not excessive.

The Demand Side of the Market

(1) In the first place, the demand for foreign exchange is certain to be negatively inclined, since it directly reflects the demand for imports. This being a demand for commodities (and services), it obeys the normal rule that a lowering of price will induce increased purchases. If the demand for foreign exchange is of this kind, depreciation will always contribute something to the elimination of a deficit, since as the exchange rate rises, less foreign currency is demanded.

(2) In most circumstances, we can expect the demand for imports to be quite elastic. Even if the demand for import-type goods is inelastic, the presence of home-produced substitutes guarantees that the demand for imports proper will have a much higher elasticity.

If this elasticity is to be felt fully, however, prices in the exporting center must remain constant, so that import prices will vary with the rate of exchange. Our study suggests that, after account is taken of the price-

[7] Clearly, the size of the deficit is related to the amount of depreciation needed to correct it. An enormous deficit would require far more depreciation for its elimination than a moderate one. A reasonable statement of the problem is whether foreign exchange elasticities are sufficiently large to make depreciation a feasible remedy for situations that are not so abnormal as to require desperate measures.

moderating effect of foreign demand for a country's imports, manufactured products, at least, are not likely to vary greatly in price, whatever the level of employment. This is the more true, the smaller the market of the depreciating country.

Agricultural prices are subject to greater short-run variations. The price of a major crop, however, is unlikely to change much in response to some decline in the demand of a single customer, unless it is a very large one. But the demand for agricultural products is typically less than unity. Hence if farm products count heavily in a country's imports, this could greatly reduce the average elasticity of import demand.

(3) The aggregate demand for imports is not a demand for an array of commodities fixed once and for all. As the exchange rate rises, and import prices consequently go up, more and more domestic producers, who at lower exchange rates could not meet foreign competition, become able to do so. One after another, additional imports are pushed out of the market by new domestic competition. This gives to the aggregate demand for imports an elasticity greater than that for any single import or for any fixed group.

(4) As the time period under consideration is lengthened, import demand is certain to be more elastic than in the short run we have had in mind. Over a longer period, more and more import substitutes will appear on the market, for it takes time to make plans and assemble productive resources into a going concern. Moreover, as time passes and the depreciation sticks, potential producers become reassured and determine to enter the field.

For all these reasons, it appears very likely that the demand for imports will normally have a rather high elasticity, especially if manufactures bulk large among imports. This elasticity will be enhanced if the economy is well diversified, with a wide range of import-competing production. And it will be increased with the passage of time.

The Supply Side of the Market

Although the supply of foreign exchange is simply the demand for exports turned around, it will contribute nothing—in the event of depreciation—to the elimination of a deficit unless the export demand has an elasticity greater than unity. For with that value, foreign outlay, which *is* the supply of exchange, remains constant at all rates of exchange. This gives a vertical exchange supply curve—elasticity is zero. With depreciation, although demand (autonomous payments) contracts, supply (autonomous receipts) stays unchanged.

Considerations analogous to those underlying demand, however, suggest that often, at least, we can expect something better than this rather unsatisfactory outcome.

(1) There is even more reason than in the case of imports to expect export demand to have a relatively high elasticity, probably greater than unity. For a single country facing the rest of the world is almost certain to find its exports encountering substantial competition from foreign suppliers. As depreciation permits our country to lower its prices abroad, it displaces some competing suppliers and commands a larger share of the market. This is true even of as large a country as the United States; it is even more true of smaller countries whose exports are but a small proportion of world consumption.

(2) Moreover, as the exchange rate rises (our country's currency depreciates), the range of domestic commodities able to enter into export competition constantly widens.

The combined operation of these two factors should in most cases be sufficient to give the demand for exports, as distinct from the demand abroad for goods such as our country exports (export-type goods), an elasticity greater than 1. This would mean a supply curve of foreign exchange that was positively inclined.

(3) Were we to consider a period longer than the short-run, with its assumption of a fixed amount of productive resources, then just as with imports, the supply of foreign exchange would, without doubt, expand still more rapidly. For with more time, the supply of exports can be adjusted to demand, exporters can develop their market connections, and foreign competitors can complete their adjustment to the new competitive situation.

Thus, there is a good prospect that the demand for a single country's exports will be quite elastic (greater than unity), so that the supply curve of foreign exchange will be positively inclined. With depreciation, the expansion in the supply of exchange will contribute its share to bridging the gap in the balance of payments. This auspicious outcome is the more likely, the larger is the share of manufactures in a country's exports, for being generally in more elastic supply than agricultural products, substantial price increases are less probable. A diversified list of exports and potential exports is also an advantage, as is the presence abroad of a wide range of competing products. A country with one or two commodities dominating its exports, on the other hand, is at a disadvantage, a disadvantage that will be increased if that country is also the chief supplier, as Brazil with its coffee.

It should be clear that although general considerations support the view that for most countries, exchange market elasticities are fairly high, there are many special combinations of circumstances that could produce a very different result. In any concrete situation, detailed analysis is essential to sound judgment.

Market Stability

The answer to our second question, whether the foreign exchange market—so far as it depends on exports and imports of goods and services—is likely to be stable, is now fairly obvious. The demand for a country's exports must be quite inelastic for its foreign exchange supply curve to have a negative inclination. As for imports, unless they are predominantly necessities, and encounter little competition from substitutes, there is small likelihood that the demand curve for foreign exchange will be steeper than the supply curve, so that above their point of intersection the former will lie above and to the right of the latter. Unless this especially unfavorable combination of circumstances is encountered, the foreign exchange market will be stable.[8]

CAPITAL MOVEMENTS AND THE FOREIGN EXCHANGES

In addition to transactions involving the purchase or sale of goods and services, those arising from the desire to effect international transfers of capital may be quantitatively important in a country's balance of payments and in its foreign exchange market. It is necessary to consider them separately, since the demand and supply of foreign exchange to which they give rise respond differently to variations in the exchange rate.

Capital movements can be classified in various ways. For our purposes, it is important to distinguish between those undertaken for investment purposes—for the sake of the interest or dividends to be gained; and those whose motivation is speculative, where the object of the transfer is to gain from appreciation in the capital value of the investment. Fear-motivated flights of capital in search of a safe haven are a special category. The usual

---

[8] This special relation of the two curves can be expressed in terms of the elasticities of demand for exports and imports. Instability will exist when the sum of the elasticity of demand for imports and of the elasticity of demand for exports is less than 1 ($n_m + n_x < 1$). (This is known as the Marshall-Lerner condition. See, for example, Abba P. Lerner, *The Economics of Control,* pp. 377-9.)

This theorem, however, assumes that, initially, exports and imports are equal. If imports exceed exports to begin with, as when a country is running a deficit, the critical value is not 1, but less than 1. The theorem also assumes that the elasticity of supply of exports and imports is infinite. Lower values of these elasticities would be more favorable if n_m and n_x are both small.

distinction between short-term and long-term investments is of secondary interest only.

Transfers for Investment Purposes

International transfers of capital to take advantage of an attractive yield may be invested in stocks, bonds, and physical assets such as manufacturing plant, all of which are long-term in character, or in such short-term securities as bills, notes, and acceptances. And such movements, it is clear, may, from the point of view of any country, be in either direction—they may give rise to a demand for or a supply of foreign exchange.

Let us consider first investment by the residents of a particular country, say the United States, in the stocks, bonds, and similar assets of other countries. Funds must be transferred from the United States to the foreigners who are offering these assets for sale; hence the process of investment brings into the foreign exchange market a demand for foreign currencies, say pounds sterling. How is this demand expressed? Stocks of corporations, physical assets, and short-term securities are always priced in the currency of the country where they are issued or where they exist. Earnings from such assets will be payable in the same currency. Bonds, however, may be issued with principal and interest stipulated in the issuing country's currency or in the currency of some other country, usually that of the principal buyers.

When the principal and interest of bonds are expressed in the issuing country's currency, let us say sterling, a decline in the dollar/sterling exchange rate cheapens the bond to the American buyer. Taken by itself, this should make additional purchases attractive. But a lower price of sterling, if it is expected to be enduring, also lowers the dollar return on the investment equally. This cancels the effect of a lower purchase price.[9] The sums invested abroad would depend upon the relative attractiveness of foreign as opposed to domestic investments; the exchange rate would be irrelevant. A fixed amount of sterling, depending upon investment considerations alone, would be demanded for the purpose of transferring capital abroad. The investment demand for sterling would be a vertical straight line (elasticity zero); added to the demand derived from transactions in goods and services, it would give a total demand curve for foreign exchange a fixed distance to the right of the former.

Suppose, however, as sometimes occurs, the principal and interest of bonds are expressed in the buying country's currency (dollar bonds). Here

---

[9] If the lower exchange rate is expected to be only temporary, speculative considerations take over; all sterling holdings would become attractive for speculative purchase.

the exchange rate is irrelevant from the very beginning. U.S. investors would determine, on the basis of the attractiveness of the various foreign investments, how many dollars they wished to invest in any given period. This sum in dollars would be offered for sterling whatever the exchange rate. (Extreme depreciation of sterling might arouse fears as to the ability of the security issuers to service and repay the debt, and thus reduce the sum invested. This is equally true when securities are issued in terms of sterling.) Here we have total outlay in dollars on foreign exchange constant. The demand for foreign exchange for investment purposes has an elasticity of unity. The total demand for sterling would lie to the right of the transactions demand by an ever increasing amount.

Sales of U.S. securities or property to foreigners for investment purposes give rise to a supply of foreign exchange. Stocks, physical assets, and short-term securities, always priced in the issuing country's currency, may be considered together with bonds whose principal and interest are quoted in dollars. As with goods and services, the supply of foreign exchange arising from the sale abroad of U.S. assets will depend upon the foreign demand. This will be determined by investment considerations alone, since depreciation or appreciation of the dollar will affect principal and yield in the same direction and to the same degree. Foreigners will demand the fixed quantity of dollars so determined, whatever the exchange rate. Translated into a supply of exchange in the United States, this would mean that at a high dollar-sterling rate, a relatively small amount of sterling bills would need to be drawn to yield a given sum in dollars, and that at lower rates, the sum to be drawn in sterling would increase in inverse proportion to the fall in the exchange rate. (One million dollars would require only £200,000 to be drawn at $5/£; at $2/£, £500,000 would be necessary.) This is a supply of foreign exchange with a negative elasticity of 1, which would be added to the supply from goods and services transactions.

Should the United States issue bonds with principal and interest payable in sterling, the foreign investment in sterling would be that amount determined by investment considerations. This gives a fixed supply of sterling, to be added to the supply from merchandise transactions to get the total supply of foreign exchange.

At this point, we may add that all types of gifts and one-sided payments like reparations would give rise to a demand or supply of foreign exchange corresponding precisely to the above analysis. For although donations are not undertaken to earn an income, like transfers of investment capital, the criteria on which they are based bear no relation to the exchange rate.

Capital Flight

At times of great political and economic insecurity, owners of capital are likely to want to transfer their funds abroad for safety. Although once they have transferred them, they will doubtless sooner or later invest them in earning assets, considerations of income have nothing to do with the original capital movement. It is motivated by fear; the owners of capital sought for it a safer haven. During the disturbed years before World War II, huge amounts of capital were exported from Europe for this reason. Estimates place the amount coming to the United States alone, between 1935 and 1939, at well over $5 billion.

When fear spurs people to send their wealth abroad, the dearness or cheapness of the currency into which they are converting is of little moment. The demand for foreign exchange in the exporting centers tends toward zero elasticity; in the receiving country, the corresponding supply will have a negative elasticity of 1.

Speculative Capital Movements

International transfers of capital with the aim of profiting from an increase in the value of the principal, rather than to earn an income, may be like rifle shots, directed at specific long-term assets, or like the scattered discharge of a shot gun, directed at foreign assets in general. Purchase for appreciation of a particular long-term foreign asset, such as the stock of a corporation, would not be undertaken unless the buyer were reasonably certain that the exchange rate would remain stable, or that any change would be favorable. For an adverse movement of the exchange rate could wipe out any gain from the appreciation of a specific asset. On the assumption, therefore, that any change in the exchange rate will be upward, the foreign exchange demanded would be a fixed amount at all rates—whatever amount was justified by the prospects of appreciation of the particular foreign assets involved. For similar inward capital movements, since the demand abroad would be for a fixed amount of dollars, for example, the supply of foreign exchange reflecting this foreign demand would have a negative elasticity of 1.

The most common object of international speculation, however, is not particular foreign assets, but holdings of some country's currency. It is the shot gun case. Such speculation may be stabilising in character; that is, it may supplement and support non-speculative forces and thus tend to establish a stable exchange rate—or its influence may be highly disruptive and destabilising. Whether it is the one or the other depends on how speculators react to changes in the exchange rate.

If speculators on balance anticipate that a drop in the price of a particular currency is accidental and transitory, speculative sentiment will on balance be "bullish," and demand from this source will support the exchange rate, effecting a prompter return to normal. But when the other, more permanent determinants of the exchange rate are adverse, and especially when they are expected to become increasingly adverse, foreshadowing a currency's depreciation, speculative opinion will become preponderantly "bearish." (When underlying conditions indicate currency appreciation, the opposite will be true.) Those with holdings of the currency in question will sell them and move into stronger currencies, thus reenforcing and speeding up the currency's tendency to depreciate.[10]

Thus after World War I, most people thought Europe, including Germany, would soon return to normal prewar conditions. Through 1920 and 1921, speculation (reenforced by the speculative activity of large numbers of amateurs) supported the mark. Momentary declines in its price in terms of dollars and other currencies led promptly to increased purchases and reduced supplies.

But in 1922 and increasingly in 1923, as it became apparent that German recovery was being delayed and that the government was unable to check inflation, speculative opinion rapidly changed. Confidence in the stability of the mark vanished; the bulk of speculators became convinced that it would depreciate; and a decline in the dollar price of the mark, instead of stimulating increased purchases, caused buyers to withdraw from the market. The demand curve acquired a "perverse" elasticity; it became positively inclined.

Also, those who held marks (both in Germany and abroad) took each decline in their value as a presentiment of further weakness, and offered larger and larger quantities for sale. The supply curve became negatively inclined.

So strong were speculative forces at this time that they dominated the market. Reenforced by unchecked inflation in Germany, they pushed the

[10] At the same time, speculators who do not possess holdings of the depreciating currency will sell it forward; that is, enter into contracts to deliver the currency later at a price specified now. Though this price will, if prospects are unfavorable, be lower than the current price, it will be higher than the price at which the speculator believes he can in the future buy "spot" exchange with which to cover his forward commitment. For further discussion of the operation of the forward exchanges, see the Appendix to Chapter 15.

international value of the mark lower and lower until in early 1924, it became virtually worthless.

Such an extreme situation is of course exceptional. In this instance, inflation and other disruptive forces were constantly pushing the German demand for imports and other payments to the right, while at the same time diminishing the availability of exports. Underlying conditions justified the increasing pessimism of speculators. More frequently, speculators might anticipate that a country's currency would be weak below a certain level of the exchange rate, but that after a certain degree of depreciation, a country's receipts and payments would be brought into balance. Below this equilibrium rate, speculative demand and supply would tend to be perverse in character. As that rate was approached, speculative opinion would become more evenly divided; at the estimated equilibrium rate and above, speculative demand and supply would resume their normal shape, with demand diminishing and supply expanding as the price of foreign currency rose.

Such conditions existed in the months prior to September 1949 with respect to the pound sterling. Speculators and other traders had become convinced that the pound, at a price of about $4.03, was overvalued, and that devaluation was imminent. Holders of sterling balances converted them into dollars, while those with payments to make in sterling postponed them. Owing to the existence of exchange controls in the United Kingdom, these speculative transactions could not affect the rate of exchange; they merely widened the gap between British receipts and payments. When, in September, the pound was devalued to $2.80, confidence returned. It was felt that further depreciation was unlikely, so the demand for sterling strengthened and the supply became less abundant.

Speculation: Conclusion

What can we say in conclusion? Under reasonably normal circumstances, speculation will operate as a stabilising force. Speculators will support a currency's international value, when it is falling, by increasing their purchases and reducing their sales. They will act to check a rise, when a currency's international value is increasing, by reducing their purchases and increasing their sales.

But when conditions underlying ordinary commodity and security transactions foreshadow weakness, so that speculators expect a decline in the exchange rate to be followed by further decline, a speculative demand for and supply of foreign exchange may become perverse. Changes in exchange rates will be aggravated, since total demand and supply of exchange are both less elastic than before. When extreme pessimism reigns, speculative forces completely dominate the market, causing the exchange rate to become unstable.

SELECTED REFERENCES

Alexander, Sidney S., "Effects of a Devaluation on a Trade Balance," *IMF Staff Papers,* Vol. II, No. 2 (April 1952). Suggests the replacement of the elasticities approach to exchange-rate problems by the income-absorption approach, which is then developed.

Chang, T. C., *Cyclical Movements in the Balance of Payments* (Cambridge University Press, 1951). Chapter 2 discusses average and marginal import propensities and their determinants; estimates are given for these propensities and for price elasticities of demand for several countries.

Chang, T. C., "A Statistical Note on World Demand for Exports," *Review of Economics and Statistics,* XXX (May 1948). Examines income elasticities of demand for different categories of goods, and price elasticities for different countries, with generally unfavorable results.

Haberler, Gottfried, "The Market for Foreign Exchange and the Stability of the Balance of Payments, *Kyklos,* III (1949). Discusses the derivation of demand and supply curves for foreign exchange, *a priori* considerations relating to their elasticity, and their relation to a deficit.

Machlup, Fritz, "The Theory of Foreign Exchanges," Chapter 5 of *Readings in the Theory of International Trade* (The Blakiston Co., Philadelphia, 1949). A lucid presentation of the theory of foreign exchange.

Machlup, Fritz, "Elasticity Pessimism in International Trade," *Economia Internazionale,* III (Feb. 1950). A vigorous criticism of the pessimism reflected in measures of demand elasticities in international trade.

Metzler, Lloyd A., "The Theory of International Trade," Chapter 6 of *A Survey of Contemporary Economics,* Howard S. Ellis, editor (The Blakiston Co., Philadelphia, 1948). Section III is devoted to fluctuating exchange rates, with particular emphasis on the stability condition.

Orcutt, Guy, "Measurement of Price Elasticities in International Trade," *Review of Economics and Statistics* XXXII (May 1950). Criticises elasticity estimates in terms of the price data used, the bias introduced by large variations in prices of goods in inelastic demand, and the small degree of price changes actually observed.

17

DISEQUILIBRIA IN THE BALANCE OF PAYMENTS AND THEIR ADJUSTMENT

DIFFERENT KINDS OF BALANCE

A balance of payments must always balance. This is required by the rule of accounting, that debits must always equal credits. Such an accounting balance can plainly be realised—*must* be realised—under any conceivable circumstances: with exports rising or falling, with capital moving into or fleeing from a country, with prices fluctuating or stable. No country, therefore, need concern itself with whether its balance of payments balances—this is unavoidable.

A country must, however, concern itself with *how* this balance is achieved. It may be attained easily and without effort; if so, there is no cause for worry. On the other hand, the balance may be realised only under conditions of severe strain. To ease the strain, strong remedial measures may be necessary.

An Analogy

Consider the balance of payments of an individual—of you or me. Each of us has a balance of payments with the rest of the world; it consists simply of his total receipts and expenditures. So long as one's income equals his outgo, he is in a stable position that can continue indefinitely; his balance of payments is in equilibrium. But let him begin to spend more than he earns, and he will have to draw on his savings or run into debt. His payments and his receipts still balance, in an accounting sense, but his changed situation cannot continue indefinitely. Sooner or later he will exhaust his savings; sooner or later his creditors will refuse to extend further loans. Then he will have to make a radical adjustment, either increasing his earning power or cutting his spending down to his income.

Similarly with a nation: so long as it lives within its international means, all is well. Its balance of payments is not only in accounting balance, but in equilibrium too. But let the expenditures its residents wish to make abroad exceed the expenditures foreigners choose to direct toward this country, and it will have to draw on its international reserves to meet the resultant deficit.

This condition of disequilibrium cannot continue; the drain on reserves must be checked before they are exhausted. Some kind of adjustment is necessary.[1]

Rephrasing the foregoing statement in more technical terms, we can say that a country's reserves will not change if its autonomous receipts equal its autonomous payments. Autonomous transactions on both sides of the international account include *all* transactions undertaken for their own sake—not only imports and exports of goods and services, but inward or outward movements of capital as well.

Balance of Payments Equilibrium

Beyond indicating that disequilibrium is present in a country's balance of payments when it is forced to draw upon its international reserves, which implies as a corollary that equilibrium exists when reserves do not change, we have done little to clarify these concepts. In other words, we have given one important criterion of equilibrium—absence of changes in international reserves—but have not explained the concept itself. Let us now turn to this problem.

What must be true if equality of autonomous receipts and payments, once established, is to continue? The answer to this question will specify the conditions of stable balance of payments equilibrium.

Consider first a country's exports of goods and services. These will tend to remain constant when the forces that determine them are in a stable relationship with one another. Summarily, this means that the supply of exports is adjusted to the demand for them at stable prices. More specifically, the prices of the productive factors and the amounts of them used to produce exports have achieved stable adjustment to the wants of consumers at existing levels of income. Similarly, imports will be stable when the forces determining their supply are adjusted to consumers' demands. When a stable adjustment of all these interrelated forces is reached, there will be no tendency for exports or imports to increase, nor for resources to move from one industry to another.

---

[1] If a nation's current international receipts exceed its current payments, it will develop a surplus in its balance of payments, marked by an inflow of gold and foreign exchange. This is a condition favorable for the country immediately concerned, yet it does not reflect equilibrium. It too must be corrected, if only because a surplus in one country's balance of payments implies a deficit in those of some of its trading partners. Much depends, of course, upon the relative size of the surplus country. We shall focus upon the problems of deficit countries, however, for that is where the real difficulties lie.

In a static world, we would have to concern ourselves with nothing but exports and imports of goods and services. There would be no capital movements, because there would be no saving and no investment. But in the real world there is growth: population expands, people save, and these savings are invested in increasing a community's capital resources. And there are movements of capital from countries where accumulation is relatively rapid and returns to capital comparatively low, toward regions where capital is less abundant and its earning power (after allowing for risk) is greater. Given the differential in the return to capital in various parts of the earth, a steady flow of capital will reflect balance between the desire of investors for a higher return, and the retarding effect of such obstacles as ignorance of investment opportunities, differences in laws and customs, the greater difficulty of supervising foreign investments, and a natural fear of the unknown.

Growth would, of course, mean changes in exports and imports, as well as capital movements. Stability in a country's balance of payments could be preserved by small but continuing adjustments through changes in factor prices, in volume of output, in the allocation of resources, and in the rate of capital flow.

The world we live in, however, does not behave in this smooth and orderly fashion. Change takes place, not only slowly and gradually, but often violently and unexpectedly. When such changes affect a country's exports, its imports, or its lending or borrowing, equilibrium in its balance of payments is disturbed. A deficit or a surplus develops. Adjustment becomes imperative for a deficit country, and this adjustment must be reasonably prompt. We shall consider two alternative methods by which a nation can adjust to disturbances in its balance of payments later in this chapter. But first let us see what kinds of disturbance are likely to be encountered.

DISTURBANCES OF EQUILIBRIUM IN THE BALANCE OF PAYMENTS

Our discussion of balance of payments equilibrium enables us to say, with some suppression of detail, that a country's exports depend upon three things: (1) the total volume of purchasing power available to foreigners for expenditure on all conceivable items, including this country's exports; (2) the particular kinds of commodities and services wanted by foreigners, as determined by their tastes; and (3) the prices at which goods such as our country exports are available. Similarly, a country's imports depend upon:

(1) the total purchasing power its residents can command; (2) their specific desires or tastes: and (3) the prices of imports and possible domestic substitutes.

In sum, any change in the level of income, at home or abroad, tends to affect imports or exports, since it alters total expenditure in one place or the other. And any change in demand or supply conditions, either at home or abroad, will influence the volume of specific imports and exports, and through these, their aggregate value. Long-term capital movements depend principally upon international differences in the return to capital. As new opportunities for investment appear in some countries, they raise the relative rate of return there. Similarly, returns may decline relatively or even absolutely where capital accumulates faster than new investment outlets appear. Such changes will cause the direction and rate of flow of capital to vary.

One important source of disturbance to a country's balance of payments thus resides in income changes. The rest may be classified as structural changes, if we define "economic structure" as the way in which the parts of a country's economy are put together and how they are related to the external world. A structural change thus implies an alteration in some specific sector of a nation's economy; its effect on the balance of payments will generally be limited to one or a few of its component items. By way of contrast, income changes affect exports or imports in their totality, though not necessarily in equal degree throughout their entire range.

Short-Run Disturbances

We can simplify our analysis by eliminating some causes of disequilibrium as relatively unimportant. To begin with, a distinction can be made with respect to the duration of disequilibria. Some are short-run in character, lasting only for a few months or perhaps a year or so. Such are purely seasonal disturbances, commonly encountered by agricultural-exporting countries.

Thus Australian wool floods the market between November and March. During this period, Australia's exports greatly exceed her imports and foreign balances accumulate rapidly. In subsequent months, there is an excess of imports and foreign balances are drawn upon. Since this is a recurring pattern, it poses no problem. The sensible way of meeting the deficits between April and October is to draw upon international reserves, since their prompt replenishment is assured.

A crop failure, leading either to reduced exports or increased imports, is more serious. But it is usually a temporary disturbance, to be succeeded by a return to normal. A nation, like an individual, can justifiably draw on its reserves when confronted with such unusual and short-run emergencies.

We shall pay little attention to phenomena of this kind, and consider only situations which continue or threaten to continue for some time and thus tend to exhaust or reduce to the danger point a country's international reserves.

Changes in Money Income

Let us first consider changes in money income as a cause of balance of payments difficulties. Two types of income variation need to be distinguished: those that occur independently in one or more countries, and those that are linked together through the international propagation of the business cycle.

An independent change in income in a given country may be inflationary or deflationary. Only the former need concern us here, since a decline in national income (deflation) will cause imports to decline and thus lead to a surplus in the balance of payments.

Inflation is present when the total demand for goods and services exceeds, at current prices, total domestic output plus any normal long-term capital inflow. Usually, inflation will be accompanied and made possible by a flood of money, newly created by the banking system or the government. But inflation may also occur when increased spending is financed by dishoarding of existing money. Inflation is usually accompanied by, and its existence is proved by, a rising price level. Eventually, there will be some changes in the pattern of relative prices. Relative price changes may fail to appear, however, if the inflation is mild or if price controls suppress significant price increases.

Any inflation tends to bring about a deficit in the balance of payments, for increased expenditures are bound to affect exports and imports. The seriousness of the resultant deficit depends very largely on the degree to which a country is involved in international trade. If, like the United States, it is comparatively self-sufficient, rising demands may be largely concentrated on home goods. A country whose exports and imports are a large proportion of national income, on the other hand, like the United Kingdom, Belgium, or Norway, will feel the international impact of excess demand more promptly; it will quickly develop a serious balance of payments deficit.

When an inflation is serious, to the direct impact on exports and imports of increased expenditure must be added its indirect effect through its influence on internal prices. Home goods are likely to rise first and most. Increased costs of living stimulate wage demands. As wages rise, the cost of producing exports goes up too, reenforced by higher prices for home-produced raw materials and other components of exports. Exporters will find sales abroad diminishing, the more so if competing products are available from many sources. They may even be forced to contract output. Imports, in the meantime, will have become increasingly attractive substitutes for domestic goods.

The immediate causes of the higher spending of inflation, whether mild or severe, vary widely. There may be a war, which results in enormous outlays on military equipment and troops. Inflation can result, as in western Europe after World War II, from an attempt by government to maintain both consumption and investment at levels beyond the reach of the country's resources. It will come about, as in many underdeveloped countries, if the country undertakes a rate of investment in excess of domestic saving and normal capital inflow. Or it may simply be the consequence of a lax or ineffectual central bank, unable or unwilling to resist the demands of consumers or producers for expanded credit. Whatever the cause, the results are the same: excess of demand over available production, rising imports, falling exports, and a continuing balance of payments deficit.

The business cycle and the balance of payments. In all the instances so far considered, disequilibrium in a country's international accounts resulted from an absolute rise in that country's money income, independently of what was happening elsewhere. But similar difficulties may arise even though incomes in all countries rise or fall together, due to a common cause, provided these variations in national incomes are not synchronised. If all nations entered the phase of prosperity together, though each would find its imports increasing, its exports (which are the imports of others) would keep in step. Similarly in depression: each country's imports and exports would keep pace with one another. In fact, however, such perfect correspondence in timing does not exist. A depression, for example, generally gets under way first in one country, then is transmitted abroad in the manner shown in Chapter 13.

If all of the ninety-odd nations of the world were of equal economic importance, this phenomenon would cause little trouble.[2] For a decline (or rise) in the income of a sector of the world economy with a weight of

---

[2] Such an assumption of the equal importance of nations underlies much reasoning about international trade. It is well to be on guard against it, especially when it comes to applying theoretical analysis to practical problems.

only about 1 per cent would be spread so thinly as to have little effect. But when a few nations are of outstanding importance, the situation is very different.

This has been particularly true since the United States became the economic giant it is today. Various estimates indicate that the U.S. comprises, economically speaking, some 40 per cent of the entire free world. Small wonder then that when, between 1929 and 1932, our national income fell by half, and our imports and foreign investments by even more, our trading partners faced balance of payments deficits of huge proportions. Their levels of income, employment, and production were dragged down by the decline in ours, which was bad enough. But added to this was a severe balance of payments problem, brought about mainly because their income contraction lagged behind ours, so that their imports fell less promptly and drastically than their exports.

Cyclical disequilibrium in a country's balance of payments may be either aggravated or moderated by differences in national propensities to import. It will be aggravated if the country has a lower marginal propensity to import than the average of its trading partners, for then its imports will decline less than its exports during depression, independently of any income lag, while during prosperity they will rise by a smaller proportion. It would be unwise to generalise on the basis of this point, however, since we know relatively little about variations in the propensity to import during the different phases of the business cycle, except that they are probably very substantial.

Structural Changes

A structural change can originate at home or abroad, and on the demand or on the supply side. Thus a *domestic change in supply conditions* occurs when the depletion of a natural resource raises an industry's costs, or when an invention or improved processes give rise to a new production function permitting a lowering of costs or the introduction of a new product. An illustration of the former is the gradual exhaustion of the better coal seams in Great Britain, which in spite of improved mining methods has raised costs. Combined with the difficulty of attracting sufficient labor to the mines, this has caused a shift in the country's status from a net coal-exporting to a net importing basis. New products and improved processes are legion. We need mention only nylon, dacron, and other synthetic fibers, which have affected especially the world market for silk; synthetic nitrates; synthetic rubber; and transistors to replace radio tubes. Among noteworthy new processes are the use of mechanical cotton pickers, of mechanical handling equipment, and the introduction of "automation" in the manufacture of automobile engines.

A *domestic change in demand* occurs when tastes alter, either in favor of or adversely for a domestic industry, with a consequent shrinkage or expansion of imports. The shift in the diet of the United States and other western nations, as the standard of living has risen, from cereals and toward meat and dairy products may be mentioned.

The conversion of ocean shipping from coal- to oil-fueled engines brought a *shift in world demand* that contributed to declining British coal exports. The development and spreading use of nylon in the United States reduced that country's demand for imports of silk; the reverse side of the coin was its effect on Japanese exports.

Any of these changes in demand and supply conditions, whether they originate at home or abroad, affect a country's economic structure in relation to that of the rest of the world and therewith its balance of payments. If many such changes occur at once, the relative prices of its exports and its imports as a whole may be affected. We then get a change in its *terms of trade*. If a country's imports consist predominantly of raw materials and foodstuffs, while its exports are principally manufactured goods, a rapid increase in world population and in manufactures, set against scarce supplies of minerals and more intense cultivation of land, could raise the prices of its imports relatively to its exports. The resultant worsened terms of trade would require it to export larger quantities of manufactures to obtain the same volume of raw materials and food imports, thus presenting it with a serious problem of adjustment.

In addition to structural change resting on altered demand and supply relations, we must consider *variations in the rate of international capital flow*. The discovery of important new resources in a country that has been importing no or little capital is likely, by raising the expected returns from investment, to stimulate the inward movement of capital. Venezuela is a good example; first came oil, which led to huge investments by some of the world's leading oil producers during and since the 1920's. More recently the uncovering of large deposits of rich iron ore has induced heavy investment by Bethlehem and U.S. Steel. Discovery of new resources may play a less striking role, as when a gradual growth of a country's population and wealth create a market and cause its resources to be developed to the point where investment becomes attractive to foreigners. The United States attracted foreign investment in this fashion during much of the nineteenth century. So has Canada, both before World War I and, conspicuously, since World War II.

Changes in the rate of international investment from an established level to a new, higher one have a direct impact on its balance of payments. The export of securities expands, perhaps suddenly, creating an international surplus to which the country must become adjusted. In the investing or lending country or countries, adjustment is required to the deficit caused by the importation of securities.

A *special case* of structural change traceable to altered debtor-creditor relations is that exemplified by Britain's loss of overseas earning assets during World War II and the subsequent incurring of heavy international indebtedness. Britain's international investment income shrank sharply for a time; this and the need to liquidate outstanding debts (notably the so-called "blocked sterling balances") added to the strain on a balance of payments which for other reasons already constituted a grave problem.

Finally, we should note a particularly puzzling kind of structural disequilibrium, what Kindleberger calls *"structural disequilibrium at the factor level."* [3] This is typified by an inappropriate relation between factor prices and their relative supplies. As an illustration, Kindleberger cites Italy, where wages, though low relative to most other countries of western Europe, are high relative to Italy's endowment with labor, while interest rates appear to be too low relative to the amount of capital available. Too much production uses capital-intensive methods, too little is carried on by labor-intensive methods, with the result that there is a constant shortage of capital alongside of chronic unemployment of labor. Although since the early postwar years, Italy's balance of payments problem has not been severe, it has been prevented from becoming so only by substituting internal disequilibrium in the form of chronic unemployment for external disequilibrium. In the absence of a readjustment of factor prices more in line with factor endowment, or vice versa, any attempt to employ labor more fully is almost certain to lead—through the consequent rise in income and imports—to an open balance of payments disequilibrium. In the meantime, it is concealed or disguised by being transformed into an unemployment problem.

THE ADJUSTMENT OF BALANCE OF PAYMENTS DISEQUILIBRIUM

Ever since the dawn of modern times, constant change—at least in

[3] C. P. Kindleberger, *International Economics,* Richard D. Irwin, Inc., Homewood, Ill., 1953. See pp. 461-9 for a more extended discussion, in particular of the "dual economy" problem, when factor prices differ substantially between the developed and undeveloped sectors of an economy.

western Europe and the countries settled by Europeans—has been a leading characteristic of the economic order. More recently, the profound stirring in the hitherto relatively stagnant, undeveloped areas of the world has shaken them loose from their traditional patterns and introduced a dynamism hitherto lacking. The changes are of the types we have been examining—in incomes, either of the inflationary or cyclical variety, and in economic structures.

Whatever the cause of a specific alteration in income or structure, in an "open economy" (one linked to the rest of the world by trade and by factor movements), it is bound to affect international receipts and payments. It will generate balance of payments surpluses in some, deficits in others.

When such a disequilibrium is enduring, especially if it involves a deficit, it must somehow be halted. Something must give, and bring to an end the loss of international reserves a deficit imposes. But what? Are there any alternatives, and if so, which entails the least difficulties? These are the questions to which we must now turn.

A clue is provided by commodity markets. In these, a disturbance of an equilibrium position, owing say to an increase in demand, leads—through the operation of the price mechanism—to a new position of equilibrium. Now we know that the various national economies are related through the prices of goods and factors and the exchange rates which link those prices together. The possibility suggests itself that a process of adjustment analogous to that in a commodity market may be set in motion—that a change in demand or supply may lead, through its effect upon the relevant prices, to a restoration of equilibrium.

Other "natural" or automatic adjustments are suggested by our study of national income, where we saw that a rise in exports generates an expansion of income and therewith a parallel but smaller change in imports. We already have at our command a considerable analytical equipment with which to tackle problems of this kind. Our task now is to use them appropriately.

Any country has a choice as to how its own currency shall be related to those of other nations. It can adopt a completely independent currency system, determining the internal value or purchasing power of its money by its own monetary policy, while allowing its external value in terms of other currencies to be settled by the free interaction of demand and supply upon the foreign exchange markets. No attempt is made to influence exchange rates—they are permitted to fluctuate freely.

Or one nation may join others in establishing a fixed relationship between the different national currencies. This is accomplished by expressing each currency in terms of some objective standard, such as gold. If each country sets a price, in national currency, at which it will buy and sell gold without limit, then exchange rates between the various gold standard currencies are fixed at the relative gold value of each pair of currencies. As we shall see, adoption of such an international system implies the sacrifice of monetary autonomy.

Finally, a country may try to obtain the best of both worlds, and so enjoy both independence of monetary policy and stable exchange rates. It can do so by establishing direct controls over the demand and supply of foreign exchange.

We shall examine the process of adjustment to a balance of payments disturbance under each of these different systems. What the cause may be is irrelevant to the operation of the adjustment mechanism. Later on, we shall consider whether different methods of adjustment are appropriate or inappropriate to specific types of disturbance.

ADJUSTMENT WHEN CURRENCIES ARE INDEPENDENT AND EXCHANGE RATES ARE FREE TO FLUCTUATE

Meaning of An Independent Currency

The first case to consider is that of a country with an independent currency, whose exchange rates are subject to no control and hence fluctuate freely. Transactions leading to a demand for or supply of foreign exchange will be limited to those derived from exports and imports of goods and services, which means that both short-term and long-term capital movements are ruled out. Since short-term capital movements include changes in foreign balances, these too are excluded. It is this proviso that makes our country's currency completely independent; its importance will be indicated in the next section.

To make our argument as concrete as possible, let us take France as our country, and let the franc/dollar exchange rate epitomise foreign exchange relations between France and the rest of the world. We start from an equilibrium position, with the demand for and supply of foreign exchange as represented in Figure 17.1 (D_m and S_x) effecting a balance of international payments and receipts at a rate of exchange of 350 francs per dollar. At this rate exports are equal in value to imports, in terms either of dollars or francs. (The dollar value of each is $200 million; the franc value is 350×200 million or 70,000 million francs.)

Now suppose that (owing perhaps to an increase in tariffs abroad, to more intense competition with French exports, to the depletion of re-

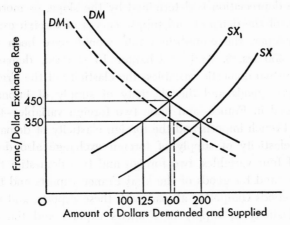

Fig. 17.1: Adjustment via Free Exchange Rates.

sources upon which France's exports have relied, or to many another possible cause) the country experiences a decline in its exports. The specific nature of the adverse change is irrelevant here; all we need is that there shall be a disturbance of equilibrium. The supply of foreign exchange shifts to the left, to the new position S_{x1}. If nothing else happened, the value of exports (in dollars) would fall to $125 million, while imports remained unchanged at $200 million. A gap or deficit of $75 million in the balance of payments would emerge.

Adjustment Through Depreciation

Since the exchange rate is free to move, however, it will rise to 450 francs, at which demand and the new supply schedule are in equilibrium. At this new rate, since imports are now more costly in domestic currency, certain buyers of dollars withdraw from the market—there is a movement along the demand curve from a to c. Similarly, France's exports are now cheaper abroad, so there will be a partial recovery of exports, shown by a movement along the new supply curve from b to c. Exports and imports are brought to equality at the 450 frs./$ exchange rate, and the potential deficit in the balance of payments is prevented from appearing. The change in the exchange rate, or currency depreciation, performs the entire task of adjusting to the disturbance in the balance of payments.

Why did the franc depreciate (the exchange rate rise) only as much as it did, no more and no less?

Assuming that the amount by which we shifted the supply curve accurately reflects the initial decline in the demand for French exports, the extent of the depreciation is determined by the slope, or more accurately, the elasticity, of the demand and supply curves of foreign exchange. Had both been steeper, the equilibrium rate would have been considerably higher than 450 frs./$. And as Chapter 16 showed, demand elasticity depends upon two domestic variables—the elasticity of the French demand for import-type goods and the elasticity of supply of import-competing goods produced in France—and upon two foreign variables—the elasticity of supply of French imports and the foreign elasticity of demand for these goods. The elasticity of supply of foreign exchange also depends on a similar set of four variables, two foreign and two domestic: the elasticity of foreign demand for goods of the kind France exports and the elasticity of supply of goods competing abroad with these exports, and on the other hand, the elasticity of supply of France's exports and the elasticity of French demand for these goods.

No change in France's income other than that attributable to the changed value of exports will be set in motion, since any alteration in the value of exports (in terms of francs) is matched by an identical change in the value of imports. (The franc value of exports and imports, at the old 350 fr. rate of exchange, was 70,000 million francs. At the new rate of 450 frs./$ it is 72,000 million francs.) Though French exporters take in 2,000 million francs more than before, any stimulus this might give to a further expansion of income is offset by the diversion of an identical sum toward imports. Only if this diversion of income is at the expense, not of domestic consumption, but of saving, would there be any net additional expansionary effect.

Internal Effects of Depreciation

Certain aspects of the inevitable changes in price relationships must now be taken into account. The *direct* effect of higher import prices, and of possibly higher (franc) export prices too, upon the home demand for imports and the foreign demand for exports, has already been reckoned with in arriving at determinate values for the elasticity of the foreign exchange curves. But as we saw in the preceding chapter, if imported raw materials are used in producing exports, their costs will be raised. Moreover, if imports enter significantly into the cost of living, demands for wage increases are almost certain to be heard. If such increases are granted, export costs will be further raised.

To reflect the worsened conditions under which exports are supplied, the supply curve of foreign exchange (S_{x_1}) would have to be raised somewhat above the position shown in the diagram. Depreciation of the franc would be slightly greater than originally shown, but unless these price changes set off a wage-price spiral of inflation, the foreign exchange market and the balance of payments should come to rest at a somewhat higher rate of exchange.

Need for Monetary Restraint

Clearly, a policy of monetary restraint would be needed to offset the inflationary tendencies. If the supply of credit were held constant, employers would be unable to finance wage increases and would have to refuse them, possibly at the cost of strikes. Furthermore, at the expense of some actual contraction of credit and diminution of income, even the adverse effect on the balance of payments of higher prices of imports used to produce exports could be counteracted, for any reduction of income would cause the demand for imports to fall.

The need for a restrictive monetary policy to offset the adverse, indirect price effects of currency depreciation depends, of course, upon how much export prices are raised. A study by staff members of the International Monetary Fund [4] indicates that this rise is only 5 to 6 per cent of the amount of the depreciation under conditions of depression. If the depreciation were 20 per cent, the rise in export prices would be insignificant—only about 1 per cent; with a 50 per cent depreciation, it would still be only 2½ to 3 per cent. With prosperity, however, the rise of export prices appears to be much greater—30 per cent or more of the amount of depreciation. This means a rise of export prices of 6 per cent or more if the depreciation is 20 per cent, of 15 per cent or more if it is 50 per cent.

The danger is negligible if depreciation occurs when the economy is depressed, but under conditions of prosperity it could be serious, especially if the depreciation is substantial. Clearly, if depreciation is to be relied upon as a means of adjusting to an adverse change in the balance of payments, and if it occurs during a period of prosperity, a policy of monetary restraint will be in order. But that is precisely the time when it will do the least harm to the economy. It is also clear that at such a time the extent of the depreciation should be minimised.

[4] See J. J. Polak and T. C. Chang, "Effect of Exchange Depreciation on a Country's Export Price Level," *Staff Papers*, Vol. 1, No. 1 (1950-51), International Monetary Fund, Washington, D. C. The results of this study are rather inconclusive with respect to conditions of prosperity, owing partly to the small number of case studies and to the admixture of other price-raising forces in the main example (France, 1936-37).

THE EQUILIBRIUM RATE OF EXCHANGE

Our study of how, with freely fluctuating exchange rates, a disturbance to a country's balance of payments is adjusted has shown that equilibrium between autonomous international receipts and payments is restored by a rise in the exchange rate. Since the new rate establishes a new equilibrium in the balance of payments, it may appropriately be called an equilibrium rate. Are we, then, to mean by an equilibrium rate of exchange whatever rate exists when autonomous international receipts and payments are in balance?

What the Term Means

On a superficial level, the equilibrium rate may be described as the one that clears a nation's foreign exchange market, thereby bringing its autonomous international transactions into balance and restoring equilibrium in the balance of payments. Since this outcome requires a balanced relationship between a country's factor and commodity prices, its income, and its demands, and prices, incomes, and demands in the rest of the world, an equilibrium rate of exchange may be defined, in a more fundamental sense, as one that establishes this kind of balance.

An equilibrium rate will remain the same only so long as these underlying determinants are unchanged. Thus, if a given country's factor prices are altered, commodity prices will be different; so will the distribution of income. With changed commodity prices and a new distribution of income, expenditures at home and abroad will be affected, shifts will occur in the demand and supply of exchange, and balance of payments equilibrium will require a different exchange rate. Changes in real or money income in any part of the world will have similar consequences.

When Is An Exchange Rate An Equilibrium Rate?

So much for definition. But how are we to tell when an equilibrium exchange rate, so defined, is realised? Is the absence of a deficit (or surplus) in the balance of payments an adequate test? And must this balance be attained every day, every month, every year? What is the relevant time period?

The time period. Let us consider the last question first. To what time period should an equilibrium rate of exchange refer? Changes in demand occur almost continually, price changes are frequent, and national incomes vary somewhat even from month to month.

Strict logic would seem to require, in a free exchange market, an equilibrium exchange rate varying almost from day to day. No country, however, would permit such instability. If stabilising speculation did not counteract casual and seasonal disturbances, the monetary authorities would use the country's international reserves for this purpose. This implies, of course, that complete monetary independence, with completely free rates, would not be tolerated.

Suppose we take a year as the minimum period to which an equilibrium exchange rate is to refer, on the ground that a period of this length eliminates from consideration seasonal and casual disturbances. Then some specific rate should preserve international balance over that interval. Reserves will ebb and flow within this period in response to short-term fluctuations. But there should be no appreciable net change in a country's international reserves if the exchange rate is at the appropriate level. Over longer periods than a year, the equilibrium rate would vary with changes in prices, incomes, and demands.[5]

Restrictive measures. Restrictions on trade or payments can eliminate a deficit just as effectively as the establishment of an equilibrium rate of exchange. They are a substitute for an appropriate change in the exchange rate (or in internal prices and incomes). The mere fact that a country has no deficit in its balance of payments is therefore no proof that its exchange rate is at the equilibrium level. Were we to restore the restrictions to their pre-deficit condition, the reappearance of a deficit would clearly show that the controlled rate was not an equilibrium rate.

Unemployment. Finally, we know that deflation is an effective means of eliminating a deficit. With mass unemployment and a low national income, an economy might balance its international payments; with full employment, that same economy would have to depreciate its currency to preserve balance of payments equilibrium. Thus different levels of employment are consistent with balance of payments equilibrium only at differing exchange rates.

Taking this fact into account, which of several exchange rates are we to regard as the equilibrium rate—only the one that will establish balance of payments equilibrium at full employment? Since full employment, or some-

[5] Nurkse has suggested that a period of five to ten years, sufficiently long to include a complete business cycle, is the appropriate period of reference for an equilibrium rate. But maintenance of a stable rate over such a long period, in the face of a major cyclical swing, would require the use of international reserves on a scale unattainable by most countries. See Ragnar Nurkse, "Conditions of International Monetary Equilibrium," *Essays in International Finance*, No. 4, Spring 1945 (International Finance Section, Princeton University); reprinted in *Readings in the Theory of International Trade*.

thing closely approaching it, is a universal goal of national policy today, the answer has to be "yes." A country whose (autonomous) payments balanced only because of heavy unemployment would then be said to have an overvalued rate.

Great Britain in the years 1925-1930 affords a good illustration of this point. There was little sign of disequilibrium in the British balance of payments, yet the pound was rightly regarded as overvalued. There was practically no net change in the British gold reserve during that period. . . . If we apply our definition of the equilibrium rate literally, the pound cannot be said to have been overvalued. The British balance of payments was kept in equilibrium, however, only at the cost of depressed conditions at home compared with conditions in the outside world.[6]

Conclusion. To conclude, we have three criteria of an equilibrium rate of exchange: (1) It refers to a period of at least a year; during that period there must be no major change in international reserves. (2) Balance of payments equilibrium must be achieved without introducing new or intensifying old restrictions on trade. (3) This equilibrium must not require the existence of a significant volume of unemployment.

Purchasing Power Par

An attempt was made, after the first World War, to develop a concept of the equilibrium rate of exchange that would permit its measurement by readily available data. This concept is known as "purchasing power par." It holds that the equilibrium rate is one that equalises the purchasing power of two currencies, and that the actual rate, if free to move, will approximate this rate.

Thus if in a given year, as compared with a base year when balance of payments equilibrium prevailed, prices in the United States have trebled, while in the United Kingdom they have risen only 50 per cent, the new equilibrium rate of exchange between the dollar and the pound will be double the old rate. Assuming that in the base year the exchange rate was $4 a pound, the purchasing power rate for the later year will be:

$$\$4 \times \frac{150}{300} = \$8.$$

Rigorously interpreted, the purchasing power par doctrine assumes that relative commodity prices are the sole determinant of international transactions. We know this is not true. We have encountered many causes of balance of payments disequilibrium besides changes in commodity prices.

[6] *Ibid.*, pp. 6-7.

We need only mention variations in the rate of flow of capital, in service payments, and in the level of real income.

Nonetheless, purchasing power par may be a useful first approximation to an equilibrium rate for periods dominated by price changes. To get a more accurate evaluation, one would then have to take into account concurrent changes in tastes, techniques, capital movements, and real income.

(For references, see end of Chapter 18.)

18

BALANCE OF PAYMENTS ADJUSTMENT: ADDITIONAL METHODS

ADJUSTMENT WHEN CURRENCIES ARE INTERDEPENDENT AND EXCHANGE RATES ARE STABLE

Interdependence of Monetary Systems

We shall now alter our model by allowing short-term capital movements to take place, in the form of changes in foreign balances. This is a step toward greater realism, for even when exchange rates are not anchored to gold or controlled, a country's banks build up and deplete their foreign balances; in-payments and out-payments are not instantly and automatically equalised by exchange rate variations, as in the preceding model.

Go back now to the initial disturbance of equilibrium, arising from the decline in France's exports. They fell in value (in terms of foreign currency) to $125 million, while imports remained for the moment unchanged at $200 million, thus giving rise to a deficit of $75 million. Let us assume that this is financed by drawing down foreign balances, the necessary foreign funds being supplied by the Bank of France if the commercial banks have inadequate deposits abroad. In other words, the banks are discounting bills of exchange brought to them by exporters to a value of $125 million; by this action they are *adding* 43,750 million francs (350 × 125 million) to the supply of *domestic* money. Simultaneously, they are selling bills of exchange drawn against their foreign balances in the amount of $200 million; this action causes the domestic money supply to *diminish* by 70,000 million francs; this is the value of the checks drawn by importers against their bank accounts. There is thus a net diminution in the French money supply of 26,250 million francs. Abroad, balances to the net amount of $75 million have been transferred from the ownership of French banks to foreign exporters. France's currency is no longer completely independent—a reduction in foreign balances implies a parallel reduction in the domestic money stock, whereas an addition to foreign balances causes the domestic supply of money to increase.

The Income Effect

Now consider the consequences of this shrinkage in the money supply. Where will its impact be felt? In the export industries, of course; they are selling fewer goods abroad, and their total receipts, in domestic money, have fallen by 26,250 million francs. There is a fall in income equivalent to the reduction in the value of exports. But the decline in income does not stop here; we must reckon with the multiplier. Its value will depend upon the marginal propensity to consume or its converse, the marginal propensity to save (s), and upon the marginal propensity to import(m). If s is ¼ and m also ¼, the multiplier $\left(\dfrac{1}{s+m}\right)$ will have a value of 2. The ultimate decline in income will be double the decline in exports, or 52,500 million francs. (If we allowed for foreign repercussions—the effect of the reduction of imports abroad upon incomes there and the stimulus this gives to French exports—it would be somewhat less.) Assuming that the reduction of French exports is lasting, France's income will remain at this lowered level just so long as the banks finance the deficit in the balance of payments by drawing upon their foreign balances.

But with the decline in income, this deficit will not remain unchanged. If the marginal propensity to import is ¼, then with a decline in income of 52,500 million francs, imports will ultimately fall by 13,125 francs.[1] After the multiplier and the propensity to import have done their work, a new situation emerges in the foreign exchange market. The dollar value of imports has fallen by $37.5 million (the franc value of the decline in imports, 13,125 million francs, divided by the rate of exchange, 350 frs./$). Diagrammatically, this can be shown (see Figure 17.1) by a shift to the left of the demand curve for foreign exchange such that at 350 frs./$, $162.5 million of imports are demanded. If the supply of exports is unchanged, this means that the balance of payments deficit has been correspondingly reduced—from $75 million to half that amount, or $37.5 million.

The Price Effect

When we also take into account the price effects that generally accompany deflation, the total correction of the deficit will be still greater. As income, production, and employment shrink in France, producers' cost curves will tend to shift downward. Prices are likely to fall; even wages may decline, though under modern conditions they are resistant to downward pressure.

---

[1] "Ultimately" here means the length of time it takes the multiplier to work out its full effects. Except for a very small residue this will be in a year-and-a-half to two years. (See Chapter 13.)

With prices lower, French exports are more attractive to foreign buyers; the supply curve of foreign exchange is likely to move to the right—more foreign exchange is supplied at the exchange rate of 350 frs./$. Imports will now be relatively more expensive; the demand for foreign exchange is likely to shift further to the left. These opposite, price-induced movements of the demand and supply curves will narrow the deficit still further, perhaps, together with the income effects, eliminating it completely.

The Gold Standard

This famous international currency system is simply a special case of interdependent currencies, one where fixed exchange rates are maintained, not by the deliberate action of banks in depleting or accumulating foreign balances, as in the case just discussed, but by the device of equating currencies to gold at a fixed price and then buying and selling gold in unlimited amounts at that price.

Thus the United States is today on the gold standard, since the Treasury or its agent, any one of the Federal Reserve banks, stands ready to buy all gold offered at a price of $35 an ounce, and is equally ready to sell (though only for international shipments or use in manufacture) at the same price. If the Bank of France were to set a price for gold of 12,250 francs per ounce, and would buy and sell without limit at that price, a gold par of exchange of 350 francs per dollar would be established ($\frac{12,250}{35} = 350$). So long as both countries remained on the gold standard, actual rates of exchange could never deviate from this rate by more than the cost of shipping gold from New York to Paris and vice versa. When the practice of earmarking gold is followed rather than shipping it, the cost of transferring gold from the ownership of one country to another is zero.

In terms of the foreign exchange market, this situation means that, since no French buyer of dollars would ever have to pay more than 350 francs for the gold equivalent of that currency, and no seller would have to take less, the only point on each demand and supply schedule that could be realised would be that corresponding to an exchange rate of 350 frs./$. If, as in the preceding illustrations, we started with France's balance of payments in equilibrium at this rate, with the demand for and supply of dollars both amounting to $200 million, we should have to represent both schedules as being hypothetical at any other rate, using dashed lines for this purpose. The loss of French export markets, leading to a shift of the supply curve to a new position (S_{x_1} in Figure 17.1) could be similarly represented by drawing a new hypothetical supply curve, whose only realisable point would be that on the 350 frs./$ line at the $125 million point.

The deficit in the balance of payments could be financed by the commercial banks or the Bank of France drawing down their dollar balances, if they had them. If not, or if they were insufficient, the gap would be filled by the Bank of France, which would sell the desired amount of dollars. It would obtain them by earmarking gold in its possession (in Paris) in favor of the Federal Reserve Bank of New York and cabling that institution that it had done so.[2] The latter would thereupon provide dollars in New York with which to honor the dollar bills of exchange sold by the Bank of France.

The mechanism of adjustment to the balance of payments disturbance is in all its essentials the same as in the previous more general case. It operates through a decline in income, starting (if the disturbance originates in a slump of exports) in the export industries and spreading from there throughout the economy. Imports fall, to the extent dictated by the marginal propensity to import, thereby narrowing the balance of payments deficit.[3] Further aid toward adjustment is likely to come from the decline in prices which usually accompanies a deflationary trend of income, stimulating exports and retarding imports.

Another feature shared by all forms of interdependent currencies, including the special case of the gold standard, is the change in the supply of money that always occurs when the balance of payments is disturbed. If a deficit develops, foreign balances or gold equal in value to the size of the deficit are sold to importers and domestic money of this amount is extinguished. It is this dependence of the money supply upon the state of the balance of payments that accounts for the use of the term, "interdependent currencies," or the alternative, "international monetary system."

Enforced Contraction of Credit

The initial contraction of the money supply and the decline in income generated by a slump in exports (or by an increase in imports) may, under an international monetary system, be followed by a further restriction of credit and a consequently accelerated decline in income as a result of deliberate action on the part of the monetary authorities. Such a delib-

---

[2] If the Bank of France already held gold earmarked to its account in New York, it would simply send a cable transferring this to the Federal Reserve Bank of New York and requesting that dollar deposits be made available instead.

[3] The outcome would be similar were the disturbance to originate in a shift in demand from domestic goods to imports, owing say to a reduction of the French tariff. Working through the steps in adjustment to such a change furnishes a useful exercise.

erately imposed contraction is not, however, an essential feature of the gold standard or of any other kind of interdependent or international currency system. It may be invoked to hasten the adjustment of the balance of payments or to protect the reserves of the central bank. On numerous occasions during the nineteenth century, the Bank of England, anticipating a loss of gold or wanting to stop it, raised its discount rate, sold securities to the money market, and thus forced up market rates. This prevented or checked the loss of gold in two ways: by setting in motion a decline in income and prices and thus starting the adjustment to work, and by attracting short-term capital to London. These short-term capital movements increased the supply of foreign exchange in London, thus serving in the stead of gold to fill in the gap in the balance of payments.

Multiple Contraction of Credit

If a country's banking system incorporates the fractional reserve principle, whereby the minimum required reserves of the commercial banks are set at, say, 10 per cent of demand deposits, then a loss of gold may cause reserves to fall below the required minimum. To the extent that they do, it then becomes necessary, if the prescribed ratio between reserves and deposits is to be restored, to set in motion—through higher discount rates and other restrictive measures—a multiple contraction of credit. This consequence cannot be attributed to the gold standard as such, however; it is due to the incorporation of the fractional reserve principle in the country's banking system. This is proven by the fact that the severity of the credit restriction induced by the loss of gold will vary inversely with the reserve proportion, being tenfold if this is 10 per cent, fivefold if it is 20 per cent, and only twofold if it is 50 per cent.

A DIGRESSION ON INTERNATIONAL TRANSFERS OF CAPITAL

International transfers of capital, in their effect on a nation's balance of payments, are no different from any other kind of disturbance. A burst of long-term international lending, or the remission of tribute or reparation, increases the payments a country has to make, just as does an increase in its imports. Capital transfers, however, have received special attention in the literature of international economics. This is justified, in part, by a peculiar relation between capital movements and the business cycle that complicated the analysis. Because of this complication, we undertake this brief digression on the special problem of international capital transfers.

Transfer Mechanism: The Gold Standard

Under a gold standard or international currency system, what happens when a country undertakes substantial long-term international lending depends mainly upon the source of the funds used to acquire the foreign securities. If these come from savings that would otherwise have financed domestic investment, the consequent decline of home investment will set in motion a multiple contraction of income. Additional investment abroad, made possible by the foreign loan, takes place and raises income there by some multiple. Imports of the lending country contract, its exports expand, and a substantial part of the loan is transmitted in the form of goods. Price effects accompanying the income changes work toward the same end. If the initial loss of reserves induces credit contraction, to the initial fall in income and prices inaugurated by the decline of investment will be added a secondary fall in income and prices. The entire loan may be transferred in the form of an excess of exports over imports. That is, the foreign exchange derived from the excess of exports is purchased by the buyers of foreign securities and turned over to the sellers in the borrowing country.

Transfer Mechanism: Fluctuating Rates

Adjustment to an international capital transfer would be much smoother under a system of fluctuating exchange rates. The demand for foreign exchange with which to pay for the foreign securities, added to the normal demand for imports of goods and services, would force the exchange rate up. Foreign prices of the lender's exports would fall, and, with elasticity of demand for these exports greater than 1, foreign exchange receipts would rise. In Figure 18.1, the initial position is one of equilibrium, with the demand for (D_m) and supply of (S_x) foreign exchange arising out of current transactions equal to one another at an exchange rate of r_1. Foreign investment now begins. The demand for foreign exchange shifts to the right by a distance reflecting the additional outlay on foreign securities (to D_{m+1}). The exchange rate rises to r_2. The supply of foreign exchange derived from exports expands, moving along the supply curve from **a** *to* **b**. Import prices in home currency rise; the demand for import exchange shrinks, moving along the demand curve from **a** to **c**. The excess of the supply of foreign exchange over the demand for imports of goods and services (M_2X_2) would provide the amount needed to transfer the loan (equal to the difference between D_m and D_{m+1} at the new exchange rate, r_2).

As for income and employment, the original decrease resulting from the

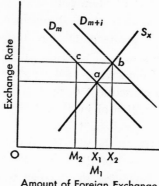

Fig. 18.1: Transfer of Capital
with Free Exchange Rate.

shrinkage of domestic investment would release resources. Some of these resources would find employment in the export industries, and through the operation of the multiplier, some would be drawn into other occupations.

If these were the only alternatives, we might conclude that a country on the gold standard ought not to allow any appreciable international transfer of capital to take place, because of its adverse effects on income and employment. If the transfer is to be permitted, it might be preferable to abandon the gold standard and to rely upon adjustment through a rise in the exchange rate. But the harshness of the fixed exchange rate mechanism arises only if funds for foreign investment are diverted from domestic investment, thus inducing depression in the lending country. There remains the possibility that foreign investment may be financed with newly created money.

Transfer Made Easy

The historical record shows that international investment, like domestic investment, follows a cyclical pattern, rising to a peak during prosperity and falling sharply, even ceasing altogether, during recession and depression. A wave of international lending typically starts at a low level, when unemployment is still substantial. Planned investment, both domestic and foreign, is financed in large part by credit expansion, and exceeds planned saving. Hence international lending is not the crippling rival of home investment, but its companion.

The lending country need not suffer unemployment and depression, but may enjoy rising business activity in company with the borrower.

Smooth international transfer of capital requires only that expansion be more rapid in the country receiving the loan. Then the demand of the lender for the borrower's currency puts at the latter's disposal foreign balances or gold which can be promptly used either to buy investment goods in the lending country itself or for investment in physical assets at home. With its reserve base enlarged, the borrower can expand credit to support a further rise of income, while the creditor's reserve losses suggest the need for a more cautious advance.

Since the bulk of long-term international loans are made by relatively rich, developed countries to relatively poorer, less developed ones, the borrower's marginal propensity to import tends to be high; large quantities of investment goods, in particular, unobtainable at home, are needed to carry out the purpose of the loan. With rapidly rising income and a high propensity to import, imports into the borrowing country expand sharply. Very soon, the lending country's increased demand for foreign exchange with which to purchase foreign securities is matched by increased supplies from the growing exports to the borrower. Capital is transferred, not as at first, in the form of bank balances and gold, but in the form of goods.

Price changes may, and with the income changes outlined, probably will, facilitate the transfer mechanism. Prices in the borrowing country will tend to rise more than in the lending country; prices of domestic goods, subject to little or no foreign competition, will probably rise most, export prices less, and import prices, determined primarily by forces abroad, least of all.

Illustration: Canada

This sequence of adjustment is well illustrated by Canadian borrowing between 1900 and 1913. In this period, Canada borrowed—principally from England—approximately $2.5 billion, of which $1.5 billion was net borrowing. (The difference of $1 billion was required to provide for rising interest and amortisation payments.) Of the $1.5 billion, 92 per cent entered the country in the form of an excess of imports of commodities and services over corresponding exports. Although national income statistics are not available, data on business activity indicate that except for relatively brief and mild depressions in 1902-03 and 1908, conditions were generally prosperous in both England and Canada, with more rapid growth occurring in the latter country. Price changes corresponded to theoretical expectations; Canadian domestic prices rose from 100 in 1900 to 162 in 1913, export prices to 134, and import prices only to 114.[4]

---

[4] See Jacob Viner, *Canada's Balance of International Indebtedness 1900-13;* also his *Studies in the Theory of International Trade,* Ch. VII. Price data are from James W. Angell, *The Theory of International Prices,* Appendix B.

In circumstances such as those described above and as exemplified in the Canadian case, international transfers of capital under gold standard conditions can be and have been effected with a minimum of disturbance. But when the transfer is attempted under less favorable circumstances (say, during a depression), the mechanism of adjustment either works badly or is not allowed to function at all. For example, between 1935 and 1939, when business conditions in most of the world were far from prosperous though improving, some $5 billion of capital was transferred to the United States in the form of gold.[5] Though the inflow greatly increased U.S. gold reserves, these reserves were already adequate to support a large credit expansion. The movement of capital was primarily motivated by fear; its purpose was not investment in American industry but in U.S. bank balances. Moreover, with the level of business confidence low, there was a dearth of borrowers who might otherwise have put some of these funds to work. In the countries where the capital flight originated, exchange and other controls insulated their economies from the normal effects of severe balance of payments deficits.

German reparation payments after World War I provide another illustration of the relevance of the surrounding conditions to the operation of the adjustment mechanism. We shall consider it in some detail later.

OBJECTIONS TO DEPRECIATION AND DEFLATION

The foregoing analysis has shown that adjustment to a balance of payments disequilibrium may be reached by either one of two distinct paths.

If a country maintains a completely independent currency, taking no steps to finance a deficit by drawing upon foreign balances and allowing exchange rates to be determined exclusively by market forces, the balance of payments will be adjusted (in the absence of destabilising speculation) via a rise in exchange rates. No important change in national income need occur.

At the other extreme stands the case of an interdependent currency. Here the entire initial deficit is financed by sacrificing foreign balances or gold reserves; the exchange rate is not allowed to vary, but is held constant. In the course of time, the deficit is eliminated by the effect upon imports of the induced decline in income, reenforced by the effect upon both imports and exports of the accompanying decline of prices. This

[5] The total inflow of gold into the U.S. in these years was close to $9 billion, the excess over capital transfers being due to a favorable U.S. current account balance.

mechanism may be still further intensified by a multiple contraction of credit or by credit restriction deliberately imposed by the central bank, though such phenomena are no necessary part of the adjustment mechanism.

Each of these methods of adjustment has aroused strong opposition. Exclusive reliance on variations in exchange rates encounters the objection that it implies, in practice, constantly fluctuating rates. An orderly, once-and-for-all shift from one equilibrium rate to another is held to be, in a world of constant change in demand and supply conditions, and in levels of income, highly improbable, a purely theoretical expectation based on unreal assumptions. Under the unstable, ever-varying conditions of the real world, exchange rates would fluctuate incessantly, increasing the risks of trading and therefore penalising the conduct of trade. Even though well-organised forward exchange markets, by providing facilities for hedging, could greatly reduce this risk, it is contended—with some reason—that they could never encompass all trade and that they could not eliminate the risk entirely. Moreover, with fluctuating exchange rates, speculation is sure to appear, and when a currency is under pressure and there is no foreseeable limit to its depreciation, speculation is likely to be a destabilising force. Finally, there is the fear that currency depreciation, through its effects on internal prices, may set off a spiral of inflation. For all these reasons, with the notable exception of Canada since 1951, no country has for long tolerated completely free exchange rates.

Opposition to the income-and-price method of adjustment typified by the gold standard has been even more vigorous. For this adjustment mechanism eliminates a balance of payments, or external disequilibrium, by replacing it with internal disequilibrium in the form of income deflation, unemployment, and reduced production. The cure, it is held, is worse than the disease.

To combat the deflationary effects of a decline in foreign exchange or gold reserves, many central banks in the 1920's adopted a policy of neutralising or sterilising these movements. When a balance of payments deficit caused a contraction of deposits and a loss of bank reserves, this was offset by the purchase by the central bank of open-market securities. Thereby bank reserves were replenished, leaving the credit base, at least, relatively unaffected. A similar offsetting of gold inflows was effected through the open-market sale of securities. By this practice, a country's money supply and, to a degree, its national income, were insulated from influences originating in the balance of payments.

A COMPROMISE SOLUTION: CONTROLLED DEPRECIATION AND DEVALUATION

A compromise solution to the problem of international adjustment was sought in the 1930's in attempts to combine both methods of adjustment in a workable mixture.

One such effort places principal reliance upon exchange rate variations. But these are either held within certain limits or else depreciation is allowed to take place only in a gradual and controlled manner. An instrument to achieve this end is needed; most countries found it in a fund specifically set up for the purpose of exchange stabilisation.[6] These *exchange stabilisation funds* smooth out seasonal and speculative fluctuations in exchange rates by buying foreign currencies when these rates fall and selling them when they rise. Rate movements due to the more basic forces of demand and supply of exchange for goods, services, and long-term capital transfers are moderated, even sometimes offset, in a similar manner. The various funds also to a large degree insulate the domestic money supply against change by the manner of their operation.

Thus the British Exchange Equalisation Account, when the balance of payments is under pressure and the pound tends to depreciate, supports the pound by exchanging gold in its possession for foreign exchange, which it supplies to satisfy the excess demand for foreign exchange at the existing rate. It receives pounds sterling from importers and speculators.

If it hoards these pounds, the effect is of course deflationary. But the Account usually turns them over to the money market through the purchase of short-term Treasury bills. Thus the domestic supply of money remains constant; all that happens is a change of ownership.[7] Only to the extent that changes in the supply of money and in national income are consistent with the objectives of monetary policy are they allowed to occur.

Britain used this technique exclusively from June 1932 until early 1940, since when it has been combined with exchange controls. From about the end of the first year of the prewar experience, fluctuations in the crucial dollar/sterling rate were held within a range of only slightly over 10 per cent. France's record was similar, though over a shorter period. Between November 1933 and September 1936, the franc/dollar rate remained within approximately the same range.

[6] As, for example, Belgium, Canada, France, the Netherlands, Switzerland, the United Kingdom, and the United States.

[7] This is subject to some qualification so far as the Exchange Equalisation Account transactions are with banks rather than with the public or non-banking institutions.

Devaluation

A second compromise between stable exchange rates and freely fluctuating rates has been worked out gradually, coming to prominence since World War II when it was officially embodied in the charter of the International Monetary Fund. This is devaluation of a currency that is under pressure, from its overvalued level to a lower level that, it is hoped, will restore equilibrium. A sharp and definitive downward revision of a currency's value is substituted for gradual and controlled, but somewhat indefinite depreciation.

To correct a balance of payments disequilibrium, devaluation relies upon the stimulus to exports and the check to imports characteristic of currency depreciation (rising exchange rates). It avoids the deflationary contraction of income typical of adjustment when exchange rates are fixed. But since devaluation would only be used to combat a severe disequilibrium, it is to be presumed that changes in exchange rates would be infrequent. Thus it combines the merits of the relatively easier adjustment process of fluctuating rates and of stability of exchange rates over considerable periods.

As with freely fluctuating and flexible rates, the effectiveness of devaluation depends upon the elasticity of the demand and supply of foreign exchange. If, for special reasons, these are very low, devaluation either would not restore equilibrium at all, or would have to be excessive. As we have suggested, however, it seems reasonable to expect that, for any single country, these elasticities are likely to be substantial, especially if sufficient time is allowed for the full effect of revised price relationships to register.

Because stable exchange rates are maintained except when the balance of payments is under severe pressure, speculative short-term capital movements would normally be stabilising in character. With an upper limit to exchange rate fluctuations established either by attachment of the currency to gold or by strong official support, speculators would be eager to sell foreign currencies as balance of payments pressures forced rates toward this limit, confident that they could be repurchased later at a lower price. Their support would thus minimise gold losses or the need for official sales of foreign exchange. This is an advantage not available with freely fluctuating rates, where—with no official intervention to limit rate variations—a rise in rates would be likely to induce destabilising speculation, or the purchase of foreign currencies on the assumption that rates would go still higher.

On the other hand, when there is a major disturbance to the balance of payments, accompanied by a continuing deficit, the near certainty of devaluation would provoke destabilising speculation. Short-term capital would flow out of the country, as it did from the United Kingdom prior to the devaluation of the pound in 1949, being returned at a substantial profit after the devaluation had occurred. In this respect, the method of devaluation is similar in its effects to flexible rates or controlled depreciation, under which short-term capital movements would tend to be stabilising in the face of moderate balance of payments pressures but destabilising as the pressure became more severe and depreciation more likely.

Devaluation, with its combination of the merits of depreciation and of stable exchange rates, has much to commend it as a remedy for the balance of payments difficulties of a single country. Since it affects the trade of other countries adversely, however, there is a danger, especially when many countries suffer from such difficulties, that devaluation may become competitive. This possibility suggests the need for international consultation and agreement, a topic we shall explore more fully when we consider the provisions of the International Monetary Fund.

SELECTED REFERENCES

Alexander, Sidney S., "Effects of Devaluation on a Trade Balance," *IMF Staff Papers*, Vol. V, No. 2 (April 1952). An extension of the income analysis that stresses the favorable effect of devaluation as consisting in its reduction of absorption (real expenditure), which permits the release of goods for export. An original and important contribution.

Hawtrey, R. G., *The Gold Standard in Theory and Practice*, 5th edition (Longmans, Green & Co., New York, 1947). A standard brief work on this subject.

Kindleberger, Charles P., *International Economics* (Richard D. Irwin, Inc., Homewood, Ill., 1953). Chapters 21-24 provide an extended and relatively advanced discussion of cyclical, secular, and structural disequilibrium.

Lary, Hal. B., *The United States in the World Economy* (Government Printing Office, Washington, D. C., 1943). Still one of the best treatments of the U. S. balance of payments during the inter-war period.

League of Nations, *International Currency Experience* (1944). The interwar experience with international monetary relations. Chapters IV and V are especially relevant to this chapter.

Machlup, Fritz, "The Analysis of Devaluation," *American Economic Review*, XLV (June 1955). Challenges the view expressed by Alexander, and insists on the continued relevance of price elasticities in the analysis of devaluation.

Meade, James E., *The Balance of Payments* (Oxford University Press, 1951). A book of broad scope, with its central concern the means of realising both internal and external balance.

Tarshis, Lorie, *Introduction to International Trade and Finance* (John Wiley & Sons, New York, 1955). In Chapters 13 through 19, this book has an extended discussion of capital movements and their determinants.

Whale, P. B., "The Working of the Prewar Gold Standard," *Economica*, **IV**, new series (1937). An enlightening discussion of the gold standard before 1914.

19

EXCHANGE CONTROL

CONVERTIBILITY AND ADJUSTMENT

A common feature shared by the two major methods of adjustment we have examined, flexible exchange rates and the gold standard, is that neither of them involves any direct interference with the operation of market forces. Purchases can be made in the cheapest market and sales in the dearest, or where they are most badly needed. Moreover, international payments can be made in any currency, in any amounts, and for any purpose. Thus whether adjustment is via fluctuating exchange rates or stable rates with deflation (or some combination of the two), currencies remain fully convertible. Any intervention, as when a government supports the value of its currency by sales of foreign exchange, is indirect, affecting the results of market forces, but leaving those forces themselves free to function in their normal manner.

Exchange control, the remaining alternative means of dealing with balance of payments difficulties, differs radically in that in essence it disregards market forces and substitutes for them the arbitrary decisions of government officials. Imports and other international payments are no longer determined by international price comparisons, but by considerations of national need. Not only is government intervention direct rather than indirect, but since the core of exchange control is a set of restrictions on international payments, convertibility is also sacrificed.

LEADING FEATURES OF EXCHANGE CONTROL

A full-fledged system of exchange control aims at establishing complete government domination over the foreign exchange market. All receipts from exports and other sources must be surrendered to the control authorities. To ensure against evasion, export licenses, which certify the delivery of foreign exchange to these authorities, must be presented to customs officials before shipment is permitted. The available supply of foreign exchange is then allocated to the various competing buyers according to the criterion of relative national importance. Capital exports are frequently banned, interest and amortisation payments severely limited. Imports of goods essential to the functioning of the economy, such as basic foodstuffs, petroleum products, and raw materials of industry receive relatively liberal rations of exchange, while luxuries and non-essentials fare poorly.

Not all systems of exchange control are so rigorous. If the balance of payments pressure is not severe, and especially if it is limited to moderate capital exports, the controls may involve no more than general supervision of applications for foreign exchange, together with informal limitations of certain categories of demand. For example, at the time Great Britain departed from the gold standard in 1931, it banned capital exports but set up no government control apparatus. It left the enforcement of this prohibition to the commercial banks.

Such mild forms of exchange control have generally been shortlived; they have been removed with the disappearance of the difficulties that brought them into being. Where the balance of payments pressure has continued, and especially when it has been severe, limited restrictions have given way to comprehensive and rigorous controls.

WHY EXCHANGE CONTROL?

Why should a country faced with a deficit in its balance of payments not rely upon the automatic mechanism of fluctuating exchange rates or of deflation, or upon some compromise between the two? Why should it, instead, sacrifice both convertibility of its currency and reliance upon the self-regulating forces of the market, and erect a cumbersome bureaucracy to enforce arbitrary judgments? There must be powerful reasons to explain the great popularity of exchange controls, which since World War II have in one form or another been all but universal, and even before the war were used by many European and most South American countries.

Defects of Automatic Methods

The answers to these questions are to be found in defects, real or fancied, in the automatic methods of adjustment, and in the superior effectiveness of exchange control for coming to grips with certain types of disturbances.

As we have already noted, the gold standard, the archetype of the system of fixed exchange rates, requires in the deficit country a decline of income and employment, accompanied by a contraction in the supply of money and by falling prices. This is a severe discipline, submission to which implies—unless the disturbance and the consequent adjustment are relatively mild—a degree of fortitude and an ability to ignore outraged opinion that no democratic government possesses.

Freely fluctuating exchange rates, by restoring an equilibrium relation between internal and external prices, afford a solution that avoids disturbance of the deficit country's economy. But as we know, they are subject to the grave danger of setting off destabilising capital movements and thus inducing excessive depreciation. And even in the absence of speculation, depreciation may have to be excessive for the exceptional country whose demand and supply of foreign exchange are both of fairly low elasticity. Finally, some countries have bitter memories of depreciation accompanied by inflation, and wrongly attribute causation to the former. For them, even devaluation or flexible but controlled exchange rates are remedies to be shunned.

Exchange Control as a Check to Capital Exports

Such rational or irrational objections to the available alternatives go far to explain the adoption of exchange control. But in addition, exchange control possesses one positive advantage. This is its special effectiveness for dealing with capital movements. Many exchange control systems of the 1930's originated because of this specific advantage, notably those of Germany, Denmark, and Argentina, among others.

If the government acquires an effective monopoly over the foreign exchange market, it can eliminate capital movements simply by refusing to make foreign exchange available for such transfers. In the event that the incentive to export capital is strong, measures supplementary to the basic technique of rationing will be necessary. For the requirement that all foreign exchange be surrendered to the control authorities can be evaded by under-billing exports or over-billing imports. A shipment, in fact worth $10 thousand, may be billed to the foreign importer at $8 thousand, with the understanding that the difference will be paid into a foreign bank account in the exporter's name. Or, by prior agreement an exporter abroad bills the domestic importer at an excessive value; on the basis of his invoice the importer obtains the foreign exchange and pays the exporter, who deposits the excess in the importer's foreign bank account. To block these methods of exporting capital requires a constant study of markets by commodity experts and the checking of invoices against this information.

How effectively can fluctuating exchange rates discourage capital exports? Although the cost of acquiring foreign currencies rises with depreciation, this rise is no serious deterrent to capital in search of a safe haven. Price is no object when safety of one's principal is in question.

With stable rates, on the other hand, the only check to capital export comes from a relative increase in interest rates in the deficit country. This may attract an equilibrating or stabilising movement of capital if the country's balance of payments problem is not severe and if confidence in the maintenance of the exchange rate (i.e., the gold standard) is consequently high. But if the pressure of international payments is intense, a rise in discount rates may simply generate uncertainty, thereby stimulating what it was aimed to prevent. And if a fear-motivated capital flight is already under way, even large differences of interest rates will be of small consequence.

As a means of checking a flight of capital, exchange control is clearly superior to either fluctuating exchange rates or the deterrent of high discount rates.

In general, exchange control deals with balance of payments disequilibrium by suppressing the deficit that is a symptom, not the basic trouble. When the deficit is due to capital flight, suppressing the deficit does not cure the underlying cause: political or economic uncertainty, fear of war, or expected devaluation. In all other situations, also, exchange control fails to come to grips with basic causes.

Even so, it may be the only possible choice for some countries, especially if their reserves are inadequate to support a fixed exchange rate while deflation takes hold or if the factors underlying their demand and supply of foreign exchange are exceptionally adverse. In such circumstances, exchange control can be justified as a temporary measure, to gain time while other steps are taken to restore equilibrium.

THE LOGIC OF RESTRICTIONISM

Once exchange controls are introduced, they are apt to set up a train of increasing restrictions. As we shall see, trade is forced ever more into bilateral channels, more and more countries are drawn into the system of controls, and convertibility of currencies becomes increasingly limited. If no check is interposed, these developments are likely to continue until exchange control becomes practically universal—the world market is fragmented into a number of isolated regions among which the kinds of things traded are determined by availability of supplies without much regard to comparative cost, and the volume of trade is shrunk down to a minimum.

Insulation Removes Restraints

What sets this logic of restrictionism into operation is the insulation that exchange control gives an economy against outside forces. The external deficit that led to the imposition of controls has been removed, the balance of payments is in a strait-jacket, and any loss of reserves can be checked or eliminated. The country has acquired freedom of action with respect to internal policies that might affect the balance of payments.

No government is apt to delay very long using this newly found freedom, usually in a way that increases the supply of money and credit. Monetary and fiscal disciplines are difficult and unpopular, and there are many attractive national goals—maintenance of full employment, economic development, postwar reconstruction, raising the standard of living—whose pursuit inevitably leads along the path of monetary expansion. Some countries will follow this primrose path reluctantly and slowly, some rapidly.

Overvaluation

Let us assume that the initial disequilibrium that forced the introduction of exchange control in one or a number of countries was due to capital flight. Current accounts—the trade and service items—were in equilibrium—which means that costs, prices, and incomes in the different countries were also in equilibrium at the existing level of exchange rates. Even so, if easy-spending monetary and fiscal policies are followed, prices and incomes in the insulated countries will rise. Exports are overpriced abroad and tend to shrink, imports are underpriced at home and tend to expand. Imports rise the more because people's money incomes have risen. Currencies become *overvalued* at the controlled rates. Controls over imports are now necessary.

Producers of goods competing with imports (whose types and quantities are now determined by administrative decision rather than by international price comparisons) have less incentive to keep a close watch on costs, since the threat of foreign competition has been removed. Moreover, with rising money incomes, pressure from the demand side also tends to raise their prices. And restriction of imports is itself directly inflationary: with quantitative limits on their supply, imports rise in price. Overvaluation of the currency becomes ever greater unless offset by deflationary measures.

Bilateral Channeling of Trade

A country in this spot almost inevitably is forced to search for new outlets for its exports and for new sources of imports. The accustomed markets, so far as they are in countries with convertible currencies, become increasingly constricted. Because of its overvalued currency, its exports are overpriced, its imports are cheap, attractive, but insufficient. If some other countries have introduced exchange controls, they are probably in the same fix. What is more natural than that two or more such countries should get together? All have a common interest in augmenting both imports and exports; all that is required is some device making it unnecessary to pay in scarce, convertible currencies.

Out of such shared difficulties and interests have arisen various forms of bilateral trading arrangements, the essence of which is agreement to accept one another's inconvertible currencies in payment for exports and to use them to acquire imports. (We shall examine some of these arrangements in more detail shortly.)

If only one country adopts controls, its currency becomes inconvertible by the very fact that use of that currency is restricted. This inconvertibility is non-discriminatory, however; restrictions apply equally to the purchase of any other currency. But with the spread of exchange control and of its inevitable companion, bilateral trading arrangements, restrictions quickly become discriminatory. Applications for foreign exchange are granted readily if the currency desired is that of a bilateral trading partner, where balances can be easily acquired. But if it is a free or convertible currency, applications are rigidly restricted. The world becomes divided into "hard" and "soft" currency areas, one with convertible currencies, the other regulating convertibility with varying degrees of discrimination.

This division of the world encourages the further spread of exchange controls. For a country still adhering to convertibility finds that although its balance of payments, as a total, is an over-all balance, it has a surplus with the soft currency bloc, a deficit with the hard currency area. To deal with the latter, depreciation or deflation would be appropriate, but either policy would tend to increase its surplus in inconvertible currencies. The country needs to reduce exports to and increase imports from the soft currency area and the reverse with respect to the hard currency countries. It may find that to do this it is obliged to introduce exchange controls itself.

BILATERAL TRADING ARRANGEMENTS

Private Compensation

Among the earliest forms of bilateral trade were barter deals undertaken by private firms. These were common in the 1930's; although largely superseded by more formal arrangements, they continued to be used after the war. Thus in the early thirties, German coal producers arranged for the export to Brazil of 9 million marks worth of coal, obtaining in exchange an equal value of coffee. German fertilizer was similarly exchanged for Egyptian cotton.

Somewhat more complicated arrangements, having the advantage of releasing the exporter from also performing the unaccustomed functions of an importer, involved an export and import firm in *each* country. Agreement had to be reached on what commodities would be exported, in what quantities, and at what values. Upon receipt of the goods, the importer in each country paid the exporters *in the importing country's currency,* and the transaction was completed.

All such arrangements require the approval of the exchange control authorities, even though they avoid the need to apply for an allocation of foreign exchange. For not only are exports and imports both subject to license; it is also the duty of the authorities to see that exports that can, in spite of difficulties, be sold for scarce, free currencies are not needlessly diverted from these markets. Hence it has generally been necessary for firms engaging in such deals to show that their exports were "additional"—i.e., that except for some such special arrangement, they could not be sold. This tends to give weight in this type of trade to relatively unimportant or fringe items in the exports of each partner.

Private compensation requires that the individual exports and imports of each transaction offset each other. This puts upon the exporter wishing to consummate such a deal the responsibility of ascertaining what imports are acceptable both to the exchange control authorities and to buyers in his country. Even when a fellow countryman among importers is drawn into the arrangement, it is still necessary for the two parties to find one another. To overcome such difficulties, specialised brokers emerged before the war in Germany and other countries, devoting their energies to uncovering possibilities of mutually advantageous and permissible trade, and to finding and bringing together potentially interested parties.

Clearing Agreements

A more satisfactory solution to these problems was found with the development of *exchange clearing,* which broadens and generalises the offsetting procedure. Each country enters into an agreement to establish, usually in its central bank, an account through which all payments for imports and exports shall be cleared.[1]

---

[1] Some clearing agreements are limited to certain categories of commodities, the rest of the trade being carried out in the normal manner.

Argentina and Italy in 1952 entered into a five-year agreement of this type. All imports from Italy into Argentina require that payments by importers shall be made into the Argentine clearing account in pesos. Similarly, Italians importing Argentine goods make payments into the Italian clearing account in lire. Exporters in each country are in turn paid in local currency from the balances deposited by importers.

Such an arrangement eliminates the need for applications for import licenses, for checking the prices of exports and imports to prevent over- or undervaluation, and thus greatly reduces the amount of red tape. So long as exports and imports are equal in value, clearance is complete and there is no problem of keeping the account in balance.

Since precise equality is not to be expected, some provision to meet such a divergence is necessary. The commonest method is to establish a "swing" credit of a fixed amount. Thus in the Italian-Argentine agreement, exports may exceed imports in either direction by as much as $100 million. Any further excess must be settled in gold or dollars. Another device is to alter the exchange rate applied to the clearing transactions, which is always specified in the agreement. Since it is an arbitrarily determined rate, it may overvalue one of the currencies and thus be responsible for the trade imbalance. Before the war, Germany deliberately used its superior bargaining power vis-a-vis the Balkan nations to force their acceptance of an overvalued rate for the mark. This gave it advantageous terms of trade and led also to the accumulation of large mark balances, which it was willing to liquidate only by exporting relatively unwanted commodities. Hence the large Balkan imports of aspirin and harmonicas.

Without a "swing" limit to the net excess of trade in either direction, not only might large unusable balances accumulate, but the monetary effects in each country could be serious. In the country with an excess of imports, substantial net payments of local currency would be made into the clearing account, thus retiring money from circulation. As with any excess of imports over exports, this is deflationary. In the country whose exports exceeded its imports, in-payments by importers would be insufficient to compensate the exporters. If the central bank were willing to advance credit to pay them, the money supply would be increased immediately by this amount, and ultimately, after these central bank funds had been deposited with commercial banks, perhaps by the full amount made possible by reserve requirements. Without such advances, the exporters would have to wait for payment until their turn came, which would dampen their enthusiasm to export.

Payments Agreements

Another type of bilateral arrangement, somewhat wider in scope than the clearing agreement, is the *payments agreement*. It is no different from the former in principle or in mechanism, but simply extends clearing facilities to additional categories of payments. The most important of these is outstanding debts, although the various service transactions, including the service of debt, are usually included.

Countries that build up substantial credits in exchange control countries, either prior to the introduction of controls, as a result of the operation of a bilateral accord, or simply because of the rashness of exporters, acquire a frozen asset. A payments agreement provides the means to thaw it, by prescribing that a certain per cent of payments for imports into the creditor country's clearing account shall be earmarked for the liquidation of accumulated debt. The creditor country need exercise no control over imports from the debtor, since only if imports exceed exports can accumulated debt be paid off. The debtor country, on the other hand, must hold imports from the creditor down sufficiently so that the agreed proportion of the value of its exports actually becomes applied to debt retirement.

Since World War II, most bilateral agreements have been of this broader type, including provisions not only for the settlement of debt, but also for payments for shipping charges, debt service, tourism, and the whole range of service items. With the gradual liberalisation of trade, strictly bilateral accords have given way more and more to arrangements that permit a considerable degree of multilateral clearing. We consider these more recent developments, especially the Sterling Area and the European Payments Union, in Chapter 23.

DISORDERLY CROSS RATES

In addition to causing a bilateral channeling of trade, exchange control tends to disturb the orderly relationship between exchange rates, replacing it with disorder.

So long as currencies are convertible, the whole system of interrelated exchange rates between different currencies must remain consistent. Any tendency, for example, for the cross rate between the franc and the pound to diverge from the rate between the dollar and the pound and between the franc and the dollar will be promptly corrected by the activity of exchange arbitragers.[2] With the introduction of exchange control and in-

[2] See above, p. 264.

convertibility, exchange arbitrage—the simultaneous purchase and sale of exchange in different markets—becomes impossible. Since the rate on any and every currency is arbitrary—being set by the authorities and maintained by quantitative restrictions—then, unless consistent cross rates are consciously sought, they will generally become disorderly or disparate. This is particularly true if a country has a deficit with one trading partner, a surplus with another, for then it will be tempted to depreciate its currency vis-à-vis the first and appreciate it vis-à-vis the second.

Suppose, with the dollar/pound rate at $2.80, the rates on the dollar and the pound in French francs are consistent, at 350 frs./$ and 980 frs./£ respectively. Encountering a deficit in its balance of payments with the United States and a surplus with the United Kingdom, the French exchange control authorities now depreciate the franc against the dollar to a 400 franc rate, appreciate it relative to the pound to 960 francs. The corresponding cross rate is $2.60 per pound (960/400 = 2.60), inconsistent or disparate as compared with the actual cross rate of $2.80 per pound.

This inconsistency provides an opportunity for Americans (or perhaps the nationals of other countries) to purchase sterling cheaply. At a 400 frs./$ rate, they can buy 960 francs for $2.60, and with these francs acquire £1—a saving of 20¢ over the rate on sterling in New York. Even though the British exchange control authorities permit sterling so obtained to be used only for goods shipped to France, these can be transshipped to the United States, or the destination can be changed after they have left a British port.

Situations of this kind arose frequently in the years after World War II, and were the basis for official protests against the establishment of inconsistent exchange rates which led to the emergence of disorderly cross rates.

MULTIPLE EXCHANGE RATES

In our discussion of exchange control, we have repeatedly stressed how an overvalued exchange rate depresses exports and requires the strict regulation of imports. In the search for relief from this constriction of trade, Germany in the 1930's originated and developed to a high degree the bilateral arrangements which soon became widespread.

Another device serving the same purpose—*multiple exchange rates*—also originated in Germany in the early thirties. Its effectiveness in opening up hitherto closed markets, together with other advantages that appeared as time went on, led to its rapid extension, especially in Latin America.

In the years immediately after the war, some twenty-odd countries used multiple exchange rates in one form or another.

Dual Rate Systems

The simplest, though not historically the earliest, of multiple exchange rate systems is one employing only two rates, an official rate (usually an overvalued one) for permitted transactions, and a free rate for all others. Ordinarily the official rate is confined, on the supply side, to exports capable of holding their markets even at an overvalued rate. These are typically commodities in which the country's position as a supplier is strong, even semi-monopolistic, as with Brazil in coffee or Chile in copper. Part or all of the foreign exchange from these exports must be surrendered at the official rate. Under Thailand's exchange control system, for example, 100 per cent of rice proceeds had until recently to be turned over to the government; for rubber, the surrender quota was 20 per cent; and for tin it has been, successively, 50, 40, and 20 per cent.

On the demand side, imports of basic necessities alone are usually permitted at the official rate. If the list of these commodities is narrowly restricted and if sufficient foreign exchange is allotted to satisfy demand at the import price plus the normal importer's profit, their prices can be held down. If, however, the exchange made available is insufficient, low prices can only be maintained in the face of shortages with supplementary price controls. Otherwise, importers will charge prices high enough to ration the scarce supplies and will gain a windfall profit.

All transactions other than those permitted at the official rate take place at the free rate. These include exports needing encouragement, non-essential and luxury imports, and usually all invisibles as well as capital exports and imports. With a truly free rate, the competition of these various demands and supplies establishes a rate that clears these transactions. There is, it should be noted, a possibility that this competition may drive the rate up to the point where costly luxuries are imported at the expense of semi-essentials needed by the lower and middle income groups. This is especially true where, as in some underdeveloped countries, income distribution is highly uneven, with a large share in the hands of the wealthier classes.

If the free rate fluctuates violently, the government may attempt to stabilise it by entering the market as a buyer or seller. To avoid the need for this, or to limit depreciation thought to be excessive, it may limit the transactions allowed at the free rate. This is almost certain to lead to the emergence of a "black" market where deals excluded from other markets are transacted. Because they are difficult to detect, these transactions are usually confined to such invisible items as tourists' expenditures, remission of profits, and transfers of capital.

Advantages of Multiple Rates

An interesting and important feature of a multiple exchange rate system, whether only two rates or several are in force, is that it permits the abandonment of quantitative restrictions and licensing. This is obvious if the exchange furnished importers at the lower rate or rates is adequate to satisfy their demands. If it is insufficient, the problem can be solved simply by limiting still further the imports granted preferential treatment. Clearly, this makes possible a great reduction in the complexity of the administrative apparatus, as well as a considerable saving in cost.

The most important single feature of multiple exchange rates is that they substitute a system of rationing demand by cost or price for rationing of imports by quantitative restrictions on supply. The currency is devalued in a partial or piecemeal fashion; imports not obtainable at the overvalued rate or rates can be purchased, but only at relatively higher prices. To the price mechanism is restored some, at least, of its regulatory function. And the area of purely administrative decision is considerably restricted.

Fixed Multiple Rates

While there has been a movement toward simplification of multiple exchange rate systems, with the establishment of dual rates as a common outcome, the trial and error procedure of prewar days often resulted in the emergence of a number of distinct exchange rates, one for each of several categories of transactions. A few of these complex systems still survive, notably (as of 1957) in Afghanistan, Bolivia, Brazil,[3] Nationalist China, Indonesia, Paraguay, Uruguay, and Yugoslavia. The lowest rates are commonly applied to exports in the strongest competitive position, or perhaps (as a percentage surrender quota) to only part of them, and to imports of the greatest importance to the economy. On the ascending scale of higher rates, the position of any export depends upon the degree to which it is felt necessary to stimulate it, of any import, upon its relative importance. The highest of all rates usually applies to invisibles, including

---

[3] Brazil's multiple rate system was established only in 1953, and has some unique features. See Alexandre Kafka, "The Brazilian Exchange Auction System," *Review of Economics and Statistics,* **XXXVIII** (August 1956).

capital transfers. As an illustration of an actual multiple rate system, the following table exhibits the rates in force in Chile at the end of 1955. (The system has since been greatly simplified.)

Table 19.1

EXCHANGE RATES IN CHILE

(as at January 24, 1956;
pesos per U. S. dollar)

BUYING   SELLING

19.37
Sales of exchange from nitrate exports up
to US $0.50 per ton.
                                    110.00
                                    Applies only "to a few outstanding com-
                                    mitments."

                                    203.00 *(Banking Rate)*
                                    Government imports and payments. Im-
                                    ports of raw sugar, kerosene, and some
                                    antibiotics.

300.00 *("Free" Banking Rate)*   303.00 *("Free" Banking Rate)*
Most exports and invisibles.   Most imports and invisibles.

519.00 *(Fluctuating Free Brokers' Rate)*   529.00 *(Fluctuating Free Brokers' Rate)*
Other invisibles, including travel receipts.   Other invisibles, including travel ex-
Exports of fish and fish products. Private   penses. Private capital.
capital.

573.00 *("Special Area" Fluctuating*   583.00 *("Special Area" Fluctuating*
     Rate) °   *Rate)* °
Exports of wine and crystallised nitrate.   Specified less essential imports. Some
Percentages of some other exports, e.g.,   invisibles.
iron ore from small mining companies.
Some invisibles.

° This rate is essentially the brokers' rate, but generally it is moved only once a week and is based on the average brokers' market quotation of the previous week.

   Other effective buying rates result from a mixing arrangement applied to certain export proceeds, all or part of which receive the benefit of the "special area" fluctuating rate, with the balance at the "free" banking rate.

(Source: *Seventh Annual Report on Exchange Restrictions*, International Monetary Fund, Washington, D. C. 1956.)

Effects of Multiple Rates

   Take the average of all the various exchange rates used by a given country as a base for comparison. Those below the average overvalue the currency. They have the effect of a tax on exports and a subsidy on imports. Higher than average rates, on the other hand, undervalue the currency. They resemble a subsidy on exports and a tax on imports.[4]

   [4] Unless we can assume that, under a free exchange rate system, the average of multiple rates would be the equilibrium rate, there is a difficulty here. If, as has some-times appeared to be the case, the equilibrium rate would approximate the highest of the multiple rates in effect, then *all* lower rates would provide varying subsidies to

Overvaluation (low exchange rates) tends to discourage the use of a country's more productive resources, both in export and in import-competing lines. With respect to exports, only the strongest export producers—that is, those whose resources have the greatest international advantage—are able to sell at these low rates. And the subsidy to imports provided by low rates of exchange discourages domestic production of substitutes that could easily compete at the average rate.[5] On the other hand, under-valuation (higher than average rates) encourages the use of inefficient resources, through the subsidisation of marginal exports and the protection of inefficient import-competing industries.

In addition to these protective and subsidy effects, there is also a revenue effect if the supply of exchange at the lower rates exceeds sales to importers at these rates. For then the government can make a profit by selling this surplus of cheaply bought exchange at higher rates. A common device for ensuring such a revenue to the government is to establish an appreciable spread between the buying and selling rates in any given category. (See Table 19.1 for an illustration of this.)

EVALUATION OF MULTIPLE EXCHANGE RATES

Administrative Simplification

Multiple exchange rates are in essence a form of partial devaluation. Consequently, foreign exchange is less scarce than it would be with a single but overvalued rate. If the imports permitted in each of several categories are limited to the exchange forthcoming at the corresponding rate, and especially if residual demands can find an outlet at a free rate, the whole complex apparatus of quantitative control can be dismantled. This reintroduction of rationing by price greatly reduces the area of administrative decision—the need for determining: the amount of each commodity to be imported, the source from which it may be obtained, and which importer is to get the business. The huge bureaucratic staff required

---

imports and impose taxes of varying severity on exports. Since it is impossible to generalise *a priori* with respect to where in a range of multiple rates a free equilibrium rate would lie, and difficult even to estimate such a rate in a concrete situation, we adopt the average rate merely as a provisional and convenient benchmark.

[5] The scheduling of imports of essential foodstuffs at subsidy rates greatly handicapped Chile's agriculture. From being a net exporter of agricultural products in the 1930's, by the late 1940's, the country had become a net importer. Although this shift was partly due to growing domestic demand for agricultural products not suited to Chile, it was aggravated by rising imports of such commodities as wheat and meat, whose production was made unprofitable by the low export and import exchange rates applied to these products.

to carry out such detailed regulations can be heavily pruned, to the substantial benefit of the government budget.

Since the efficiency of the control apparatus depends upon the honesty and ability of the administrators, elimination of quantitative restrictions is a particularly great boon to a country lacking a first-rate civil service. For incompetence compounds errors in judgment, serious enough in the best of circumstances. And corruption means that exports and imports will be determined largely on the basis of graft and favoritism.

Complexity and Uncertainty

Despite these advantages over exchange control with no devaluation whatever, multiple exchange rates have their own shortcomings. They introduce an additional element of complexity, and if either the rates themselves or the transactions permitted at each rate are frequently changed, as has often been true, further uncertainty is created. Further, unless positive action is taken to prevent it, disorderly cross rates are very likely to emerge.

Inefficient Use of Resources

The increased ease of importing and the stimulus to favored exports are, of course, a gain to the country adopting multiple rates. Against this must be set the inefficient use of resources resulting from the combination of taxes and subsidies implicit in such a system. This effect can be quite serious; [6] it is, moreover, haphazard, in that the various subsidies and penalties are not determined with reference to prospects of long-run industrial efficiency, but by balance of payments considerations.

Discriminatory Effects on Competitors

Also to be taken into account is the effect of multiple exchange rates on other countries. Particularly important in this respect is the fact that when a subsidy rate is introduced for exports, it applies only to a limited number of exports, and thus concentrates its impact upon a few competing countries. This is rightly regarded as a form of unfair competition, which is aggravated by resort to further changes in such rates. With uniform,

[6] Thus, not only Chilean agriculture, but that of Peru and Ecuador (and doubtless of other countries as well) suffered serious contraction because of the penalty rates on certain foodstuffs. Before Peru introduced multiple rates, domestic production of meat was sufficient for home consumption; with imports of meat permitted at the (low) official rate, home production fell to less than half of total consumption. Ecuador had a similar experience with wheat flour. E. M. Bernstein, "Some Economic Aspects of Multiple Exchange Rates," *International Monetary Fund Staff Papers*, Vol. 1, No. 2 (September 1950), p. 230.

over-all depreciation, on the other hand, the impact on competitors is spread "as broadly as the diversity of the economy of the depreciating economy permits." [7]

EXCHANGE CONTROL IN REVIEW

Reviewing the system of exchange control, as a method of safeguarding a country against an adverse balance of payments, we find it to have serious consequences both for the economy immediately affected and for the world economy as a whole.

Due to the insulation it provides against outside forces, the nation practicing exchange control is free to adopt policies with an inflationary bias which tend to convert an equilibrium exchange rate into an overvalued rate, or to increase any initial degree of overvaluation. There is a strong temptation to use this freedom, since nation-centered objectives normally have a stronger political appeal than more cosmopolitan goals.

When overvaluation has occurred, trade is gradually forced into bilateral channels, to ensure markets for overpriced exports and adequate supplies of scarce imports. Because countries with overvalued currencies are eager to obtain imports if they can pay for them with their own inconvertible money but are reluctant to draw upon scarce free exchange, convertibility of the controlled currencies becomes not only limited but discriminatory. Soft currencies are made available with relative liberality, hard currency allocations are severely restricted.

Once exchange control becomes widespread, the world market slowly developed during the nineteenth and early twentieth centuries is destroyed. The system of multilateral trade and convertibility of currencies upon which that world market rests are replaced by bilateral trading arrangements and inconvertibility. Hence the gains from trade, both for the uncontrolled as well as the controlled regions, are reduced. Goods can no longer be bought freely where they are most efficiently and cheaply produced, nor can they be sold where the need is greatest and prices are consequently highest. Ability to buy, as always, is determined by ability to sell. Exports priced in overvalued currencies have limited access to free markets; disproportionate amounts must be exchanged for the similarly overpriced exports of other nations that have hedged themselves in with restrictions.

With trade determined in considerable part not by comparative costs but by availability of means of payment, the allocation of resources becomes more and more uneconomic. Export industries come into being or

[7] *Ibid.*, p. 234.

are expanded, not because they are efficient, but because their markets are sheltered. Quantitative restrictions on imports give effective protection to high-cost substitutes.

To the reduction in the gains from trade must be added the direct cost of supporting a sizeable bureaucracy and the more intangible, indirect costs of errors in judgment, magnified manyfold if the administrators are incompetent and corrupt.

Resort to multiple exchange rates can mitigate some of these deficiencies. Multiple rates are, however, only a halfway house to devaluation, and introduce uncertainties and distortions of their own.

A country facing a balance of payments disequilibrium and forced to choose between depreciation, deflation, and exchange controls should weigh carefully the desirable and undesirable consequences of each. Exchange control furnishes no solution to the problem. It deals only with the deficit, not its causes, and it exacerbates those causes, tending to create a more basic disequilibrium.

Unless restrictions can be kept moderate or are to be used as a temporary stopgap while other, more fundamental adjustments are made, resort to exchange control is likely to be a costly and disappointing choice.

SELECTED REFERENCES

Bernstein, E. M., "Some Economic Aspects of Multiple Exchange Rates," *IMF Staff Papers*, Vol. I, No. 2 (1950). A brief theoretical discussion of the effects of multiple exchange rates.

Bloomfield, Arthur I., *Speculative and Flight Movements of Capital in Postwar International Finance*. (Princeton University Press, 1954). In addition to much factual material, this book considers methods of avoiding exchange controls and possible means of dealing with capital flight.

Chalmers, Henry, *World Trade Policies* (University of California Press, 1953). A continuing account of events in the field of international commercial policy in the form of a collection of current articles.

de Looper, Johan H. C., "Current Usage of Payments Agreements and Trade Agreements," *IMF Staff Papers*, Vol. IV, No. 3 (August 1955). An extended discussion of the main features, effects, and problems of trade and payments agreements.

Ellis, Howard S., *Exchange Control in Central Europe* (Harvard University Press, 1941). Examines the operation of control schemes in the 1930's.

League of Nations, *International Currency Experience* (1944). Chapter VII deals with exchange control.

Meade, James E., *The Balance of Payments* (Oxford University Press, 1951). Part V contains a good discussion of direct controls, both financial and commercial.

Mikesell, Raymond F., *Foreign Exchange in the Postwar World* (Twentieth Century Fund, New York, 1954). The best source for a general discussion of the postwar system of controlled trade and payments, with much illustrative material.

20

CHOOSING THE BEST WAY OUT

In the last two chapters we have seen that a nation confronted with a serious disequilibrium in its balance of payments can resort to any one of three distinct methods of dealing with it. (1) It can allow exchange rates to fluctuate freely, relying upon the resultant changed relationship between the prices of exports, imports, and domestic goods to eliminate the deficit. (2) It can maintain stable exchange rates, permitting the decrease in exports or the increase in imports that brought about the deficit to induce a decline in income and in domestic prices; if these changes are insufficient to restore equilibrium, they can be reenforced by a contraction of the supply of money, either deliberately engineered by the central banking authorities or caused by the effect of reserve losses upon a fractional reserve banking system. (3) Or it can subject the foreign exchange market to controls, limiting exchange allocations to the supplies made available to the control authorities.

These alternatives are not mutually exclusive, but can be combined in various ways. We have noted how flexible exchange rates and devaluation may combine, in different degrees, reliance upon rate changes and upon internal deflation to effect adjustment. And exchange control need not imply refusal to devalue in some degree, either piecemeal or at one stroke. Moreover, internal economic policies may, as we shall see, be used to supplement these adjustment mechanisms.

THE PROBLEM OF CHOICE

A country confronting a balance of payments problem has a choice among alternatives. Which should it choose? And what criteria should determine its choice? Does it make any difference what caused the disturbance, or is the cause irrelevant? These are the questions to which we must now address ourselves.

The criterion for the determination of *any* economic policy should be the attainment of maximum results at minimum cost. In our particular setting, this criterion means elimination of the balance of payments deficit with the least disruption of the national economy. As will soon become apparent, success in treating the disease of balance of payments disequilibrium depends in large measure upon the nature of its cause.

Our analysis of the various methods of adjustment up to this point has focused entirely upon mechanisms; the cause of the initial disturbance has been assumed to be irrelevant. We must now discard this assumption. A deficit is a deficit, whether caused by internal inflation or by more intense competition with a country's exports. But to restore equilibrium with the least friction requires a quite different kind of treatment for each situation.

DIAGNOSIS

We might now proceed to prescribe, for each major type of disturbance, the appropriate remedy. But diagnosis, as in medicine, comes first. We have, it is true, described the main causes of balance of payments disequilibrium, and have classified them according as they are due to income changes or structural changes. But how is one to recognise them in practice?

The policy-determining official, who must choose the measures to be adopted, confronts a going economy in all its complexity. A balance of payments deficit stands out clear and obvious in statistical data readily available in most countries today. But what lies behind it? Is it due to price disparities caused by past inflation, to rising costs in his country's principal export industries, to technological change abroad, to depression in a major export market, or perhaps—and most likely—to a mixture of these and possibly other causes? The government official, with an important decision to make, must answer this question as best he can. The answer is not clear and self-evident, but is buried in the mass of statistics that he and his staff have to work with. These relate to income, employment, prices, bank credit, industrial and agricultural production, inventories, construction activity, exports, imports, capital movements, and many other economic phenomena. Here is a real problem of diagnosis—of knowing what symptoms to look for and where to find them. Some clues to the solution of these problems can be given.

Income Changes

Easiest of all the possible causes of balance of payments disequilibrium to identify is *rampant inflation*. It will stand out clearly in rising prices, expanding currency and bank credit, and government budget deficits; in over-full employment and in shortages of labor and raw materials. Chile since the mid-1930's is a good illustration. It has had either an actual balance of payments deficit or a potential one, held in check by rigorous exchange controls and moderated from time to time by piecemeal devaluation. Between 1937 and 1955, currency and bank deposits expanded at annual rates ranging from a minimum of 6 per cent to a maximum of 70 per cent. Prices roughly kept in step with the money supply, rising at annual rates that averaged almost 23 per cent. Though other causes played a role in Chile's balance of payments difficulties, inflation was far and away the most important.

Mild inflation is less easy to spot. There is almost certain to be less than the normal frictional unemployment—that is, employment is over-full. Aggregate demand exceeds supply available from production at current prices, but the pressure on prices may not be severe enough to overcome rigidities, or controls may suppress their tendency to rise. Credit expansion may be negligible, the excess demand being financed by past accumulations of cash, as in the United States immediately after World War II.

Nevertheless, with full employment the existence of a balance of payments deficit is a clear indication of current inflation. When a country absorbs in consumption and investment more than its own output and any ordinary capital inflow, without offsetting unemployment, aggregate demand must be excessive to the extent of the balance of payments deficit.[1]

During a mild inflation, investment would tend to be high in relation to income as compared with previous, non-inflationary periods. So would the whole range of imports, while exports in general would be relatively low. Reports of materials and labor shortages should also provide confirmatory evidence.

A balance of payments deficit may be due, not to current inflation, but to *price-cost disparities* caused by a preceding period of inflation. If inflation is serious and continues for some time, a country's costs and prices are almost certain to be raised substantially in relation to those of other countries. Prices of domestic commodities, in particular, are likely to be especially out of line, since they are not restrained by competition with foreign producers. Clearly, a comparison of the relative trend in the recent past of prices and wages at home and in other countries is called for. A deficit resulting from a price-cost disparity is likely to be characterised by large imports and small exports relative to the size of national income. There is likely to be substantial unemployment because of the price disadvantage suffered by both export and import-competing industries.

Cyclical disequilibrium in the balance of payments would be reflected,

[1] E. M. Bernstein, "Strategic Factors in Balance of Payments Adjustment," *International Monetary Fund Staff Papers*, Vol. V, No. 2. August 1956, p. 158. Much of this chapter is heavily indebted to Dr. Bernstein's analysis.

in the early stages, by a sudden drop in exports, while imports, income, and employment remained relatively unchanged. Data for the country or countries where the depression originated should show declining income and imports. As the depression spread, deficit countries would also experience rising unemployment and declining income.

Structural Changes

Structural changes causing balance of payments disequilibrium are of many different kinds. Those due to *altered demand or supply conditions* would share the common trait of affecting specific exports or imports, so it is primarily detailed trade data that the analyst would want to examine. If particular exports had declined, this might be due to a shift in foreign demand, to a worsened competitive position of domestic exporters, or to an improved position of foreign competitors. Inquiry should be directed to discovering whether trade barriers abroad had been increased, whether there had been a change in tastes, or whether foreign competitors had introduced new processes lowering costs or improved or totally new products. If exports remained substantially unchanged but certain imports were abnormally large, inquiry should center upon such possibilities as a shift in domestic tastes, improved efficiency and lower costs of suppliers of imports, or the introduction of new types of imported goods.

To illustrate the points at issue here, we may cite a Tariff Commission study requested by President Eisenhower in 1955. The briar pipe industry had experienced declining sales, which it (and the Tariff Commission in an earlier report) ascribed to rising foreign competition. The requested study showed that the major cause of the industry's difficulties lay not in the competition of imports but in the changing habits of smokers, who were turning steadily away from pipe smoking to cigarettes. A similar study of the difficulties of the felt-hat industry showed the villain to be, not the foreign producer, but the American male: he was determined to go bareheaded.

Changed debtor-creditor relationships are another type of structural change that can cause a balance of payments deficit. These could include an upsurge in long-term lending, a sudden decline in long-term borrowing, flight movements of capital, or the loss of overseas earning assets. For a country with good balance of payments statistics, these changes would be evident in the data for capital movements or, for the last-named case, in declining yields from past overseas investments. In the absence of such statistics, inquiries of banks doing a foreign business should provide some corroborative evidence.

TREATMENT

In the practice of medicine, treatment of symptoms is rarely effective in eliminating the disease that causes them. The case is no different in economics. A balance of payments deficit is simply the manifestation of some deeper malady. The deficit can be suppressed by direct controls, but unless corrective measures attack its causes, it will break out again with their removal. *To be effective, remedies must be specific.*

Inflation

The truth of this is most easily seen with a deficit caused by inflation, whether severe or mild. To free exchange rates to rise or to devalue the currency would be useless or worse if the inflation itself were to go unchecked. For the continuing excess demand would merely generate a recurring deficit, requiring for its correction a steadily rising free rate or ever new doses of devaluation. Moreover, either form of depreciation would aggravate the inflation by stimulating exports and checking imports.

The appropriate remedy is clearly deflation, at least to the extent necessary to destroy the excess demand: Maintain fixed exchange rates, and allow the pressure of the deficit upon income to do its work. With moderate inflation, unaccompanied by any appreciable rise of prices, little if any positive deflation would be necessary. With severe inflation, accompanied by a marked rise in the price level, reliance upon deflation would require a substantial decline of income and prices.

Since, in the social context of the mid-twentieth century, deflation would be sure to encounter stiff political opposition, the checking of inflation ("disinflation") might well represent the limit to the use of this classical remedy. To restore balanced price relationships, devaluation would now be appropriate, accompanied by sufficient restraints on credit to prevent a reemergence of the inflationary trend. Devaluation and credit restraint would also be suited to an existing price-cost disparity left over from previous inflation.

Cyclical Disequilibrium

Cyclical disequilibrium in the balance of payments is more difficult to cope with. The deficit has been caused by declining exports, traceable to a depression originating abroad. Under the gold standard, the decline in exports and the loss of reserves would be followed by income and price deflation. Eventually the balance of payments disequilibrium would be corrected, but at the cost of severe depression.

Devaluation may appear to offer a less costly remedy. But with a world-wide decline in incomes, demands tend to become inelastic, especially for commodities whose consumption is readily postponable. In the face of inelastic and shrinking demand, devaluation, unless very substantial, is unlikely to stimulate exports or check imports appreciably. Moreover, so far as it does retard imports, the depression is aggravated in other countries. Retaliation is almost certain.

As we indicated earlier, the solution much to be preferred in this situation is *the concerted adoption of expansionary monetary and fiscal policies*, especially in the economically more important countries. If, whether by agreement or by accident, the larger countries simultaneously generate a recovery of income and employment, their imports will increase, spreading the impulse toward expansion throughout the world. The exports of each will increase as income and imports rise in the other countries following an expansionary program. Although, in these countries, imports are likely to exceed exports, as the major trading nations their reserves are also likely to be relatively large; these can be drawn upon to support the program of expansion. As recovery spreads, balance of payments deficits will gradually be eliminated and equilibrium restored.

In view of the political importance of preventing unemployment, it may not be too optimistic to hope that, even without international agreement, the onset of depression would today be promptly countered by vigorous monetary and fiscal action. Although to foresee the complete elimination of depressions would be utopian, their duration and severity should be greatly moderated. Domestic expansionary measures together with use of their international reserves might well enable the major countries to weather the storm at tolerable cost.

If this hope is not realised—and lack of international reserves by one or more of the larger countries might frustrate it—neither deflation nor devaluation have anything to offer. The prescription for any country facing depression abroad, with declining exports and income, remains internal expansion—but accompanied by exchange and trade controls to suppress the deficit and avoid exhaustion of its reserves. All the better if these controls discriminate against imports from the country where the depression originated, for then its spread can be minimised. Moreover, the pressure of such discrimination may, by intensifying the depression at its focus of infection, help force the adoption there of an expansionary policy.

Structural Disequilibrium

A change in specific demand or supply conditions affects only one or a few exports or imports. The affected country has either lost an advantage in the production of exports or its disadvantage in some import-competing industry has increased, with the consequence of a deficit in its balance of payments. What is clearly called for here is not general deflation, nor even necessarily a change in the relative prices of the whole range of exports and imports, but a shift of resources into a new export line or into the production of additional import substitutes.

A good deal depends upon the degree to which the economy in question is specialised. If it is already well diversified, the easiest solution may well be a moderate amount of devaluation to effect an across-the-board stimulus to exports and import substitutes, accompanied by a policy of credit restraint to inhibit inflation. If, however, the economy has been heavily dependent upon one or a very few exports—like Chile on copper and nitrates, Malaya on rubber and tin, or Ceylon on tea and coconuts—and its exports have lost out to new products or to a more efficient competitor, devaluation is unlikely to be of much help. This is even more true if there are few domestic substitutes for imports. There is little in the way of domestic industry, either on the export or the import-competing side, to stir into action; the whole burden of the devaluation falls on the shoulders of the consumer of imports.

A country in this situation desperately needs to reallocate its unemployed resources to the most productive remaining uses. Use of all the techniques of economic development is suggested. These include government aid, both financial and technical, to promising industries; appeal to international agencies for similar help; carefully chosen infant-industry protection; possibly a measure of devaluation once progress is under way; and quite probably the introduction of exchange controls to safeguard the country's reserves while the internal changes are taking place.

Conclusion

This chapter should have made clear the relevance, both to the diagnosis of a country's problems and to the choice of a suitable remedy, of economic analysis. Theory has a real task to perform. It is a tool needed to isolate the causes of difficulties, to determine what policies can be used to combat them, and to judge which is appropriate. Without analysis, facts alone are refractory and meaningless. With it, they become orderly, tractable, and significant.

SELECTED REFERENCES

Bernstein, E. M., "Strategic Factors in Balance of Payments Adjustment," *IMF Staff Papers*, Vol. V, No. 8 (Aug. 1956). A fine example of the application of economic analysis to balance of payments problems.

Haberler, Gottfried, "Some Factors Affecting the Future of International Trade and International Economic Policy," in S. E. Harris (ed.), *Economic Reconstruction;* reproduced in *Readings in the Theory of International Trade.*

Kindleberger, Charles P., *International Economics* (Richard D. Irwin, Inc., Homewood, Ill., 1953). Ch. 26, on the "Means to Equilibrium," compares the different remedies, and stresses the contribution of competition, mobility, high income elasticity, etc., to their efficacy.

League of Nations, *International Currency Experience* (1944). Ch. IX contains a review of adjustment methods in the light of interwar experience.

Meade, James E., *The Balance of Payments* (Oxford University Press, 1951). See Chapters IX, X, XV, and XXIV for a comparison of the different methods of adjustment.

Polak, J. J., "Exchange Depreciation and International Monetary Stability," *Review of Economics and Statistics*, **XXIX** (Aug. 1947). Urges devaluation as especially suited to income and price disequilibria, but as quite unsuited for dealing with structural disequilibrium.

21

STRUCTURAL WEAKENING OF THE WORLD ECONOMY

THE WORLD ECONOMY OF 1913

The hundred years between the Napoleonic wars and the war of 1914-18 witnessed the creation of a true world economy, with most of its member nations closely integrated through a highly developed network of trade and finance. The numerous facilities essential to the operation of this complex system of interrelated markets were centered in London, but their influence was spread throughout the globe by means of branch offices, correspondents, and contractual relationships. These facilities included specialised export and import firms, commodity brokers, commercial banks and investment banks, acceptance and discount houses, insurance companies, shipping lines, and last but not least, a worldwide system of telegraphic communications.

Specialisation of national production, based on widely varying factor endowments, was intense. Although tariffs to some extent obstructed trade and retarded specialisation, their effect was not too serious, for they were changed infrequently and only a few were high. Because each of the various kinds of specialised production was concentrated in a very few geographic localities, multilateral trade was essential. Fortunately, since all the principal and many of the less important countries were on the gold standard, there existed the universal convertibility of currencies so necessary for the operation of a multilateral trading system.

This was not a static world, but one of rapid change. Technology advanced with great speed, bringing into existence new methods of production and totally new products. Heavy migration of labor and large movements of capital progressively altered relative factor endowments, the very foundation of international trade. Nor were these movements themselves constant—they ebbed and flowed and changed their direction without warning. Intermittently, too, the channels of trade were interrupted and diverted by changes in the commercial policy of nations.

All these phenomena introduced disturbances of varying severity, to which the balance of payments of each nation affected had somehow to become adjusted. The means to that adjustment was furnished by the automatic mechanism of the gold standard, which the opinion of the day accepted and allowed to work. Through its operation, the many and recurring changes were assimilated with a remarkable smoothness and lack of friction.

FORCES OF DISINTEGRATION

This happy combination of economic institutions, market forces, and harmonious climate of opinion was rudely shattered after 1914. The balance of power in Europe, carefully nurtured by a century of British diplomacy, ended abruptly with the challenge of German expansionism. Four years of bitter war, with entire nations in arms, wrought terrible destruction and loss of life.

Despite all the damage and disruption, within a few years the worst of Europe's wounds had healed. Production recovered to prewar levels and then began, after a brief interruption, a steady climb. A deep nostalgia for the past bred a sincere attempt to reconstruct the international framework. The gold standard was restored, the wartime restrictions on trade were abandoned, trade connections were reestablished, and a new agency —the League of Nations—was created to ease international tensions and to facilitate agreed solutions for common problems.

For a time, success appeared within reach. The middle and later twenties were years of great prosperity; production and trade advanced steadily and standards of living improved. Yet the international structure on which all this rested had been greatly weakened in ways little appreciated at the time, ways that made the world economy less resilient and less capable of smooth adjustment to further change. Moreover, that structure was subjected to a series of disturbances far greater than any it had hitherto been forced to face. Even before the great upheaval of a second World War, the impact of these developments destroyed the highly articulated but feebler successor to the world economic system of the late nineteenth and early twentieth centuries.

This chapter depicts the sources of weakness in the international economy of the inter-war years, indicates the structural and other changes to which adjustment had somehow to be made, and shows how failure to meet this challenge brought about collapse.

A WEAKENED INTERNATIONAL STRUCTURE

Monetary Developments After the First World War

The pressures of war had caused most of the belligerents and many of the neutral nations to abandon the gold standard. Although the sharpness and extent of the break varied from one country to another, free movements of gold ceased during and for some years after the war. Thus, the close link between national price systems was broken, and prices in different countries were free to move independently. Inflation went to varying lengths, depending upon the balance of payments situation confronting each nation and the fiscal policies it followed. It was most intense in Germany, Russia, and Austria-Hungary, where currencies became, within a few years after the war, virtually worthless and had to be replaced by new issues. In France, wholesale prices rose to more than eight times the 1913 level; in Italy, the rise was about sevenfold. Even the United Kingdom and the United States witnessed a postwar peak of prices of 330 and 272, respectively.

To bring some order into this chaotic situation was one of the first postwar concerns. Except where currencies had become virtually worthless, the earlier long attachment to the gold standard bred a strong desire for its restoration. Its abandonment during and after the war was generally regarded as but a temporary break with the past.

But if gold was again to be the base, there arose immediately the question of what the metallic content of each currency should be, and thus the level of exchange parities. The United States, which during the war had modified its attachment to the gold standard only to the extent of requiring licenses for the export of gold, merely abolished this requirement in 1919 and returned to gold at the old parity. With ample gold reserves, it could do so. Germany and Austria scrapped their worthless currencies and adopted new ones—the Reichsmark, with the prewar gold parity relative to the dollar of 23.8 cents, and the schilling, with the relatively high parity of about 14 cents. Rigorous controls over the supply of money in both countries kept the internal value of these new currencies in line with their external or gold value, while international loans provided the reserves needed to meet adverse swings in the balance of payments. Many countries, however, had to make do with their existing but badly depreciated currencies. For them to have restored the relatively high prewar gold parities would have meant exchange rates that seriously overvalued their currencies. It would have required ruinous deflation to bring down internal costs and prices sufficiently to effect an appropriate balance between exports and imports. The only alternative for these countries was to devalue their currencies in terms of gold—to bring their external value into line with the existing and depreciated internal value. Some nations—notably the United Kingdom—stood in an intermediate position, with prices and costs high in relation to 1913, but not so much higher than in the United States that the gap could not be eliminated by moderate deflation.

Restoration of the Gold Standard

Great Britain, the center of the prewar gold standard, approached the problem of restoration gradually, yet with its course set in advance. The British decision rested on a report (in 1918) of the famous Cunliffe Committee, which assumed that the gold standard still existed in Great Britain, that its continuance was imperative, and advocated its restoration "without delay."

The Committee's recommendations were followed, however, only slowly and tentatively. Exchange restrictions were removed gradually, the Bank of England pursued a cautious deflationary policy, and British prices became more closely aligned with prices in the United States. As a result, the dollar/sterling exchange rate recovered from a low of $3.18 in early 1920 to $4.36 two years later. An embargo on the placement of foreign loans in Britain, and American credits of $300 million, gave sufficient support to the pound to permit Parliament in 1925 to put the currency back on gold at the prewar parity of $4.866.

At this time the index of wholesale prices in the United Kingdom stood at 159, in the United States at 155 (1913 = 100), a fairly close correspondence. But because the wholesale index is heavily weighted with the prices of internationally traded commodities (which must meet foreign competition and therefore cannot differ much across national boundaries), it failed to reflect adequately the fact that British costs remained relatively high. Restoration of the old parity is generally conceded to have overvalued the pound by at least 10 per cent and to have subjected the island's economy for the next seven years to continuous deflationary pressure. Because prices and costs were quite rigid, they failed to decline appreciably. Instead, Britain suffered from chronic unemployment, which throughout the twenties never fell below the figure of a million.

Between 1925 and 1928, more than forty countries returned to gold, some at their prewar parity, others at a devalued level. Switzerland and the Netherlands were among the former group; France and Italy, on the other hand, where even postwar deflation left prices far higher than in 1913, cut the gold content of their currencies by approximately four-fifths and three-quarters respectively. By the end of 1928, an extensive international currency system based on gold had been recreated.

Hopes and Expectations

With the reconstruction of a broadly inclusive international gold standard, that prewar pillar of stability and cohesion, it was widely assumed that the most essential aspect of reconstruction had now been achieved. The world, it was felt, could look forward once more to the attainment of a stable international equilibrium, subject of course to temporary disturbances or even to changes of a deeper, more enduring character, but sufficiently limited or gradual so as to permit adjustment by the old familiar processes. It is hardly surprising that statesmen, weary of the burden of unaccustomed problems, should have regarded with relief the restoration of an automatically functioning mechanism. That mechanism, it was believed, would take from their shoulders the responsibility for thought and for difficult decisions.

As it turned out, their hopes rested in large part on illusion. They had, they thought, reconstructed a well-understood and efficient piece of machinery. They overlooked the fact that parts of this machinery beyond their control had changed in ways that seriously hampered its operation. And they could not foresee the excessive burdens to which it would be subjected.

Formal Changes in the Gold Standard

The gold standard established in 1925-28 differed somewhat from that of 1914. To alleviate an impending shortage of gold, its coinage had been generally discontinued, except in the United States, and assets in the form of balances in gold-standard countries were permitted to count as reserves of a country's central bank. These changes, known as the gold bullion system and the gold exchange system, were comparatively unimportant. Under the former, currencies were convertible into gold bullion rather than coins, and vice versa, at a fixed price; under the gold exchange system, local currencies could be used to acquire the currencies of gold standard countries. Gold exports and imports were unrestricted.

It was in the basic or vital rather than in the purely formal or external characteristics of the system that serious change had taken place. The prewar efficiency of the gold standard had depended upon the centralisation of international transactions in London and upon adherence to well-established rules of international conduct. These essential foundations had been eroded.

Prewar Features of the Gold Standard

Before the war, the gold standard had centered in London. By the simple process of adding to and subtracting from the sterling balances owned by the banks of practically every nation, the great bulk of international transactions was *cleared*. The London market also played the role of a world central bank. When other countries suffered an adverse balance of payments, the London market advanced short-term loans that supplemented their dwindling gold reserves. When Britain lost gold, the London market borrowed from the entire world. With gold movements in part replaced by short-term capital, the extent of the accompanying contraction or expansion of credit was moderated. If the underlying disturbance proved short-lived, this was all to the good; if, however, a fundamental readjustment were needed, London's lending or borrowing interposed no obstacle, but merely gave more time for deep-seated forces to assert themselves.

Finally, London had for long been the principal source of long-term investment abroad. From their experience in this exacting business, her bankers developed a high degree of skill and judgment. Moreover, the well-organised London investment market was very sensitive to international influences. When exports exceeded imports, foreign balances were transferred to British ownership and gold moved in, easing the money market. For a time, short-term foreign lending might absorb part of the additional funds now available. But the scope of such lending is limited; if the balance of payments surplus continued, the lending would come to a halt, with a resumption of gold movements and a further easing of the money market. The continuance of easy credit conditions would now stimulate long-term foreign lending. An inward movement of foreign securities replaced the flow of gold, and the purchasing power put at the disposal of foreigners supported and made possible the continuance of the large volume of exports. International investment thus played an essential part in and greatly facilitated the adjustment mechanism.[1]

Substantive Change: Divided Responsibility

Because of events transpiring during and after the war, these substantive

---

[1] This account is confirmed by direct evidence. "In London interviews granted the writer it was repeatedly stated by investment bankers that before the war they never concerned themselves with the position of the balance of payments, but that when money was knocking around, looking for employment, they felt that to be a good time for bringing forward foreign issues." William Adams Brown, Jr., *The International Gold Standard Reinterpreted*, p. 55. Copyright 1940 by the National Bureau of Economic Research, New York.

aspects of the gold standard had undergone radical change. The Federal Reserve System, established in 1915, gave the United States a central banking structure that stabilised the hitherto erratic money markets, as well as an acceptance market which soon came to rival that of London. The growing importance of this country as a source of supplies, both during and after the war, supported this market and also made increasingly necessary the maintenance of substantial dollar balances in New York. Though negligible in 1914, these balances as early as 1926 amounted to nearly $1.5 billion. Moreover, the New York Stock Exchange at no time imposed restrictions on trading in foreign securities, while the United Kingdom at various intervals had to place an embargo on foreign issues. This fact, together with the availability of credit for long-term borrowing in New York, brought additional deposits and a large and growing business of distributing securities.

Two heads may be better than one, but two clearing centers certainly are not. For the efficiency of a clearing center is in direct proportion to its centralisation of transactions. When there is more than one, after the transactions are cleared in each center, those between the centers must be offset. More foreign balances must be maintained, and more labor devoted to the clearing function.

Two *financial centers,* on the other hand, can strengthen the international economy if they work in harmony, not at cross purposes. The additional resources, both short- and long-term, that the rise of New York made available, were all to the good, the more so since London's ability to finance foreign investment was declining. On the debit side, however, must be set the inexperience of New York bankers and the greater sensitiveness of its money market to domestic and speculative forces than to the pressures of a changing balance of payments. It is to be expected that the financial center of a nation continental in extent and comparatively self-sufficient in production, whose foreign trade is a small fraction of its total turnover, should be relatively unaffected by surpluses and deficits in its international accounts. Less predictable was the dominating influence in New York of the rate of interest on stock market loans (the call loan rate), responding to speculative influences rather than to movements of trade.

In such a money market, if active speculation drives up the call loan rate, commercial interest rates, including that on acceptances, will also rise, for competition for funds is pervasive. If at the same time there exists a surplus in the U.S. balance of payments (which means deficits in those of other countries), short-term international lending by New York would be appropriate to the international needs. Yet a contrary inward movement of funds may take place, attracted by the high return on stock market loans. Precisely this combination of circumstances arose during the 1920's. The stock market boom made it impossible for New York to perform its function of short-term international lender.

Despite this contradiction, the United States did engage in substantial *long-term* foreign lending. Yet these loans (totalling nearly $5 billion between 1922 and 1928) were not closely related to the state of our balance of payments, but to inflationary forces within the country. Moreover, the inexperience of New York bankers had unfortunate results: excessive attention to the immediate gains from bankers' commissions rather than to the underlying soundness of the loans themselves. Hence, there were many loans to dubious borrowers, and for unproductive purposes. Financing of foreign investment also tended to be sporadic rather than steady.

Changes in the Rules

The sharing of London's functions with another, less well-adapted financial center, was not the only substantial alteration in the prewar gold standard. The "rules of the game" according to which it operated had also been changed. Though unwritten, these rules had previously been well-understood and observed. For the system to work, an inflow of gold had to be allowed to effect an expansion of the supply of money; an outflow, a contraction. Otherwise, the changes in income and prices so essential to adjustment simply could not occur. Moreover, with fractional reserve systems, it was accepted that monetary expansion and contraction would be a *multiple* of the initiating gold movement.

After the war, independent national determination of the supply of money supplanted its dependence on the ebb and flow of gold. Inward movements of the metal were neutralised by central bank sales of securities to the market: the additions to commercial bank reserves from abroad were offset by domestic withdrawals. Losses of reserves due to a gold outflow were similarly replaced by central bank funds devoted to the purchase of open-market securities. Thus, between 1920 and 1924, the Federal Reserve authorities offset a considerable part of the large gold receipts of these years, attributing their action to the need (1) to maintain sound credit conditions (*domestic* stability), and (2) to ensure that this gold would be available for export again when the need arose.[2] The Bank of

[2] The gold came from countries that were off the gold standard, and whose trade was still disorganised; its movement was therefore regarded as abnormal. For an official explanation of the policy of neutralisation, see the *Tenth Annual Report of the Federal Reserve Board* (1923), pp. 20-22.

England, too, after 1925, followed a systematic policy of gold neutralisation by varying its security holdings inversely with gold movements—a policy whose net effect was deflationary. Although, in view of all the circumstances, and especially in view of *domestic* conditions in both countries, these actions may have been wise, they clearly went counter to traditional gold standard practice.

Many reasons underlay this substitution of national goals for reliance on the automatic operation of an international monetary system. Among them was a growing concern for internal economic stability, induced by increasing industrialisation and urbanisation, which subjected ever more and more people to the hazards of unemployment. The advance of economic knowledge also played a role. Confronted with the monetary disturbances of the war and postwar years, economists had studied these phenomena intensively; out of their studies came greater understanding and increased powers of control. In particular, schemes for the stabilisation of prices and therewith of economic activity through central bank action acquired a wide following. Furthermore, the means to make these schemes effective increased apace. Central banks, formerly confined to a few countries, now arose all over Europe, in several Latin American nations, and in Australia and South Africa.

The Changing Climate of Opinion

The trend toward independent national action in monetary affairs was only an eddy in a much broader current. Especially since World War I, but starting much earlier, there has been an unmistakable movement toward increasing government intervention in economic life. This was an inevitable reaction against some of the unfortunate consequences of laissez faire.

Economic freedom brought striking increases in productivity and therewith in standards of living. For it released the energies of business men to amass capital, to form new enterprises, and to adopt new techniques, and thus to expand output at a phenomenal rate. But it also enabled the strong and well-informed to take advantage of the weak and ignorant. The result was long hours of labor, widespread employment of children, dangerous working conditions, insecurity, and filthy slums. These consequences had not been foreseen by the early supporters of laissez faire, for they assumed all participants in economic activities to be equal—equal in bargaining power, in knowledge of their interests, in capacity to distinguish good wares from bad, and equal, too, in available alternatives as to occupation, place of work, or housing. Since this necessary equality was patently absent, individual and social interest failed to coincide. The actual situation was aptly suggested by an oft-quoted parody of the mid-nineteenth century: " 'Every man for himself and God for all of us,' as the elephant said when he danced among the chickens." [3]

The response to the anti-social effects of industrial change in a framework of individualism varied widely. Some thoughtful and sensitive people, like the Tory humanitarians in Great Britain, introduced specific reforms for particular evils such as child labor and long hours of work. Others rejected the individualist philosophy in its entirety and sought to formulate a new and more adequate social theory. These included utopian socialists like Robert Owen in England and St. Simon and Fourier in France, Christian Socialists like Charles Kingsley, and most important of all, Marx and Engels and their followers.

With the spread of industry and with it the growth of cities and an urban working class, the numbers subjected to the hazards of unemployment, industrial accidents, a weak bargaining position, and slum living constantly rose. There developed a basis of mass support for reforms directed toward these deficiencies and for the new collectivist ideas. Political parties broadened their appeal by introducing reform measures, trade unions organised the workers for more effective bargaining, and socialist and labor parties emerged to promote their political interests. Legislatures enacted laws to regulate public utilities, to outlaw child labor, to regulate the conditions of work, and to protect the consumer. Generally somewhat later to appear were the various forms of social insurance: workmen's compensation, old-age insurance, unemployment insurance, and finally, health insurance. Also to be included under the heading of social legislation are slum clearance and public housing and our old acquaintance, central banks, established to permit the more effective control of credit.

These new laws all had two things in common: they aimed at improving conditions of life in modern industrial society, and to accomplish this, they required ever more intervention by the state in the operation of the economy. The role of the state took on ever-increasing importance. In changing social conditions and the response made to them there existed a solid foundation for an ever larger exercise of national authority.

Economic Nationalism

Reenforcing this trend toward independent national action were the

---

[3] Attributed by W. Jethro Brown, *The Underlying Principles of Modern Legislation* (1912), to Charles Dickens.

forces of nationalism bred of economic rivalry. We have shown how they led, after about 1870, to rising tariffs and to colonial expansion. After the first World War, economic nationalism was reenforced, quite naturally by the inflammatory effects of war itself, artificially by the creation of Poland and the Baltic states and of the succession states of the Austro-Hungarian Empire. Moreover, during the war, in belligerent and nonbelligerent nations alike, new industries arose or old expanded to replace supplies cut off by the war. With the war's end, motives of security and of self-interest combined to exact protection against the original and more economical centers of production.

Thus, free-trade Britain continued duties established in wartime on certain luxuries and inaugurated the "Key Industries" duties (with rates of 33⅓ and 50 per cent) on a number of militarily important items. The United States abandoned the policy of low duties embodied in the Underwood Tariff of 1913 and in 1922, enacted a new high tariff. In Japan, India, Australia, and Latin America, the disappearance of European competition for four years in many lines of industry called forth local production. Some of these war infants died a natural death as trade was reopened, but many clamored for and obtained protection.

Resurgent economic nationalism not only raised barriers to trade; it also interfered with the international movement of labor. The United States, though it remained the principal destination of immigrants, restricted immigration sharply and in 1924, introduced quotas based on national origin. These quotas favored immigrants from northern Europe, and discriminated against those from southern Europe and the Orient where population pressure was greatest. The total numbers entering the United States, which had averaged 880 thousand a year in the decade ending with 1910, fell to an annual average of 411 thousand in the 1920's.

All the developments to which we have drawn attention in the last few pages—the rise of New York as a second and less suitable world financial center, the national determination of monetary policy, the increased role of the state in economic affairs, and the resurgence of economic nationalism —weakened the delicately balanced international economic system, making it more rigid and less sensitive to changes calling for adjustment. Our next task is to examine the increased burden this mechanism was called upon to meet.

THE BURDEN OF STRUCTURAL CHANGE

War Debts and Reparation

Prewar capital movements, at least since the Franco-Prussian war, had been the result of the free choice of individual investors, and were mainly in response to the attraction of a more promising yield. Though they varied from year to year, and altered their direction as time passed, these shifts were seldom violent. Between each lender and borrower, too, the current of lending generally began slowly, rose gradually to a peak, and then tapered off, thus giving time for balances of payments to adjust to the flow of capital.

The situation was very different after 1918, for the war left a heavy legacy of international debt. At the end of the paying line was Germany, saddled (in 1921) with a reparation burden of $33 billion, most of which was to be paid to Great Britain and France. Italy, France, and Belgium were in debt to one another and to Britain. All of these countries, together with several others, owed the United States at the time of the armistice a principal sum of a little over $7 billion.

For the chain of payments to move smoothly all along the line, two requirements had to be met: large sums in marks had to be extracted annually from the German people, and these sums had to be transferred regularly into other currencies—ultimately a large proportion into dollars.

The first of these problems was one of taxable capacity—an internal problem. The capacity of Germany to pay reparation from this point of view would amount to the difference between the maximum taxable capacity of the country and the minimum needs of government. In the late twenties, German taxes were 25 per cent of the national income, while reparation obligations comprised 10 per cent of these taxes, or 2.5 per cent of the national income. Though heavy, the burden would not appear to have been insuperable.

The transfer problem was more complex and difficult. After the sums in money had been raised in Germany, they had to be remitted to the reparation recipients. Over any but a brief period of time and for relatively small amounts, such international transfers could only be made in the form of goods and services. Under the restored gold standard, it was essential to set in motion an expansion of incomes and a rise of prices in the creditor countries, a decline of incomes and prices in Germany, sufficient to cause Germany's exports to exceed its imports by the amount of annual reparation to be transferred.

To some extent, the extraction of additional taxes from the German people helped set this mechanism in operation. By reducing their personal consumption, this taxation released goods, or the factors to produce goods, for export, and also caused some diminution of imports. In addition, however, an expansion of incomes and spending was needed in the creditor countries. This could have been started had Germany been able to make a sizeable transfer of funds. Had the receiving governments then spent these sums on reconstruction, in addition to similar expenditures out of domestic resources, a rise in incomes would have resulted. Imports would also increase, to the direct or indirect benefit of German exports.

The catch was that Germany had insufficient reserves of gold or foreign exchange with which to make the needed initial transfers of purchasing power. Moreover, the Dawes Plan protected Germany against any serious loss of international reserves, and also prohibited any devaluation of the newly stabilised mark as a means of making her exports more attractive. The essentials for setting the transfer mechanism in motion were therefore lacking.[4]

The problem of war debts and reparation continued to plague both creditors and debtors throughout the twenties and early thirties. Although the British government owed the United States only about half as much as was due it from its allies, at the peace conference in 1919 it unsuccessfully urged the cancellation of all war debts. Three years later, the British offered to scale down payments from their debtors to what they in turn had to pay the U. S. But the American government met these overtures with stubborn resistance, and steadily refused to concede the existence of any connection between allied war debts and German reparation. Its attitude was tersely expressed in President Coolidge's famous dictum: "They hired the money, didn't they?"

Not until 1927, some three years after the Dawes Plan arranged a settlement of German reparation, did all the countries involved finally reach agreement on the amounts owed and the terms of payment.[5] Capital sums were scaled down considerably, and annual payments were to be spread over a period of 62 years. At least, some degree of certainty replaced the earlier bickering and confusion. Yet the former European belligerents

---

[4] The fullest discussion of the German transfer problem is to be found in the controversy between Keynes and Ohlin, which appeared in 1929. Keynes stressed the need for a fall in German costs and prices to make her exports more attractive — the classical aspects of the adjustment mechanism — while Ohlin emphasised the effect upon international demands of initial transfers of purchasing power. But as Keynes finally pointed out in a reply, the means of starting the transfer of purchasing power was lacking. "If Germany was in a position to export large quantities of gold or if foreign balances in Germany were acceptable to foreign Central Banks as a substitute for gold in their reserves, then it would be a different matter." (J. M. Keynes, "Mr. Keynes' views on the transfer problem: III, a reply," *Economic Journal*, XXXIX (1929), pp. 404-8.) The two original articles, though not the subsequent discussion, have been reprinted in *Readings in the Theory of International Trade.*

[5] No settlement was ever reached between the U.S.S.R. and its major creditors, owing to the Soviet unwillingness to assume debts incurred by the Czarist government.

were left with a burden of payments reflecting a debt not based on productive assets, but representing a sheer dead weight.

International Investment

International investment revived after the war; by the end of the decade, the United States, the United Kingdom, and France had each lent substantial sums. Between 1919 and 1929, the United States invested abroad approximately $7 billion, France about $600 million, while Britain restored her foreign investments, which had fallen about a quarter, to the prewar level of some $19 billion.

Although this international lending of the twenties provided foreign exchange needed by many countries, it was not as large in proportion to income as in prewar days, nor directed to as productive uses. Instead of going mainly into railways, public utilities, and other capital equipment to increase the output of the relatively undeveloped areas, a major share went to European national and municipal governments, notably in Germany, where it was used for building and other public works. Though serviceable, these investments yielded no saleable output which could earn foreign exchange with which to meet interest payments. Moreover, particularly after 1925, to these long-term investments was added a large volume of short-term lending, much of which was actually used to finance long-term projects. These short-term loans created an unstable situation, in which the danger of default was serious.

In one important respect, international lending of the 1920's created an illusion of soundness and stability that simply did not exist. Some countries used the proceeds of new loans to pay the interest on past loans. It was only in this way that Germany, which borrowed almost three times as much abroad as it paid in reparation, was able to transfer the required payments. These, in turn, enabled European governments to meet their war debt payments to the United States.

The Changing Structure of Industry and Trade

The postwar years also witnessed a change in the relative industrial strength of different countries that both imposed an additional burden of adjustment and rendered the international economy less capable of meeting that burden. These developments were the consequence partly of the war and the economic disruption that followed in its wake, partly of differences in long-term trends of economic growth.

Industry in the European belligerents, faced with the implacable demands of war, had to convert from the production of peacetime goods to the manufacture of munitions and military supplies. Exports naturally suffered, in the case of Britain declining to about half the prewar volume. Even this reduced volume was more precarious and uncertain, being subjected to constant interruption by Germany's unrestricted submarine warfare. And after the conflict was ended, to the difficulty of restoring broken trade connections were added the uncertainties caused by inflation and by the losses in shipping.

In this interval of some eight years or more, many countries began themselves to produce goods no longer available, or available only intermittently and uncertainly, from Europe. We have already noted this development; suffice it to say that it was very widespread. Another alternative was to place orders with neutral suppliers, especially those outside the area of combat. Japan benefited particularly from such sales; her output of manufactures doubled between 1913 and 1921-25. This need not have been and was not, a total loss to European countries, since the economic growth of their customers meant higher incomes and a greater ability to import than before. But if this opportunity was to be met, it required rapid adaption of supplies to the new types of goods for which demand was increasing.

Pressure on Britain

The effects of industrial expansion abroad were felt with particular severity in Britain. Japanese and Indian production of cotton piece goods increasingly displaced British sales in Far Eastern markets. By 1937, these were less than 10 per cent of the 1913 figure. Like cotton, the woolen textile industry lost heavily to protected domestic industries in foreign markets, and to a lesser extent to rising Japanese competition. Exports of woolen tissues fell from 219 million square yards in 1913, to 156 million in 1929. In the same interval, coal exports declined almost 20 per cent. This industry faced additional competition from newly opened mines in Russia, China, India, and South Africa at the same time that fuel conservation and the use of petroleum and hydroelectric power were reducing the demand. The iron and steel industry barely held its own; to do so, it was forced to concentrate more and more on finished products, where its disadvantage was least, while pig iron lost ground to the new, larger plants in Germany and the United States.[6]

Faced with declining demand for her traditional staples and with many markets lost to new competitors, Britain clearly had to undertake a major

---

[6] Data in this paragraph from Alfred E. Kahn, *Great Britain and the World Economy*, ch. VI. Copyright 1946 by the Columbia University Press, New York.

shift of resources. This she did with considerable success—even though hampered by an overvalued currency and the restrictive credit policy this implied. While output of cotton and woolen textiles and of coal were lower in 1930 than before the war, a rapid expansion took place in the production of motor cars and motorcycles, electrical machinery and equipment, and chemicals. Exports of these and other products replaced coal and textiles, with the result that in 1929 the total value of exports was some 15 per cent greater than in 1913.

Even so, Britain—and to a lesser degree, other European countries as well —lost ground relatively. Between 1913 and 1929, the total value of world exports increased by two-thirds. The British increase of only 15 per cent is small by comparison; so is that of Belgium, of 22 per cent. Germany fared somewhat better, with her exports rising 33 per cent. France almost held her own with a 50 per cent increase. In contrast with Europe, Canada, Japan, and the United States forged ahead. Canada's exports multiplied three-and-a-half times between 1913 and 1929, Japan's increased threefold, and those of the United States doubled. Expressed in terms of percentages for continents, the distribution of world exports had changed as follows:

1913: North America, 15.8; Europe, 50.9; Asia, 12.5; Other, 20.8
1929: North America, 19.5; Europe, 47.4; Asia, 14.9; Other, 18.2

Although Europe remained the world's greatest exporting region, it was losing ground. Moreover, the changes that occurred in the twenties were, as we shall see, only the beginning of a continuing trend.

Increasing Dominance of the U.S.

A particularly interesting and important feature of the industrial change going on in the world was the increasingly important position occupied by the United States. We have already noted that in the interval 1870-1913, that country came to surpass Great Britain as a manufacturing power, its share of world manufactures rising from 23 to almost 36 per cent, while Britain's declined from nearly 32 to only 14 per cent. (Germany's share of manufacturing output also rose from a little over 13 to just under 16 per cent). This phenomenal increase reflected the rapid economic growth of a young country; its roots are to be found in a steady natural increase in population, supplemented by a large volume of immigration, and in a high rate of capital accumulation and investment. Between growing numbers and rising incomes, more and more opportunities for the domestic production of manufactured goods appeared and were exploited.

Immigration and the natural increase in the population added less to growth in the 1920's than formerly, although total population increased from 106 to 123 million during the decade. Investment, that dynamic factor in economic expansion, continued at an extremely high level. Gross capital formation averaged 20 per cent of gross national product from 1919 to 1929. Technology, most visible in new and improved products, also continued its advance. Thus, it is not surprising to find that industrial production simultaneously rose by 51 per cent. This was the period when the automobile industry grew from infancy to adulthood, carrying with it petroleum extraction and refining and tire production. This decade also saw the output of electrical equipment and of the power to drive it more than double. This rate of industrial growth was unmatched by any other country, although Canada, Japan, and South Africa, each starting from a much smaller base, came close.

As a result, the United States increased its lead as a producer of manufactures still further. In 1926-29, it accounted for 42.2 per cent of the world total, as against 11.6 per cent for Germany and 9.4 per cent for the United Kingdom. Other estimates tell a similar story: of the consumption by the fifteen most important commercial nations of the nine principal raw materials and foodstuffs, the United States accounted for 39 per cent. Its national income was equal to that of twenty-three other nations, including its most important rivals. When we add to these facts that in the twenties the U. S. became the world's first exporter and its principal investor, though still second to Great Britain as an importer, its dominant position is striking.

The meaning of these facts is clear. As the world's outstanding manufacturing power, its largest creditor, and one of its two largest traders, the economic health and the economic policies of the United States were of the greatest significance to the suppliers, customers, and debtors of that country.

Ready access to the U. S. market, stable U. S. income and employment, and a steady flow of U. S. lending were not only important but vital. Sudden changes in the U. S. tariff, capriciousness in its lending, or instability in its business could disrupt economic life in most of the rest of the world. Its position of leadership, so suddenly achieved, imposed responsibilities. These unfortunately, the nation was not prepared to assume.

Agricultural Overproduction

If the expansion of industry in various new lands created an unbalanced situation, even greater instability resulted from the growth of agricultural production. The 1914 war greatly increased the demand for many raw materials, as well as for some foodstuffs, while it removed from production or from contact with world markets important sources of supply, especially of wheat and sugar. Consequently, production in accessible regions bounded upward. With the return of peace, supplies from older producing areas gradually reappeared. But the newer producers did not retire from the field. The result was an accumulation of stocks, downward pressure on prices, and agricultural discontent.

Producers of rubber, wheat, sugar, and coffee attempted to deal with the situation by establishing various types of control schemes. Although details of these projects varied, they all shared one common weakness: the controls could be made effective over only a portion, though usually a major share, of the producers. Each scheme foundered because it made expansion profitable outside the area under control. Thus, rubber restriction applied only to Malaya: additional plantings in the Netherlands East Indies brought its ruin. Coffee control was limited to Brazil, but production in Colombia, Venezuela, and other regions increased rapidly. Cane sugar producers tried restriction, but beet sugar output, aided by tariffs and subsidies, continued to rise.

Thus, at the end of the 1920's, overproduction of important agricultural products, and of such raw materials as timber, copper, and nitrates, as well, both contributed to world instability and presented a problem of structural disequilibrium that would take years to correct.

The World Situation: 1929

Reviewing the developments of the decade 1919-29, we may put on the credit side the re-creation, after the disruptive effects of World War I, of a working international system. Though the world's monetary arrangements were less effective than formerly, they were still truly international in character. Currencies practically everywhere were convertible into one another at stable exchange rates, thus making possible the continued existence of a truly open or multilateral trading system. It is true that tariffs were considerably higher than in prewar days and that, therefore, less advantage was taken of the possibilities of international specialisation. Yet trade was large and growing, and it continued, with minor exceptions, to be free of those particularly repressive barriers, direct quantitative controls. And international lending was once again providing, in large volume, badly needed foreign exchange.

Yet the painfully reconstructed international economy labored under great difficulties. The new gold standard was less efficient than the old, and the rules whose observance had made it such an effective engine of adjustment had been discarded in favor of nationally more congenial, but internationally far more questionable practices. The same forces that had led nations to assert greater monetary independence—the increasing role of government and the rising tide of economic nationalism—also led to greater self-assertion in policies concerned with employment, taxation, trade, and immigration. A huge dead weight of war debts and reparation had somehow to be collected and fitted into balances of payments, and although the large volume of international lending contributed to the momentary solution of this problem, it did relatively little to increase the capacity of debtors to service these loans. Major shifts in the location of industry required a vigorous response in the older countries: though this adjustment had begun, it was proceeding at a rather sluggish pace. The increasing dominance of the United States forced it into a position of leadership for which its isolationist tradition equipped it most inadequately. And to the structural changes in industry were added serious maladjustments in important sectors of agriculture.

It is possible that, given time, even the weakened international structure could have carried through the necessary adjustments and that some difficulties would have yielded to sensible negotiations—if only a reasonably high level of world demand had been maintained. The gradual and piecemeal changes that normally occur, involving the transfer of labor and capital from unprofitable to profitable lines of production, would have had a chance to operate.

Such a gradual solution of its problems, however, was denied the world by the outbreak of the worst depression in history. Even the most profitable industries became unprofitable. There was nowhere for surplus resources in the overexpanded industries to go, no incentive to build up new fields of employment, and no opportunity for lending to improve by continued experience.

(For references see end of Chapter 22.)

22

FORCES OF DISINTEGRATION

Beginning with 1929, new difficulties piled on top of old. The precariously balanced international economy collapsed under their weight.

THE GREAT DEPRESSION OF THE 1930'S

Its Origin and Spread

The great depression of the 1930's throws a strong light upon the dominant economic position of the United States, and reenforces the view that economic conditions in this country go a long way toward determining the level of activity in the rest of the world. For there can be little doubt that the major forces that transformed the prosperity and optimism of 1929 into the unemployment and pessimism of 1932 had their origin in the United States, and that declining activity and demand here spread outwards in all directions until they encompassed most of the globe.

Although it is true that a downturn in economic activity got under way in half a dozen of the less developed countries (and in Germany) at various points in time between late 1927 and the middle of 1929, their collective economic weight was not sufficient to spark a worldwide collapse. It was not until the downturn of industrial activity in the United States in July 1929, followed by the stock market collapse in October, and therewith the puncturing of the bubble of overoptimism, that conditions became rapidly worse in ever-widening circles.

The main support of generally prosperous conditions over most of the world had been a high level of income, employment, and production in the United States, dating from 1922. Underlying and making possible this eight-year stretch of prosperity was an investment boom of record proportions. Investment, the dynamic factor in any modern economy, attained unprecedented heights. Besides this large and continuing investment, induced principally by the rapid growth of industries related to the automobile and to the use of electric power, the country enjoyed its greatest building boom in history.

What brought this era of good times to an end? There can be little doubt as to the principal factors responsible for the onset of depression, even though any brief explanation is bound to involve serious oversimplification. It was simply that major fields of investment, whose activity primed that of the whole economy, had become saturated. The capacity of the automobile industry to produce cars, by 1929, far exceeded its ability to sell them. The tire industry, too, was overbuilt. Many other producers of durable goods faced a similar situation, and encountered serious sales resistance early in 1929. Investment in additional plant and equipment to produce still more of all these goods was not needed and was unlikely to be needed until demand had caught up with existing capacity.

Ever since the beginning of 1928, residential construction had been falling off sharply; it was clear that the supply of houses and apartment buildings, whose numbers the building boom had immensely augmented, was adequate to meet even a growing demand for some time to come.

The decline in activity was swift, especially after the shock to confidence administered by the stock market collapse. With only brief interruptions, investment, industrial production, employment, and national income plummeted downward for three disastrous years. Investment, the key to industrial activity, virtually ceased. In real terms, the gross national product shrank by one-third; in current prices, by nearly half. Industrial production fell to less than half the 1929 level, and that of durable manufactures, reflecting both industrial goods and consumer goods like automobiles whose consumption could be long postponed, to less than a fourth.

The collapse of the huge American economy reacted swiftly and violently upon other countries. As our income declined, so did our outlay on imports. Indeed, as Figure 22.1 shows, the quantity of our imports went down almost precisely in accord with our income. Over the entire period covered by the chart, there is a close correspondence between physical imports and the level of industrial production, understandable because two-thirds of U. S. imports consist of primary products and semi-manufactures used in industry.

In terms of purchasing power directed toward foreign countries, our outlay on imports fell from $4.4 billion in 1929 to $1.3 billion in 1932. This meant reduced activity in the export industries of our trading partners, and by the well-known mechanism of the multiplier, a decline in their incomes and levels of employment. But this was not all. Payments by the United States for service transactions were cut almost in half—from just under $2 billion in 1929 to $1 billion in 1932. Even more important, American long-term lending not only ceased entirely, but turned into an import of capital (mainly a repatriation of American funds). Long-term foreign loans by the

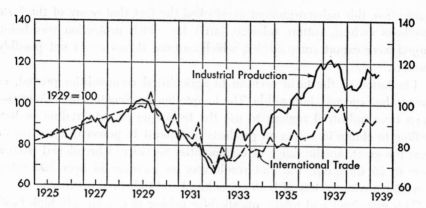

Fig. 22.1: World Industrial Production and International Trade Indexes
on Base 1929 = 100.

United States averaged $978 million from 1927 to 1929; in 1932, there was
an inflow of $251 million of long-term funds from abroad.

Taken together, the amount of dollars spent or invested abroad by
Americans

dropped from a level of about $7,400,000,000 for the 3 years 1927 to 1929 to a
mere $2,400,000,000 in 1932 and 1933—a reduction of 68 per cent over a span of
only 3 years.[1]

This in itself was a terrific shock to the economies of other countries.
Added to the difficulties already encountered by agricultural producing
nations, it sufficed to pull the entire world (outside the insulated and
planned Russian economy) down with us.

The Smoot-Hawley Tariff of 1930

To the depressing effect on world trade of a sharp decline in our national
income there was added, in June 1930, a substantial increase in our tariff.

Discussion of tariff revision had been underway in Congress for some
time. It started as a means of providing relief to agriculture, many branches
of which, because of declining prices, did not share fully in the general
prosperity of the 1920's. The general argument seemed to be: Since industry
is prosperous, and industry has protection, therefore agriculture will be
made prosperous if it is granted protection. Quite aside from the fact that the
prosperity of industry depended mainly upon the high level of investment
and the high level of production induced thereby, and hardly at all on

[1] Hal B. Lary and associates, *The United States in the World Economy*, p. 173,
Economic Series No. 23, U. S. Department of Commerce, Washington, D. C. 1943.
This excellent study is also the source of the data cited above.

protection, this naive argument overlooked the fact that many of the farm products (wheat, cotton, tobacco, lard) for which protection was being urged were export commodities, which customs duties could not possibly protect.

Limitation of the tariff revision to agricultural commodities proved, as was to be expected, impossible. The temptation for Senators and Congressmen from industrial regions to use the technique of vote-trading or logrolling to obtain increases on products of interest to powerful constituents was too great. So the range of commodities considered broadened from a few to 25 thousand; the end result was an increase in over 800 rates, covering a wide variety of both agricultural and industrial goods.

This gratuitous and totally uncalled-for raising of our already high tariff produced nothing but unfortunate results. It evoked widespread protests, and precipitated prompt tariff increases in a dozen nations, notably of duties on products of particular importance to the United States.

How much the Smoot-Hawley Tariff reduced our imports is impossible to judge, though there is no doubt that it had an appreciable effect. At least as serious was that it nullified completely efforts of the League of Nations, in progress since 1927, to halt the upward trend of tariffs, and instead accelerated that movement.

Why Not Insulation?

With the shrinkage in U. S. imports and foreign lending, in each of a large number of countries there set in a decline of production and employment. Reenforced by the operation of the multiplier, their incomes and imports fell sharply, spreading depression in ever-widening circles. Because of the lag between the initial decline in their exports and the induced fall in their imports, these countries experienced an adverse shift in their balances of payments that caused a large outflow of gold. To the primary deflation of income due to falling exports there was added a secondary deflation in response to the contraction of reserves.

With the wisdom of hindsight, we might now recommend as a preferred policy for these countries the prompt introduction of exchange control, coupled with discriminatory restrictions on imports aimed at the source of depression. These external measures should have been combined with increased government outlays to sustain income and employment. The United States would then have been left to stew in its own juice, while the rest of the world maintained a relatively high level of economic activity and thereby arrested the downward spiral of production and employment.

There are many reasons why such action was impossible at the time. It was a type of policy that would have required international agreement, and this agreement would have been impossible to achieve. Moreover, devotion to the principles of laissez faire was still too strong. In spite of the enlargement of the area of state action, no government as yet accepted responsibility for the level of economic activity and employment. At most, it was felt that government should attempt, through central banking policy, to check booms and to moderate depressions. The very fact that no depression comparable in severity to that of 1929-33 had been experienced in the memory of living man tended to reenforce this view, as also did the rapidity of recovery from the postwar slump of 1920-21 and the success attending the use of monetary policy in the twenties.

Finally, there existed as yet no general agreement, even among economists, as to the principal causes of the business cycle or as to means of combating it. It was the great depression of the thirties that directed attention forcibly to the problem, and led to the development of the modern theory of employment and income, with its stress on anti-cyclical fiscal policy.

Varying Reactions

Instead of acting together to insulate the depression and counteract its effects, each nation was left to face its mounting difficulties as best it could. One alternative was to adhere to the gold standard and allow the deflationary forces to tighten their grip, while perhaps restricting imports by higher tariffs. Another was to abandon the gold standard and permit the currency to depreciate. Still a third was to subject the balance of payments to direct control, either by quantitative restrictions on imports or by outright exchange control.

Each nation's response varied with its financial strength, its dependence on foreign loans, and the degree of its attachment to the gold standard. The countries of western Europe without exception chose fixed exchange rates plus deflation. They allowed their balances of payments to deteriorate, their gold reserves to shrink, and the level of economic activity to contract.[2] This solution proved impossible for certain primary producing countries

---

[2] Contrary to the general trend, France throughout 1928 to 1932 added heavily to its gold holdings. This may be explained largely in terms of the calling back to France of overseas balances, the liquidation of French security holdings, and the attraction to France of foreign short-term capital in search of a safe haven. Germany's imports declined more rapidly than its exports, thus giving rise to a surplus in its current international account which made possible the continuance of reparation payments and the service of foreign debt.

whose export prices had been under severe pressure and which were hard hit by the decline in foreign lending. Thus even before the end of 1929, Argentina, Brazil, Paraguay, and Uruguay all depreciated their currencies. Australia, New Zealand, Bolivia, and Venezuela followed them in 1930. Only Turkey and Iran introduced exchange controls.

By the spring of 1931, it looked as though deflation, even if a painful method of readjustment, was doing its work. The gold standard was still intact in western Europe and the United States. Exchange depreciation had not spread beyond the original nine countries, nor had controls been extended. There were even some hopeful signs on the horizon: in the early months of 1931, industrial production recovered slightly in Germany and the United States. Money rates were low even in Germany, and credit was easy in all the principal centers. There was some prospect that recovery might finally take hold.

The International Financial Crisis of 1931

The hesitant optimism of the spring of 1931 was shattered by the outbreak of an international financial panic. It began, not in a major financial center, but in little Austria. A revaluation of the assets of the Credit-Anstalt, the largest commercial bank in Vienna, showed that they had depreciated to the point where the bank was technically insolvent. This revelation led immediately to the withdrawal of foreign short-term credits. A "standstill" agreement with creditors, followed by restrictions on withdrawals, stopped the run on Austria, but did nothing to stem the anxiety that lay behind it.

Worried creditors shifted their withdrawals to Germany, which was a net short-term debtor (see p. 371) to the amount of 5 billion marks (over a billion dollars). Although a one-year moratorium on reparation payments, initiated by President Hoover, caused withdrawals to slacken, it did not end then. An important German bank failed early in July, the run intensified, and by the end of the month nearly three billion marks of short-term funds had been transferred abroad. Rather than see the gold and foreign exchange reserves of the Reichbank exhausted, the government introduced exchange control by a series of decrees, a step followed by eleven other countries in eastern and northern Europe before the year ended.

Germany's choice of exchange control was dictated by the fact that the public had been schooled to believe that exchange depreciation would lead to extreme inflation. Also, exchange control was especially suited to blocking capital flight. The traditional weapon—a high discount rate—had proven its ineffectiveness, for the Reichsbank had raised it to 15 per cent without producing the slightest effect.

Britain Abandons Gold

Capital withdrawal now shifted to England. It was known that British bankers had lent heavily to Germany and other central European countries and that now these credits were tightly frozen. On the other hand, foreigners had claims on London totalling £560 million. Adding to the uncertainty of Britain's position was the probability of a large government deficit, as well as the steady worsening of the country's balance of payments.

Foreign withdrawals mounted rapidly. Despite advances of £130 million from the Bank of France and the Federal Reserve System, these and more were soon paid out. With further credits unavailable, on September 21, Parliament suspended the Bank's obligation to sell gold.

During the crisis, Bank Rate had been raised only to 4½ per cent. Critics claimed that had a rate of 8 to 10 per cent been established, the run on London might well have been halted. This argument is nonsense. What are earnings of 10 per cent against a possible loss of 30 or 40 per cent of one's capital? In the circumstances of 1931, a Bank Rate of 10 per cent would far more likely have been interpreted as a sign of weakness than as the exercise of a bygone power "to pull gold from the earth."

With the abandonment of gold, sterling exchange rates were freed to reflect the country's weak balance of payments position. Gradually, sterling depreciated, reaching a point 30 per cent below the old parity in December. Within five months, the pound began to rise again. In June 1932, with the establishment of the Exchange Equalisation Account, Britain inaugurated a period of flexible rather than freely fluctuating exchange rates. The Account, or stabilisation fund, received certain foreign assets from the Bank of England, together with £150 million in Treasury bills (in 1933 increased by £200 million) which it could sell in the market for sterling, using the proceeds for the purchasing of gold or foreign exchange. By alternately buying and selling foreign currencies, it could keep fluctuations of the pound within bounds, subject of course to a limit on support imposed by previous accumulations of gold and foreign exchange.

Formation of Currency Blocs

In abandoning gold, Britain carried with her a large number of countries which, because Britain was their major market and London their reserve center, could not afford to see sterling depreciate against their currencies. They too left the gold standard, tied the value of their currencies more or less closely to the pound, and continued to keep the major part of their international reserves in the form of sterling assets. Here we have the beginnings of the present-day sterling area.[3] London, as the principal reserve center of the members, also performed most of their clearing, although until the outbreak of war, their currencies remained on the whole freely convertible. Each member kept the value of its currency stable in terms of the pound by official purchase and sales of sterling; and the British Exchange Equalisation Account moderated fluctuations of the pound against the dollar and other gold currencies. Stability of the pound was also enhanced by an informal but very effective control of foreign lending by the Treasury, which confined capital exports to sterling area members.

After the depreciation of sterling and the formation of the sterling area, only five countries remained solidly on the gold standard. These were the United States, France, Switzerland, Belgium, and the Netherlands.

Most other nations adopted some form of exchange control, whereupon their currencies immediately became inconvertible. The European members of the exchange control bloc kept their exchange rates stable at the old gold parities, while others, especially in South America, allowed their currencies to depreciate heavily, then held the new exchange rates absolutely or relatively fixed.

Disintegration of the World Trading System

The introduction of exchange control and inconvertibility over a rather large area set in motion the tendency toward the bilateral channeling of trade to which we drew attention in Chapter 19. Depreciation by the sterling area and by certain countries outside it (notably Japan) reenforced this tendency, especially among the nations that used exchange controls to maintain unchanged the nominal gold value of their currencies. For quite independently of monetary developments within these nations, their currencies now became over-valued relative to those that had depreciated. Their exports were depressed, their imports stimulated. Controls had therefore to be tightened, and alternative markets for exports and sources of imports sought by means of bilateral trading arrangements.

The members of the gold bloc were, of course, similarly affected. As their balances of payments became increasingly adverse, they attempted to check rising imports by raising tariffs or by introducing quantitative restrictions. France, in particular, relied heavily upon import quotas, a form of trade restriction that sets a fixed limit to the amount of imports of different categories permitted to enter the country.

---

[3] With later additions to the membership, the prewar sterling area included all British Commonwealth countries except Canada, plus the Baltic nations, Egypt, Eire, Iraq, Palestine, Portugal, the Scandinavian countries, and Thailand.

Even Great Britain, in spite of the relief from the pressure of falling world prices afforded by depreciation, embraced protection. Earlier duties, imposed during and immediately after the war, had been limited in scope. In 1931 and 1932, the Conservative Party, now dominant in a coalition government and since the onset of the depression strongly committed to a protective policy, pushed through a comprehensive tariff. Duties ranged from 20 per cent on a wide variety of manufactures to 30 per cent on many luxuries and to 33⅓ per cent on the products of "key" industries.

For a long time the Conservative Party had cherished the ambition of uniting the Empire more firmly by a system of *Imperial Preference*. Since the new tariff did not apply to Commonwealth countries, a basis now existed for the negotiation of mutual concessions. The Ottawa Conference of 1932 was called to explore the possibilities.

Being mainly an exporter of manufactured goods, Britain wanted freer access to dominion markets for these products. But the Dominions were keenly interested in developing further their growing manufactures. These objectives appeared irreconcilable. They could only be realised, in part, if the Dominions raised the duties on foreign goods, while leaving them more moderate, though still protective, on British goods. In general, this is what they did. For her part, Britain maintained a number of existing preferences and imposed new "Ottawa" duties on foreign supplies of certain products of particular interest to the dominions. Thus, after Ottawa, Commonwealth tariffs were higher against the foreigner.

We can summarise the effects of the international financial crisis by saying that it led, first, to the breakdown of the international currency system and its replacement by three fairly distinct blocs, consisting of five countries still on the gold standard, a much larger group with fluctuating but convertible currencies, and another large group subject to exchange controls. Second, largely because of the effects of this division, but partly for extraneous reasons, the world trading system itself began to disintegrate as tariffs multiplied and climbed, as quantitative restrictions spread, and as trade became increasingly diverted into bilateral channels.

World Economic Conference: 1932

By the summer of 1932, the opinion was widespread that general and lasting recovery required measures to combat the breakdown of international trade and finance, and that such measures could only be undertaken through intergovernmental cooperation. Plans were laid for a World Economic Conference to be held in June, 1933. A Preparatory Commission of Experts worked out an elaborate draft agenda dealing with tariffs, quantitative trade restrictions, agreements on raw materials and foodstuffs, and a wide variety of monetary problems, including, particularly, currency stabilisation. It was hoped that by restoring stable currency conditions, the revival of international trade would be facilitated, through "making it possible to abolish measures of exchange control and remove transfer difficulties." Shortly after the Conference had convened in London, however, and before it could achieve any concrete results, these hopes were dashed by the destabilisation of the American dollar.

Devaluation of the Dollar

Deflation in the United States had been especially severe. Between 1929 and 1932, wholesale prices fell 32 per cent, while the national income was cut in half. As prices fell, the banks liquidated commercial loans rapidly. Total loans of all banks had by the end of 1932 been contracted by 42 per cent. Real estate loans, however, shrank only 10 per cent. As property values declined, the security behind this paper evaporated, and more and more banks were forced to close their doors. Some 5,100, about a third of the total, did so between 1930 and 1932.

As the weak position of the banks became more apparent, a wave of currency and gold hoarding got under way, rising to panic proportions early in 1933. President Roosevelt declared a national banking "holiday" on March 16. At the same time he imposed an embargo on gold and silver exports except under license from the Treasury. A month later, the President announced that our departure from the gold standard would continue indefinitely. Simultaneously, Congress passed legislation permitting him to lower the gold content of the dollar by 50 per cent. The dollar was left to fluctuate uncertainly.

The reason for this drastic step had nothing to do with our balance of payments, which was stronger than that of any other country, but reflected our obsession with the credit and price squeeze. Some of President Roosevelt's advisers held the naive view that if the price of gold were raised, commodity prices would automatically rise in direct proportion. Won over to their position, he was determined to put their policy into effect. Therefore he rejected a specific proposal of the World Economic Conference aimed at exchange stabilisation; the Conference dragged on in futile discussion for some three weeks more, but accomplished little.

For a time, depreciation of the dollar and rising prices went hand in hand. At first, speculators, anticipating further government action, bid up foreign currencies. Then the Reconstruction Finance Corporation used its newly acquired authority to buy gold, gradually raising its price. By July, a weighted average of exchange rates had risen 32 per cent over the February level, export prices had climbed 33 per cent, import prices 27 per cent, and purely domestic prices 12 per cent.

The rise of export prices was considerably more than theoretical considerations would appear to justify, for in the existing conditions of depression, the supply of exports was very elastic. Moreover, a large proportion of U.S. exports being consumed at home, any appreciable increase in their dollar price would reduce home purchases and divert production abroad.[4] As for U. S. imports, these are predominantly raw materials and crude foodstuffs whose supply is inelastic in the short run. And the huge U. S. market is highly important to their producers. For both these reasons, foreign suppliers of our imports would tend to cut their prices as the dollar depreciated, thus leaving prices in the United States relatively unchanged.

The apparent contradiction between theoretical expectations and what actually happened can be explained by other contemporary developments. The National Industrial Recovery Act of 1933 prohibited price cuts and set floors under and raised wages. In anticipation of higher wages, manufacturers expanded output halfway to the 1929 level. Agricultural legislation paid farmers to reduce output, generating speculative buying of farm products. In these purely domestic events, not in exchange depreciation, is to be found the main explanation of the rise of export prices. Reenforcing the rise of export prices and stimulating an increase in the price of U. S. imports was a temporary improvement in the world situation, accompanied by an upward movement of the wholesale price level in several important countries.

During the next several months, the picture changed. Between July, 1933 and February, 1934, export prices rose only two points, to 135. Import prices climbed a bit more, from 127 to 131, while the average of exchange rates went on up from 132 to 146. Without any firm support, the earlier expansion ceased and turned into a slump. Industrial production, income, and consumption fell. Foreign prices stopped rising and moved downward, probably in part reflecting the deflationary influence of exchange depreciation in this country.

It is difficult to justify the depreciation of the dollar by the results. This

---

[4] Since the United States is a large country, exporting only a small part of its production, increased foreign sales resulting from lowered foreign prices would add relatively little to total demand. Also, the large U. S. economy contributed a relatively large proportion to the total world supply of many goods; any increase in its exports would therefore tend to have a seriously depressing effect on prices abroad. (For a review of the various factors involved, see Chapter 16.)

policy served badly the price-raising objective of the administration. Nor is that objective itself above criticism, for it represented a treatment of a symptom rather than the cause, which was the collapse of private investment expenditure. Later recovery measures relied much more heavily upon government outlays to replace this shrunken component of income, and were more successful.

In any event, on January 31, 1934, our experiment with currency depreciation came to an end when the price of gold was fixed at $35 an ounce, as compared with the pre-depreciation price of $20.67. The dollar was now definitely devalued relative to gold and gold standard currencies by approximately 41 per cent.

THE RESULTS OF EXCHANGE DEPRECIATION

Effects on Trade and Production

Devaluation of the dollar, added to the depreciation of sterling and related currencies, intensified deflation in the remaining gold standard countries and increased the pressure on the balances of payments of those with overvalued currencies supported by exchange controls. As the ability of the gold countries to resist devaluation became more doubtful, a speculative flight of capital developed, reenforced by growing fears of war. With the dollar stabilised, most of these funds sought safety in the United States. Between 1934 and 1936, the inward flow of gold, closely paralleling the inflow of capital, surpassed $4 billion, almost half of this amount coming from the reserves of the gold standard nations.

At first these countries responded by raising tariffs and tightening quantitative restrictions on trade. Then, early in 1935, Belgium devalued her currency 28 per cent; Switzerland, France, and the Netherlands followed in September, 1936, with devaluations of approximately 30, 25, and 19 per cent respectively. France, with gold losses continuing, found herself unable to hold the fort. Two further downward readjustments of the franc were succeeded, in 1938, by abandonment of gold altogether and stabilisation of the franc in terms of sterling. Germany and other exchange control countries in eastern Europe and South America stiffened their controls, and to stimulate exports, began to experiment with multiple exchange rates.

Although world industrial production mounted steadily from 1933, reaching at the end of 1936 a level 20 per cent above 1929, world trade recovered but haltingly. In December, 1936, it was still 10 per cent below 1929, reflecting the intensification of restrictions in both the gold standard and exchange control areas.

Partially offsetting these adverse developments was the stimulus exchange depreciation and abandonment of gold gave to internal expansion. By releasing countries following this policy from the fear of losing reserves, it permitted them to introduce more liberal credit and fiscal policies. Early in 1932, the Bank of England lowered Bank Rate from 6 to 2 per cent and added to commercial bank reserves by open-market security purchases. Sweden also adopted a cheap-money policy and stepped up government expenditures. In these and other sterling area countries that took similar steps, industrial production recovered rapidly, by 1936 reaching levels substantially above the previous peak of 1929. Rising production and incomes in these countries also brought an increase in their trade, especially with one another.[5]

Insulation against outside forces permitted a comparable internal expansion where exchange controls were in force, as in Germany, though these same controls held the advance of trade in check. But in those nations that still adhered to gold, economic recovery was but slight; 1936 production levels remained well below those of 1929.

A New Structure of Exchange Rates

When, in 1938, the period of devaluation and depreciation came to an end, a new structure of currency relationships emerged. At least roughly, the new pattern corresponded to the relative degree to which prices fell during the depression and rose again during the subsequent recovery. Compared to the United States dollar, the Latin American currencies and the Japanese yen had depreciated most, closely followed by the French franc. The amount of depreciation ranged from two-thirds of the 1929 value to one-third. In these countries, prices fell less from 1929 to 1932-33, and rose substantially more thereafter than in the United States.[6]

The Swiss franc, the Belgian franc, and the Dutch guilder, though devalued in terms of gold, had appreciated relative to the dollar. In these countries, the price decline was similar to or greater than in the United States; the following increase of prices less. Internal price developments thus offset the relative currency appreciation after 1934. Sterling currencies occupied an intermediate position, three close to the value of the dollar, the others in the list down less than 25 per cent. Price movements were

[5] The temporary abandonment of gold by the United States, though not the forced depreciation that followed, can be defended as a precondition of expansion. For efforts earlier in 1933 and in 1932 to expand the credit base had been accompanied by outward movements of gold.

[6] The price decline in France during the depression was approximately the same as in the U.S.; the succeeding rise, however, was much greater.

also intermediate in intensity, the decline being less precipitous and the rise somewhat greater than in the United States.

THE WORLD ECONOMY PRIOR TO WORLD WAR II

Although the trend toward higher tariffs, the wider use of quantitative restrictions, and the intensification of exchange controls continued after 1932, thus tending further toward the disintegration of the world economy, the picture just before the outbreak of the second World War was not one of unrelieved gloom.

Exchange-Rate Equilibrium Approached

While three distinct currency areas still existed, the period of recurring devaluation and exchange rate instability was at an end. Since final devaluation of the dollar, the dollar/sterling rate had varied within a range of approximately three per cent ($4.90 to $5.05), and some sixteen other currencies were pegged to sterling. Exchange rates, except on the controlled currencies, had approached equilibrium levels, and even those subject to controls were being brought more in line with reality by the fractional depreciation that goes with the introduction of multiple exchange rates.

The Trade Agreements Program

Even in the field of trade policy, a modest program of tariff liberalisation got under way. Sponsored by Cordell Hull, the U.S. Secretary of State, a bill to permit gradual tariff reduction was passed by Congress in 1934. Known as the Reciprocal Trade Agreements Act, it authorised the President to sign commercial agreements with other countries reducing existing U. S. duties by as much as 50 per cent, in exchange for parallel concessions. Since the study of proposed concessions and counter-concessions, as well as the actual negotiations in which they became realised, were to be carried out by committees made up of representatives of executive departments, this measure removed the making of tariffs from the political arena of Congress and made possible the beginning of a rational approach to this problem.

Especially in the depressed conditions of 1934, the bill could probably never have been sold to Congress had it not stressed the expansion of American exports by reduction of foreign duties. And since the Trade Agreements Act transferred from Congress to the executive responsibility for alterations in our tariff, there can be little doubt that this abdication of power was made attractive by the memories that many Congressmen had of their nightmarish experience in the year-long legislative tussle preceding the enactment of the Smoot-Hawley Tariff Act of 1930. For then they were subjected to the constant pressure of innumerable lobby groups and were "asked to pass judgment on the wisdom of thousands of different rates defined in the esoteric jargon of hundreds of different trades."[7]

In no sense did the Reciprocal Trade Agreements program contemplate the abandonment of protection, for a provision known as the "peril point clause" specified that duties were not to be cut if such action threatened serious injury to American industry. Moreover, an "escape clause" required an upward adjustment of a duty reduced as a result of negotiations if serious injury were shown to have resulted from that reduction. Yet in spite of these limitations, the Trade Agreements Act was a step toward the liberalisation of trade—as Sumner Welles later characterised it, "one spot of sanity in a world outlook that seemed wholly and hopelessly dark."[8]

Originally enacted for a span of three years, the Trade Agreements Act was periodically reenacted (though modified somewhat after the war) and is still (1957) in effect. Before war broke out, twenty-one agreements had been signed, under which average rates of duty on dutiable imports into the United States were substantially reduced, and corresponding reductions on our exports granted by other parties to these agreements.[9] By setting in motion a reversal of the trend toward ever higher barriers, the program funished the basis for a renewed and broader attack upon the problem in the years immediately after the war.

[7] Raymond Vernon, "America's Foreign Trade Policy and the GATT," *Essays in International Finance, No. 21,* October 1954. (International Finance Section, Princeton University.)

[8] Sumner Welles, "Postwar Trade Policies of the United States," *International Conciliation,* May 1943, p. 394.

[9] For estimates of the extent to which the U.S. tariff has been reduced as a result of the Trade Agreements program, see pp. 450-1.

SELECTED REFERENCES

Ashworth, William, *A Short History of the International Economy, 1850-1950* (Longmans, Green & Co., London, 1952). Chapters VII and VIII provide, in brief compass, an excellent review of the major events between 1914 and 1950, together with an evaluation of their significance.

Bank for International Settlements, *Annual Reports* (Berne). For a review and evaluation of current developments, these reports are extremely useful.

Beyen, J. W., *Money in a Maelstrom* (Macmillan, New York, 1949). A lively account of monetary disturbances of the inter-war period, by an insider.

Brown, William Adams Jr., *The Gold Standard Reinterpreted, 1914-1934* (National Bureau of Economic Research, 1940). A thorough study of the gold standard that focuses upon the changes it underwent after the first World War.

Harrod, R. F., *The Life of John Maynard Keynes* (Macmillan, London, 1952). The middle chapters of this book provide a vivid account of events of the inter-war period from the point of view of one who was an active and influential participant.

Interim Report of the Committee on Currency and Foreign Exchanges after the War, reprinted in *British Banking Statutes and Reports, 1932-1928*, Vol. II, edited by T. E. Gregory (Oxford University Press, 1928). The report of the Cunliffe Committee, which officially set the stage for Britain's return to the gold standard in 1925.

Kahn, Alfred E., *Great Britain in the World Economy* (Columbia University Press, 1946). A well documented and readable account of the post-1914 changes in the British economy and how they affected Britain's international position.

Keynes, J. M., "The End of Laissez Faire," in *Essays in Persuasion* (Harcourt Brace; New York, 1932). Reflections of a great economist on "possible improvements in modern Capitalism through the agency of collective action."

———, "The German Transfer Problem," *Economic Journal*, XXIX (1929); reprinted in *Readings in the Theory of International Trade*. One side of a famous debate on the operation of the adjustment mechanism with stable exchanges.

Lary, Hal B. and Associates, *The United States in the World Economy*, Economic Series No. 23, U. S. Department of Commerce (Washington, 1943). A detailed analysis of the international transactions of the United States during the inter-war period.

League of Nations, *International Currency Experience*, (Geneva, 1944). Especially good for its discussion of the changes in the operation of the gold standard, the history and effects of the devaluations of the 1930's, and the purposes and operation of exchange control.

———, *World Economic Survey*, annually (Geneva, 1932-40). A current analysis of events during the years of the great depression.

Ohlin, Bertil, "The Reparation Problem: A Discussion," *Economic Journal*, XXXIX (1929); reprinted in *Readings in the Theory of International Trade*. The other side of the debate inaugurated by Keynes (see above).

Report of the Committee on Finance and Industry, Cmd. 3897 (H.M.S.O., London, 1931). An analysis by Britain's leading experts of the monetary problems posed by the depression, and of alternative policies.

23

POSTWAR DISEQUILIBRIUM

Our review of the interwar period has shown it to have been dominated by the legacy of war and by the impact of the depression. World War I brought in its train disruption and disequilibrium. Looking back nostalgically to the simplicity and certainty of a world firmly bound together by a gold standard centering in the London money market, the world's political and economic leaders struggled uncertainly to reconstruct the past. Their efforts, however, were overbalanced by structural and political changes as yet imperfectly understood. They restored the gold standard, but not London's position of pre-eminence, nor the prewar "rules of the game." They sought to free trade from its increasing shackles, but were repeatedly balked by the irresistible forces of nationalism unleashed by the war.

Because its great economic strength was now apparent, the United States might have led in forging a world economy more suited to the changed circumstances. Yet its people, having just completed a long period of internal development, shrank from the responsibilities their new position thrust upon them. The automobile age had arrived, and they exploited to the limit the opportunities it afforded.

From the point of view of what forces were to be allowed to determine the course of trade, the decade of the 1920's was inconclusive and contradictory. Impulses and efforts toward establishing greater freedom for comparative costs competed with nationalistic policies with respect to money, trade, and immigration. Less free than in the Victorian Age, far more free than under Mercantilism, the world economy moved uncertainly toward reliance upon the impersonal price mechanism.

This phase ended suddenly with the outbreak of the Great Depression. One of its chief manifestations, the sharp decline in income, now seized the center of the stage. Imports followed the curve of production; the ranks of the unemployed swelled everywhere. To combat unemployment and to safeguard its currency, one nation after another adopted more and more stringent controls. With few exceptions, goods or capital could move only when governments gave their permission. The forces of nationalism dominated almost all channels of international trade and payments.

Again during the second World War, the channels of trade and even
its composition were shaped by the division of the world into warring
blocs and by the insatiable needs of the armed forces. Because more
nations and more people were drawn into this struggle, and because the
complexity and costliness of armaments had greatly increased, the demand
for goods to feed the war effort was far greater and more disruptive to
the peacetime structure of production than in 1914-18. On the other hand,
to obtain the needed supplies became more difficult, because the Axis
powers dominated most of Europe, north Africa, and the East beyond
India. The consequent search for substitutes for rubber, tin, quinine,
hemp, and a long list of strategic materials furnishes a vivid illustration
of the vital role played by international trade.

EFFECTS OF THE WAR

Despite the wholesale reorganisation of production and severance of
markets and suppliers occasioned by six years of global war, restoration
of market connections and reconversion to peacetime production occurred
with remarkable speed and without any general interruption of employment. It was the impact of war upon productive capacity, upon the conduct
of national finances, and upon the pattern of international debt that had
the most disruptive consequences for the functioning of an already badly
weakened world economy. Some of these effects, and the degree of recovery as compared with the 1914 war, are shown in Table 23.1.

Table 23.1

RELATIVE RECOVERY IN THE SECOND FULL YEAR
AFTER THE TERMINATION OF THE FIRST AND
SECOND WORLD WARS

	INDUSTRIAL PRODUCTION	AGRICULTURAL PRODUCTION	LIVESTOCK NUMBERS	POPULATION
1913	100	100	100	100
1920	76	63	90	99
1938	100	100	100	100
1946/7	80	75	81	97

Source: United Nations, Department of Economic Affairs, *A Survey of the Economic
Situation and Prospects of Europe,* Geneva, 1948. Tables 8, 11, and 16. The data refer
to Europe, and cover the same countries for both periods. Population comparison from
United Nations, Economic Commission for Europe, *Growth and Stagnation in the European Economy,* Geneva, 1954. Table A.4.

In the second full year after the termination of the last war (1946/7),
industrial production was still 20 per cent below prewar, agricultural

production 25 per cent, and livestock numbers 19 per cent. Figures such as these spelled shortages of goods both for home consumption and investment and for export. The record, however, appears on the whole to have been clearly better than after World War I, except with regard to the number of livestock. Moreover, although industrial production did not attain the prewar level until the fourth year after the last struggle (1948/9), the same relative degree of recovery was not attained until the seventh year after the 1914-18 conflict (in 1925). This difference is in considerable part explained by the fact that employment and income remained high after 1945, whereas there was worldwide depression from late 1920 until early 1922.

INTERNATIONAL PAYMENTS DIFFICULTIES

It is in western Europe's balance of payments that the international consequences of subnormal production and other war-induced changes are mirrored. (See Table 23.2). With production low and income and employment high, goods that might have been exported were retained for domestic use, and imports were badly needed to supplement scanty domestic production. For the first three years after fighting stopped, Europe's trade deficit exceeded $5 billion; in the three years before the War, the trade deficit had been only $2 billion. And whereas the current account as a whole was in balance in 1938, for five years after the war it showed a large though gradually diminishing deficit.

Table 23.2

EUROPE'S BALANCE OF PAYMENTS ON CURRENT ACCOUNT
1938 AND 1946-50

(in billions of current dollars)

	1938	1946	1947	1948	1949	1950
Imports, f.o.b.	$ 5.8	$ 9.4	$ 13.7	$ 14.4	$ 13.5	$ 12.5
Exports, f.o.b.	3.7	4.3	6.4	8.8	9.4	9.6
Balance on trade account	$ −2.1	− 5.1	− 7.3	− 5.6	− 4.1	− 2.9
Income from Investments (net)	1.4	0.5	0.4	0.4	0.4	0.5
Other current invisibles (net)	0.7	− 1.2	− 0.5	0.3	− 0.1	− 0.1
Balance on services account	2.1	− 0.7	− 0.1	0.7	0.3	0.4
Balance on current account (goods and services)	0.0	− 5.8	− 7.4	− 4.9	− 3.8	− 2.5

Sources: United Nations, *A Survey of the Economic Situation and Prospects of Europe*, p. 54; *Economic Survey of Europe in 1949*, p. 109; *Economic Survey of Europe in 1950*, p. 114.

Since almost three-fourths of Europe's cumulative deficit (1946-50) of $24.4 billion was with the United States alone, the deficit was often called simply "the dollar shortage." This phrase did not mean, of course, that Europe was spending more dollars than it had, for that would be impossible. What it did mean was that Europe was unable to earn enough dollars from normal sources to meet its expenditures, and so was forced to draw heavily on reserves, borrow what it could, and rely on large extraordinary grants to make up the balance.[1] Nor was this so-called dollar shortage a purely European phenomenon. Until 1950, Canada, Latin America, and all the major areas of the world had a dollar deficit on current account.

Sources of Trouble

Inasmuch as Europe's current account was in balance in 1938, but in a condition of serious disequilibrium during the years after the war, we could say that its payments troubles were war-induced. This is true but trite. For "war" in this context implies not only military operations and the destruction they wrought, but also the effects of trade dislocation and of wartime finance, both during the war itself and for years thereafter. To evaluate Europe's problem, and in particular to estimate to what extent it is likely to be enduring, we must distinguish the different ways in which the events of wartime impinged on that continent's balance of payments.

Let us begin by examining the separate components of Europe's current account, to see how much each part contributed to the over-all deficit. A study of the forces affecting each of these components should then lay bare the roots of the trouble. We shall focus at first upon the year 1947, when the deficit was at its maximum.

Merchandise account: Note first that while, between 1938 and 1947, the value of exports nearly doubled, import values rose far more. Hence a trade deficit of only $2.1 billion before the war, by 1947 reached the huge amount of $7.3 billion, an increase of $5.2 billion. Thus much the greater part of the over-all dollar shortage of $7.4 billion—some 70 per cent—is traceable to this cause alone.

Part of the great rise in the trade deficit must be attributed to real changes in exports and imports—to changes, that is, in their physical

[1] Neither should "dollar shortage," applied to this period, be taken to imply an insufficient supply of dollars made available by the United States through normal channels. Europe's payments difficulties arose from inadequate amounts of goods and services available for export, combined with an exceptional need for imports. Because its dependence upon the United States as a source of supplies was unusually great, its deficit was focused primarily upon this country.

volume—and part to price changes. It has been estimated that had prices remained constant from 1938 on, the trade deficit would have been larger than prewar by $1.5 billion, for while the volume of imports increased, that of exports actually fell.[2] Approximately a quarter of the rise in the trade deficit is thus accounted for. All the rest must be laid at the door of price changes. The prices of both exports and imports approximately doubled.

At this time (1947), there was virtually no alteration in the terms of trade. Imports were dearer in terms of exports by only 2 per cent. But later on, especially after the outbreak of the Korean war, the relative rise in the price of imports helped to perpetuate the trade deficit.

Services. Subtracting from the 1947 over-all current deficit of $7.4 billion the $5.2 billion due to Europe's relatively larger outlay on imports leaves $2.2 billion to be accounted for. Of this the larger part was caused by a decline in the income from shipping and other services. These sources yielded Europe a net income of $0.7 billion in 1938; by 1947, this had been transformed into a net expense of $0.5 billion, thus contributing $1.2 billion to the deficit. Investment income, which stood at $1.4 billion in 1938, fell by $1 billion, thus accounting for the remainder.

CAUSES OF EUROPE'S DEFICIT

The foregoing examination of Europe's international accounts tells us how the deficit was apportioned; it reveals little about what caused it. To understand the causes, we must probe deeper.

Forces Affecting Trade

So far as concerns the increase in the passive balance on trade account, we have seen that nearly three-fourths of this was due to an approximately *equal rise in the prices of both imports and exports,* a rise resulting from inflation which was world-wide in scope. (That this augmented the trade deficit is simply a matter of arithmetic: doubling each term of a subtraction doubles the difference).

As for the real changes in exports and imports that account for the remainder of the trade deficit, their causes are more complex. A number of forces converged to stimulate imports and depress exports. (1) *The reduction of European productive capacity* as a result of war damage and

[2] *Economic Survey of Europe in 1948,* Economic Commission for Europe, Table 41. (Reprinted for House Committee on Foreign Affairs, U.S. Government Printing Office, 1949.) Citations are from this reprint. The original was published by the United Nations.

inadequate maintenance made imports more necessary and exports less available. (2) Similar in its effect was the heavy domestic pressure to maintain and increase standards of living after several years of austerity and hardship, as well as to restore and improve capital equipment. This pressure led governments to *finance excess demand* instead of scaling it down to correspond to the resources available. Inflationary finance, in other words, added to demands without correspondingly stimulating supplies; the excess demand withdrew domestic production from export channels and also sucked in imports. Moreover, since the excess demand raised domestic prices, it tended also to result in (3) *overvalued currencies*, relative at least to such countries as the United States and Canada, where inflation was less severe. This had an important effect on the direction of exports: it was easier to sell them in soft-currency markets than in the dollar area. Hence the dollar deficit rose further.

Another factor affecting the physical volume of exports was (4) *the loss of overseas markets.* Some of this loss proved to be but temporary, so that a recovery of trade awaited only the restoration of trade connections. Some, however, resulted from the expansion of production by former customers (as of steel in Australia), or from the replacement, especially in Latin America, of European suppliers by American and Canadian firms. Similarly on the side of imports: Soviet Russia and the countries of eastern Europe, which formerly supplied western Europe with much of her timber, wheat, and other grains, could no longer be counted on after the war. The growth of population and the urge toward industrialisation in these nations so increased domestic consumption of these commodities that little was left for export. Hence western Europe was forced to rely more heavily on Western Hemisphere sources for them.

The adverse shift in receipts from shipping and other services had a very simple explanation. (1) Heavy *wartime losses of tonnage* left the European nations with far fewer ships to carry an increased volume of freight; they had to depend on the recently constructed (and heavily subsidised) American merchant fleet to bring their imports from overseas. Among "other" services, (2) *credits earned from supplying tourists' wants were low* just after the war, while Britain and the Netherlands, in particular, had to continue large military expenditures in the Middle East and in Southeast Asia.

(3) *Net income from overseas investment,* as we have seen, *fell sharply.* In 1947 it stood at half the prewar figure. Partly this fall was due to the liquidation, during and immediately after the war, of many of these investments to pay for needed imports, partly it is explained by impaired

earning power of other investments, and partly by an increase in the foreign indebtedness of Europe.

Types of Disequilibrating Forces

If we classify the forces responsible for western Europe's deficit according to their type, it will be seen that most of them were *structural* in character, involving a change affecting Europe's ability to supply exports, the world's demand for these products, or Europe's demand for specific imports. Such was the destruction and deterioration of productive resources, which greatly reduced the output of her export industries. The loss of shipping tonnage was similar in its impact. The rise of domestic industries overseas and the displacement of European exporters from foreign markets by new competitors, as well as increased American competition in shipping, banking, and the like also effected a structural change, for these developments reduced the demand for Europe's goods and services. Liquidation of overseas investments, together with increased European indebtedness to the outside world, must be set down as a shift in the structure of financial relationships. The decline of East-West trade forced Europe to transfer its demand for timber and certain foodstuffs into channels leading principally to the Western Hemisphere.

How much of Europe's deficit should be attributed to these diverse structural changes is impossible to say. Certainly the share was large. But some part, and probably a substantial part, of the disequilibrium must be allocated to *income changes—that is, to inflation.* Because of the demands of reconstruction and the political need to maintain and to increase as rapidly as possible the standard of living, all European monetary authorities permitted or even encouraged an expansion of credit more than sufficient to take off the market, at stable prices, the current output of goods and services. Some of this excess demand spilled over directly into increased imports, some diverted exports into domestic consumption, while the remainder raised domestic prices and caused currencies to become overvalued at existing exchange rates.

EUROPEAN RECONSTRUCTION

A deficit must, of course, somehow be financed. During 1946 and 1947, the means of meeting Europe's huge excess payments came from an assortment of loans and grants and from further drafts on her badly depleted reserves.

Stop-Gap Aid

Much of this balance of payments financing was the incidental result of measures whose immediate purpose was to provide relief and reconstruction to Europe's damaged economy. Thus while the war was still in progress, it was clearly realised that Europe would need large-scale assistance if starvation, disease, and total economic collapse were to be avoided. In late 1943, forty-four of the nations allied against the Axis Powers agreed to establish the United Nations Relief and Rehabilitation Administration, to which each was to contribute one per cent of its income. This great humanitarian agency supplied nearly $4 billion of relief aid, mainly in the form of food, clothing, and medicine, though a considerable part went as seed, livestock, and equipment to get agricultural and industrial production started in areas where physical destruction had been greatest. Its salvage work completed, UNRRA was dissolved June 30, 1947.

Another rescue operation, undertaken in 1946, arose out of Britain's mounting balance of payments difficulties. Heavy military and financial commitments in Germany, Greece, and elsewhere, combined with a slow recovery of exports and a continuing need for heavy imports from the dollar area, threatened to exhaust Britain's international reserves. Outside financial assistance was essential to avert chaos. In the Anglo-American Financial Agreement, reached after close bargaining, the United States undertook to advance $3,750 million in the next four years.[3] Canada at the same time provided $1,250 million. But as a condition of the loan, the U.S. negotiators, obsessed with a desire for the prompt resumption of multilateral trade, insisted that exchange controls over current transactions be removed immediately and that within a year the pound sterling be made convertible. Although the first of these steps contributed heavily to a rapid use of the loan (over $2 billion was used up within twelve months), the British stuck to their agreement and took the second step of making the pound convertible. Then owners of sterling throughout the world converted their holdings into dollars. The American credit melted like ice in the Sahara. After less than two months' trial, convertibility was suspended.

Additional stop-gap aid came from various sources: $400 million to Greece and Turkey for military and economic assistance; Export-Import Bank loans of approximately $2 billion; and nearly another billion from the International Bank and the International Monetary Fund.

---

[3] Consolidation of outstanding obligations totalling $650 million raised the total amount of the debt to $4,400 million.

The European Recovery Program

By the summer of 1947, it had become clear that relief works and emergency loans were totally inadequate means for coping with Europe's difficulties. The mounting international deficit, inadequate supplies of fuel and raw materials, slackening industrial production, and a shortage of foodstuffs intensified by the worst harvest in years—all pointed to the need for a more drastic and far-reaching attack. This the European Recovery Program, or the Marshall Plan, aimed to provide.

In his commencement address at Harvard University on June 5, 1947, Secretary of State Marshall, after reviewing the breakdown of the European economy, stated the concern of the United States for this condition and its willingness to cooperate fully in a coordinated recovery effort. Insisting that "the initiative . . . must come from Europe," and that they should agree on requirements and on the action they would take, he pledged U. S. aid in drafting a program and in later financial support thereof.

The response was immediate. Out of a conference lasting all summer, there emerged a Committee, later crystallised as the Organisation for European Economic Cooperation (OEEC), whose report analysed Europe's problems and formulated a program of recovery to extend over the four years 1948-51. Financial aid needed was estimated at $22.4 billion, most of which would have to come from the United States. As their contribution, the participating countries[4] undertook to do everything in their power to make Europe productive, so that it could sell enough to pay its way in the world. This meant raising output and increasing efficiency of production, both of exports and of articles hitherto bought outside the European trading area. As means to this major goal, OEEC members were to cooperate in every way possible, in particular to eliminate restrictive trade barriers, and each was to check inflation as a precondition to the effective use of Europe's resources.

Parallel committees in the United States wrestled with cost estimates, the availability of American resources for aid, and the probable impact of a major aid program on the U.S. economy. From $12 to $17 billion was suggested as the necessary American contribution to a really effective undertaking. Congress was persuaded to advance some $600 million of

[4] The participating countries, all of which became members of the OEEC, were: Austria, Belgium, Denmark, France, Greece, Iceland, Ireland, Italy, Luxembourg, Netherlands, Norway, Portugal, Sweden, Switzerland, Turkey, and the United Kingdom. Western Germany was always included in the proposals made, and became a member upon achieving independence of Allied military control.

interim aid and $4 billion for the first year's operations of the Economic Cooperation Administration, the administrative counterpart of the OEEC in Europe.

The story of the ERP is a fascinating one. A flood of American administrators and experts, including business men, college professors, industrial and agricultural technicians, and publicity agents crammed into offices in the European headquarters, Paris, and in the capital of every OEEC member country. Their job was to schedule Europe's needs in cooperation with the OEEC, to approve orders for goods ranging from wheat to tobacco, from tractors to locomotives and freight cars, and to see that these goods got to where they were needed.

By late 1951, although the recovery program was not yet completed, mutual defense against Communist aggression overshadowed economic aid and the ECA was merged in a new organisation, the Mutual Security Administration, which administered both military and economic assistance. The cause of this change in direction and in organisation was, of course, the outbreak of the Korean war in June 1950 and the resultant emphasis on rearmament.

Up to mid-1951, the ECA had spent a total of $10.3 billion. Approximately 90 per cent of this was in the form of outright grants, only $1.1 billion being advanced in the form of loans. Expenditures were about equally divided between agricultural and industrial products, most of the former going for food, the rest for cotton and tobacco. Industrial products consisted about a third each of fuels, raw materials, and machinery and vehicles.

EUROPE'S RECOVERY

With the crucial aid supplied by the United States, Europe made rapid progress. This can be seen in each area attacked by the recovery program—in the record of production, in price statistics, in the expansion of intra-European trade, and in Europe's balance of payments.

Production

Table 23.3 tells, in cold figures that average-out movements in different countries, the productive accomplishment of the seventeen OEEC nations. From a point some 17 per cent below the prewar level in 1947, the output of industry almost recovered to pre-war in 1948. From then on production rose about 10 per cent each year until 1951, when it stood 35 per cent above the level in 1938. Except for a period of hesitation in 1952, the earlier progress has continued, with industrial output 70 per cent above prewar in 1955.

Table 23.3

THE LEVEL OF INDUSTRIAL AND AGRICULTURAL PRODUCTION

(OEEC countries, including West Germany)

	PREWAR[a]	1946	1947	1948	1949	1950	1951	1952	1953	1954	1955	1956
Industrial Production	100	72	83	98	110	123	135	136	142	156	170	177
Agricultural Production	100	90	88	97	106	114	117	122	131	130	134	131

[a] For industrial production, 1938 = 100; for agricultural production, 1934-38 = 100. Figures refer to crop years ending June 30th; thus the 1950 figure is for the crop year 1949/50.

Source: Annual Reports of the OEEC. Data converted to a prewar base.

Agricultural production has moved in a similar direction, though at a slower rate. Starting from a figure some 12 per cent below prewar in 1947, the prewar output was nearly reached in 1948. From then on progress was fairly steady, averaging approximately 5 per cent a year, or almost exactly half the rate of increase of industrial production.

Control of Inflation

In terms of the situation that existed in 1947, inflation demanded immediate attention. In some countries, notably France and Italy, inflationary forces were open and unrestrained. Forced after the war to continue heavy outlays for demobilisation, reconstruction, or the suppression of colonial revolt, yet unable to increase their revenues at a similar pace, these governments issued more and more money. Prices rose at an accelerated rate. In other countries, like England and the Netherlands, inflation was "suppressed." Price controls and rationing kept the excess supply of money in search of goods from driving up the prices of the latter. But whether inflation was open or suppressed, so long as it continued, production suffered and the balance of payments problem was intensified.

Due to a combination of forces, inflation came increasingly under control. In six participating countries, wholesale prices reached a peak in 1948, in another six the peak was attained early the following year, while in three others prices remained relatively constant. This was partly the result of deliberate monetary or fiscal policy, partly of the increasing abundance of goods as production rose, and partly of a decline in demand accompanying a mild business recession in 1949. Both Germany and Austria carried through drastic currency reforms, replacing badly depreciated currencies with new ones, and in the process cancelling the larger part of the old issue. Italy applied stringent credit controls, while France and the United Kingdom used fiscal policy to good effect, cutting government expenditures and maintaining or increasing taxes. The data in Table 23.4 show the almost universally good results achieved up to 1950.

Table 23.4

WHOLESALE PRICES IN EUROPE, 1937 AND POSTWAR

1953 = 100

	1937	1948	1950	1951	1952	1953	1954	1955	1956
Belgium	26	94	93	113	107	100	99	101	103
Denmark	35	74	86	109	107	100	100	103	107
France	3.36	64	78	100	105	100	98	98	102
Germany*	46	90	85	101	103	100	98	101	103
Italy	1.78	104	93	106	100	100	101	101	102
Netherlands	29	75	87	107	104	100	101	102	104
Norway	37	66	76	94	100	100	101	102	110
Portugal	37	86	91	97	99	100	95	95	97
Sweden	38	72	76	100	106	100	100	104	109
Switzerland	58	102	95	107	104	100	101	101	104
Turkey	22	92	88	100	98	100	109	123	139
United Kingdom	33	67	80	97	100	100	101	104	——

* 1938 figure. For Germany, industrial prices only. Source: International Monetary Fund, *International Financial Statistics*, May 1957.

With the commencement of fighting in Korea in June, 1950, the fear of shortage generated a spurt of buying, which included not only traders and governments trying to increase their stocks, but also ordinary consumers. The increase in demand was especially marked for raw materials; because their short-run supply was inelastic, prices rose sharply, those of wool, rubber, tin, Egyptian cotton, hides, and pulp climbing from 100 to 200 per cent in less than a year. Through their effect on costs, there occurred a rise in the cost of living, which in turn led to a demand for higher wages. By the second quarter of 1951, wages in Austria, France, Germany, and Sweden had risen by 20 per cent or more; in other European countries the increase was smaller.

With renewed inflation a reality that could seriously worsen their balance of payments position, most European countries took prompt action. Monetary policy came into its own again. Fairly generally, central banks raised their discount rates and increased reserve requirements or otherwise limited the credit available to commercial banks. Varying with the promptness and firmness with which monetary policy was used, the rise in prices slowed down and came to a halt. In five OEEC countries, prices reached a peak in 1951; in seven others, the rise was checked during the following year. Thereafter, until 1956, wholesale prices remained relatively stable except in Turkey.

Intra-European Trade

Because production, both industrial and agricultural, was so low immediately after the war, there was a great shortage of goods, whether for domestic consumption or export. Production remained especially low in Germany and Austria. These inequalities in the ability to produce completely disrupted the prewar pattern of trade, which depended upon a large export surplus of Germany with other European countries and the large export surplus which these in turn had with the U.K. Nor, given the imbalance in production, could any new multilateral trading pattern emerge. Instead, some countries, better able to supply goods, became heavy creditors to the rest of Europe, like the United Kingdom, Belgium, Italy, and Switzerland, and others (notably France, the Netherlands, Norway, and Sweden) heavy debtors. With reserves of gold and foreign exchange, which might have made possible the settlement of these surpluses and deficits, approaching exhaustion, there developed a general tendency toward the close bilateral balancing of accounts between European trading partners. By 1948, some 200 bilateral agreements, backed up by rigorous quantitative restrictions, governed intra-European trade.

In 1947, trade among western European countries was only about 60 per cent of its prewar volume. Partly because the ERP furnished new credits, but mainly because of the increase in production, intra-European trade grew both absolutely and relatively to total trade during the next two years. (See Table 23.5). To accelerate this movement, the OEEC in July, 1949, requested members to remove quantitative restrictions on 50 per cent of all private trade. (Some exceptions were allowed for members with especially severe balance of payments difficulties). With the entry into force in July, 1950, of the European Payments Union,[5] the "liberalisation quota" was to

Table 23.5

VOLUME OF INTRA-EUROPEAN TRADE

(1938: 100)

1948	74
1949	91
1950	125
1951	138
1952	133
1953	150
1954	169
1955	189
1956	192

Source: Annual Reports of the O.E.E.C.

[5] For a discussion of this important institution, see Chapter 24.

increase to 60 per cent. At that time, in order to formalise the principles and procedure of their approach to freer trade, OEEC members subscribed to a Code of Liberalisation, under which each committed itself to comply with the percentage of liberalisation announced by the Organisation. Early in 1951, this was raised to 75 per cent and in January, 1955, to 90 per cent. Some members regularly exceeded the degree of liberalisation required; others felt obliged to take advantage of safeguarding clauses in the Code which granted exceptions for balance of payments or certain other compelling reasons. Undue use does not appear to have been made of these exceptions; by 1952, the average percentage liberalisation for all members was close to two/thirds, by the end of 1953, it exceeded 75 per cent, and by December, 1955, was approximately 84 per cent.

The liberalisation proceedings have applied only to private trade. From the end of the war until 1952, a substantial share of Europe's trade was carried out by the state, principally to ensure stable supplies or to facilitate rationing. With the steady disappearance of shortages, state trading has subsided. By 1954, the French government alone bought as much as one-third of the country's imports; in no other country did state-conducted trade account for more than 10 per cent.

Widespread Devaluation in 1949

In the early postwar years, people throughout the world were eager to obtain goods that for several years had been denied them. Supply lagged behind demand, especially in Europe. A typical seller's market came into existence: almost any producer could find willing buyers, even at high costs and prices—the chief problem was to get the materials and labor with which to satisfy the pressing demands, almost regardless of costs. Attention to costs was also subordinated by the network of payments-agreements that insulated much of Europe's trade, for these agreements channeled exports into sheltered, soft-currency markets.

This seller's market lasted through 1948. Then, as European production mounted, and as supplies became more abundant, too, in the United States and Canada, a seller's was rapidly transformed into a buyer's market. Price considerations again became important. European countries, which had experienced a greater degree of inflation than their competitors across the Atlantic, found their goods overpriced, not only in American and Canadian markets, but also in third markets. Currency overvaluation, not a serious hindrance to exports so long as supplies were short, now became a primary obstacle. It became increasingly clear that currency values simply must be revised.

On September 18, 1949, Britain took the plunge, devaluing the pound sterling by 30.5 per cent. Within a few days, some 27 nations followed her example, including all the sterling area (except Pakistan) and 11 western European nations. Most of the countries devalued by the same amount; a few—notably Belgium, France, Western Germany, and Italy—chose a substantially smaller figure.

Europe's Balance of Payments

During the ten years from 1947 to 1956, there has been steady progress toward a position of stable balance in Europe's international accounts. Consider first the period through 1950. (See Table 23.2). Although imports increased moderately, a larger proportion were obtained from within Europe or Europe's dependencies. With industrial production up sharply, not only were more goods available for export; exports actually rose from 1947 to 1950 by over $3 billion. As a result, the trade deficit declined from $7.3 billion to only $2.9 billion.

Investment income remained low, only about a third as large as prewar. Receipts from shipping and from tourism, however, rose steadily, accounting for a net gain of $0.4 billion. With the improvement in both trade and invisibles (together with a decided decline in private capital outflow), total net financing needed was cut from over $7.4 billion in 1947 to only $2.5 billion in 1950. For the entire five years after the war ended, the cumulative deficit of $24.4 billion was financed very largely by foreign government grants and loans.

From 1952 on, the trade deficit greatly diminished, owing mainly to the maintenance of the value of exports, while imports declined from the high level of 1951.[6] On balance, international income from services rose, due to steadily increasing transportation earnings and receipts from tourists; investment income turned down in 1952-4 because of higher United Kingdom payments on amortisation of foreign loans and the resumption by Germany of payments on its public debt. Military expenditure (which had involved western Europe in net outlays in 1950 and 1951) yielded steadily rising receipts, as the United States spent increasing sums on military procurement, troop supplies, and "infra-structure" in Europe.

After including the contribution from military expenditures, the OEEC countries from 1952 through 1955 had a surplus on current account. Since economic aid continued to be received, though in diminishing amounts, it

[6] For balance of payments data after 1950, see Table 23.6. This table is not directly comparable with Table 23.2, since the latter is for *all* of Europe except the U.S.S.R., the former for OEEC countries only.

Table 23.6

OEEC COUNTRIES: BALANCE OF PAYMENTS, 1949-55 [1]

(in billions of U. S. dollars)

	1949	1950	1951	1952	1953	1954	1955[2]
A. Goods and Services [3]							
Exports f.o.b.	10.2	9.9	14.2	14.2	13.81	14.65	15.97
Imports f.o.b.[3]	−13.3	−12.4	−17.2	−14.9	−14.42	−15.74	−17.37
Trade balance	−3.1	−2.5	−3.0	−0.7	−0.61	−1.09	−1.40
U.S. military expenditures [4]	0.3	0.2	0.3	0.7	1.17	1.44	1.61
Other services [3]	0.2	0.7	0.6	0.5	0.55	0.90	0.59
Total	−2.6	−1.6	−2.1	0.5	1.11	1.25	0.80
(Military goods and services imported under aid, net)[4]	(−0.2)	(−0.6)	(−1.3)	(−2.4)	(−3.69)	(−2.61)	(−1.82)
B. Private Donations	0.2	0.2	0.2	0.2	0.27	0.18	0.21
C. Private Capital	−0.5	−0.2	−0.6	−0.1	−0.18	−0.54	−0.66
D. Miscellaneous Official Donations and Capital [3]	−0.3	−0.3	−0.8	−1.0	−0.79	−0.89	−0.82
E. Net Errors and Omissions	−0.3	—	0.1	0.3	0.23	0.27	0.79
F. Cumulative Balance (A through E)	−3.5	−1.9	−3.2	−0.1	0.64	0.27	0.32
G. Economic Aid [3]							
Grants and loans received	4.7	3.0	2.4	1.6	1.03	0.90	0.72
Grants and loans extended by U.K.	−0.1	−0.1	−0.1	−0.1	−0.07	−0.10	−0.15
Total	4.6	2.9	2.3	1.5	0.96	0.80	0.57
H. Monetary Movements							
Repurchases from IMF	—	—	—	—	−0.15[5]	−0.14	−0.08
Overseas sterling holdings	−0.5	0.9	0.3	−0.8	0.68	0.53	−0.16
Gold and U.S. and Canadian dollar holdings (increase −)							
EPU	—	−1.9	0.1	−0.2	−0.11	0.03	0.05
Countries	−0.2	—	0.4	−0.4	−2.11	−1.95	−0.87
Other short-term capital	−0.4	—	0.1	—	0.09	0.46	0.17
Total	−1.1	−1.0	0.9	−1.4	−1.60	−1.07	−0.89

[1] No sign indicates credit; minus sign indicates debit.   [2] Preliminary.

[3] Imports of military goods and services under aid programs (shown in parentheses in the table) are excluded from Group A, and the corresponding grants are excluded from Groups D and G.   [4] These data have been derived from U.S. sources.

Source: International Monetary Fund

was possible to add to reserves of gold and foreign exchange. These climbed steadily from $9.8 billion at the end of 1951 to $15.5 billion in June, 1956.

IS THERE A CHRONIC DOLLAR SHORTAGE?

In spite of the great improvement in western Europe's balance of payments, the view is rather widespread that the gain is partial and inadequate, resting on the one hand upon uncertain American military expenditure and on the other hand upon quantitative restrictions on dollar imports. Those who hold this view believe there is a persistent tendency toward a dollar shortage which would break out into the open with any decline in U.S. expenditure or with the removal of the import restrictions that hold it in check.

Evidence of Chronic Dollar Shortage

The evidence in support of this position is impressive. In the first place, if we look back over the period since 1914, it is apparent that the United States has run a continuous surplus in its balance of payments on current account. (See Table 23.7). Since one country's surplus is a deficit to the rest of the world taken together, all during this period, the rest of the world has had a current account deficit with the United States. This in itself, of course, is no indication of balance of payments disequilibrium. So long as the United States finances its current surplus, or the corresponding deficit of its trading partners, by lending or investing abroad according to normal economic motives sufficient to cover this deficit, the balance of payments as a whole is in equilibrium.

Supporters of the view that there has been chronic imbalance in the payments relations between the United States and the rest of the world note, however, that in only seven years (from 1923 to 1929) out of some four decades was the U.S. surplus financed by normal lending or investing abroad—that is, by private capital movements in search of a higher return. In that period, total net financing required was fully provided by ordinary private investment. Besides, foreigners added some $3 billion to their holdings of gold and dollar balances.

By contrast, in each of the other periods shown in Table 23.7, special financing was required. During and after the 1914 war, it came principally from extraordinary U.S. loans and from the liquidation of foreign-owned gold and dollar assets. In the depression decade of 1930-40, transfer of gold and dollar balances to the tune of $12 billion—a heavy reduction of the outside world's international reserves—financed the current account surplus

Table 23.7

THE U. S. BALANCE OF PAYMENTS ON CURRENT ACCOUNT AND MEANS OF FINANCING IT, BY PERIODS

	7/1/14-12/31, 1918	1919-22	1923-29	1930-40	1941-45	1946-51	TOTAL, 7/1, 1914-1951
Exports, gds. & services	$24,793	$31,529	$44,498	$42,422	$75,510	$102,121	$320,873
Imports, gds. & services	14,022	20,030	36,868	35,033	37,156	62,467	205,576
Excess of exports	10,771	11,499	7,630	7,389	38,354	39,654	115,297
Means of financing excess of exports:							
Liquidation of gold and dollar assets	3,229	1,260	-3,019	12,027	-5,258	3,113	11,352
Net dollar disbursements by:							
International Monetary Fund						720	720
International Bank						632	632
U.S. Government aid:							
Grants (net)	-312	343	93	181	40,253	22,231	62,789
Long- and short-term loans (net)	7,680	2,442	-309	-79	1,971	8,444	20,149
Remittances (net)	711	2,230	2,445	2,152	1,381	3,437	12,356
Long- and short-term private capital (net)	1,520	2,133	6,946	-2,676	480	4,809	13,212
Total net financing	12,828	8,408	6,156	11,615	38,827	43,386	121,210
Errors and omissions	-2,057	3,091	1,474	-4,226	-473	-3,732	-5,923

Sources: Economic Cooperation Administration, *Report of the ECA-Commerce Mission* (Washington, D. C., October 1949), Table 8, p. 42. Data for 1946-51 from U. S. Department of Commerce, *Balance of Payments of the United States, 1949-1951* (Washington, D. C., 1952), Table 3, p. 134.

of more than $7 billion and most of the inward movement of capital. The latter consisted of the $2,676 million listed, plus most of the $4,226 million shown as "errors and omissions." As in each period, a substantial balancing contribution came from remittances, which includes immigrants' remittances, charitable contributions, and the like. Finally, during and after World War II, down through 1951, the major share of the huge current account surplus (or world dollar deficit) was covered by extraordinary U.S. government grants and loans. Drafts on international reserves and private capital movements contributed appreciably only in the postwar years.

Chronic Imbalance or Recurring Disturbance?—The Evidence

The evidence cited proves one thing conclusively: that over the whole 37 years between 1914 and 1951, international transactions between the United States and Europe in particular (as the major economic portion of "the rest of the world") were seriously disturbed. It does not prove that the balance of payments of the United States or of Europe was in a state of chronic disequilibrium. To establish this, it would be necessary to show that a common cause or set of causes underlay the recurrent payments difficulties.

Each period's troubles, however, can be traced to a distinct set of factors. From 1914 to 1923, it was the first World War and its aftermath: Europe's resources were devoted primarily to the prosecution of the war and to reconstruction. That continent made heavy demands on the United States, but lacked the means to finance the resultant deficits. This was not, to speak accurately, a period of dollar shortage, but rather of a temporary unavailability of real resources abroad combined with exceptional need for U.S. aid. Deficits were necessary for the conduct of the war and for reconstruction; the United States made them possible by providing additional resources.

Beginning with 1923, European recovery had progressed far enough so that with normal U.S. lending, for some seven years the accounts between the United States and the rest of the world were in balance. But with the onset of depression in 1930, U.S. spending and investing, as we saw in the last chapter, fell catastrophically. For a few years what could truly be called a dollar shortage appeared. Because of low income and employment, the United States spent fewer dollars on imports than in the immediately preceding years, and its international lending almost ceased. Europe's demand for imports from the U.S. decreased rather than increased, and that continent suffered no shortage of real resources. What was lacking was enough dollars to enable foreigners to pay for the U.S. surpluses on current account. Until 1933, these were financed mainly by short-term borrowing and use of dollar balances.

The middle thirties are more debatable. During 1935, 1936, and 1937, the United States ran a small current deficit. There is no convincing evidence that insufficient dollars were being supplied for normal purchases of U.S. exports. These were years, however, of huge gold movements, which were the means by which the fear-induced flight of capital from Europe was financed. But if capital flight is an undesirable and unwanted component of any country's balance of payments (it is so treated in the IMF Agreement), neither it nor the gold flow that effected the capital transfer should be taken into account in arriving at conclusions regarding balance of payments equilibrium or disequilibrium. As for the two years 1938 and 1939, U.S. sales of goods and services again greatly exceeded its purchases; the current account surplus, together with a continued capital inflow, was financed by a large movement of gold into the United States. But now, Europe was preparing for war; its demands for raw materials, armaments, and related goods was voracious. Again, it was not an inadequate supply of dollars but excess foreign demand that caused the payments imbalance.

Finally, we have the war and immediate postwar years included in the decade 1941-51. Again the source of payments difficulties was scanty resources and immense needs, not a lack of dollars.

Thus of three major periods of imbalance in the payments relations of the United States and Europe (or, more generally, the rest of the world), two are attributable to war and its aftermath, and the third—whose character varied during its course—to a collapse of employment, income, and foreign lending in the United States. Moreover, a more detailed analysis of the two postwar periods, 1919-22 and 1946-51, would reveal both great variety in the relative payments position of different countries and in the forces that were dominant at any time. We need merely recall the relative importance of inflation and of shipping losses between 1946-48 and the Korean war "scare" buying and consequent higher prices of primary products in 1950-51.

Recurring Disturbance Is Indicated

There can be no denying that in the four decades encompassing the years 1914-1951, payments difficulties have been recurrent, for the very good reason that these have been years of unusual political and economic turbulence. Recurring difficulties have caused recurring disequilibrium, each instance of which can be explained in terms of a unique set of causes.

To characterise the entire period as one of chronic disequilibrium, in which there was an "inevitable and inveterate" shortage of dollars due to a single, continously operating cause or set of causes, would appear to twist the facts unduly. Professor Ellis has expressed the matter in an apt analogy:

If an unfortunate citizen were to fall victim to yellow jaundice, then to an automobile accident, then to a plunge into icy water while skating, next to pneumonia, and finally to a fall from a step-ladder while trimming roses, we *might* call him a "chronic" invalid. But I doubt it.[7]

The evidence to me, at least, is conclusive. Before 1914, there was no sign of chronic disequilibrium in the balance of payments of the United States or of any European country. Within the next 40 years, the two costliest wars in history—covering nine of those 40 years—devastated much of Europe and shook its economy to its foundations. The worst depression on record accounts for another seven years (1930-36). One need not look beyond these three shattering forces to find the explanation of Europe's recurrent and severe balance of payments troubles since 1914.

The Contrary View

Perhaps historians of the future will view the events of this entire period as the death throes of western civilisation. If so, all our difficulties are but the symptoms of a chronic ailment. Even if this turns out to be true, it is irrelevant to the present argument. For those—and there are many—who uphold the view that there is and has been a chronic dollar shortage do not go this far. They attribute the alleged dollar shortage to a quite different and much more specific set of causes. Their position is well expressed by Professor Williams:

It is true that this period can be broken down into a succession of critical situations, and much that has happened can be blamed on the two wars. My own view, however, has been that the wars hastened processes of change already under way, and that the successive short-run crises have been primarily the symptoms of longer-run and deeper-seated maladjustments in international relationships that go back for at least three-quarters of a century.[8]

American Technological Progress

As the principal cause of deep-seated maladjustment, attention has been increasingly focussed upon the superior competitive position of American

[7] Howard S. Ellis, "The Dollar Shortage in Theory and Fact," *Canadian Journal of Economics and Political Science,* Vol. 14 (1948), p. 364.

[8] John H. Williams, *Trade not Aid: a Program for World Stability,* Harvard University Press, Cambridge, 1953, p. 9.

industry, due, it is alleged, to its more rapid technological progress.[9] Evidence often cited in support of this interpretation shows U.S. trade expanding between 1899 and 1950 at the expense of other nations, but especially of the United Kingdom and France.[10]

The facts are reasonably clear. The United States has continually increased its relative share of world trade since 1899. It has also been a highly dynamic economy, with a most progressive technology. Over much of this half century, and in many lines of American industry, though not in all, technological progress may have been more rapid than that of its foreign competitors. (But see below, p. 418). And finally, since 1914, international payments difficulties have been recurrent, severe, and much of the time concentrated upon the United States.

[9] This view was originally expressed by Thomas Balogh, in "The United States and the World Economy," *Bulletin of the Oxford Institute of Statistics,* Vol. 8 (1946); also "The United States and International Economic Equilibrium," Ch. 25 of *A Foreign Economic Policy for the United States* (Seymour E. Harris, Editor), Harvard University Press, Cambridge, 1948. It was taken up and elaborated by Professor Williams in his Stamp Memorial Lecture, cited above. J. R. Hicks, "An Inaugural Lecture," *Oxford Economic Papers,* N. S. Vol. V (1953), has formulated this view most logically and clearly, while one of its most persuasive presentations is that in *The Political Economy of American Policy, Report of a Study Group* (William Y. Elliott, Chairman), Holt, New York, 1955, pp. 77-96.

The principal critics of this explanation of the "chronic" dollar shortage are Howard Ellis, cited above; Gottfried Haberler, "Dollar Shortage?" Ch. 24 of *A Foreign Economic Policy for the United States;* Fritz Machlup, "Dollar Shortage and Disparities in the Growth of Productivity," *Scottish Journal of Political Economy,* Vol. I, No. 3 (1954); and E. M. Bernstein, "American Productivity and the Dollar Payments Problem," *Review of Economics and Statistics,* Vol. XXXVII (1955).

[10] The original source of the data usually cited is H. Tyszynski, "World Trade in Manufactured Commodities, 1899-1950," *The Manchester School of Economic and Social Studies,* Vol XIX (1951). The crucial table, showing the share of different countries in world exports of manufactures, is the following:

	1899	1913	1937	1950
United States	11.2	12.6	19.6	29.1
United Kingdom	32.5	29.9	22.4	25.0
Germany [a]	22.2	26.4	22.4	7.1
France	15.8	12.9	6.4	10.2
Belgium	5.6	4.9	5.9	5.8
Italy	3.7	3.6	3.6	3.8
Japan	1.5	2.4	7.2	3.3
Canada	0.3	0.6	5.0	6.1
Other [b]	7.2	6.7	7.5	9.6
	100.0	100.0	100.0	100.0

If we leave out 1950 as unduly influenced, especially as regards Germany and Japan, by temporary postwar dislocations, and focus upon 1937, it still appears that the United States has forged ahead vigorously, while the U.K. and France have retrogressed, and Germany and Italy have stayed about constant.

[a] After 1937, West Germany.   [b] Sweden, Switzerland, and India.

Analysis of the Problem

The question to be resolved is whether more rapid technological progress in the United States has made this nation such a formidable competitor that Europe's recurring payments problems must be regarded as reflecting a deep-seated and intractable problem.

Let us consider, first, the effects of a *uniform relative increase in American industrial productivity.*[11] Suppose U.S. productivity increases at the same rate in all sectors of industry, and that money incomes (for simplicity, wages) rise in the same proportion. Abroad, productivity remains unchanged and money incomes are constant. Prices in the United States and elsewhere are therefore unchanged and the competitive position of foreign industry remains the same. With higher U.S. incomes, however, the demand for imports will increase; the United States will develop a deficit in its balance of payments. This could be prevented by a monetary policy that limits the rise in wages to something less than the increase in productivity, the extent of this limitation being discovered by trial and error. American prices would then fall slowly, other countries would share the gain in productivity in improved terms of trade, and both American exports and imports would rise together.

Now modify this simple model by assuming that *productivity also increases outside the United States at a uniform rate, though more slowly than here,* and that wages everywhere increase in proportion to rising productivity. Again, there will be no change in competitive relations. If, however, the income elasticity of demand for imports—the proportionate increase in imports relative to the proportionate increase in income[12]—is higher abroad than in the United States, purchases from the U.S. can rise more rapidly than purchases by the U.S., and payments difficulties might arise. These could be prevented, however, by anything that causes incomes in the U.S. to rise sufficiently more rapidly than abroad to counteract the effect of higher income elasticity. This can be a still greater increase in productivity in the U.S., which is not amenable to deliberate policy measures, or a slower increase in money incomes abroad, which is. As before, if the monetary authorities outside the U.S. restrict the money supply sufficiently so that money incomes rise less than productivity, the previous balance of exports and imports can be preserved.

Finally, let us postulate *a model that does impair the competitive position*

[11] The approach adopted here is a condensation of that followed by E. M. Bernstein in the article cited above.

[12] Symbolically: $\dfrac{dM/dY}{M/Y}$, or $dM/dY \times Y/M$.

of foreign producers. Assume that productivity in U.S. export industries increases uniformly and more rapidly than in import-competing and domestic industries, while abroad, productivity rises less rapidly in the export industries. If, now, wages in both regions rise in proportion to the *average* increase in productivity in *all* industry, the costs and prices of U.S. exporters will fall, those of foreigners will climb, and the competitive position of the latter will be impaired in third markets. So far as the effects of price changes on demand are concerned, foreign producers will be at a disadvantage—sales of their products will tend to fall, of competing American products, to rise. Yet because American incomes are rising more rapidly than elsewhere, the income effect of increasing productivity may offset the price effect. American purchases may increase sufficiently to compensate foreigners for the displacement of their products in third markets by cheaper American goods.

If, however, the income elasticity of demand in the United States is less than abroad, there may be trouble. As before, however, the means of dealing with this problem are in the hands of foreign monetary authorities. By restraining the rise in money incomes to something less than the rise in average productivity, both the disadvantage of rising costs may be minimised and the tendency for expenditure on imports from the U.S. to increase too rapidly may be offset. Since productivity is increasing, such a policy of monetary restraint would not involve positive deflation and should, therefore, not be too difficult to achieve. If, however, the pressure to raise wages is too great, recurrent devaluation or steadily depreciating free exchange rates could limit foreigners' purchases to their ability to sell exports.

The point of this rather abstract discussion is that where changes in productivity are uniform, though occurring at divergent rates, the relative rise in American incomes helps to avert payments difficulties. But if U.S. income elasticity of demand for imports is relatively low, tending to cause such difficulties, these are amenable to treatment by monetary policy, which, in circumstances of rising money and real incomes, would not be unduly harsh.

Actual Changes Have Diverse Effects

In actual fact, increases in productivity are never uniform throughout a whole range of industry, and they do not affect all countries in the same way. Bernstein expresses the matter clearly:

The increase in productivity cannot be uniform for all American exports. Instead, there are certain industries which from time to time, and even over long periods, show a more rapid increase in productivity than output generally, so that no conceivable wage policy could prevent those goods from falling in price, even if the average level of all prices or of all export prices in the United States were constant. Some countries are producers of the same or competitive goods; other countries are consumers of the same or competitive import goods. The balance of payments effects cannot be the same for all countries and these differences require special emphasis.[13]

When we inquire into the effects of a specific improvement, we cannot generalise. The introduction of rayon and nylon severely injured the Japanese silk industry, but it benefited suppliers of wood-pulp in Canada. Technological progress in the machine tool industry may undercut sales of Britain, Germany, and other competing manufacturers, but it helps lower the costs and expand the markets of foreign producers who use these machines. The development of capital-intensive methods of cultivating rice increased the world supply of that foodstuff and lowered its price, to the disadvantage of Burma and Thailand, but it cheapened the imports of western European countries and contributed something to the easing of their balance of payments problem.

Technical progress in general, in the sense of basic research and its applications to industry, is of course going on all the time and in a fairly steady fashion. Its over-all effect is to raise incomes, and so far as this effect is absolutely greater in the United States than elsewhere, it eases rather than worsens the payments position of the rest of the world. As for the specific embodiments of technological progress, these may affect some countries adversely, some favorably, and the countries injured or helped will not always be the same. At times the injury may be focused on a single country and cause it serious payments difficulties. *But a cause with such diverse effects and such changing impact can hardly serve as the explanation of a general world payments problem.*

U.S. Exports Are in the Expanding Groups

It is noteworthy that the gain in the share of world trade achieved by the United States has been concentrated in certain groups of industries for which world demand has been expanding. Between 1899 and 1937, the U.S. gained 13.6 per cent in its share of the trade of these groups,[14] while Japan increased its share only 2.7 per cent and the United Kingdom lost to the extent of 22.9 per cent. Canada, which gained in every group, increased its share most in the stable category—by 10 per cent—primarily in non-ferrous metals and paper. Japan, on the other hand, improved its position by the

[13] Bernstein, *op cit.*, p. 105.
[14] These comprised motor vehicles, industrial equipment, iron and steel, and electrical goods. Data from Tyszynski, *op. cit.*, Table XI.

largest percentage (6.2 per cent) in the declining group of industries, mainly in textiles and apparel.

The fact that technological progress in the United States appears to be concentrated in products for which world demand is expanding complicates the problem, but does not change its character. It suggests that a changing pattern of trade requires a reallocation of resources, including a shift in the direction of research. The situation is not unlike that presented in the latter part of the nineteenth century, when Germany's industrial progress challenged Britain's position. It may be that today the adjustment is more difficult to make. But the fact that, since the war, Britain's income has been rising at close to 5 per cent a year would seem to indicate that that nation is not a laggard. In particular, it is hard to reconcile this material progress with an explanation of her payments problem that runs in terms of over-all competitive decline. It may be, however, that a shift in the character of exports is needed.

"Dollar Shortage" and Inflation

Our detailed analysis has shown that more rapid technological progress in a single country, even one as large as the United States, is not likely to explain a payments problem that is worldwide in character. Technological change affects specific industries at different times, and its effects on various countries are diverse. For an explanation of the recurring "dollar shortage" and its wide extent, we need look no further than to the impact of two world wars and a depression of unparalleled severity.

Inflation—the inevitable accompaniment of war and its aftermath—must bear an especially large share in accounting for the payments difficulties of the past several decades. Recall, for example, that 70 per cent of Europe's 1947 over-all deficit was in the trade account, and that three-quarters of this was attributable to an equal rise in the prices of imports and exports. Add to this the fact that inflation was more severe in western Europe than in the United States and Canada, that European currencies consequently were for some years overvalued, and the larger part of that continent's recent difficulties are explained. Much the same could be said of the period 1914-23.

More Rapid Technological Advance in U.S.?

If our refutation of the "superior American productivity" doctrine of chronic dollar shortage does not convince you, consider this: A recent careful study of relative changes in productivity by Sir Donald MacDougall raises serious doubt as to whether technological progress in the United States is really any more rapid than in the rest of the world. It shows that in normal peacetime years, the rate of increase of productivity per capita and per worker in the United States, between 1900 and 1953, was no greater than in the rest of the non-Communist world.[15] This is true of food, raw materials, and manufactures. That over the entire period of 53 years, American productivity rose more than in other countries is not denied—the data show this. But the difference is accounted for by the continued rise in American productivity during both world wars, when productivity in the rest of the world stayed about the same.

Although Sir Donald admits that some of the figures are "based on shaky estimates and of doubtful comparability," he justly says:

These may with justice be criticized as statistically unreliable—and individual estimates could certainly be improved—but it would appear necessary to produce a completely different set of figures to prove that productivity does increase substantially faster in the United States. While our statistics do not conclusively prove that it does not, neither do they confirm the more commonly held belief.[16]

[15] G. D. A. MacDougall, "Does Productivity Rise Faster in the United States," *Review of Economics and Statistics,* XXXVIII (May 1956). The statistics for countries other than the United States exclude Russia and China throughout, and "usually the countries of Eastern Europe after 1939," (p. 155). Although the data presented are in per capita terms, evidence relating to hours of work and to the proportions of populations engaged in production indicate that changes in per worker productivity probably were closely similar.

[16] *Ibid.,* pp. 155, 175.

SELECTED REFERENCES

Balogh, Thomas, *The Dollar Crisis: Causes and Cure* (Basil Blackwell, Oxford, 1950). Contains the author's most extended treatment of the problem of "dollar shortage," together with his remedial suggestions.

———, "The United States and International Economic Equilibrium," in *Foreign Economic Policy for the United States,* edited by S. E. Harris (Harvard University Press, 1948). Argues that American instability and rapid technological progress create a chronic dollar shortage, and suggests as a remedy a region-grouping and strengthening of the European economy.

Economic Commission for Europe, *Economic Survey of Europe in 1949,* and annually since then (United Nations, New York). An analytical discussion of current developments in Europe.

———, *Economic Survey of Europe Since the War* (United Nations, New York, 1953). A thorough review of Europe's progress through 1952, and an analysis of its problems of trade and payments and of industrial development.

Elliott, William Y., chairman, *The Political Economy of American Foreign Policy, Report of a Study Group* (Henry Holt, New York, 1955). Undertakes a searching diagnosis of the economic ills of the western world, with considerable emphasis on the competitive superiority of American industry; argues forcefully for economic integration of the Western World under American leadership.

Ellis, Howard S., *The Economics of Freedom* (Harper & Bros., New York, 1950). A comprehensive study of the European Recovery Program, covering needs, problems, and prospects with special chapters on the United Kingdom, Western Germany, France, and Italy.

Haberler, Gottfried, "Dollar Shortage?" in *Foreign Economic Policy for the United States*, edited by S. E. Harris (Harvard University Press, 1948). Challenges the concept of dollar shortage, and attacks the view based on superior American productivity.

Harris, Seymour E., *The European Recovery Program* (Harvard University Press, 1948). A critical discussion of the ERP and the major issues it raised, as of the beginning of that program.

Hicks, J. R., "An Inaugural Lecture," *Oxford Economic Papers*, new series, V (1953). An able, theoretical formulation of the case for viewing Europe's payments problem as attributable to the superior productivity of the American economy.

International Monetary Fund, *The Revival of Monetary Policy* (Washington, 1953). An informal discussion of the renewed use of monetary policy in several countries.

Lubell, Samuel, *The Revolution in World Trade* (Harper & Bros., New York, 1955). A lively discussion of the impact of the war on international trading relations and of the needs of American trade policy under conditions of cold war. Chapters V and VII effectively challenge the view that the U.S. tariff is responsible for Europe's balance of payments difficulties.

Machlup, Fritz, "Dollar Shortage and Disparities in the Growth of Productivity," *Scottish Journal of Political Economy*, I (Oct. 1954). Reviews the discussion of this issue at the hands of Balogh, Haberler, Williams, and Hicks; attributes the shortage of dollars to the economic policies of the deficit countries.

MacDougall, G. D. H., "Does Productivity Rise Faster in the United States?" *Review of Economics and Statistics*, XXXVIII (May 1956). See discussion at end of this chapter.

Organisation for European Economic Cooperation, *Annual Reports*, since 1951 (Paris). Reviews economic conditions and changes in Europe each year. The OEEC's first *Interim Report on the Recovery Program* (1948) provides estimates of problems and needs; its second report, *European Recovery Programme* (1950), reviews the accomplishments of the first year-and-a-half.

Robertson, Sir Dennis H., *Britain in the World Economy* (George Allen & Unwin, London, 1954). A series of four delightful essays on the position of Britain, the sterling area, the dollar shortage, and the use of discriminatory restrictions on U.S. imports.

Williams, John H., *Economic Stability in a Changing World* (Oxford University Press, New York, 1953). Part II consists of Professor Williams' Marshall Plan papers, which criticise and evaluate the progress of that Plan from a contemporary viewpoint.

——, *Trade not Aid: a Program for World Stability* (Harvard University Press, 1953). Persuasively presents the author's views with respect to world imbalance in the context of a single lecture.

24

POSTWAR MONETARY ARRANGEMENTS

THE INTERNATIONAL MONETARY FUND

Unable to withstand the shocks and stresses of the world depression and international financial crises, the international gold standard disappeared in the early thirties. Therewith the world lost the efficient automatic machinery upon which it had for decades relied to preserve balance once disturbed. No substitute mechanism emerged to take its place. Instead, each nation dealt with its balance of payments problems in its own way—with solutions that often aggravated the difficulties of other countries, caused the volume of trade to shrink, and contracted the range of international specialisation. The pressures of World War II extended the area and intensified the severity of arbitrary restrictions on trade and payments.

It was therefore clear, in view of the disruption and dislocation certain to exist when the war ended, that if exchange arrangements were to be orderly, a deliberate and concerted effort would have to be made to create them.

Origins of the Fund

Sharing such convictions, experts in the United States and the United Kingdom during the War prepared plans for international monetary cooperation on a comprehensive basis to be put into effect as soon as hostilities ended. At first working independently, they soon began close and frequent consultations, later extending these to include the representatives of other countries. Finally there emerged the elements of a common plan proposing the establishment of an International Monetary Fund.

The U.S. government invited 44 nations to meet and discuss this proposal in a United Nations Monetary and Financial Conference at Bretton Woods, New Hampshire, in July, 1944. Out of its deliberations came the Articles of Agreement of the International Monetary Fund as well as the Agreement for the International Bank for Reconstruction and Development.

The creation of the Fund represents a major effort at international cooperation. Though by no means the first in its field, it is the most detailed attempt deliberately to organise the conduct of international monetary affairs. Before World War I, there was international cooperation, but it relied upon impersonal market forces and not upon the establishment of specific institutions with directors, staff, and powers of action. The cooperation between central banks of the 1920's was informal and relatively loose. The IMF, however, strikingly embodies the trend that has become so prominent in recent years, of deliberate and conscious organisation to achieve certain agreed international goals.

Purposes

The purposes of the Fund clearly reflected the lessons of the interwar period. These may be summarised under three heads.

(1) Perhaps most apparent was the need for worldwide convertibility of currencies, for this would re-create a multilateral system of payments and therewith a trading system which would permit the fullest advantage to be taken of the possibilities of international specialisation. Since it is the restrictions on international transfers implicit in exchange controls that destroyed convertibility, to restore free exchange markets the Fund must work to eliminate these controls.

(2) The experience of more than a decade showed that unstable exchange rates were highly undesirable. Few countries had tolerated them for more than a brief period, for they increased risks and unsettled trade, stimulated unwanted and uneconomic capital movements, and tended to generate competitive depreciation. Another task of the Fund, therefore, was to bring about reasonable stability of exchange rates.

(3) The goal of high and stable employment had come to be universally accepted. This goal requires a large degree of national independence with respect to monetary and fiscal policy. Yet such independence is inconsistent with any truly international currency system with stable exchange rates, such as the gold standard, for any system of that kind automatically adjusts balance of payments disturbances by invoking deflation or inflation, which it is the object of a stable employment policy to prevent. The Fund, therefore, had to devise a means of international adjustment that would preserve exchange stability while at the same time guaranteeing national monetary and fiscal independence.

Provisions: General

To realise these difficult and somewhat contradictory objectives, the provisions of the Articles of Agreement of the IMF had to be firm but conciliatory. In broad terms, they replaced free-wheeling national exchange and payments policies with a code of reasonable behavior in these matters by which the Fund members—39 nations in the first year of operations, 68 some ten years later—agreed to abide.

Thus the totally independent and destructive national action of the thirties was to give way to international agreement and cooperation. To attain the specific goals of currency convertibility and a multilateral system of payments, generally stable exchange rates, and an adjustment mechanism consistent with national monetary independence, the Fund Agreement established four sets of provisions.

Elimination of exchange restrictions. To eliminate foreign exchange restrictions and thus eventually to restore convertibility, Article VIII stipulates that "no member shall, without the approval of the Fund, impose restrictions on the making of payments and transfers for current international transactions." In other words, one principle in the new code of behavior requires that a member shall not adopt exchange controls without permission, but shall submit any proposals of this sort to an international agency for scrutiny.

It was fully recognised, however, that in the disturbed, postwar conditions, many members might not be able to cope with acute balance of payments problems by any other means. Therefore, Article XIV provides that "in the postwar transitional period members may . . . maintain and adapt to changing circumstances . . . restrictions on payments and transfers for current international transactions." After an initial five-year period, which ended in 1952, members were required to consult periodically with officers of the Fund with respect to continuance of exchange restrictions. When we come to review the Fund's record, we shall see that it has been forced to adopt a tolerant attitude toward this problem.

Stability of exchange rates. In approaching the twin problems of restoring stable exchange rates and providing an acceptable means of international adjustment, the Fund Agreement showed great ingenuity. It borrowed some elements from the gold standard, and some from the rival system of fluctuating exchange rates, combining them in a compromise solution—one achieving flexible stability of exchange rates.

Gold is retained as a base by the requirement that each member shall establish, in cooperation with the Fund, a par value for its currency expressed in terms of gold or the U.S. dollar. To ensure that these par values are maintained, members must not permit maximum and minimum spot rates of exchange to vary from them by more than 1 per cent.

Adjustment through devaluation. Once established, however, these par values need not remain indefinitely rigid. They may be changed, in consultation with the Fund, whenever a member confronts a "fundamental disequilibrium" in its balance of payments. If a proposed change does not exceed 10 per cent of the initial value, "the Fund shall raise no objection." If the proposed change is greater, it is up to the Fund to determine whether or not the change is necessary. Should this be found to be the case, approval would be automatic; if not, approval would be denied. Should a member revalue its currency in defiance of the Fund, it could be denied use of that agency's resources and ultimately expelled from membership.

Thus, the Fund provisions rely for adjustment to major balance of payments disturbances, not upon the painful and objectionable deflation or inflation required by a true international monetary system, but upon readjustment of price relationships through definitive devaluation. Since major disturbances may be presumed to arise, for any given country, only at rather long intervals, the par value of its currency and therefore its exchange rates would remain stable over considerable periods.

Fundamental disequilibrium.   Difficult questions could arise if a country, confronting what it thought to be a fundamental disequilibrium, requested permission to devalue in excess of 10 per cent. The Agreement states that the Fund must concur "if it is satisfied that the change is necessary to correct a fundamental disequilibrium." But it also stipulates that "provided it is so satisfied, it shall not object to a proposed change because of the domestic social or political policies of the member proposing the change."

A considerable area of possible disagreement exists here. First, there is the question of deciding whether *fundamental disequilibrium* is or is not present. What are the criteria for its identification? Second, devaluation must be *necessary* to correct such a disequilibrium, which presumably means that devaluation must be an appropriate and effective method of adjusting the particular disturbance. Again, according to what criteria is this to be decided? Finally, nothing a country may do in the realm of domestic "social or political policies" is to stand in the way of the Fund's approval if the first two conditions are met. But what if a nation's domestic policies—an overzealous expansion of credit, for example, in support of a program of economic development—are the cause of its balance of payments difficulties?

Because these questions are complex and difficult, with the answers varying with particular circumstances, it was impossible to prescribe means for dealing with them in advance. They will have to be resolved through discussion as each occasion arises. Economic analysis, applied by the Fund's capable experts to the circumstances of each concrete case, will have to be used to determine whether fundamental disequilibrium is present and whether devaluation is likely to be a suitable remedy.

Evidence of Serious Disequilibrium

In most instances where a country requests devaluation in excess of 10 per cent, serious disequilibrium should be evident in the form of a continuing and serious deficit in its balance of payments. The disequilibrium might, however, be potential rather than actual, its impact taking the form of excessive unemployment in the affected country. It might then be wise, as Professor Haberler has suggested, for the country to take domestic action to counteract the unemployment, and allow devaluation "only after there is objective evidence of a deterioration in the balance of payments." [1] If, on the other hand, the symptoms of disequilibrium were prevented from appearing by the use of exchange controls, this in itself would constitute evidence of serious disequilibrium.

Appropriateness of Devaluation

As for the appropriateness of devaluation as a corrective measure, substantial agreement is being reached with regard to broad categories of problems. In terms of the classifications adopted in Chapters 17 and 19, devaluation is best suited to correct an income disequilibrium caused by inflation or by price disparities left over from past inflation, provided that any current inflation is first checked by internal measures. Where the disequilibrium is cyclical in origin, devaluation by one country tends to become a means of exporting unemployment. The problem is worldwide in character and requires a different approach, which is indeed provided in the Articles of Agreement. The causes and nature of structural disequilibrium, on the other hand, are so diverse as to leave much room for judgment; the suitability of devaluation in any concrete situation can only be determined by careful study and consultation between officials of the Fund and of the government concerned.

The most delicate issues arise when external disequilibrium results from internal inflation. For, there, it is domestic policy that is responsible for the difficulty, and the Fund may not object to a proposed devaluation "because of the domestic social or economic policies of the member proposing the change." A serious dilemma could emerge: devaluation would

---

[1] Gottfried Haberler, "Currency Depreciation and the International Monetary Fund," *The Review of Economic Statistics*, Vol. XXVI, No. 4 (November 1944), pp. 180-1. For a contrary point of view, see Robert Triffin, "National Central Banking and the International Economy," in *International Monetary Policies, Postwar Economic Studies No. 7*, Board of Governors of the Federal Reserve System, Washington, D. C., 1947.

be useless unless the inflation is stopped, yet the Fund cannot insist on appropriate domestic policies, since this would constitute unauthorised interference. Solution of this problem might be achieved through consultation and persuasion. We shall see that this is precisely the approach taken by the Fund.

Resources of the Fund

A change in par value, or devaluation, is reserved for coping with fundamental disequilibrium. To deal with less serious, presumably short-run disturbances, or with the early stages of more deep-seated difficulties, the sizeable resources of the Fund may be used. These consist of its holdings of the currencies of the various members, which constitute in effect a supplemental reserve upon which any member may draw.

The total resources of the Fund amount to approximately $9 billion, of which about $1.7 billion is in gold, the rest in the currencies of members. They were acquired as a condition of membership. As each country joined the Fund, it was given a *quota* based on its relative size and economic strength. Of this quota, it had to subscribe 25 per cent in gold or dollars, the remainder in its own currency.

Each nation's quota determines how much financial assistance it can normally obtain in case of need—that is, when it suffers an adverse balance of payments which its own reserves are insufficient to meet. It may in effect borrow from the Fund by purchasing with additional deposits of its own currency, the currencies of other members with which it is running a deficit. Such purchases are limited, in the first year, to 25 per cent of its quota; they may be increased each year by the same percentage until they amount to 125 per cent of its quota. Thus at the end of five years of such purchases, the Fund would hold national currency of the member equal to 200 per cent of its quota (125 per cent representing the sums borrowed, 75 per cent, the share of the original subscription in national currency).

Quota limitations on purchases or borrowing may be waived, and often have been. Additional flexibility is provided through stand-by arrangements, under which the IMF guarantees the availability for a determined period of an agreed amount of resources, which may exceed the usual initial 25 per cent.

Limitations on Use of the Fund's Resources

To discourage excessive or prolonged use of the Fund's resources, a scale of charges is levied. For current purchases not in excess of a member's quota, or for any purchases not lasting more than three months, there is a service charge of ½ per cent. For sums larger than the quota and continuing more than three months, charges start at 2 per cent per annum and rise progressively.

Since the Fund's resources are tantamount to a secondary reserve for the use of members, it is important that they be replenished after being drawn upon, just as with ordinary reserves, so that they may be available when needed again. Hence a member is required to repurchase its currency held by the Fund (i.e., repay loans) if its regular gold and convertible currency reserves increase, or if these decrease less than the Fund's holdings of its currency has increased.[2]

Drafts on the Fund's resources are regarded as a means of meeting temporary payments difficulties. It would be as inappropriate for a member to use them to postpone action when confronted with an enduring source of disequilibrium as it would be to exhaust its normal reserves in the same circumstances. As a deterrent to such use, in addition to the graduated charges and the repurchase provisions, members are required to consult with the Fund after three years' continuous use of its resources.

The Scarce Currency Provision

It is important to note that the total resources of the Fund, equivalent to some $9 billion, *do not* represent its ability to provide financial assistance to members in the likely event that their need is for a particular currency, say the American dollar. Balance of payments disequilibria are not haphazard in direction, but can be focused upon a single country—in the years since the war, predominantly upon the United States. The great bulk of the Fund's resources, however, are in the form of the national currencies of 68 different countries. Were several members simultaneously to require dollars, the Fund has available to meet this demand only the gold and dollars subscribed by the United States (its quota), amounting to $2,750 million, plus the 25 per cent of the quotas of the other members subscribed in this form, which is about $1.5 billion. The total of gold and dollars with which it could provide members, therefore, is $4,250 million.

In the event of a severe depression originating in the United States—the kind of disturbance hitherto considered most likely to lead to a sudden and widespread demand for dollars—the rest of the world might easily

---

[2] Half of any increase in reserves must be exchanged for the member's currency, or half the difference between the decrease in its reserves and the increase in Fund holdings of its currency. These "repurchase provisions" do not apply when a member's reserves are less than its quota, nor, of course, do they apply to the original 75 per cent of its quota subscribed in national currency, which remains permanently in the possession of the Fund.

run a deficit well in excess of this amount within a single year.[3] Normal reserves would of course be drawn upon first, but a continuance of any such deficit would soon exhaust both these and the Fund's resources.

The Fund's scarce currency provisions were designed to meet such a situation. When the demand for a member's currency becomes so great as to threaten the Fund's ability to supply it, the Fund "shall formally declare such currency scarce and shall thenceforth apportion its existing and accruing supply of the scarce currency with due regard to the relative needs of members, the general international economic situation, and any other pertinent consideration" (Art. VII. 3.). The issuance of such a formal declaration automatically authorises any member to impose exchange controls over the use of the scarce currency. Such controls, however, are to be no more restrictive than necessary to balance the member's demand for it with its supply of the scarce currency, and they are to expire with the ending of the scarcity.

It should be noted that before the scarce currency provision can be invoked, the scarcity of the currency in question must be *general*. This is implicit in the specification that the Fund's holdings of the currency must be inadequate. So long as these were ample, the Fund could meet all reasonable demands for this currency, or even large demands from one or two countries. But if the demand were large and general, the Fund's holdings would soon become exhausted. Should only one or two countries be short of dollars, it would appear that they were suffering from a "fundamental disequilibrium" whose correction might well require devaluation of their currencies.

In establishing the scarce currency provision, the Articles of Agreement borrow some of the techniques of exchange control—but only for a severe emergency and for a limited period. This provision also embodies the principle of insulating affected regions from a depression originating elsewhere. With dollar payments subject to control, reserve losses of the countries involved would be minimised, and they would be free to pursue, singly or in concert, full employment policies within their borders.

Control of Capital Flight

The Fund Agreement also permits another use of exchange control. This is to check unwanted capital movements, that is, speculative or politically

---

[3] U.S. imports in 1956 totalled approximately $17 billion, while its postwar international lending has been at an annual rate of about $2 billion. Were imports to decline as rapidly as they did during the sharp recession of 1938, when they fell by 31 per cent, and were international investment to collapse, the supply of dollars could shrink by as much as $7 billion within a single year.

motivated flights of capital. The Articles prescribe that: "A member may not make net use of the Fund's resources to meet a large or sustained outflow of capital." Moreover, "the Fund may request a member to exercise controls to prevent such use of the resources of the Fund" (Art. VI. 1.). If it fails to do so, it may be refused use of these resources.

Ordinary capital movements, either long or short-term, are in no way affected. They may be financed out of a member's own gold or foreign exchange holdings, or even with the aid of the Fund's resources if the capital transactions are of reasonable amount.

Whether exchange controls could be confined to capital transactions, or would have to be extended to cover current transactions as well, is open to question. We have already noted (Chapter 19) some of the numerous devices by which capital movements can be concealed. But if a country's currency were not overvalued, then even though the *machinery* of control might have to be extended to current transactions to prevent disguised exports of capital, restriction of such transactions themselves should not be necessary. This would be consistent with the Fund's prohibition against the exercise of controls "in a manner which will restrict payments for current transactions."

THE TEST OF EXPERIENCE

Par Values and Changes in Par

In September 1946, 32 countries communicated to the Fund the initial par values of their currencies. These reflected the exchange rates current at the time and were agreed generally to contain a large element of overvaluation. Although there was, therefore, serious doubt as to their compatibility with international balance and thus as to their permanence, the Fund raised no objection, feeling that in view of the worldwide shortage of goods, overvaluation would not be a serious handicap to exports nor an undue stimulus to imports.

As time went on and goods became more plentiful, a number of countries began, as we noted in the last chapter, to experience increasing difficulties in exporting. Although the Fund could not formally *propose* changes in par value, it was not debarred from privately discussing the matter with members and of urging such a move if convinced it would promote a more balanced payments position. Prior to the extensive devaluation of 1949, involving countries accounting for some 65 per cent of world imports, Fund officials engaged frequently in such discussions. Since these devaluations received the Fund's approval, it may be presumed that the appropriate amount of change in par values and the problem of unfair competitive depreciation were thoroughly considered. Subsequent to September, 1949, nine other currencies were devalued in agreement with the Fund.

Not all members had declared an initial par value by the end of 1956; nine nations were in this group. Their failure to comply with this requirement has been tolerated by the Fund, subject to consultation if they contemplate changing the artificially maintained official exchange rates. Canada since 1950, and Peru since 1949, have allowed the value of their currencies to fluctuate more than the permitted 1 per cent. With respect to such fluctuating rates, as well as the use of multiple rates, the Fund's attitude has also been tolerant. While not approving them, it has recognised that special circumstances may make them temporarily necessary; but it continues to press for adoption of a single stable rate as soon as possible. In one instance, when in 1948, France changed its par value on its own initiative and adopted a dual rate, the Fund, which objected to the French action, had no choice but to declare the French change in par value unauthorised and to deny France the use of its resources.

Removal of Exchange Restrictions

In the last chapter, we traced the improvement in the world payments situation after 1948. This permitted a gradual relaxation of the severe exchange restrictions with which most countries emerged from the war. In considerable part, this relaxation did not involve abandonment of the machinery of exchange control, but rather, increasing liberality in the application of its provisions. Belgium-Luxembourg, Western Germany, the Netherlands, and the United Kingdom all greatly reduced the restrictive effect of their controls, especially with regard to transactions in raw material markets. Along with the liberalisation of payments restrictions has gone a diminution in bilateral trading practices and a rapid growth in the volume of world trade.

Though by no means solely responsible for these changes, the Fund has pressed continuously for them in consultations with members and is certainly entitled to some of the credit.[4]

Convertibility

Considerable progress has also been made toward the restoration of convertibility. Although only 10 currencies in the dollar area were formally

---

[4] Beginning with 1950, the Fund has regularly published an *Annual Report on Exchange Restrictions,* in which all changes introduced during the year are described.

convertible as of 1957, sterling area currencies acquired increasingly wide transferability, extending to almost all non-dollar countries, and the establishment of the European Payments Union made its own members' currencies fully convertible with one another.

The advance toward convertibility received a severe check, however, late in 1956, with the outbreak of the Suez crisis, for the interruption of oil supplies from the Middle East and the derangement of shipping because of the closing of the Canal both increased the need of western Europe for oil from the dollar area and retarded exports.

Use of the Fund's Resources

Relatively little use was made of the Fund's resources in the first nine years after it began exchange operations in March, 1947. Total assistance to members in this period amounted to $1,236 million. A large proportion of its advances came before the Marshall Plan went into effect, in 1947 and 1948, and again during 1949. During the life of that Plan (1948-50), participants were denied access to the Fund, which desired to conserve its resources for use after European reconstruction had been completed. Thereafter, the growth in the reserves of non-dollar members and the strengthening of their balances of payments reduced the need for resort to the Fund. It was not until the Suez crisis seriously threatened to weaken the pound sterling that significant action was required. Then the Fund supported the pound vigorously by undertaking to provide Britain, through a combination of drawing rights and stand-by credit, with automatic recourse to its resources to the full amount of Britain's quota, $1,300 million. France also obtained a stand-by credit of $262.5 million, equal to half of its quota.

The greater part of the Fund's operations have been in dollars and sterling, since these are the two principal currencies used in international payments. Before the middle of 1956, over $1 billion in dollars and almost $200 million in sterling were sold to members, lesser sums in Belgian francs and German marks.

By the end of April, 1956, $1,049 million of the total transactions of $1,236 million had been repaid, mostly after 1951, when members began to accumulate gold and dollar reserves. The larger part of these repayments was made by repurchase by members of their own currencies, though $203 million of member obligations were cancelled by the Fund's selling their currencies to other members. Figure 24.1, showing changes in the Fund's holdings of members' currencies by major areas, traces the record of its financial assistance.

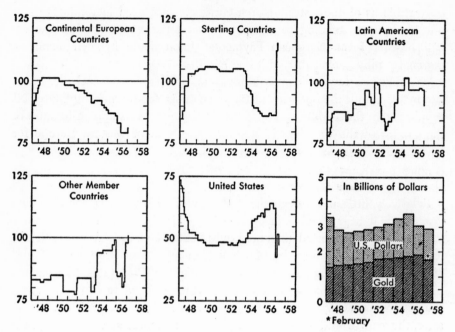

Fig. 24.1: Fund Holdings of Member Currencies & Gold
(In Per Cent of Quota)

Persuasion and Advice

To deal with the dilemma presented by a conflict between a member's domestic financial policy, over which the Fund has no control, and the maintenance of exchange stability, which is one of its major objectives, the Fund has relied mainly on persuasion. If a member pursued a continuously inflationary policy, as some have done, this would be contradictory to its undertaking "to collaborate with the Fund to maintain exchange stability" (Art. IV. 4a.). The Fund would have the right to refuse permission to devalue or to deny the member access to its resources. As it stated in one of its reports, however, "it would be unfortunate if the Fund were to content itself with such a negative role. In fact, the Fund has regarded its responsibility as a positive one—to study the problems of its members, to advocate financial policies necessary to cope with the problems, and to provide technical assistance in the application of such policies." [5]

The Fund has a highly competent technical staff, which continuously reviews the economic situation in each member country, prepares reports on specific problems, and provides the personnel for missions to members

[5] *The First 10 Years of the International Monetary Fund*, p. 36, Washington, D. C., 1956.

who are in difficulties. With the information and understanding at their disposal, Fund officials can, through consultations with member governments and through discussions at annual meetings, exert a great deal of influence. Partly as a consequence of this, there has been increasing recognition of the importance of exchange stability and a balanced payments positions, and of the close relation to these goals of domestic financial policies. Along with the reduction in exchange restrictions, consolidation of multiple rates, and elimination of bilateral trading practices has come a gradual improvement in national monetary behavior. The conflict between internal policies and external stability is by no means ended, but it is certainly being steadily moderated by the facilities for international monetary cooperation embodied in the Fund.

THE STERLING AREA

Changes in Its Character

The sterling area in its various transformations may perhaps not inaccurately be characterised as the shrinking residue of the once worldwide system of international payments centered in London and using the pound sterling as its currency. From 1931, when Britain went off gold, until 1939, the sterling area consisted of a motley group of countries which found it convenient, because of their trading or financial connections with the United Kingdom, to tie the value of their currencies to that of sterling and to keep the bulk of their foreign exchange reserves in London. The pound remained convertible into gold and dollars, though at a varying rate of exchange, and transactions of members with most of the world were cleared through London. Membership was comparatively large, including, besides the British Commonwealth (but *not* Canada), the Irish Republic, Portugal, the Scandinavian nations, the Baltic countries, three Middle Eastern countries, Argentina, and Thailand.

With the outbreak of war in 1939, the prewar sterling area shrank in size, while its formal and easygoing arrangements gave way to an increasingly more complex and restrictive set of exchange controls. Besides the British Commonwealth plus Ireland and minus Canada, from now on it included only a few relatively small countries.[6] This smaller area became subject to a common set of exchange controls, decentralised in administration but everywhere patterned on the British regulations.

Restrictions on sterling area payments became necessary because of

[6] These are today (1957) Burma, Iceland, Jordan, and Libya. During the war Argentina, Egypt, and Portugal retained their membership.

the tremendous volume of purchases that could only be made in the dollar area. The system that grew up and continued into the postwar years with the persistence of the dollar shortage had two main purposes: (1) to conserve gold and dollars available to members; and (2) to retain for sterling as wide use as possible for making international payments. In seeking to realise these objectives, four principal means were used.

Mechanics of the Sterling Area

First, *members of the sterling area agreed to pool their reserves* of gold and hard currencies. In practice this meant surrender of all current earnings of gold and dollars to the Bank of England and control of their use by that institution. This was essential if scarce currencies were to be economised and allocated to the most pressing needs.

Second, *dealings in foreign exchange by residents of the area had to be confined to authorised banks*. Thus concentrated in the hands of institutions responsible to central banks or other monetary authorities, they could be more readily policed.

Third, *payments* from one part *of the sterling area* to any other part, or to a resident of a non-member country, *were centralised in London*, as before the war. Now, however, only intra-sterling area payments could be made freely by transfers from one sterling area balance in London to another. Payments from a sterling area resident to any other part of the world required the permission of the London authorities. This proviso made it possible, so far as needs and resources could be foreseen, to plan the use of hard currencies and thus to prevent a drain of reserves. Changes in prices, in markets, and in requirements, however, made it impossible to predict accurately the need for dollars or how many would be available.

When, as happened from time to time, events belied previous estimates and a dollar deficit emerged, a fourth and final means was used to cope with such an adverse development. This consisted in a *tightening of import restrictions* by the United Kingdom and the independent sterling area members. Agreement on the extent of restriction has been reached informally or, since 1949, at formal meetings. Thus, in the fall of 1949, all members agreed to a 25 per cent cut in dollar imports.

The Sterling Accounts System

Maintenance of sterling balances or accounts in London is by no means confined to sterling area members. Banks and firms in many other countries (over 60 since the war) have long kept such balances as a convenient means of clearing transactions with the sterling area or an even larger part of the world. Their existence has made possible the use of sterling for international payments outside of as well as within the sterling area.

When the war began and exchange controls were imposed on sterling area members, a sharp distinction had to be drawn between the accounts of sterling area residents and those of non-residents. Transfers from resident to non-resident accounts could not be freely permitted. At first, transfers between different non-resident accounts or from non-resident to sterling area accounts were unrestricted. As time went on, however, the accounts of different non-sterling countries came to be classified in increasingly complex categories according to the freedom permitted in their use, which varied with the degree of control exercised over transfers in the country of the owner. During the first nine years after the war, there were five sets of accounts: resident, American and Canadian, transferable, ordinary, and bilateral. The general principle respecting their use has been to prevent sterling deposits from getting into hands that might try to convert them into dollars. In practice, this has meant prohibiting transfers from any account into a dollar account (except from another dollar account) or into a less well-controlled account (where the sterling might surreptitiously be sold for dollars). Thus payments could be freely made *to* resident (sterling area) accounts *from* any other account, but transfers *from* resident accounts were limited to other, similarly controlled resident accounts.

Transfers within the sterling area (from one resident account say in New Zealand to another in India) could be made freely, whether for trade, service, or capital items. Holders of other kinds of sterling could use them for *current* but not for capital transfers. Such current payments could be made automatically and without question anywhere in the sterling area, to owners of the same type of account, and to other types as permitted by British regulations. In addition, special permission was granted fairly readily to make other transfers (except to American and Canadian accounts). These (administrative transfers) considerably increased the flexibility and usefulness of the sterling account system to participants. In 1951, half the international transactions of the world were being carried out in sterling.

In 1954, the system was greatly simplified and liberalised. Two kinds of accounts—resident, and American and Canadian—continued unchanged. All others—involving the acounts of 51 countries—were merged into the class of transferable accounts. Now, sterling held anywhere outside the dollar or the sterling area could be transferred anywhere in the sterling area or to any of the 51 transferable account countries in payment of current transactions.

Since the inception of exchange controls, capital movements from Britain to countries outside the sterling area have been closely regulated. British capital exports and repatriation of foreign-owned capital in the United Kingdom have been prohibited except for special cases, and the proceeds of sales of foreign-owned British securities have been placed in special "security sterling" or blocked accounts, to be used only for the purchase of other British securities. These regulations have, however, been progressively relaxed, either administratively or through changes in the rules.

Partial Convertibility Realised

The principal element of liberalisation introduced in 1954 was the release of foreign central banks from their obligation to police the use of transferable sterling, an obligation hitherto made a condition for the establishment of a transferable rather than a more restricted type of account. With this abolition of controls over the disposal of non-convertible sterling, it now began to be sold freely for other currencies, including dollars. Transferable pounds were now in fact convertible in overseas exchange markets.[7] In London, however, they could not be transferred to dollar accounts, nor converted into gold or dollars, so this *de facto* overseas convertibility imposed no drain on British reserves.

During the latter half of 1954, owing to strength in the British balance of payments, transferable sterling sold for dollars at a very slight discount from the official rate for convertible sterling. So long as this discount was no more than about 2 per cent, commodity shunting—the purchase of British goods with transferable sterling for ostensible shipment to a transferable account country, but with diversion or shunting of the shipment to the dollar area—did not pay.[8] But as in early 1955 the discount rose to about 3 per cent, these activities became profitable. Americans could buy transferable pounds for approximately $2.70, as against $2.78 for official sterling, and use them to buy shunted commodities. The dollars spent on such transactions became the property of the sellers of transferable sterling instead of being added to British holdings. To counteract this, the Exchange Equalisation Account began to support transferable sterling in foreign

[7] Blocked accounts became negotiable abroad for dollars or other currencies at the same time.

[8] Owing to additional costs involved in shunting as opposed to direct purchases.

markets, buying these pounds with dollars. From early in 1955 to mid-1956, this action kept the rate for transferable sterling about 1 per cent below spot sterling. Commodity shunting ceased, but at the cost of some loss in British reserves.

The Rationale of Sterling Area Membership

Membership in the sterling area has involved submission of each member's international payments to a common set of exchange controls, surrender of hard currency earnings to a common pool, reliance for gold or dollars needed for international payments upon decisions strongly influenced by Britain's exchange requirements, and continuous and occasionally severely tightened restrictions on hard currency imports. Why should independent nations of the Commonwealth, like South Africa or New Zealand, have been willing, after the imperative needs of war had passed, to submit to such limitations on their action? The answer, in the most general terms, is that no available alternative had as much to offer. Sterling area membership carried with it not only obligations, but also rights and privileges.

(1) In the first place, the sterling area constitutes a large region within which payments are fully multilateral. A member can buy or sell anywhere in this region as freely as he ever could.

(2) Closely related to this is the freedom to transfer capital, which has been a distinct advantage to peripheral members but a drain on Britain's resources, both financial and real.

(3) Before the war, the overseas sterling area earned a large dollar surplus, but that has since melted away. Lacking the dollars to pay for various kinds of manufactured goods, many of them important for their development, the overseas sterling countries have been able, through their ready access to the U.K. market, to obtain them there instead.

(4) During the war, Britain bought food, military supplies, and services in large quantities by simply adding to the sterling deposits of the suppliers, all sterling area members at the time. She had the great advantage of having a huge charge account with which to obtain these resources. After the war, these deposits were put into blocked accounts, and agreements reached with the various holders to release them as rapidly as possible. While they are being liquidated, their owners benefit from being able to draw upon Britain's resources, while that nation suffers the disadvantage of shipping "unrequited exports" which might otherwise be exchanged for goods or foreign currencies or used at home.

(5) Finally, the pooling of reserves has worked sometimes to a par-

ticular member's advantage, sometimes to its disadvantage, depending upon whether at a particular time the pool was financing its hard currency deficit or whether it was contributing a hard currency surplus to the reserves. For most countries, this shoe has alternately been on one foot and then the other. Having the shoe available, however, has been better than going barefoot.

Problems of the Sterling Area

Operation of the sterling area has by no means always been clear sailing. Allocation of hard currencies from the pool has been a particular source of recurring dissatisfaction. Members who have contributed to the pool have often felt that their needs were slighted, and that too often, policy has been determined overmuch by the payments position of the United Kingdom. South Africa actually withdrew from the dollar pool in 1948, convinced that it could do better by financing its dollar requirements with exports of its large gold production. It agreed, however, to sell gold to the Bank of England in amounts sufficient to cover its net payments through London to creditors outside the sterling area.

Intermittent dollar payments difficulties of the area as a whole, sometimes chargeable to the United Kingdom, sometimes to the overseas sterling area, have made necessary, as we have noted, the intensification of discriminatory restrictions on dollar imports. At times, an adverse balance of payments has even developed between different parts of the sterling area, requiring the introduction, as in 1952, of restrictions on intra-sterling area trade. The latter type of disequilibrium, in particular, and to some degree the former as well, has been due to the divergent monetary policies of members. Being independent countries with their own national goals and their own central banks, there has not been the coordination of policy that is essential to the preservation of equilibrium within a unified monetary area.

Administration of the reserve pool, too, has often been made difficult by lack of the knowledge necessary to estimate dollar needs and availabilities, and thus to make suitable allocations. Some countries have been dissatisfied with the rate at which the United Kingdom has been willing and able, in view of the conflicting claims on her resources, to liquidate the blocked wartime balances. And finally, there has been discontent with the degree of policy control exercised in London.

A partially successful attempt to deal with these problems took the form of improved organisation and of more frequent and regular consultation. In 1947, the sterling area Statistical Committee was set up. It consists of staff officials from the more important member governments. The Committee prepares statistical information relevant to the decisions that have to be made, and meets in London at frequent short intervals. Another coordinating body is the Commonwealth Liaison Committee, which studies member governments' needs in relation to available resources and formulates suggestions as to policy. Finally, meetings of the Commonwealth Finance Ministers, hitherto only occasional, after 1952 became regular annual affairs at which all matters relating to the working of the sterling area are discussed and joint decisions taken.

THE EUROPEAN PAYMENTS UNION

The Need for Multilateral Clearing

During the years immediately after the war, damage to Europe's productive equipment, together with its deterioration due to a long period of inadequate maintenance, had so reduced output that there was a great shortage of goods, whether for domestic consumption or for export. There was no common international monetary system, nor even an organised system of payments. To obtain badly needed imports, each country entered into a series of bilateral trading agreements, under which the trading partners undertook to supply each other with defined amounts of specified lists of goods. Since currencies were inconvertible, no country could afford to accumulate large holdings of other currencies, which meant that under each bilateral arrangement, trade had to be balanced or nearly balanced, at a level determined by the export capacity of the weakest partner. Besides the tendency toward a bilateral balancing of trade at a low level, Europe's postwar trading arrangements meant that some countries, able to provide relatively ample supplies of commodities in most urgent need, could obtain other essential commodities in adequate amounts, while other nations, less able to furnish articles in strong demand, had to struggle along on short rations of vital goods.

A multilateral system of payments would have done away with these undesirable effects of bilateral trade, and facilitated as well the removal of the innumerable quantitative restrictions imposed to safeguard balances of payments. For when a country can use the proceeds from its exports to buy the imports it needs wherever it can obtain them cheapest, it is under no compulsion to hold its exports down to some arbitrary limit. As, therefore, its exports expand, it can afford to spend an increasing part of its receipts even on luxuries, thus furnishing countries which produce such commodities (wines, perfumes, subtropical fruits) with the means of acquiring—perhaps in a third market—basic industrial supplies needed by their economies, such as machinery, coal, and petroleum.

Establishment of the European Payments Union

To restore a multilateral payments system within Europe, the nations adhering to the OEEC established successively, between 1948 and 1950, two intra-European payments schemes. Though partially successful, they contained serious flaws; moreover, the continuance of inflationary conditions and of inadequate levels of output impeded their operation. By the summer of 1950, rising production and success in curbing inflation provided the conditions needed for a more thoroughgoing attack on Europe's trade problem. Following months of discussion, the members of the OEEC agreed to a Code of Liberalisation and to the establishment of a European Payments Union. The former committed them to eliminate, by stages, the quantitative restrictions on intra-European trade and services; the latter provided the machinery for a European-wide clearing of international payments.

Quotas and Drawing Rights

To make possible the automatic clearing of member's deficits and surpluses with one another, the EPU set up a system of drawing-rights. Each member was allotted a *quota* based on its relative importance as a participant in intra-European trade. It undertook to extend credit to the Union, up to 20 per cent of its quota, whenever it had a balance of payments surplus against other members. Should its surplus exceed this proportion of its quota, half the excess was to be settled by a further extension of credit to the Union, half by the payment of gold and dollars, up to a total amount equal to the member's quota. On the other hand, the Union undertook to extend credit to each member with a deficit, in the form of an overdraft facility, in an amount equal to 20 per cent of the member's quota. Larger deficits were to be settled partly in gold and dollars, partly by a further overdraft, with the proportion of hard currency settlement gradually increasing until 100 per cent of the quota was reached, above which all payments were to be in gold or dollars.

Through these arrangements, members obtained in the form of automatic overdraft facilities, a supplement to their inadequate gold and dollar reserves.[9] This serves the purpose of making possible the liberalisation of

---

[9] It should be noted that the overdraft facilities provided to the EPU by members correspond to the subscriptions made by members to the IMF, while the overdraft rights compare with the purchase rights of the Fund.

intra-European trade without imposing an intolerable loss of hard currency reserves on the weaker members.

For purposes of reckoning the value of transactions with the Union, each member's currency was expressed, at a rate of exchange reached by mutual agreement, in units of account having a value equal to the U.S. dollar. All the accounts of the EPU are kept in these units.

Settlement of Balances

Settlements of members' accounts with the Union occur each month. When the cumulative deficit or surplus of each one is computed, any available overdraft is granted or taken, and the necessary gold or dollar payment is made. Since a country with a continuing deficit is permitted overdrafts and must make payments on a scale determined by its *cumulative* rather than merely its *current* deficit for a given month, its payments gradually increase in amount. This means that such a member not only receives help in *meeting* its deficit, but is also under steadily increasing pressure to *correct* it. The EPU mechanism thus contains a built-in element of adjustment.

Miscellaneous Features

The management of the EPU is in the hands of a board of experts appointed by the Council of the OEEC. It supervises the operation of the Union; continually reviews economic developments in member countries, including their financial and economic policies; and makes recommendations to members for actions it regards as necessary to avoid "undesirable consequences." The actual clearing operations are carried out by the Bank for International Settlements[10] as the agent of the European Payments Union. The Union, originally established for two years, has had its life extended by annual renewals since 1952. To provide it with needed working capital, it received an initial "kitty" of $350 million from the Economic Cooperation Administration.

Toward Convertibility

During 1950-52, the Korean war and the subsequent drive for rearmament by the Western nations introduced price disturbances and imposed additional balance of payments burdens on many members of the EPU. Some ran deficits with the Union in excess of their quota limit, while others, more

---

[10] This bank was originally established in Basle to receive and transfer German reparation payments to the creditor countries. After the collapse of these payments in 1931, the B.I.S. continued in operation on a greatly reduced scale.

fortunate, accumulated large surpluses. Rather than require full payment of these large sums in gold and dollars, the Union arranged special credits. Thus, Western Germany, with a heavy deficit in 1951-2, received a supplementary credit of $120 million, while France, in 1952, obtained a $100 million credit. Belgium-Luxembourg, which had a surplus of $458 million in excess of its quota, extended a credit to the Union of $223 million.

In 1953-4, despite a generally improved balance of payments situation and the accumulation by members of more adequate reserves, some countries (notably the United Kingdom, France, Turkey, Greece, and Norway) had maintained a deficit position continuously for three to four years, while others (Western Germany, Belgium, the Netherlands, and Switzerland) had run a continuous surplus. Supposedly short-term credits were unintentionally becoming long-term credits. To remedy this situation, in June, 1954, a large proportion of these outstanding debts and credits were *funded,* or converted into long-term debt, with repayment to be made over a term of years.

This difficulty out of the way, the improved turn of events made possible a step toward convertibility. From mid-1954, it was agreed that all deficits and surpluses would be settled on the uniform basis of 50 per cent credit and 50 per cent gold and dollars. A year later, the hard currency share of settlements was increased to 75 per cent. Balance of payments transactions between members thus began to approximate those ruling under conditions of convertibility. (This development had the incidental effect of reducing the incentive to discriminate against dollar imports, which had to be paid for fully in gold or dollars).

Trade Liberalisation

The first stage of the Code of Liberalisation (1950) called for the removal of quantitative restrictions on intra-European trade up to 60 per cent of private as contrasted with government-administered trade, with exceptions for some countries. By 1955, liberalisation of 75 per cent had been requested by the OEEC; achievement was even better, at an average of 85 per cent of a larger absolute and relative volume of trade, since the area of state-trading had substantially diminished. Considerable progress was also made in the reduction of discriminatory restrictions on imports from the dollar area.

Supplementing the efforts of the OEEC, the EPU simultaneously helped bring about a relaxation of foreign exchange controls. "In sum," to quote from the Fifth Annual Report of the European Payments Union (p. 70), "it is fair to say that the E.P.U. with its successive adjustments has contributed to the fundamental progress made during the last five years, particularly by enabling Member countries to break away from bilateralism, to promote the liberalisation of transactions of all types between each other and to move gradually closer to full multilateral trade and the general convertibility of currencies."

The European Monetary Agreement

Looking toward the day when the EPU may cease to exist, and when convertibility for at least its stronger members may become a fact, plans were laid in 1955 to preserve some features of the Union which might continue to be of benefit under these new conditions. These are embodied in the European Monetary Agreement, to which all OEEC countries subscribed in August 1955, and which will come into effect upon the demise of the European Payments Union.

Two provisions are of primary interest. (1) The Agreement establishes a European Fund of $600 million, made up of the capital in the hands of the EPU when it terminates, plus gold contributions of the OEEC countries. Credits are to be granted from this Fund to members to help them overcome temporary balance of payments difficulties that might otherwise undermine the liberalisation of trade. These credits are not to be available automatically, as has been true of the EPU drawing rights, but are to be granted only upon application and a showing of need. Moreover, each such grant of credit will carry the obligation of the borrower to comply with recommendations made with respect to its financial and economic policies by the European Fund's Board of Management. (2) The Agreement sets up a multilateral system of payments which obliges members to fix limits to their exchange rates in terms of gold and dollars, and to exchange their currencies freely with one another at rates not exceeding these limits. It is expected that most OEEC members will use the regular foreign exchange markets for payments, but this provision assures any member holding the currency of another that it can exchange that currency for gold or dollars at a fixed rate.

SELECTED REFERENCES

Bell, Philip W., *The Sterling Area in the Postwar World* (Oxford University Press, 1956). A careful study of the sterling area mechanism, of the strength of sterling area ties, and of prospects for the future.

Conan, A. R., *The Sterling Area* (Macmillan, London, 1952). A relatively brief and lucid analysis of the operation of the Sterling Area and of the changing relations of its members.

Economic Cooperation Administration, *The Sterling Area, An American Analysis* (London and Washington, D. C., 1951). Chapter 1 provides an excellent analysis of the economic interdependence of the Commonwealth countries; Chapter 4 traces the changes in the mechanics of the sterling area system down to 1951. Other chapters give a large amount of detailed information on the resources and trade of the sterling area, with exceptionally fine diagrammatic illustrations.

Gardner, Richard N., *Sterling-Dollar Diplomacy* (Oxford University Press, 1956). An illuminating study of Anglo-American collaboration in the attempt to reconstruct multilateral trade after the war.

Mikesell, Raymond F., *Foreign Exchange in the Postwar World* (Twentieth Century Fund, New York, 1954). Chapters 10 and 11 contain a good account of the practices and policies of the United Kingdom down to 1953. Part IV surveys international currency problems in their postwar setting.

Organisation for European Economic Cooperation, *Annual Reports of the Managing Board* (Paris). These reports review developments in trade and production since the war.

———, *The Liberalisation of Trade* (Paris, 1955). An account of this aspect of the OEEC's work.

Tew, Brian, *International Monetary Cooperation, 1945-1952* (Hutchinson's University Library, London, 1952). An excellent, brief discussion of the machinery and operation of the IMF, the sterling area, and the EPU.

Williams, John H., *Postwar Monetary Plans and Other Essays*, 3rd edition (Knopf, New York, 1947). Chapters 2 through 8 present Professor Williams' views on postwar monetary stabilisation, with particular attention to the discussions leading up to the establishment of the IMF and the World Bank.

25

GATT AND U.S. TARIFF POLICY

For nations as highly specialised and oriented toward foreign trade as those of western Europe, such makeshift arrangements as the bilateral agreements that sprang up after 1945 were thoroughly inadequate. Even the formation of regional unions, such as the sterling area and the European Payments Union, within which the convertibility of currencies permits much greater freedom of trade and payments, is but a halfway house to the worldwide exchange of goods such economies need so badly.

Proposal for An International Trade Organisation

In view of the success that attended the discussions leading up to the Bretton Woods Conference, which eventuated in the deliberate organisation of international monetary and financial relations through the establishment of the International Monetary Fund and the World Bank, the question naturally arose: if international cooperation can work here, why not in the field of international trade itself?

Officials of the allied governments exchanged views on this topic over a prolonged period. Finally, toward the end of 1945, when the Anglo-American Financial Agreement was concluded, the U.S. State Department followed up these discussions by publishing a thin brochure entitled "Proposals for Expansion of World Trade and Employment." [1] These proposals covered a wide range of topics in the realms of commercial policy: tariffs, preferences, quotas and licensing systems, invisible protection, subsidies, commodity agreements, restrictive business practices, the maintenance of full employment, and the establishment of an International Trade Organisation to administer any agreements that might be reached. In a joint statement, the executive branch of the U.S. government and the government of the United Kingdom fully endorsed these proposals.

The next step was to get action. Copies of the proposals were sent to all members of the United Nations, and at the first meeting of its Economic and Social Council, they were made the agenda of a committee that was to

[1] Department of State Publication 2411, Commercial Policy Series 79 (Government Printing Office, Washington, D. C., 1945).

formulate plans for a Conference on Trade and Employment. This Conference first met in London in the autumn of 1946; discussions were resumed in Geneva the next year, and concluded at Havana in the winter of 1947-48. Some 53 nations there signed the resulting Charter for an International Trade Organisation (ITO), which would go into effect upon its ratification by a prescribed number of nations.

The ITO never became translated from provisions on paper into a functioning organisation. Probably the main reason for the failure to obtain its ratification by Congress was that it tried to solve too many problems. Instead of concentrating on means of dealing with tariffs, quotas, and subsidies, and thus complementing the IMF's attempt to eliminate exchange controls, the ITO Charter included provisions to compromise national action concerned with full employment, to harmonise opposing views with regard to international cartels, and to reconcile producer and consumer interests while stabilising the prices of primary products. To generate public support for such a complex and highly technical document, which involved answering the arguments of the opposition it inevitably aroused, proved impossible. It was never ratified by the U.S. Congress, and since the ITO would have been meaningless without our adherence, it never obtained the necessary support from other countries.

THE GENERAL AGREEMENT ON TARIFFS AND TRADE

Origins

When the State Department sent out its original "proposals," it simultaneously issued an invitation to fifteen countries, under the provisions of the Trade Agreements Act, to participate in negotiations to reduce tariffs and other barriers to trade. These countries, later joined by eight others, began discussions in Geneva concurrently with those on the ITO. Participation promised to be fruitful, for although the United States had before the war exhausted most of its authority to reduce duties by 50 per cent from the Smoot-Hawley level, when the Trade Agreements Act was renewed in 1945, the administration received the further power to reduce duties by 50 per cent from the level then ruling.

Bargaining at Geneva proceeded on a product-by-product basis between pairs of countries. Each pair confined its attention, as has been usual under our trade agreements procedure, to products of which each party was the other's principal supplier. The concessions agreed on such products were then generalised, that is, extended to all members of the negotiating group. Altogether, there were 123 sets of negotiations covering approximately 50,000 items. The results were incorporated in a single General Agreement on Tariffs and Trade (GATT), signed on October 30, 1947.

Provisions of Gatt

GATT is a curious hybrid. It is fundamentally a trade agreement among 35 nations (since 1955), but it is also a loose sort of international organisation. When the "contracting parties" signed the agreement on duty concessions, they also adopted as a set of general rules that part of the ITO Charter dealing with commercial policy. One of these provides for non-discriminatory or most-favored nation treatment, which means that concessions granted, for example, by the United States to France in our agreement with that country are generalised, or made applicable to all the other contracting parties. Another basic rule outlaws the use of quantitative restrictions. Other subordinate rules provide for the free movement of goods in transit, for equality of internal taxation of imported and domestic goods, for curbing excessive customs red tape, and for subjecting export subsidies to periodic scrutiny.

Because the nations participating in GATT include both advanced and relatively undeveloped regions, countries with serious balance of payments problems and others to which such problems are of little concern, and still others with agricultural price-support programs, reconciliation of these divergent interests required the introduction of many qualifications to the basic rules. Thus underdeveloped countries can use protection rather freely in order to develop infant industries. Also, import restrictions are permitted to safeguard a country's balance of payments. And nations confronted by agricultural surpluses can, within limits, use import restrictions to buttress price-support programs.

In spite of these qualifications, which would appear to sabotage GATT's avowed goal of eliminating quantitative restraints on trade, the organisation has functioned surprisingly well. It has provided a forum for bringing pressure upon members for better international behavior, for the airing of grievances, and for the settlement of disputes. Its positive accomplishments have been realised even though GATT has no full-time governing body nor any secretariat of its own. It has had to rely upon annual meetings of the contracting parties and upon the exertions of an ad hoc committee between these meetings. Without a budget or a permanent staff, it has operated with a small secretariat borrowed from the United Nations.

Settlement of Disputes

Greatest success has been achieved in the settlement of disputes. In the early years of GATT, if one member felt that another had violated the rules, withdrawn a valuable concession, or otherwise acted in a manner conflicting with the agreement, it brought its complaint to the annual meeting. The disputants were urged to attempt to settle their differences bilaterally. If this failed, the contracting parties formed a working committee, which after studying the matter would make a recommendation or a ruling. If then the offending member refused to change its ways, the aggrieved party could retaliate by withdrawing some concession. More often than not, offending members could and did comply with a recommendation by some change in administrative procedure. Thus Chile, which exports a large volume of natural nitrate, complained that an Australian subsidy on the production of a competing artificial fertilizer was nullifying a Chilean tariff concession to Australia. Upon the recommendation of GATT members that Australia modify its subsidy arrangements, it complied.

Although many such instances could be cited, there were many failures, too. One of the most conspicuous of these was the continuing refusal of the United States to modify its import restrictions on dairy products. It was agreed that these impaired concessions granted to certain members by the United States, and the Netherlands was authorized to impose a compensating restriction on imports of wheat flour from that country.

Yet GATT had proved so useful in bringing issues to a head and in settling a reasonable proportion of them that, in 1953, the contracting parties set up a panel to act as an informal court to handle disputes. This panel listens to the disputants, formulates and considers the issues, and drafts a report—all the while consulting with the disputing parties. With this change in procedure, the number of complaints brought before GATT and successfully resolved has increased markedly.

Moderation of Quantitative Restrictions

In dealing with quantitative restrictions to protect a country's reserves, GATT's record is less impressive. The exception to the rule against quantitative restrictions merely obliges a nation to relax restrictions as its position improves, to avoid unnecessary damage to others, and to consult with members on request.

GATT's principal power is the weak one of requiring consultation, although it may permit injured members to impose specified countermeasures. The organisation must rely mainly on persuasion and education. Any nation intent on doing so could ignore any suggestions made. Yet the fact that the use of quantitative restrictions is under continuous review, and that these practices are subject to constant pressure, has given strong support to their opponents within countries following these practices. The mere fact that offending governments must justify their action before a broad forum has made them more sensitive to their behavior. As one participant in its work has said,

In sum, the GATT has neither surrendered the field nor carried the day in mitigating the use of quantitative restrictions. Fortuitously, it has succeeded in surviving the post-war period of general balance-of-payments difficulties without surrendering the principle that such restrictions were to be allowed only as exceptions to a general rule and that the rule itself should be applied as soon as circumstances permitted.[2]

Agricultural Provisions

Under the agricultural exception, a country may impose quotas on imports of agricultural or fishery products provided equally restrictive production or marketing controls are applied to like domestic products. This makes it possible for countries like the United States to maintain price-support programs, which would be impossible if imports were not restrained. So long as both imports and domestic production are subject to controls of similar severity, foreign sellers can expect to retain their normal share of the market, whereas without restriction of output, increasing domestic supplies would create unmanageable surpluses and crowd foreigners out of the home market altogether.

The United States has been the principal offender against this rule. This is because changes in our agricultural legislation greatly extended the range of agricultural programs to which import restrictions became applicable without at the same time including production controls in their provisions. Although our government has removed import restrictions on some commodities (notably oats, barley, and nuts), those on dairy products continue to be a chronic source of friction.

Unless we bring our agricultural policy into line with GATT's rules by introducing production controls wherever import quotas are applied, the only alternative solution of the dilemma would be to relax the GATT provision so as to permit the general use of such quotas without accompanying production controls. This solution, however, would aggravate our domestic farm problem. For the United States exports about an eighth of the value of its agricultural production; for a number of important

---

[2] Raymond Vernon, *America's Foreign Trade Policy and the GATT, Essays in International Finance,* No. 21. (Princeton University, October, 1954).

crops, the proportion is much higher.[3] Were import quotas to be used with comparative freedom by other countries, the consequent loss of overseas markets would cause land now devoted to raising export crops to be shifted to products sold on the domestic market, thus intensifying the problem of oversupply there.

Tariff Negotiations

GATT has achieved its most concrete results in the five tariff-negotiating sessions it has conducted.[4] By including 30-odd nations in each set of negotiations since the first, it has provided, in the potential range of concessions realisable, a stimulus to initiate bilateral negotiations. Although it is impossible to measure the gain to members from the concessions made, the range of trade covered has been large, close to two-thirds of world commerce, and more than 60,000 tariff rates have been involved.

Some idea of the degree of tariff change achieved may be derived from considering the effects of the trade agreements on the American tariff. Since our tariff has been reduced only on the condition that others make equivalent concessions, probably the tariffs of at least other major nations have been affected in roughly the same proportion.

Before the United States inaugurated its Trade Agreements program in 1934, the average duty on dutiable imports was 46.7 per cent. The decline in the average duty since that time has been the result of two principal forces: (1) the effect of rising prices on specific duties; and (2) tariff concessions. Changes in the composition of imports have had a minor effect.

The larger part of U.S. duties are specific rather than ad valorem— that is, the duties are expressed as so many cents per pound or per unit rather than as a percentage rate. Thus in the 1930 tariff, the rate on garlic was 1.5¢ a lb. Converted into an ad valorem figure, it amounted to 40 per cent. By 1950, the price of garlic had risen to the point where the 1.5¢ duty amounted to only 22 per cent.

As of 1947, the *rise in prices* since 1934 had alone reduced the average rate of duty from 46.7 per cent to 28.3 per cent. By the end of 1948, the trade agreements negotiated before the war plus those consummated at

---

[3] Thus, in 1952, the shares of domestic production exported were: rice, 59 per cent; wheat, 43 per cent; dried whole milk, 42 per cent; cotton, 30 per cent; grain sorghums, 30 per cent; lard, 24 per cent; tobacco, 22 per cent. Committee on Foreign Economic Policy, *Staff Papers*, p. 154.

[4] At Geneva in 1947; at Annecy in 1949; at Torquay in 1950-51; and in Geneva again in 1955 and 1956.

Geneva in 1947, further reduced the average rate to 15 per cent. *Tariff concessions* therefore caused a lowering of our effective tariff rates in this interval by 47 per cent. In the next five years (up to the end of 1952), price increases had further lowered pre-agreement duty rates from 28.3 to 24.4 per cent. The additional but more limited agreements concluded at Annecy and Torquay brought the average rate of duty at that date down to 12.2 per cent. Thus a net reduction of U.S. duties of 50 per cent had been achieved by tariff concessions alone.[5]

Additional benefits have accrued to members of GATT from the stability of the rates established through negotiations, without which the concessions would be relatively meaningless. These concessions were bound by agreement for definite periods which have from time to time been extended. The last extension was from June 1955 to January 1958.

Proposal for An Office for Trade Cooperation

At the ninth session of GATT, held in the winter of 1954-55, the contracting parties reviewed the provisions of the Agreement. Several important decisions were taken. Members agreed to continue the basic rules with only minor alterations, they concluded that GATT's organisation should be improved, and they admitted Japan to membership. To strengthen GATT, it was proposed that an Organisation for Trade Cooperation (OTC) be created.

What this would amount to is the substitution of a formal organisation, with a continuously functioning executive committee with its own permanent staff, for the improvised and informal arrangements under which the "contracting parties" have operated in the past. The OTC would have no powers not already possessed by GATT. It would merely administer those it already has. It would sponsor tariff negotiations, settle disputes, and carry out studies essential to its work.

Establishment of OTC as the administrative arm of GATT would, however, considerably increase the efficiency and importance of that organisation. Ratification of the new agency is necessary before it can start to work, and the act of ratification would give to GATT a stamp of approval and hence a degree of permanence that protectionists and other opponents of international cooperation do not wish to accord it. It was opposition of this type that prevented action by the U.S. Congress in 1956 and that threatens to sabotage ratification in 1958.

[5] Data from Don D. Humphrey, *American Imports* (Twentieth Century Fund, New York, 1955), p. 129.

The Future of Gatt

GATT represents an attempt, on the whole successful, to introduce some degree of order and reason into the trade practices of the nations of the free world. Its future effectiveness rests, in considerable part, upon the direction in which United States trade policy and practice moves. Failure to ratify the OTC Agreement is likely to be taken as representing a victory of the forces of protectionism and isolation and a rejection of the path leading toward freer multilateral trade and a better-integrated world. Even if this Agreement were ratified, unwillingness to continue to reduce duties through negotiation, especially if combined with more frequent invocation of the escape clause in our existing agreements, would certainly be subject to the same interpretation. Let us therefore examine and evaluate the attitudes that have been current in the United States in recent years.

U.S. participation in GATT has been based on the fact that it is an agreement, negotiated by the President under authority conveyed by the Trade Agreements Act. Nonetheless it has been criticised, especially by those anxious to curb the powers of the President, on the grounds that Congress may not delegate its legislative power, that negotiation of multilateral agreements exceeds the authority granted under the Trade Agreements Act, and that the President has unconstitutionally "redelegated" his authority to GATT.[6]

Although, under our Constitution, Congress may not delegate its legislative power, the Supreme Court has held that Congress is not engaging in such delegation of powers if it enacts laws which lay down a policy embodying an intelligible principle, leaving it to the executive to use its discretion in administering the law. As for multilateral as contrasted with bilateral agreements, the Trade Agreements Act contains no limitation that would exclude the negotiation of multilateral agreements, but merely authorises the President "to enter into foreign trade agreements with foreign governments or instrumentalities thereof." The principal answer to the charge that the President has redelegated his authority to GATT rests on his exclusive power to conduct foreign relations.

All in all, the legal case for attacking our participation in GATT is weak. Although in part it reflects the attitude of those elements in our government opposed to a strong presidency, it is also in part a smokescreen for protectionist opposition. For the main issue that divided both Congress and the public on such matters as the Trade Agreements program and its

[6] For a fuller discussion of these legal issues, see: *G.A.T.T.: an Analysis and Appraisal of the GATT* (U.S. Council of the International Chamber of Commerce, February, 1955), pp. 73-9.

multilateral version in GATT is the old tariff issue—the question as to whether the United States should pursue a liberal trade policy or should invoke protection whenever American industry is threatened by the competition of imports.

THE TARIFF ISSUE AS AN ELEMENT IN U.S. FOREIGN POLICY

The tariff issue, or more specifically, the issue between a liberal or low tariff policy and one which provides substantial protection, cannot be considered alone, but only as part of our entire foreign economic policy. There is general agreement that this should promote the prosperity and security of the United States. It is also generally agreed that our position will be improved by a strengthening of the economies of the free world. Therefore, because of the predominant position of the United States in that world, it is imperative that we consider the effects of our economic policies upon our friends and allies, for if they are injured, so are we.

Is the U.S. Tariff Low?

It is contended by some that as a result of the duty reductions made under the Trade Agreements Act, our tariff is now one of the lowest in the world. Superficially, the figures seem to support this view. We have seen that, by the end of 1952, the average rate of duty on dutiable U.S. imports was only slightly above 12 per cent. Since that time, the relatively limited negotiations that have occurred at Geneva have reduced this average a little further, perhaps to about 10 per cent.

The trouble is that averages are misleading. First, an average duty is simply the arithmetic result of a computation applied to a mixture of duties, some of which are high, some low. It gives no idea of the proportion which are high, or how restrictive of imports these are. In particular, it gives no weight whatever to duties that are so high as to exclude *all* imports. Second, even duties that are low percentagewise may still be definitely and effectively protective. To judge the restrictiveness of a tariff, it is necessary to estimate the extent to which goods would enter the country *if* the tariff did not exist.

A careful estimate of this sort has been made, covering 80 per cent of all dutiable imports entering the United States in 1951.[7] On the assumption of

---

[7] *Staff Papers Presented to the Committee on Foreign Economic Policy*, February 1954 (Washington, D. C.), pp. 293-301. The figures cited in the following paragraphs are taken from this source. See also Howard S. Piquet, *Aid, Trade and the Tariff*. (Thomas Y. Crowell Co., New York, 1953).

total suspension of our tariff (but not our quotas) for a period of five years, it was calculated that imports would increase by a minimum of approximately $800 million to a maximum of $1.8 billion. This would represent an expansion of 18 to 38 per cent of our dutiable imports, which in 1951 were $4.8 billion out of a total of $10.8 billion. (The remaining $6 billion of imports, principally raw materials and foodstuffs not produced in this country, are free of duty.)

The effects of tariff suspension would by no means be uniform. Some 40 per cent of dutiable imports would be but little affected, mainly because they are non-competitive with U.S. products. Of the remainder (aggregating something over $2 billion), a small proportion—about $53 million of 1951 imports—would increase from 100 to 300 per cent or more. Duties in this category are relatively high and significantly protective. The group includes such products as earthenware and chinaware, hand-blown glassware, leather gloves and handbags, fur-felt hats, clay tile, clocks, canned tuna fish, scissors and shears, pocket knives, and a limited range of textile products. A more moderate percentage increase in imports—from 50 to 100 per cent—but a much larger aggregate increase, would occur for products subject on the whole to less drastic protection (over $800 million of 1951 imports, including wool, woolens and worsteds, fish fillets, sewing machines, optical instruments, and bicycles). The remaining dutiable imports, estimated to increase less than 50 per cent, comprised almost $1.3 billion in all, and included such important products as watches, whiskey, cotton cloth, cattle and beef, aluminum, and structural steel. Duties in this category are predominantly in the range of 10 to 25 per cent.

It should be stressed that these estimates are based on the assumption of a temporary, five-year suspension of our tariff. The effects of its permanent removal would, of course, be more drastic, since foreign suppliers of the American market would then expand their capacity, advertise in this market, and establish branches and service facilities in the United States. An unofficial estimate by the U.S. Treasury Department of the effects of *permanent* removal of the U.S. tariff *and* quotas places the increase in imports at $2.5 billion in the first three to five years and at $3.5 billion over a ten-year period.

A temporary suspension of the tariff would make little sense as a policy move.[8] But the impact on U.S. producers and workers of total tariff removal would be heaviest in the short run. Over a longer period, there would be more opportunity to adjust to the gradually diminishing effects of a definite and enduring free trade policy. Therefore, if we consider the estimated

[8] This particular assumption was necessary to limit the range of considerations to be taken into account in arriving at an estimate of effects.

injury from a five-year suspension, we shall take into account the most important and severest part thereof.

Injury from Tariff Suspension

There can be no doubt that removal of U.S. duties would injure a considerable number of people. A change in any important government policy usually hurts someone. When the Federal Reserve authorities restrict credit to check inflation, borrowers generally are injured, and when taxes are increased to finance heavy defense expenditures, taxpayers are injured.

A responsible government will not hesitate to incur the cost if this is necessary to realize a substantially greater benefit. As with countering inflation or supporting an adequate national defense, the fundamental questions arising out of a change in tariff policy are, on the one hand, how many individuals are injured by the change, and how badly, and on the other hand, to what extent is the nation as a whole benefited?

Our immediate concern is the degree of injury. We shall return to the matter of benefit later.

Even the total suspension of all import duties would affect only a small proportion of the American market, while the area within which domestic production would actually be displaced would be even smaller. Total dutiable imports in 1951 [9] were less than 1.5 per cent of GNP and only about 3 per cent of total private expenditures on movable goods. Moreover, almost two-thirds of dutiable imports are not highly competitive with domestic production; the "area of maximum import competition" would be limited to the remaining third of such imports (some $1.6 billion in all). It is these alone that would tend seriously to displace U.S. production. The great bulk of our industry, agriculture, and mining would be relatively unaffected by tariff suspension.

Another measure of the extent of possible injury runs in terms of the number of workers potentially affected by expanded imports. Assuming the maximum increase in imports within five years of tariff suspension of $1.8 billion, it is estimated that only 150,000 workers would be directly affected in the "area of maximum import competition." Another 105,000, engaged in supplying or servicing that area, would be involved, for a total of 255,000. (Total employment in the United States in 1951 was 61 million.)

Suppose imports were to increase by the nearly $2 billion after tariff suspension. This does not mean that American production to that value would

---

[9] Although the absolute amount of dutiable imports increased in later years, the proportion thereof to GNP and its components varied but little. Conclusions based on later data would probably be but little altered.

cease, nor that the 255,000 workers directly and indirectly affected would lose their jobs. How seriously production and employment in this sector (and to a far less degree, in the much less competitive sectors of U.S. industry) would be influenced would depend upon a member of considerations, among the most important of which are the elasticity of demand for a particular product and whether its market is expanding or contracting.

Where demand is elastic, a substantial increase in imports could be absorbed with relatively little decline in price. If the American producer could introduce new economies and intensify his sales efforts to meet the additional competition and the lowered price, he might retain or increase his relative, as well as his absolute, share of sales. Where demand is inelastic, a small rise in imports could seriously depress price, confronting the American producer with a difficult problem of adjustment.

Where an industry's market was expanding, the effect of additional imports would be minimised, whereas it would be aggravated where the trend of demand was downward. The fur-felt hat industry is a good illustration of the latter; increasing numbers of people have been going hatless. Watch sales, on the contrary, have been expanding.[10]

The facts indicate that not even the complete abolition of the U.S. tariff would cause serious injury to more than a small segment of American industry. Moreover, the data on the volume of production and the numbers of workers affected make no allowance for such adjustments to increased competition as the improvement of methods, elimination of lines of production made unprofitable by import competition and concentration on lines relatively unaffected, and diversification of production or a shift to distinct but related products.[11]

And finally, there is much that could and should be done to facilitate and make easier adjustment to increased imports. Thus the companies affected could be helped by accelerated depreciation on investment in plant and equipment to diversify their production, by loans from the Small Business Administration for this purpose, and by technical assistance in conversion. Workers released from employment because of import com-

[10] "Even though the domestic industry has protested vigorously against imports there is no evidence that increased imports have brought about an absolute curtailment of domestic production. Even though the domestic producers of watches do not supply as large a share of the domestic market as they did previously, the fact remains that so many more watches are now sold than were sold in the last two decades that both importers and domestic producers enjoy a larger market than ever before." *Staff Papers, op. cit.*, pp. 309-10.

[11] As from watch movements to cases, wrist bands, and jewelry. This shift had begun to take place before President Eisenhower raised the duty on watches under the provisions of the Defense Act.

petition could be helped by extended unemployment insurance, by special allowances for retraining and for moving, and by accelerated retirement pay for older workers.[12]

Present U.S. Policy Is Basically Protective

Granted that some industries, some workers, and some communities would be injured by removal of our tariff, or even—to a far lesser degree—by a selective reduction of duties—the real question is whether the over-all benefit to the country of a more liberal tariff policy would justify this cost, or the alternative cost of minimising this injury. Our present policy, embodied in the "peril point clause" and the "escape clause" of the Reciprocal Trade Agreements Act, is in the opposite direction. It seeks to avoid injury to each and every producer. Under the "peril point" provision, no duty may be reduced if such reduction would threaten serious injury to any domestic industry, while the "escape" clause permits the restoration of a duty if its reduction has caused such injury.

Although the escape clause has been used sparingly, applications for relief under its provisions have been rather numerous, and increasing in frequency.[13] Its very existence, coupled with its occasional use, is a source of apprehension to exporters to the United States, who feel that were they to invest money and effort in developing the American market, their success would surely cause the escape clause to be invoked.

Means to and Benefits from a Liberal Trade Policy

Clearly the first step toward a more liberal tariff policy would be the repeal of the peril point and the modification of the escape provisions. Repeal of the peril point clause is essential, for as long as it stands, no really significant liberalisation of our tariff is possible. As for the escape clause, it should be either repealed, or limited to serve a real emergency purpose, perhaps by confining it to cases where a change in a duty causes excessively rapid adjustment, with compensatory rate increases made for a temporary period only.[14]

[12] For an excellent discussion of the various possibilities of easing adjustment, including assistance to communities heavily dependent on industries injured by imports, see *Staff Papers, op. cit.*, pp. 384-426.

[13] As of early 1957, 77 applications for relief had been filed under the escape clause. The Tariff Commission, which determines whether injury has occurred, has recommended relief in 20 cases and been evenly divided in 5. The President, who takes all factors into account in reaching a final decision, invoked the escape clause in 7 of these. Three of these decisions in favor of escape action were taken by President Truman, 4 by President Eisenhower.

[14] These suggestions of modifying the escape clause have been made by the U.S. Council of the International Chamber of Commerce.

Further action toward liberalising our trade policy would involve either relatively generous concessions in future negotiations under the GATT, or, better yet, a unilateral reduction of U.S. duties, especially of those that effectively restrict imports. Such action would help to realise two of our declared and consistently pursued foreign policy objectives: the restoration of as wide as possible a system of multilateral trade, and the strengthening of the economies of the free world.

Whether there is or is not a chronic tendency toward a "dollar shortage," many nations still maintain, principally for balance of payments reasons, quantitative restrictions on imports. Easier access to the American market would make possible their removal, which, indeed, might well be coupled with reduction of our tariff as a compensatory concession. Moreover, as American military expenditures abroad gradually decline, their replacement by increased sales in our domestic market would help to sustain foreign purchasing power over U.S. exports.

Most important of all, however, western Europe and Japan need an expanding volume of imports of raw materials and foodstuffs, which implies expanding markets for their exports. The United States, as the largest and most rapidly expanding market in the free world, can alone provide, on the scale needed, the growth and stability the export industries of these regions require. Politically and psychologically, too, adoption of a liberal tariff policy could be of the greatest importance, in that it would assure our allies and friends that our leadership was positive and constructive.

A liberal trade policy would by no means imply abolition of our tariff. This would be politically impossible. But a decision to move steadily in the direction of greater trade liberalisation by a gradual reduction of restrictive duties might be attainable.

It would require strong leadership, willing to stand up to the exaggerated outcries of concentrated and vocal protected interests. It would require a carefully thought-out program of easing the difficulties of adjustment for industries adversely affected by duty reductions. But a program along these lines would be a vital component of an American foreign policy geared to the needs of our times.

SELECTED REFERENCES

Brown, William Adams Jr., *The United States and the Restoration of World Trade* (Brookings Institution, Washington, 1950). A thorough analysis and appraisal of the ITO Charter and GATT.

Commission on Foreign Economic Policy, *Report to the President and the Congress,* January 1954 (Government Printing Office, Washington, D. C.). Report of the Randall Commission, which reflects a shift toward protectionism from the Bell (Public Advisory Board) report a year previous.

——, *Staff Papers* (Government Printing Office, Washington, D. C., 1954). A series of papers prepared by staff experts of the Randall Commission dealing with all aspects of the tariff question.

Diebold, William J., *The End of the ITO, Essays in International Finance,* No. 16, October 1952 (Princeton University Press). Analyzes the opposition to the ITO and the reasons for its failure, and raises the question of future American foreign trade policy.

G.A.T.T.: an Analysis and Appraisal of the General Agreement on Tariffs and Trade. Prepared by the William L. Clayton Center for International Economic Affairs of the Fletcher School of Law and Diplomacy for the U. S. Council of the International Chamber of Commerce (February 1955). An excellent statement of the pros and cons.

Hoffman, Michael L., "The Future of GATT," *Lloyd's Bank Review,* New Series No. 34, October 1954. A review of the problems confronting GATT.

Humphrey, Don D., *American Imports* (Twentieth Century Fund, New York, 1955). A thorough study of the American tariff, its restrictiveness, and the effects of and the problems raised by a further substantial lowering of duties.

International Trade, 1955, The Contracting Parties to the General Agreement on Tariffs and Trade (May, 1956). GATT's annual report (preceded by others); it provides an excellent critical survey of changes in the structure and pattern of world trade and in commercial policies, together with GATT's own activities.

Knorr, Klaus, and Patterson, Gardner, *A Critique of the Randall Commission Report* (International Finance Section and Center of International Studies, Princeton University, 1954). Record of a round table discussion of the report cited, in which both that report and U. S. foreign economic policies are vigorously criticised.

Kravis, Irving B., "The Trade Agreements Escape Clause," *American Economic Review,* **XLIV** (June, 1954). Criticises the function and use of the escape clause.

Lloyd, Lewis E., *Tariffs: The Case for Protection* (Devin-Adair, New York, 1955). A protectionist's views on the level of U.S. duties, GATT, and a desirable U.S. trade policy are presented in Chapters VIII, IX and XI.

Public Advisory Board for Mutual Security, *A Trade and Tariff Policy in the National Interest* (Government Printing Office, Washington, 1953). An excellent analysis of U.S. trade problems and policy, with recommendations for a simpler and more liberal tariff.

U. S. Tariff Commission, *Operation of the Trade Agreements Program* (Government Printing Office, Washington, D. C.). Annual reports since 1949; they cover all aspects of the topic, including actions of the U.S. Government, of GATT, and of individual countries having trade agreements with the United States.

Vernon, Raymond, *America's Foreign Trade Policy and the GATT, Essays in International Finance,* No. 21, October 1954 (International Finance Section, Princeton University). A useful, brief discussion of how GATT originated, how it works, and its future prospects.

——, "Organising for World Trade," *International Conciliation,* No. 505, November 1955 (Carnegie Endowment for International Peace, New York). Similar to the above, but somewhat fuller; includes a discussion of the OTC.

26

ECONOMIC DEVELOPMENT

Decade by decade, as the problems that confront the world and its governments alter with changing circumstances, the attention of economists is directed first to one area of study, then to another. Each such shift of interest, with the intensive work that goes with it, extends our knowledge, results in the refinement and consolidation of theoretical advance, and leads to practical measures of reform.

In the 1920's, following the violent price disturbances during and after the first World War, attention was focused upon the problem of price level stabilisation and the role of monetary policy therein. With the mass unemployment of the depressed years of the 1930's, when it became apparent that economic stability encompassed more than the stabilisation of prices, economists became concerned with variations in investment and savings as causes of cyclical fluctuations. In the hands of John Maynard Keynes, these forces became the crux of a new theory of employment. Fiscal policy assumed a dominating position among remedial measures.

Economic Development to the Fore

During the years immediately following World War II, Europe's balance of payments difficulties overshadowed all other problems. The impetus given to studies in this field led to great advance in our understanding of the forces underlying international equilibrium and disequilibrium, while the practical needs of the day brought into being the massive European Recovery Program. As the impact of this program restored levels of production and as Europe's payments difficulties gradually subsided, a new and urgent problem—the economic development of the world's underdeveloped areas—occupied the center of attention.

Within the short span of less than a decade, economic development already promises to outdo all problems of the preceding half century or more in its power to enlist the efforts of economists, statesmen, and philanthropists. The literature its discussion has called forth is immense, comprising hundreds of books, pamphlets, and articles, and even specialised journals devoted to the continuing analysis of developmental problems.

Students have flocked to the universities in increasing numbers seeking a "major" in the field of economic development. To meet their demands, specialised courses and seminars have been developed. Technical experts numbered in the thousands have been dispatched to Southeast Asia, Africa, the Middle East, and Latin America, to place their services at the disposal of the governments of underdeveloped nations. And loans, credits, and grants totalling billions of dollars have flowed to these regions to support the work of technicians and to carry out irrigation projects, install power plants, build roads, and establish new industries. There is every indication that the need for concentrated study, for the services of experts, and for an enlarged flow of funds will not soon abate. And in view of the urgency of the need, we hope that both the human and the financial requirements will be met.

Urgency of Economic Development

Economic development has become an urgent problem because it embodies the aspirations aroused by a social, economic, and political revolution in the underdeveloped areas of the world. These comprise the nations and colonial dependencies that, in the past century and a half, have not participated in the increase in productivity and rise in standards of living enjoyed by the more advanced countries, but instead, have suffered relative, and in some cases absolute, economic stagnation. Recent improvements in communication, such as air travel and the ubiquitous movies, worldwide news services, and the radio have spread a knowledge of the differences in their material standards and those of the West. Increasing literacy has reenforced the impact of these improved media of communication. Direct contact between the people of underdeveloped areas and the superlatively equipped armies of the advanced countries has further emphasized the contrast.

The result has been a ferment of discontent, a growing conviction of the possibility of change, and a determination to act to bring that change about. Along with this "revolution of rising expectations" has gone a revolution in the political status of these countries, as one by one they have achieved independence of their former colonial masters, and in the political status of the people themselves, as they have acquired the ballot and therewith attracted the solicitous attention of politicians.

Some idea of the differences in well-being that accompany different stages of development may be gleaned from Table 26.1. This lists, for four groups of countries ranged according to per capita income level, certain data pertaining to nutrition, health, literacy, and investment. Notice that

Table 26.1

MEASURES OF MATERIAL WELFARE, 1955

	NATIONAL PRODUCT PER HEAD (dollars)	CALORIC INTAKE PER PERSON PER DAY (numbers)	PROTEIN CONSUMPTION PER DAY (grams)	INFANT MORTALITY (number of deaths per 1000 live births)	LITERACY (per cent of population 10 years and over)	INHABITANTS PER PHYSICIAN (number)	PER CENT OF GROSS INVESTMENT OF GNP (1954)
I. Countries with per capita incomes above $750	1,288	3,078	90	33	98	953	18.8
II. Countries with per capita incomes between $750 and $300	470	2,761	84	57	84	782	20.7
III. Countries with per capita incomes between $300 and $150	229	2,369	70	72	55	4,129	14.9
IV. Countries with per capita incomes below $150	97	2,048	55	114	38	14,388	9.8

Note: The countries included in the income groups are as follows: I. United States, Canada, France, United Kingdom, Denmark, Germany; II. Uruguay, Israel, Austria, Italy, Argentina, Cuba; III. Turkey, Brazil, Japan, Greece, Philippines, Iraq, Mexico; IV. Egypt, Indonesia, Ceylon, Syria, Thailand, India, Burma, Pakistan.

Source: *The Role of Foreign Aid in the Development of Other Countries*, a study prepared at the request of the Special Committee To Study the Foreign Aid Program, United States Senate, by the Research Center in Economic Development and Cultural Change of the University of Chicago, 85th Congress, 1st Session (Government Printing Office, Washington, D. C. 1957).

as you move from the highest to the lowest income level, caloric intake, protein consumption, and literacy all fall, while infant mortality and number of inhabitants per physician rise. The percentage of national income invested also is smaller, the lower one goes in the income scale. (There are only two exceptions, both in the second income group. They relate to inhabitants per physician and per cent of GNP invested).

Change Under Way

India stands out as the nation in which newborn nationalism and a consciousness of the potentialities of economic development have most spectacularly combined to set in motion the forces of change. Her first comprehensive five-year plan was completed in 1955; the second is already under way. But India is by no means alone. Turkey has made great strides in modernizing its agriculture and in creating a sizeable industrial structure. Burma is engaged in putting into effect projects suggested by private consultants employed by the government. Pakistan, Ceylon, and Malaya—each has dozens of development projects under way. And in Latin America, there is not one of the twenty nations that does not have its development corporation, its planning board, or its ministerial council at work on coordinated schemes for economic improvement.

What this all adds up to is that the underdeveloped countries are officially on the move. The idea of economic progress has seized the imagination, if not of all their people, at least of a sufficient number of those who count politically. They are determined to end their long period of stagnation, with the low standard of living it has imposed, and to exchange antiquated and inefficient methods of production for those of the twentieth century.

The task they confront is one of great difficulty. Without substantial outside aid, there is danger that the hopes and aspirations now fully aroused will be frustrated. This could only result in political turmoil and instability, excessive nationalism and isolation, and pressure to resort to the ruthless totalitarian methods of Communism to achieve their goal. It is this possibility that makes of economic development not just a domestic problem of the underdeveloped nations, but a world problem of the first magnitude, posing grave questions of policy for the advanced nations of the West.

This chapter examines some of the difficulties involved in promoting rapid economic development, and inquires in what ways the United States and other western countries can best help to overcome them.

Economic Development Means Westernisation

Economic development of a magnitude sufficient to bring appreciable change within a reasonable period requires a deliberate and massive effort. The reason this is so is that such economic development involves no less than the reconstruction of the entire society. For the kind of growth experienced by the nations of western Europe (broadly interpreted) during the past century and a half is something unique in history. There was, of course, expansion and progress before that, but never on the scale or with the rapidity of this particular period. In this part of the world, at this particular time, historic forces converged to produce a type of society that embodied the conditions essential to rapid economic growth. If the underdeveloped countries of today are to become developed, they must incorporate these essential conditions into their structure, which means that they must become westernised. Let us see why this is so and what it involves.

Components of Western Progress

When one thinks of the causes of the economic progress of the last century or so, the first thing that is almost certain to come to mind is the tremendous alvance in technology. And this certainly was one of the crucial factors.

But the technology that was so productive would have been nothing but ideas in books and in the minds of men except for its embodiment in the furnaces, the engines, the lathes, the buildings, and all the complex and costly equipment of modern industry. And these physical capital resources could never have come into existence had people somewhere not denied themselves the pleasures of consumption and chosen the satisfaction of thrift instead. Moreover, without skilled workers to operate them, these capital instruments are inert and unproductive. Just as vital to the huge and growing output of recent times are the skills of workers and of the managers who direct them.

The rapid advance of the West, however, depended not alone on a progressive technology and a high rate of investment and saving to incorporate technological changes in increasingly efficient instruments of production. New inventions are not transferred from the drafting board to the shop automatically; someone must raise the capital essential to make this transformation possible, and he must first decide it is worth his while to do so. This is equally true of those more intangible inventions such as improved methods of accounting, better methods of keeping track of inventory or of routing materials through a factory, more efficient forms of organising an enterprise—all of which have contributed substantially to the rise in productivity of past decades. Such changes, too, require the presence of enterprising individuals who can foresee the benefits from the improved methods, make the decision to introduce them, and then see that their decisions are carried out. One of the chief factors underlying the rapid economic progress of the West was its possession of a large class of entrepreneurs who had the imagination to see what innovation could accomplish, the enterprise to introduce change, and the willingness to risk their own capital, and the ability to persuade others to risk theirs in carrying through innovations.

Historic Origins of Western Progress

Western society alone possessed, at the beginning of the nineteenth century, these principal requisites of rapid industrial change: *a progressive technology, a rate of capital accumulation sufficient to make a speedy economic transformation possible,* and *a supply of entrepreneurs adequate to this task.*

That it had these requisites was not accidental; it was the consequence of historic forces that had shaped the structure and institutions of that society in a manner favorable rather than antagonistic to the emergence of these three carriers of economic advance. As we noted earlier, the Renaissance brought an awakening of interest in the behavior of nature that led to the later scientific discoveries which were the foundation of modern technology. It also turned men toward secular affairs, with a consequent flowering of commercial activity in the city states of northern Italy which spread over the Alps into northern Europe. The business man achieved in this period important status—he was respected in a way that had been true during the Middle Ages only in the free cities of the Hanseatic League. The increased respect accorded business men helped attract more and more of the brighter young men toward industrial and commercial pursuits, thus developing the large class of merchant-capitalists that in the sixteenth and seventeenth centuries broke the bonds of custom and established laissez faire for enterprise as the guiding principle.

Along with the Renaissance, the Reformation also inculcated new attitudes needed for an era of economic expansion. This was especially true of the Calvinist and Puritan branches of Protestantism, with their stress on the duty of work and the virtue of thrift. "Money-grubbing" became respectable, as it never did in Spain or the Spanish colonies, where the aristocratic ideal of gracious living on a large, landed estate remained predominant well into the twentieth century.

Finally, the preservation of the Roman concept of law and order and the reintroduction of the rule of law at the end of the Middle Ages provided a legal framework that enforced contracts, gave stability and certainty to business endeavor, and so guaranteed the effectiveness of thrift and effort.

Characteristics of Underdeveloped Countries

The underdeveloped areas of the world generally possess few of these social characteristics. They are predominantly agrarian, with from 65 to 75 per cent of the population employed on the land. Cultivation is carried on either on small-scale, peasant plots, as in most of Asia and Africa, or on large semi-feudal estates, as in the major part of Latin America and in such countries as Iran and Egypt. In both these types of agricultural society, tradition and status determine one's conduct and one's place in life.

Farming methods of 2,000 years ago continue to be practiced. With these methods sanctified by custom, there is little stimulus to innovate. In the towns and cities, trade and money-lending are principally in the hands of "outside" groups—the Chinese in Indonesia, Thailand, and Malaya, the Indian or Arab in Ceylon, the Levantine or newly arrived European until recently in much of Latin America. This is partly because loyalty to one's kin, in the traditional family-oriented society of Asia, precludes the impersonal relations so essential to business success, partly because the low prestige accorded to business occupations deters entry by indigenous members of the dominant group.

Since most underdeveloped countries are poor, the margin for saving is small and the proportion of the smaller income saved is less than in the richer, more advanced nations. Productive domestic investment tends to be even smaller, since a considerable share of what savings there are go into the purchase of land at inflated prices, into investment in the relatively safe securities of more stable and more developed countries, into gold and silver ornaments, or into weddings and other ceremonies. Consequently, industry is scanty and almost always short of funds.

Development Requires a Social Revolution

Since no other method of effecting rapid economic progress has ever been devised than the one that depends on work, thrift, and constant innovation, it is clear that if the stagnation of the past is to give way to speedy economic development, the economically backward nations must undergo a far-reaching and drastic revolution. Inadequate savings must by every possible means be increased, so that the money capital so necessary for irrigation and power dams, for roads and railways, for more abundant and efficient agricultural equipment, and for factories, trains, buses, and urban housing, can be provided. There must be a great deal of investment, too, in the human skills needed if these capital installations are to be used efficiently, as well as in raising the level of literacy and in swamping ignorance and superstition with knowledge. Those social values that now put a premium on success through conformity must be replaced by others which give high rewards for successful innovation. This means, too, that the business man must be accorded at least as much prestige as the heriditary landowner or the government official.

The obstacles to the kind of revolutionary change needed thus include more than a lack of savings and inadequate numbers of enterprising business men to be the agents of economic development.

The more deep-seated obstructions are qualitative in nature: social values unsuited to an industrial age, and habits and traditions hallowed by time but cursed by inefficiency. To eradicate these is a delicate, difficult, and time-consuming task.

Moreover, it is likely to arouse deep-seated opposition, for in changing over from a peasant- or latifundia-dominated society to the modern, commercial-industrial economy, not only must long-established habits be disrupted, but powerful vested interests must be challenged.

Government Has a Major Role to Play

It is clear that the social transformation implicit in economic development can only be undertaken by the people of the country in question. This means, in practice, their government.

For only the government is in the commanding position to exert the pressure—through example, through the establishment of new institutions, and through enactment of laws—necessary to effect this kind of change. By these and other means, it must, to stimulate young men to enter the ranks of business, exert every effort to gain for the business man as much recognition as the army officer, the professional man, or the landed proprietor. It must also induce people to save more, and to invest their savings in a manner more beneficial to the country. Unless such changes as these in values and habits are officially sanctioned and pushed by the government they will come so slowly as to be imperceptible except over decades.

The governments of the underdeveloped countries must also take the lead in dealing with those two more tangible shortcomings of underdeveloped areas—their lack of capital and of modern technological "know-how." Investment is needed in practically every sector of the economy, as is, likewise, the application of more efficient techniques of production. A few illustrations will serve to give point to this statement.

The Crucial Role of Investment and Technology

Except in the production of a few important export crops, such as tea, rubber, coffee, and sugar, the agriculture of underdeveloped countries is generally inefficient and often downright primitive. To increase yields, better methods of cultivation, better seed, more extensive use of fertilizers, and irrigation are all badly needed. These mean not only dams and irrigation channels, but also experimental stations to determine which seeds, which fertilizers, and which methods are best adapted to local conditions. They mean, in addition, extension services to communicate the findings to the cultivator and to persuade him to use them, as well as roads and railways to get his crops to market, warehouses to store them, and credit to finance their production.

At every point, investment is essential, either in physical equipment or in the skills of those who are to use it, and the services of technical experts to transmit modern techniques and help in adapting them to local circumstances.

Development also means industrialisation, both to absorb the labor released from agriculture as it becomes more efficient and to provide goods to be exchanged for the increased output of the farmer. Expanding industry requires investment all along the line, in buildings and machinery, and in technical training as well. The worker accustomed only to hand-tools must learn totally new techniques when he exchanges the hand-saw for the power saw, the hand-loom for the power loom, the bullock cart for the truck. And if he is to stay in town as a permanent worker instead of going back to his village as soon as he has made a stake, town living must be made attractive to him. This means decent housing, good water and sewage disposal, and facilities for recreation, all of which require capital.

Moreover, investment in industry will generally be unattractive to the investor, whether domestic or foreign, unless there exists a background of facilities essential to the operation of industry. These facilities, or the "social overhead capital" of the community, include roads and railways, electric power, warehouses and docks. Then there are the schools necessary to provide literate workers, able to read and follow written instructions, and hospitals and doctors to care for their health. Everywhere one turns, there is a pressing need for investment in the physical instruments of economic progress and for the technical training of their human counterparts.

Since incomes in underdeveloped countries are generally low, only a small proportion is saved, and as we have seen, much of that is diverted into unproductive channels. The shortage of investible funds is therefore acute. Everything the governments of the less developed lands can do to increase the rate of saving—increased taxation, the establishment of suitable savings institutions, and carefully controlled deficit finance—or to channel savings into productive outlets, will still provide only enough additional capital resources to speed up the pace of economic change moderately.

FOREIGN AID FOR ECONOMIC DEVELOPMENT

It is in sharing their capital and technical knowledge, which they have in relative abundance, that the more developed nations can furnish to their less fortunate neighbors the most tangible and effective aid. These important requisites of economic development can be transmitted with comparative ease, whereas the changes in social values and customs, equally necessary for accelerated economic progress, can only be brought about by the governments and institutions of the underdeveloped countries themselves.

Nonetheless, the provision of capital and technical assistance themselves raises many troublesome questions. How much aid of this kind, for example, is needed to make a real difference in the rate of economic progress of the underdeveloped areas? In what volume is such aid now going to these countries? Are there limitations on the rate at which capital and technical knowledge can be assimilated? By what means can their flow be increased? Is it to the interest of the United States and other Western nations to give strong support to economic development? If so, what conditions, if any, should be attached to this support? We shall devote the next part of this chapter to an attempt to answer these questions.

Capital Needs of Development

How much foreign assistance the underdeveloped countries need depends, first, upon what rate of progress is regarded as desirable, and second, at what rate that goal is being approached today. With respect especially to the first of these criteria, there is much room for the exercise of judgment. A number of estimates have been made, of which one of the most reasonable and conservative, in my view, is that of Millikan and Rostow.[1]

Since capital requirements for development vary with the stage of advance a country has reached, it is necessary to start with some reasonable classification of countries. Nations in the earliest phase of development, which have scarcely "got off the ground," will lack most of the preconditions of development, such as efficient transport, communications, a moderately good educational system, and even a modest supply of hospitals and doctors. Until these needs are met, progress will be slow or negligible. Capital requirements to get off dead-center are large, and will continue to be so for at least four to five years after plans are put into effect before an appreciable rise in income occurs. Millikan and Rostow estimate that foreign funds amounting to 30-50 per cent of current annual investment in such countries will be necessary for some such period.

During the next stage, that of transition, the effects of the earlier investment and accompanying technical assistance make themselves felt. Commerce, including the export-import trade, expands; agriculture produces better yields; urban population grows; and new opportunities for investment in local industry appear. Savings rise from around 5 per cent of national income to around 10 per cent. With appropriate governmental effort to keep development going, new credit institutions (savings banks, mortgage banks, agricultural credit cooperatives, perhaps a development corporation) channel a larger proportion of the increase in income into productive investment. Higher taxes and borrowing should enable the government itself to raise substantial funds for development projects.

In this stage, experience indicates that the maximum attainable rate of growth of physical output, under the most favorable conditions, ranges from 3 to 5 per cent a year. Even this requires a rate of investment of 10 per cent or more of national income per annum if reasonably conservative assumptions are made as to how much additional income a dollar of investment will generate. The latter figure—the marginal capital-output ratio —is taken to be 3:1, which is relatively, but certainly not excessively,

[1] Max F. Millikan and W. W. Rostow, *A Proposal: Key to an Effective Foreign Policy,* Harper & Bros., New York, 1957. Their calculations are based on statistical data that vary widely in reliability, but are the best available. The resultant estimates may err by as much as 20 to 25 per cent, but they probably give a fairly good idea of the orders of magnitude involved. See especially the Appendix of their book for the methods used. I find the approach of these authors to the problem of aid to underdeveloped countries so congenial to my own views that this section not only presents their method of arriving at an estimate of capital needs, but also parallels their analysis at other points.

conservative.[2] But since populations are increasing throughout the under-developed nations at rates of 1.5 to more than 2 per cent per annum, a gross annual increase in income of 3 to 5 per cent becomes only 1 to 3½ per cent per capita. The average annual percentage increase in income would thus be approximately 2 per cent. If economic growth is to become self-sustaining, so that the developing countries can become independent of foreign aid, a substantial part of this annual increment of income must be captured—via taxes or induced savings—for additional investment. It is desirable and probably feasible that this proportion should be as high as 25 per cent, which would leave the average rate of increase in income available for enhanced consumption (i.e., a rising standard of living) at 1.5 per cent a year. This means a modest improvement of the lot of the individual in 10 years—not a great deal, but at least sufficient to generate hope.

Foreign Financial Aid Needed

To attain even these results during the period of transition, however, substantial foreign aid will be required. Take the available data for South Central Asia (India, Pakistan, and Ceylon) as an illustration. National income in 1953 was approximately $28 billion.[3] Gross capital formation is estimated at $2.8 billion. Part of this, however, is needed merely to maintain existing capital intact. Deducting the amount estimated for depreciation and other forms of capital maintenance ($1.1 billion) leaves only $1.7 billion of *net* investment. To raise net investment to even 10 per cent of national income would require foreign capital assistance in the order of a billion dollars a year, which is 60 per cent of current net domestic investment of South Central Asia.

Some of the underdeveloped countries are investing a somewhat larger proportion of national income than India, Pakistan, and Ceylon. Millikan and Rostow estimate that to ensure a rate of net investment of 10 per cent a year for all the underdeveloped countries of the free world, the foreign capital provided would have to be only about 40 per cent of current net investment. Added to the amounts required for countries going through the preliminary stage of development, this gives a grand total of $3.5 billion

[2] A marginal capital-output ratio of 3:1 means that it takes $3 of investment to generate a continuing flow of $1 of additional income. Therefore, if 10 per cent of income is invested, this should cause income to increase by 3⅓ per cent. Were the capital-output ratio as high as 4:1, a 10 per cent rate of investment would, of course, yield only a 2.5 per cent annual increase in income.

[3] This and the other figures in this paragraph are taken from Millikan and Rostow, *op. cit.,* Appendix, Table 1.

a year. Assuming that all countries make the maximum use possible of such foreign aid, this annual sum would be required for a period of about 10 to 15 years. Probably after 10 years, some countries now in the transitional stage would move onto the stage of self-sustained growth, so that the amount of aid then required would taper off appreciably.

It is important to note that this estimated sum of $3.5 billion per annum of needed capital inflow into the underdeveloped areas is in addition to existing investment there. For current foreign loans and grants are included in the base (total current investment in underdeveloped countries) on which the additional requirement was computed.

The data on which the foregoing estimates are based are far from precise. Few countries have accurate national income statistics, and for many, such information is very sketchy. Figures on gross capital formation are even scantier and information on net capital formation is hardly more than rough notions of what might be reasonable. Enough is known with some accuracy, however, and enough scraps of evidence are available to permit intelligent guesses, so that these estimates can be taken at least as representing the order of magnitude of the total volume of investment needed to speed up economic development appreciably, and of the amount of foreign financial aid required to make this possible. Even if the correct figure for foreign aid is not $3.5 billion, but only three-quarters of this ($2.65 billion), it is still a great deal more than is now forthcoming, as we shall see.

Technical Assistance

In addition to providing capital to finance the construction of all the innumerable aids to greater productivity we have indicated as necessary, the more advanced countries can make another important contribution to economic development—by transmitting to the underdeveloped countries their knowledge of improved methods of farming, of better industrial techniques, and their methods of discovering new improvements or of adapting techniques already known to different situations. This can be and is being done in many ways—by sending experts into the field to show how their knowledge can be applied, by placing them on the staffs of agricultural colleges and industrial institutes, by sending students from the underdeveloped countries to foreign universities for advanced work, and by establishing and setting in operation research organisations to study the specific problems of the underdeveloped areas.

On the whole, this need is being met much more adequately than the need for investment funds. In the nine years, 1948-56, the United States spent over $300 million on "technical cooperation" alone. The United Nation's Technical Assistance Board, which has been in operation since mid-1950, devoted approximately $100 million to this kind of work up to the end of 1955. In addition, other United Nations agencies, such as the Food and Agriculture Organisation, the World Health Organisation, the International Labour Organisation, have contributed the services of their specialised experts. Others have been provided by European governments, as through the Colombo Plan, or to colonial dependencies, as especially by France and the United Kingdom.

Potential Sources of Funds

Suppose for the moment that additional foreign loans and grants of $3.5 billion a year, continued over a period of ten years and combined with adequate technical assistance, could provide the support necessary to put most underdeveloped countries well on the road to self-sustained growth. Where can sums of this magnitude be obtained? With further improvement in the conditions of private investment, which it would be part of a concerted program to bring about, a half billion dollars additional might come from this source. Nearly this much additional might come from the International Bank, since its annual loan disbursements in recent years, averaging about $150 million, have been limited mainly by the lack of sufficient sound projects rather than any shortage of funds. With a vigorous broad program under way, a substantially larger volume of bankable projects would be forthcoming. Of the remaining $2.5 billion, which would have to be public capital, the major share, about $2 billion, would have to come from the United States. Millikin and Rostow give the following breakdown of possible sources:

These figures represent, the authors of the Report point out, a maximum of funds whose availability should be assured. In practice, because of un-

Table 26.2

POSSIBLE SOURCES OF ADDITIONAL CAPITAL AID FOR ECONOMIC DEVELOPMENT

Grants:	
U.S. contribution	$ 360 million
Other country contributions	240
Direct Private Investment	500
Additional International Bank Loans	400
Public Loans:	
U.S. contribution	1,700
Other country contributions	300
Total	3,500 million

avoidable lags in getting national development programs under way and because the estimate assumes a rate of absorption that is unlikely to be fully realised, actual use of funds would probably not be more than approximately 60 per cent of this amount. Although funds adequate to support the full program in case things went exceptionally well should be guaranteed, this would reduce the probable claims substantially. The annual contribution of the United States, the largest of all, would drop to $1.2 billion a year, the need of the entire program to $2 billion.

Importance of Economic Development

In these days of overloaded national budgets and high taxes, any suggestions for additional expenditures must be supported by cogent argument if they are to avoid becoming objects of derision, let alone receive serious consideration. The resistance to spending is especially strong against programs aimed to help other people, when there are so many things that need to be done at home. Thus in the United States in the spring of 1957, urgent claims have been advanced for federal aid for the construction of much-needed schools, redevelopment of our blighted urban areas is attracting increasing attention, and a huge federal highway program is about to get under way. After the multi-billion dollar outlays on European recovery and mutual security, and with annual appropriations for military and economic aid of $3 to $4 billion still continuing, it would be an understatement to say that Congress takes a dim view of further expenditures on foreign aid.

Sustained Effort Is Vital

Yet many share the conviction that a really bold and purposeful program to underwrite economic development should be a main component of the foreign economic policy of the United States and of its Western allies. Present outlays are no more than a holding operation, which prevents a serious loss of ground, but which lacks strong forward momentum. These outlays shift their focus from place to place as local tensions become acute or as military conflict breaks out—to Formosa after 1949, to Korea after 1950, to Viet Nam in 1954, to the Middle East in 1957. *They represent essentially a scattered and uncoordinated series of efforts with no sustained objective* other than countering actual or threatened Communist aggression, and they depend upon recurring annual appropriations.

A real program capable of giving momentum to economic development must be positive, adequate in size and scope, coordinated, and sustained. Such a program would clearly be in the interest of the underdeveloped areas. But it would equally serve the vital interests of the United States and the Western members of the free world because it affords a good prospect of transforming unstable and poor nations dangerously close to frustration into stable, progressive, and responsible ones.

The direct threat of military aggression by the Communist powers has been met by the defense buildup, including military and economic aid to our allies. Equally important, however, is the character of the rest of the non-Communist world, which contains 71 per cent of the free world's population. For harmonious and relaxed relations, it is essential that it should consist of stable and democratic societies, for only such societies share our outlook and our values and are capable of being our unsolicited friends.

Contrariwise, the security of the West will be undermined if the aspirations of Asia, Africa and Latin America for economic betterment, independence, and political equality are frustrated by a lack of resources to build viable and productive economies. There would then be a serious danger of resort to totalitarian methods as a means of extracting from the people the resources needed for development. The example of Russia is a constant reminder that poor countries *can* achieve a kind of economic development by themselves, provided their governments are willing and able to force their values on the public, compel the necessary tightening of the belt, and reshape the structure of society.

Purpose of Economic Aid

Some people hold strongly to the conviction that economic aid should be closely tied to the receipt of some compensating advantage. The compensation may be concrete, as in the provision of stipulated amounts of strategic materials, or undertaking to train and maintain a military force of a given size, or it may be more intangible, as entering into a military alliance or adopting a foreign policy desired by the grantor of funds. Much aid has been advanced on this sort of *quid pro quo* basis, and doubtless will continue to be. It has a strong appeal to the hard-boiled legislator, who wants to get some tangible return for every outlay.

As the basis for a broad program of economic aid, however, the conditional principle is inappropriate. The principal aim of such a program, as we have outlined it, should be to promote more rapid economic development over a wide area with a view to replacing stagnation with progress, frustration with hope, and weak and unstable economies with strong and stable ones.

Economic development sets a goal which challenges the energies of all classes of a nation and provides outlets for the exercise of the talents of its people. New opportunities constantly unfold, new abilities are needed, and technical assistance programs provide means for their acquisition. Successful prosecution of a development program will also improve living conditions; this material gain is an important result of economic development, and one of the reasons for undertaking it, but it is probably less important than the effect of the program in mobilising the energies of a nation's people in a great cooperative endeavor.

The compensation to the countries supplying aid are very real, though not directly sought. They are the satisfaction from participating in a challenging and rewarding task, and the creation of political, economic, and social conditions in the underdeveloped countries likely to make them willing members of the free world.

The attempt to link economic aid closely to compensating favors has, moreover, serious positive drawbacks. Many of the underdeveloped nations have but recently emerged from colonial status. They are understandably jealous of their sovereignty, and regard efforts to make technical or economic assistance conditional upon participation in a military alliance or adoption of a specific foreign policy as a renewed attempt at colonial domination. And even when it is possible to buy collaboration with economic aid, there is always the danger that what one party can purchase, another can win away for a higher price.

Conditions for a Successful Aid Program

If the purpose of a foreign aid program is simply the realisation of economic development and the mutual benefits this confers, enough has been said to indicate the conditions of its success. First, *it must be adequate in size*. On the basis of previous estimates, resources of the order of $2 billion above those currently forthcoming would likely be needed, and considerably more than that should be available. Second, *the program must be a continuing one*. It cannot be made to depend on annual appropriations subject to recurring review, debate, trimming, and possible defeat. Continuity is essential if there is to be intelligent planning and if governments are to be enabled to make the necessary long-term financial commitments. Governments participating in the program should therefore appropriate sufficient funds for a 5- or 10-year period in advance, though they would not have to be raised and disbursed until the need for them arose. Third, *the condition of aid should be detailed evidence that the aid received will be used in the most productive manner possible*. This point requires some elaboration.

The Test of Productivity

A request for aid may be limited to a single project, or it may (and as the program develops, doubtless will) include several related projects. The success of each such project depends upon the availability, from domestic or foreign sources, of adequate financing, of the physical resources for construction, and of the managerial capacity for its operation. The beneficiary should be able to produce convincing evidence that all these requisites will be met. If it can not do so, further preparation is necessary, which may well include a revision of plans to include setting up facilities to train technicians or skilled labor essential to the project's success.

Assurance would also be required that services or facilities independent of but essential to the project's success are also available. Thus, for example, a program to stimulate increased production of rice by means of irrigation, the use of improved seed and implements, and the application of more efficient methods can founder if such complementary needs as storage facilities, transport, marketing arrangements, and production credits are not provided at the right time and the right place.

Finally, the test of maximum productivity requires that all the projects proposed be mutually consistent, and that the particular combination of projects chosen, and not some other, represents the best use of resources. In other words, some degree of national planning is called for, to be sure that each element of a program contributes the maximum to the country's economic development. As one aspect of such planning, attention would need to be given to the probable effects of the program on the country's balance of payments. This would include ensuring that any national program did not put such heavy demands on the country's resources as to generate serious inflation; also that in the financing of the program, foreign debt was not incurred beyond the country's ability to service it.

Evaluation of Projects and Plans

A fourth and final condition for the success of an augmented aid program is that there be some agency capable of evaluating projects both in their individual form and as components in a national scheme of development. If the availability of aid is to be made conditional upon its productive use, someone, somewhere, has to decide whether each application meets this test. If no specific institution is set up to make that decision, the present loose-jointed "system" will be magnified manyfold. Now, each country tries to get outside financial aid from any one of the alternative sources open to it—the International Bank, the Export-Import Bank, or the government of one of the more developed countries.

So long as funds are as scarce as they are relative to the needs for them, the situation is tolerable. But with relatively ample funds, it would be in danger of becoming chaotic, with one source being played off against another. Standards of allocation would be sure to suffer, and coordination of national plans would be totally lacking. There would be an obvious need for a sort of clearing house where individual projects could be considered on their merits, where their articulation into a national program could be evaluated, and where some coordination even of the plans of different countries might be suggested.

To have the desired influence, such an agency must command the respect and confidence both of the nations seeking aid, and of those supplying it. This means that its personnel would have to possess high competence and a reputation for rigorous objectivity. It is scarcely imaginable that any national organisation could qualify as wholly objective; the implication is clear that the only type of body capable of meeting this test would be one with international status, like the International Bank or some direct agency of the United Nations. The initial staff of such an organisation would have to be drawn from the ranks of those experienced in the current work of economic development—the International Bank, the United Nations Technical Assistance Administration, the Food and Agriculture Organization, the International Labour Organization, the regional committees of the United Nations (ECAFE, ECLA, ECE). and qualified civil servants now in the employ of various governments. As time went on, of course, additional staff members would be trained within the organisation.

Ideally, perhaps, if such an organisation were created, it should also be entrusted with the additional public funds to be made available. Since a substantial part of these funds would be needed for grants or low-interest loans to finance such non-self-liquidating projects as roads, harbor works, schools, and health facilities, it is unlikely, to put it mildly, that any subscribing government would be willing to surrender control over their allocation to an international agency. Possibly such an arrangement would become acceptable if the proposed review agency develops the necessary reputation for objectivity. At first, and perhaps indefinitely, the functions of the agency would be those of review and coordination, together with that of suggesting the most appropriate source of finance. This does not imply that such an organisation would have veto power over the allocation of funds, for this power would require a grant of authority from both recipients and suppliers of aid that is not likely. Yet if properly organised, and particularly if it were closely associated with the International Bank, which has developed an expertise and a reputation for competence, its voice should carry great weight, both with those applying for aid and those granting it. Moreover, it could render valuable assistance to countries in drawing up individual projects and in fitting them together into an effective development program.

PRIVATE INVESTMENT IN UNDERDEVELOPED AREAS

Private investment, which during the nineteenth century played the major role in the transmission of capital from the older, more advanced nations to the outlying and more undeveloped regions of the world, has in the last half-century undergone a heavy decline in relative importance. This has been closely associated with an accompanying change in the character of foreign borrowers and with the United States' replacement of Great Britain as the world's principal capital market. In view of the insistence of the United States government that private investment should carry the main burden of economic development, close attention to these significant changes is imperative.

Declining Importance of Private Investment

In the decade before the first World War, total foreign investment reached an annual rate of about $1.5 billion, of which the United Kingdom supplied roughly half. This amounted to some 7 per cent of her national income.

During the 1920's the flow of capital approximated the prewar rate. The United States supplied half of this, but it comprised only about 1 per cent of national income. But with prices in the U.S. and the U.K. some 50 per cent above the prewar level, the purchasing power of foreign investment was only $1 billion a year as compared with prewar. Moreover, nearly half of this reduced volume of real investment was going to Germany; not over a third of the total went to underdeveloped countries.

During the 1930's, international lending came to a standstill.

Since 1946, private international investment has been running at an annual rate of about $1.8 billion, or somewhat higher in dollar terms than in the 1920's. Again, the United States has accounted for close to half, or about $900 million a year. (This is less than one-half of 1 per cent of our postwar national income). But with prices now twice as high as the 1926-29 level, the current dollar figures for international investment must be reduced by half to make them comparable with the data for the 1920's. This means that in dollars of similar purchasing power, private foreign investment in recent years has been only about 60 per cent of what it was in the 1920's, and less than half of the pre-World War I level. With total world production at least double the 1913 figure, this clearly represents a substantial shrinkage in the contribution of private international investment to its traditional role of promoting economic growth in the developing areas of the world. If international investment bore the same relation to world production and income today that it did in 1913, the annual figure would be somewhere in the neighborhood of $8 to $9 billion.

In tracing the decline in the relative importance of private capital movements, we have at the same time noted that the United States has replaced the United Kingdom as the principal source of funds. This is explained in large part, of course, by the steady growth in the wealth and income of the United States. Britain, on the other hand, has become less important, both absolutely and relatively, as an international investor, because her income has expanded less rapidly, and because, especially since 1945, she has not been able to spare resources for foreign investment to the same extent as formerly. High rates of taxation have reduced the proportion of income saved, and postwar reconstruction and expansion have put heavy demands on these savings and on the physical resources required for investment.

Changed Conditions of Borrowing

Along with the reduction in the relative importance of international investment and the replacement of the United Kingdom by the United States as the principal investor, there has also occurred a change in the character of international borrowing. Together with the transfer of the role of major capital supplier to the United States, this has been an important cause of the reduced importance of private international investment.

In our discussion of the international flow of capital in the nineteenth century (see Ch. 10), we noted that nearly half of this flow went into railways and other public utilities. Another 30 per cent was invested in government bonds, of which a considerable portion was also used for these purposes. Increasingly in recent years, governments of underdeveloped countries have taken from private enterprise the task of providing public transportation and other similar services. Many have nationalised existing systems, while others have assumed the responsibility for new construction. Argentina's purchase of its railway and telephone systems from British investors is merely an extreme example. Financing of these undertakings must now rest upon the sale of government bonds, whereas formerly, funds were raised from the issue of the securities of public utility corporations.

Unfortunately for the borrowers seeking capital for this still vital field of investment, government bonds have a poor market today. Widespread defaults in the 1930's created a profound distrust of the bonds of all but the most reputable borrowers, particularly in the United States, where the lax bank administration of loans in the 1920's produced especially unhappy results. Moreover, many states of the Union have laws which prohibit the investment of the funds of insurance companies, banks, and other institutional investors in the bonds of foreign governments.[4]

As a consequence of these developments, only about 10 per cent of U.S. private foreign investment now goes into portfolio investment, as contrasted with an approximately equal division between portfolio and direct investment in the 1920's.[5] Private capital today is thus largely confined to providing resources for direct investment alone. This limits it pretty much to trade, manufacturing, mining, and plantation agriculture. In fact, approximately 60 per cent of U.S. private foreign investment in the decade, 1947-56, was in petroleum extraction and refining.

Factors Limiting Direct Investment

Direct investment, which now accounts for the lion's share of private international investment, is itself subject to a number of limiting forces. For one thing, its principal source tends to be the funds of corporations engaged in international trade. Possessing a good knowledge of conditions abroad and anxious to expand their business, such corporations direct a substantial portion of their investment into branch plants or the plants of associated companies, or into exploiting mineral deposits required by their operations.

The ordinary private investor, who in the United States accounts for two-thirds or more of net savings, is not attracted by the possibility of similar investments in foreign firms. He generally knows little of the opportunities available. Even if he does, he is in no position to assess their merits.

This acute disadvantage has occasionally been partly overcome, as particularly in the case of British investment in South African gold mining, in tin mining in Malaya, and in tea and rubber plantations in various parts

[4] These laws made it impossible for the International Bank for Reconstruction and Development to sell its bonds in these states. It required many months of effort by President Eugene R. Black of the International Bank to obtain the enactment of special statutes removing this handicap from the bonds of that institution.

[5] U. N. Department of Economic Affairs, *The International Flow of Private Capital 1946-1952* (New York, 1954), p. 10. By direct investment is meant investment in physical plant or in the stock of foreign corporations which carries control over the enterprise. Portfolio investments include mainly the bonds of foreign governments and corporations, which do not involve any element of control.

of South Asia, where British financial houses have acted as sponsors of a number of individual operating enterprises. This provided a sufficient guarantee for their securities to find a favorable market among small investors.[6]

Direct investment is, moreover, hampered by the policies adopted by the underdeveloped countries. Some of these have an ideological basis, as when governments with a socialist bias reserve large areas of investment to the state. The threat of the extension of the range of state investment, possibly involving expropriation of existing private enterprise, has at times constituted a serious obstacle to foreign private investment. Discriminatory taxation of foreign firms, insistence on the employment of nationals in technical and managerial posts, and such social legislation as that limiting the discharge of employees or requiring high dismissal pay are similarly discouraging through their effect on profits. Restrictions on the transfer of earnings or of capital, introduced to protect the balance of payments, have also operated to depress foreign investment.

Possible Remedies

Many of these difficulties could be, and some are being, overcome. Thus, new intermediaries, capable of performing the supervisory function earlier furnished by British financial houses, have sprung up in recent years. The governments of many underdeveloped countries have established Development Banks, which raise capital by the sale of their own securities and relend the funds to domestic enterprises. If these banks develop a good reputation, they should be able to attract some capital from abroad.

The newest and most promising institution in this category is the International Finance Corporation, established in 1956 as an affiliate of the World Bank. Its task is to discover likely outlets for investment, enlist the financial participation of both domestic and foreign investors, and make loans from its own capital of $100 million. As ventures mature and become self-sustaining, it is expected that the IFC will sell its participation to private investors, thus permitting its capital to function as a revolving fund.

The governments of the underdeveloped countries can improve the climate for direct investment by moderating the policies that have proved adverse. Governments can specify exactly the area reserved for state investment and assure fair compensation in case of nationalisation. They

[6] See W. Arthur Lewis, *The Theory of Economic Growth* (George Allen & Unwin, Ltd., London, 1955), p. 261. Professor Lewis' Chapter V, on Capital, is a particularly good discussion of this subject. I have found many of his points most helpful.

can permit firms to employ foreign personnel when qualified people are not available locally. They can assure equitable standards of taxation. They can guarantee the free transfer of earnings and at least the gradual repatriation of invested capital. Some governments, notably those of India, Turkey, and Israel, and a few of Latin America, have already acted to improve conditions in these respects.

The United States government, through the Export-Import Bank, has for its part provided guarantees (up to $500 million) against losses from inconvertibility and expropriation. This action has, however, stimulated but little response, partly perhaps because to obtain the guarantee involves costs running up to 5 per cent.

The Capital Needs of Development

Even if we were to adopt a most optimistic estimate for the effect on direct foreign investment of more helpful policies and of more adequate intermediaries, this source of foreign capital could not possibly meet the requirements of the underdeveloped areas. For direct investment, to which private foreign investment is now mainly confined, and with respect to which alone the suggested remedies are relevant, can never furnish more than a small part of the financial resources needed. In the underdeveloped countries, the heaviest investments are required to provide all-around community facilities of the character indicated earlier. Few projects in these areas are self-liquidating. They cannot, therefore, be financed by the World Bank or the Export-Import Bank. Their financing must rely upon loans or grants to governments. As we have seen, however, the possibility of greatly increased private lending to governments is, for a number of reasons, very unlikely in the foreseeable future.

Indeed, one can go further, and say that future self-liquidating projects that might appeal most strongly to foreign investors, such as manufacturing industries, will be severely limited *until* these essential community facilities are made available. What is needed, therefore, is a substantial increase in the volume of lending to the governments of the underdeveloped nations, and in the existing state of the world's capital markets, the only large potential source of such loans or grants is the governments of the Western nations.

Despite these considerations, and in the face of a relatively minute volume of private developmental lending since the war except to petroleum-rich countries, the U.S. government continues to stress private international investment as the chief source on which reliance should be placed in economic development. This view has been reiterated *ad nauseam* in statement after statement of high administration officials and in government report after government report. One refreshing exception is the Gray Report,[7] which states:

Taking into account the known obstacles, and the uncertain effectiveness of the limited measures that can be taken to overcome them, it must be frankly recognized that private investment cannot be expected to solve the problem of financing development alone.

If the external contribution to the financing of economic development is to meet the requirements of United States foreign policy, public funds will have to play a substantial role. The probable inadequacy of the total volume of private foreign investment available for most areas is not the only reason for this conclusion. Economic development requires funds for the construction of facilities to provide basic services which are ordinarily not attractive to private capital and therefore in most cases must be financed by public funds. The provision of such facilities where they are now absent or inadequate may be expected to increase opportunities for profitable investment abroad of private capital in other types of enterprises.

[7] *Report to the President on Foreign Economic Policies* (Gordon Gray, Chairman), Washington, D. C., Nov. 10, 1950, p. 63.

SELECTED REFERENCES

Baran, Paul A., *The Political Economy of Growth* (Monthly Review Press, New York, 1957). Parts I, II, V, VI, and VII deal with the problems of underdeveloped areas from a Marxist point of view. Parts III and IV consider the growth of the mature industrial economies and Part VIII the growth of the Communist economies in the same frame of reference.

Buchanan, Norman S., and Ellis, Howard S., *Approaches to Economic Development* (Twentieth Century Fund, New York, 1955). A good general introduction to the problems of economic development.

Frankel, S. Herbert, *The Economic Impact on Underdeveloped Societies* (Blackwell, Oxford, 1953). Part I contains some stimulating critical essays, Part II, reflections on some aspects of development in Africa.

International Bank for Reconstruction and Development, reports of economic survey missions, available as of 1957 for Ceylon, Colombia, Cuba, Guatemala, Iraq, Jamaica, Malaya, Nicaragua, Nigeria, Surinam, and Turkey.

Kuznets, Simon S., "International Differences in Income Levels," and "National Income and Industrial Structure," Chapters 6 and 8 of *Economic Change* (Norton, New York, 1953). Pointed discussions of the relation between national income and its determinants.

Lewis, W. Arthur, *The Theory of Economic Growth* (George Allen & Unwin, London, 1955). A stimulating study of some of the more important factors underlying economic growth.

Millikan, Max F., and Rostow, W. W., *A Proposal: Key to an Effective Foreign Policy* (Harper & Bros., New York, 1957). A vigorous defense of a substantial and sustained program of economic assistance to underdeveloped countries.

Myrdal, Gunnar, *An International Economy* (Harper & Bros., New York, 1956). Principally a discussion of the relations between the more advanced and the underdeveloped nations, with emphasis on ways and means of promoting fuller integration of the latter in a true international economy.

Nurkse, Ragnar, *Problems of Capital Formation in Underdeveloped Countries.* (Blackwell, Oxford, 1953). A trenchant analysis of the reasons for the lack of capital in underdeveloped countries, together with a discussion of possible remedies.

Staley, Eugene, *The Future of Underdeveloped Countries* (Harper & Bros., New York, 1954). Contrasts Communist and democratic methods of realising economic development; noteworthy for its discussion of the political and social aspects of the problem.

United Nations, *Report on a Special United Nations Fund for Economic Development* (New York, 1953). A much-discussed proposal for supplementing existing sources of capital with funds available for long-term loans at low rates of interest, as well as outright grants.

Viner, Jacob, *International Trade and Economic Development* (Free Press, Glencoe, Ill., 1952). Chapters III, V, and VI deal critically with widely accepted views on economic development, particularly the vogue for industrialisation and for planning.

Zinkin, Maurice, *Development for Free Asia* (Chatto & Windus, London, 1956). A lively discussion of the political, social, and economic obstacles to development in Asian societies, and of the policies suitable for overcoming these obstacles. Contains vivid illustrations; most readable.

In addition to these references, there is a large United Nations' literature in the form of special reports and monographs dealing with land reform, financing economic development, cooperation, industrialisation, etc. Titles of possible interest may be found in the annual list of U.N. publications. Special mention also may be made of *Economic Development and Cultural Change,* published by the Research Center in Economic Development and Cultural Change of the University of Chicago since 1952. This journal contains articles dealing with practically every aspect of economic development, including a large number concerned with concrete experience.

27

TOWARD RESTORATION OF A WORLD TRADING SYSTEM

Contrasting Trade Policies: 1500-1939

In the course of our historical survey, we have encountered three periods during which the attitude of governments toward international trade has differed widely. The first of these, the Mercantilist era, was a phase of close regulation and control, with the regulation undertaken in the interest of supporting the power of the state. In the course of the two-and-a-half centuries during which Mercantilism held sway, the middle class of merchants and manufacturers, hitherto small in numbers and of little importance, became increasingly numerous and prosperous. Yet because the restrictive features of Mercantilism hampered expansion and enterprise and held down their profits, the new middle class came more and more to oppose and evade its prohibitions and requirements. The merchant-capitalist class, steadily growing in economic and political influence, found its interest better served by economic freedom. Under its pressure, the internal restrictions of Mercantilism gradually broke down. Finding wider and wider acceptance, the new laissez faire philosophy was given vigorous expression in the writings of Adam Smith. In Britain, it became the dominant point of view, and even on the continent found increasing numbers of influential adherents.

After the Napoleonic wars, the steady shift in the political strength of conflicting economic interests led to the extension into foreign trade of the liberal ideas hitherto applied only to the internal economy. Trade was freed from its centuries-old bonds by one country after another. The nineteenth century saw trade freer than it had been since Roman times. Both the direction of trade and the character of national specialisation became dominated almost exclusively by market forces. Under the new regime, the volume of international commerce expanded by leaps and bounds, making it possible for western Europe to become a highly specialised manufacturing center and thereby to support a huge increase in population.

This remarkable era was marred toward its close by a resurgence of nationalism, which brought with it the beginnings of a return to trade restriction. This movement became intensified with the outbreak of war in 1914 and the inflammation of nationalist sentiments that this entailed. The nostalgia of the 1920's for the comparative simplicity of the Victorian era met only disappointment in the mounting forces of nationalism, of growing economic rigidity, and of a widening range of sensitivity to disturbance. The shock of world depression speeded the disorganisation of the world economy and ended in the dominance of nationally oriented policies. Although demand and supply still continued to function, they did so within narrowly constricted areas; the broad world market, which had served so well before 1914 to allocate production and to ensure steady supplies of every imaginable commodity, no longer existed.

Cooperation to Restore a World Economy

The difficulties encountered during the 1930's showed conclusively that the specialisation of the nineteenth century and the growth of population it had engendered had gone too far to permit this disorganisation to continue. The dependence of western Europe and Japan upon a wide-flung network of trade made efforts to repair that network imperative. Even while World War II was raging, extensive discussions were undertaken and plans laid to reconstruct a wider market area, and at the same time, to effect the minimum essential compromises between the requirements of a multilateral trading system and national demands for reasonable economic stability.

Some of these efforts were on a regional scale, some much broader. We have devoted some attention to the sterling area, which provided a degree of financial unity, stability and convertibility of currencies, and comparative freedom of trade and payments over a large area. We are also acquainted with the efforts of the OEEC to liberalise the trade between European nations, and with the role played by the European Payments Union in easing their payments problems. And the European Recovery Program not only made the last two institutions possible by assisting European reconstruction, but set the EPU in operation with a grant of funds. Moreover, in its administration, the European Recovery Program constantly stressed the need for the liberalisation of trade and for a closer integration of the European nations.

As institutions serving to restore a more efficiently operating world economy, we have noted the contributions of the International Monetary Fund, the International Bank for Reconstruction and Development, and the General Agreement on Tariffs and Trade. The first of these aimed to replace chaotic currency conditions with some degree of stability, and by constant pressure on members to eliminate exchange controls and encourage a movement toward convertibility. The principal function of the International Bank is to foster the development of the less advanced nations: Indirectly, economic growth will enable them to lower their trade barriers and to move toward currency convertibility. GATT, of course, embodies an effort to make the price system more effective over a near-global area.

Interest in European Union

Interest in binding the European nations closer together has not been confined to American officials connected with the Recovery Program. European Union has been a persistent dream of many residents of the area. They feel that the present national economies are too small for efficient operation, and that if western Europe were economically united, the greatly increased size of the market would permit the realisation of economies of scale, as well as many external economies, that would add greatly to its prosperity and viability.

Discussion of European Union was immensely stimulated by the rising threat, after 1947, of Soviet domination. Although this threat led directly to the adoption of military measures, in particular the formation of the North Atlantic Treaty Organisation, and to proposals for the establishment of a European army, it also stimulated interest in economic union as a further means of strengthening Europe.

The Schuman Plan

The first concrete step toward economic integration came with the proposal and then the adoption of the *Schuman Plan for a Coal and Steel Community*. This was a bold and imaginative proposal, which aimed, through the elimination of trade restrictions and the encouragement of the free movement of resources, to stimulate the concentration of the coal and steel industries in the hands of the most efficient producers. With a common market kept competitive by the policing action of a central authority, it was hoped that members [1] would be assured of abundant and cheap supplies of these essentials of modern industry.

Before the war, an international steel cartel, which united monopolistic national organisations, also regulated production, restrained competition, and fenced off national markets from outside competition. Inefficient plants were kept alive by the high price policies of the cartel, as well as by

---

[1] The members of the Community are Belgium, France, Germany, Italy, Luxembourg, and the Netherlands.

government subsidies. Investment in modern facilities was restrained. Fear of a revival of this cartel supplied one motive for advancing the Schuman Plan; another was that, while it would require some sacrifice of French sovereignty, it would give France some control over the German coal and steel industries.

Rather than merely abolish tariffs and quantitative restrictions on trade in coal and steel, the Schuman Plan set up an international Authority with substantial powers. It was to do away with all tariffs and other restrictions on trade, eliminate a maze of discriminatory transport rates and establish an equitable system, and allocate funds to alleviate the impact of the common market during a five-year transitional period. To police the common market once established, it was authorised to prohibit mergers and even to dissolve existing combinations and to set maximum prices. Finally, the Authority has important powers over investment: It may require the submission of information about plans, forbid a firm to seek outside finances for any project it deems unwise, and make loans to firms for modernisation or expansion.

Established in 1952, after four years the European Coal and Steel Community (ECSC) has important achievements to its credit. Its operation, however, has revealed a number of serious obstacles that have still to be overcome. The common market was opened promptly among all countries but Italy (which was allowed to eliminate its tariffs gradually over a five-year period). "Double pricing," or the practice of charging one price to domestic consumers, another to foreign customers, was abolished, and a more rational system of railway rates was established. The chief gain has probably come from the impetus the Community has given to investment, for the European steel industry was badly in need of modernisation.

Some progress has been made in eliminating sub-marginal plants, though many still remain. The probability of any considerable relocation of production facilities appears slim, however. This is largely owing to the formidable resistance to movement on the part of workers.

Labor mobility is further hampered [in addition to the difficulties imposed by a severe housing shortage] by the unwillingness of most European workers to leave their native locality. The effects of this reluctance to move were strikingly apparent in the efforts to transplant some 5,000 French miners who were scheduled to be laid off in the process of modernizing Cevennes mines. As provided in the Treaty, the High Authority and the French government agreed in 1953 to share the expense of moving and readapting the workers, and jobs were arranged for them in Lorraine. Despite this assistance, the resistance both of the workers and of the whole community was very stubborn . . . real or imagined differences in dialect, climate, temperament, and social customs combined to discourage the workers from taking advantage of the new jobs that had been offered them. As a result, by the beginning of 1955 only 258 of the 5,000 had volunteered to leave . . .[2]

Nor does it appear that anything approaching truly competitive conditions is likely to emerge, owing to the small numbers of producers in each national market and their consequent reluctance to engage in price-cutting. To forestall the reemergence of private, restrictive cartels, the ECSC is likely to have to continue to operate as a supranational public cartel, establishing maximum prices in periods of rising demand, and enforcing minimum prices and establishing production quotas when demand is falling.

In spite of these defects, the statistical record of accomplishment is good. In the five years 1952-56, the Community's internal trade in steel has trebled, while steel production has risen by more than a third. Coal production has lagged, with only a four per cent increase. In the next three years, however, the Community plans to raise hard coal production by 25 and coke by 50 per cent.

EUROPEAN ECONOMIC UNION

Another move in the same direction as the Coal and Steel Community is the broader proposal for a *Common Market*, which reached the status of a draft treaty in March, 1957.[3] Ratified later in the year, the treaty went into effect on January 1, 1958. After a year allowed for dealing with the problems of organisation, it is to come into actual operation at the beginning of 1959.

Purpose

The purpose of the Common Market is mainly the realisation of the advantages of increased specialisation. It is hoped that a market embracing a population of over 160 million people will permit the more rapid development of the most economical sectors of each industry, as well as the use of the most modern production techniques. At present, it is contended, national markets are too small for economical operation of certain industries except as monopolies. A larger market area will make possible mass production without this drawback. Attainment of these ends should, the sponsors of the plan feel, make the unified area a more powerful unit,

---

[2] Derek Curtis Bok, *The First Three Years of the Schuman Plan, Princeton Studies in International Finance, No. 5* (Princeton University, 1955), pp. 53-4.

[3] Again, the participants are the Six: Benelux, France, Germany, and Italy.

ensure continual expansion, increase economic stability, raise standards of living, and develop harmonious relations between its component states.[4]

Customs Union

The crucial provision of the Common Market is the one establishing a customs union of the six nations. This means that all tariffs between members are to be abolished, and a uniform tariff adopted vis-a-vis other nations. Existing duties on the trade between members are not to be eliminated at once, but in three stages of four years each, in installments of 30, 30 and 40 per cent in the successive stages. These reductions are not to be uniform for all goods. Commodities are to be grouped according to the height of current duties, with the average level of duties on each group reduced by the specified percentage—a proviso that leaves room for flexibility that in practice is likely to mean postponing as long as possible cuts that will affect powerful interests adversely.

It is likely to be harder to get safely past the first stage of duty reductions than to continue the process once it is well under way. Perhaps for this reason, the treaty provides that the transition from the first to the second stage may be delayed for two years upon the request of a member. At the end of six years, however, inauguration of the second stage can be made compulsory by a majority vote of the Community's executive body, the European Economic Council.

Primarily at the insistence of France, overseas territories of members are to be associated with the Common Market. Imports from these territories are to be treated in the same fashion as those from the metropolitan country, while territorial duties (with exceptions for local overseas industries) are to be gradually reduced to the level applying to imports from the parent country.

The uniform external tariff is to be no higher than the average of the previous tariffs of members. Attainment of such equality of rates is to be gradual, just as with the elimination of the internal tariff. Quantitative restrictions, which the OEEC has succeeded in eliminating on nearly 90 per cent of intra-European trade, will be gradually enlarged until they are no longer restrictive. (The legal framework of quantitative restrictions apparently will remain in existence, capable of being swiftly rehabilitated in case of emergency).

Agricultural products present an especially difficult problem because

[4] Organisation for European Economic Cooperation, *Report Prepared by the Heads of Delegations of the Intergovernmental Committee Set Up by the Messina Conference to the Ministers of Foreign Affairs* (Paris, 28th August 1956).

of the prevalence in member countries of price supports, production controls, and special market arrangements. Although these products are not to be exempted from the provisions of the treaty relating to customs duties and quotas, the present national policies are to be merged, during the period of transition, into a common market policy for all of the six nations. The difficult task of formulating such a common policy is to be undertaken by the Council.

Other Aspects of the Common Market

The Common Market involves more than a customs union, however. It looks toward a much broader economic union of the six states. Free movement of both labor and capital within the Community is a declared goal. It is to be reached by the gradual removal of existing obstacles, through consultation and cooperation leading to the adoption of agreed measures.

Common rules of competitive behavior are to be established, prohibiting the division of markets, price fixing, and concerted restriction of production, and aiming to prevent "abusive" domination of the market by a single concern. Similarly with subsidies: It is proposed that a code of uniform behavior compatible with the principles of a common market be worked out. Discrimination in freight rates is to be eliminated, and a uniform transport policy formulated.

None of these items of a common code of behavior is specified in the treaty. They all involve too many details for that. Much prior study is needed to permit the rules to take into account the wide variance in conditions in the different countries. Formulation of this code is to be the task of the Council, which, if the treaty is ratified, promises to be the busiest official body on the continent.

Another problem requiring gradual resolution is that of dealing with national distortions in cost-price relationships caused by the differing industrial incidence of such burdens as social security taxes. These, as well as other taxes and government regulations, can raise a particular industry's costs relative to its competitors, as for example high social security taxes in a labor-intensive industry. It may be necessary to suggest and press for changes in national legislation so as to "harmonise" the policies of the different countries, or to permit escapes through subsidies or deferred duty reductions.

Special Aid Funds

If the gradual abolition of tariffs is carried through according to schedule, industries hitherto dependent on protection are likely to be injured, even though they may be able to adjust over time by intensifying their specialisation, improving efficiency, or converting to other lines of production. To help workers in these industries over their difficulties, a European Social Fund is to be established which will meet half the costs of retraining employees and, if necessary, of moving them to new locations.

Aid to industrial proprietors is to be part of a larger project. This is the *European Investment Fund,* which is to have one primary and two secondary functions. Its most important task promises to be furnishing aid to improve conditions—as by financing basic community facilities—in the underdeveloped regions of member states. In addition, it is to help finance projects of European importance that are too large to be handled alone by the individual states, and to advance funds to firms encountering difficulties in reconversion. The Fund is to have a capital of $1 billion, supplemented by loans raised in international capital markets.

Another fund with a special appeal to France, the "reluctant dragon" of the Six, puts up nearly $600 million for investment during the first five years in the overseas territories. France is to contribute only $200 million, the same as Western Germany, but her territories are to get the lion's share of the expenditures—over $511 million.[5]

Payments Problems

Finally, the treaty recognises clearly that if members follow divergent monetary and financial policies, the Community is sure to face stubborn balance of payments difficulties. Therefore each state agrees to follow economic policies that will maintain balance in its over-all international payments and confidence in its currency, and at the same time preserve a high degree of employment and price stability. To attain these ends, the six states agree to coordinate their policies through an Advisory Monetary Committee that will watch over balances of payments and advise the two main administrative agencies of the Community, the Council and the European Commission. If balance of payments troubles do develop, the Commission must immediately examine the situation and recommend remedies, which may include aid to a member in distress.

Organisation

With the entry into effect of the Treaty of Rome in 1958, the European

---

[5] The capital of the fund is to be $581,250,000. Belgium and the Netherlands are to contribute $70 million each, Italy $40 million, and Luxembourg $1¼ million. Belgian territories are to benefit from investment to the extent of $20 million, those of the Netherlands are to get $35 million, and of Italy, $5 million.

Economic Community immediately confronted a great variety of tasks—establishing administrative agencies and their procedures, determining rules for the regulation of competition, and agriculture, and preparing for the first installment of duty reductions. The Community will be a sort of super-government with respect to economic affairs, and like any government, will require specific agencies to act, to legislate, and to settle disputes. The treaty provides for a full complement of the necessary agencies.

The principal administrative body will be the European Council, a sort of economic cabinet of the six states. It is to consist of one member from each state, and will be the executive agent of the Community, making daily decisions, formulating rules of conduct, preparing new legislation, and prodding members to carry out the provisions of the treaty. Aiding the Council in its work will be a nine-man European Commission, which will oversee the application of the treaty, study special problems, and make recommendations to the Council. As an advisory body, in addition to the Monetary Committee already mentioned, there will be the European Economic and Social Committee, consisting of representatives of industry, workers, farmers, retail trade, and the liberal professions.

The legislative branch is to consist of an Assembly of 106 members, which will take final decision on recommendations of the Council, embodying these in new laws. The Assembly is also to become the legislative body for the European Coal and Steel Community and for Euratom, the organisation proposed to plan and administer the development of atomic energy resources for the six states.

Finally, there is to be a Court of Justice to adjudicate disputes, also shared in common with the Coal and Steel Community and Euration.

PROPOSAL FOR A FREE TRADE AREA

Still in the stage of discusison is a proposal to broaden the European common market by establishing a larger free trade area. This would include, in addition to the six, as many OEEC members as care to join.

Interest in a free trade area was stimulated by the fact that the OEEC's program of liberalising trade had about reached its limit. Some OEEC members have relatively high tariffs, others relatively low ones. Those with moderate tariffs are unwilling to go further in removing quotas unless the high tariff countries bring down their duties. In view of the progress of the idea of a common market, it was only natural to think of extending in some way the application of that idea. The OEEC established a working party to study the matter; its report is the basis of current discussions.[6]

The proposed free trade area is like the common market in that all trade barriers between members would be abolished, but differs in that each member would maintain its own tariff against the rest of the world.

Problems of a Free Trade Area

Many of the problems involved in establishing a free trade area would be the same as those confronting the common market. These include the need for setting a time table, with sufficient time to make adjustments, but not enough to put them off indefinitely; establishing area-wide rules of competition; and coping through escape clauses with special hardships, yet limiting such clauses to the inescapable minimum.

Besides such common problems, a free trade area encounters some special worries due in particular to the divergent tariffs of its members. Of these, the chief is how to define the origin of goods imported from within the area, which yet in fact originate in part in non-member countries. To allow them to enter free of duty, like fully indigenous products of the area, would permit evasion of the importing member's tariff. An objective standard for verifying origin is needed, both to reduce difficulties of enforcement and to minimise disputes. Such a standard could be based on the percentage of value added in the area of origin, or on a definition or origin in terms of the processes of manufacture through which a commodity had passed.

These special problems should be capable of resolution through negotiation. A more difficult issue was raised by Britain's insistence on excluding agricultural products from the list of freely traded items. She is a big importer of food from the Commonwealth, and is also Europe's best customer for such commodities. Forced to choose between a free trade area with a uniform tariff on agricultural products and existing preferences on Empire products, Britain would have to choose the latter. On the other hand, such European agricultural exporters as Denmark strongly support the removal of all barriers to trade in agricultural products between the free trading group.

In addition to the problems specific to a free trade area, serious issues have arisen with respect to the relationship between the broader free trade area—which presumably would include all or most OEEC members—and

[6] Organisation for European Economic Cooperation, *Report on the Possibility of Creating a Free Trade Area in Europe* (Paris, Jan. 1957).

the smaller but more compact common market, as well as between each of these regions and outside countries. Potential members of the free trade area fear that the tariff of the common market countries may be so high as to be unduly restrictive of trade with the outside world. Within the common market group, which would join the free trade area so far as mutual trade is concerned, France especially is concerned lest the low tariffs of some of the latter group give them an unduly strong trading position. Some of the underdeveloped countries, which have found in western Europe a good market for their primary products, have worried lest the common market's preferences for the overseas territories of members might work to their disadvantage. Other countries, such as Australia and Argentina, have feared that common market regulations applying to trade in agricultural products would reduce their sales to Europe. The re-casting of Europe's trading arrangements, in short, is no easy matter, but will require years of negotiation and adjustment before it is brought to a successful conclusion.

THE BENELUX ECONOMIC UNION

Some light on the difficulties to be surmounted in the course of making a going concern of a common market or a free trade area can be obtained from the experience of a much more modest project, the *Belgium-Netherlands-Luxembourg Economic Union,* or Benelux for short. This began with an agreement between the three governments-in-exile during the war (1944) to establish, first, a tariff community, with a common external tariff and lowered duties on Benelux trade; second, a customs union; and third, a full economic union.

It was hoped that movement to the last stage of full economic union would be smooth and prompt. But the difficulties proved to be much greater than anticipated. A common external tariff was established in 1948; by 1957, customs union had not been altogether completed, considerable obstacles to the free movement of capital and labor still remained, and domestic economic and social policies had by no means been fully coordinated.

Delay in Union: Causes

The chief obstacles to elimination of duties on internal Benelux trade came from the special problem raised by agricultural products and from the difficulty in unifying differing rates of excise duties, especially on beer. This is the most popular beverage in Belgium; its people want the excise duty kept low. In the Netherlands, on the other hand, beer carries a considerably higher tax and yields substantial revenue; there, spirits are more popular and carry low excise rates. Equalisation of these duties has till now (1957) been unattainable. As for agriculture, this is a relatively high-cost industry in Belgium and Luxembourg. The governments of these countries have considered it politically impossible to eliminate restrictions on agricultural imports from the Netherlands, though its products do receive preference.

The principal reason for delay in achieving economic union appears to have been a failure to appreciate promptly and to come to grips with the need for *coordinated commercial and financial policies.* Thus in the early postwar years, when the Dutch balance of payments was under severe strain, imports and interest payments were closely restricted. Belgium, with a comfortable balance of payments position, followed a relatively liberal import policy. In contradiction to the movement toward economic union, Dutch restrictions had to be applied to Belgian goods to prevent a leakage of payments through the mild Belgian controls. On the other hand, Belgium, to check the sale of imports from the dollar area to Holland for soft guilders, had to control exports to that country. Again, wide differences in internal economic policies caused difficulties in intra-Union payments. Until after 1948, the Netherlands made wide use of direct controls over prices, interest rates, investment, and use of materials, and had an extensive system of subsidies. Belgium relied principally on such more indirect methods as varying discount rates and easing or restricting the availability of credit. Variations in either country's policies wrought sudden changes in the balance of payments, and in addition, subsidies, price controls, and rationing by one partner made a common market impossible in products so affected. An agreement reached in 1948, which prescribed gradual abandonment of direct controls by the Netherlands and the substitution of indirect measures, brought real progress. This was speeded in 1953, when each partner agreed to pursue a financial policy aimed at avoiding either inflation or deflation.

WILL EUROPEAN ECONOMIC UNION SUCCEED?

Prospects of Achieving Union

Taking the establishment of a common tariff in 1948 as the concrete beginning of the Benelux Economic Union, it took nine years to achieve a large degree of customs union, partial freedom of movement of capital and labor, and partial coordination of economic and financial policies. Attainment of the same extent of unification among the six members of the common European market, which differ with respect to costs, scale of production, industrial traditions, and social and economic policies far more than the three smallest members that have already undertaken unions, will be a formidable task. Certainly the twelve years of transition will be needed. If they are to be fruitful, there will have to be the same constant consultations and official meetings, the same dogged determination to reach the prescribed goal, as have characterised the efforts of Benelux authorities.

The Common Market will have the advantage of a distinct organisation dedicated to its realisation. Clearly, much will depend on the quality of its leadership. Even more important, however, is the strength of the desire for union on the part of the political leaders, the parliaments, and the people of the six nations, which will have to offset the inevitable appeals to national sentiment by interests injured by economic union. There is considerable evidence that the desire for union is fairly wide and strong. Realisation of that goal should be greatly aided by prompt and effective use of the financial provisions for easing readaptation.

Suppose that the Common Market is actually established, and that free movement of capital and labor are also gradually realised. What tangible economic gains, in addition to the less tangible political one of six nations working together to achieve a mutual goal, can be expected?

Possible Gains and Losses in Trade

As Professor Viner has pointed out,[7] a customs union may create trade, or it may divert it. When it causes one member to import from another, at lower cost, a product hitherto produced at home behind a protective tariff, a customs union creates trade. Since this results in a more economic allocation of resources, it is an advantageous change.

But when a customs union causes one member to import from another a product previously bought from a third country, where costs are lower, trade is diverted into less economical channels and resources are allocated less efficiently.

To illustrate, suppose that before union, wheat costs $2 a bushel in the United States and Canada, $3 in France, and $5 in Italy, and that Italy now levies a 200 per cent duty on imports. No imports will enter the country; Italians will satisfy their wants entirely with high-cost Italian wheat. If a

[7] Jacob Viner, *The Customs Union Issue* (Carnegie Endowment for International Peace, New York, 1950).

common European market is established, Italy will now shift her purchases to France, obtaining wheat at the lower price of $3. Beneficial trade has been created.

Suppose, however, that the initial duty had been only 100 per cent. Italy would then have relied on imports from the lowest cost source. After payment of the duty, American and Canadian wheat would have sold in Italy for $4 a bushel. With the formation of a common market, French wheat, now free of duty, will sell in Italy for $3 a bushel, and will displace American and Canadian wheat. Here trade is diverted from a lower to a higher cost source. Though the Italian consumer gains, there is a more uneconomic allocation of resources (and a loss of revenue to the Italian treasury to set against the consumer's gain).

Whether, taking into account both the creation of trade and its diversion, a customs union results in net gain to its participants, could only be determined by a careful study of both effects. Merely adding up the total value of goods obtained from more economical sources and comparing it with the total diverted to more costly suppliers would be insufficient. For there is the question of the relative size of gains and losses.[8]

Suppose, for example, that before union, Italy imports 100 million bushels of overseas wheat; it cost $200 million to produce, but with a 100 per cent duty, sells at $400 million. After union, French wheat takes over the Italian market; its wheat (assuming a fixed Italian demand) costs $300 million to produce. The costs of producing Italy's wheat have risen by $100 million. This is the measure, in this simple case, of the real loss caused by the diversion of trade.

But Italy may have been producing most of its steel at home. Suppose that a given grade costs Italy $30 a ton to manufacture, and that Italian consumption is 10 million tons, or a total value of $300 million. If Germany can make this steel for $10 a ton, after the abolition of intra-European tariffs Italy can purchase 10 million tons there for $100 million. Although the formation of the customs union caused an uneconomic diversion of trade worth $200 million, and the creation of trade worth only $100 million, there was not a net loss of $100 million, as these total figures would suggest. Instead, Italy gains $200 million in the saving on costs from the steel trade, and loses only $100 million on the diversion of trade in wheat from the United States and Canada (cost: $200 million) to France (cost: $300 million). It enjoys a net saving in cost of $100 million.

[8] This point is elaborated in J. E. Meade, *The Theory of Customs Unions* (North-Holland Publishing Co., Amsterdam, 1955).

This is, of course, by no means the whole story. Demand is not fixed and unalterable, as we have assumed, nor are costs likely to remain constant. These and other refinements would have to be taken into account in a complete analysis. [9] But the qualifications they require do not substantially affect the argument.

Unless a customs union raises costs on the trade diverted more than it lowers costs on the intra-union trade created, formation of the union will result in a net gain to its members. A favorable outcome is more likely, in general, the more competitive are the economies of the customs union members before the removal of tariffs, and the more complementary after their removal.

To illustrate, suppose that France, Germany, and Italy are relatively low-cost producers of wheat, steel, and textiles, respectively, but that before union each produced all these behind a wall of protection. Their economies were then very similar. After union, each specialises on its cheap product and supplies the others with it. A high degree of potential complementarity has been realised. Under such conditions, a customs union will greatly expand trade between the members of the union without causing a large diversion of imports or exports from other markets.

Economies of Scale?

There is a possibility upon which the architects of the common market appear to place considerable reliance, that customs unification will so expand the market for many commodities that substantial economies of scale can be realised. Thus the OEEC Report to the Ministers of Foreign Affairs says:

This merging of markets will create outlets large enough to permit the use of the most up-to-date production techniques. There are already certain branches which require such enormous production resources that they are already more than a single national market can cope with. But what is more, in many sectors of industry, national markets do not allow firms to develop to their optimum size unless they enjoy a virtual monopoly. The advantage of the wide market is that it makes possible mass production and at the same time does not create a monopoly.[10]

It is doubtful if this optimism is fully warranted. As Professor Viner has noted, even in industries in which large-scale plants are common, there are usually plants of moderate size that are as efficient as the giant plants.[11] Only rarely does optimum size of plant imply enormous size.

Moreover, even though in some industries the more efficient plants are

---

[9] Meade, *op. cit.*, goes into these matters with great thoroughness.
[10] *Op. cit.*, p. 1.
[11] *Op. cit.*, p. 46.

very large, there is no insuperable obstacle to the location of such a large-scale plant in a small country. Table 27.1 shows, for a number of U. S. industries, the proportion of total national capacity contained in a single plant of optimum size, and the approximate cost of constructing and equipping such a plant. The industries chosen (from a longer list) are those in which the optimum size plant was relatively large.

Table 27.1

ESTIMATED SIZE OF OPTIMAL PLANTS IN CERTAIN
U. S. MANUFACTURING INDUSTRIES

INDUSTRY	PERCENTAGE OF NATIONAL INDUSTRY CAPACITY CONTAINED IN ONE OPTIMAL PLANT	CAPITAL REQUIRED FOR ONE EFFICIENT PLANT (in millions)
Distilled liquor	1.25 to 1.75	$30 to 42
Petroleum refining	1.75	193 (ex transport facilities)
Metal containers	0.5 to 3	5 to 20
Steel	1 to 2.5	265 to 665
Tires and tubes	3	25 to 30
Rayon	4 to 6	50 to 135
Soap	4 to 6	13 to 20
Cigarettes	5 to 6	125 to 150
Fountain pens	5 to 10	6
Automobiles	5 to 10	250 to 500
Tractors	10 to 15	125
Typewriters	10 to 30	No estimate

Source: J. S. Bain, "Economies of Scale, Concentration and Entry," *American Economic Review*, XLIV (Mar. 1954), pp. 30, 36.

If an optimal plant in these industries comprises, say, 10 per cent of national production in a market as large as the United States, it stands to reason that plants of similar efficiency will dominate national output even more completely in a small or medium-sized European country. Despite this fact, and in spite of the high capital requirements for a single plant in some of these industries, *there is not one of them that does not already exist in some European country.* It may be, of course, that optimum size is different in Europe, perhaps made smaller by a more intensive use of labor and less intensive use of capital than in the United States. The point is, however, that these are typical large-scale industries, and that each of them is operating today in an un-unified Europe. Moreover, these industries are apparently operating successfully—the products of many of them are encountered in markets all over the world (Olivetti typewriters, Dunlop tires, Courtauld's rayon, Lever Brothers soap, and Volkswagen, Fiat, Renault, and Austin cars, to mention only a few of the better known names).

The very fact that the European firms engaged in these industries produce for an international market both helps account for their ability to attain large scale and provides assurance against national monopoly in a single market—unless such monopoly is deliberately established by some form or other of protection.

Bases for Increased Efficiency

The possibility of realising increased efficiency and lower costs will be improved if the six nations of the common market achieve full economic union, with substantially increased mobility of labor and capital. Any such heightening of efficiency is unlikely to come because greater factor mobility introduces economies of scale, however. If the argument stated above is correct, the common market countries are now *each* quite capable of supporting plants of optimum size, with perhaps rare exceptions.

But under the Common Market, increased mobility of labor and capital should permit the relocation of some industries, to take advantage of readier access to markets or raw materials and thus to reduce transport costs. More economical combinations of the factors could also probably be attained if labor and capital were free to move. With more capital, Italy's industries would be able to make better use of modern techniques, while with more labor, Britain's coal mines could be worked more efficiently. Finally, concentration in a single locality of industries that are now scattered would tend to make possible the realisation of such external economies as specialisation within each industry and the provision of specialised services not now available.

The greatest gains in efficiency, however, would probably come through the invigorating effects of increased competition. Many of Europe's industries are now controlled by formal or informal cartel arrangements, under which output is restricted and price maintained at a level that permits the high-cost producer to survive. In France, especially, the typical business is small, dominated by a single family, with security of its position a more potent consideration than growth.[12] The introduction of competition from the outside, together with the establishment and enforcement of common market rules against the restriction of competition, could force the liquidation of high-cost producers and the scrapping of antiquated methods. In this direction lies one of the greatest potential gains of the Common Market—and one of its greatest dangers, for the threat of competition is precisely what many fear, and will organise and fight to prevent.

[12] Landes, David D., "French Business and the Business Man: A Social and Cultural Analysis," Ch. 19 of Edward Mead Earle, *Modern France: Problems of the Third and Fourth Republics* (Princeton University Press, 1951).

In Conclusion

We cannot assess in advance the economic gains to be expected from economic union. But unless there is much displacement of imports from outside Europe by second-best suppliers from within, the possibility of improving the location of some industries, of attracting to others complements of labor and capital now lacking, and above all, of forcing inefficient and cartel-supported producers to change their ways, should yield substantial benefits. Extending the area and increasing the intensity of competition has in the past generally produced good results, as the example of the United States bears witness.

SELECTED REFERENCES

Bok, Derek Curtis, *The First Three Years of the Schuman Plan*, Princeton Studies in International Finance, No. 5 (International Finance Section, Princeton University, 1955). A critical review of the early years of the European Coal and Steel Community.

"Towards Freer Trade in Europe," special supplement to *The Economist*, Oct. 12, 1957. A good discussion of the issues raised by the proposed free trade area, especially in their relation to Britain and the Commonwealth.

Meade, James E., *Negotiations for Benelux: An Annotated Chronicle 1943-1956*, Princeton Studies in International Finance, No. 6 (International Finance Section, Princeton University, 1957). A study of the difficulties encountered in establishing a common market for three small countries.

——, *Problems of Economic Union* (George Allen & Unwin, London, 1953). An analysis of the problems of commercial policy, international payments, and factor mobility that are due to arise when economic union of national economies is attempted.

——, *The Theory of Customs Unions* (North-Holland Publishing Co., Amsterdam, 1955). A brief but thorough discussion of the welfare effects of a customs union.

Organisation for European Economic Cooperation, *Report Prepared By the Heads of Delegations of the Intergovernmental Committee Set Up By the Messina Conference to the Ministers of Foreign Affairs* (Paris, August 28, 1956; mimeographed). This report contains the proposals that formed the basis for the draft treaty for a Common Market.

——, *Report on the possibility of creating a Free Trade Area in Europe* (Paris, January 1957).

Viner, Jacob, *The Customs Union Issue* (Carnegie Endowment for International Peace, New York, 1950). Chapter IV is of greatest interest; it deals with various aspects of the economics of customs unions. Chapters II and III consider the relation between customs unions and the most-favored-nation principle.

AUTHOR INDEX

SUBJECT INDEX

Index